CADOGAN
guides

SCOTLAND

P9-DTA-509

Cadogan Books plc
Letts House, Parkgate Road, London SW11 4NQ

The Globe Pequot Press
6 Business Park Road, PO Box 833, Old Saybrook,
Connecticut 06475–0833

Copyright © Richard Miers 1987, 1989, 1991, 1994
Illustrations © Charles Shearer 1994

Book design by Animage
Cover by Animage
Maps © Cadogan Guides, drawn by Thames Cartographic Ltd

Proof Reading: Lorna Horsfield
Indexing: Ann Hall
Production: Book Production Services
Mac Help: Jacqui Radisic, Winning Design

Editing: Robert Sneddon
Managing: Vicki Ingle
Series Editors: Rachel Fielding and Vicki Ingle

A catalogue record for this book is available from the British Library
ISBN 0–947754–63–6
Library of Congress Cataloging-in-Publication-Data
Miers, Richenda
    Scotland/Richenda Miers.   4th ed.   p. cm. -- (Cadogan guides)
    Includes index
    ISBN 1–56440–461–7
    1. Scotland--Guidebooks.   I. Title. II. Series.
    DA870.M54 1994
    914.1104 859--dc20
                                                     94--3019
                                                     CIP

The author and publishers have made every effort to ensure the accuracy of the information in this book at
the time of going to press. However, they cannot accept any responsibility for any loss, injury or
inconvenience resulting from the use of information contained in the guide.

Typeset in Weidemann and entirely produced on Apple Macintosh with Quark XPress, Photoshop, Freehand
and Word software.

Printed and bound in Great Britain by Redwood Books, Trowbridge, Wiltshire, on Jordan Opaque
supplied by McNaughton Publishing Papers Ltd.
Output by Cooling Brown.

Acknowledgements

I owe a great debt of gratitude to the following people, who have given me invaluable help. First, to my daughter Mary for her remorseless and very necessary red pen; also to David Murray, Ann and Christopher Thompson, Angus Fairrie, Alasdair Maclean, Peter Carthew, Francis Pearson, Penny Holt, Zilla Tuck and James Murray.

I would also like to thank the staff of the area tourist boards who have given their precious time to help, advise and amend: Donald Pow, James McMillan, Margret Sutor, G. Taylor, C. Good, Scott Armstrong, Gwen Sinclair, Fiona Meikle, Isobel Reid, Angus Macmillan, Fiona Grant, Alistair MacPherson, Liz Allan, Fiona Ramponi, Anne Burgess, Patrick Laughlin, Hilary Fleming, Gordon Henry, Helen Cheyne, Ann Jones, Alan Reid, Liz Grant, Tara Campbell, Moira Dyer, Riddell Graham, Susan Donaldson, F. Jarvie and Douglas Richie.

I would like to thank my editor, Robert Snedden, for his patience and hard work on this edition. Finally, I am most grateful to the following contributors: David Murray, for the Topic on piping; Michael Wigan, for his piece on fishing in Scotland; Bruce Critchley, for his expert guide to Scotland's golf courses; and Chris Hines for his personal account of surfing in Scotland.

The publishers would like to thank Alex, Lorna, Horatio and Kicca for their skills, and, especially, Charles Shearer for the drawings.

About the Author

Richenda Miers is a novelist, freelance journalist and travel writer. Part English and part Scottish, she divides her time between the two countries, and has spent many years living 'north of the border'. She has many ties to the country she loves: her husband served in a Highland regiment; her son was born in Inverness; two of her daughters went to school in Aberdeen; and two of her children studied at Scottish universities. The Miers family share a home in the Outer Hebrides.

Contents

Maps

In 1975, amid bitter controversy, Scotland was divided into regions, some of which are obvious, others less so. Now, nearly 20 years later, the regions are again being redrawn, and the new boundaries should be in effect by 1996. This book is divided into the 1975 regions; now and then, therefore, the reader must turn to a different section that crosses a regional boundary.

Each of Scotland's regions has its own unique character and attractions to captivate the visitor. Whether you dip in to just one of the regions or you have the leisure to explore the whole country, careful planning should ensure that you get the best from your trip. Where you choose to go is, of course, up to you, but these brief sketches of the regions may help you to decide which places are most likely to suit you.

Borders

The region was fought over time and again as control switched back and forth between the Scots and the English, and the Border reivers quarrelled amongst themselves, their exploits recalled today in the many Common Riding Festivals that are a feature of this part of the country. Ruins dotted across the landscape give mute testimony to the violence of the times. The Borders are rich in salmon and trout rivers, and offer excellent walking over the Southern Uplands.

Dumfries and Galloway

This is a major centre for Robert Burns enthusiasts; after spending some time as a farmer near the town he became an exciseman in Dumfries itself. The mild climate of the region makes it a magnet for a number of rare bird species, and for the people who want to see them. If you are not amongst them, you may simply enjoy walking over the hills of the Galloway Forest Park or along the coast of the Solway Firth.

Lothian

Lothian's jewel is Edinburgh, capital city of Scotland, and it is set in countryside that is well worth exploring. The Lammermuirs and Pentland Hills and Lothian's varied coastline offer much to the walker. The Royal Burgh of Linlithgow, birthplace of Mary, Queen of Scots, is well worth a visit. Edinburgh itself is a city it is is difficult to tire of, the skyline of the Old Town seen from the New is unparalleled.

Strathclyde

Here, perhaps, is the heart of Scotland. And at the heart of Strathclyde is Glasgow, a sprawling city full of of canny, rumbustious people. Much of the region is far from being urban—from the calm spirituality of Iona in the north to the Ayrshire farmlands, the other end of the Burns axis, in the south; from the islands in the west, to the legendary 'bonny banks' of Loch Lomond in the east.

Central

Central is the physical heart of the country. Much of it is urbanized but it is easy to find your way to the country, particularly to the wooded Trossachs. Stirling, rich in history, is the ideal centre from which to explore further.

Fife

Fife, across the Firth of Forth from Lothian, juts out into the North Sea yet enjoys a surprising amount of sunshine. Once known as the Kingdom of Fife, it has rich pickings for the historian, particularly in Dunfermline and St Andrews. The Royal and Ancient Golf Club at St Andrews will require no introduction for sporting readers.

Tayside

Across the Firth of Tay, Tayside is the ancient home of the Picts, that mysterious vanished race. Their hill forts and stone circles abound. Festivals at Perth and Pitlochry and Highland Games at places such as Blair Atholl entice the tourist. Tayside offers several challenges for the walker, including the imposing Ben Lawers and Schiehallion.

Grampian

This is an attractive region, with the North Sea on one side and magnificent mountains on the other. Speyside malt whiskies are justly famous and a happy time may be had wandering the Whisky trail. Aberdeen, the Granite City, is worth a visit and makes a good starting point for your explorations.

Highland

The remoter parts of the Highland region seem untouched by time. It is here, particularly in the islands, that you will find the majority of Scotland's Gaelic speakers. It is said with some truth that Scotland divides into two nations across the Highland Line. This is walking country that is unexcelled anywhere in the world. Delights are everywhere.

Western Isles

The Western Isles have a character all their own. There are literally hundreds of them, although not all are inhabited. Skye, Uist, Harris and Lewis all command attention and a warm welcome is practically guaranteed. If you have access to a boat this is idyllic sailing territory.

Orkney and Shetland

Far to the north, these island outposts are scarcely 'Scottish' at all. These were the bastions of the Vikings and still retain much in the way of Norse character. A birdwatchers' paradise where seabirds throng the cliffs and islands.

Ruins

Castle Tioram, Castle Campbell, Tantallon Castle, Hermitage Castle, Linlithgow Palace.

Antiquities

Maes Howe, Mousa Broch, Callanish Standing Stones, Traprain Law, Iron Age hill fort on Barry Hill near Alyth, Ruthwell Cross.

Preserved Castles and Mansions

The castles of Cawdor, Eilean Donan, Blair, Floors, Glamis, Fyvie, Crathes, Edinburgh and Stirling; Traquair House, Hopetoun House, Abbotsford, Fasque.

Gardens

Finlaystone, Castle of Mey, Crathes Castle gardens, Royal Botanic Gardens, Edinburgh, Crarae Woodland Garden, Inverewe Garden, Pitmedden Garden, Threave Gardens.

Churches

Croick Church, the Italian Chapel; Orkney, Dalmeny Church, Ladykirk.

Art Galleries and Collections

In Edinburgh: the National Gallery of Scotland, the Scottish National Gallery of Modern Art; in Glasgow: Glasgow (Museum) and Art Gallery; Hunterian Art Gallery, the Burrell Collection.

Museums

Royal Museum of Scotland, Edinburgh, including its separate Antiquities collection; Glasgow Museum (and Art Gallery); the Highland Folk Museum, Kingussie; Angus Folk Museum, Glamis village; Gairloch Heritage Museum; Strath Naver Museum, Bettyhill.

Festivals

Edinburgh International Festival, Glasgow Mayfest. Jedburgh, Selkirk and Hawick Common Riding Festivals.

Activities

Sheepdog trials, piping competitions; Highland games and gatherings; curling; Malt Whisky Trail.

Restaurants

Peat Inn, Fife; Champany Inn, Linlithgow; La Potinière, Gullane; Loch Fyne Oyster Bar, Cairndow, Loch Fyne.

Places to Stay

Gleneagles; the Summer Isles Hotel, Auchiltibuie; Inchnadamph Hotel, Loch Assynt; Loch Melfort Hotel, Arduaine; Crinan Hotel; Greywalls, Gullane—where the food is so outstanding that the King of Jordan pinched their last chef; Philipburn House Hotel, Selkirk; Gleddoch House, Langbank; Altnaharrie Inn, Ullapool; Knockinaam Lodge Hotel, Portpatrick.

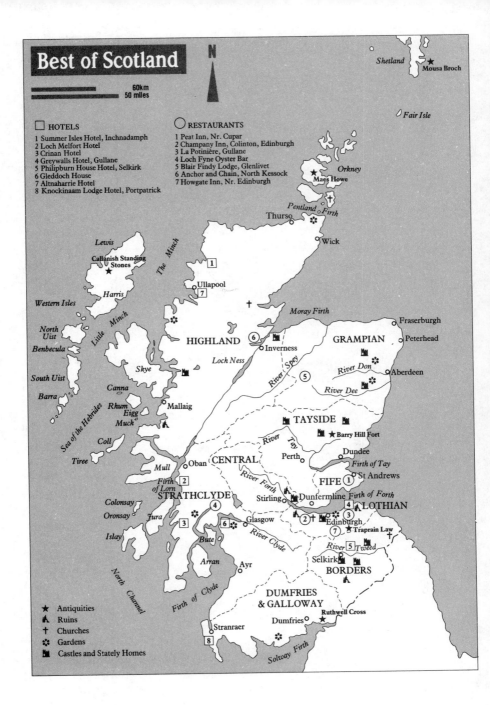

Best of Scotland

60km
50 miles

N

☐ HOTELS
1 Summer Isles Hotel, Inchnadamph
2 Loch Melfort Hotel
3 Crinan Hotel
4 Greywalls Hotel, Gullane
5 Philipburn House Hotel, Selkirk
6 Gleddoch House
7 Altnaharrie Hotel
8 Knockinaam Lodge Hotel, Portpatrick

◯ RESTAURANTS
1 Peat Inn, Nr. Cupar
2 Champany Inn, Colinton, Edinburgh
3 La Potinière, Gullane
4 Loch Fyne Oyster Bar
5 Blair Findy Lodge, Glenlivet
6 Anchor and Chain, North Kessock
7 Howgate Inn, Nr. Edinburgh

Shetland
★ Mousa Broch

◌ Fair Isle

Orkney
★ Maes Howe

Pentland Firth
Thurso
Wick

Lewis
Callanish Standing Stones ★
The Minch

Western Isles
Harris

North Uist
Little Minch
Benbecula

South Uist
Barra

Ullapool ☐7

Moray Firth

✝

HIGHLAND
Loch Ness
◯6 🏰
Inverness

GRAMPIAN
Fraserburgh
Peterhead

River Spey
River Don
◯5
River Dee
Aberdeen

Sea of the Hebrides
Skye
Canna
Rhum
Eigg
Muck
Mallaig

Coll
Tiree
Mull
Oban

TAYSIDE
★ Barry Hill Fort

River Tay
Perth
Dundee
Firth of Tay
St Andrews ◯1

Firth of Lorn
☐2
CENTRAL
River Forth
Stirling
FIFE
Dunfermline
Firth of Forth
LOTHIAN

Colonsay
Oronsay
Jura
Islay
☐3
◯4
☐6
Glasgow
STRATHCLYDE
River Clyde

◯2 ✝ ◯3
Edinburgh
◯7 ★ Traprain Law

Bute
Arran
Ayr

River ☐5 Tweed
Selkirk 🏰

North Channel

Firth of Clyde

BORDERS

DUMFRIES & GALLOWAY
Dumfries ◌
Ruthwell Cross ★

★ Antiquities
🏰 Ruins
✝ Churches
❀ Gardens
🏰 Castles and Stately Homes

Stranraer
☐8

Solway Firth

xi

Introduction

romantic visions

O Caledonia! stern and wild,
Meet nurse for a poetic child!
Land of brown heath and shaggy wood,
Land of the mountain and the flood,
Land of my sires! what mortal hand
Can e'er untie the filial band
That knits me to thy rugged strand!

Sir Walter Scott

Even Scotland's most ardent advocate failed to capture the essence of his native land. No poem can perfectly evoke the evening sun, dipping below the horizon beyond islands that stand out in dark relief against a blazing sky, nor the heart-stopping sound of a lone piper playing a grave-side lament in a remote highland glen. And no artist, not even McCulloch, has yet done full justice to the scenery: smoke-grey hills; stark mountain ranges; wild moorland carpeted with mulberry-red heather; mossy glens shaded by rowans and gnarled oaks; rivers and burns swirling over slabs of granite, and slicing through steep-sided gorges into lochs where peat-coloured water is overlaid by fragments of mist.

Ceud Mìle Fàilte! You'll see this poster all over Scotland; it means 'A Hundred Thousand Welcomes!' But don't expect the Scots to gush over you; their hospitality comes from the heart, with quiet dignity tempered by shrewd wit. To find their true nature, you must peel away layers of tartan, haggis, monsters and whimsical blether. The Romans called them Caledonians, failed to subdue them, and went away. Brave, proud and fiercely independent, they have been fighting for freedom from England since their earliest history; yet when Bonnie Prince Charlie swept through Scotland, rallying the clans to his father's standard and offering them an alternative to Hanoverian rule, far more fought against him or remained neutral than fought with him. The Scots defy classification—they are canny, yet generous; taciturn, yet eloquent; dour, yet witty; realistic, yet unashamedly romantic. A piper, decked out in kilt and plaid, will serenade a captive audience in a loch-side lay-by, and expect a tip, but if you break down and a Highlander comes to your rescue with a tractor, petrol or makeshift fan-belt, reward him with a dram or a bottle, don't insult him with a fiver. A Gaelic-speaking bard will sit on a bench outside his cottage surrounded by picture-postcard scenery, beguiling you with Celtic tales, while round the back there's a tangle of rusting machinery, and empty cans and bottles lie strewn like confetti in the heather.

Whatever sort of holiday you want, you'll find it in Scotland. You can climb in the Cuillins with crampons and ropes, reel in a salmon as it thrashes about in the Spey, or play golf at St Andrews. You can sail among the islands on the west coast at the helm of a sturdy ketch, anchor for the night in a sheltered sea-loch, and fall asleep to the eerie wailing of seals. You can explore the blanket bog of the Flow Country, spotting rare birds and insects and carnivorous plants. You can sit in a croft-house kitchen, pungent with acrid peat-smoke, and listen to Gaelic songs and stories of the past that have been passed down by word of mouth over many generations. You can gaze at paintings in Edinburgh's 'finest small gallery in the world', or marvel at priceless tapestries in Glasgow's Burrell Collection. If you are a gourmet you can dine on smoked salmon or local oysters, followed by a succulent lobster, fresh from the Minch, or an inch-thick Aberdeen Angus steak, and finish off with raspberries from the Carse of Gowrie. And for your picnic lunch, you can buy scampi off one of the fishing boats, boil them up in a billycan over your camp fire, and eat them still warm with wholemeal bread. You can go north and look for that elusive cosmic stunt, the Aurora Borealis (Northern Lights), when shafts of coloured lights, mostly green and red, flash across the sky like a pageant of searchlights. If none of these attractions are to your taste, you can rent a bothy on a remote island and curl up in front of a peat fire with a glass of whisky and your favourite companion (or, failing that, the complete works of Sir Walter Scott). *Ùine gu leòir* is Gaelic for 'time enough' and the word 'whisky' comes from *uisge-beatha*—water of life.

This book is for my husband, Douglas, with thanks for his patience during its creation and subsequent updating. It is also for Paula Levey, to whom I owe so much.

Travel

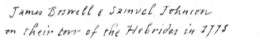

James Boswell & Samuel Johnson on their tour of the Hebrides in 1775

1

By Air

Scheduled flights serve Scotland from all over the world, some direct, some via London.

From the US, there are direct services with Northwest Orient to Prestwick Airport, 30 miles (48km) south of Glasgow. Free coaches connect with frequent trains to Glasgow.

From Canada, Air Canada flies from Toronto and Halifax to Prestwick.

European airlines with direct scheduled services to Scotland include: British Airways, from Milan, Paris, Frankfurt, Dusseldorf, and Munich; Air UK, from Amsterdam, Bergen, Copenhagen, Oslo, Stavanger; KLM Royal Dutch Airline, from Amsterdam; SAS from Copenhagen, Oslo and Stavanger; Lufthansa, from Dusseldorf; Scandinavian Airways from Oslo, Stavanger and Copenhagen; Icelandair Airways, from Copenhagen and Reykjavik. Visitors from other countries must travel via England.

From England

British Airways and **British Midland Airways** fly direct to Edinburgh and to Glasgow (Abbotsinch), from London Heathrow. British Airways also fly to Inverness via Glasgow. **AirUK** fly to both cities from Gatwick. Flights take just over an hour and there are frequent buses and plenty of taxis into Edinburgh or Glasgow. All airlines offer economy fares with conditions, such as having to book and pay ahead, with no cancellation refund. For example, British Airways offer non-refundable return fares, London to Edinburgh or Glasgow, booked at least two weeks in advance, for from £107 (full fare £218, standby £148) and London to Inverness £120 (full fare £244, standby £142). Offers change frequently so it is always worth checking. There are also many special 'package' offers, some of which include return fare, self-drive car, insurance and a tank of petrol.

Heathrow Airport, ✆ 081 759 4321   **British Airways**, ✆ 0345 222111

British Midland, ✆ 071 589 5599   **Air UK**, ✆ 0293 517654

British Airways, Inverness, ✆ 0463 232471

By Train

British Rail run regular train services from London to Scotland from Kings Cross and Euston stations. The inter-city trains are modern and comfortable and it is a good idea to book seats in advance during the tourist season. The journey to Edinburgh or Glasgow takes from four to five hours and there are at least 15 trains a day to both cities. Special-offer tickets, with all sorts of extras such as free parking, a free dram and free breakfast, are frequently available. London to Edinburgh/Glasgow: Superapex, booking at least 14 days ahead, £29 return; Supersaver, not travelling on a Friday, £59 return; normal return, £69. London to Inverness, Supersaver, £72; normal return, £80. These prices are only a guide.

In addition, there are direct trains to Scotland from several other towns and cities, and convenient connections from Edinburgh and Glasgow. Overnight sleeper connections from London and Bristol operate to Edinburgh, Glasgow, Dundee, Perth, Aberdeen and

Inverness. A second-class sleeper costs £25 (first-class costs £30 but you must then have a first-class ticket). During the holiday season you should book sleepers well in advance.

Freedom of Scotland Rover tickets allow you to travel anywhere in Scotland: 15 days costs about £100. There are other travel passes worth enquiring about. North Americans can buy a Brit Rail Pass through their travel agents. There is also a motor-rail service to the main cities.

Kings Cross Station, London, ✆ 071 837 4200

Euston Station, London, ✆ 071 387 9400

Waverley Station, Edinburgh, ✆ 031 556 2451

Buchanan Street Station, Glasgow, ✆ 041 332 9811

Central Station, Glasgow, ✆ 041 204 2844

Aberdeen Station, ✆ 0224 594222

Inverness Station, ✆ 0463 238924

By Bus or Coach

Several coach companies operate between London and Scotland, usually running at least one day coach and one overnight. The journey from London to Edinburgh or Glasgow takes about six hours, with an hour's stop at a service station. The coaches are reasonably comfortable, with toilets. Some have a snack service and show a film. Prices vary and there are often special offers. Average midweek return, London to Edinburgh or Glasgow, costs from £24.

Eastern Scottish Coaches, Victoria Coach Station, London, ✆ 071 730 0202

Scottish City Link, Victoria Coach Station, London, ✆ 071 730 0202 and Glasgow, ✆ 041 332 9191

By Car

An excellent network of motorways means that you can drive comfortably from London to Edinburgh in 7 hours, sticking to the 70 mph limit. The M1, A1(M) and A68 is the quickest route to Edinburgh, and the M1, M6 and A74, to Glasgow.

Specialist Tour Operators and Special Interest Holidays

Tour operators offer many travel-inclusive packages: golfing holidays, fishing holidays, historic trails, scenic tours, etc. Consult your travel agent for details.

in the US

Abercrombie and Kent, ✆ 800 323 3602, run tours through lovely Highland scenery in The Royal Scotsman, a restored steam train. **Caravan Tours**, ✆ 800 621 8338, offer a 15-day holiday for Americans which includes the air fare from New York, escorted motor-coach tours of Scotland and Ireland, free entrance fees, evening entertainment and first-class hotels.

Alternatively, there are package tours arranged from all over Britain, ranging from luxury coach tours with scheduled itineraries and first-class accommodation, to cheaper tours with less ritzy accommodation. National Holidays operate from all over the country with an extensive choice of tours, ✆ 0924 383838 (West Yorks) or 0942 44246 (Lancs). The Scottish Tourist Board publish a free brochure, *Scotland*, with details of over 300 good-value holidays, all of which can be booked at an ABTA Travel Agent.

Special Interest Holidays

If you like to build your holiday round a theme or particular activity, the Scottish Tourist Board publishes an excellent free brochure, *Adventure and Special Interest Holidays in Scotland*, with details of dozens of ideas for 'different' holidays, and addresses to contact. Write for a copy to the Scottish Tourist Board, PO Box 15, Edinburgh EH1 1UY. You can, for example, go on an archaeological holiday (Dumfries and Galloway Tourist Board, ✆ 0387 53862), and be introduced to the many prehistoric sites on the Solway Coast, and the Early Christian remains at Whithorn. For creative people there are arts and crafts courses offering instruction as well as relaxation. Subjects range from painting and music to woodcraft, silversmithing and stone-cutting. Outdoor holidays include: birdwatching, camping, canoeing, climbing and walking, cross-country and downhill skiing, cycling, diving, fishing, gardening, geology, gliding, golf, riding, shooting and stalking, skiing, swimming and watersports.

cruising holidays

If you want to see the west coast of Scotland from the sea, haven't got your own boat, and prefer an experienced hand on the helm, try STA Schooners, ✆ 0705 832055. They run week-long voyages in the *Malcolm Miller*, a 300-ton topsail schooner, and part of the experience is that you are one of the crew—a pleasure for which you pay quite a lot. There are many more, smaller and mostly cheaper: Sinbad Charters, for instance, ✆ 0346 842247, or Yacht Corryvreckan, ✆ 0631 64371. Western Isles Sailing & Exploration Company, ✆ 0208 851457, operate out of Oban. Their *Marguerite Explorer* is a beautiful gaff-rigged ketch with a highly competent crew who are only too happy to teach passengers the complexities of sailing as they cruise in some of Scotland's most beautiful waters. Hebridean Island Cruises, ✆ 0756 701338, offer cruises on the western seaboard in the *Hebridean Princess*, a floating luxury hotel with a crew of 30 serving 40 passengers. If you are lucky with the weather and can afford luxury prices, this is an ideal holiday for hedonists. There are plenty of opportunities for a 'run ashore'. Serenissima, ✆ 071 730 9841, do a cruise in MS *Caledonian Star*, starting from Edinburgh and going up the east coast to Orkney and back down the west coast via the Outer Hebrides to Greenock.

outdoor holidays

For an outdoor activity holiday try Garry Gualach Country Holidays, Invergarry. In a relaxed family atmosphere, you can do a variety of things including pony-trekking, sailing and windsurfing, fishing and field sports. There are boys' and girls' dormitories, and two family rooms, and the rates are cheap. Holidays here are unique and never forgotten. Contact Jane Isaacson, ✆ 08092 230.

touring holidays

Touring holidays range from luxury transport and accommodation to spartan. Try Landrover Expeditions, ✆ 03552 30385, which gives a good selection of Scottish scenery and attractions and a choice of hotel, farmhouse and camping accommodation. Other tours include Scottish Heritage tours of castles and historic sites, Whisky Tours—where someone else drives you home—and scenic tours. There are also holidays for those who prefer a more cerebral break. English language courses, for example, with outdoor activities laid on, such as English Écosse, run by Fiona Wyllie, Arduaine, Oban, Argyll, ✆ 085 22227. Or, if you really want to stretch yourself, the College of Sabhal Mor Ostaig, in Skye, runs short courses in Gaelic and in piping at all levels, as well as courses in fiddle, clarsach, accordion, song and dance, ✆ 07414 373.

working holidays

There are 'working' opportunities, such as Farmhouse Holidays where you can help with anything from peat-cutting to cheese-making: try Hi Line House, ✆ 0349 63434. Or go on a conservation project, learning drystone walling, fencing, tree-planting and lots more, ✆ 0786 79697. For impoverished students, a fruit-picking holiday in Perthshire can be fun. With free accommodation and acres of strawberries and raspberries to pick, there are worse ways of making holiday money, ✆ 0250 3707.

Getting Around

By Air

British Airways and Loganair operate services around the mainland and out to the islands.

Loganair
Aberdeen Airport, ✆ 0224 723306
Glasgow Airport, Abbotsinch, ✆ 041 889 3181
Inverness Airport, ✆ 0463 62332
Kirkwall Airport, Orkney, ✆ 0856 3457
Lerwick Airport, Shetland, ✆ 059 584 246
Stornoway Airport, Lewis, ✆ 0851 3067

British Airways
Aberdeen Airport, ✆ 0224 722331
Edinburgh Airport, ✆ 031 333 1000
Glasgow Airport, Abbotsinch, ✆ 041 887 1111
Inverness Airport, ✆ 0463 232471
Wick Airport, ✆ 0955 2215

By Train

As well as the main inter-city routes, branch lines run through the very best of highland scenery. Trains run as far as Thurso and Wick via Inverness and Lairg, in the far northeast, and to Oban, Fort William, Mallaig and Kyle of Lochalsh in the west. Aberdeen–Inverness, Glasgow–Stranraer, Glasgow–Oban and Perth–Inverness are all very attractive journeys. The Kyle Line runs from Inverness across Scotland to Kyle of Lochalsh, a lovely stretch of country which links up with the five-minute ferry crossing to Skye. The famous West Highland Line from Glasgow to Fort William and on to Mallaig is worth doing just for the beauty of the journey, and the trains themselves—beautifully preserved locomotives and coaches. British Rail offer all sorts of excellent bargain tickets; check at any station.

By Bus

Buses serve most of Scotland. In very rural areas there is usually a 'postbus' service in the mail mini-bus—an experience often memorable for the social outing as much as for the transportation. Enquire locally or at tourist information centres.

By Car

Car hire firms operate from the airports and stations, and there are always local firms: the more rural, the better the bargain usually. Arnold Clark are very reasonable, from about £16 a day. You drive on the left in Scotland, as in the rest of the British Isles, and it is law in Britain for drivers and all passengers to wear seat belts. Road signs are similar to those in Europe. There is a mandatory speed limit of 70mph on all motorways. Parking in towns is usually restricted to parking meters and car parks. A single yellow line by the kerb means you can't park by day; a double yellow line, and zigzag lines by pedestrian crossings, mean no parking at any time.

Main roads are generally good, although many are not dual carriageways. In rural areas there are many single-track roads with passing bays. These should not be used for parking; they are also for slow cars to pull into, to allow faster ones to overtake. When touring in the far north, remember there are not many petrol stations and some close on Sundays.

Hitch-hiking

It is neither more nor less chancy to thumb a lift in Scotland than anywhere else. In populated areas, be extremely wary. In the islands, however, locals will invariably stop and offer a lift without being thumbed; it is part of their instinctive hospitality.

Ferries

Caledonian MacBrayne serve the west coast and the Western Isles. They publish a comprehensive brochure with details of schedules, prices and special offers, some of which change seasonally as well as annually. Write to Caledonian MacBrayne, The Ferry Terminal, Gourock PA19 1QP, ℰ 0475 33755. P&O serve Orkney and Shetland. For their comprehensive brochure, write to: PO Box 5, Jamieson's Quay, Aberdeen AB9 8DL, ℰ 0224 57 2615.

Practical A–Z

You can choose between *haute cuisine* that will satisfy any gourmet, good plain cooking at a reasonable price, and fast-food. In the cities, meals are served at fairly flexible hours, but in smaller places you should aim to have lunch between 12.30 and 2pm, and dinner between about 7 and 9pm. If you know you will be late it is wise to make arrangements in advance. 'High tea' is an alternative to dinner, usually served between 4.30 and 6.30pm, and is an extremely sustaining meal consisting of a main course (usually fried) followed by bread, cake, biscuits, etc., washed down by cups of tea—a very British meal. Some of the country's best restaurants are to be found tucked away in out-of-the-way places. These are mentioned in the relevant sections within this book.

national dishes

> *Fair fa' your honest, sonsie face,*
> *Great chieftain o'the puddin'-race!*
> *Aboon them a' ye tak your place,*
> *Painch, tripe, or thairm:*
> *Weel are ye wordy o' a grace,*
> *As lang's my arm.*

from 'Address to a Haggis', by Robert Burns

Scotland has an unmatched reputation for salmon, both fresh and smoked. The development of fish farming has increased the availability but it has to be said that 'wild' salmon is usually nicer than that which has been reared in a farm. Apart from the salmon, national dishes include trout, sea fish, shellfish, game, beef and lamb. Almost without exception you should go for these served simply in the traditional ways. Poached salmon with mayonnaise, new potatoes and cucumber; a freshly caught mackerel, fried so that its skin is crisp and curling, with wedges of lemon and watercress; an Aberdeen Angus fillet steak, medium-rare, an inch thick, with a green salad of lettuce, chives and a hint of garlic; well-hung roast grouse with game chips, fresh petit pois, fried breadcrumbs, bread sauce, and gravy. These will linger on the taste buds as well as in the memory long after any dish wrapped up in an exotic sauce and given a pretentious name.

Everyone should try haggis—if only once. It is made of the heart, liver and lungs of a sheep, mixed with suet, oatmeal and onion, highly seasoned and sewn into the sheep's stomach. Traditionally, it is eaten with 'bashed neeps' (mashed turnip; turnip, in Scotland, is what the English call swede) and washed down with neat whisky. Try black pudding, too: its unusual flavour is strangely addictive.

the celebrated haggis

Fair fa' your honest, sonsie face,
Great chieftain o' the pudden race!

Arbroath smokies are fresh haddock, dry salted and smoked in pairs; a delicate, mild flavour makes them particularly delicious and the best way to eat them is cold, with brown wholemeal bread and butter, a generous squeeze of lemon juice and plenty of freshly ground black pepper.

Porridge is no longer a national habit but you can always get it in hotels. The popular myth that Scotsmen eat their porridge with salt, standing up or walking about, is quickly disproved when you discover how many of them sit down and tuck into it heaped with sugar and cream and sometimes even black treacle. If you have to add salt, it has been badly cooked.

Scottish cheeses are worth pursuing. Crowdie is unique to Scotland, a creamed cottage cheese, made from skimmed milk. Dunlop cheese, originally made in an Ayrshire village of the same name, is now also made in Orkney, Arran and Islay. Caboc is a rich double-cream cheese rolled in pinhead oatmeal. Galic and Hramsa are both soft cream cheeses flavoured with wild garlic and herbs. Pentland and Lothian cheeses are like Camembert and Brie.

Oatcakes are unsweetened biscuits made with oatmeal. Brand-named oatcakes can be dull compared with delicious local and home-made varieties that crumble and melt in the mouth. Best eaten with cheese, honey or marmalade. Shortbread originated in Scotland and is known all over the world. You will find many local variations of the standard buttery biscuit: Yetholm Bannock, for instance, a very rich shortbread with crystallized ginger, to be found in the Borders. Dundee cake is a rich, dark fruit cake with split almonds on top, indispensable for cold, wet picnics.

Soups include cock-a-leekie, made with chicken and leeks; Scotch broth, made with mutton stock and barley; cullen skink—delicious—made with smoked haddock, and partan bree, made with crab.

Scotch pies are to be found all over the country; small round pies made of hot-water pastry filled with minced meat, eaten hot. Bridies are pies made with a round of pastry folded over, filled with meat, sometimes padded with potatoes and vegetables.

Cranachan, if properly made, is memorable; double cream, and sometimes crowdie, is mixed with toasted oatmeal, sweetened and eaten with fresh soft fruit, preferably raspberries—another of Scotland's specialities.

The Scottish Tourist Board brings out a *Taste of Scotland* booklet every year offering details of over 200 hotels and restaurants specializing in good Scottish cooking.

drink

Inspiring, bold John Barleycorn!
What dangers thou canst make us scorn!
Wi' tippenny, [ale] we fear nae evil;
Wi' usquabae, [whisky] we'll face the devil!

from 'Tam o' Shanter', by Robert Burns

Among the myths that need to be taken with a pinch of salt is the whisky myth. The average canny Scot will go for the two bottles of cut-price blended whisky that he can get for the price of one bottle of vintage malt. On the whole, except among the rich, malt whisky is kept for special occasions, bought as presents for other people—or exported. There are over a hundred malts and every connoisseur will swear to the unquestionable superiority of his particular fancy. However, experiments involving the transfer of a 'favourite' malt into a bottle with a rival label will often prove that it is the eye rather than the taste buds that dictate preference. Most of the distilleries are on Speyside, northeast of Aviemore, in the north, or on the islands of Islay and Jura and a large number of them run guided tours, complete with a free dram, showing the process of whisky making. The Malt Whisky Trail, on Speyside, is a 70-mile (110km) voyage of discovery, taking in eight distilleries. Guided tours last about an hour and you can get details from the tourist information centres.

Traditionally, malt whisky should be drunk neat or with a little water—any other additions spoil the flavour. No other country in the world has the essential ingredients for that unique taste that makes Scotland's whisky so special: a blend of snow melt, peaty water and carefully malted barley. A true Scotsman drinks whisky, or asks for 'a dram'; he will never ask for 'Scotch'—unless he is abroad and in danger of being served with a foreign imposter.

Drambuie is a whisky liqueur, very drinkable for those who enjoy 'stickies'. Gingermac or whisky-mac is a mixture of whisky and ginger wine which slips down easily on cold days.

Scotsmen prefer to drink seriously, in bars, though wine bars and English-type pubs are mushrooming in the towns. You may hear, in a true bar, someone ordering 'a pint of heavy and a chaser'. This will be a pint of bitter and a dram of whisky—the accepted way to spin out the precious *uisge-beatha*—the 'water of life'. Often the dram is not sipped and savoured, but tossed down in a single reviving gulp. In the old days, when the licensing laws were restrictive, there was no time for leisurely drinking. Now, licensing laws in Scotland permit public houses to stay open for 12 hours a day, or longer with special extensions, but not all of them choose to do so. Generally, a bar will be open from 11am to 2.30pm, and from 5pm to about 11pm, with reduced hours on Sunday. Most city centre bars will stay open till at least midnight and residents in licensed hotels can buy drinks at any time. Children under 18 may not be served drink in a public house or restaurant, nor may they be sold alcohol in a shop. Some establishments provide special family rooms where children can join their parents, but they must not drink alcohol here. Landlords risk losing their licences if they break the law in this respect.

Slàinte (pronounced slahn-tchuh) is Gaelic for 'health' and is often heard as a toast.

Historic Scotland

Historic Scotland is a division of the Scottish Office Environment Department, responsible for the care and upkeep of many of the country's historic ruins, buildings and sites. Some castles and historic houses open to the public are privately owned and each has its own opening times and admission charges. Wherever possible, this book gives an idea of opening dates but these change from year to year and should be checked in advance. There is an 'open to view' ticket which entitles you to free entrance to 563 places of historic interest: castles, abbeys, stately homes, famous gardens, etc., in Scotland, England, Wales and Northern Ireland. These can be bought from major tourist information centres. Many castles, historic houses and smaller museums close for the winter.

Doors Open Day is Scotland's contribution to 'Heritage Days'; two weekends every September when Europe's finest buildings are open free to the public. You can explore historic churches, towers, country houses, breweries, power stations and many more. Find out dates and details from local tourist information centres

Maps

Good maps are essential if you are to enjoy your holiday to the full. Bartholomew's half-inch maps are good but you need many of them and they are expensive. There is a very adequate *Ordnance Survey Motoring Atlas,* 3 miles: 1 inch (Scottish Highlands and Islands, 7 miles: 1 inch), available from most garages and bookshops. A 'tourist map' of the whole of Scotland, marking special attractions, is useful. Maps of each region are obtainable from the relevant tourist information centre. If you plan to walk or climb then you should get the appropriate Ordnance Survey sheets, scale 1:50000. One of the best places to get maps and travel books is Stanford's, 12–14 Long Acre, London WC2E 9LP, © 071 836 1321.

National Trust for Scotland

Many of Scotland's historic buildings and conserved land are under the care of the National Trust for Scotland (NTS), a charity formed in 1931 to promote the preservation of the country's heritage. Over a hundred properties, including castles, small houses, islands, mountains, coastline and gardens come under the protection of the NTS. Most are open from April to October, and admission charges vary. Annual membership admits one person free to all NTS properties, and to all National Trust properties in England, Wales and Northern Ireland. Write to the National Trust for Scotland Head Office, 5 Charlotte Square, Edinburgh EH2 4DU, © 031 226 5922.

Packing

Because of the unpredictability of the weather, sweaters and waterproof clothing are essential all year round if you are to enjoy the country to the full, as are comfortable, sturdy shoes. Remember Scotland is famous for its woollen industry so if you intend to buy Fair Isle, Shetland, Cashmere and tweed, pack the minimum. Rubber boots are useful but uncomfortable for walking long distances—they are cheap to buy locally if wet weather looks relentless. Go prepared for rain and cold; the chances are you will have hot sunshine and drought. Scottish waters are cold, but if the sun shines you might regret not bringing bathing things. Very summery clothes are seldom needed.

New Year's Day is the only statutory public holiday in Scotland. Bank Holidays are mainly for banks only and include: 2 January, the Friday before Easter, the first Monday and last Monday in May, the first Monday in August, 30 November (St Andrew's Day), 25 December (Christmas Day), and 26 December. Most towns and districts have local public trades' and other holidays which vary from place to place and from year to year. It is worth asking at one of the Area Tourist Board Information Centres for the annual leaflet, *Public Holidays in Scotland.*

Shopping

tweed and wool

As well as the tourist-traps, there are sheds and cottage parlours where weaving is still done on hand looms, mostly in the islands and parts of the highlands. They are invariably signposted from the road. Hardwearing Harris tweed is acclaimed all over the world: to be authentic it should be woven in the home of the crofter on a hand loom with Scottish wool (but not necessarily wool from Harris). Most of the textile mills in the Borders have their own shops selling knitwear, tweed, tartans, etc and some, like Pringles, have centres further north. Perhaps the most tempting of the first-class establishments is Campbells of Beauly, Inverness-shire.

glass and pottery

Some Scottish glass is beautiful. At Edinburgh Crystal in Penicuik and Caithness Glass in Perth, Oban and Wick, factory tours show all the processes of glass-blowing, moulding and engraving, and there are shops selling the finished products. Pottery can be found all over Scotland, often within the potter's workshop.

hoots memorabilia

Traditional accessories to Highland dress, set with cairngorms and amethysts, in wrought silver and gold, can be bought from most jewellers. Jewellery made from local stones can be found in workshops and craft shops throughout the country. With such a large deer population, both decorative and functional objects carved from horn are made all over Scotland. Take home a shepherd's crook, called a *crommach*, with a handle carved from ramshorn or, if your luggage isn't designed to take something of five feet or more in length, go for a horn salt spoon or drinking bowl.

food and drink

Try and squeeze a side of smoked salmon into your suitcase but make sure it is well wrapped. It isn't cheap: for good quality and the most reasonable price go to Clark Brothers, The Harbour, Musselburgh, © 031 665 6181. Buy shortbread, oatcakes and Dundee cake, in tins. They are a good reminder of a Scottish holiday. In the duty-free shop at the airport your choice lies between the malt whisky you have adopted as your 'special' (if in doubt, Glenmorangie won't let you down) and Drambuie, Scotland's whisky liqueur.

Sports and Activities

canoeing

This is possible all round the coast and on many of the rivers, where the fast flow is often ideal for 'white water' canoeing. There are many water-sport centres. The Scottish Sports Council, 1–3 St Colme Street, Edinburgh, © 031 225 8411, runs outdoor training centres where courses include canoeing.

climbing

Climbing in Scotland can be an energetic scramble, suitable for anyone who is reasonably fit and sensible, or skilled rock-climbing, which should only be undertaken by experts with proper equipment. There are more than 270 mountains over 3000ft (914m) high, nicknamed 'Munros' after Sir Hugh Munro, who collated these hilltops in his 'Munro's Tables'. It has become a popular sport to climb as many Munros as possible. The Cuillins, in Skye, have provided a testing training ground for some of the world's top mountaineers. From Glasgow and Edinburgh there are several high hills within easy reach by car for a day's outing. The Arrochar Alps, the peaks northwest of Loch Lomond, particularly the Cobbler, 2891ft (867m), are an example. The Trossachs are popular, as is Ben Vorlich, 3231ft (969m), near Lochearnhead. North of Loch Tay, Ben Lawers, with its exceptional alpine flowers, is another Munro at 3984ft (1195m), looked after by the National Trust for Scotland. Perthshire has a number of hills, including Schiehallion, 3554ft (1066m), near Loch Rannoch. The hills around Glen Lyon are also good and Glencoe has a variety of challenging peaks. Further north, Ben Nevis, 4406ft (1322m), is Scotland's highest mountain, with several routes up including a well-marked tourist route. There are a number of other high hills in Lochaber. To the northwest, the highest peaks of the Grampians are truly arctic in the winter, but splendid for experienced climbers. The eastern edge of the Grampians, around Glen Clova, and the Lochnagar area, accessible from Deeside, are also popular. North of the Great Glen, Torridon, in the west, offers spectacular rock scenery, equalled only by the peaks of the Inverpolly Nature Reserve north of Ullapool, including the distinctive Stac Polly, 2009ft (603m), Canisp, 2779ft (834m) and Guilven, 2399ft (720m). Ben Hope, southwest of Tongue, is Scotland's most northerly Munro, at 3042ft (913m).

The following advice may seem nannyish and bossy to those accustomed to hill-climbing, but there are a great many idiots whose ignorance has put the lives of mountain rescue teams at risk. However settled and fine the weather may look, there are certain precautions that should always be taken if you are going any distance off the road. Bear in mind that the weather changes rapidly in the hills and that other lives can be lost if you get into difficulties and have to be rescued. Always tell someone where you are going, what time you are leaving and what time you expect to return. Display a note in your parked car with this information. Consult someone local about your planned route and keep an eye on the weather. Carry a compass and a good map. Wear warm, waterproof clothing and suitable footwear. Wellington boots are not comfortable for long-distance walking and climbing.

curling

Scotland's traditional winter game is usually played on indoor rinks these days. It has been played in Scotland for over 450 years and is described as 'a sort of bowls on ice'. For information on where you can go to watch or participate contact the Scottish Sports Council, 1–3 St Colme Street, Edinburgh, © 031 225 8411.

diving

The wonderful clarity of the sea around the coast, full of highly coloured sea animals and plants, makes Scottish waters among the best in the world for diving. There is a wide choice of good places where you can dive. The four places listed here are outstanding. In the north there is Scapa, in Orkney. Four ships of the sunken German fleet, scuttled at the end of the First World War, lie untouched below the clear waters of this huge anchorage and offer marvellous scope for wreck diving. You can charter boats and get air from several places around the coast. On the east coast, St Abbs Head is well known for its exceptional sub-aqua quality. This stretch of coast, down to Eyemouth, is good for beginners, being reasonably shallow with lovely marine life. The weather can be bad, so you must be prepared to hang around sometimes. On the west coast the waters around Oban are excellent, with a good air supply and boats to charter in Oban. The Sound of Mull is littered with wrecks, and there is sub-aqua cliff scenery. Ailsa Craig and the Firth of Clyde are also good diving sites. The Summer Isles, in the northwest, are also ideal for diving. For more information contact Scottish Sub-aqua Club, 16 Royal Crescent, Glasgow, © 041 332 9291.

fishing

Lord, suffer me to catch a fish,
So large that even I,
When talking of it afterwards,
May have no need to lie.

'A Fisherman's Prayer', Anon

In the first half of the 19th century southern fishermen began making the stagecoach trek to Scotland to ply for salmon with rod and line. The industrial revolution had begun to pollute England's great salmon rivers, and was to wipe the salmon out in many of them by the turn of the century. The Scottish lairds had been accustomed to sending forth their 'sealgairs' (hunters) to procure fish and game for them, frequently disdaining such activities themselves. They were amazed and delighted to be paid by these newcomers for the right to dangle their baits in the water.

Much has changed since Scotland made its name as the world's best fishing venue. The night-time revellers who hunted spawning salmon in their breeding places with lamps and pronged spears have been replaced by fishermen and women throwing out high-tech fishing lines with rods made of supremely light, flexible and strong new materials. Where once the huge bulk of Scottish salmon were caught by estuary nets, now salmon nets (challenged by the low price of farmed salmon) are becoming uneconomic; many have fallen into disuse, or been bought up and laid to rest by the rod angling fraternity. The silver king of the river is chiefly valuable as a game fish, and the value of fishing rentals to Scotland, apart from the benefits fishing brings to many sideline economies, is enormous. The capital value of salmon fishing in Scotland has been calculated at close to £1 billion. It is no exaggeration to say that in the valleys of some of the great rivers like the Spey and Tay, the way of life is chiefly determined by the fishery. Fishing hotels and lodges occupy strategic positions above the precious waters, and ghillies' and water bailiffs' houses are never far from the fish that sustains their livelihood. In many villages on rivers the focal point is the tackle shop, trading not only in fishing paraphernalia, but also in gossip about pools in which fish have been caught and the flies that have caught them. The news of big hauls is particularly influential with trout fishermen, and round any little loch in which someone has struck lucky large concentrations of anglers are to be observed days later, trying in vain to repeat an individual's one-off glory.

The joy of a river is that its course connects contrasting parts of the country. The sources of many of Scotland's great rivers are swampy spring-fed patches in hanging valleys high in the mountains, or even springs in the floors of lochs. Many Scottish rivers can be fished from the mountain burns near the headwaters right through to the wide sleepy stretches flowing through farmland nearer the coast. In some places fishermen use rod and line to spin for migratory fish in the sea off the river mouths, usually for seatrout. Seatrout are the members of the native brown trout family which choose to migrate to sea, but unlike the Atlantic salmon, which forage as far as the Greenland shelf to feed, seatrout winter offshore, generally returning in spring and early summer. In seeking enjoyment from duping fish many methods have been devised to balance the challenge of a catch with applications of physical dexterity and manual skill. Fishing is an outwitting art, and man delights in playing the deceiver.

Salmon fishing in Scotland is classically associated with the wet fly, a contraption of feathers and other titbits which need bear no resemblance to any known insect or creature, but for certain well-tested reasons rouses fishes' aggressive urge. On the bigger rivers spinning is practised in slow, wide pools; but fly fishing is in the ascendancy, and spinning increasingly frowned on. The ancient practice of worming, which is suited to the tails of deepening pools where the worms twirl enticingly in the current, is discouraged even more.

Dapping is a technique developed for catching seatrout and brown trout in windy conditions on lochs. By deploying a loose silky cord from a pole-like rod the fly can be made to dance over the surface like an insect blown from land and trying unsuccessfully to rise. Nymph fishing employs a wingless body in imitation of the fly at larval stage. When a trout takes a nymph it is capitalizing on the momentary opportunity offered by a fly as it rises from the river-bed prior to hatching on the surface. Dry fly, like nymph, is imitative, and although in most Scottish salmon rivers the water is too cold for dry fly to be successful, trout fishermen use it productively on warm evenings on the lochs, when the puffed-up wings of the dry fly keep it popped up on the surface.

The water surface to all fishermen is a hypnotic thing, always moving, always changing with the shifting light in the sky. Cunliffe Pearce has written evocatively of 'the top of the water, that magic looking-glass through which trout and man mysteriously make acquaintance with each other'. In Scotland there is the extra factor of supreme scenery. The Highland lochs—Loch Lomond, Loch Awe—are famed for beauty, yet also loved in a different way by the connoisseurs for the fishing they offer. Some of the far north rivers—Helmsdale, Brora, Naver, Dionard—open out through heather moorland, and become faster as they drop through rocky passages before entering the sea. The outer isles have magnificent salmon and seatrout fishing, and it is on the magical Grimersta, where running fish can stream by in a seemingly endless flow, that the British record catch by one man in a day was recorded—52 salmon. Some of the most exciting trout lochs are those gem-like bodies of water in the far north, famous for being dour and unco-operative in one mood, then exploding into action the next. A hundred fish in a day to two rods is not unimaginable.

Scottish rivers come in all styles and sizes. The Tay and Tweed fishermen waddle to the bank in chest-waders, bearing aloft 18-foot rods capable of throwing 45 yards of line, to brave the heavy waters. If the width of the river completely defeats them, ghillies row the boat to the most productive lies. Alternatively there are the restricted lies of smaller, more intimate and secretive rivers, like the Stinchar in the southwest, or the Laxford in the northwest. Fishermen speak with bated breath and condign respect of these illustrious names; rivers more remarkable in their great catches for the small water the fish have come out of.

Scottish salmon fishing is not, as is sometimes said, the preserve of rich tenants on famous water. There are thousands of miles of fishing in Scotland, and many opportunities for those who seek them out. The game fishing magazines, *Trout and Salmon* and *Salmon Trout and Seatrout*, advertise plenty of rentable fishing, and once embarked on the salmon fishing circuit, chances spring up for keen fishermen through contacts made along the way. Some local councils own water, and many rivers are open to day-ticket fishermen either through angling associations, fishing hotels, local river boards, or private riparian owners. Salmon fishing permits start at around £10 per day. Trout fishing is available in greater supply than is ever utilized, particularly in the far north and west of Scotland, and some of the famous fishing hotels have access to numerous remote lochs which never see a fisherman year-round. A boat on a loch costs around £10 a day, bank fishing around £8. Tourist information centres circulate fishing information, and details of self-catering accommodation which is accompanied by trout fishing. The more expensive salmon fishing possibilities are marketed through the main sporting agencies, and often sold in exclusive packages based in neighbouring fishing lodges.

The salmon fishing season varies from river to river; starting from January in some places and as late as March in others. Trout fishing is from 15 March to 6 October. Sea fishing is extensive, with such a length of coastline. Porbeagle shark, halibut, cod, bass, hake, ling, skate and turbot are but a few of the many species of fish you can expect to find. There is never a shortage of charter boats or, in most places, of experienced locals to take you out. There is no closed season: weather and availability are the only limitations. Again, ask at your hotel, or in the tourist information centre.

Useful Addresses for Fishermen

Central Scotland Anglers Association, 53 Fernieside Crescent, Edinburgh, ✆ 031 664 4685.

Scottish Anglers National Association, 307 West George Street, Glasgow, ✆ 041 221 7206.

Scottish Federation for Coarse Angling, TighnaFleurs, Hill o' Gryfe Road, Bridge of Weir, Renfrewshire, ✆ 0505 612580.

The Scottish Federation of Sea Anglers, 18 Ainslie Place, Edinburgh, ✆ 031 225 7611.

Scottish Sports Council, 1–3 St Colme Street, Edinburgh, ✆ 031 225 8411.

gliding

Gliding is possible in some areas and most clubs offer temporary membership and instruction. Consult the Scottish Sports Council, 1–3 St Colme Street, Edinburgh, ✆ 031 225 8411.

golf

The origins of the game of golf are lost in the mists of time. Some say golf, or a form of it, was first played in Holland; but no one denies that the Scots nurtured the peculiar habit of knocking along a pebble with an old stick and are mainly seen as the founding fathers of the game we know today.

Fortunately the best terrain for golf is usually land of little use for agricultural purposes. So it is that many of the oldest courses evolved along the sea-shore on salt-laden land reclaimed from the sea; in other words, links. Golf on this sort of terrain is almost unique to the British Isles and traditionally our major championships, including the Open, are played on links courses and the majority of them in Scotland. That said, there are some pretty spectacular inland courses as well.

The Borders and Lothian

The rolling countryside between Edinburgh and the border is not to the forefront of Scotland's golfing heritage, but there are one or two gems, none more so than **Hawick** where the views from the higher parts of the course are breathtaking. **Minto** and **St Boswells** are two others worth taking in should you be in the vicinity.

Lothian positively teems with courses and East Lothian in particular contains some of the finest links courses to be found anywhere. Furthest to the east is **Dunbar**, not as widely known as some of the more famous championship venues, but the 14 holes that run along the sea-shore are on a par with the best. While at Dunbar, and if looking to play 9 holes after tea, pop inland to **Gifford** and sample one of the least-known delights in this part of the world. Moving north and east to **North Berwick,** a collector's item for any acquisitive golfer is West Links, probably little changed from when it came into being in 1832. Shots over ancient walls and across bays confirm that courses, then, materialized rather than were designed, and at least two of the holes here have been copied elsewhere .

Five miles closer to Edinburgh lies **Muirfield**, the home of the **Honourable Company of Edinburgh Golfers** and for many the best seaside course of all. The Open Championship has been coming here regularly since the course was founded towards the end of the last century. For those wishing to play, a letter to the secretary beforehand is a must, preferably endorsed by the applicant's own club secretary. Muirfield lies on the eastern edge of the town of Gullane, which has three courses of its own. **Gullane No 1** is a fine test and, like North Berwick, is used as one of the qualifying courses when the Open is at Muirfield. **Nos 2 and 3** get progressively shorter and easier, but all are a stiff test when the wind blows. Alongside the three Gullane courses lies **Luffness New**. Not as visually striking as the Gullanes and Muirfield and flatter, it is nevertheless quite a test and is more exposed to the wind, such an important element of seaside golf.

The courses round Gullane are the cream of those situated on the southern shores of the Firth of Forth. Closer to Edinburgh, this seam of golfing country continues unabated with **Kilspindie** and **Longniddry** upholding the area's reputation almost to the city boundary. Just when you might think that nothing more of importance could exist in the urban fringes, you will come upon Musselborough Race Course. The original links at **Musselborough** was on the site of the race course and the 9 holes still exist. The second home of the Honourable Company (the first being in Leith), Musselborough was one of the early venues for the Open until Muirfield was developed in the late 1800s. Two other clubs which shared the Musselborough Links with the Honourable Company, have established courses of their own in Edinburgh. The **Bruntsfield Links Golf Society** and **The Royal Burgess Golfing Society** have adjacent parkland courses in the western suburbs of the city, and a joy to play they are too. To the west of Edinburgh are a number of mostly parkland courses and undoubtedly the best is **Dalmahoy**. The scene of several national and international tournaments, Dalmahoy has 36 holes and is the centre of a fine new hotel and leisure complex.

Fife and Tayside

Across the Firth of Forth from Gullane lies Fife, as blessed as East Lothian both in the quality and the quantity of its golf courses. If golf did start in Scotland, then it probably began somewhere along the shores of Fife or Tayside.

St Andrews is the golfing capital of the world. It is from their clubhouse overlooking the first and last holes of the Old Course that the **Royal & Ancient Golf Club** look after the customs of the game and mastermind the world's premier golf event, the Open Championship.

The **Old Course** is unique. There are huge double greens; the 17th, the Road Hole, is probably the most famous hole in golf; and the massive shared fairway of the opening and closing holes is seemingly in the middle of the 'Old Grey Toun'. The other courses of St Andrews, the **Jubilee**, the **Eden** and the **New**, lie deep in the shadow of their famous sister, but are all well worth a game.

A few miles to the south are a number of fine links courses, some whose origins go back over 200 years. The nearest is the **Crail Golfing Society** who play over the Balcomie Links, a course built over sloping terrain and looking out over the Firth of Forth towards North Berwick. On round the corner, and perhaps best known after St Andrews, lies **Elie** where the members of the **Golf House Club** play. No par 5s and only two par 3s make this a tough course to score on, but once again the knowledgeable golfer can only marvel at the way holes have been conjured out of the sandy humps and hollows left by the departing sea. Further west still and you come to the links of **Lundin** and **Leven**. Lundin is the more links-like in character and, to be honest, more fun. Also Lundin is good enough to be one of the final qualifying courses when the Open is at St Andrews. To the north and over looking the Firth of Tay towards Dundee, **Scotscraig** is another course good enough to have helped sort out those anxious to play in the Open proper.

The inland courses of Fife should not be ignored and amongst the likes of **Glenrothes** and **Dunfermline**, **Ladybank** stands out as a course that has evolved from its 6-hole inception in 1879 into a first-class heathland course. Across the Tay, **Carnoustie** is to Tayside what the Old at St Andrews is to Fife. On the Open Championship rota until 1975, when lack of sufficient good hotel accommodation caused its removal, Carnoustie is one of the toughest championship layouts of them all. There are five more links course within the proverbial 'drive and pitch' of Carnoustie, with the longer **Monifieth** and **Panmure** being the pick of the bunch.

Further up the coast, **Montrose** is a must. One of the oldest of the lot, the current layout is largely unchanged since the middle of the last century. Of inland character, the **Downfield Club** at Dundee is a fine, relatively modern course and is a most pleasant change from the staple diet of links golf. To the north, **Forfar** has an excellent 18 holes, not very long, but full of interest. While on the subject of inland courses, it is vital to take a swift drive to the west and visit the glorious rolling hills of **Perthshire**. **Rosemount** at Blairgowrie is ranked amongst the most beautiful courses in the world, set amongst heather and pine. Another in a stunning setting is **Pitlochry** and while not very long, its hill-top situation gives panoramic views.

The monarch in these parts is **Gleneagles**, in the lee of the Ochils. The **Kings** and the **Queens** are as fine a pair of courses as you will come across in a day's march, and the combination of great golf and good living is hard to beat, if you can afford it.

The Highlands

Golf in the Highlands is concentrated around the east coast. Aberdeen boasts 11 courses of which **Royal Aberdeen** and **Murcar** stand out, both classic links and right next door to one another. **Cruden Bay** is a splendid seaside course and, were it a little longer and more accessible, could be a great test for a full blown professional tournament. From **Fraserburgh**, the fanatic could have a fortnight of golf before he got to Inverness, without ever playing the same course twice. While Fraserburgh is a pure links and great fun, Banff sports a couple of titled courses in **Royal Tarlair** and **Duff House Royal**. Neither are really links courses but should not be bypassed if the itinerant golfer is taking his time about sampling all the delights of Highland golf.

In Morayshire, **Moray (Lossiemouth)** and **Forres**, both next to the sea, are the pick, together with **Elgin** some 12 miles (19km) inland. Still moving west, at **Nairn** there is a highly regarded links course, which on more than one occasion has played host to the Scottish Championships. **Boat of Garten**, in the Spey Valley, is a relatively short course, but a joy to play. James Braid designed it, and there are superb views—making it a must!.

North of Inverness, **Fortrose and Rosemarkie**, **Muir of Ord** and **Strathpeffer Spa** all offer a pleasant 18 holes, but **Tain** is the choice if time is short. A new bridge at Tain has cut an hour from the journey north to **Royal Dornoch** and made this magnificent links more accessible. But for its location, Dornoch would be the choice for the most important championships and indeed the Amateur Championships were played there for the first time in 1985.

Carrying on through **Wick** to **Thurso** and **Reay** will enable the collector to say he has played the most northern courses on the British mainland. As for the islands, **Orkney**, **Shetland**, **Skye** and **Lewis** have courses well worth playing.

Strathclyde, Dumfries and Galloway

In the west, the Ayrshire coast is as blessed as Fife and East Lothian both in terms of quality and quantity. Once again, standards are measured in terms of the Open Championship. The top of the heap are those that host the Open, followed by the courses that are used for the final qualifying rounds. This great golfing stretch begins just south of the town of Irvine with **Western Gailes** and **Glasgow Gailes**. Of the two, Western Gailes just has the edge, perched as it is on a narrow strip of land between the Glasgow to Ayr railway line and the sea. Glasgow Gailes is flatter, but both have served with distinction in the qualifying stages when the Open is held at Troon. Immediately south is **Barassie**, also a 'qualifier' but perhaps a little gentler than the Gailes courses. Barassie is just north of Troon, a town ringed with courses. **Royal Troon** is the Championship course and typical of many old links courses in that it runs straight out and back along the sea-shore, with the 9th at the farthest point. Flattish at start and finish, the best holes are through the dunes around the turn. It also has the distinction of having the longest and shortest holes in British Championship golf, the 6th measuring nearly 600 yards (550m) and the 8th, the 'Postage Stamp', just 126 yards (116m).

Prestwick is neither on the Open Championship rota nor is it used in the qualifying events. It no longer has the space to cope with the paraphernalia of big tournaments and has anyway done its share as the venue for the first dozen Opens when it all started in the mid-19th century. However, it remains one of the pearls of Scotland's golfing heritage and should be the first choice of any golfer visiting these parts. Right from the start along the railway line, you can see these holes being played over the centuries with gutty ball and hickory shaft. The final four holes should be preserved behind glass in a museum. **Prestwick St Nicholas,** but for its more famous sister, would be the choice course in this town. Some 20 miles (32km) south of Ayr, the splendidly isolated **Turnberry Hotel** looks out over the **Ailsa** and **Arran** courses—very much a Gleneagles-by-the-sea. Indeed, both Turnberry and Gleneagles were the creation and, for most of their lives, the property of the railway companies. The Ailsa is the senior course and takes its name from the rock standing proud out in the bay.

Golf on the islands should not be ignored. **Arran** has seven courses of which **Blackwaterfoot, Lamlash** and **Brodick** are the pick. Then there is **Machrihanish** on the **Mull of Kintyre** and the **Machrie** on **Islay**. Islay has just the one course and eight distilleries, so care is needed with your priorities if the golf is to be enjoyed.

Back up the coast from Irvine, **Greenock**, **Gourock** and **Largs** are all fine courses and the sheer volume of courses close to Glasgow almost defy selection. If pressed, **Haggs Castle** and **Pollock** would be two not to miss.

Dumfries and Galloway is not thought of as being somewhere to go in pursuit of golf, but along the northern shores of the Solway Firth there are some gems. **Portpatrick**, a little fishing port, has a stunning golf course. Long it is not, but with the west winds constantly blowing, it is a test for the very best; that is if they can avoid being distracted by the views. A few miles east, next to Port William, is **St Medan**, just nine holes, but a must. Finally, and almost due south of the town of Dumfries, lies **Southernes**, perhaps the best seaside course of the lot. Only opened since the war, it is a true mixture of links and heathland, with heather and gorse standing alongside wispy grass-covered dunes.

Scotland has more to offer the golfer than perhaps any other country on earth. Most of the courses are not too difficult to get on, but the more famous they are, the more crowded they are likely to be in season. Any golfing trip should be carefully planned, with letters to the secretaries of clubs you intend to visit. This way starting times will be guaranteed and caddies, if required, may be booked in advance. The *Golfers Handbook* is invaluable for addresses. One other piece of advice. Plan to eat at the clubhouses you visit. There are no better places to sample the best of local Scottish fare at reasonable prices and in an atmosphere almost untouched by time. Good golfing! I wish I was coming with you.

Golfing Holidays

A number of tourist organizations organize specialist holidays. The Scottish Tourist Board, 23 Ravelston Terrace, Edinburgh, © 031 332 2433, will send full details.

leisure centres

All over Scotland centres offer facilities for squash, tennis, badminton, bowls, table tennis, ice hockey, aerobic dancing, judo, karate, skating, etc.

ornithology

For a number of reasons, including terrain, climate and vast tracts of land both unpopulated and remote, Scotland's birdlife is unsurpassed. Some regions harbour birds so rare many people have never even heard of them. There are dozens of nature reserves and bird sanctuaries all over the country. Fair Isle, staging post on a number of migratory routes, is probably the best place for serious ornithologists. For details, write to Fair Isle Lodge and Bird Observatory, Fair Isle, ✆ 03512 258. Other ornithological information is available from RSPB Scottish Office, 17 Regent Terrace, Edinburgh, ✆ 031 556 5624.

pony trekking

This is a pleasant way of seeing the country and you don't have to be an experienced rider. There are lots of pony-trekking centres, offering a choice of day trekking or trekking and camping. The local tourist information centres will give you addresses: most tourist maps mark them with a horseshoe. The Scottish Tourist Board publishes a leaflet called *Pony Trekking and Riding Centres in Scotland.*

shinty or shinny

Scotland's version of Irish hurling is said to derive from cries used in the game: shin ye, shin t'ye. It's like hockey, with a leather ball and curved sticks.

shooting and stalking

The terrain is ideal, with farmland, mixed woodland and moorland, and Scotland has a long tradition of good game management. The estuaries and marshes provide excellent scope for wildfowlers, and there are plenty of deer. Stalking, for the uninitiated, involves spending all day wriggling through wet undergrowth until your prey is within range and then, at a signal from the keeper, missing it, or wounding it and spending the night following it to administer the *coup de grâce*. Stalking with a camera instead of a rifle can be infinitely more rewarding. Game-shooting species include pheasants, snipe, grey partridge, woodcock, grouse, capercaillie and ptarmigan. Permitted wildfowl species include many varieties of duck and geese. Rough shooting is for wood pigeon, rabbit and hare. Deer species include red deer, roe, fallow and sika. All other species of wildlife, both bird and mammal, are strictly protected in Scotland by the Wildlife and Countryside Act. No game shooting is allowed on Sundays and a certificate is required by anyone owning or using either a rifle or a shotgun. Before you shoot game you must get a game licence, which is available in all main and branch post offices throughout the country. Some hotels will arrange shooting and stalking and local tourist boards will advise on contacting estates and on shooting seasons.

Resorts, with groomed runs and lift networks, are developing rapidly but first-timers should note that picture-postcard conditions are less common in Scotland than in the Alps. At times only the more experienced skier will enjoy this sport, when the slopes are icy, balding and pitted with rocks, visibility is nil and a piercing wind invades even the most thermal of clothing. The main centres are at Cairngorm, Glencoe, Glenshee and the Lecht, with cross-country as well as downhill skiing. The Scottish Tourist Board booklet, *Ski Holidays in Scotland*, gives details of the many skiing packages on offer and you can book in London, at 19 Cockspur Street, London SW1Y 5BL, ✆ 071 930 8661. There are dry-ski slopes at Hillend, in the Pentlands, just outside Edinburgh—the largest in Britain— Aviemore, Glasgow, Aberdeen, Bearsden, Cairnwell and Polmont.

surfing

Surfing in Scotland hardly conjures up images of Hawaiian shores and hot weather, but the north of Scotland can lay claim to some of the best surfing waves in Europe. In fact, the European Amateur Surfing Championships were held in Thurso in 1981. Any exposed part of Scotland's long coastline has the potential for excellent waves; but the northern-most section, from Bettyhill almost to John O'Groats, has a reputation for the most consistent swells and variety of breaks. There are waves to suit everyone, from gentle beachbreaks to massive reefs, point breaks and river mouths. This is wild-frontier surfing against stunning back-drops of mountains and castles.

The water is a slightly off-putting brown, but don't be alarmed because it's only coloured by peat washed down from the hills. There are very few local surfers but those there are are really friendly.

walking

There are coastal footpaths, nature trails, woodland trails, city strolls and long-distance footpaths. Long-distance footpaths include the **West Highland Way**, which runs for 95 miles (150km) from Milngavie on the outskirts of Glasgow to Fort William on the south end of the Great Glen. It includes a marvellous range of lowland and highland scenery, on the old drove roads, forestry tracks, an old military road and a railway track bed.

The **Speyside Way** runs for 30 miles (48km), from Tugnet to Ballindalloch, then a further 15 miles (24km) to Tomintoul, with splendid and very varied scenery along the route.

The **Southern Upland Way** runs from Portpatrick in Dumfries and Galloway, east to Cockburnspath in the Border Region, and is 212 miles (340km) long. It is signposted and well marked all the way and there are leaflets to make it more interesting. Ski lifts for walkers are available at Cairngorm, Glencoe and Glenshee. These chair-lifts are open for hill walkers in the non-skiing season only and give easy access to the higher terrain.

Scotland: Walks and Trails, gives details of a selection of walks which need no special equipment and are suitable for children. *Scotland: Hillwalking* gives details of over 60 more difficult, higher level walks. Both can be obtained from Scottish Holidays, Telelink, 56 Belhaven Road, Wishaw M12 7BN. The Wayfarers, Brayton, Asputria, Cumbria CA5 3PT, © 06973 22383 (or 172 Bellevue Avenue, Newport, RI 02840, US, © 401 849 5087), organize excellent walking holidays in Mull and Iona, and in the Borders. Everything is laid on for you, luggage is moved forward everyday, the accommodation is excellent, and the walks are well planned.

water sports

Water sports are available all over the country, including sailing, windsurfing, waterskiing and swimming. Coastal resorts invariably have sailing clubs where you can get tuition and hire boats and equipment. There are a large number of inland water sport centres on the lochs. For full details get the *Scotland Holiday Afloat* booklet from the Scottish Tourist Board or © 0382 21555 or 0577 62816.

Tourist Offices

For tourism purposes, Scotland is divided into regions covered by **Area Tourist Boards**; each has its own **Tourist Information Centre** and publishes its own free brochure with local information and a fully comprehensive accommodation guide. Readers are strongly advised to use these brochures to supplement the recommendations made in this book. Information centres will also advise on routes, sporting permits and local events, and will book accommodation.

The Scottish Tourist Board's Scottish Travel Centre, 19 Cockspur Street, London SW1 5BL, © 071 930 8661 (open Mon–Fri throughout the year) provides a full range of information, advice and literature. They also help with route planning, and have a travel agency where you can make reservations for accommodation and book for events such as the Edinburgh Military Tattoo.

Also in London is the **British Travel Centre**, 12 Regent Street, Piccadilly Circus, W1, © 071 730 3400 (open daily, no telephone service on Sundays). Here, the British Tourist Authority, British Rail, American Express and Roomcentre combine to provide a comprehensive booking service covering rail, air and sea travel, sightseeing tours, theatre tickets and accommodation. They also change currency.

For drivers using the M6 route north, **Southwaite Tourist Information Centre**, in the Southwaite Service Station, a few minutes south of the border near Carlisle, offers full information on all areas in Scotland, and accommodation services.

The main Tourist Information Centre for the whole of Scotland is **Edinburgh Marketing** in Waverley Market, 3 Princes Street, Edinburgh (open daily, except Sundays, Oct–May, personal callers only). Run in partnership with American Express and Europcar, they offer advice to tourists in all areas, accommodation and travel booking, route planning, a Scottish bookshop, currency exchange and car hire. The head administrative office of the Scottish Tourist Board is at 23 Ravelston Terrace, Edinburgh, EH4 3EU, © 031 332 2433.

Tracing your Ancestors

For many reasons, not least the Highland Clearances in the 17th and 18th centuries, a large number of exiled Scots, and descendants of exiled Scots, return to the land of their origins hoping to trace their family history. Write to the Keeper of the Records of Scotland, Scottish Record Office, Her Majesty's General Register House, Princes Street, Edinburgh EH1 3YY, ✆ 031 557 1022. Send all the information you have on your ancestors. Many clans have their own clan historian/library and will give advice. Alternatively, try a good researcher. Probably the best to set your feet on the right path is Census Searches, The Lady Teviot, The Knoll, Stockcroft Road, Balcombe, West Sussex RH17 6NG, ✆ 044 4811 654.

Where to Stay

The choice of accommodation in Scotland is enormous, ranging from (a few) superb, luxury hotels to simple bed and breakfasts, or self-catering. The price is not always a reliable guide. The accommodation guides in the local brochures give full details of price and facilities. This book gives only a very small selection and tourists should always try and get one of these publications for each area they want to visit.

As little as £10 a night can buy bed and breakfast in a clean house, with a warm welcome and a thumping good breakfast. £120 can buy a night in a four-poster bed or £150 a suite with a jacuzzi. You can rent a whole house or cottage from as little as £60 a week to over £600. Prices often vary seasonally: single rooms are usually more expensive, per head, than double. You can get good value in a hotel for as little as £15 a night in some areas.

A static caravan costs from £40 a week upwards, and campsites charge from about £3 a night for visiting caravans. Campsite facilities vary enormously. Some are good, others not, but often the scenery makes up for primitive plumbing. The one at Braemar is excellent.

Many bed and breakfast places serve an evening meal and all hotels provide full service. In the more rural areas, and indeed in the towns, don't be put off by the lack of en suite bathrooms in the smaller hotels. What they lack in modern facilities is invariably made up for in the friendly hospitality of the staff. Very often 'public bathroom' means sole use of a bathroom across the passage.

Prices

Prices change frequently. In this guide accommodation is loosely graded into three categories, based on the price of bed and breakfast for one person in a single room—double rooms are almost always cheaper per person—as charged in 1994. Many hotels do special bargain breaks, so it is well worth enquiring about these.

expensive:

You won't see much change from £60 at the bottom end of this range, and the ceiling is out of sight.

moderate:

From about £30–50 should buy you a comfortable night.

inexpensive:

As little as £10 a night, if you are lucky, up to about £30 and some of the cheapest are often surprisingly good.

Scottish Tourist Board accommodation gradings

An impartial team of inspectors visits hotels, guest houses, bed and breakfast, and self-catering establishments, to assess their quality. They award classifications ranging from 'Listed' to five crowns, and gradings from 'Approved' to 'Highly Commended', depending on the standard and facilities. Full details can be obtained from the Scottish Tourist Board, 23 Ravelston Terrace, Edinburgh EH4 3EU, © 031 332 2433. Visitors should be aware that these awards are based on a set range of standards and facilities such as: TV, shoe-cleaning kit, full-length mirror, trouser press, luggage stand, hospitality tray, etc. , as well as the more obvious requirements such as heating and towels. They do not apply to character and soul. It is therefore possible to opt for a Highly Commended, five-crown hotel only to find yourself in a sweltering, double-glazed bedroom crammed with gadgets and electric goodies, totally lacking in atmosphere. Equally, an old fashioned, slightly shabby ex-shooting lodge, as full of highland character and hospitality as you could ever wish for, with blazing log fires instead of central heating, pure cotton sheets, early-morning tea brought to you, and delicious home cooking, may be excluded from the Scottish Tourist Board's list because of its lack of tangible 'facilities'.

As well as the individual publications you can get free from area tourist centres, the Scottish Tourist Board publish a number of useful brochures covering the whole country, with details of accommodation, sports, special holidays, etc.

youth hostels

There are 80 youth hostels in Scotland, marked on most maps by a triangle. They fall into three grades, A, B and C, some having central heating, hot showers, carpets, etc., and all offering dormitory accommodation and self-catering facilities. Anyone over the age of five may use a youth hostel. The one on Loch Lomond is very high class and so is Carbisdale Castle, near Bonar Bridge. For full details, you can write to SYHA, 7 Glebe Crescent, Stirling FK8 2JA, © 0786 72821.

History

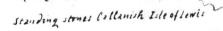

Standing stones Callanish Isle of Lewis

Scotland, wild and fiercely independent, was always a thorn in England's flesh. No one wants hostile neighbours and inevitably Scotland's history has been a continual struggle to remain independent. The Romans tried to occupy it for a few years, found it invincible and slunk away. The English spent centuries trying to annex it until eventually they had to accept a Scottish king on their throne. Intrepid younger sons, black sheep, political exiles and the dispossessed sailed from Scotland to leave their mark on the world.

John Logie Baird invented television; Alexander Bell invented the telephone; Alexander Fleming discovered penicillin; James Watt invented the steam engine. James Clerk Maxwell, the Scottish physicist, demonstrated the existence of radio waves in 1873, before Marconi pioneered their use for communication; Lord Reith of Stonehaven greatly influenced the early development of the BBC and was its first general manager. John Paul Jones founded the American Navy. David Hume, the 18th-century philosopher and historian, has influenced thought up to the 20th century. Patrick Gordon was a general to Tsar Peter the Great; James Keith was a field-marshal to Frederick the Great. 'Adam' is a household word used to describe the style of architecture designed by brothers Robert and James Adam. Thomas Telford's bridges, roads and canals, Robert Stevenson's lighthouses, Carnegie's benevolent institutions, are all renowned. Gladstone, Ramsay MacDonald, Harold Macmillan and Alec Douglas-Home each served as prime minister of Britain. Eleven of America's presidents were of Scottish descent, as were 25 of the 73 Americans honoured in their Hall of Fame, a third of their secretaries of state and half their secretaries to the treasury. John McDouall Stuart was the first man to cross Australia, through the central desert, in 1866; John Macarthur laid the foundations of Australia's agricultural system; Lachlan MacQuarie was responsible for turning the penal colony of Botany Bay into Sydney. These are but a few of the Scots who spread their talents across the world.

Prehistory

The Ice Age eradicated evidence of any previous habitation in Scotland. **Stone Age** settlers, at least 7000 years ago, were the first to leave clues to their existence. Burial sites and middens (rubbish heaps) from those times have thrown up enough to tantalize archaeologists, but not enough to leave more than a shadow of the identity of those nomadic tribes. They came from Asia and Europe, through England and Ireland, wave after wave of them, creeping up the coast in dug-out canoes, settling for long enough to leave traces of their culture and way of life, before vanishing into obscurity. They lived off deer and wild boar, fish and crustaceans. Some only stayed a short time, living in caves. An excavated house in Grampian dates from 7000 BC, a round stone building about 25 feet (8m) across. Later, farmers came from the Continent and introduced agriculture. People settled for longer periods, burning forests and enriching the land with potash.

After the hunters and gatherers came the **Beaker People**, who laid beakers in the tombs of their dead. They were skilful engineers and historians puzzle over their mysterious stone circles and monoliths, and over the true purpose of their brochs (massive stone towers built near the sea in the far north, about 2000 years ago). Metal was introduced about a thousand years before Christ, and with it the sword and shield. Scotland, on the trade route between Ireland and Scandinavia, was able to barter food and hides for bronze and copper. During this millennium the Celtic-speaking Britons arrived, a sturdy, fair-haired race, combative and quick to attack in order to acquire precious land. The local people built defensive forts, with ditches and ramparts, such as the ones on Berry Hill and Finavon, and skirmishing became part of life.

The Romans: AD 82–4th century

The Romans arrived in AD 82 and with them came the first record of Scottish history, written by the historian **Tacitus**. Tacitus describes how his father-in-law, **Agricola**, defeated an army of tall, red-haired men on an unidentified hillside in the northeast, in the **Battle of Mons Graupius**. The exact location of this battle is debatable, but it was some-where in today's Grampian, so called from a misprint of 'Graupius' by a 16th-century chronicler. Roman remains were found as far north as the Moray Firth and Tacitus recorded that they 'discovered and subdued' Orkney.

The Romans called their victims *picti*, the painted ones, from which the name 'Picts' is thought to derive, and failed to subdue them. Highly trained legionnaires could not compete with hostile tribes who faded into the mountains, forests and marshes, refusing to fight army-to-army, preferring to lay cunning ambushes for their aggressors. The Romans fell back having, it has long been believed, lost the entire Ninth Legion in a savage massacre. In fact, evidence of their having been merely posted elsewhere was unearthed recently when traces of their later existence were found around the Danube.

In 121 **Hadrian** built a wall between the Solway and the Tyne, hoping to contain the barbarians in the north, but the wall was so frequently attacked that another was constructed between the Forth and the Clyde in 141–2—the **Antonine Wall**. This proved to be no more effective and was soon abandoned. Exasperated, the Romans with-drew to Hadrian's Wall. In 208, **Emperor Severus** sailed into the Firth of Forth and laid waste Fife and the land around the Tay. In spite of the devastation he caused, the barbar-ians refused to be conquered. The old emperor died, the Romans withdrew again and an uneasy peace existed between the north and south until the middle of the 4th century. The Picts then resumed their ferocious attacks while Saxons began to invade from the northeast. The Roman Empire was in decline: more and more legions were being recalled to fight nearer home. By the end of the 4th century the Romans abandoned Scotland completely, leaving the untamed Picts to defend themselves against new invaders. They not only failed to subdue their foes, but also failed to impose any of their sophisticated culture on them. The only evidence of their occupation is a few straight roads, a number of forts and the remains of the Antonine Wall.

The Coming of Christianity: 397–7th century

Four races dominated Scotland, then called Alba, or Alban. The **Celtic Picts** were the most powerful, occupying the land from Caithness to the Forth; the **Teutonic Angles**, or **Anglo-Saxons**, occupied Bernicia, south of the Forth; the **Britons**, another Celtic race, occupied the western lands south of the Clyde. Finally there were the **Scots**: Celts who had come over from Ireland during the 3rd and 4th centuries and settled north of the Clyde, establishing the **Kingdom of Dalriada** and eventually giving their name to all Scotland. **St Ninian** founded the first Christian centre at Whithorn, near the Solway Firth, in 397, and started the daunting task of converting the pagans. Then came **Columba**, a clever man of royal birth, who was exiled from Ireland and arrived in Scotland in 563. He established himself on the island of Iona, continuing St Ninian's work, and sent missionaries to the mainland and to the other islands. They penetrated further and further into Pictland. Columba's influence was political as well as religious and he did much to consolidate the strength of the Scots.

For those who believe there is some historic truth in the Arthurian legends, King Arthur led his army north at some time in the 5th or 6th century and had a crack at the Picts and Scots. That intrepid romancer, Geoffrey of Monmouth, in his *History of the Kings of Britain* describes the **Battle of Loch Lomond** in graphic detail. The loch, with its islands, streams and crags, and its eagles who foretold 'any prodigious event which was about to occur in the kingdom by a shrill-pitched scream emitted in concert', provided sanctuary for the barbarians. They fled to the islands where Arthur besieged them for 15 days until he had reduced them to such a state of famine that they died in their thousands. The Irish arrived with a fleet and a 'huge horde of pagans' to help the Scots, but Arthur cut them to pieces mercilessly and forced them to return home. He then continued to massacre the barbarians until they 'fell on their knees and besought him to have mercy'. The king was moved to tears and pardoned them. True or false, it is stirring stuff and well worth a read.

By the end of the 7th century the four kingdoms of Alban were nominally converted to Christianity—a Celtic Christianity, not yet in line with that dictated by Rome.

Norse Invasion: 8th century

At the end of the 8th century Norsemen began to attack from the north, conquering Orkney and Shetland, the Western Isles, Caithness and Sutherland, while the four kingdoms continued to fight amongst themselves, weakening their resistance to outside attack.

The Birth of Scotland: 843–1034

In 843 **Kenneth Macalpine**, King of the Scots, achieved some sort of union between Scots and Picts, making himself king over all the territory north of the Forth and Clyde, which then became Scotia. The Picts, who had been dominant for more than 1000 years, vanished for ever. They remain an enigmatic people whose history is unrecorded and unknown; an elusive ghost-race who will perhaps never be fully understood. It was not until 1018, however, that **Malcolm II** defeated the Angles and brought Bernicia, or Lothian, into the kingdom. He was succeeded in 1034 by his grandson **Duncan I** who already ruled the Britons, and so the four kingdoms were finally united into one Scotland, except for those parts occupied by the Norsemen. The country was divided into seven main kingdoms, of which Fife was the strongest, plus a few smaller ones, each ruled by a *mormaer*. The *Ard Righ* or High King was their overlord—King of the Scots, but not of Scotland, for each *mormaer* owned his land (see 'Stone of Destiny', 'Topics'). In those days, under a remarkable clan system in which no one was subservient and each played an important part, Scotland was truly democratic.

The Norman Influence: 11th century

Duncan I was killed in 1040 by **Macbeth**, the last Celtic king. Shakespeare portrayed Macbeth as a weak man, but in fact he ruled for 17 years and his reign was chronicled as a time of plenty. He was killed by Duncan's son, **Malcolm Canmore**, with the help of the English, in 1057. *Ceann Mor* is Gaelic for big head, referring to Malcolm III's status rather than any anatomical defect, or conceit.

It was Malcolm Canmore's second wife, **Margaret**, who made his 36-year reign memorable. She was an English princess, sister of Edgar Atheling—Edward the Confessor's heir, usurped by William the Conqueror. She and her brother had taken refuge in Scotland after the Norman Conquest in 1066. Margaret, who was extremely pious and later canonized, set about anglicizing the Celtic church. She brought in English clergy and established an English court, and it was her influence that civilized Scotland and transformed it into a kingdom similar to Norman England. It was now that the Lowland clans gave up their democracy: *mormaers* became earls and established a feudal system, while the Highlands and Islands retained the old, patriarchal clans.

Inspired by the presence in his court of his English brother-in-law, Malcolm coveted the English throne. He made several border raids into Northumberland and Cumbria, forcing William the Conqueror to invade Scotland to subdue him. In order to prevent the subsequent destruction of Scotland, Malcolm was then forced to pay homage to William at Abernethy in 1071. He continued to harass the English until he was treacherously killed while laying siege to Alnwick Castle in 1093. Queen Margaret, already mortally ill, survived him by only three days. She died thanking God for her grief, believing that it purified her soul.

David I: 1124–53

David I, ninth son of Malcolm Canmore, inherited the throne in 1124 from a succession of unremarkable monarchs and ruled for nearly 30 years, bringing many beneficial changes to Scotland. He had been brought up in England and most of his friends were Norman. His wife was a Norman heiress: his sister, Maud, was married to King Henry I of England. He gave large Scottish estates to his Anglo-Norman friends among whom were the ancestors of the Balliols, Robert the Bruce and the Stewarts. The old Celtic families merged with

French-speaking incomers, establishing families in the Lowlands and the northeast, whose names are common throughout Scotland today: Frasers, Maxwells, Gordons, Crichtons and many more. The Highlanders retained their traditional clan system and took little notice of these southern interlopers.

David led an army against England in 1138. Although the outcome of the **Battle of the Standard** was inconclusive, subsequent negotiation won him Northumberland and Cumbria. He encouraged Flemish weavers to settle along the east coast, granting them special privileges, rights and monopolies. These ancestors of the Flemings and the Taylors introduced new fabrics and taught new skills, and their foreign ways were absorbed by their new neighbours.

David had little time for vows of poverty: he founded a number of lavish cathedrals, churches and monasteries, including the Border abbeys, importing religious communities from Europe and urging the monks to establish commercial interests to the glory of God. He granted royal charters to towns, permitting markets and fairs; he tried to establish a national judiciary; he encouraged foreign trade and selected a body of advisers from his court to help him. He died in 1153, heartbroken from the death of his son and heir the year before.

The Treaty of Falaise: 1174

Malcolm IV was 13 when he inherited the throne from his grandfather David I. Known as Malcolm the Maiden, he was nevertheless a brave young man, whose courage inspired many of his followers. Gentle and religious, he ruled for only 12 years before he died, to be succeeded by his brother, **William the Lion**. William was ambitious and ruthless in his desire to recover parts of his kingdom annexed by England. An ill-conceived expedition into Northumberland in 1174 failed and William was taken prisoner. He was sent to Normandy, where he was forced to sign the humiliating **Treaty of Falaise**. This placed Scotland under feudal subjection to England. Fifteen years later, when the English king Richard Coeur de Lion needed money for a Crusade, he agreed to annul the Treaty of Falaise in return for 10,000 marks.

The End of the Norse Occupation: 13th century

England and Scotland were at peace, then, for over 100 years. **Alexander II** succeeded to the throne in 1214, and directed his attention to the Western Isles, whose lords gave their allegiance to Norway. It was his son, **Alexander III**, however, who managed to expel the Norsemen from the Hebrides. He did this by defeating old **King Haakon IV** of Norway in the **Battle of Largs** in 1263. The Hebrides became part of the Kingdom of Scotland again, though the Lords of the Isles paid little heed to any authority but their own.

Alexander continued to enrich Scotland, emulating his great-great-grandfather, David I. He married the English Princess Margaret, daughter of Henry III. Their daughter, also Margaret, married King Eric of Norway and thus links were forged with both countries.

Alexander had a long and successful reign. He outlived his first wife and three children and married again, desperate for an heir. He was, however, killed six months later, in 1286, when thrown from his horse, leaving his grand-daughter **Margaret of Norway** to succeed him, under the regency of John Balliol. Balliol was a powerful Norman-Scot whose wife, Devorguilla, founded Balliol College in Oxford.

The Auld Alliance: 1295

Edward I of England, determined to unite Scotland to England, immediately proposed a marriage between his son Edward and the 8-year-old **Maid of Norway**. The little queen died of seasickness on her way to Scotland, and Edward declared himself to be overlord of Scotland. There were several claimants to the throne, the strongest being **John Balliol**, son of the regent, and **Robert the Bruce**. Both were Anglo-Norman nobles with estates in England and Scotland, given to their ancestors by David I. They were descended from David's youngest son and had both fought in Edward's army. In 1292 Edward gave the crown to John Balliol in Berwick Castle, believing him to be more easily manipulated than Robert the Bruce. He ordered Balliol to pay homage to the English throne and accept himself as Scotland's overlord. He also insisted that Scotland should contribute to English defence costs and join with them in an invasion of France. Rather than do this the Scots instead formed an alliance with France in October 1295. The **Auld Alliance**, as it became known, was between two independent kingdoms, rather than being forced by a stronger state on a weaker one, as England had sought to do to Scotland. Edward saw it as practically a declaration of war.

In 1296, Edward's army laid waste to the town of Berwick, slaughtering almost every male inhabitant. The Scots army that advanced against him was heavily defeated at Dunbar and King John was captured a few months later. He was humiliated by Edward at Montrose Castle, being ritually stripped of his royal trappings. This episode earned King John the epithet 'Toom Tabard', or 'Empty Coat'. Edward, 'The Hammer of the Scots', progressed through Scotland, compelling nobles and lairds to sign the **Ragman Roll** acknowledging him to be their king. He then returned to England, taking with him what he thought to be the Stone of Destiny, brought from Ireland seven centuries earlier and believed to embody special powers of sovereignty. It had always been used in the coronation of Scottish kings (see Topics). Edward was convinced he had finally conquered Scotland.

William Wallace: 1274(?)–1305

William Wallace was a young Scot from the southwest, outlawed in 1297 for killing the Sheriff of Lanark in revenge for the murder of his wife. In exile Wallace became the leader of a fast-expanding resistance movement against English repression. In September 1297 he defeated the English at the **Battle of Stirling Bridge**, kindling new hope in Scottish hearts, and paving the way to freedom. Wallace was made Guardian of the Realm, but

the following year he was defeated by Edward at the battle of Falkirk and had to go into hiding. Wallace evaded capture for seven unhappy years before he was betrayed. He was paraded through the streets of London, tried on a series of trumped-up charges and condemned to death. It was a particularly vicious execution. He was hanged, drawn and emasculated, his entrails being burnt before his eyes as he died. Quarters of his body and his head were displayed throughout Britain.

Robert the Bruce: 1306–1329

Robert the Bruce, grandson of John Balliol's rival, replaced Wallace as Guardian of Scotland, alongside Balliol's nephew, **Red John Comyn**. Bruce resigned the guardianship in 1302 and went over to Edward's side. In 1306 Bruce and Red Comyn met at Greyfriars Kirk, in Dumfries. They quarrelled and Bruce killed Comyn, possibly because of his refusal to help Bruce in a campaign for the Scottish throne. Bruce was excommunicated for this sacrilege and hounded by the powerful Comyns. Seizing the initiative, he went to Scone and had himself crowned King of Scotland in March 1306.

Edward hurried north and defeated Bruce, a month later, at Methven. Outlawed, his friends and allies dead, Bruce went into hiding. During this time of exile, probably on the island of Rathlin, off the Irish coast, he encountered the legendary spider, whose persistence enabled it to swing from one rafter to another on its frail homespun web. If the spider could succeed, then so could he.

Bruce returned to Scotland in 1307, overcame all other claimants to the throne and defeated Edward I's successor Edward II, at **Bannockburn** in 1314. Excommunicated by the Pope, Bruce's sovereignty was not recognized by Europe. In 1320 his Council decided to send a petition to the Pope, asking him to tell Edward to lay off Scotland and acknowledge Bruce as the rightful king. Bernard, Abbot of Arbroath, who was Chancellor, composed a defiant letter to the Pope which was signed by eight earls and 38 barons. This passionate plea for freedom from English harassment, emphasizing the ancient Celtic line of the Scots and playing down the Anglo-Norman blood that had infiltrated their veins, states, 'For as long as one hundred of us shall remain alive, we shall never under any conditions submit to the domination of the English. It is not for glory or riches or honours that we fight, but only for liberty, which no good man will consent to lose but with his life'. The Pope was sufficiently impressed by the spirit of the appeal and advised Edward to leave Scotland alone.

On the day of Edward III's coronation in 1327, the Scots launched a raid into England and Edward was almost captured by the Scots when he led a retaliatory expedition the following year. A peace treaty was concluded in 1328 in which Scotland's independence was acknowledged. Bruce's four-year-old son, David, was married to Joan, Edward III's seven-year-old sister. Bruce died at Cardross Castle on the Clyde in 1329 following a long illness. It is said he always wore a hair shirt in penance for his act of sacrilege.

Struggle for Power: 1331–71

Bruce was succeeded by his young son, **David II**, with **Thomas Randolph, Earl of Moray**, as regent. The 42 years of David's reign were troubled times for Scotland. Encouraged by Edward III of England, who declared the peace treaty void, the Scottish nobles who had been disinherited earlier by Bruce for backing the English, tried to put Toom Tabard's son, **Edward Balliol**, on the throne. Moray was killed, as was his cousin the Earl of Mar, who succeeded him as regent, and Balliol was crowned King of Scotland, at Scone, in 1332. David was sent to France for safety with his child-wife Joan. By 1337, Andrew Murray, Guardian of David's kingdom, had practically driven out Balliol's supporters. David and Joan returned to Scotland in 1341 and made a series of raids into England. He was captured by the English at the **Battle of Neville's Cross**, in 1346, however, and spent the next 11 years in England as a captive. Following his ransom and release in 1357, David was offered easier terms for the ransom's repayment if he would name Edward III or one of his sons as his successor. Not surprisingly, the Scottish parliament rejected this notion. David reigned until his death in 1371, to be succeeded by his steward, Robert.

The Stewarts: 14th–15th century

The Stewarts took their name from their hereditary position as stewards to the kings of Scotland. Robert, the first Stewart king, was better as regent than monarch. Anarchy, rebellion and internal squabbles disturbed the peace he strove for. Border raiding was rife, causing continual devastation in the south, and the whole country seethed in a turmoil of lawlessness. Robert II died in 1390 and was succeeded by his son, **Robert III**. Crippled by a kick from a horse, Robert was in poor health and much of the responsibility of government passed to his brother, the **Duke of Albany**, as Guardian of the realm. In 1399 Albany gave way to Robert's son, **David, Duke of Rothesay**, but three years later had him arrested and imprisoned. Within two months Rothesay was dead and Albany once again took over. The ailing Robert III sent his son and heir, **James I**, to France in 1406, fearing Albany had plans to remove him from the succession, but the young prince was captured by pirates and handed over to the English. Too shocked to go on living, Robert died a month later, leaving Albany in full power for 18 years while James was held hostage. Powerful nobles seized the opportunity to consolidate their strength. They expanded their estates and built up private armies, many of them becoming as powerful as kings. Most notable among them was the **Douglas** family, whose lands and subjects rivalled those of the king. Meanwhile, in the northwest, the Lords of the Isles allied themselves with the English and continued to live their own lives with little regard for central government.

Anarchy: James I, 1406–37

James I returned to his throne in 1424, aged 29, with an English bride, Joan Beaufort, cousin of Henry VI. Reared and educated in England, he had a good grounding in statesmanship and in military strategy. He found his country in turmoil. His nobles were too powerful, and anarchy, poverty and lawlessness were rampant. His first step was the execution of the Albany family in 1425 and the seizure of their considerable estates. In 1427 he summoned the Highland chiefs and arrested 40: Alexander of the Isles retaliated by burning Inverness. Further rebellion from the west was subdued and James redressed the balance of power in the Lowlands by annexing many of the earldoms that had threatened his supremacy.

James achieved much for Scotland, restoring order and introducing a number of reforms. Inevitably, his decisive methods won him enemies and in 1437 three of them stabbed him to death, leaving his six-year-old son **James II** as his heir.

The Douglases: 15th century

Scotland was once again ruled by regency, and once again the nobles, in particular the Douglas family, became too powerful. In 1440, Sir William Crichton, who had custody of the young king, invited the 14-year-old Earl of Douglas and his younger brother to dine with the eight-year-old King at Edinburgh Castle. This became known as the **'Black Dinner'**—the two Douglas youths were seized and summarily executed. For a while, the Douglas family was subdued.

James II came to his throne in 1449 at the age of 19. He continued the reforms so dear to his father, but was threatened by an alliance between the Douglases, Crawfords and John of the Isles. The King summoned the Earl of Douglas to Stirling Castle and stabbed him to death. With English help the Douglases attempted revenge and James defeated them at the **Battle of Arkinholm**, killing three of the murdered earl's four brothers. The power of the Douglas family, known as the Black Douglases, was squashed. James was killed in 1460 when a cannon exploded during the siege of Roxburghe.

James III: 1460–88

James III was nine when his father died so Scotland was once more ruled by regents, until his accession at the age of 19. He married the King of Norway's daughter, whose dowry included Orkney and Shetland. James was an intellectual, better fitted for academic life than a crown. He antagonized his nobles, who rose against him. They hanged his favourites and imprisoned him in Edinburgh Castle. James survived this attempt to dethrone him but six years later his son led a successful coup against him, becoming James IV in his place. James III was killed in mysterious circumstances at the decisive battle of Sauchieburn, a parliamentary inquiry recording simply that the King 'happinit to be slane'.

James IV: Renaissance, 1488–1513

James IV, most popular of the Stewart kings, was 15 when he came to the throne. He was clever and charming, a good leader, pious and energetic, generous, flamboyant and sensual. His mistresses bore him a number of bastards. His reign brought the Renaissance to Scotland: the arts and education blossomed and James led the way. He authorized the building of palaces and churches. His court was elegant and cultured and the country was peaceful and prosperous. But the peace was not absolute: on the doorstep the Lords of the Isles continued to live as they always had, fiercely patriarchal, their loyalties rooted in their clans and chieftains. James, who had learnt Gaelic, decided to visit the Western Highlands and Islands, hoping to win the friendship of the clans. His attempts were viewed with suspicion, so he desisted and appointed overlords to rule them. This resulted in an uprising of the Macdonalds and Macleans who stormed and burned Inverness in 1503.

In that same year James married 12-year-old Margaret Tudor and signed a Treaty of Perpetual Peace with England. But in 1511, his brother- in-law, Henry VIII of England, joined the Pope, the King of Spain and the Doge of Venice in a Holy League against France. James passionately desired a united Europe. Determined to maintain a balance of power, therefore, he renewed the Auld Alliance with France and tried, in vain, to mediate. In 1513, threatened from all directions, France appealed to Scotland for help. James in turn appealed to Henry, who replied with insults.

Against advice, in August 1513, James led a Scottish army across the Tweed, to **Flodden Field**, where they were massacred by the superior forces of the English. The king, his nobles and most of Scotland's best men were killed in a battle as pointless as it was valiant: it was perhaps Scotland's greatest tragedy. The country was left leaderless, its army slain, its new king **James V**, a toddler and its regent, Margaret Tudor, with divided loyalties.

James V: 1513–42

There followed a period of more turmoil until the king was old enough to take office and try to restore order. Ignoring several offers of brides, he chose French Madeleine, who only lived two months after their marriage. The following year he took a second French wife, **Marie de Guise-Lorraine**, who bore him two sons, both of whom died. James was an ingenuous man. He liked to disguise himself as a commoner and mingle with his subjects, posing as the Guidman of Ballangeich, fooling no one but himself, and getting into several unfortunate escapades. He squabbled with the English, aggravated his nobles, and tried to invade England. His pathetic, mutinous army, quarrelling amongst itself, was defeated by Henry VIII's army at **Solway Moss** in 1542. Sick and despairing, James returned to Falkland Palace to hear that his wife had just given birth to a daughter. The news was too much for him and he died, leaving as his heir Mary, Queen of Scots, only a few days old.

Mary, Queen of Scots: 1542–67 (*d. 1587*)

Henry VIII, determined to absorb Scotland, proposed a marriage between Mary and his delicate son, Edward. A marriage treaty was arranged by the Governor of the Realm, the Earl of Arran, but the Scottish parliament rejected such a treaty with England and renewed instead the Auld Alliance with France. Furious to be thus snubbed, Henry began what Sir Walter Scott later named the **Rough Wooing**. He devastated the south of Scotland and earned the bitter hatred of the Scots. Mary, aged five, was sent to France for safety, where she stayed for 15 years, marrying the French Dauphin.

While she was away, learning French ways, Protestantism was gaining power in Scotland. In 1554, Marie de Guise-Lorraine replaced Arran as Regent. The presence of a great many French officials in the Regent's government greatly upset a number of the Scottish nobility. Several of them, calling themselves 'The Lords of the Congregation', declared their support for the Protestant religion. Fear of French domination increased when Mary's husband became King Francis II of France on his father's death. In 1559, with the support of much of the nobility, **John Knox**, a powerful Reformer, delivered a fiery sermon in Perth, denouncing the Church of Rome. A series of armed conflicts between the Lords of the Congregation and Mary de Guise-Lorraine's French and Scottish forces ensued, which led to her being deposed. In 1560, the Regent died, after an illness, in Edinburgh Castle and shortly afterwards the Treaty of Edinburgh was concluded between England and France, bringing about the removal of all foreign troops from Scotland.

Mary's French husband died at the end of 1560 and she returned to her country as queen in 1561—no longer Mary Stewart, but Mary Stuart, the French form of her name which was adopted in England. French in education and attitude, a devout Catholic, high-spirited, passionate, sensual and beautiful, she had the best intentions. She had no desire to tangle with the Protestants. She was not a bigot; she merely wished to be allowed to practise her own religion in peace. This horrified John Knox and his followers, who found her light-hearted ways obnoxious.

In 1565, she married her cousin, **Henry Stewart, Lord Darnley**, a dissipated Catholic youth, four years her junior, and mistrusted by all. Within a year, when Mary was six months pregnant, Darnley became jealous of her Italian secretary, Rizzio, and helped to murder him, in Mary's presence. She never forgave him. When he himself was murdered, in 1567, some hinted that Mary may have known of the plot.

Eight weeks later, Mary married **James Hepburn, Earl of Bothwell**, a buccaneering Protestant of great charm and little honour. Bothwell had been heavily implicated in the murder of Darnley and this ill-advised marriage sparked off an inferno of protest from both Catholics and Protestants. Mary was imprisoned and Bothwell forced into exile. Humiliated, Mary was forced to abdicate in favour of her baby son, **James VI**. Her half-brother, **James Stewart, Earl of Moray**, bastard son of James V, was proclaimed Regent.

Mary escaped from her imprisonment the following year, 1568, and Scotland was torn by civil war for the next five years as her supporters fought the Reformers. Mary fled to England and threw herself on the mercy of her cousin, Elizabeth I. But they never met. Elizabeth, without an heir, could not forget Mary's claims to the English throne. Mary was imprisoned for 20 years, and then beheaded.

James VI/I: 1567–1625

After another spell of regency, James proclaimed himself king in 1585 and found himself to be head of a country divided between Catholics and Protestants. He aspired to impartiality, incurring the animosity of both factions. A Protestant in name, if not belief, James had no wish to antagonize his Protestant cousin Elizabeth of England and spoil his chances of inheriting her throne. He concluded an alliance with England and made no more than a formal protest when Elizabeth agreed to the execution of his mother in 1587.

The Protestant religion in Scotland now presented problems. It was divided between the extreme Presbyterians, who wanted a religion of the purest simplicity with equality of ministers and no bishops or elaborate ritual, and James' English form of Protestantism, with bishops appointed by the Crown and a formal liturgy. He tried to impose his will on the Kirk, but failed. Presbyterians grew more and more averse to Episcopacy and their religion became less and less formal, with extempore prayers replacing those in the prayer book.

In 1603, Elizabeth I died, appointing James her heir. Thus, he became James VI of Scotland and I of England. He hurried to London and only returned to Scotland once, preferring the magnificence of the English court, and the ritual of the Church of England. But he still tried to foist Episcopacy on his northern subjects and reinstate formal worship. He died in 1625 and his son, **Charles I**, succeeded him.

The Last of the Stewarts: 1625–88

Charles, reared in England, a devout Anglican and Episcopalian, had no love for the Kirk. When he went north for his Scottish coronation, his subjects were scandalized by the 'Popish' practices he brought with him. He authorized the revision of the English prayer book in an attempt to produce one for Scotland that might replace extempore prayer. This produced violent opposition, riots and protest. Important men rebelled against the enforcement of the use of the new prayer book. Thousands flocked to Greyfriars Kirk in Edinburgh in February 1638 to sign the **National Covenant**, condemning all Catholic doctrines and upholding the 'True Religion'. Copies of the Covenant were carried all over the Lowlands and signed amidst strong national feeling. The Covenant, however, was somewhat ambivalent: its signatories swore, not only to uphold the True Religion, but also to be loyal to a king who demanded the Episcopacy they shunned. Thus, loyal subjects of the Crown found themselves torn between obedience to the king and obedience to their new religion.

When civil war broke out in England, the Covenanting Scots agreed to help the English Parliamentarians, on condition that Presbyterianism was adopted throughout England and

Ireland, as well as Scotland. In 1649, Charles I was defeated by Cromwell and executed. The Scots grasped this opportunity to advance their quest for stability and invited his exiled son, **Charles II**, to Scotland as king, on condition that he supported the Covenant. Furious, Cromwell invaded Scotland. Charles went back into exile and Cromwell ruled both countries until he died in 1658. The **Restoration** in 1660 brought Charles II back to the throne. He ignored the promises he had made, and sought to reintroduce Episcopacy. This rekindled the fervour of the Covenanters, who fled to the hills and worshipped in secret 'Conventicles'. In 1670, these conventicles were declared treasonable, and there followed the **Killing Times**, when thousands of Covenanters were slaughtered.

Charles II died of apoplexy in 1685 and was succeeded by his brother, **James VII/II**, Scotland's first Catholic sovereign for 120 years. During his brief reign, James tried unsuccessfully to introduce tolerance for all religions. He was deposed in 1688 by his Protestant daughter Mary and her Dutch husband, William of Orange. He fled to France and **William and Mary** were crowned King and Queen. Some Scots, mostly Highlanders, remained true to James. The **Jacobites**, as they were called, rose, under **Graham of Claverhouse** and almost annihilated William's army in a savage battle at **Killiecrankie** in 1689. But Claverhouse was killed, leaving them leaderless, and they lost heart and returned to their Highlands.

The Massacre of Glencoe: 1692

The government, uneasy about the rebellious Highlanders, issued a proclamation, ordering all clans to take an oath of allegiance to the Crown by the first day of 1692. Circumstances prevented **Alisdair MacIain of Clan Donald** from taking the oath until after the deadline. This provided the government with a chance to intimidate the Highland clans. A company of Campbell soldiers, commanded by a relation of MacIain's, **Captain Robert Campbell of Glenlyon**, billeted themselves on the MacDonalds in Glencoe. Under orders from higher authority, they rose at dawn and slaughtered their hosts. The barbarity of the Massacre of Glencoe produced public outcry, not so much because of the number killed—38 out of about 150—but because of the abuse of hospitality. The king denied all foreknowledge: as a gesture, he sacked his Secretary of State, the Master of Stair, who had instigated the deed.

The Union of Parliaments: 1707

Between 1698 and 1700 Scotland's economy was shattered by an unsuccessful attempt to colonize the Darien coast on the isthmus of Panama. The **Darien Scheme** failed as a result of deaths from fever and inhospitable natives, Spanish hostility and the withdrawal of English investment in what was seen as a rival to the East India Company. Scotland, bankrupt, and plunged into political crisis, was forced to accept the **Treaty of Union**, in 1707, uniting the parliaments of England and Scotland. This carefully worded document brought advantage to both countries: in particular, it gave Scotland a badly needed boost to her economy and the right to Presbyterianism, and removed the threat of further war between the two countries.

The Jacobite Rebellions: 1708–46

The signing of the Treaty of Union forced the Scots to accept a Hanoverian succession, but Jacobite loyalties still prevailed in the Highlands. **James Edward Stuart**, son of the deposed James VII/II, was regarded by many as Scotland's king. The Old Pretender, as he was called by the Hanoverians, made three unsuccessful attempts to regain his throne. (Pretender is from the French *prétendre*—to claim, not from the English word for make-believe.) His expedition from France in 1708 only got as far as the Firth of Forth. In 1715, the Earl of Mar, upset by his treatment at the hands of the Hanoverian George I, raised the Pretender's banner and proclaimed James king. The rising looked promising but following the inconclusive battle at **Sheriffmuir** support for it fell away. The Old Pretender put in a brief appearance in Scotland but soon returned to France. In 1719, a final attempt was made, backed by the Spanish; but the supporting fleet was lost in a storm and the Highlanders dispersed.

Stringent measures were taken to quell the clans. Between 1726 and 1737 **General Wade** built military roads and forts, opening up the Highlands and linking strategic strong points, at Fort William, Fort Augustus and Fort George. He raised a regiment of clansmen loyal to the Whig government, the **Black Watch**, whose duty was to keep order among the resentful clans.

George I was an unattractive German who disliked the British as much as they disliked him. When he died, his son, **George II**, equally Germanic and unsuitable to rule over Highlanders who still clung to their Jacobite dreams, gave them excuse enough. Exiled in Rome, the Old Pretender's son, **Prince Charles Edward Stuart**, was a brave young man with charisma and magnetism. He pawned his mother's rubies, set sail for Scotland and landed in Eriskay on 23 July 1745, determined to win the crown for his father.

At first his reception was daunting: Macdonald of Boisdale told him to go home. 'I am come home', he retorted. MacLeod, and Macdonald of Sleat, refused to help, but Macdonald of Clanranald stood by him. Cameron of Lochiel was reluctant to encourage what he believed to be romantic folly, but he was won over and on 19 August the standard was raised in **Glenfinnan** and the Old Pretender proclaimed King James VIII/III, with Prince Charles as his regent. Subsequent events are well known. The prince picked up support as he advanced on Edinburgh but his army probably never exceeded 8000 men. Capturing Perth on the way, he held glorious court at Holyrood, defeated General Cope's soldiers at **Prestonpans** (inspiring the song 'Hey Johnny Cope, are you wauking yet') and gathered enthusiastic support.

On 1 November Prince Charles led his motley army of 5000 men south, hoping to attract more Jacobites on the way, with the intention of taking London. Meeting little resistance, but picking up little support, they reached Derby, only 127 miles from their target, on 4 December. At this point Charles's prudent advisers insisted that to go further was madness. On 6 December he agreed reluctantly and the Highlanders turned round to march in an orderly retreat back to Scotland.

On 17 January 1746, the Jacobites won their last battle, defeating Cope's successor, General Hawley, at Falkirk. Hearing news of the advance of the Duke of Cumberland's army from England, the Prince took his army back into the Highlands, capturing Inverness on 21 February. On 16 April, Cumberland marched towards Inverness, his forces meeting the Jacobite army on Drummossie Moor, south of **Culloden**. Out-numbered and out-gunned, the Jacobites were soon defeated. Defeat turned into a rout in which Cumberland's men showed no mercy to their opponents.

The Prince escaped, with a price of £30,000 on his head, and spent the next five months in hiding in the Western Highlands and Islands. Aided by brave **Flora Macdonald**, he escaped eventually to Europe, where he lived in squalid exile for the rest of his life, dying in Rome in 1788.

The Aftermath of Culloden: 1746–1860

The English and the Lowland Scots were determined to squash the rebellious Highlanders for ever. They enforced the **Act of Proscription** in 1747, banning Highland dress and the bearing of arms. Jacobites who had not died at Culloden were either executed or transported. The old way of life was dead. The act was repealed in 1782, but by this time it was no longer relevant; the **Highland Clearances** had begun (see 'Topics'). Between 1780 and 1860, thousands of crofters were evicted from their homes in the Highlands and Islands to make way for sheep. Many others emigrated voluntarily, to escape persecution, to Canada, America, New Zealand and Australia. In the mid-19th century Ireland's potato famine reached the Highlands, resulting in appalling hardship and causing further emigration. By the end of the 19th century, the rural Highlands and Islands were almost deserted.

The Scottish Enlightenment: 18th–19th centuries

Meanwhile, the Lowland aristocracy drifted south, seduced by London, leaving room for a burgeoning middle class. Unfettered by the inhibitions of social mores, without the blinkered vision and moribund minds of a nobility which had grown complacent, a new intelligentsia emerged in a surge of genius to dazzle the world. Egalitarian social clubs became centres for debate and the free exchange of views. Philosophy and literature flourished. David Hume, Adam Smith and Thomas Carlyle were but a few of the great names that contributed to the Enlightenment. Sydney Smith, though not a Scot, taught in Edinburgh and helped to found the *Edinburgh Review*. The poet Allan Ramsay lived long enough to see the birth of the Enlightenment. Robert Burns was a product of the period, Sir Walter Scott was a leading influence. Others were: James Thomson the poet, Tobias Smollett the writer, James Boswell, biographer of Dr Johnson, James Watt the engineer who invented the steam engine. These remarkable men, and many more, achieved an astonishing record of success in all fields of human accomplishment. Scottish physicians, engineers and inventors led the world. The Enlightenment spanned about a century, from after Culloden until Queen Victoria discovered Scotland in the mid-19th century and herds of nobility stampeded north to smother the blasts of innovation with cosy convention.

A flourishing cotton industry collapsed in the 1860s when the American Civil War cut off supplies of raw cotton and heavy industry developed instead. Glasgow, once the biggest tobacco importer in Britain, led the world in shipbuilding. Expanding industries meant expanding labour forces; there were concentrations of population in industrial areas, fed by refugee Highlanders and Irish.

20th-century Scotland

Shipbuilding and engineering developed rapidly from the mid-19th century until, by the beginning of the 20th century, some 100,000 jobs were related to Clydeside shipbuilding alone. The Steel Company of Scotland, founded in 1871, replaced iron, and the entire economy of west and mid-Scotland depended on Glasgow's heavy industry. The First World War took its toll of Scottish manhood, but it needed a constant supply of arms and ships and machinery and there was more than enough work for those left behind. It was the Great Depression in the 1920s and 1930s that dealt Scotland a mortal blow. After the Wall Street Crash in 1929, the global wave of economic disaster washed over Clydeside and by 1936 the output from the shipyards had fallen from three quarters of a million tons to less than 60,000, with at least two-thirds of the workforce unemployed. In order to try to increase efficiency and generate more trade, firms merged and pruned their labour forces still further, resulting in more job losses. Not surprisingly, socialism flourished, passionately fuelled by leaders like James Maxton and Emmanuel Shinwell. Public opinion favoured the plight of the workers and by the end of the 1930s, things were beginning to look up. The Second World War brought with it a fresh demand for armaments and ships: Clydeside boomed and Scotland grew prosperous again. But after the war, competition from abroad began to steal trade. Instead of looking ahead and seeing the need to modernize and revitalize old methods, the Scots, led by militant unions, grumbled and groaned and went on strike, refusing to accept innovations which could have kept them in the forefront of the world's industry. Strikes led to failure to meet deadlines and buyers went elsewhere for their goods. Shipyards, steelworks and factories closed. Less coal was needed so coalmines closed. Sullen Scots queued for their dole cheques and blamed their employers. The oil boom in the 1970s brought new prosperity for a while but this was short-lived affluence.

A new generation of enterprising minds, particularly from Glasgow, is turning the tide of apathy. Diversification has spread a rash of light industry throughout the country and workers are more inclined to negotiate for rights than to cripple their livelihood with strikes. The Scottish education system is more democratic and more effective than that of England. When England had but two universities, Scotland had four. The legal system is also different: rooted in Roman and Germanic customary law, it is more logical than English law and is based on common law. Politically, Scotland leans to the left and juggles with nationalism. Those in favour of autonomy hold that they are the poor relations of politicians at Westminster, whose survival-of-the-fittest policies make no allowance for Scotland's circumstances. But when, in 1979, they were invited to vote for Devolution, over 36% didn't bother to vote and the Nationalists lost through the nation's apathy.

There were further stirrings of nationalist feeling prior to the General Election of 1992 when it seemed likely that the Conservative Party's 13-year grip on government would be loosened. The opposition parties were united in offering greater or lesser degrees of autonomy to the Scottish people but these promises came to nothing when the Conservatives, although winning a mere 11 of Scotland's 72 seats in Parliament, were once again returned to power in the south.

Genetically proud and independent by nature, Scotland bides its time. Who can say when the Stone of Destiny will be brought from its hiding place?

Topics

Climate

A popular postcard shows someone sitting in a deck chair under an umbrella in pouring rain, with the caption 'Having plenty of weather here in Scotland'. In fact, with a bit of luck, you can return from a holiday in Scotland with a tan not entirely inflicted by wind, and photographs showing idyllic blue skies and brilliant sunshine. Unpredictability is the main drawback and it is common to get wide contrasts in one place in one day. When the weather is good, there is no country better. When the weather is bad and people struggle against piercing winds and relentless rain and a damp chill pervades to the marrow, Siberia would be preferable. It is worth remembering that places in the north of the country have an average of 18 to 20 hours of daylight in the summer, and resorts on the east coast are noted for their hours of sunshine. In the far north, in the middle of the summer, it is never completely dark. In spite of the Gulf Stream, whose warm waters are alleged to lick the western shores of Scotland, the sea is gelid.

In general, the west is wettish, and mild enough in some coastal regions to support palm trees and tropical vegetation. The east is drier with a more bracing climate and colder winds. (Edinburgh has almost exactly the same rainfall as London and Rome.) Winter in the Highlands, when the precipitation is mainly snow, can be very beautiful, with clear skies and sun, though temperatures may seldom rise above freezing.

An unfortunate side-product of the moist, mild weather in the west is the 'midge', a particularly virulent breed of gnat unequalled in persistence anywhere else in the British Isles. Grown men have been reduced to gibbering wrecks under their vicious attacks. They are at their worst in warm, humid conditions; they hide when it is windy and sometimes, though not always, in very bright sunshine. Anyone contemplating camping or picnicking during the midge season should have lots of the strongest possible repellent. In truth, midges can completely ruin an outdoor holiday; even the natives retreat indoors when they are marauding. The only good thing about them is they won't follow a boat off-shore.

Religious Differences

In the Highlands and Islands, where communities tend to be slow to change, there are predominantly Catholic areas, where they rejected the Reformation and reconverted, while others, following the laird, became Protestant. On the whole, Catholics and Protestants live together perfectly happily with few of the sectarian problems experienced in Ireland. The football field proves an occasional exception, particularly when fans of the two Glasgow teams, traditionally Catholic Celtic and Protestant Rangers, meet. Sometimes, too, an innovation conflicts with the strict Sabbatarian beliefs and practices of a small proportion of Presbyterians, and invariably member of the media will manage to stir up an 'incident'.

In the Outer Hebrides, South Uist, Eriskay and Barra are almost entirely Catholic. In their belief God belongs to every day and Sunday is for celebration, both in church and out. North Uist, Harris and Lewis are Presbyterian and the most rigid Protestants in Britain. Their interpretation of the Fourth Commandment is stringently enforced by the Lord's Day Observance Society, who exert moral, social and political pressure. Sunday is for long sermons in church, full of the threat of damnation; for reading the Bible and holy tracts; for dark clothes and solemn faces. No work must be done, not even cooking; the washing must come in off the line; the fishing boats must lie at anchor and swings are padlocked.

Until recently, no ferries ran to the islands on Sundays. Then Caledonian MacBrayne announced a changed schedule including some Sunday sailings. The uproar was clamorous. There were huffings and puffings and threats of barricades. Running in tandem with this dispute, there was friction over a new £12 million school, built at tax-payers' expense, on the island of Benbecula, mid-way between the Catholic south and Protestant north and serving both. The predominantly Protestant Western Isles Council would not employ supervisory staff on Sundays, so no one could use the school's leisure facilities—swimming pool, cafeteria, games hall, library, etc. Catholics protested that their beliefs allowed them to have fun on Sundays and they saw no reason why Sabbatarian rules should prevent them from doing so. The situation was satisfactorily resolved in the end, but not without lasting damage to the hitherto dignified, *laissez-faire* attitudes that enabled such extreme creeds to live side by side in harmony.

The majority of Scots belong to the Established Church of Scotland, or Presbyterian Church and its many breakaway sects. The Episcopal Church, with its bishops, is the equivalent of the Church of England. The Free Presbyterian Church of Scotland (Wee Frees) is a tiny, fundamentalist sect who believe that the Pope is 'Antichrist' and the Mass . . . 'the most blasphemous form of religious worship that Satan ever invented; an offence unto God and destructive of the souls of men.' In 1989, Britain's Lord Chancellor, Lord Mackay of Clashfern, a member of this strict sect, was castigated by fellow members of his congregation because he attended requiem masses for two of his Catholic friends. The Free Church Synod suspended him from his position as a senior Elder of the Kirk, and from Communion. Lord Mackay, who once said his Church gave 'the most tender love that has ever been described', was forced to resign from it.

Clans and Tartans

The Scottish clan system was once an integral part of the Highlands and Islands. Every member of the clan bore the name of the chief, whether related by blood or by allegiance, and each was an equal member of the clan family (Mac means son of). The chief was the father, ruler and judge and the strength of the clan lay in his justice, kindness and wisdom, and in the loyalty of the members of the clan, to him and to one another. Rents were mostly paid in kind or man-rent, and in return for his patronage and protection, the chief could call on his people at any time to form an army and fight for him.

It is known that Highlanders wore some sort of brightly coloured, striped and checked material as far back as the 13th century, though whether the designs, or 'setts', were related to clans or to territories is not known for certain. The Suppression of the Highlands after Culloden in 1746 broke up clans, forbade tartan and highland dress to all civilians, and led to the death of the clan system. During the 36 years Highland dress was banned, many of the old setts were lost or forgotten.

The highland regiments were exempt from the ban so it is through them that the kilt survived. The early regiments all wore the Government, or Black Watch, tartan, sometimes introducing coloured overstripes to differentiate one regiment from another. It was not until Hanoverian George IV appeared at Holyrood in 1822 in an astonishing Highland outfit, that the fashion for tartan was revived. In a wave of enthusiasm, a large number of tartans were hastily designed, and adopted by clans who had for many years been kindred in name only. They were also keenly worn by Lowlanders whose ancestors would have died rather than be seen in Highland dress. It is these relatively modern patterns that make up most of today's enormous range of tartans, which can be seen all over the world, not only in cloth but also adorning luggage, footwear and a staggering range of knick-knacks. The average Scotsman doesn't stride over his native hills swathed in tartan. On the whole, kilts are kept for ceremonial or formal occasions, or for 'Sunday best', and a great many Scotsmen don't even own one.

Clan feelings still run strong, especially in the veins of expatriates, but the clan name is now no more than an umbrella for museums, annual gatherings and ceremonial, with the chief as a figurehead, in a tartan costume redolent of moth balls. The mystique that has grown up round clan tartans is put into perspective by the apocryphal story of the irate chieftain, towering over one of a coach party, visiting his ancestral castle:

> 'By what right are you wearing my tartan, my man?'
> 'By the ri' o' purrchis, at fifteen pounds a yard, my lord.'

See also 'Clans and Families' at the end of the guide.

The Highland Clearances

The Clearances are an emotive subject and it has to be remembered that the first emigration ship sailed out of Fort William as early as 1773, almost 20 years before *Bliadhna nan Caorachd*—the year of the sheep. There were several reasons for the depopulation of the Highlands after Culloden. Some Jacobites who had escaped execution found it expedient to go abroad for a few years; others were transported. Many Catholics, unable to practise their religion publicly at home, sought liberty across the ocean. The suppression of the Highlands and the breaking up of the clan system deprived chiefs of their hereditary status as patriarchs, and many drifted south to become London Scots. Away from the womb of the clan and the benefits of feudality, however, they felt the pinch financially. Vast, infertile estates in the north, overpopulated by impoverished peasants, brought in little or no revenue. Rents paid in kind were of little use to those trying to keep up with society in fashionable assembly rooms or pay off gambling debts in gentlemen's clubs. Sheep farmers from the south offered good rent for sheep-runs in the north but they wanted land free of people. Highland landowners, desperate for money, began to evict their tenants. Some built resettlement towns and villages for them and established new livelihoods such as fishing; some merely served eviction notices and employed agents to enforce them; some offered to assist with fares to new countries. Hundreds of crofting communities—those which relied entirely on their smallholdings for a living—broke up and scattered. Those who didn't emigrate flocked to the cities in the hope of finding work or to settlements, mainly on the coast, where the land was unsuitable for sheep.

Meanwhile, in the islands, landlords basked in a false prosperity from the kelp industry. Seaweed, of which there was a seemingly inexhaustible supply, was collected after each tide, burned in kilns, processed into valuable fertilizer and exported. All that was needed was a huge labour force to cut, carry and burn it. Island proprietors with an eye to the main chance offered tiny plots of land to dispossessed crofters from the mainland. They charged high rent and deliberately ensured each tenant had not enough land for self-sufficiency, forcing them to work at the kelp. By 1812 the islands were crammed with people entirely dependent on kelp for their living . After the Napoleonic Wars, import duty was abolished and cheap foreign kelp flooded the market: prices plummeted; people starved. Proprietors and politicians, faced with the problem of destitute multitudes, offered inducements to encourage emigration and many people went. The final blow came in 1846. The potato famine, which had already decimated Ireland, drifted across the sea in wind-born spores and descended on Scotland, half of whose population lived on potatoes. For the already starving Highlanders and Islanders, the effect was catastrophic. Many of those who had managed to stay on, often surviving several evictions, were now forced to join their compatriots in Canada, America, Australia and New Zealand. By the end of the 19th century, the rural Highlands and Islands were almost deserted.

Gaelic

Gaelic is still the first language in the Outer Hebrides, but even there, with an influx of non-Gaelic speakers and television, the children are growing up speaking English among themselves. Elsewhere it is no longer a living language, though many people are trying to revive it and there are many great Gaelic scholars. Sabhal Mor Ostaig, in Skye, is a popular and very successful Gaelic college; television and radio have a lot of Gaelic slots. It is taught in schools and in adult classes and there are a large number of Gaelic publications. It is an almost impossible language to 'pick up' by ear and eye because the spoken word bears little resemblance to the written. Recently, a crop of new notices appeared in some of the islands, proclaiming placenames in Gaelic. They must have cost a fortune: local people don't need them, and visitors can neither understand, nor pronounce them.

Gaelic, which is much older than English, stems from the Goidelic branch of Celtic languages, which were an offshoot from the earlier Indo-European language. Scottish Gaelic became a distinct dialect separate from Irish around the 13th century, and there are still many similarities. With the revival of Gaelic has come a revival of Gaelic culture.

Groups like Runrig and Capercaillie who perform modern style Gaelic music are enormously popular and an important part of the Scottish music scene.

Crofting

Since the Highland Clearances, croftland tenure has been strictly controlled to protect the rights of the tenant. A croft is a smallholding in the Highlands, with a few acres, as many sheep as the land will support, and sometimes cows and poultry. If there is arable land it will be tilled. In the old days, *feannagan*, or inappropriately named lazy-beds, were dug for potatoes, involving much hard work, deep digging and the carting of heavy creels of seaweed for fertilizer. Some of the work on the croft is still done communally—sheep-dipping and shearing for instance, and cutting the peat and haymaking. Peat is still used as fuel in some areas. Composed of partially-rotted vegetation, compressed in waterlogged conditions in temperate or cold climates, it takes 3000 years to form a depth of one foot, so peat-bogs are getting scarce. It is cut in the spring in oblong slabs with a special digger and stacked *in situ*, on end like miniature wigwams, until dry. In a wet summer the peat can still be lying late into the year. Once dry, it is built into neat beehives. As recently as the 1970s, hay was cut by hand, with scythes, and it is still turned with pitchforks until dry.

The family dwelling is the croft-house—often mistakenly called the croft. Less than 50 years ago, many Highlanders still lived in a *tigh dubh* or black house, now almost extinct except as a folk museum or byre. It had thick, double walls, about 6 feet (1.8m) high, made of local stone and packed with earth and rubble. Unlined on the inside, it had rounded corners, no gables, and a reed- or heather-thatched roof anchored by boulders tied to ropes of plaited heather. Inside, the furniture was functional: a dresser, box-beds, a bench, stools, rat-proof meal chests, coffers and a spinning wheel. A peat fire was laid on a stone slab on the earthen floor in the middle of the room, the smoke escaping out of a hole in the thatch. In earlier times, light came from a *crùisgean*—a lamp fuelled with fish liver oil burning on a wick of plaited rushes. Even within this century, in some island communities the beasts shared the family house, penned at one end with the floor sloping down towards them and the effluent running out through holes in the wall.

The crofter is the owner or tenant of the croft. Most crofters have a subsidiary job as well: fishing, building or public works. Since the Clearances, the Crofting Commission has kept very careful control of crofters' rights.

Céilidh

Céilidh (pronounced kayly) is a Gaelic word meaning visit. In winter, when nights were long, crofters used to gather in one of the houses when darkness fell, packed in round the central fire. One of the older members, often a bard or musician, acted as the master of ceremonies and everyone was expected to contribute to the entertainment. The women knitted or spun, men repaired fishing nets or whittled wood; everyone listened. Stories, songs, poems, proverbs and legends were recited, passing their history, folklore and tradition from one generation to the next. Their music stirred the soul: mouth-music, straight from the heart; Gaelic songs; pipe, harp and fiddle music. Children grew up steeped in the past and could tell you who their great, great, great grand-uncle was and whose sweetheart he had run off with. The practice is dying now, thanks to television, and *céilidhs* tend to be commercial shows, staged in halls and hotels.

Piping

Two kinds of bagpipes are played in Scotland these days, the 'warm wind' and the 'cold wind'. The Highland bagpipe, being mouth blown, is 'warm wind'; the Lowland or Border bagpipe is blown by a bellows operated by the piper's right elbow, hence 'the cold wind pipes'. The Highland bagpipe is designed to be played out of doors; the Lowland is essentially an indoor instrument. Recent improvements in the manufacture of the Highland bagpipe along with the higher standards now being demanded by audiences have altered the tone of the instrument until it can be listened to with pleasure indoors, where the most prestigious piping events are held. The Highland bagpipe no longer 'skirls'. The 'Small Music' of the Highland bagpipe includes marches and dance tunes in differing tempi; the *ceòl mor*, the 'Great Music' (usually anglicized as 'pibroch' from *pìobaireachd*, meaning piping) comprises tunes constructed on a theme followed by up to ten variations.

Pibroch pieces date from the late 15th century and their names commemorate great events in Highland history. Pibroch is listened to in silence. It is unwise for the visitor to interrupt, even by a whisper. The Lowland pipes are intended to accompany social events indoors and fit in well with the folk music groups now popular in Scotland and beyond. Their tone is sweet and mellow and the repertoire includes the ancient Border ballads from the days of the cross-border raids and feuds as well as a wide range of dance music and song airs. Both instruments are taken seriously in Scotland, for their own sake as well as for their traditional connotations. Derogatory comment is not appreciated, especially if voiced in the accents of South Britain. The pipes were never specifically proscribed by the Disarming Act of 1747, but it would have been a brave piper who would have played within earshot of a Government post. The oldest thesis on pipe music was written during the proscription and there are several pibroch pieces that were composed while the Act was still in force.

Sorcerers and Superstition

Communities lived in terror of Devil-worshippers and sorcerers, whom they believed could control the elements and cause plague, famine, drought, miscarriages and crop failure. In the Middle Ages, fertile Celtic minds were fed by inherited paganism, folklore, ignorance and religion. This was particularly so in Galloway and the Highlands, where remote communities were separated by vast tracts of moor, hill and loch, far from urban influence, schools and the steely eye of the Church. Every act, from pre-birth to death was vulnerable and the power of evil had to be propitiated. Offerings of food, herbal potions, benisons, gestures, talismans and rites were employed in the hope of warding off super-natural ills. Curiously shaped stones had magic properties. Certain lakes and wells were thought to be especially efficacious. Pilgrims brought their sick and their petitions and tied votive offerings to trees and bushes. People still go to some of the *Clootie Wells* as they are called. There is one at Culloden where coachloads of people arrive on or around May Day, the Celtic Beltane, and throw money into the well. Superstition or not, when the Highland Division was being pounded on the beaches of St Valery-en-Caux, in the summer of 1940, the Culloden Clootie Well attracted throngs of petitioners. Another, on a back road in Ross-shire, is so festooned with squalid old rags it looks like a tinkers' tip, yet even today, no one removes them for fear of reprisals from the god of the well.

It was by no means just ignorant peasants who believed in sorcery. Macbeth's encounter with the three witches was not a figment of Shakespeare's rich imagination. His source for the story was Holinshed, the 16th-century chronicler, who describes 'three women in strange and wild apparell, resembling creatures of eldritch world', who 'vanished immedi-atlie' having delivered their prophecies. King James VI/I was terrified of witches. He believed his political enemies hired them to try to kill him and comforted himself with the theory that the sacred oil with which he was anointed at his coronation made him immune from their sorcery. One of his enemies was half-mad Francis Stewart, Earl of Bothwell, nephew of Mary's Bothwell, commonly believed to be the Satanic overlord of several covens of witches. When the king nearly drowned in a freak storm off the Bass Rock, he claimed to have seen one of Bothwell's covens sailing round his foundering ship in a sieve. He ordered their arrest and they were discovered in the graveyard of the Auld Kirk in North Berwick, having an orgy presided over by their 'Devil' Bothwell. James attended their trial and wrote a treatise on witchcraft. The last execution for witchcraft in Scotland was believed to be in Dornoch in 1727, when a mother was found guilty of riding upon her daughter, who had been transformed into a pony and shod by the Devil. She was burned in a barrel of pitch having first warmed her cold feet at the fire that was to consume her.

Seers

The second sight, *taibhsearachd* in Gaelic, goes hand in hand with sorcery and among the many seers who emerged from the Celtic mists were Thomas the Rhymer and the Brahan Seer. Thomas, born in 1220, lived for nearly 80 years, and earned himself the title 'True Thomas'. He predicted the death of Alexander III and the Battle of Bannockburn. Traditionally, he had a passionate affair with the Fairy Queen and went off to live with her for three years in Elfland, deep in the Eildon Hills.

The Brahan Seer, Còinneach Odhar, is an enigmatic figure from the 17th century, known for the uncanny accuracy of many of his prophecies about the Highlands, some of which are still to be fulfilled. He fell asleep, so it is said, on an enchanted hillside: when he awoke he was clutching a stone with a hole in it, through which he could see the truth and the future. Among the events he foretold that have already happened are the depopulation of the Highlands, the demise of crofting, the arrival of rich landowners, and the making of the Caledonian Canal. He said that when it was possible to cross the River Ness in Inverness dryshod in five places, a terrible disaster would strike the world. There were four bridges over the Ness until a fifth was erected to replace one about to be demolished. This was opened at the end of August 1939: on 1 September Hitler marched into Poland.

The Brahan Seer met his death by antagonizing his patroness, the Countess of Seaforth. The Earl visited France, soon after the Restoration of Charles II in 1660, and had not returned. The Countess sent for the Brahan Seer and asked what her husband was doing. When he was reluctant to say, she pressed him until he revealed that the Earl was in a sumptuous gilded room, grandly decked out in velvet, silk and cloth of gold, with a voluptuous lady on his lap. The Countess was furious, accused him of malice and ordered him to be burnt in a barrel of tar at Fortrose. Before he died he predicted the downfall of the Seaforth Mackenzies, whose line came to an end after a dramatic chain of events, precisely following the prophecy, in 1815.

The Stone of Destiny (Stone of Scone)

Traditionally, the Stone of Destiny was the pillow on which Jacob laid his head when he dreamt about the ladder of angels reaching from earth to heaven. Its subsequent history is shadowy. It floated round the world carrying mystical powers of sovereignty until it arrived in Ireland, whence it was brought to Dunadd by early missionaries and used as a throne in the coronation of Scottish kings.

In those days, *mormaers* owned their kingdoms and the High King was their overlord, King of the Scots but not of Scotland. At the coronation, each *mormaer* filled a shoe with earth from his kingdom and poured a little into a footprint carved into a rock. The King sat on the Stone of Destiny and put his foot over this cocktail of Scottish soil.

From here the Stone was moved to Dunstaffnage. In the 9th century, Kenneth Macalpine took it to Scone where it continued to be a coronation throne for the united Scots and Picts. Edward I, believing firmly in its mystical powers, pinched what he thought to be the Stone of Destiny during one of his ravages of the north and whisked it off to become part of the Coronation Chair in Westminster Abbey. It has been there ever since, except for a brief hiatus in 1950 when Scottish Nationalists kidnapped it and hid it for about three months in Arbroath. The canny Scots had almost certainly hidden the original stone—the one in London, a rather dull lump of plain sandstone, is not even a replica, because the true stone was intricately carved. It is safe, in a secret cavern, and will be brought out by its hereditary guardians when the time is right.

Two Enlightened Men

Walter Scott (1771–1832)

A woman who knew Walter Scott as a child described him as sweet and intelligent and 'the most extraordinary genius of a boy'. One of his tutors described him as an incorrigibly idle imp but never a dunce. In maturity he was worldly, genial, magnanimous, never jealous or petty, patriotic and loyal. He was a combination of romantic and practical and his integrity was much admired. Scott was one of 12 children, son of a Writer to the Signet in Edinburgh and a physician's daughter. A childhood illness affected his right leg. From the age of three he spent much of his youth at his grandparents' farm, Sandyknowe, in the Tweed valley, where his grandparents tried every sort of cure for his lameness, such as wrapping his leg in the fleece of a newly killed sheep, but without success. He sat for hours listening to the Border shepherds and country people, and to the songs his grandmother sang for him and her endless fund of legends. The essence of the land seeped into his soul to become his inspiration.

When stronger, he was sent to Edinburgh High School, where, though lazy, he excelled at Latin. In spite of his deformity, he was physically brave and was renowned for climbing on the dangerous crags of the castle rock. He was also quick to square up to the 'town boys' who used to taunt their more privileged peers. Growing too fast in adolescence, he became weak and was sent to Kelso for six months' convalescence. Here he read Percy's *Reliques*, a collection of ancient ballads, songs, sonnets and romances discovered, restored and edited by Percy, and these, together with the romances of 16th-century Torquato Tasso, and Spenser's *Faerie Queene*, fired his imagination. He also studied the old romantic poetry of France and Italy, and modern German poetry. Even in his teens he had the gift of spinning a good yarn and he would ramble over Arthur's Seat, in Edinburgh, swopping stories with a friend.

He went to Edinburgh University where he was no less idle, but continued to collect material to feed his passion for romantic ballads and songs. By the time he was a law clerk in his father's office, he was tall and strong, with a graceful figure and 'the chest and arms of Hercules'. His features were 'not handsome but singularly varied and pleasing', with bright eyes and a 'brilliant complexion'. He fell deeply in love with a girl of 16 called Williamina Belsches, but because of her age her father forbade their friendship. His friends believed this was the strongest passion of his life and that Williamina appears in several of his novels.

He was called to the Bar in 1792 and travelled the country, always listening, observing, absorbing. His first visit to the Highlands, second only to the Borders as background for his stories, was while he was on a case, directing one of the evictions of the Clearances. In 1796 he published, anonymously, a collection of translations of German ballads. On holiday in Cumbria, he met Margaret Charlotte Carpenter, daughter of a Royalist émigré from the French Revolution, who was taking the waters at Gilsland Spa. She was high spirited and beautiful with an entrancing French accent, dark brown eyes, masses of black hair and a 'fairy-like figure'. They fell in love and were married in Carlisle Cathedral on Christmas Eve 1797.

Two years later he was appointed Sheriff of Selkirkshire, a position he held for 27 years, during which time he wrote the majority of his books. To begin with he stuck to ballads and romantic poems. His first publication was *Border Minstrelsy*, three volumes of ballads he had collected and edited, and this was followed by his first original work, the romantic poem 'The Lay of the Last Minstrel'. He became a partner in James Ballantyne's printing business. In 1811, with the money rolling in from his prolific (but still anonymous) output and his post of Sheriff, he bought land on the Tweed and built himself a fanciful baronial castle, described by Ruskin as an incongruous pile. The place was originally called Clarty Hole—*clarty* being the Scots word for dirty or muddy—so he changed it to the more digni-fied Abbotsford, in memory of the days when it was just that.

About this time, Byron hit the headlines with 'Childe Harold' and Scott, recognizing without rancour a greater talent than his own, decided to turn his pen to prose. He was self-deprecating about his poetry: when someone asked his daughter if she had read 'The Lay of the Last Minstrel', she shook her head and answered demurely: 'Oh no, Papa says there is nothing so injurious for young people as reading bad poetry.' Indeed, when he was offered the laureateship, in 1813, he turned it down, suggesting Southey as an alternative, although many would argue that his loose, flowing verse was preferable to Southey's rather stilted, plodding style. *Waverley* was Scott's first novel, published in 1814, a stirring Jacobite tale in which the turncoat hero is rescued from reprisals after Culloden by an English colonel whose life he had saved. In the following 16 years he published 29 stories. When he had milked Scottish history dry, he turned to England in the Middle Ages, and rattled off *Ivanhoe*. Among the many places and periods he wrote about was 15th-century France, in *Quentin Durward*, and he frequently returned to his beloved Scotland as in *Redgauntlet*, the imaginative story of Prince Charlie's abortive return, some years after 1745, to have another crack at the throne. Scott entwined his extensive knowledge of the minutiae of history with romance and adventure and he brought the past vividly to life by endowing it with the present. He was not always strong on character, though some of his simple country people were brilliant, and his plots were a bit shaky, but his sense of place was outstanding and his passion for history gave him a limitless supply of stories. His books were good clean fun and as such were loved by the reading public. As well as novels, he wrote and edited a number of learned publications including histories, essays, biography and the delightful children's history: *Tales of a Grandfather*.

Scott's influence as a novelist was unquestionable. He established the form of the historical novel and was a model to such other novelists as Mrs Gaskell, George Eliot and the Brontës. *The Two Drovers* and *The Highland Widow* were, in themselves , a new form of short story. Abbotsford became a popular meeting place for all the learned men of the day. Scott was liked and admired and had many friends. In maturity he was described as a straightforward man who got on equally well with dukes and peasants, a delightful companion, not only to his contemporaries but also to his children. Growing up as he had during the Scottish Enlightenment, his circle included many of the great men who created Scotland's Golden Age. He contributed to the *Edinburgh Review* until its Whiggish lean-ings outraged his Tory heart, when he promoted the rival *Quarterly Review*. In 1818 he instigated a successful search for the 'Honours of Scotland' as the Crown Jewels were called. Tucked away in a chest at the Union of Parliaments in 1707, they had been forgotten. Scott's passion for history embraced a passion for the trappings of the past and the Scottish Regalia were the oldest in Europe. In 1820, he was created a baronet and in 1822 he had an enthusiastic hand in George IV's flamboyant visit to Edinburgh. He was always surrounded by a crowd of dogs and thoroughly enjoyed gentlemanly sport. It was a period of prosperity and happiness until 1826, when disaster struck.

Due partly to the inefficiency of James Ballantyne the printer and partly to rash borrowing, the firm went bankrupt, together with Scott's publisher, Constable. As a partner, Scott himself was liable for some £114,000. Determined to repay every penny to his creditors, he threw himself into an even greater frenzy of work, breaking his health and shortening his life. In 1827, no longer Sheriff of Selkirkshire, he emerged from the anonymity he had previously sheltered behind and poured a torrent of words into several more books, some of which reflect the rapid decline in his health. Scott's own pathetic *Journal* shows how anguished his last few years were. He died in 1832 at the age of 61, within sight and sound of the River Tweed, surrounded by his family. All his debts were paid as a result of his labours, and Abbotsford, which had been restored to him by his creditors, was preserved as a monument. It is an apt memorial to a man whose passion for Scotland was unrivalled and who himself epitomized the things he admired most about his beloved country.

Perhaps the most informative biography of Scott is *Memoirs of the Life of Sir Walter Scott* by his son-in-law, John Gibson Lockhart, a comprehensive account full of personal anecdotes but perhaps a little too tender in some details.

Robert Burns (1759–96)

> *Immortal Robert Burns of Ayr,*
> *There's but few poets can with you compare;*
> *Some of your poems and songs are very fine:*
> *'To Mary in Heaven' is most sublime;*
> *And then again in your 'Cottar's Saturday Night',*
> *Your genius there does shine most bright,*
> *As pure as the dewdrops of night . . .*

tribute from 'Scotland's worst poet', William McGonagall

Burns, the ploughman-poet, came from a very different background to that of Walter Scott, but he was no less remarkable a product of the Scottish Enlightenment. He was a genius. He cut through elegant devices and rhetoric and went straight to the heart of mankind. No subject was sacrosanct: 'Holy Willie's Prayer' is a blueprint for satire. Nothing could be more tender than his 'To a Mouse', that 'Wee, sleekit, cowrin', tim'rous beastie' he turned up in her nest with his plough, nor more romantic than his love who was 'like a red, red rose, that's newly sprung in June'. Nationalism blazes in 'Scots, wha hae wi' Wallace bled' and the revolutionary spirit was so strong in 'A man's a man for a' that' it had to be published anonymously.

Burns' admirers shroud him with an almost mawkish sentimentality, personified in the statue in Dumfries High Street of a languishing beau clutching a posy of flowers. In fact he was an earthy man with a wicked sense of humour, contemptuous of the hypocrisy of Kirk and officialdom, as his satirical poems show. He was sensitive and perceptive and his heart frequently ruled his head, but he was not sentimental. On the contrary, he was extremely down to earth. He was fiercely humanitarian; loathed oppression; despised privilege through birth and wealth; hated cruelty. His easy wit and natural charm endeared him to peasant and noble alike. He was convivial and thoroughly enjoyed tavern life and a night out with the boys, but was by no means a reeling drunkard. James Currie, three years his senior, was a reformed alcoholic and his biography of Burns was strongly influenced by his vehement abhorrence for the Demon Drink. Burns liked his dram but most of the time poverty and a weak heart kept him fairly abstemious. He was extremely good-looking with dark hair, large dreamy eyes, a straight nose and a quirky, sensual mouth. Sir Walter Scott said of him: 'There was a strong expression of sense and shrewdness in all his lineaments: the eye alone, I think, indicated the poetical character and temperament. It was large and of a dark cast, which glowed, I say literally glowed, when he spoke with feeling or interest. I never saw such another eye in a human head, though I have seen the most distinguished men of my time.' Women found him irresistible and fell like skittles. He fathered 15 children, six of whom were bastards, but he made no distinction and was a good father to them all. He had an easy morality, believing that 'the light that led astray was light from Heaven'. But in spite of his many infidelities and the rough passage of their early years together, he loved Jean Armour more than any of his mistresses and their marriage was happy. He farmed for all but the last five years of his life and was far more at home on the end of a plough than in an Edinburgh drawing room. Tough work on the land when he was undernourished and still growing led to recurring bouts of rheumatic fever which strained his heart.

Oldest of the seven children of an impoverished market gardener, he grew up hungry, always labouring, barely subsisting at times. He went to the village school when he was six and his retentive memory impressed his teachers. He learnt some Latin and French and devoured any book he could lay hands on. *The History of Sir William Wallace*, borrowed from the blacksmith, 'poured a Scottish prejudice into my veins which will boil along there till the floodgates of life shut in eternal rest.'

He wrote his first song, 'Handsome Nell', to Nelly Kirkpatrick, a 'bewitching creature' who worked in the fields with him and probably initiated him into that 'delicious passion which I hold to be the first of human joys.' In 1775 he went to Kirkoswald to study surveying, but 'a charming filette who lived next door to the school overset my Trigonometry and set me off on a tangent from the sphere of my studies.' It was here he developed a liking for tavern life and learned 'to look unconcerned on a large tavern bill'. His cronies in the inn were Douglas Graham of Shanter Farm—model for Tam o' Shanter—and John Davidson the cobbler—Souter Johnnie .

When he was 18, he joined a dancing class at Tarbolton, against his father's wishes, 'to give my manners a brush'. A year later he helped found the Tarbolton Bachelors' Club, and he and his friends sat debating long into the night. These were exciting times to be growing up in and his sharp mind was uncluttered by received opinions and prejudices. The French Revolution was ten years ahead but its labour pains were starting. Poverty made him sympathetic towards any movement against oppression. The Scottish Enlightenment was in full bloom: new ideas were burgeoning. Men were arguing, inventing, abandoning moribund conventions. Burns was ripe for rebellion. When he was 26 he met Jean, one of 11 children of stonemason James Armour, and declared her his common-law wife. At the beginning of the following year, however, desperate for money, he made plans to emigrate to Jamaica to work on a plantation. Before departing, he arranged for some of his poems to be published in Kilmarnock. James Armour renounced him as a son-in-law, and issued a writ against him, although Jean was by now pregnant. Robert in his turn renounced Jean and went into hiding. In July 1786, *The Kilmarnock Poems* was published. Six days later he was hauled up before the Kirk in Mauchline and ordered to sit on the Penitential Stool in chastisement for his irregular marriage. (He stood, defiantly, beside it and such was his magnetism that no one insisted on the full humiliation.) For all his failings, he was a religious man, but his clear, revolutionary mind despised the hypocrisy of strict Calvinistic discipline.

Three weeks later he exchanged a pledge of marriage with Mary Campbell of Auchnamore, near Dunoon. A wistful apotheosis has left the impression that Highland Mary was a pure, virginal maiden whose tragic death, five months later, left him heartbroken. In fact, if rumour is to be believed, she was little more than a local floozie and a number of writs and claims for paternity settlements soon after her death indicate that he was not slow to seek solace in other arms. In September, Jean Armour gave birth to twins, Robert and Jean, who did not survive long.

The Kilmarnock Poems was an instant success. Burns cancelled his plans for Jamaica and went to Edinburgh where he was lionized by society and the *literati*. After a second edition of his poems appeared, he was asked if he would help collect old Scottish songs for the Scots Musical Museum. He threw himself into this venture and during the last ten years of his life collected, edited and wrote over 200 songs. He travelled in the Highlands and the Borders to find material and accepted no payment, saying it was his patriotic duty. In January 1787 the Grand Lodge of Scotland (Masonic) hailed him as 'Caledonia's Bard'. That same year he met Mrs Agnes McLehose and started a passionate correspondence of high-flown letters, addressing her as Clarinda and signing himself as Sylvander. In February 1788, he left Edinburgh, bought Jean Armour a mahogany bed, and set up house with her in an upper room in Mauchline, publicly declaring them to be married (again). Just over a week later, Jean gave birth to another set of twins, neither of whom survived the month. The couple moved to Ellisland and while trying his hand at experimental farming, Burns trained as an excise officer. The Kirk Session finally acknowledged the authenticity of the marriage but eight months after the birth of the twins, a Jenny Clow bore him a son and claimed paternity settlement.

In 1790, Burns was posted to Dumfries as Excise Officer. He moved his family to the town and for the last six years of his life continued to write, procreate, and pay up for his indiscretions. An inquiry was launched at the end of 1793, to investigate his revolutionary leanings. He was acquitted, and when the French declared war on Britain in 1795, he was the first to join the Dumfries Volunteers and he wrote several patriotic songs. He died in July 1796 at the age of 37, from a heart defect contracted after rheumatic fever. On the day of his funeral Jean, with not a shilling in the world, gave birth to his son Maxwell.

Borders

St Abbs

March, march, Ettrick and Teviotdale,
Why the deil dinna ye march forward in order?
March, march, Eskdale and Liddesdale,
All the Blue Bonnets are bound for the Border.

from 'Blue Bonnets Over the Border', by Sir Walter Scott

Most routes into Scotland top a summit from which you look across a chequerboard of fertile farmland, laced with wooded river valleys within a rim of undulating hills. In contrast is the savage, rocky coastline with cliff-hung fishing towns and villages. This borderland was bitterly fought over, from prehistoric times until the middle of the 17th century: many ruins bear witness to those violent times. Buildings and towns were sacked and hastily rebuilt: most settlements were fortified. The four abbeys, at Melrose, Jedburgh, Kelso and Dryburgh, built within a few miles of each other in the fertile river valleys by David I in the 12th century, were destroyed and repaired often before the Reformation led to their final decay.

It was not just the invading English who caused havoc: the Border Reivers, powerful border families, warred amongst themselves, raiding each other's territory and stealing cattle. Ballads and folk tales romanticize them: in reality they were savage and barbaric.

The fast-flowing rivers, internationally famous for salmon and trout, were harnessed in the old days to drive woollen mills: today, though the mills may be powered by more modern means, the Borders are still famous for their textiles. Farming and horse-breeding also play an important part in the economy of this fertile land and the annual agricultural shows provide robust local colour. Much has been written in prose, poetry and song, trying to capture the elusive spirit of the Borders. Perhaps Sir Walter Scott, who made the Borders his domain, wrote most.

In several towns the turbulent days of the Border Reivers are revived with annual **Common Riding Festivals**, remembering the days when the men rode out to check the boundaries. These celebrations provide light-hearted entertainment and pageantry and take place throughout the summer months. They usually commemorate some event in local history, as well as a 'ride' when a cavalcade of riders streams out of the town to 'inspect the marches'. Some of the Border Ridings and festivals to look out for in June include: the Peebles Beltane Festival, West Linton Whipman Play, Galashiels Braw Lads Gathering, Hawick Common Riding, Melrose Summer Festival, and Selkirk Common Riding. In July there are: Earlston Civic Week, Jethart Callants Festival, Jedburgh, Duns Summer Festival, Kelso Civic Week, Innerleithen St Ronans Border

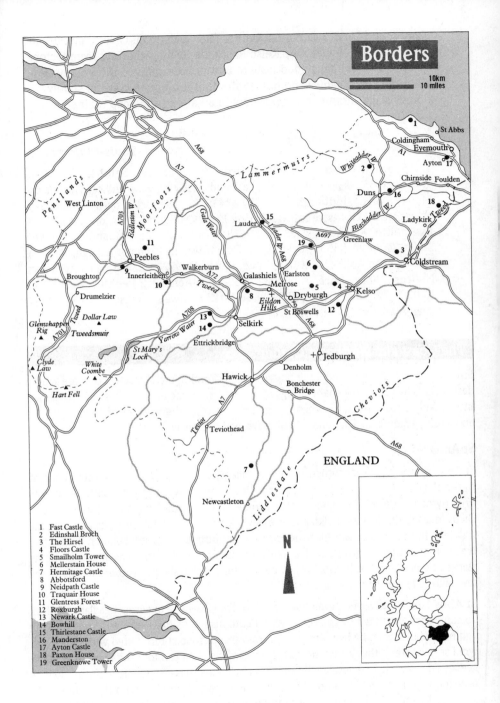

Borders

10km
10 miles

St Abbs
Coldingham
Eyemouth
Ayton 17
Chirnside Foulden
Duns 16
Blackadder W. 18
Ladykirk Tweed
Greenlaw
Coldstream
Lammermuirs
Whiteadder W.
2
Lauder 15
Leader W. A68
19
A697
6
3
Earlston
Galashiels
Melrose
5 4
Dryburgh Kelso
St Boswells
8 Eildon Hills 12
Walkerburn
A72 Tweed
Peebles
11
West Linton
Pentlands
Eddleston W.
Moorfoots
Gala Water
A68
A7
A703
Broughton
Innerleithen
10 9
Drumelzier
Dollar Law
Tweed
A701 Tweedsmuir
Glenwhappen Rig
Clyde Law
White Coombe
Hart Fell
St Mary's Loch
Yarrow Water
A708
13
14
Selkirk
Ettrickbridge
Denholm
Jedburgh
Hawick
Bonchester Bridge
Cheviots
A68
Teviot
A7
Teviothead
Liddlesdale
ENGLAND
A68
7
Newcastleton

N

1   Fast Castle
2   Edinshall Broch
3   The Hirsel
4   Floors Castle
5   Smailholm Tower
6   Mellerstain House
7   Hermitage Castle
8   Abbotsford
9   Neidpath Castle
10   Traquair House
11   Glentress Forest
12   Roxburgh
13   Newark Castle
14   Bowhill
15   Thirlestane Castle
16   Manderston
17   Ayton Castle
18   Paxton House
19   Greenknowe Tower

61

Games, and Lauder Common Riding. The Coldstream Civic Week usually takes place in August. The Kelso Races are lively gatherings from October to April and you get a good taste of Border atmosphere at the many agricultural shows, games and horse sales that proliferate. Several stately homes stage summer extravaganzas in an attempt to keep their stately roofs on.

Tourist Information

The **Scottish Borders Tourist Board**, 70 High Street, **Selkirk**, TD7 4DD, © 0750 20555 is open all year with a 24-hour answerphone service. The office at Murray's Green, **Jedburgh**, © 0835 863435/863688, is also open all year. Local offices are at: **Coldstream**: Henderson Park, © 0890 882607, open April–Oct; **Eyemouth**: Auld Kirk, © 08907 50678, open April–Oct; **Galashiels**: St John's Street, © 0896 55551, open April–Oct; **Hawick**: Common Haugh, © 0450 72547, open April–Oct; **Kelso**: Town House, © 0573 223464, open April–Oct; **Melrose**: Abbey Place, © 089682 2555, open April–Oct; **Peebles**: High Street, © 0721 720138, open April–Nov; **Selkirk**: Halliwell's House, © 0750 20054, open April–Oct.

The Coast and Northeast Corner

Fishing and smuggling played an important part in forming the characters of those whose descendants live along the coastal fringe of the Borders. Some of the towns and villages are little changed since the days when smugglers teemed in the warrens of twisting wynds and closes, evading the excisemen in underground hideaways.

St Abbs

St Abbs, on the northeast corner, is a pretty village, almost Cornish in character, clinging to the cliffs, with narrow zigzag streets running steeply down to the harbour, lined with brightly painted terraced fisher cottages, some of which still have quaint 'doll's house' sheds in front. St Abbs is a holiday village now, with just a few lobster boats replacing the trawlers that used to go out for haddock, cod and turbot. Boats still come in during bad weather for shelter. Down in the harbour there are upturned boats, piles of nets, tottering stacks of creels and fish boxes, backed by old stone tackle-sheds. St Abbs has one of the few sandy beaches on this coast.

St Abbs Head is a rugged promontory north of the village—a towering headland of black volcanic rock, pounded by the sea, with a lighthouse at its tip. Parking is limited at the lighthouse but it is an invigorating walk, across sheep-cropped turf dotted with whins and wind-stunted trees, the restless sea in the background. You can tour the lighthouse at the keeper's discretion. This desolate headland is a wildlife reserve and there are many species of seabird: guillemots, like a host of chattering waiters; razorbills, with their cut-throat-razor beaks and their endearing courting ritual; shags stretching out their black wings to dry their feathers, and many more. The air is vibrant with their noise. There is a visitors' centre at Northfield Farm Steading, with information about the reserve.

Fast Castle, about 3 miles (5km) to the west, on Wheat Stack, attached to the mainland by a terrifying gangway, is a lovely walk along the cliffs, but take care where you put your feet—the path approach is hazardous. All you can see now are the tattered remains of what was once a notorious fortress, used by wreckers and robbers, perched halfway up the cliff. It is easy to see why Scott used Fast Castle as the model for 'Wolf's Crag' in *The Bride of Lammermoor*. It is accessible, with care, from the cliff above. It was a stronghold of the Home family by the end of the 14th century, but its origins are not known. Margaret Tudor, Henry VIII's sister, stayed here on her way to marry James IV, leaving her entourage of 1500 attendants at Coldingham Priory. She was fourteen years old: what can have been her thoughts as she stood in her bedchamber, fresh from the magnificent English court, and looked out across that bleak sea? The year was 1503: in ten years' time in an upstairs room in Linlithgow, she was to weep for her faithless husband, one of the many flowers of the forest that were 'a' wede awae' on Flodden Field.

Coldingham

Coldingham, a mile (1.5km) inland, is an attractive, twisting village with the remains of a 13th-century priory, the choir of which is now the parish church. A soaring arch rises from the ruined foundations, ancient gravestones and fragments of carved masonry scattered at its feet. The priory makes an impressive foreground to a distant seascape. It was mostly demolished by Cromwell in 1648. It offered the right of sanctuary for lawbreakers, the boundary within which they were safe being marked by crosses. On the beach you can collect pretty coloured pebbles which make unusual ornaments, polished and displayed in glass jars.

Eyemouth

Just down the coast, Eyemouth is a small seaside town with a busy commercial fishing industry that includes the export of shellfish. When James VI/I granted it a Free Port Charter in 1597, it became a thriving centre for smugglers. The intricate design of the older part of the town provided a maze of hiding places and escape routes and many of the houses still have hidden chambers and secret passages: it is said that more than half of Eyemouth is underground. The cliffs around are honeycombed with caves.

Stand on the harbour wall, looking out to sea and think back to Friday 14 October, 1881. The fishing fleet sailed on a day that dawned too bright and too still, with the barometer reading too low. At noon there was a dark stillness, followed by a sudden storm—a tornado that devastated the fleet. Many drowned at once; others, struggling home, were smashed on the rocks outside the harbour in sight of their helpless families. Only six boats got back safely; 23 were lost; 129 Eyemouth men were drowned, leaving 107 widows. Other fleets up and down the coast suffered in the same way.

The Eyemouth Museum (open daily April–Oct) is in the converted Georgian Auld Kirk, which is in the Market Place near the harbour. It was opened in 1981 as a centenary memorial to the fishing disaster. Look for the tapestry, a most striking piece of contemporary work with pictures of the storm, sea scenes and the names of all the boats that were lost and of the men aboard them. There is also the wheelhouse of a modern fishing boat as well as local fishing and farming history.

Eyemouth Harbour, recently improved and enlarged, is long and narrow and teeming with maritime life. Fish boxes are stacked in open-sided sheds surrounded by all the clutter of the sea: nets and derricks and craft of all sizes, and great ribbed skeletons of hulls propped in cradles. For those who find the North Sea rather chilly, there is a swimming pool with sauna and sunbed at The Shore. Trampolines, one of those huge outdoor chess and draughts boards and a children's playground can also be found there. **Gunsgreen House**, opposite the harbour, is alleged to have secret passages leading to the water. Every July, Eyemouth holds a Children's Picnic and Herring Queen Festival.

Where to Stay

There are several not very inspiring hotels and guest houses in Eyemouth, some overlooking the harbour, all quite cheap.

Eating Out

You won't find much in the way of haute cuisine around this unpretentious area, but if you want a warm welcome and local atmosphere, try **The Contented Sole**, in Harbour Road, Eyemouth, ✆ 08907 50268. It's open all day and you can get bar meals. Try Eyemouth Pale, a lighter, more delicate version of smoked haddock, and Eyemouth Tart, a delicious confection made with walnuts, currants and coconut.

Ayton

Ayton is a crossroads village, southwest of Eyemouth. Prominent here is **Ayton Castle** (open 2pm–5pm on Sundays in the summer, or by appointment, ✆ 08907 81212), a vast red Victorian pile, clearly seen from the road and the railway. This architectural extravaganza is so ostentatious it is easy to believe the local legend that it developed from its foundations without plans or architect, its creator crossing the river each day to order the erection of yet another turret or crow-stepped gable according to his mood. This splendid example of Scottish Baronial at its most fanciful was in fact designed by Gillespie Graham in 1846, on the site of an ancient fortalice destroyed by the English in the 15th century.

Beyond the church, near the imposing entrance to the castle, in a graveyard that is a carpet of snowdrops in early spring, are the ruins of a pre-Reformation church. Among these ivy-covered stones, emissaries of Scots and English kings often met to arrange short-lived truces during the years of the border wars. Many ancient bones lie buried far below the present layer of graves in this tranquil resting-place, and the ugly castle, standing high on the skyline, intrudes like a brash newcomer on the ancient ruin.

Foulden

Foulden, to the south, is little more than a row of cottages on a cobbled terrace on one side of the road, facing a green beyond which the land falls gently away to the Cheviot Hills on the southern horizon. The Flemish-style cottages gaze out over the magnificent view, their gabled eyebrows for ever raised in surprise. To the left of the row, in the old schoolhouse, the door to the post office is set back behind four delightfully incongruous fluted columns.

By the church is a restored two-storey **tithe barn**, with an outside stair and crow-stepped gables, where the minister stored the grain given him by his parishioners as a stipend.

Chirnside

Chirnside, due west of Foulden, is where the racing driver Jim Clark was born and is buried. The **church** has a 12th-century Norman doorway on the south wall. Inside, a plaque dated 1572 tells you to 'Helpe the Pur'. In 1674, the Chirnside minister's wife was buried in this churchyard, wearing a valuable ring. The sexton, returning at night to rob the grave, tried to hack off the ring with a knife. The corpse sprang up, screamed and rushed to the manse, yelling: 'Open the door, open the door, for I'm fair clemmed wi' the cauld'. (She later mothered two sons who founded the Original Secession Church!)

Duns

Heading inland towards the heart of the Borders you come to the small county town of Duns, straggling uphill from a solid-looking church on a green mound with narrow streets behind, where buildings seem to jostle each other, all set at odd angles in no apparent order. Duns was designed as the capital of Berwickshire and has some very fine buildings. The town hall was intended to be the county hall.

Duns has a horse show in May, a Summer Festival in July, which is their Common Riding Celebration, and the Berwickshire Agricultural Association Show in August.

Duns Nature Reserve is reached by a footpath from the top of Castle Street. It has pleasant walks and a short, steep climb up **Duns Law**. The town used to cling to the southwest slope of this hill until the English completely destroyed it in 1545 during Henry VIII's Rough Wooing. It was rebuilt in its present position within 50 years. On top of the law is a stone with a hole in it. A Covenanter army flew its standard here in 1639, awaiting a battle that never took place. Their general, Leslie, is thought to have had his headquarters in **Duns Castle**, at the foot of the hill. The stone at the castle gate was erected by Franciscans, claiming Duns to be the birthplace of Johannes Duns Scotus, a great medieval scholar who questioned the teachings of Thomas Aquinas.

The Jim Clark Memorial (open in summer: adm) is clearly signposted on the west side of the town. It displays the trophies of the world champion racing driver who was killed in 1968.

Crumstane Farm Park (open daily except Tuesdays, Easter–Sept: adm), 2 miles (3km) east of Duns, offers farm walks and has rare breeds of farm animals and poultry.

Edinshall Broch

Edinshall Broch, 4 miles (6.5km) north of Duns on the northeast shoulder of Cockburn Law, is the sturdy remains of one of the Iron Age towers that are unique to Scotland and rare so far south. The 20–30-minute climb from a pine wood by the road is clearly marked. It crosses a bridge over Whiteadder Water, which cascades down over gleaming slabs of granite below, the sound of its turmoil carrying far across the bleak moorland. Scattered piles of stones on the grassy slopes are relics of those settlers who roamed the desolate hillside with their beasts, huddling for refuge within the tall, double-walled tower, honeycombed with chambers and galleries. The massive walls were the base of a tapering tower about 40ft (12m) high, its one passage-entrance easily defended.

Manderston

Manderston (open Thursday and Sunday afternoons; Bank Holiday Mondays; mid-May–Sept: adm), 2 miles (3km) east of Duns, is one of the finest Edwardian stately homes in Scotland, with 56 acres of gardens. The rhododendrons are especially worth seeing. In the house is what is believed to be the only silver staircase balustrade in the world—actually silver plated. Spare a thought for whoever has to keep it clean. To judge by the 56 bells in the servants' quarters, there were plenty of silver cleaners when the house was built.

Greenlaw

Greenlaw, a little town 7 miles (11km) southwest of Duns on the Blackadder, has a remarkable **church** whose spire actually contained the prison. Known locally as **Hell's Hole**, it has a sinister gridiron gate, or *yett*, and barred windows. Originally, the court-house was also joined to the church as if to emphasize the connection between the wrath of God and justice.

Where to Stay

moderate

The following will give you bed and breakfast for less than £30 in Duns. **Barniken House Hotel**, 18 Murray Street, ☎ 0361 82466, is a Georgian house in its own grounds in the town, family-run, with only a few bedrooms. There is a putting green in the garden and you can get bar-food all day. **The Black Bull**, Black Bull Street, and the **White Swan,** in the Market Square, both have a few bedrooms for those who like to be at the centre of things.

Greenlaw has several hotels of which **The Castle Hotel**, ☎ 03616 217, a family-run Georgian coaching inn, is friendly, and **Bridgend Guest House** in West High Street, built in 1861, is by the river and has trout fishing. There is also the **Waterloo Arms Hotel** in Chirnside, ☎ 089081 520, a village inn with a mention in the *Good Pub Guide*.

The Tweed Valley

The River Tweed is one of Scotland's most famous salmon-fishing rivers, and also one of its most delightful. It rises in the hills above Moffat, quickly gathering strength to flow through a wide, mostly wooded valley until it reaches the sea at Berwick-upon-Tweed, across the border in England. (The name 'tweed', as in the cloth, incidentally, comes not from the river but from a printing error by an English clerk employed by James Locke of London in 1829, who misread a blotted word—tweels— on a consignment note, 'tweels' being the Scots word for cloth.)

Paxton House

Just outside Berwick-upon-Tweed (open daily, Good Friday–31 Oct: adm), Paxton House is a perfect example of an 18th-century Neo-Palladian mansion. Built in 1758 to designs by John and James Adam and later embellished by Robert Adam, it was intended as the home of Patrick Home of Billie, later 13th Laird of Wedderburn, in anticipation of his marriage to the natural daughter of Frederick the Great of Prussia. The marriage never took place. The house contains Chippendale furniture and important paintings and there are gardens, parkland, riverside walks and an adventure playground.

Ladykirk

Ladykirk, a few miles southwest of the mouth of the Tweed, is just a handful of houses surrounding a pale rose-coloured cruciform **church** that is worth travelling a long way to see. Built in 1500, its solid buttresses, topped by carved finials, support the tremendous weight of an overlapping slabbed-stone roof. The curiously oriental tower was added in 1743 by William Adam. The delicate blush of the exterior seems to glow in daylight as if lit from within. James IV was almost drowned crossing the Tweed here and he vowed to build a shrine to Our Lady in gratitude for his survival. Ladykirk was the fulfilment of his promise: a magnificent rarity in a land where the house of God, since the Reformation, is so often austere. Inside this well-restored gem, a spiral stair leads up to the original living-quarters of the priest, with a small window from which he could watch the altar. James often visited Ladykirk, and he knelt at prayer here before the Battle of Flodden in 1513. Sit in one of the pews for a moment and catch an echo of that poignant lament, composed by Jean Eliot over two hundred years after Flodden, that enshrines the whole tragedy of the battle:

> *I've heard the lilting at our yowe-milking,*
> *Lasses a-lilting before the dawn o' day;*
> *But now they are moaning on ilka green loaning;*
> *'The Flowers of the Forest are a' wede awae.'*

Coldstream

Literally a border town, Coldstream clings to the banks of the Tweed a few miles south-west of Ladykirk, seeming to ignore the rumble and grind of the traffic that thunders up its narrow main street. The Tweed, winding through its broad valley, casts a spell over this area, each bend and pool and cascade having its own character and beauty. The fast, dark currents slide and whirl seawards carrying memories of the past when the mingled blood of Scots and English so often stained the water. Coldstream was the first place where it was easy to cross the river: many armies passed this way and camped on the banks.

The Common Riding Celebrations take place at the beginning of August, during Coldstream Civic Week.

In the middle of the bridge that spans the Tweed, a plaque marks the spot where Robert Burns first put a foot across the border into England in 1787. On the north side of the bridge is a tiny 'marriage house', used by fugitive lovers from England in the 18th century. The figure in a frock-coat, just beyond, who stands Nelson-like on a fluted column, dispatch papers in hand, lightning-conductor pointing heavenwards from the back of his head, was a Victorian MP—Charles Marjoriebanks.

Henderson Park is a formal garden overlooking the river off the Main Street. The engraved stone, erected by the Coldstream Guards, records how, in 1660, their predecessors crossed the Tweed nearby, following their beloved General Monk, to crush Cromwell and establish Charles II on the throne. Although they were not raised here, they adopted their title of Coldstream Guards in honour of this historic event.

Coldstream Museum (open daily, Easter–Oct: adm) is in General Monk's Headquarters in the town's asymmetrical Market Square, rebuilt in 1863. This simple building houses regimental and local history exhibits. Abbey Road leads down from the Main Street to where a Cistercian priory stood for four centuries until it was destroyed by the English in 1545. Human bones were excavated in 1834, which may have been the remains of the bodies that arrived here, piled on waggons, in 1513: Flodden's dead, brought to the Lady Abbess for burial.

The Hirsel, on the western edge of the town, is the seat of the Douglas-Home family. Lord Home (pronounced Hume) of the Hirsel was Prime Minister when President Kennedy was assassinated in 1963. He made history by renouncing his peerage and fighting a by-election at Kinross, during which, although Prime Minister, he was technically not a member of either the House of Lords or the House of Commons. The house is not open to the public but visitors can walk in the park at any time of the year, leaving a donation in the honesty box in the car park. A picturesque stableyard has been converted into a Homestead Museum, craft centre and workshops, each stall containing domestic displays: wash house; joiner's shop; forestry; archaeology. Maps and guides are sold and there are toilets and a coffee shop.

With one exception, the best hotels around Coldstream are across the river—in England. The exception is the **Wheatsheaf Hotel** in Swinton, © 0890 880257, an attractive country inn with only three bedrooms. They won the Scottish Borders Tourist Board Competition for Best Eating Place in the Borders in 1990, so even if you can't get a room it's worth eating there.

Otherwise, you are advised to sneak back over that bridge to Cornhill-on-Tweed in Northumberland: it is still a Coldstream telephone number, if that makes it feel better. **Tillmouth Park Hotel**, in Cornhill-on-Tweed, © 0890 882255, is an imposing Victorian baronial pile in 1000 acres with salmon fishing. Antique furniture gives a country-house atmosphere and the food is good.

The Collingwood Arms, also in Cornhill-on-Tweed, © 0890 882424/882556/882265, is a nice old inn. At Crookham, just outside Cornhill and cheaper, **The Coach House**, built round a sunny courtyard, is very comfortable with good home cooking.

Eating Out

There's not much in the way of gourmet restaurants around here, apart from the Wheatsheaf (see above).

Kelso and Around

Two famous border rivers, the Teviot and the Tweed, meet under the walls of Kelso, a compact market town facing south across green plains towards the Cheviots. Originally called Calkou (Chalk-hill), Kelso was never strongly fortified, relying on its status as an abbey town for immunity from attack. However, being on the threshold of Scotland, it was frequently sacked by the English; it was also the last staging post for Scottish armies on their way south. The Old Pretender was proclaimed king in the market place in 1715 and his son, retreating north after his march on London in 1745, stayed here.

In spite of shocking architectural vandalism in the 19th century, when the town hall's piazza was filled in and a monstrous bank was built, the elegant Georgian square is still very fine, almost Flemish in style, its spaciousness a contrast to the narrow streets of most border towns, crammed behind defensive walls. It was the first central square in any Border town.

The Kelso Races take place in the winter months, from October to May. The Berwickshire Hunt has its point-to-point in Kelso in February, and the Buccleuch and Jed Forest point-to-point takes place in April. The Kelso Dog Show is in June. In July, Kelso Civic Week celebrates the Common Riding Festival, followed by the Border Union Agricultural Show. In September there are the Kelso Horse Sales and the Kelso Ram Sales. (These dates can vary.)

Kelso Museum (open April–Oct: adm) is in one of Kelso's oldest buildings, Turret House, Abbey Court, off Bridge Street, owned by the National Trust for Scotland. It covers Kelso's history as a market town whose main industries were skinning and tanning. By 29 Roxburgh Street a horseshoe set into the road marks the spot where Prince Charles's horse cast a shoe in 1745, during his progress south to Derby. The graceful five-arched bridge over the Tweed was built by Rennie in 1801 as a model for the now demolished Waterloo Bridge, two of whose lamps adorn it.

Kelso Abbey

Kelso Abbey (open daily: free) was founded by David I in 1128, the monks having been moved there, inexplicably, from Selkirk. All that can be seen today is the façade of the northwest transept, the tower and a small part of the nave. This was once the most powerful ecclesiastical establishment in the land and one of the most wealthy, collecting revenue from dozens of parishes, manors, granges, mills and fisheries. The infant James III was crowned here in 1460. In 1523 the English began their attacks on the abbey, tearing off the roofs and firing the monastic buildings. In 1545 they completed the work, slaughtering a hundred brave defendants, including twelve monks.

Floors Castle

Two miles (3km) northwest of Kelso, Floors Castle (castle and grounds open Sun–Thurs, Easter; May, June, Sept; daily July–Aug; Sun and Wed in Oct: adm) is the home of the Duke of Roxburghe. Built by William Adam between 1721 and 1725, and added to by William Playfair in 1849, this immense, eastern-looking, castellated mansion, flanked by vast pavilions, with minarets and cupolas, is best appreciated from a distance. A tree in the grounds marks the spot where James II was killed by an exploding cannon in 1460. Inside are fine tapestries, porcelain and paintings. Floors Castle is the largest inhabited castle in Scotland.

Mellerstain House

Seven miles (11km) northwest of Kelso, Mellerstain (open Easter and 1 May–30 Sept, daily except Sat: adm), the home of Lord Haddington, was partly built by William Adam in 1725 and finished by his son Robert in 1778. It is one of Scotland's finest Georgian mansions, approached down a mile-long avenue of giant beeches, oaks and firs, with formal Italian terraced gardens at the back sloping down to an ornamental lake. Inside are original Robert Adam ceilings and plaster work, especially in one of the two libraries. There is Chippendale, Sheraton and Hepplewhite furniture and paintings by Gainsborough, Allan Ramsay, Constable and Veronese.

A brief liaison between a son of the house, Robbie, and Pippin, a lady of easy virtue who lived in one of the estate cottages, resulted in the birth of a jaunty, wolfish Borderer known as Tam o' Shanter. Picaresque tales of his life as a maverick hunter became legend, even in his lifetime.

Smailholm Tower

Smailholm Tower (open daily in summer: adm) is a couple of miles south of Mellerstain, off the B6404, a fine example of a 16th-century Border peel tower. Well restored, it stands, gaunt and forbidding, 57ft (17m) high on a turf-carpeted crag above a small, weed-choked loch, overlooking flat arable land. To the south, Great Cheviot, guardian of the border, dominates the horizon. Monks from Dryburgh Abbey were given these lands in 1160 and grazed their sheep here. In 1799, the tower was a ruin. Walter Scott, who had spent many holidays with his grandparents at Sandyknowe Farm just to the east, made a deal with the owner, Scott of Harden, who agreed to save the tower if Sir Walter would write a ballad about it. *The Eve of St John* was the result and Smailholm also got a mention in *Marmion*. It seems incongruous that such a stern-faced fortress should contain a museum of dolls and tapestries, but the theme of the display is Scott's *Minstrelsy of the Scottish Border*. With piped 'atmospheric' music to fuel the imagination, it isn't difficult to picture the five storeys as they were, with store rooms below and living quarters above, despite the present exhibitions. When the wind is howling outside one almost hears the warcries of marauding clans and the clash of broadsword and pike.

Smailholm Tower

Kirk Yetholm

Kirk Yetholm, about 7 miles (11km) southeast of Kelso on the B6352, is the northern terminus of the Pennine Way, a 250-mile (400km) hike down into Yorkshire. This was the gypsy capital of Scotland, where all gypsy queens were crowned, until 1883, when the last one, Esther Faa Blythe, died. You can still see the Gypsy Palace, a tiny cottage in the village. Many of Flodden's dead were buried in the churchyard here, in 1513, around an earlier church.

Where to Stay

expensive

If you're after luxury, then it has to be **Sunlaws House Hotel**, Heiton, Kelso, © 05735 331. Owned by the Duke of Roxburghe, Sunlaws is 18th-century baronial, in 200 acres on the banks of the Teviot. Conversion to hotel has not spoiled its family home atmosphere, with antique furniture and excellent food and wine. They offer fishing on the Tweed and the Teviot, shooting, tennis and even croquet.

moderate

Cross Keys Hotel, The Square, Kelso, ✆ 0573 223303, is one of Scotland's oldest coaching inns, completely modernized, in the middle of the town overlooking the square. More peaceful, **Ednam House Hotel**, Bridge Street, Kelso, ✆ 0573 224168/9, is a comfortable 18th-century mansion overlooking the Tweed. Modern extensions haven't spoiled the original ceilings, fireplaces and woodwork.

Eating Out

For a lunch out, try the restaurant in the old stable courtyard at **Floors Castle**, Kelso, ✆ 0573 223333, overlooking the Tweed. Try Floors Kitchen Pheasant Pâté, or the fresh or smoked local salmon. Good home baking comes from the castle kitchen, too, none of it expensive. A local speciality to look out for is Yetholm Bannock, a very rich shortbread with crystallized ginger.

Dryburgh Abbey

Returning to the Tweed, Dryburgh Abbey (open daily; adm), 10 miles (16km) west of Kelso, is one of the quartet of 12th-century Border abbeys founded in the reign of David I, all within a few miles of each other. Built in 1150, it is a beautiful ruin, standing in a loop of the Tweed. Its cloister buildings are more complete than those of other Scottish monasteries, though little remains of the church itself, built with the pinkish, warm-coloured local stone. In common with the other abbeys, Dryburgh was continually ravaged by the English until 1545 when Hertford, acting for Henry VIII, left it a smoking ruin. It was robbed of its usefulness, but not of its tranquil beauty and atmosphere of sanctity. Look for Walter Scott's tomb, behind a railing: his great-grandfather owned the abbey lands at the beginning of the 18th century. Earl Haig, the First World War leader, is also buried here. The stately cedars of Lebanon that throw their shade across the grass were brought back from the Holy Land during one of the Crusades.

Scott's View

A detour from Dryburgh, 5 miles (8km) north up the B6356, to Earlston, takes in Scott's View from below the crest of Bemersyde Hill. This typical Borders' panorama, across a chequerboard of woods and fields, to distant hills, with the Tweed sparkling below, was such a favourite of Sir Walter's that when his mile-long funeral cortège passed by on the way to Dryburgh Abbey, his horses paused here of their own accord. For the history of the Eildon Hills, the three nearest hills to the southwest, see Denholm and Rubers Law, p.85. Legend has King Arthur and his knights sleeping below the Eildons, awaiting summons back to the world.

Earlston

Earlston (with a Summer Festival in June) was the home of Thomas the Rhymer, the 13th-century seer whose gift of prophecy, given by the Fairy Queen, was so effective that he was known as True Thomas. A stone, worn almost bare, in the east wall of the church, is carved with his name and the chunk of ruined wall behind the café to the south of the village is said to be all that remains of his tower. Sorrowlessfield in Earlston was so called because it was the only farm in the Borders to which all the men returned safely after the tragic battle of Flodden in 1513.

Lauder

Go on up the valley of Leader Water, 6 miles (10km) or so northwest to Lauder—a one-street town with a market place in the middle, once an important staging post. The pink stuccoed church, built in 1673, is in the form of a Greek cross with each arm equal and the pulpit in the middle under the tower. Lauder Common Riding is in August.

Thirlestane Castle

Thirlestane Castle (open May, June, Sept, Wed, Thurs and Sun only; July–Aug, daily except Sat, afternoons only: adm), home of the Maitland family for four hundred years, is on the outskirts of Lauder. This huge pile, built on to in many different styles over the centuries, was originally a 14th-century fortress, Lauder Fort, though most of what you see today is late Tudor and early Victorian. William Maitland, Secretary of State to Mary, Queen of Scots, converted the original fortress into a home; John Maitland was Secretary and Chancellor to her son, James VI. A lot of the rich decoration inside was the work of the architect Sir William Bruce in the 17th century, commissioned by John Maitland's grandson, the Duke of Lauderdale who was Secretary of State for Scotland to King Charles II. Among the treasures in the magnificent staterooms are paintings by Gainsborough, Lawrence, Hoppner and Romney. The nurseries are a delight, with old toys on display. There is a Border Country Life Museum in the grounds, a tea room and gift shop.

Melrose

Melrose is an unpretentious town best known for its ruined abbey, fragments of which are incorporated into a few of the older houses. The Melrose Summer Festival, in June, brings the inhabitants out *en fête*: some of the ceremonies, re-enacting history, take place among the ruins of the abbey. The Southern Upland Way passes close to the north of the town—a delightful walk along the Tweed.

Melrose Abbey (open daily: adm) was the most beautiful of the four abbeys founded by David I in the 12th century. Established in 1136 to replace a Celtic monastery at Old Melrose nearby, it was, like its sisters, sacked frequently by the English and as frequently rebuilt by its monks. Much of its mellow stone remains, soaring upwards, a harmony of arches, towers and windows, splendidly decorated. Don't miss the carving of a pig playing the bagpipes.

Heart of the Bruce

Robert Bruce's heart is believed to be buried here in a casket. In fulfilment of a vow, Sir James Douglas cut out the king's heart and set off to the Holy Land, where it was to be buried. But Douglas was killed on the way, fighting the Moors in Spain, and the heart was returned to Scotland and buried in the abbey. An embalmed heart, excavated in this century and hastily reburied, is claimed to be the royal organ.

The abbey has a **museum**, in the Commendator's House, with local history and a room devoted to excavations from the Roman fort at Trimontium.

The **Trimontium Exhibition**, in The Square, (open daily, Easter–Oct: adm) is 'a celebration of Romans and Celts at Newstead'. Here are Roman artefacts from Trimontium, which was the headquarters of the Roman army in Scotland. There are models of forts, an audio visual room, photographs and other displays including a children's corner.

The **Melrose Motor Museum** (open daily in summer: adm), 200 yards (190m) from the abbey towards Newstead, is a private collection of about 20 vintage cars, motor-cycles and cycles, old signs, posters and memorabilia.

While motor enthusiasts sigh over vintage cars, horticulturalists should slip across to **Priorwood Gardens** also by the abbey (open daily April–Oct, and 7 Nov–24 Dec: adm), owned by the National Trust for Scotland. The flowers are all suitable for drying. For anyone who has tried to grow everlasting flowers and then tried to tease them into chic, fashionable arrangements, there is inspiration in these gardens. If you feel daunted, there is a shop where you can buy them. There is also an NTS Visitor Centre, an orchard walk and picnic area.

Abbotsford House

Abbotsford House (open daily late March–31 Oct: adm) lies less than 2 miles (3km) west of Melrose and was Sir Walter Scott's home for the last 20 years of his life. He bought a farm here in 1811 but wasn't happy with its name, Clarty Hole ('clarty' being a Scots word meaning dirty), and decided on Abbotsford in memory of the monks from Melrose who used to cross the river nearby. He demolished the farmhouse and, bit by bit, as the money came in from his books, built the house. When financial disaster struck, his creditors made him a present of the house. Scots Baronial, it is Sir Walter's monument to himself with ideas borrowed from many sources: a cloister from Melrose; a porch from Linlithgow; a ceiling from Roslin. Now a museum, it is a must for Scott enthusiasts. Visitors can see his personal possessions, the rooms just as they were, and the extraordinary range of things he collected: a lock of Bonnie Prince Charlie's hair, for instance, and one of Robert Burns's drinking tumblers. The most romantic names in history seem to be represented. When you've had enough nostalgia, inspect the 9000-volume library. There is also a teashop and gift shop. Before tracing the Tweed further, detour 2 miles (3km) southwest and follow the Yarrow Water a few miles to Selkirk.

Selkirk

Selkirk means 'kirk-of-the-shieling', a peaceful, rural connotation that no longer applies to this town on the hillside above the valleys of the Ettrick and Yarrow, its spires and gables visible for miles, its textile mills tucked away along the river banks. These valleys were once extensive forests, hunting ground for kings and refuge for fugitives. Selkirk men are still called 'Souters' (shoemakers) from the days when cobbling was the main occupation: Prince Charles ordered 4000 shoes from Selkirk for his barefooted army in 1745.

Of the 80 Selkirk men who rode out to fight at Flodden in 1513, only one returned, throwing down a captured English standard at the feet of the waiting families in silent tribute to his fallen friends. The standard is preserved in the library, and the Selkirk Common Riding, in June, culminates in a ceremony re-enacting the 'casting of the colours'. Most of the mills round Selkirk have mill shops, selling tweed and woollen goods.

The triangular **Market Place** has a statue of Sir Walter Scott on a 20ft (6m) pedestal in front of the town hall. Scott was county sheriff here for 33 years. In the town hall (open weekday afternoons in summer or by arrangement) where court sessions were heard in the days of Sir Walter's jurisdiction, there are mementos of him and of other famous 'Souters'.

Halliwell's House Museum and Gallery (open daily April–Oct; weekday afternoons, Nov–Dec: free) is off the main square. This row of 18th-century houses has been renovated to recreate Selkirk's history, the history of the buildings and an ironmonger's shop. The Robson Gallery has art exhibitions. The statue at the east end of the High Street is of **Mungo Park**, the 18th-century explorer. He was born 4 miles (6.5km) away at Foulshiels and gave up medical practice to devote himself to exploring the River Niger, in Africa, in which he was drowned while escaping in a canoe from hostile natives.

The Flodden Monument, just beyond Mungo Park's statue, depicts a standard bearer, with the inscription 'O Flodden Field'.

Selkirk Glass, on the A7 just north of Selkirk, has a visitors' centre and gives demonstrations of making glass paperweights. A plaque over a shop doorway in West Port marks where Montrose lodged in 1645 before his defeat at the battle of Philiphaugh a couple of miles to the west. After the battle, General Leslie and his Covenanters butchered the remains of Montrose's army, including hundreds of women and children, in the name of their God.

Newark Castle

Newark Castle, west of Selkirk (apply: Buccleuch Estates, © 0750 20081), is where a hundred of these luckless victims were shot. Even without its grim history—and you find yourself looking for bloodstains and shot-scars on the walls, and listening for the echo of screams—it is an impressive ruin. It stands five storeys tall, a tower house within a curtain wall on a green mound above the fast-flowing river, once a royal hunting seat for the

Forest of Ettrick, with the 15th-century arms of James I on the west gable. This was the setting for Walter Scott's *Lay of the Last Minstrel*.

Bowhill (grounds open daily in the summer, except Fri; house only open in July: adm, ring 0750 20732 to avoid disappointment) is 3 miles (4.5km) west of Selkirk. This Georgian mansion, built in 1812, is the home of the Scotts of Buccleuch, surrounded by wooded hills that dazzle the eye in autumn. Here are paintings by Leonardo da Vinci, Gainsborough, Reynolds, Claude, Canaletto, Guardi and Raeburn; proof copies of books by Walter Scott; relics of the Duke of Monmouth, and a good deal more. While culture vultures sigh over these treasures, more philistine visitors are offered an adventure playground, nature trails, a riding centre, an audio-visual show, mountain-bicycle hire, a gift shop and a licensed tea-room.

St Mary's Loch

Before returning to the Tweed, follow the Yarrow Valley to St Mary's Loch, 14 miles (22km) southwest of Selkirk. This 3-mile (4.5km) stretch of reed-fringed water set among hills is a popular spot for sailors and fishermen. Stop for refreshment at Tibbie Shiel's Inn, on the southeast shore of the loch, called after the innkeeper who served Walter Scott, Thomas Carlyle, Robert Louis Stevenson and James Hogg. These literary giants came here for convivial gatherings. Hogg lived nearby and his statue overlooks the inn from the other side of the loch. An annual service is held in the churchyard of **St Mary's of the Lowes** overlooking the loch on the northwest, celebrating the Blanket Preaching, when the preacher delivered his message from a tent made from a blanket. The church has gone now.

One of the most beautiful stretches of the Southern Upland Way skirts the eastern shore of the loch and the walk north from here, about 8 miles (13km), to Traquair House (see below) is not stiff and worth the effort. There is also a route from Cappercleuch, on the west side of the loch, about 9 miles (14.5km) to Tweedsmuir, steep, twisting and remote, with panoramic views. This goes past **Megget Reservoir**, long and wide, cradled below hills and winner of a major design award. This valley was once part of the Forest of Ettrick, a favourite hunting ground in the days of David I.

Where to Stay

moderate

You won't go far wrong in **Philipburn House Hotel**, a mile out of Selkirk on the A708 to Peebles, © 0750 207 47/21690. This homely 18th-century country house in five acres of grounds with outdoor swimming pool, has a cuisine that has won acclaim in most of the good food guides and first prize in the dinner section of the Scottish Borders Tourist Board competition. Try saddle of roe deer in port, and bilberry sauce. Packages include riding, mountain-biking, walking, fishing and excursions.

Ettrickshaws Hotel, Ettrickbridge, © 0750 52229, 6 miles (10km) southwest of

Selkirk, is a family-run Victorian mansion in ten acres of the Ettrick valley beside the river. Fishing is free and riding is available. **Dryburgh Abbey Hotel**, St Boswells, © 0835 22261, is an imposing pile in wooded grounds next to the abbey, on the Tweed. Recently renovated and upgraded it is Highly Commended by the Scottish Tourist Board, and not cheap. **The Buccleuch Arms** in St Boswells, © 0835 22243, is a restored 17th-century coaching inn overlooking the village green with arrangements for fishing, golfing, shooting and pony-trekking.

There are several hotels in Melrose, of which the refurbished **Bon Accord** in the Market Square, © 089682 2645, is probably the best value. More imposing is **Burts Hotel**, © 089682 2285, also in the Market Square.

inexpensive

Black Bull Hotel, Lauder, © 05782 208, is a restored coaching inn with good bar meals and a nice atmosphere.

Eating Out

Apart from Philpburn House (above), **Cross Keys Inn,** Selkirk, **Hoebridge Inn**, Gattonside, Melrose, and **Tibbie Shiels Inn**, St Mary's Loch were all runners up in the Scottish Borders Tourist Board Best Eating Place competition in 1990, though reports on Tibbie Shiels have subsequently been less favourable.

Galashiels

On another tributary of the Tweed, the Gala, 6 miles (10km) or so north of Selkirk, Galashiels (**Shieling-on-the-Gala**) is a busy town concentrating on the manufacture of textiles. Plain and unpretentious, it lies among hills and fast rivers. Involved in milling since 1622, Galashiels built the first Scottish carding machine in 1790 and is famous for its tweed and woollen hosiery. The **Scottish College for Textiles** is in the town, launching pad for many aspiring designers. Galashiels' Common Riding celebrations are in June, with the Braw Lads Gathering.

The Galashiels **War Memorial** is a reconstruction of a peel tower with a death-roll engraved on a bronze tablet in the wall, serving as a backdrop to a statue of one of the Border Reivers sitting on his horse, proud and vigilant. The town crest, on a wall of the municipal buildings, consists of a fox, reaching up for some plums, with the motto 'Sour Plums'. It commemorates an incident in 1337 when men of Galashiels disposed of a band of English soldiers who were looking for wild plums in the woods.

Old Gala House has a visitor centre with the history of the lairds of Galashiels and an art gallery with sculpture. **Galashiels Museum**, attached to Peter Anderson's Woollen Mill, runs guided mill tours, and has displays tracing the history of Galashiels' textile industry. At the **Borders Wool Centre** there is a collection of rare breeds of sheep, spinning demonstrations, a display of fleeces, and a shop.

Kingsknowes Hotel, Selkirk Road, Galashiels, ✆ 0896 58375, is a 19th-century mansion house full of Victorian character, overlooking the Tweed and Abbotsford. For an activity holiday, try **Tweed Valley Hotel**, Walkerburn, ✆ 089687 220. This Edwardian country house overlooking the Tweed offers fishing, walking, bicycling, golf, bird-watching and wildlife, as well as courses in sketching and watercolours, a sauna and solarium. Try their Tweed Valley Game Casserole.

Scottish Museum of Woollen Textiles

The Scottish Museum of Woollen Textiles (open weekdays all year, and daily in summer: free) is at Walkerburn, halfway to Peebles on the A72 from Galashiels. It covers the development of the wool industry from a humble cottage industry, with the original wool and cloth patterns, through to the thriving enterprise it is today. There is also a mill shop.

Innerleithen

When Walter Scott's *St Ronan's Well* was published in 1824, his readers identified the spa in the novel as the mineral spring above Innerleithen and flocked there to take the waters. The contemporary Earl of Traquair who owned the land, a canny Scot, built a pump room to exploit his natural resources and you can buy a gulp of the water, and see the well. One of the earls, perhaps an urbanite at heart, named the streets: Bond Street, The Strand, Princes Street, etc.

Robert Smail's Printing Works, in Innerleithen, restored by the National Trust for Scotland, is a working printing museum with vintage machinery including a 100-year-old press once driven by water, and an NTS Visitor Centre.

Traquair House

Traquair House (open Easter, daily May–mid-Sept; grounds and restaurant daily from Easter: adm) is 3 miles (4.5km) southwest of Walkerburn. The name comes from *Tra*—a dwelling or hamlet, and *quair*—a winding stream. Dating from the 10th century, Traquair is said to be the oldest mansion in Scotland continuously inhabited by the same family: William the Lion held court here in 1209. The house hums with domesticity, unlike most stately homes. The grey harled walls rise to four storeys with corbelled turrets and a steeply pitched roof, like a French château. Twenty-seven monarchs visited Traquair, notably Mary, Queen of Scots, with Darnley and their infant son, whose cradle you can see. Mary's rosary, crucifix and purse are also displayed.

At one time the Tweed ran so close to the house that its owner could fish from his windows. Finding that unfortunately he could also swim in his cellars, James Stuart, the 17th-century laird, diverted the river's course so it now flows a quarter of a mile away. The grounds offer woodland walks, a maze, craft workshops and exhibitions. Ale is produced in the 18th-century brewhouse and the Traquair Fair is in August. The Southern Upland Way passes close to Traquair.

The Bear Gates

 Prince Charles Edward Stuart was the last person to leave through the 'Bear Gates', which bar the entrance to the avenue, on his march to Derby in 1745. They were then clanged shut by the Jacobite Fifth Earl of Traquair, who vowed they would never be reopened until a Stuart ruled Scotland again. Another version of this story is that in the days when Catholics were not allowed to own carriages, but continued to do so clandestinely, an unfriendly neighbour of the Catholic Earl of Traquair told the authorities. His carriage and horses were confiscated and he slammed his gates in protest. Whichever story is true, the gates remain closed.

Glentress Forest

Glentress Forest is about 3 miles (5km) northwest of Traquair on the way to Peebles, with signposted walks, one of which leads to **Cardie Hill Fort**, with grass-covered ramparts, and another to **Shielgreen Tower**, of which little now remains. At the entrance to the park a trio of tall wooden figures stand, unornamented and graceful in their simplicity, carved from local wood.

Peebles and Around

Flanked by wide greens, the River Tweed hurries through Peebles, a peaceful old town with narrow streets leading to quaint yards and buildings with carved lintels. The name is derived from *pebylls*, meaning tents, which refers to the tents of the nomadic Gadeni, the first inhabitants of the town. St Mungo came in the 6th century, baptizing converts in the well that bears his name. Traces remain of the wall built to protect the town from the destructive English. Cromwell garrisoned troops here.

The Beltane Festival in June has pagan roots and incorporates Peebles' celebration of the Common Riding of the Marches. There are sheepdog trials in June, an agricultural show in August, and in September, the Peebles Highland Games and an arts festival.

The **Tweed Bridge**, with five elegant stone arches, decorated with ornate lamp standards, dates from the 15th century. **The Chambers Institute** (open weekdays: free), once the townhouse of the Queensberrys, was given to the town by William Chambers, the publisher. With the help of a grant from Andrew Carnegie, it was enlarged to house reading rooms, libraries, two museums and an art gallery. **The Cornice**, Innerleithen Road, is a museum of ornamental plasterwork, with a re-creation of a plasterer's casting shop, cornices, corbels, mouldings, gargoyles, statues, and all the tools of the craft.

Cross Kirk (open daily: free, key from the custodian next door) is the 13th-century ruined nave and west tower of a Trinitarian friary, with the foundations of the cloister buildings. When the English burnt down the collegiate church of St Andrew, Cross Kirk was used as the parish church.

Neidpath Castle

L-shaped, 13th-century Neidpath Castle (open Easter and daily in summer: adm), west of the town, stands on a green mound overlooking the Tweed. Continuously inhabited for almost seven hundred years, it has just been given a grant for essential repairs. Its ochre walls, nearly 12 feet (3.6m) thick in places, withstood the bombardment of Cromwell's troops in the mid-17th century for longer than any other castle south of the Forth. You can see the pit prison hewn out of the rock and some of the original vaults, and climb on to the roof and look out over wooded hills and valleys. Along the grassy path to the castle are a few yew trees. These are all that remain of a once famous avenue (the Neidpath Yews) from which bows were made for crusaders. The majority of the yews were cut down to pay the gambling debts of that debauched reprobate 'Old Q', William Douglas, Duke of Queensberry, in 1795. Wordsworth was so shocked by this vandalism that, during his tour of Scotland in 1803, he wrote the sonnet 'Composed at Neidpath Castle' starting:

> *Degenerate Douglas! oh, the unworthy Lord!*
> *Whom mere despite of heart could so far please,*
> *And love of havoc, (for with such disease*
> *Fame taxes him,) that he could send forth word*
> *To level with the dust a noble horde*
> *A brotherhood of venerable Trees.*

Neidpath stages one of the ceremonies of the annual Beltane Festival, when the Warden of Neidpath—someone in high office—is proclaimed from the castle steps.

Kailzie Gardens

Kailzie Gardens (open daily, April–Oct: adm), 2 miles (3km) east of Peebles, include a rose garden, herbaceous border, shrubs, a 19th-century walled garden with greenhouses, a 'laburnum alley', an art gallery, gift shop and licensed tea room. Woods surround the gardens, along a sparkling burn, where the ground is golden with daffodils in spring, and waterfowl are abundant.

Dawyck Botanic Gardens

Dawyck Botanic Gardens (open daily in summer: adm), 8 miles (13km) southwest of Peebles, were created by Sir James Nasmyth in 1720, under the influence of his mentor Linnaeus, the great Swedish botanist. The woods are particularly magnificent: the first larches introduced into Scotland were planted here in 1725. Carpets of scented narcissi lie among rare trees and shrubs from all over the world, twisting and climbing to a Dutch bridge over a waterfall. The chapel in the woods was designed by William Burn.

Merlin's Grave

 Merlindale, in Drumelzier, 9 miles (14.5km) southwest of Peebles, is one of the legendary sites of the grave of Merlin, Britain's elusive magician. Thomas the Rhymer, 13th-century seer, said: 'When Tweed and Powsayl meet at Merlin's grave, England and Scotland shall one monarch have.'

The day Elizabeth I died, when James VI of Scotland inherited the English throne, the River Tweed burst its banks and flooded across Drumelzier into the neighbouring Powsayl.

Broughton

Broughton, 10 miles (16km) southwest of Peebles, is a village in the valley of Biggar Water, below layers of rounded hills. **Broughton Place** is a treasure which could be missed—look out for the signs, up a steep drive. It is a 20th-century castle, designed by Sir Basil Spence in the 1930s, in the style of the Border fortresses. It looks startlingly authentic against its background of blue-grey hills. Inside is a first-class art gallery, open in the summer. Many contemporary artists and craftsmen show their work here including the father-and-son proprietors, Ian and Graham Buchanan-Dunlop.

The **John Buchan Centre** (open afternoons May–mid-Oct: adm) is also in Broughton, in a converted chapel, with biographical information for devotees of the remarkable 1st Baron Tweedsmuir, writer and creator of Richard Hannay. He not only wrote more than fifty books but was also a barrister, statesman and Governor-General of Canada. Buchan grew up here and, looking around at the wild hills, it becomes clear where he got many of the settings for his Scottish novels. You will leave determined to re-read his books.

Six miles (10km) to the south, to the west of the A702, **The Crook Inn** is one of the oldest pubs in the Borders. John Buchan was a frequent customer, as were Walter Scott and his circle. In the bar, cast your mind back to the 18th century when this was the kitchen: Robert Burns sat here, drawn in no doubt by the charms of one of the kitchen staff, and dashed off one of his poems at the table!

Another mile south is the village of **Tweedsmuir**, from which John Buchan took his title.

Further south, to the east of the A702, is **Tweed's Well**, the source of the Tweed. It is hard to believe this small beginning will so quickly develop into that torrent that swirls through the Borders to the sea.

Where to Stay

moderate

The huge, château-like **Peebles Hotel Hydro**, Innerleithen Road, Peebles, © 0721 720602, might be up your street if you are more concerned with facilities than cosy atmosphere. In 30 acres, with a backdrop of rolling hills, it has a swimming pool, jacuzzi, saunas, solaria, gym, games room for badminton, tennis and squash, golf, riding and pitch-and-putt. It also offers theme holidays, such as golfing, walking. **Cringletie House Hotel**, at Eddleston, Peebles, © 0721 730233, is a privately owned, baronial mansion, festooned with turrets, 2 miles (3km) outside Peebles. It stands in 28 acres with wonderful views from all the rooms, and serves imaginative food. Try their poached salmon.

Drummore, Venlaw High Road, Peebles, © 0721 720336, perched on a hill with panoramic views, specializes in mountain biking. If castles appeal to you, try **Venlaw Castle Hotel**, Peebles, © 0721 720384. Built in 1782 in the Venlaw Hills, with magnificent views, this baronial pile is family-run with a reputation for good cooking.

Kingsmuir Hotel, Peebles and **Kailzie Garden Restaurant**, Peebles, were both runners up, and **Riverbank Restaurant**, Innerleithen, a winner in the Scottish Borders Tourist Board Best Eating Place competition.

The Teviot Valley

The River Teviot rises in the hills south of Teviothead, on the border of Dumfries and Galloway, descending rapidly to cut a beautiful valley northeastwards to Kelso, where it joins the Tweed.

Roxburgh

Roxburgh was once a mighty walled royal burgh, built round the fortress of Marchmount, about a mile southwest of Kelso, so large that in the 12th century some of its inhabitants had to be rehoused outside the town. This metropolis was so bitterly fought over and so frequently annexed by the English that in 1460 the Scots decided the only way to keep it permanently from their enemies was to remove it from the map. They made a pretty good job of it: all that remains are the earthworks of the castle, and you have to search for them. (The present village of Roxburgh, further southwest, dates from more recent times.)

Jedburgh and Around

Jedburgh lies in the valley of Jed Water, a tributary of the Teviot, surrounded by fields and woods whose vivid autumn colours are a delight. Its proximity to the border made it the target of many raids and its position on one of the main routes north brought a succession of armies through its streets. Built round its abbey, Jedburgh is packed with history. The men of Jedburgh were renowned for their resistance to invasion, defending their town with gruesome tenacity. 'Jeddart Handba', a local game played with a hay-stuffed leather ball, is said to originate from when Jedburgh (or Jeddart) men returned from routing the English and played ball with the heads of their victims.

The Jedburgh Festival is held annually in July, two weeks of pageantry dominated by the Jeddart Callants—the young men of Jedburgh—who re-enact the Common Ridings of the past. The Jedburgh Border Games are also held in July.

Jedburgh Abbey

Jedburgh Abbey and Visitor Centre (open daily: adm) has a history spanning several centuries. Fragments of carved Celtic stonework, found during the restoration of the abbey, suggest that it was built on the site of a 9th-century church that appears in the records of Lindisfarne. Founded as a priory in 1138 by David I, and raised to abbey status in 1147, it was frequently sacked by the English, the most devasting attack being by Hertford in 1544 during his ruthless execution of the orders of Henry VIII. It stands on a green sward, its mellow stone supporting graceful arches and windows, including a rose window, called St Catherine's Wheel. The **Visitors Centre** gives an interpretation of the abbey's history, with displays of how the monks lived and recordings of their music and chanting.

Jedburgh Castle Jail Museum

The museum (open daily in summer: adm) was built at the top of Castlegate in 1823 as the county prison, on the site of a castle built around the same time as the abbey. It was a popular royal residence; Alexander III chose it for his wedding feast when, desperate for an heir, he married his second wife, Jolande, in the abbey in 1285. The spectre of Death is said to have appeared at this feast, prophesying the death of the king—which happened six months later when he fell from his horse. Frequently occupied by the English and in fact ceded to them under the Treaty of Falaise in 1174, it was destroyed by order of the Scottish Parliament to keep it from the enemy. The museum contains reconstructed rooms showing the 'reformed' system of imprisonment in the early 19th century—a gruelling insight into the penal and social history of those days.

Mary, Queen of Scots' House

Queen Mary's House (open daily in summer: adm) in Queen Street is haunted with memories of Scotland's tragic queen. Mary came here in 1556, still married to Darnley, to preside over the Court of Justice at the Assizes. She stayed in this house, reputedly because it was the only one with indoor sanitation. During her stay she heard that James Bothwell had been wounded and was ill at Hermitage Castle, 20 miles (32km) away. Perhaps already in love, she rode over to Hermitage and back again, in the same day, to visit him. As a result she became critically ill of a fever from which she nearly died. Her attendants opened the window at the crisis of her illness, to let her soul fly free. Years later she was to say: 'Would that I had died, that time in Jedburgh.' Darnley came to visit her while she was ill and when she was better she rode back to Edinburgh with Bothwell, now also recovered, in her entourage. The ochre-coloured house has high crow-stepped gables and a turret stair; the steep roof was once thatched. It has been restored and is much as it was when Mary was there: you can see the great hall, withdrawing-room and fireplace and the stuffy little room where she lay so ill for a month, near the chamber occupied by her four Marys: Mary Beaton, Mary Seton, Mary Carmichael and Mary Hamilton. The **Visitor Centre** was up-graded to mark the 400th anniversary of her death in 1987, and presents an interpretation of her life and times. Among the exhibits are one of the rare portraits of Bothwell, done in 1565; a facsimile of Mary's death-warrant, signed by her cousin Elizabeth, and her watch, apparently found in the marshy land near Hermitage Castle 200 years after she lost it on her impulsive visit to Bothwell. There is also a gift shop.

Harestanes Countryside Visitor Centre is 3 miles (4.5km) north of Jedburgh off the A68 (open daily, April–Oct: free). A Discovery Room, in converted farm buildings, describes the flora and fauna on the signed walks on the estate. There is also a play area, tearoom, shop, exhibitions, audio visual display and games room. **Jedforest Deer and Farm Park** (open daily May–Oct: adm), 4 miles (6km) south of Jedburgh, is a working upland farm with deer, many breeds of animals, an adventure playground, walks, information centre, café and shop.

Hermitage Castle

Although closer to Hawick than Jedburgh, it is really from Jedburgh you should visit Hermitage Castle (open daily; weekends only in winter: adm), so you can appreciate Mary's frantic ride (see Mary, Queen of Scots House). Twenty miles (32km) southwest, it stands stark and indestructible, on a grassy platform surrounded by earthworks; an angular fortress with frowning arches. On all sides, moorland rises in peaks whence watch could be kept in every direction, including across the border. Even in sunshine, with the sparkling Hermitage Water at its feet, it has a grim aura. The 14th-century tower, built round a small courtyard, has later additions of massive square towers and walls, set with holes and corbels that once supported a continuous walkway, high on the exterior walls, reached through rectangular doorways. Close by are the ruins of St Mary's Chapel and traces of the medieval village that grew up round the castle.

Legends of such horror and cruelty surround this melancholy lump of history that locals believed the weight of its iniquities would eventually cause it to sink into Hades, though it shows no sign of doing so yet.

The first man to build on the site was Nicholas de Soulis, in the 13th century. He was so cruel and evil that his neighbours and servants carted him off to Ninestone Rig, a mile to the northeast, wrapped him in a sheet of lead, and boiled him to death.

The 11-foot (3.5 m) long grave outside the walls of the kirkyard beyond the castle, is believed to contain the remains of the Cout of Kielder, a giant baron who came over the hills from Kielder Castle across the border to Hermitage to slay de Soulis. He was drowned by his intended victim, in a deep pool in the river, still known as Cout of Kielder Pool. A 'gallant Scottish patriot', Alexander Ramsay of Dalhousie, was lowered into the pit-prison still visible in the castle. He existed for many days on a trickle of grain that fell from the granary above, before he starved to death.

Glenbank Hotel, Castlegate, Jedburgh, ℂ 0835 862258, is a Georgian house in attractive gardens, 5 minutes' walk from the town centre. If it's history you are after, the **Spread Eagle Hotel**, Jedburgh, ℂ 0835 862870, is reputed to be the oldest in Scotland, and claims that Mary, Queen of Scots slept there. With such romance, you can't expect ritzy surroundings.

Denholm

Denholm, 5 miles (8km) southwest of Jedburgh, is a conservation village, its 18th-century houses built close together round a green, in the style of earlier settlements when the beasts were herded on to the green when raids were anticipated, the narrow alleyways making defence easier. The elaborate monument on the green is to Dr John Leyden, who was born in the thatched cottage just off the north side of the square, in 1775. This remarkable scholar, physician and poet, who died at the age of 36, was almost entirely self-taught, astounding his contemporaries, including Sir Walter Scott, with the range and scope of his knowledge.

The village is dominated by **Rubers Law** to the southeast, accessible from all sides and easily scaled to the remains of an Iron Age hill fort at the top. This was a Roman signal station, within sight of a similar one on nearby Bonchester Hill. There is a rock on the law, known as Peden's Pulpit, from which Alexander Peden preached to huge congregations of Covenanters during the Killing Times.

It is said that the Devil used to get so irritated at being woken every morning by the chanting of the monks in Melrose Abbey that he decided to move three of the Cheviot Hills and plant them between Melrose and the rising sun. Unfortunately, during the move, he dropped the top half of the last one. This was Rubers Law, and explains why it would fit exactly on to the flat top of one of the Eildon Hills.

Hawick

In a fold of the hills on the banks of the Teviot, Hawick (pronounced Hoyk) owes its prosperity to the textile mills along the river, many with their own shops, and to the well-stocked timber yards in the area. The hub of the town is a bronze statue in the High Street, an armoured youth on a charger, holding a standard above his head. In 1514 a band of English troops, looting through the Borders, were camped at nearby Hornshole, knowing the death-toll from the Battle of Flodden the previous year had reduced the fighting strength of the Border towns to old men and boys. The Callants—teenaged youths—of Hawick rode out in a brave, ragged band, routed the English and returned with the enemy standard. This event is enthusiastically incorporated into the Common Riding Celebrations in June.

Rugby is the town's ruling passion; Hawick has contributed players to the Scottish team over many years. The Hawick Rugby Sevens take place in April. For two weeks in August the town also holds a summer festival.

Wilton Lodge Museum (open daily April–Sept; afternoons except Sat, Oct–March: adm) in Wilton Lodge Park on the western outskirts of the town covers the textile industry, Border history, archaeology, and local natural history. There is also an art gallery. William Wallace visited here in 1297 and you can see the tree where he is supposed to have tethered his horse. The park has walks, gardens and sports facilities.

Hawick has a good **Indoor Leisure Centre**, north of the town on the A7, with swimming pool, restaurant and entertainment such as puppet shows.

Teviothead

In the village of Teviothead, 9 miles (14.5km) southwest of Hawick, is a poignant memorial. A stone set into the wall of the graveyard opposite the kirk is dedicated to the 16th-century freebooter Johnnie Armstrong and his followers. Armstrong rode to this lonely place from Langholm, further south, hoping to win the favour of his teenaged sovereign, James V. He offered the service and allegiance of his men and himself, but the young king, intent on cleaning up the lawless Borders, was not won over. Armstrong and his band were hanged from a makeshift gallows at Caerlanrig to the southwest.

Newcastleton

Newcastleton, by Liddel Water, about 5 miles (8km) south of Hermitage Castle, was founded in 1793 by the Duke of Buccleuch and has an unusual symmetrical layout. Their Traditional Music Festival, in early July, is fun.

Where to Stay

moderate

Kirklands Hotel, in West Stewart Place, Hawick, ✆ 0450 72263, is a comfortable if unexciting Victorian town house, mentioned in most guides. They have a croquet lawn, snooker room and library. For something a bit different, **Hazeldean Holidays**, Denholm, Hawick, ✆ 0450 087 373, has 12 self-catering log cabins and chalets dotted around 25 acres on the Teviot. They have horses, an indoor riding school, fishing, and golf nearby. Terms are weekly, on application.

Eating Out

The Fox and Hounds in the Main Street of Denholm is an old coaching inn. **Old Forge,** at Newmill on Teviot, south of Hawick, was a runner-up in the Scottish Borders Tourist Board Best Eating Place competition in 1990.

Dumfries and Galloway

Caerlaverock Castle

Dumfries and Galloway borders the northern shore of the Solway Firth with the dramatic hammerhead of the Rhinns of Galloway at its western tip. Apart from the extreme east, this is an isolated corner, off the main route to anywhere except Ireland, to which it is closer than to much of the rest of Scotland.

The name Galloway derives from the Gaelic *gallgaidhel*—land of the stranger. It was here, early in the 6th century, that Celtic Christian Scots from Ireland landed, drove out the Picts and moved north to establish the Kingdom of Dalriada. Earlier still, St Ninian brought the first message of Christianity to Whithorn, in AD 397. Many churches and abbeys were built in the area, becoming places of pilgrimage for Scottish monarchs, and people from distant lands. Frequent wars, the Reformation and Henry VIII's 'Rough Wooing' in the 16th century reduced most of these to ruins, but the shells of their splendour remain. Towns near the border suffered their share of hammering from the English, and settlements on the coast were fortified against invasion.

Mary, Queen of Scots, passed through in 1563, escorted by a train of nobles: a light-hearted progress in contrast to her next visit, five years later, when she fled here after her defeat at Langside and embarked from Port Mary at Dundrennan in the hope of finding sanctuary in England.

This remote corner attracts little industry; fishing and farming are important to the economy as is tourism. In early days smuggling was rife, providing employment for, among others, Robert Burns, who spent his last years in Dumfries as an exciseman.

As in the Borders, some of the towns and villages close to the English boundary have annual **Common Riding Festivals**, in memory of when the men went out to check the marches, to make sure Border Reivers hadn't been at work, stealing cattle. These festivals last for up to a week and incorporate events in local history, as well as pageantry and entertainment. Dumfries' Guid Nychburris Festival, and Lockerbie's Common Riding Festival are in June. In July there are: Annan's Riding of the Marches, Moffat's Gala Week and Langholm's Common Riding Festival. Sanquhar has a festival in August.

This is a naturalist's paradise. The mild climate of both coastal and inland habitats attracts countless rare species of birds, animals and plants. The tidal marshes are wintering grounds for barnacle geese and lots of other waterfowl. If you are lucky you may see peregrine falcons, whose breeding sites are carefully guarded by the police against avaricious crooks who sell the incubated eggs for hundreds of pounds.

The Southern Upland Way starts its 212-mile (340km) journey to the North Sea coast at Portpatrick on the west coast. It meanders through the hills of the Galloway Forest Park—some of them quite high—eastwards

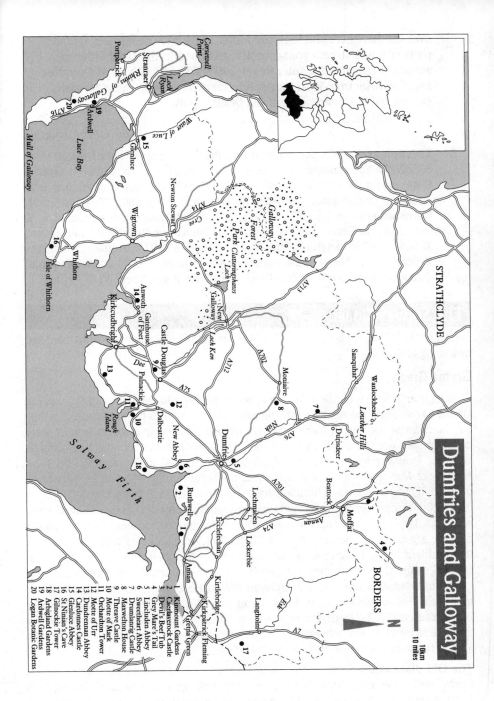

Dumfries and Galloway

STRATHCLYDE

BORDERS

N

10km
10 miles

Mull of Galloway

Corsewell Point

Stranraer
Loch Ryan
Portpatrick
Rhinns of Galloway
A716
20
Ardwell
19
15 Glenluce
Water of Luce
Luce Bay
Wigtown
Newton Stewart
A714
Cree
16
Whithorn
Isle of Whithorn

Galloway Forest Park
Clatteringshaws Loch
Loch Trool
New Galloway
Loch Ken
A713

Kirkcudbright
Anworth
14 Gatehouse of Fleet
Castle Douglas
Dee
9 Palnackie
13
11
10 Dalbeattie
New Abbey
18
6
2 Ruthwell
Rough Island

Solway Firth

A712
A75
12
A702
Moniaive
8
Dumfries
5
Annan
1
Ecclefechan
Kirtlebridge
Lochmaben
Lockerbie
Gretna Green
Kirkpatrick Fleming

Sanquhar
Wanlockhead
Lowther Hills
A76
Nith
7 Durisdeer
A74
Beattock
3 Moffat
Annan
4

Langholm
Esk
A7
17

1 Kinmount Gardens
2 Caerlaverock Castle
3 Devil's Beef Tub
4 Grey Mare's Tail
5 Lincluden Abbey
6 Sweetheart Abbey
7 Drumlanrig Castle
8 Maxwelton House
9 Threave Castle
10 Orchardton Tower
11 Motte of Ur
12 Dundrennan Abbey
13 Cardoness Castle
14 Glenluce Abbey
15 St Ninian's Cave
16 Gilnockie Tower
17 Arbigland Gardens
18 Ardwell Gardens
19 Logan Botanic Gardens
20

89

over the Lowthers and then the Moffat Hills into the Borders. Though parts of it will stretch your muscles, all is within the capabilities of anyone reasonably fit. You can get *200 Walks and Climbs in Dumfries and Galloway* from local tourist information centres. There are also guided walks around many of the beauty spots.

Tourist Information

The main tourist information centre is in the town centre of **Dumfries**, ✆ 0387 53862 (24-hour answering service); it is open all year, as is that at **Gretna Gateway** on the northbound A74, ✆ 0461 33508. The local centres, open from Easter to mid-October, are **Castle Douglas**: Markethill, ✆ 0556 2611; **Dalbeattie**: Town Hall, ✆ 0556 610117; **Gatehouse of Fleet**: Car Park, ✆ 0557 814212; **Gretna Green:** ✆ 0461 37834; **Kirkcudbright**: Harbour Square, ✆ 0557 30494; **Langholm**: Kiln Green, ✆ 03873 80976; **Moffat:** Churchgate, ✆ 0683 20620; **Newton Stewart**: Dashwood Square, ✆ 0671 2431; **Sanquhar**: Tolbooth Visitor Centre, 0659 50185; **Stranraer**: Bridge Street, ✆ 0776 2595.

The Solway Coast

Tidal mudflats and sandy beaches, fringed by woods and cut by river valleys, are bordered by a string of towns.

Gretna Green

Coming from England, on the A74, you cross the border into Dumfries and Galloway at Gretna Green. From the romance that has grown up around this famous village, it is difficult to untangle the squalid reality of an era when a great many innocent females were duped by men whose motives could not stand the test of a formal betrothal with parental consent. Runaway lovers, cheated of 'irregular marriages' in England by the 1754 Hardwicke Marriage Act, were able to cross the border until 1856 and be married by declaration before a witness. The union was 'forged' over an anvil by the blacksmith. Even in the 20th century couples came north because, until the age of consent in England was altered in 1969, Scotland was the only place where parental consent was not required after the age of 16. The border villages of Gretna and Springfield vied with each other for the considerable profit that could be made from these often disastrous unions. One blacksmith, Rennison, is said to have performed 5147 ceremonies. Today they continue to exploit that dishonourable trade by displaying the marriage houses where the ceremonies took place. Springfield lost its trade to Gretna in 1830, when the building of the Sark Bridge caused it to be by-passed by the main north–south route. At the height of the marriage industry, rivalry between the 'priests' in the area was ferocious and each had his agent, promoting his superiority in hotels in Carlisle.

The Old Blacksmith Shop, or Smithy, at Gretna (open daily all the year: adm), behind Gretna Hall Hotel, is set back off a cobbled yard, through a 'kissing gate'. Dating from 1710, it contains a museum with the marriage room, anvil, and many photographs and documents. A kilted piper may welcome you to this rather tawdry display.

Lochmaben Stone

This stone, on the shore of the Solway Firth not far south of Gretna, weighs at least 10 tonnes and is thought to be the remains of a stone circle, possibly connected with a shrine to Maponos, god of youth and music: an appropriate trysting place for runaway lovers. Fairs were held here in the Middle Ages and it was the site where border disputes were discussed and settled, under daylight truce.

Annan

Annan is west from Gretna Green, on the northern shore of the Solway Firth. Once a busy main-road town, it is now bypassed by the A75. Although its history goes back a long way, the town was too frequently torn apart in border disputes to show much sign of antiquity now. In 1317 it was recorded that 'the Vale of Annan lay so wasted and burned that neither man nor beast was left'. You may see haaf-net fishermen (from the Norse 'haf'— the open sea) standing up to their chests in the water, holding out their awkward nets, framed like soccer goal-posts. This ancient tradition, dating from Viking days and protected by Royal Charter, is restricted by licence to the men of Annan only.

Shrimp-canning is one of the town's valuable industries, and in the 19th century tea-clippers were made here. The blind poet Dr Thomas Blacklock lived here; a man who did much to promote the genius of Robert Burns and who prevented him from emigrating when times were hard. Annan celebrates the Riding of the Marches in July.

The **Brus Stone**, built into the wall of the town hall, is a carved tablet from a castle built by the Brus lords. It is inscribed with the name Robert de Brus, thought to be King Robert the Bruce. This relic was stolen in the 19th century and lost for 100 years before someone found it in North Devon in 1916.

Pinneys, at Brydhill, are high-class fish-smokers with very good smoked fish pâtés, smoked salmon, trout, mackerel, etc.

Ruthwell Cross

Ruthwell (pronounced Rivvel), 6 miles (10km) west of Annan on the coastal road B724, is the start of the Solway Coast Heritage Trail to Stranraer. In a specially built apse in the church is the 7th-century Ruthwell Cross, one of Scotland's greatest treasures, with incredibly clear sculpted figures, vine scrolls, birds and animals. The runic inscriptions, the longest and perhaps oldest known in Britain, have been deciphered by scholars and are extracts from a devotional poem, 'The Dream of the Rood', the oldest poem in the English language, written by 7th-century Northumbrian poets. The arms of the 18-foot (5.5m)high cross are modern, but they don't detract from the grace of this ancient relic. The reason why it is so well preserved is that it was buried in the 17th century by the minister, to protect it from the iconoclasm of Presbyterian reformers. The man who subsequently unearthed and re-erected it was the Rev. Henry Duncan, who also established Scotland's first savings bank, in Ruthwell, in 1810. The cottage where this first bank was founded is now a **museum** (open all the year round: free).

Comlongon Castle

At Clarencefield, just northwest of Ruthwell (open daily March–Nov: adm), Comlongon, in the process of restoration, is a well-preserved 15th-century castle with spooky dungeons, kitchen, great hall, heraldic devices and bedchambers with privies. There is a picnic area, nature trail, woodland walks, and even peacocks to add a touch of grandeur. See below for details of the adjoining hotel.

Caerlaverock Nature Reserve

West of Ruthwell, between Lochar Water and the mouth of the Nith, this reserve (open mid-Sept–April) is a great tract of wild salt-marsh and mud-flats, belonging to the Wildfowl Trust. It is the most northerly breeding ground of the natterjack toad

Caerlaverock Castle

Caerlaverock (open daily: adm) is a massive triangular-shaped ruin on the western part of the nature reserve, its moat still full, so you cross a footbridge to reach it. Its shape was governed by that of the rock on which it was built, just above the high-tide level at the mouth of the Nith. Aptly described by a medieval monk as 'shield-shaped', in 1300 the castle held off 3000 English troops under Edward I for two days, defended by only 60 men. It is surrounded by treacherous sinking-mud and swampland, adding to its impregnability. Built in 1290, the castle was a Maxwell stronghold, and it has an elegant Renaissance interior designed by the first Earl of Nithsdale in the 17th century. There is something very French about its three-storey façade, surrounding the triangular courtyard, decorated with sculpted doors and windows. Covenanters destroyed it not long after the first Earl's improvements. The Maxwell crest and motto are above the door.

Where to Stay

moderate

Warmanbie Hotel, Annan, © 04612 4015, is an elegant Georgian country house in secluded woodland grounds overlooking the River Annan with free fishing. The bedrooms are comfortable with private bathrooms and colour TV. Good food and wine, and special rates for weekend breaks and off-season holidays.

inexpensive

If castles are your fancy, try **Comlongon Castle** at Clarencefield, just north of Ruthwell, © 038787 283, open from March to December. Adjoining the original medieval castle (see above), this baronial pile, in 50 acres of parkland, is cheap and what you miss in vitality is compensated for in adjacent history.

Dumfries and Around

Dumfries, on the banks of the Nith 16 miles (25.5km) west of Annan, is surrounded by farmland, woods and beautiful gardens. Its history is as bloodstained as that of any border town, its inhabitants known for their brave opposition to invasion. William the Lion made it a Royal Burgh in 1186 and it was granted a charter in 1395 by Robert III. Bronze and Iron Age relics have been excavated nearby and it is almost certain that there was a Roman settlement with a Roman road up Nithsdale. Edward I captured the now-vanished castle; Robert the Bruce murdered Red Comyn here in 1306; Prince Charles Edward Stuart passed through in 1745. Robert Burns lived and died in Dumfries and described it as 'Maggie by the banks of Nith, a dame wi' pride eneuch'.

The name Dumfries comes from *dun*, or *drum*, *phreas*—the fort, or ridge, in the brushwood. The town was home to Norwegian exiles during the Second World War.

There is a week-long **Guid Nychburris Festival** (Good Neighbours) in June, incorporating many historic events including the granting of the charter and the Border Marches.

Dumfries Museum (open daily except Sun and Mon, Oct–March: free) adjoins a water mill—a round whitewashed tower, built about 1730. 'Period' rooms contain local exhibits: archaeological, natural history, Roman altars, early Christian monuments and costumes and, of course, Burns memorabilia. A 'camera obscura' in the old mill (adm) gives an ingeniously reflected view of the town and surrounding countryside.

The Auld Brig, a six-arched footbridge above a tumbling caul (weir) created in the 18th century to provide power for grain mills, replaced a wooden bridge built by Devorguilla Balliol in the 14th century (see 'Sweetheart Abbey', below). The present bridge dates from 1432 but was considerably restored after the 17th century when floodwater reduced it from nine, or even thirteen, arches, to the present six. This was once the gateway into Galloway. The quaint **Old Bridge House** (open daily in the summer: free), dating from 1662, is a folk museum with Victorian and Edwardian rooms.

Robert Burns

 Dumfries glows with Burns nostalgia. Listen for the echo of an ironic chuckle from that most earthy of romantic poets in the High Street, in front of Greyfriars Church where several roads meet, and look up at the splendidly sentimental statue of him. A white marble Adonis lounges against a tree-stump, hand on heart, clutching a posy of flowers, his dog resting its head on his rustic boot. He stares out over the town wearing a rather vapid expression that does not quite match his colourful life, oblivious of the swirl of traffic at his feet. **The Globe Tavern** and the **Hole in the Wa'**, two of the poet's favourite inns in the High Street, are both crammed with Burns memorabilia and it's hard to believe he died nearly 200 years ago, so alive is his memory. The barmaid at The Globe bore one of his many children. Burns lived in Dumfries for the last four and a half years of his life, working as an exciseman and writing nearly 100 of his works, including 'Auld Lang Syne'.

Burns House (open daily, closed Sun and Mon, Oct–March: adm) is a red-brick workman's cottage in what is now Burns Street but which was called Mill Vennel when he lived and died there. He called it 'Stinking Vennel' because of an open drain running down the alley, carrying effluent from the meat market to the river.

An elaborate **Mausoleum** in the grounds of St Michael's Church contains the bodies of Burns, his wife Jean Armour and five of their children. Like the statue in the High Street, this Grecian temple with the muse of poetry coming on Burns at the plough, sculpted by Turnerelli, is too mawkish for the man. It was erected early in the 19th century, costing £1450.

Robert Burns Centre in Mill Road (open daily, April–Sept: free) is the latest tribute to the poet. In an 18th-century red sandstone mill on the banks of the Nith, it has a 70-seat theatre with audio-visual shows (adm.) A model shows 18th-century Dumfries as Burns would have known it, and there are displays of his life, a bookshop and a café—Jean Armour's Pantry.

A plaque in Castle Street is all that remains of the **Monastery of Greyfriars**. It commemorates a turning point in Scottish history, when Robert the Bruce stabbed to death Red Comyn, his rival claimant to the Crown, in a quarrel. Having disposed of opposition with the double crime of murder and sacrilege, Bruce was then able to seize the throne.

The early 18th-century **Midsteeple** in the town centre was the tolbooth. A plan on the wall shows Dumfries in Burns' day. This was also the prison and ammunition store.

Lincluden Collegiate Church

Lincluden (open daily except closed Thurs afternoons and Fri in winter: adm) stands on the northern outskirts of the town on a grassy plateau within a bend of Cluden Water. It was founded for Benedictine nuns in the 12th century: in 1339 the nuns were thrown out by Archibald the Grim and the church became collegiate. Archibald's son, the fourth Earl of Douglas, son-in-law of Robert III, was killed fighting for France against England. His wife, Princess Margaret, endowed a chapel in the south transept, in memory of her husband and was herself buried in the richly decorated, canopied tomb in the ruins. There are plenty of Douglas signatures on the walls in the form of coats of arms, shields, etc., and carvings on the rood screen showing scenes from the life of Christ.

Sweetheart Abbey

Sweetheart Abbey (open daily: adm), at New Abbey, 7½ miles (12km) south of Dumfries, is one of Scotland's most poignant monastic ruins. Roofless, its grass-carpeted nave is enclosed within red sandstone arches. It was founded in 1273 by Devorguilla Balliol—mother of King John Balliol, the luckless 'Toom Tabard'—who also founded Balliol College in Oxford. Devorguilla was buried here with her husband's embalmed heart, which she had carried around with her in an ivory and silver casket since his death, her 'sweet, silent companion', and the abbey became known as Dulce Cor, or Sweet Heart. Devorguilla's tomb, marked by a raised platform of turf with a cross cut in it, lies in front of the high altar.

The shell of the abbey dominates the village of **New Abbey** with its main street lined by single-storey whitewashed cottages, curving up to the gates of what were the precincts. Part of the enormous boulder wall that once encircled the grounds remains. There is also a 19th-century corn-mill with working water-wheel. **Shambellie House Museum of**

Costume (open daily, Easter–end Sept: adm) has period costume in a Victorian house with nice gardens. **Criffel**, the highest of the coastal hills (1868ft—575m), can be climbed from here.

About 5 miles (8km) northwest, **Beeswing** village is called after a 19th-century racehorse who won a fortune for a gambling butler. He used his winnings to buy an inn and called it Beeswing; the village grew up round it. The inn is now a private house, identifiable by the large yellow butterfly by the front door.

Arbigland

Arbigland Gardens (open 1 May–30 Sept, Tues, Thurs and Sun: adm) are 12 miles (19km) south of Dumfries, on a sandy bay overlooking the estuary of the Nith. **John Paul Jones Cottage** (open April–Sept, Tues–Sat; also Mon July–Aug: adm) tells the story of this flamboyant character who was born here in 1747, son of a gardener at Arbigland. He served a prison sentence for murder and then made his home in America. A brave, dashing sailor, he fought for the Americans in the War of Independence, helping to establish their navy, and led several raids on English and Scottish territory in command of an American brig. A true mercenary, he fought for France and for Russia and died in Paris. There are many stories of his exploits, including one in which he returned some treasure, plundered by his crew, to its owner—a lady who lived on the Solway Firth.

Drumcoltran Tower

Drumcoltran Tower (open daily: free), 8 miles (13km) southwest of Dumfries just off the A711, is a 16th-century tower-house among farm buildings, three storeys high with a wheel-stair in a projecting turret. A hoard of Bronze Age rapiers was found in a ditch nearby.

Where to Stay and Eating Out

expensive

The Station Hotel, in Dumfries, © 0387 54316, is not as prosaic as it sounds, being a listed building in Lovers Walk. It is comfortable and the food is good. **Cairndale Hotel and Leisure Club**, English Street, Dumfries, © 0387 54111, is reasonably priced considering its amenities: heated pool, sauna, steam room, hot spa bath, gymnasium, health/beauty salon, toning tables etc.

moderate

Hetland Hall Hotel at Carrutherstown, 7 miles (11km) southeast of Dumfries along the A75, © 0387 84201, is a Georgian mansion with panoramic views of the Solway coast and 'Sporting Breaks' for a minimum of three days.

Dalbeattie

Dalbeattie, 14 miles (22.5km) southwest of Dumfries, is in the Stewartry, so called from the time when Balliol lands were confiscated and placed under a royal 'steward'—hence also the origins of the Stewart/Stuart dynasty. Much of the town is built with glittering granite, acclaimed for beauty and durability and used to strengthen buildings all over the world. The Eddystone Lighthouse, the Thames Embankment, lighthouses in Ceylon, paving stones in Russia and South America, are just a few constructions using this Galloway granite. Dalbeattie Civic Week is at the end of July.

The Motte of Mark and The Motte of Urr

The Motte of Mark at Rockcliffe, on the Urr Water, is a 5th/6th-century hillfort commanding such a spectacular view of the coast that few invaders could have slipped past unnoticed. The Motte of Urr, nearly 3 miles (4.5km) north of Dalbeattie, just off the B794, is an other fortified hill—the most extensive motte and bailey earthwork castle in Scotland. It is an almost circular mound, rising in three tiers, on a platform surrounded by a deep trench; a relic of Saxon-Norman occupation.

Colvend Coast

The attractive coast south of Dalbeattie, around Colvend, Rockcliffe, and Sandyhills Bay, has good walks, a bird sanctuary at Rough Island, and a picturesque harbour at Kippford. This was smugglers' territory in the old days. A good 5-mile (8km) walk is from Kippford, southeast along the coast to Castle Point, passing Motte of Mark and back past Dalbeattie Forest.

West along the coast on the A711, **Palnackie** is 3 miles (4.5km) southwest of Dalbeattie. In the silted-up harbour here, in the summer, the World Flounder-tramping Championships are held. Competitors find the flounders in the mud with their bare feet and spear them, at considerable risk to their toes. Here also you can watch glass-blowing, welding and sculpting at the North Glen Gallery (open daily, but ring 055660 200 to check).

Orchardton

Orchardton Tower, less than 2 miles (3km) south, west of the Urr Estuary, just off the A711 (open daily: free; key from the custodian who lives in a cottage nearby), is a 15th-century cylindrical tower built by John Cairns in a wooded dip. This is the only tower of its kind in Scotland, modelled on a style common in Ireland.

Screel Hill

Screel Hill, on the other side of the road from Orchardton, has a signed trail up through the forest to the craggy summit, with panoramic views.

Dundrennan Abbey

About 6 miles (10km) down the coast on the A711, Dundrennan Abbey (open daily: adm) is a must for anyone with romance in their veins. There is little left of its former splendour, but its roofless aisles and transepts, its pointed arches and blind arcades reverberate with echoes of Mary, Queen of Scots. Founded for Cistercians in 1142, and falling into ruin after the Reformation, the abbey provided the queen with her final resting place before she embarked for England from Port Mary. It is not known whether she slept here or merely rested. She arrived in tattered clothes, her head shorn for disguise, and sat somewhere in these ruins to write a final letter to her cousin Elizabeth of England, begging for sanctuary. It is heartbreaking to picture her tall, slender figure, passing through the 13th-century pointed doorway between two arched windows, into the chapter house, to the care of the abbot and his monks.

Kirkcudbright

Gaily painted houses and old streets beside the water at the mouth of the Dee make Kirkcudbright (pronounced Kir-coo-bry) one of Scotland's most enchanting towns. It was a medieval port and a royal burgh, named after the Kirk of St Cuthbert, when the saint's bones rested there on the way to interment in Durham. With its mild, almost Mediterranean climate and sea views, the town is popular with painters and has a thriving art colony. The Kirkcudbright Summer Festivities, July–mid-August, provide Scottish Nights, a raft race, a puppet festival, sports, walks and a floodlit Tattoo in front of MacLellan's Castle.

MacLellan's Castle (open daily, closed weekdays Oct–March: adm) is an impressive turreted ruin off the High Street, dating from 1582, built by Thomas MacLellan with stones from a ruined friary which once stood here. The jagged fangs of this castellated mansion draw you from across the town. In the great hall, look for the single stone lintel that spans the 10-foot (3m) aperture, and also for the small closet behind the fireplace with a peephole, hinting at intrigue in the past. MacLellan's elaborate tomb is in the 16th-century aisle of Greyfriars Church.

Broughton House (open daily in the summer, closed Sun mornings and Tues in winter: adm) in the High Street, was built in the 18th century. It was the home of E. A. Hornel, one of the first settlers of the Kirkcudbright artists' colony and a renowned artist himself. Hornel died in 1933 and left this house to the town with a collection of books and manuscripts on Galloway.

The Tolbooth, also in the High Street, dates from 1627 with an outside stone stair. Several witches were imprisoned here, as was John Paul Jones, convicted for causing the death of a seaman, but later freed. Don't miss the 'jougs' with which miscreants were tethered by the neck for public humiliation. There is also an arts centre.

The Stewartry Museum (open Mon–Sat, Easter–Oct: adm) tells of the buccaneering life of John Paul Jones. It's in St Mary Street, with a special exhibition devoted to him. There are also displays of social history going back to prehistoric times and works by local artists.

In **St Cuthbert's Churchyard** on the edge of the town is a tombstone marking the grave of 'William Marshall, Tinker', who died in 1792, aged 120. He is alleged to have fathered four of his many children after the age of 100, which may account for the ram's horns engraved on the reverse side of the headstone.

Gatehouse of Fleet

The **Mill on the Fleet Visitor Centre** (open daily, Easter–end Oct: adm) tells the story of water and has local history exhibitions. The **Murray Forest Centre** has a Log Cabin

Centre, an information office, picnic sites and forest walks. The **Fleet Forest Visitor Centre**, to the south, has a reconstructed bobbin mill and local history.

Cardoness Castle

Cardoness Castle (open daily: adm), a mile (1.5km) southwest of Gatehouse of Fleet, is a roofless, 15th-century tower-house, four storeys high above a turf mound, with a vaulted basement, original stairway, stone benches and fireplaces. At one time, the owners got so carried away celebrating the birth of an heir, it is said, that they all went skating on the loch before the ice was firm, and that was the end of them.

Anwoth

In the ruin of the old church at Anwoth, near Cardoness, less than a mile off the A75, there is a gem for anyone interested in old gravestones. On an elaborate Gordon tomb, an epitaph to a lady of Cardoness who died in 1628, reads:

> *Ze gaizers on this trophee of a tombe*
> *Send out ane grone for want of hir whois lyfe*
> *Twyse borne on earth and now is in earthis wombe*
> *Lived long a virgine now a spotless wife.*

In Glasgow Cathedral, the tomb of the Hamiltons of Holmhead (inscribed in 1616) reads:

> *Yee gazers on this trophie of a tomb*
> *Send out ane grone for want of her whose life*
> *Once born of earth, and now lies in earth's womb*
> *Liv'd long a virgin, then a spotless wyfe.*

There is an ancient Pictish stone near the church, carved with a cross, indicating that this was an early Christian settlement.

Skyreburn Aquarium

Like an underwater wildlife park, Skyreburn has local species, fresh and salt. A good way to pass a wet afternoon—though, to some, fish become rather similar after a while.

Dirk Hatteraick's Cave, on the shore just east of the mouth of Kirkdale Burn, is tricky to get at, crossed by the A75 about 7 miles (11km) west of Gatehouse of Fleet. It is the largest of several caves in this area. Hatteraick was a notorious smuggler and caves were important to him.

Barholm Castle, a 16th-century ruin in a glen to the northeast, was one of John Knox's refuges when he was a fugitive.

Half a mile up the glen of Kirkdale Burn are two Neolithic burial tombs at **Cairn Holy**. The first is a stone cist with standing stones; the second has a double burial chamber. These ancient stones, silhouetted against an evening sky, have a primal mystery that stirs the imagination. What were they like, those mourners, 4000 years ago?

If you want a sumptuous setting you will be more than satisfied at the unfortunately named **Cally Palace Hotel**, Gatehouse of Fleet, ℂ 05574 341 (open March–Jan). It is a vast Georgian mansion with original moulded ceilings, in 100 acres of parkland, with a heated swimming-pool, and many leisure facilities. **The Murray Arms Hotel** on the corner of Ann Street and the High Street, ℂ 05574 207, was one of the haunts of that discerning pub-crawler, R. Burns, and it was here that he composed 'Scots, Wha Hae', inspired, no doubt, by their fine wine and excellent cuisine. Try their local beef.

Barons Craig Hotel at Rockcliffe, south of Dalbeattie, ℂ 055663 225, open from April to October, is comfortable. This imposing Victorian country house stands in 12 acres of wooded garden, overlooking the Solway Firth. It is perhaps a little soulless, but the food is good and the staff efficient. Another imposing country house hotel, standing literally on the beach, is the family-run **Balcary Bay Hotel** at Auchencairn, ℂ 055664 217, closed December to February. The seafood is excellent. **Clonyard House Hotel** at Colvend, ℂ 055663 372, is comfortable, serves excellent food and caters for disabled guests. They do scallops very well. **The Selkirk Arms**, in Kirkcudbright High Street, has excellent food and a friendly atmosphere. Burns wrote the Selkirk Grace here.

> *Some hae meat and canna eat,*
> *And some wad eat that want it:*
> *But we hae meat and we can eat*
> *And sae the Lord be thankit.*

Creetown

Following the coast on round for about 6 miles (10km), you come to Creetown on the eastern shore of the Cree estuary, the granite gateway to Wigtownshire, a village whose public image has recently had a facelift. With hills, forests, lochs and sandy beaches all within easy reach, this is a good holiday base. Town and country walks are signposted from Adamson Square. Gemmologists should see the **Gem Rock Museum and Gallery** (open daily: adm) up the road opposite the clock tower. This collection of gems and rocks from all over the world took 50 years to gather: it is awe-inspiring to see a rock that contains water two million years old. There is a gem-cutting workshop, a tea room and gift shop. Don't miss the **Craft Centre and Fragrance Shop** in The Square, or **Creetown Gold Silversmithing Workshop**, in St John Street, where craftsmen make jewellery in gold, silver and semi-precious stones.

Barholm Mains Open Farm (open daily May–Sept: adm) has a variety of farm and other animals.

Newton Stewart

Another 5 or so miles (8km) along the A75, on the banks of the River Cree, Newton

Stewart grew around the first easy place to ford the river. It is a holiday centre and market town, surrounded by moors and farmland on the reclaimed mudflats of the estuary. From here you can enjoy walking, fishing, boating, bird-watching, sightseeing or just relaxing in the mild, often hot, sunshine. It is a good base from which to explore the enormous Galloway Forest Park, to the north.

Bargaly Gardens (open Sun, Easter–end Sept: adm) date from the 17th century, with a walled garden, water garden and exotic plants that thrive in this mild climate.

Kirrough Visitor Centre, on the outskirts of the town (open daily, April–Sept: free), covers forests and forest management with a shop, adventure playground and walks.

Creebridge Mohair Mill (open Mon–Sat, June–Sept, guided tours Easter–Oct: free) welcomes visitors to watch mohair being woven and finished, and has a shop. The privately owned, non-profit-making **museum**, in York Road (open Easter and Mon–Sat, May–June; daily, July–Sept: adm) displays local history.

Wigtown and Around

Seven miles (11km) south of Newton Stewart on the western shore of Wigtown Bay, Wigtown is another holiday resort. Here you will see two mercat crosses, the second, rather ostentatious, having been erected to celebrate the victory at Waterloo in 1816. The railed enclosure in the large town square was for penning up cattle at night, a practice necessary not only to stop them straying, but also to protect them from reivers.

Wigtown will always be remembered for its two martyrs, Margaret McLachlan, aged 62, and Margaret Wilson, aged 18. In 1685, they were convicted of having attended 20 conventicles—illegal Covenanter prayer meetings. They were tied to stakes in the estuary and drowned by the rising tide, watched by an avid crowd. Margaret Wilson was deliberately placed so that she could witness the final throes of her older companion. She was then given the chance to 'repent'. She refused, and was re-secured to her stake. The graves of these two women, the Wigtown Martyrs, together with those of six other Covenanter martyrs, are in the churchyard among the ruins of two former churches beside the present parish church. These sad memorials are food enough for thought, as is the monument on the hill above the town, but it is not until you see the simple pillar on the shore where the drownings took place, and watch the tide rising over the estuary mudflats, that the full horror of that appalling event really hits you.

Torhouse Stone Circle

The Torhouse Stone Circle, dating from about 2000 BC, some 5 miles (8km) west of Wigtown, is one of the best of this type in Britain. There are 19 roundish boulders forming a complete circle 60 feet (18.5m) in diameter with three more in the centre. As with all other standing-stone circles, historians only guess at their original purpose.

Galloway House Gardens at Garlieston, about 6 miles (9.5km) south of Wigtown on the coast (open daily: adm), is a woodland garden. Informal walks among shrubs, borders, wild flowers, fine trees and exotica lead down to a sandy bay. There is a walled garden with a camellia house. The 18th-century house, built by Lord Garlies, is not open to the public but you can get tea in the village.

Where to Stay

expensive

Kirroughtree Hotel, Newton Stewart, ✆ 0671 2141, has five crowns from the Tourist Board and is excellent value, if you can afford it, with free golf on five local courses, nice gardens and good food.

moderate

Creebridge House Hotel, ✆ 0671 2121, close to the centre of Newton Stewart, is comfortable, with weekend and short-break rates. Chris Walker, the proprietor, recently won the Taste of Scotland Chef of the Year competition.

inexpensive

Also in Newton Stewart, **Rowallan House Hotel** in Corsbie Road, ✆ 0671 2520, is an attractive country house, 5 minutes' walk from the town centre. It deservedly won a 'good room' award. **Ellangowan Hotel,** ✆ 0671 82201, is a family-run hotel with good food. In the same category is **Auchenleck Farm**, ✆ 0671 2035.

Whithorn

About 10 miles (16km) south of Wigtown, Whithorn (from the Anglo-Saxon *huit aern*— 'white house') was the birthplace of Christianity in Scotland. Born nearby, some time in the middle of the 4th century, and of royal descent, St Ninian went to Rome on a pilgrimage and returned here in 397, a consecrated bishop. He built a white stone church which became known as *Candida Casa*, and set about converting the Britons and southern Picts to Christianity. Whithorn is the oldest Royal Burgh in Scotland, its first charter having been granted by Robert the Bruce in 1329.

Whithorn Priory and Museum

Go through The Pend to get to the Priory, a deep 17th-century arch flanked by 15th-century pillars with a stone panel above carved with the Scottish coat of arms, as it was before the Union in 1707. The museum (open daily: adm), through The Pend, is worth visiting before doing anything else because it gives a description of Whithorn and the vital part it played in the birth of Christianity in Britain. There are also early Christian crosses and stones.

A ticket includes entry to the Priory on the site of Candida Casa: you can see the 13th-century nave and a doorway in the south wall, built by Fergus of Galloway who founded the priory in 1126. It was a place of pilgrimage for more than 400 years, until 'idolatry' was made illegal in 1581 by the Reformers. Many of Scotland's monarchs paid visits to the shrine: James IV walked from Edinburgh on one occasion. Mary, Queen of Scots, was the last, in 1563, during her tour of the west.

Whithorn Excavations

At Bruce Street, off George Street (open April–mid-Oct: adm), archaeologists work on extensive excavations of the original Christian community with buildings and graves going back to the 5th century, the remains of a Viking settlement with reconstructed buildings, medieval burials and even a medieval herb garden. As you watch the experts sifting through the earth, it seems miraculous that they can reconstruct history from such fragments. There is an information centre and shop, a video interpretation, and guided tours.

A mile west of Whithorn, **Rispain Camp** is a rectangular settlement defended by a bank and ditch, dating from the 1st century AD.

Isle of Whithorn

Isle of Whithorn, 3 miles (4.5km) southeast of Whithorn village, on the southeast tip of the peninsula, is a port built on what was once an island, and is still a fishing centre, with boats working out of the harbour. The ruin of a 12th-century chapel, dedicated to St Ninian, stands on the site of one probably built for the use of foreign pilgrims, for whom special safe-conducts were granted.

St Ninian's Cave

St Ninian's Cave, 3 miles (4.5km) southwest of Whithorn, is believed to have been the saint's private oratory, with early Christian crosses carved on the rock, on your left as you look in, small and quite hard to spot. There is something moving about this corner of Galloway: whether you are a Christian or not, you cannot fail to wonder at the strength of the faith of those first missionaries, working among barbaric pagans, sowing seeds that grew into the Christian church as we know it. You reach the cave by the minor road south off the A747, a mile east of its junction with the A746. There's a car park at Kidsdale Farm and the cave is signposted from there, 3 miles (4.5km) the round trip—a nice walk through Physgill woods. Be cautious getting into the cave as there have been rockfalls.

Archaeological Sites

The coast road northwest along Luce Bay from the Isle of Whithorn to Glenluce links up several antiquities on or near the shore.

The Wren's Egg Stone Circle is on the left after Craiglemine, another of those ancient remains whose purpose remains a mystery. **Barsalloch Fort**, an Iron Age fort, surrounded by a horseshoe ditch, on a cliff 60ft (18m) above the sea, is by Barsalloch Point. It's quite a steep climb up a track, but worth it for an example of how the ancient Britons defended themselves. Archaeologists found remains of Mesolithic fishermen here, over 6000 years old. In summer, the foreshore is a glorious blue carpet of saxifrage. **Drumtrodden Stones**, less than 3 miles (4.5km) inland from Barsalloch, have Bronze Age cup-and-ring markings carved in the rock. These symbols, a foot in diameter, are found on stones scattered throughout the north as well as on the Continent. **Druchtag Motehill**, to the north beyond Mochrum village, is a typical early medieval earthwork mound, steep, with traces of stone buildings.

The **Gavin Maxwell Memorial** is a life-like sculpted otter on a cliff top overlooking Monreith Bay. Maxwell grew up in this area and it is fitting that his memorial should command such an outstanding view.

Chapel Finian, little more than a few stones now, beside the A747, 5 miles (8km) northwest of Port William, was a 10th-century chapel dedicated to St Finbarr. It was built for pilgrims landing from the sea on their way either to Whithorn or Glenluce.

Glenluce Abbey

Glenluce Abbey (open daily: adm) at the head of Luce Bay, restored during this century, was founded in 1192 by Roland, Lord of Galloway. The 15th-century vaulted chapter house is almost intact, entered by a round, carved doorway. Inside, a single octagonal pillar supports the stone vaulting-ribs on carved corbels, each arch decorated with twined foliage, grotesques and emblems. All this is aesthetically satisfying, but of even greater interest to some will be the excavated baked-clay water pipes and drains, laid by those monks so long ago and still sound today. These traces of early plumbing are expertly put together and possibly a great deal more durable than modern plastic drains. A 13th-century wizard, Michael Scot, is said to have lived here and saved the community from extinction by luring a plague that attacked them into the abbey, shutting it up in a vault and starving it to death. He is also said to have commissioned witches who helped him at his work to spin the ropes of sand, revealed as broken strands of sand south of the abbey at Ringdoo Point, when the tide goes out.

Glenluce Motor Museum (open daily, March–Oct, and Wed–Sun in winter: adm) has a collection of vintage and classic cars and motorbikes. **Castle of Park**, just west of Glenluce off the A75, is a well-preserved castellated tower house built in 1590 by Thomas Hay of Park (private, but worth stopping for a look).

Where to Stay and Eating Out

moderate

For dependability and comfort, though not necessarily humming with vitality (they charge you for your dog), try **Corsemalzie House Hotel** at Port William, ℂ 098886 254. Open from March to mid-January, in 40 acres of wooded gardens, it has good food, free golf, private fishing and rough shooting. Try the smoked fish.

inexpensive

Castlewigg Hotel, 2 miles (3km) from Whithorn, ℂ 09885 213, overlooking the Galloway hills has log fires in the bar. **The Steampacket Hotel** overlooks the harbour in Isle of Whithorn, ℂ 09885 334.

The Rhinns of Galloway

The Rhinns of Galloway, the hammer-head butt on the western extremity of Dumfries and Galloway, give many panoramic views from the rugged cliffs. Sometimes Ireland looks so close you feel it would make an easy swim. Seldom more than spitting distance from the sea, you can experience fierce storms here, as well as the mild gentle climate of the rest of the region. Try and catch a sunset from the Mull of Galloway.

Stranraer

Stranraer, a busy port and market centre for the area, is a popular holiday resort. Very sheltered, at the head of Loch Ryan, 10 miles (16km) west of Glenluce, it is the gateway to the Rhinns of Galloway. Although not a beautiful town it offers many holiday amenities and numerous hotels and guest houses, golf courses, good beaches, excellent trout and sea fishing, boating and exploring. Frequent car-ferries make the two-hour crossing to Larne in Northern Ireland. High-speed catamarans also cross from Stranraer to Belfast, several times a day, in just one hour.

It is odd to think, as you walk about the modern town, that below your feet lie oystershells that were thrown out by Mesolithic settlers, 6000 years ago. Look across Loch Ryan and picture it in Roman times when they used the sheltered anchorage for their galleys, in their expeditions against the Gallovidians, calling it *Rericonius Sinus*.

Old Castle of St John, in Castle Street, is a 16th-century towerhouse, occupied by Claverhouse during his persecution of the Covenanters in 1682. His victims were imprisoned in the dungeons, where many perished. This was also the police station and prison in the 19th century. There are exhibitions on the castle, Covenanters and the jail, in the visitors' centre (open Apr–Sept, daily except Sat: free).

Wigtown District Museum, London Road, Stranraer (open Mon, Wed and Fri afternoons, 1 May–30 Sept: free), gives information about Sir John Ross (see below), and local history with the emphasis on dairy farming.

North West Castle Hotel, opposite the pier in Stranraer, was the home of Sir John Ross, the 18th-century Arctic explorer who sailed in search of the Northwest Passage and discovered the magnetic North Pole. A passionate seaman, Ross built his house as much like a ship as possible, a flamboyant, castellated mansion with the dining room modelled like a ship's cabin with rounded stern. (Hotel details below.)

Castle Kennedy Gardens

Three miles (4.5km) east of Stranraer just off the A75 (open daily in the summer: adm), Castle Kennedy Gardens were laid out by the second Earl of Stair, who was inspired by the gardens of Versailles while he was Ambassador in France. Not slow off the mark, the Earl used soldiers of the Royal Scots Greys and Inniskilling Fusiliers (who were in the area to quell Covenanters) to build his garden around Castle Kennedy, now a ruin, softened by swathes of ivy, on an isthmus between two lochs. After the castle was burned down in 1715, the gardens were neglected until 1847, when they were rescued and restored to their original design, with a sunken garden. The rhododendrons, azaleas, magnolias and embothriums are remarkable and the pinetum was the first to be grown in Scotland. The monkey puzzle avenue is one of the longest in Scotland. The present Scots–French mansion, Lochinch Castle, home of Lord Stair, was built in 1867 to replace Castle Kennedy. There is a tea room and you can buy plants. **Meadowsweet Herb Garden**, also at Castle Kennedy, has over a hundred herbs with instructive tours. **Glenwhan Gardens** (open daily, April–Sept: adm), near Castle Kennedy, include a hilltop garden with good views and a water garden.

Corsewall Point

Corsewall Point and the lighthouse are along a rough track on the northwest tip of the Rhinns. The dominating cone of Ailsa Craig rises from the sea to the north. Robert Louis Stevenson's grandfather built the lighthouse. You're a lot closer to Belfast here than to Edinburgh!

Portpatrick

Portpatrick, not quite halfway down the west coast of the peninsula, is a holiday resort and fishing village. Only 22 miles (35km) northeast of Donaghadee, in Ireland, this was once the port for the main route west, but southwesterly gales frequently made docking hazardous, so the port was moved to sheltered Stranraer. Portpatrick is an idyllic holiday centre with coastal scenery, sandy bays, a golf course, and a picturesque harbour. In summer you could easily be in a Mediterranean resort. The landscape is bright with flowers, the air deliciously scented. It is said that St Patrick landed here on a visit from Ireland.

The Southern Upland Way starts here and the least taxing stretch is the first 6 or 7 miles (10–11km) to Castle Kennedy. It meanders through the hills of the Galloway Forest Park—some quite high—eastwards over the Lowther and Moffat Hills into the Borders.

Little Wheels Toy Transport Display and Model Railway, in Hill Street (open daily except Fri, Easter–Oct; daily July–Aug: adm), is for mechanics of all ages.

Dunskey Castle, a jagged ruin dating back to the 16th century, stands on a cliff less than a mile to the south. It is one of those ruins that fire your imagination with pirates and wreckers and damsels in distress. Take care walking on the cliff paths.

The 5th/6th-century **Kirkmadrine Stones**, 8 miles (13km) south of Stranraer off the A716, are against the church wall, with a description board. Some bear Latin inscriptions and the 'ChiRho' symbol, formed by a combination of the first two letters of Christ's name in Greek. These stones prove St Ninian established Christianity in this area; they are the earliest Christian memorials in Scotland after those at Whithorn.

Ardwell House Gardens

Ardwell House Gardens (open Easter–31 Oct: adm) are 2 miles (3km) south of the stones off the A716. Go not only for the almost tropical gardens round the 18th-century house, but also for the sea views. At **Ardwell Bay**, on the west coast, there is a narrow rock spit, cut off by a wall, with one of the few brochs in the southwest, unusual in that it had two entrances, one to seaward and one to landward.

Logan Botanic Garden

About a mile (1.5km) south of Ardwell on the A716, turn right on to the B7065 to **Port Logan**, a sheltered harbour with a stone jetty, lighthouse and small beach. Logan Botanic Garden (open daily April–end Oct: adm) is just over a mile (1.5km) to the north. A branch of the Royal Botanic Garden in Edinburgh, this is a riot of sub-tropical plants, tree-ferns, cabbage palms and the Brazilian *Gunnera manicata*, the largest-leafed outdoor plant in Britain. Plants from all over the world flourish in the mild climate; you might be walking in an exotic foreign land. There is an excellent licensed salad-bar restaurant, open from 10am to 5pm.

The Mull of Galloway

The Mull of Galloway, the most southerly point in Scotland, less than 25 miles (40km) from Ireland and the Isle of Man, is a dramatic headland with cliffs 200 feet (61m) high on the southern tip of the Rhinns. Stand here, buffeted by wind and salt spray, and watch a boiling cauldron far below, at certain times and conditions, when seven currents meet. The lighthouse is unmanned and there is no public access. **Double Dykes** is the name of the trench across the western end of the point, which is said to have been the last defence of the Picts, retreating from the Scots who had driven them down the peninsula early in the 6th century.

Where to Stay

expensive

By far the best hotel in this area is **Knockinaam Lodge Hotel** in Portpatrick, © 077681 471. Open from March to December, it is a proper country-house hotel in a secluded glen with a private beach, and glorious sea views across to Ireland. The grounds are lovely and include a croquet lawn. All the rooms are elegantly decorated and comfortable, and the food is excellent. It's just like staying in a private house—except for the bill. **North West Castle Hotel** in Stranraer, © 0776 4413, is recommended if you like comfort combined with something out of the ordinary. See Stranraer for the reason why this amazing concoction is built to resemble a ship. On the seafront, it has a swimming pool, games room, saunas, sunbeds and even a curling rink. Maddeningly, they don't take credit cards. There is a splendid bar/restaurant overlooking the curling rink with a nice old fashioned atmosphere.

moderate

In Portpatrick, **The Fernhill Golf Hotel**, © 077681 220, highly commended with four crowns from the Tourist Board, stands above the harbour overlooking the Irish Sea, 400 yards (370m) from the golf course. Every dish is cooked to order. Also overlooking the harbour, **Portpatrick Hotel**, © 077681 333, with three crowns and slightly cheaper, gives good value and welcomes families; it is open from March to November.

In Portpatrick are: Mount Stewart Hotel, ✆ 077681 291, overlooking the harbour, and Rickwood Private Hotel, ✆ 077681 270, overlooking the sea.

The Valleys

Dumfries and Galloway is cut by a number of valleys bringing rivers cascading into the Solway Firth from the hills and moorland in the north. If you have time, you won't regret pausing to trace some of these rivers up to their source.

Eskdale

Many streams rise in the hills of Eskdalemuir Forest, to the north, joining above Langholm to form the River Esk, that chatters and tumbles south through gorges and ravines until it steadies its pace and flows into the Solway Firth at Gretna.

Scotsdike

On the English border, Scotsdike has a 16th-century trench and dyke dug to mark the border in the days when the 'Debatable Lands' were hotly contested.

Gilnockie Tower

Gilnockie Tower (viewable from the outside or by appointment, ✆ 0541 80976), once called Hollows, or Holehouse, is 5 miles (8km) south of Langholm, off the A7. Dating from the 16th century this was one of Johnnie Armstrong of Gilnockie's strongholds—that hero of border ballads; see Teviot, Borders, for this freebooter's history. Ruffian he may have been, but he was reputed never to do harm to any of his countrymen. It is easy to feel a twinge of affection for him, looking up at this romantic tower, with crow-stepped gables and a carved parapet-walkway round the top, standing high above the Esk valley. He would certainly have approved of his descendant, Neil Armstrong, who was the first man on the moon in 1969.

Langholm

Langholm, about 10 miles (16km) north of the border, is a mill-town where the Esk gathers up the waters of the Wauchope and Ewes. Narrow and twisting, with market-place and townhouse, the old town is quite different from the spacious, stately-looking quarter across the river that developed in the 18th century when Langholm became a flourishing textile centre. The town has Common Riding celebrations in July, with a charge of riders through a narrow bend and up the hill from the square—a dramatic stampede.

A memorial to the poet Hugh MacDiarmid is 2 miles (3km) to the northeast on the Newcastleton road. A two-fold panel stands like a great open book overlooking Eskdale with carvings of wildlife and countryside, dramatic in their simplicity. Local feeling ran high when this memorial was first commissioned after MacDiarmid's death in 1978. Although he had referred to his home town as 'my touchstone in all creative matters', he was not loved by many of his fellow Langholmites. Stuffy locals objected to some of his bawdy anecdotes and his veiled references to the sexual habits of a local citizen in his autobiography *Lucky Poet*. When the sculpture was finished, it was refused by a six to five vote from the Dumfries and Galloway Planning Committee. Fortunately, the small-minded were overruled.

There is a good walk from Langholm up to the **Malcolm Monument**—the obelisk that dominates the hill to the east. Start from the car park beside the A7, just north of the town, and go up past the golf course. The round trip is 5 miles (8km), and the view from the monument makes the final steepish climb well worth it. (Malcolm was Sir John Malcolm who, in 1782, aged 13, was commissioned into the East India Company and became Governor of Bombay 45 years later.)

Westerkirk

In 1757, Thomas Telford was born at Westerkirk, further northwest on the B709. Here, overlooking his beloved Esk, is a memorial to this giant of the Industrial Revolution, who built roads and bridges all over the country, serving his apprenticeship on his own local bridges.

Kagyu Samye Ling Tibetan Monastery

There is something inspiring about this, the largest Buddhist temple in Western Europe, just north of Eskdalemuir on the B709. Founded in 1967 and completed in the mid-80s, in the peace and tranquillity of this lovely setting, near the source of the Esk, it is a far cry from the persecution and atrocities of Communist Tibet. Whatever your creed, you won't regret taking a free conducted tour round the temple and monastery.

Where to Stay

inexpensive

If you don't mind being in the middle of the town, **Eskdale Hotel** in Langholm, © 0541 80357, is a family-run former coaching inn whose stern exterior conceals respectability and good plain cooking. They can arrange shooting and fishing. Also in the middle of the town, the more attractive **Crown Hotel**, © 0541 80247, was also a coaching inn in the 18th century and has a less hushed atmosphere.

Annandale

Follow the River Annan north along the back roads to its source just north of Moffat: the scenery gets progressively wilder and more impressive.

Kirkpatrick Fleming

Kirkpatrick Fleming, 3 miles (4.5km) northeast of Annan off the A74, has a cave where Robert the Bruce hid for three months. Accessible now by path, it was then reached by

Samye Ling Tibetan Monastery

swinging down the cliff on a rope. The cave was originally cut from rock by Stone Age people whose tools were found near the river. Locals will tell you that it was here, and not on Rathlin Island, or anywhere else, that Bruce took courage from the persevering spider we were all brought up to emulate.

Kirtlebridge

For antiquities, go to Kirtlebridge, 3 miles (4.5km) further on, off the A74, for the 15th-century Merkland Cross, 9 feet (3m) high, with intricate carvings, erected in memory of a Maxwell who was killed in battle. People alive today remember the shock of the train crash near here in the First World War, when over 200 people were killed. The **Clydesdale Horse Centre**, at Robgill Tower near Kirtlebridge, has horses and all the old harness and implements.

Ecclefechan

Ecclefechan, about 5 miles (8km) north of Annan off the A74, was Thomas Carlyle's birthplace in 1795. He was born in the white **Arched House**, now a museum (open daily, Easter–31 Oct, or by arrangement, © 05763 666: adm), so called because of its arched gateway. The house was built by his father and uncle. His parents were unpretentious people, god-fearing and eloquent. Carlyle's mother learnt to write so she could answer his letters. They sent Thomas to Edinburgh University to train for the Church in 1809. His inherited intelligence, fed by education, flowered: he developed a critical awareness and knowledge of books and men that set him apart from his peers. Among the things he wrote was *Sartor Resartus* (Tailor Repatched) in which he describes a village, 'Entepfuhl', recognizable as Ecclefechan.

A mass of memorabilia is packed into the cottage. The kitchen would have been the heart of the household and you can almost see the family, seated at the table, listening to dissertations from the young student, surrounded by the domestic clutter of country life now displayed. Upstairs, the box-bed, although not original, is a contemporary of that in which Carlyle was born, in this bedroom. Other furniture and items come from Cheyne Row, Chelsea, where the Carlyles lived for more than 30 years. The museum is of interest for its social history as well as being a memorial to a complex man.

Carlyle refused burial in Westminster Abbey and is buried below a simple sandstone slab in the churchyard behind the cottage, an unfussy monument to a brilliant man who loathed ostentation. He was a temperamental husband to intellectual Jane Baillie Welsh, with whom he shared a stormy relationship reflected in her caustic, witty letters. Although they were devoted to each other (Jane's death in 1866 'shattered my whole existence into immeasurable ruin'), she left instructions that she was not to be buried with him, but with her father in Haddington, Lothian.

Hoddam Castle

This castle, 2 miles (3km) to the southwest, was built in the 16th century by John Maxwell, 4th Lord Herries, with a watchtower on Repentance Hill to the south. (Repentance, they say, because the noble lord threw his prisoners into the sea during a storm after a piratical raid on England.) Some of the castle has been demolished and the rest of it is at risk though there are plans for developing it into a leisure complex.

Lockerbie

At 6pm on Wednesday 21 December 1988, as people prepared for Christmas, a Pan-Am Boeing 747, *en route* from Frankfurt to New York, took off from London Heathrow. It carried in its luggage hold a transistor radio packed with explosives, planted by terrorists. The device exploded over Lockerbie, at 7.19pm, killing all the crew and passengers in the plane. The wreckage fell on and around the the town and on the adjacent motorway, flattening houses in a quiet crescent, killing the residents and a number of people driving up the motorway. In all, nearly 280 people died. The town lives on, with Scottish guts and stoicism.

By the end of the 18th century, Lockerbie, 10 miles (16km) north of Annan, was a substantial town, with lamb sales held annually on Lamb Hill. These sales were great occasions for the whole of Annandale: boisterous, colourful fairs, with sideshows and booths and noisy, jostling crowds.

Birrenswark, or Burnswark as it is sometimes called, has a distinctive outline which can't be missed. It is a steep, flat-topped hill southeast of Lockerbie, visible for miles. This commanding position was the site of a large fort, many centuries BC, with circular huts inside sturdy ramparts. Along came the Romans, besieged the inhabitants and moved in, leaving the present foundations. It is worth the 940-feet (290m) climb, not just for the view from the top but for the feeling of ancient history among those ancient ramparts and ditches. In 937 a ferocious battle took place here, the Battle of Brunanburh between the Saxon-English and the united Scots and Norse armies, with victory for the English.

Lochmaben

Lochmaben, 4 miles (6.5km) west of Lockerbie on the A709, is a town with a history that goes back to the 12th century when Robert the Bruce's forebears were powerful. It is one of the places claimed as the birthplace of King Robert himself—his statue glowers down the main road. Many of the buildings were built with stone from 13th-century **Lochmaben Castle**, whose scant remains are on a promontory signposted down a track south of Castle Loch. The massive, ivy-clad walls and humpy arches, gap-toothed among saplings on a grassy mound with traces of a moat, are a travesty of what was a 16-acre concourse with four moats. It was one of James IV's favourite places in the 16th century though his preferences were often influenced by female charms available in the area. Mary, Queen of Scots, came here with Darnley and it is said she introduced vendace to the lochs—small rare fish, considered a great delicacy: they have to be netted because they won't take bait.

Spedlins Tower

 Ruined Spedlins Tower, 3 miles (4.5km) north of Lochmaben, was once haunted by a gruesome ghost. In the 17th century the local miller, Porteous, was locked in the dungeon by the laird who then rode off to Edinburgh, forgetting his prisoner. Porteous starved to death, eating his own flesh in an attempt to survive, and his ghost haunted the tower until they confined it to the dungeon by laying a black-letter Cranmer Bible on the cellar steps.

Moffat

Take the B7020 from Lochmaben, through rolling farmland with the Lowther Hills to the west and Eskdalemuir to the east, patched with forest. Moffat has a wide High Street, dissected by a double avenue of lime trees. The Colvin Fountain, at the end, a cairn of boulders with a huge bronze ram on top, underlines the town's importance as a sheep-farming centre.

In 1633, Rachel Whitford, a bishop's daughter, tasted the water from a spring to the east and recognized the tang as that of sulphur. Within 100 years, peaceful Moffat, deep in its valley among the hills, became one of the most fashionable spas in Europe, attracting the ailing rich from far afield.

It was here, in 1759, that James Macpherson produced his first 'Ossianic' Fragments, poems he swore he had 'translated from the Gaelic of Ossian, the son of Fingal'. The authenticity of these poems was hotly debated by Dr Samuel Johnson, among others, and although many scholars were convinced they were genuinely collected from oral tradition, others believed that Macpherson composed them when he was a student. The truth seems immaterial: they are excellent in their own right.

Moffat Museum, in a converted bakery, presents local history, from sheep to spa. The Moffat Toffee Shop is a first-class 'sweetie shop', renowned for its Moffat toffee.

Tweedhope Sheep Dogs, at Hammerlands, is where Viv Billingham Parkes puts her dogs through their paces. (Demonstrations are at 11am and 3pm, Easter–end Oct: adm.)

The Devil's Beef Tub

The Devil's Beef Tub, 6 miles (10km) north of Moffat, off the A701, is a natural corral, where cattle thieves hid their stolen beasts. An electric fence borders the edge but there is a gate. As you peer down the steep grassy walls into the black abyss where swirling mist rises from a stream at the bottom, you can almost hear the thudding hoofs and the harsh calls of the Johnstone men, rounding up their Maxwell neighbours' cattle. Many stories are told: when prisoners from Culloden were being marched up here in 1746, one broke away and rolled down the almost sheer sides and escaped in a thick mist. Walter Scott met this man and used his story in *Redgauntlet*:

> *It looks as if four hills were laying their heads together to shut out daylight from the dark hollow space between them. A d—d dark black blackguard looking abyss of a hole it is and goes down straight from the roadside as perpendicular as it can do.*

This is the watershed between the sources of the Annan and the Tweed—high, wild country, cut off in winter. Covenanters used to seek shelter in these hills and a memorial grave to one, who was shot opposite, stands on the lip of the Tub.

Grey Mare's Tail

Grey Mare's Tail, one of the highest waterfalls in the country, is 10 miles (16km) north-east of Moffat on the A708. The corrie was gouged out by a retreating glacier in the Ice Age. Tail Burn pours in a single cascade, 200 feet (62m) from Loch Skeen into Moffat Water. The part you see from the road seems to hang motionless in the air, but when you approach, spray fills the air like mist and the sound of water becomes a roar. In winter it can freeze solid and climbers test their skills on it with crampons and ice-axes. The National Trust for Scotland owns the land around the falls—country rich in wild flowers and supporting a rare herd of wild goats. There is a 7-mile (11km) walk from Birkhill on the A708. You can go just to the foot of the waterfall, or continue up its right side to Loch Skeen, a mist-shrouded loch surrounded by hills. Be cautious walking here; there are precipitous edges and there have been several serious accidents, some fatal. (Sir Walter Scott and his horse fell into a bog-hole round here and had the devil of a job 'to get extricated'.) On the way back to Birkhill, go left up the narrow rocky gorge of Dob' Lin.

Craigieburn Woodland Garden (open Wed–Sun, April–Oct: adm) is on the road from Moffat to the Grey Mare's Tail, with old trees and waterfalls in a natural setting.

Where to Stay

moderate

Auchen Castle Hotel and Restaurant at Beattock, near Moffat, © 06833 407, is a 19th-century baronial mansion with a modern extension, in 50 acres with a trout loch. Gracious living here, with excellent food. **Moffat House Hotel**, Moffat, © 0683 20039, is in an Adam mansion in the town centre in over two acres. It is open from March to November. Also in Moffat is **Beechwood Country House Hotel**, © 0683 20210, overlooking the Annan Valley. Open from February to December, it is friendly, with good food and wine.

inexpensive

For something a bit different, try **Corehead Farm** at Annanwater, Moffat, © 0683 20182, open from April to October. This guest house is on a 2500-acre hill farm at the base of the Devil's Beef Tub. Marvellous home cooking justifies its Farmhouse Award. Children and pets are positively welcomed. If you have children you could forget them all day among the farm animals while you slip off bird-watching. An ideal away-from-it-all holiday.

Nithsdale

The River Nith rises across the Strathclyde border, rushes through the upper moors fed by many streams and descends at a more leisurely pace into Dumfries and on out into the Solway mudflats. It is hugged by the A76, but try to stick to the back roads where you can.

Twelve Apostles Stone Circle

Newbridge, 2½ miles (4km) northwest of Dumfries off the A76, has Scotland's widest stone circle: the 11 stones are clearly visible from the gate.

Routin Brig

Follow the road along the Cairn Water from Newbridge to Routin Brig, where the river cascades down through the woods in a series of waterfalls.

Ellisland

Six miles (10km) north of Dumfries off the A76, Ellisland Farm is another Robert Burns landmark (open at all reasonable times, but ring in advance, © 038774 246: free). Burns took over the farm in 1788, built the house and made his last, abortive attempt to make a living from the soil with new farming methods. Alas, his mind was too absorbed by poetry and the ladies, and it was a dismal failure. He auctioned the stock in 1791 and moved to Dumfries to be an exciseman. He wrote some of his most famous poems here, including 'Tam O' Shanter'. In the granary you can see Burns portrayed as a farmer. There is a walk along the river, said to be where he went for inspiration. There are several open farms in this area, demonstrating farming methods both modern and extinct. One is **The Barony**, 8 miles (13km) northeast of Dumfries off the A701, which includes farm walks with a woodland bird hide, a fishery and nature reserve.

Maxwelton House

Fourteenth-century Maxwelton House (open daily, Easter–end Sept: adm), 13 miles (21km) northwest of Dumfries on the B729, was the birthplace of Annie Laurie, for love of whom the ardent Jacobite William Douglas of Fingland wrote the poem, set to music and reshaped in 1835, in which he declared that for Bonnie Annie Laurie he would 'lay me doon and dee'. She didn't put him to the test and married Mr Ferguson of Craigdarroch. You can see Annie's boudoir, an early kitchen, and dairy and farming implements. The gardens are typically Scottish.

Moniaive, 5 miles (8km) to the west on the A702, is an attractive village with brightly painted houses, narrow streets and wynds.

Thornhill

A 10th-century, Anglian cross-shaft 9 feet (3m) high can be seen at Nith Bridge, half a mile west of Thornhill along the A702.

Keir Mill, 3 miles (4.5km) southwest of Thornhill, signposted off the A702, is where the world's first pedal bicycle was built at Courthill Smithy in 1839. Kirkpatrick MacMillan, the inventor, rode his 'Dandy Horse' to Glasgow where he was fined for 'dangerous behaviour, furious driving and knocking down a girl . . .' Macmillan, who never bothered to patent his invention, is buried in the churchyard. There is a signed bicycle trail from Keir Mill to Dumfries.

Morton Castle, always accessible, 3½ miles (5.5km) north of Thornhill, is a splendid ruin on a tongue of steep, rocky ground washed on three sides by a loch that was artificially formed by a dam across the glen. The approach would have had a deep ditch across it with a drawbridge, to separate the castle from the mainland. Thought to have been built in the first half of the 15th century, on the site of an older castle, Morton has almost no recorded history. Dunegal, the Lord of Nithsdale, is thought to have had a stronghold here in the 12th century.

Drumlanrig Castle

Drumlanrig Castle, about 18 miles (29km) northwest of Dumfries off the A76 (open most days in the summer: adm), is a pink sandstone Renaissance palace on a grassy dais beside the Nith among the Lowther Hills. Owned by the Duke of Buccleuch, this pile, with its mass of turrets and windows, was built in 1689 for his ancestor, the first Duke of Queensberry. The Duke moved in, spent one night, didn't like it and moved out, having virtually ruined himself paying for his folly. When the fourth Duke, the notorious 'Old Q', inherited the castle in 1778, he sold the beautiful avenue of lime trees to help pay his gambling debts. The estate is open to the public. (It has a wheelchair lift.) There are state rooms panelled with carved oak, French furniture, paintings by Leonardo da Vinci, Rembrandt, Holbein, Murillo, Ruysdael and Rowlandson, and portraits by Kneller, Reynolds and Ramsay. There are nature trails and an adventure play area and a visitor centre in the old stable yard with gift shop and tea room. Also in the stables is a craft centre.

Durisdeer

At Durisdeer, a hamlet tucked away at the entrance to the Dalveen Pass less than 5 miles (8km) to the northeast of Drumlanrig, off the A702, don't miss the delightfully

'Baroque-Arcadian' Queensberry Aisle in the 17th-century church (key from the cottage nearby). This mausoleum contains a white marble monument, designed by Van Nost, in memory of the second Duke and Duchess of Queensberry who died in 1711 and 1709, respectively. Surrounded by twisted columns, garlands and cherubs, the duchess lies supine, with her husband propped on an elbow beside her, like lovers in a pastoral tryst. Above the romantic-looking couple there is a scroll, extolling their virtues: it doesn't mention their heir, Lord Drumlanrig, who, in 1707, murdered and tried to eat a spit-boy, in Queensberry House, Edinburgh.

The A702 continues north through the dramatic scenery of the **Dalveen Pass**, towards the A74, and can be linked with a visit to Wanlockhead.

Wanlockhead

Wanlockhead is the highest village in Scotland, 1380 feet (425m) up in the moors, off the A76 on the B797, which climbs a narrow valley beside Mennock Water, through unreal-looking, mottled green and brown hills. The village is a wedge-shaped cluster of houses built on turf mounds, in a bowl in moorland.

The Museum of Scottish Lead Mining (open daily, Easter–Nov or by appointment: adm) is in a rebuilt miner's cottage, with mining artefacts and a beam-pumping engine outside. You can follow an open-air trail and see a mine-shaft if you don't suffer from claustrophobia. There are also period miners' cottages. Gold was once panned from the streams here; a piece weighing 4 to 5 oz (approx 130g) is in the British Museum. The heather-covered moorland was a haunt of Covenanters. They held their illegal Conventicles up here, with look-outs on guard on surrounding peaks to warn of approaching soldiers, during the Killing Times in the 17th century.

The **Southern Upland Way** passes through Wanlockhead, one of its more lonely stretches with panoramic views. (For Leadhills, Scotland's second highest village, just a short distance on up the road across the regional boundary, see Strathclyde, p.196.)

Sanquhar

A small town about 27 miles (43km) up the A76 from Dumfries, Sanquhar's chief interest is historic. Two Covenanters' declarations were pinned to the mercat cross: the first, by Richard Cameron in 1680, the second, by James Renwick in 1685, both protesting against the Episcopalian leanings of Charles II during the Killing Times. An obelisk marks the site of the cross. Richard Cameron was killed but his followers were granted an amnesty by William III, and it was from them that the regiment of the Cameronians was founded— now disbanded. Renwick was also killed and there is a memorial to him near Moniaive.

The Tolbooth designed by William Adam in 1735, with clock tower and double external steps, is a visitor centre and local-interest museum. Post a letter in the **Sanquhar Post Office**—the oldest in Britain, opened in 1763, 20 years before the introduction of the mailcoach service, and still in use.

The Admirable Crichton, 16th-century genius and child prodigy, was born at Elicock Castle, 2 miles (3km) to the south. He was killed in a brawl in Mantua when he was 22.

moderate

Try **Trigony House Hotel**, Closeburn, Thornhill, ✆ 0848 31211, a cosy, family-run country house in secluded grounds with adequate food. It has salmon and sea trout fishing. **Blackaddie House Hotel**, Sanquhar, ✆ 0659 50270, is a farm-house dating from the 16th century and specializes in organic food.

inexpensive

Elmarglen Hotel. Thornhill, ✆ 0848 30558, is small. **George Hotel**, Thornhill, ✆ 0848 30326, is an old coaching inn.

The Glenkens

Bordering the eastern flank of the Rhinns of Kells and the Galloway Forest Park, the Glenkens is a string of rivers and lochs, descending through windswept moorland to Loch Ken, which narrows to become the River Dee, flowing into the Solway Firth at Kirkcudbright. Loch Ken offers fishing, birdwatching and watersports.

Tongland

Two miles (3km) north of Kirkcudbright, **Tongland Power Station** has free conducted tours daily in the summer. If you aren't tempted, wait outside, overlooking the dam. While you try to spot salmon leaping up the man-made ladder, think back to the colourful history of Tongland Abbey, which once stood here. One of its abbots was murdered as he knelt at the altar in 1235, and its most famous abbot was John Damian, an alchemist. Damian enjoyed the patronage of James IV, the king who would undoubtedly have been a leading entrepreneur today and whose enquiring mind encouraged many experiments. In an attempt to show the king that it was possible for man to fly, Damian leapt off the walls of Stirling Castle in his presence. He broke his thigh.

Castle Douglas

Nine miles (14.5km) northeast of Kirkcudbright, Castle Douglas's history goes back to when Iron Age builders created two crannogs on Carlingwark Loch below the town. These islets, built on wooden platforms submerged in shallow water, provided protection for the inhabitants of the huts on top. Horseshoes, excavated from the shore of the loch, which the Civic Park now covers, are thought to originate from a shoeing-forge that served the horses of Edward I's army when he was hammering the Scots. The town was once the village of Carlingwark, changing its name in honour of a pedlar, William Douglas, who made his fortune in Virginia and returned to his homeland in 1789, buying up the village and developing it into a prosperous cattle market.

Weather Watchers in Laurieston, nearby on the B795 (open Tues, Fri, Sun: adm), is a working weather forecasting centre with tours.

Threave Castle

Threave Castle (open daily: free, small charge for ferry), 1½ miles (2.5km) west of Castle Douglas on an island in the Dee, was a Black Douglas stronghold dating from the 14th century. It was the last of their fortresses to surrender to James II in 1455, during his struggle to throw off their powerful grip on his kingdom. James won his victory with the help of Mons Meg, that mighty cannon now in Edinburgh. The 70-foot (21.5m) tower had five storeys, each containing a single room linked by a spiral stair, surrounded by a curtain wall and four drum towers. The stone projecting above the doorway was 'The Gallows Knob' and Archibald the Grim, the aptly named 14th-century Earl of Douglas, boasted that it 'never lacked a tassel'. Covenanters stormed the castle in 1640 and demolished the interior.

The National Trust for Scotland's **Threave Gardens** (open daily, all year: adm), a mile (1.5km) south of the castle, provide a school of practical gardening. Students get a two-year training in skills that might once have been learnt at the knee of that almost extinct breed, the head gardener. They live in the Victorian house in the grounds and between them and their instructors, maintain a garden that is a joy to walk in. There is a visitor centre. The **Threave Wildfowl Refuge** has many species of wild geese and ducks. (Access to the nature reserve is limited in the breeding season: adm.)

New Galloway

Although it was only a village, New Galloway, 18 miles (29km) north of Kirkcudbright, was created a Royal Burgh in 1633, the smallest in Scotland, so that the Gordon Laird of nearby Kenmure Castle (private) could have easy access to a market. It is an attractive place, its steep main street flanked by freshly painted stone cottages. Surrounded by moorland and forest, the landscape was transformed in 1929 by Scotland's first hydro-electric development, with reservoirs where rivers and burns once ran.

Dalry is a well-kept village a couple of miles (3km) north of New Galloway. In **Carsphairn**, 8 miles (13km) to the north, there is a heritage centre with local history (open April–Oct: adm).

Kenmure Castle

Kenmure Castle is off the A762, just south of New Galloway, a shell on a hill, topped by tall chimneys, visible through trees and accessible only on foot. With 15th-century origins, this ruin is cloaked in history. The owners, staunchly Jacobite Gordons of Lochinvar, welcomed Mary, Queen of Scots during her state tour in 1563, and later sheltered her when she was escaping to England, providing her with the disguise she was wearing when she arrived at Dundrennan.

Lochinvar

If you had to learn 'Young Lochinvar', in your youth, you might feel compensatory delight in finding traces of Lochinvar's birthplace—bringing reality to what may have seemed legend. Go 3 miles (4.5km) northeast of Dalry, off the A702 and along a track to the left.

When, in Scott's 'Marmion', brave Lochinvar came out of the west, to rescue fair Ellen from having to marry a 'laggard in love and a dastard in war', it could have been from the fragment of castle on the islet that he set out.

The Galloway Forest Park

Formerly Glen Trool Forest, the Galloway Forest Park, owned by the Forestry Commission, covers 250 square miles (640 sq km). There are many walks in lovely scenery, with wildlife that includes roe deer, red deer and wild goats. Moorland, peat bog, hills, lochs and fast-flowing rivers and burns, dominated by the great bulk of Merrick, 2765 feet (850m) high, make a visit here unforgettable. In autumn the range of colour is staggering. Guide-books, sold locally, give details of the many walks as well as campsites, picnic areas and special view points. **Queensway** is the scenic drive between New Galloway and Newton Stewart on the A712, with lots of attractions on the way.

One of these is **Clatteringshaws Loch**, about 5 miles (8km) west of New Galloway. Here, the **Galloway Deer Museum** is a converted farm steading (open daily, April–Sept: free) with information about deer and other wildlife in the area, geology and history, wild goats and a live trout exhibition. An attraction in the Forest Park is **Bruce's Stone**, commemorating Bruce's victory over the English at the Battle of Rapploch Moss in 1307. It is reached either by following the National Trust for Scotland signs up into the moor northwest from Clatteringshaws Loch—quite a long haul—or from the A714, through Glentrool village. Another **Bruce's Stone** is a massive engraved boulder overlooking Loch Trool, marking the site where Robert the Bruce defeated the English by rolling boulders down on them. If the stones were anything like this, you can see why.

Where to Stay

inexpensive

In Castle Douglas you will get good value at **The Imperial Hotel**, © 0556 2086/3009; **The Urr Valley Country House Hotel**, © 0556 2188; and **Douglas Arms Hotel**, © 0556 2231. They all serve reasonable food. In New Galloway, are: **Ken Bridge Hotel**, © 06442 211, a Victorian coaching house on the river bank (and the main road), with free fishing; **Cross Keys Hotel**, © 06442 494; **Kenmure Arms Hotel**, © 06442 240; and **Leamington Hotel** in the High Street, © 06442 327, which offers sporting packages. **Lochinvar Hotel**, Dalry, © 06443 210, is friendly.

Lothian: Excluding Edinburgh

Arriving in Lothian from the Borders you come over the Lammermuir, Moorfoot or Pentland Hills and see the whole region laid out below you: an expanse of farmland punctuated with rust-red roofs and massive carbuncles of volcanic rock, with the glinting firth beyond and the blue hills of Fife on the horizon. Your eye is drawn towards Edinburgh, dark and dense in the distance, dominated by Castle Rock and Authur's Seat. There are 70-odd miles (110km) of coastline: sheer rock cliffs, wide golden sands, dunes tufted with marram grass, quaint little fishing harbours. Rivers and streams tumble from the hills and clatter across the plain to the sea. These once provided power for the mills and bring beauty and irrigation to the fertile land.

While much of East Lothian is flat farmland stretching down to the coast with some good beaches, most of Midlothian and West Lothian are industrial with historic towns and buildings scattered through them. Lothian's roots go a long way down into prehistory. Stone Age Man left traces of hill forts. When the Romans arrived it was inhabited by the Votadini, with Traprain Law as its capital. It may have taken its name from their King Loth. After they faded into obscurity, it formed the northern part of Bernicia, inhabited by Britons. Lothian men were always independent; they kept aloof from the rest of Scotland until 1018 when Malcolm II defeated the Angles and drew Bernicia into his kingdom.

When Queen Margaret persuaded her husband to move the court to Edinburgh in the middle of the 11th century, Lothian's history became bound up with that of the capital. Invading armies swept through in both directions. When the monarchy was strong, so was the surrounding land; when anarchy prevailed, it was within range of the capital that the powerful lords were most aggressive. Much of Mary, Queen of Scots' brief reign was played out in Lothian in the middle of the 16th century, and Prince Charles Edward Stuart's even briefer appearance dazzled the citizens of Lothian for six weeks when his army camped out at Duddingston near Edinburgh. When Scotland finally took on the mantle of peace, houses no longer needed to be fortresses. The cultural renaissance that erupted in Edinburgh, in the wake of the suppression of the Highlands, spread outwards in ripples of fine architecture and collections of art. Great mansions were built on vast estates, close to the capital, often financed by fortunes made from coal.

Coal-mining is Lothian's oldest industry, pioneered 800 years ago by medieval monks, whose primitive, shallow workings were the forerunners of today's deep mines. Coal was used to boil sea-water to extract the salt, essential as a preservative before the days of refrigeration, and provided fuel for castle and cottage as well as for industry. Whole families toiled in the pits, and miners were bought and sold with their mines, like slaves. Only one open-cast mine is left now where once there were hundreds. The Lady Victoria mine at Newtongrange has been cleverly exploited to create an interesting colliery museum.

With some of the most fertile land in Britain, agriculture plays an important part in the economy. In the mid-18th century, landowners started to 'enclose' the land, turning the peasants' small uneconomic 'runrig' fields into larger fields. Farm steadings were built and new villages, such as Tyninghame, were created to house the displaced peasants who became farm labourers. Some worked in textile mills built along the rivers, or went down the mines. Today, barley is the most important crop, used for malting and for feeding stock. Market gardening and vegetable growing are lucrative, with the markets of the ever-hungry capital on the doorstep. On the less fertile hill pastures to the south, cattle are bred and sold to farms on the plain to be fattened for market. Only sheep graze on the moors, often being moved down for the winter.

Tourism is important to Lothian's economy. Although the region has Edinburgh for its centre, it is by no means just the city's dormitory.

Tourist Information

The region is divided into East Lothian, Midlothian and West Lothian. The following Tourist Information Centres are open all year.

East Lothian Tourist Board: Town House, **Dunbar**, ✆ 0368 63353; Granada A1 Service Area, Oldcraighall, **Musselburgh**, ✆ 031 653 6172; Quality Street, **North Berwick**, ✆ 0620 2197.

Midlothian Tourist Association, 2 Clerk Street, **Loanhead**, ✆ 031 440 2210, extn 220.

West Lothian: Forth Valley Tourist Board, Burgh Halls, The Cross, **Linlithgow**, ✆ 0506 844600.

There are local centres, usually open from Easter to the end of September, at: **Dalkeith** Library, ✆ 031 663 2083; A1 Pencraig, **East Linton**, ✆ 0620 860063; **Musselburgh**, Brunton Hall, ✆ 031 665 6596; and at **Penicuik** Library, ✆ 09968 672340.

The Coast East of Edinburgh: Barns Ness to Musselburgh

This stretch of coast is a paradise for naturalists, with nature reserves, sandy beaches, rugged rocks and a wealth of birds. The seaside towns are like English resorts, with rows of villas staring out to sea, genteel and trim.

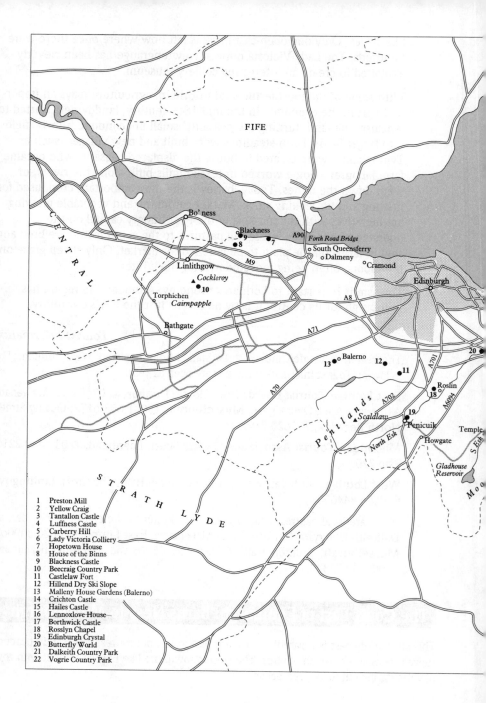

1 Preston Mill
2 Yellow Craig
3 Tantallon Castle
4 Luffness Castle
5 Carberry Hill
6 Lady Victoria Colliery
7 Hopetown House
8 House of the Binns
9 Blackness Castle
10 Beecraig Country Park
11 Castlelaw Fort
12 Hillend Dry Ski Slope
13 Malleny House Gardens (Balerno)
14 Crichton Castle
15 Hailes Castle
16 Lennoxlove House
17 Borthwick Castle
18 Rosslyn Chapel
19 Edinburgh Crystal
20 Butterfly World
21 Dalkeith Country Park
22 Vogrie Country Park

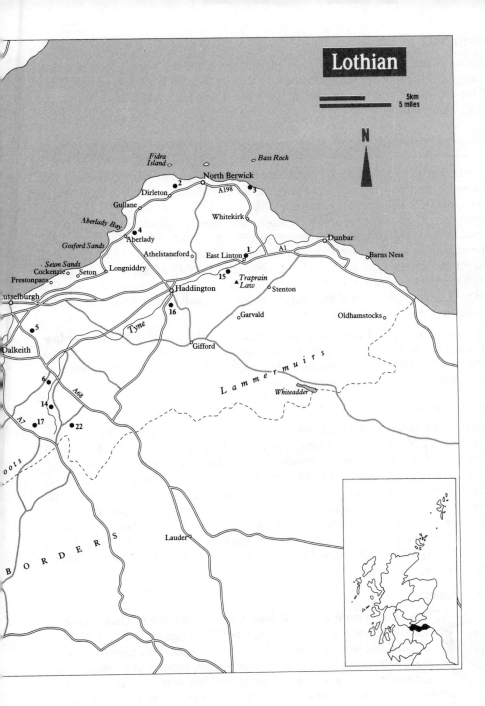

Lothian

5km
5 miles

N

Fidra Island
Bass Rock
North Berwick
2
Dirleton
A198
3
Gullane
Aberlady Bay
Whitekirk
4
Aberlady
Dunbar
Gosford Sands
Athelstaneford
East Linton
1
A1
Barns Ness
Seton Sands
Cockenzie
Seton
Longniddry
15
Prestonpans
Traprain Law
usselburgh
Haddington
Stenton
16
5
Garvald
Oldhamstocks
Dalkeith
Gifford
Tyne
L a m m e r m u i r s
6
Whiteadder
A68
14
A7
17
22
oots
B O R D E R S
Lauder

123

Barns Ness

A small detour off the A1, about 3 miles (4.5km) east of Dunbar, reaches Barns Ness: the road runs straight out to the lighthouse on a rock promontory beyond a campsite. Here there is a wildlife reserve, a geology trail with an old lime kiln, and bracing bathing from clean white sands.

Dunbar

Dunbar was an important fishing port 300 years ago, giving jobs to 20,000 workers. The harbour is quiet now, though it still has a small fishing fleet. Smuggling once flourished: in 1765, 8000 lbs (3500kg) of contraband tobacco passed through the port. Today it is a rapidly developing holiday resort with reputedly the lowest rainfall and highest sunshine in Scotland. Edward I defeated the Scots here in 1295 and his son, Edward II, escaped from the harbour by sea, 19 years later, after his defeat at Bannockburn. In 1650, Cromwell fought and defeated the supporters of Charles II in Dunbar, killing 3000 and taking 10,000 prisoners. While it was generally Cromwell's practice to order the execution of many of his prisoners, 1000 of the Dunbar men were shipped down to help Vermuyden in his efforts to drain the Fenlands.

The town sprawls round a wide High Street, squared off at the north end by **Lauderdale House,** built by Robert Adam, once used as a barracks and recently restored to flats. The 17th-century steepled **Town House,** in the middle of the High Street, is the oldest civic building in constant use in Scotland.

Dunbar Castle

The best view of the castle is from above, at the edge of Lauderdale House barrack square, and there is a board giving its history. One jagged, fang-like tower and a few scattered stones remain of what was once an extensive fortress guarding the gateway to the eastern plain, sprawled across sea-lashed rocks, overhanging the narrow entrance to the harbour. The original castle was built in the 11th century for Cospatrick, Earl of Northumbria, deposed by William the Conqueror and made Earl of Dunbar by his cousin Malcolm Canmore. When Bothwell abducted Mary, Queen of Scots, in 1567, he brought her to Dunbar Castle. It was to Dunbar that they fled, less than six weeks later. The castle was demolished by Mary's half-brother, Moray, after her final defeat. Later, Cromwell used its stones to improve the harbour.

Black Agnes

 The focus of many battles, Dunbar Castle's most stirring claim on the imagination was a siege in 1339, when Black Agnes, Countess of Dunbar, and her ladies held it for six weeks against the English. This brave woman mocked the great siege engine, called a 'sow', which was used against the castle. She and her ladies leant over the battlements and wiped the walls with their dainty handkerchiefs where the sow's missiles had hit.

Dunbar Harbour has cobbled quays round an outer and inner basin, restored warehouses, a coastguard station, working fishing boats, piles of netting and lobster creels, pleasure craft and the ever-vigilant lifeboat. Kittiwakes throng the rocks, their cries echoing above the ruined castle. In northerly and easterly gales, waves pour over the harbour walls. Picture it in the old days, the boats packed into the basins, men busy on deck, sorting and landing the catches, the quays alive with the chatter of women, gutting heaps of slithering silver herring.

The John Muir Country Park, on the western outskirts of the town, is named after a 19th-century conservationist and explorer, born in Dunbar, who founded America's national parks. Many acres of wild coastland surround the mouth of the Tyne, where you can walk along the cliffs, fish, sail, surf-ride or swim, play golf, or just enjoy the abundant wildlife.

Whitekirk

Following the coast, take the A198, 4 miles (6km) west of Dunbar, and Whitekirk is a couple of miles further on. This was once the site of a holy well, now lost in the field opposite the church. Among the pilgrims who came here in the 15th century was a papal delegate, Aeneus Silvius de Piccolomini, who later became Pope Pius II. He walked barefooted in the snow from Dunbar to give thanks for rescue from a shipwreck. This pilgrimage earned him rheumatism in his feet for the rest of his life. It is said he found the Scottish lassies 'forthcoming and eager to kiss everyone in sight'. (An amusing epilogue to this story can be seen in Sienna Cathedral: a picture in the chapel on the right, painted in memory of Piccolomini's travels, shows a romantic Italian idea of Scotland, full of fanciful flowers and fairyland scenery.)

The imposing church dates from the 12th century, well restored after it was burnt by zealous suffragettes in 1914. The name Whitekirk for such a predominantly red building is explained by the former use of whitewash or harling to cover the sandstone.

Tantallon Castle

Tantallon (open daily, except closed Wed and Thurs, Oct–March: adm) is a mile or so beyond Whitekirk. This dramatic ruin stands on the edge of a sheer cliff overhanging the sea between two bays. Dating from the 14th century, it was a stronghold of the powerful Douglas family who leased it (when it was a smaller fortalice in the 14th century) from the Earls of Fife—an unusual practice in those days. These were the Red Douglases, Earls of Angus, who 'rose upon the ruins of the Black' Douglases when they were subdued by James II. These Red Douglases became a menace to the Crown, ruling their domains with a total disregard for authority. They flaunted their personal armies and lived just as they pleased, especially when Margaret Tudor, the devious widow of James IV, married their leader, the Earl of Angus in 1514, and they became arch manipulators in the power struggle over the boy king, James V. They built on to and strengthened Tantallon, making it a perfect stronghold for this arrogantly audacious family.

The castle's massive curtain walls cut it off on its headland, making it impregnable against the impotent batterings of rivals, while supplies came in regularly by sea. It took Cromwell's artillery twelve days of devastating bombardment before Tantallon was eventually 'dinged doun'. The three ditches to landward were dug to repel siege engines and invaders. The walls are 14 feet (4m) thick and the well 100 feet (30m) deep, bored through rock. Seen silhouetted against the sea, especially as the sun comes up out of the east, Tantallon is one of Scotland's most heart-stopping ruins.

North Berwick

North Berwick, about 10 miles (16km) northwest along the coast from Dunbar, was created a Royal Burgh by Robert III around the end of the 14th century. It developed into a holiday and golfing resort during the 19th century. A compact, sunny town flanked by two bays with a rocky headland between, it is the main shopping centre for the area. Narrow, one-way streets, teeming with holidaymakers in summer, lead down to the sheltered harbour, full of boats, surrounded by warehouses converted into flats. Lobster creels, nets and fish-boxes mingle on the quay with the spars of pleasure boats and hulls of sailboards and, just beyond, an open-air swimming pool built into the rock, high above the sea.

North Berwick Museum (open daily, June–Sept; Fri–Mon, Easter–end of May: free), in School Road, on the upper floor of the old school, displays local social history, archaeology, and wildlife, with special exhibitions.

The Auld Kirk stands on a rocky spit near the harbour. All you can see of this notorious 12th-century ruin today is the whitewashed nave, south aisle and foundations. When James VI/I was nearly drowned in a freak storm off the Bass Rock, he blamed a well-established coven of witches in North Berwick, alleging that some of them had had the temerity to row round his foundering ship in a sieve. The witches were arrested one dark night as they performed some nasty rituals in and around the Auld Kirk, presided over by their 'Devil', Francis, Earl of Bothwell, nephew of Mary's Bothwell, who lived at Hailes Castle nearby. The subsequent trial of 94 witches and 6 wizards was based on confessions extracted by gruesome torture and attended by the king who was inspired to write a book on the subject.

North Berwick Law is the volcanic rock that towers 613 feet (188m) above the town. Climb its steep flank for a view out to sea, over to the hills of Fife and across the Lothian plain to the Lammermuirs, Moorfoots and Pentlands. This was one of a chain of warning beacons and in the Middle Ages was crowned by a fort. Now it is occupied by a watchtower, built to look for invaders during the Napoleonic Wars, and more modern buildings used in the First World War. There is also an arch made from the jawbone of a whale, a relic from the days of whale fishing in the North Sea.

The Bass Rock

The Bass Rock, one of Lothian's volcanic plugs, lies 1½ miles (2.5km) offshore from Tantallon. Standing 350 feet (108m) high, a mile (1.5km) in circumference, its sheer-walled wedge is a landmark for sailors. Boat trips run from North Berwick to cruise round it but permission is needed to land.

St Baldred the hermit died on the rock in the 7th or 8th century and you can just make out where his cell was, halfway up, on a terrace on the south side. Near the lighthouse are the ruins of a castle owned by the Lauder family. In 1406, James I, the 12-year-old heir to the throne, sheltered on the Bass on his way to sanctuary in France. (His subsequent capture at sea and detention in London for 18 years proved to be greatly to Scotland's advantage, for he returned well educated and able to cope with the anarchy strangling his country.) Many Covenanters were imprisoned on the rock during the Killing Times in the 17th century. Later, four fugitive Jacobites held out there for four years, provisioned by the French.

The Bass Rock is now a gannetry, as well as a haven for gulls, kittiwakes, puffins, fulmars and guillemots. You may even see seals. If you are sailing near its guano-whitened cliffs on a hot day, you won't miss it.

Dirleton

Three miles (4.5km) west of North Berwick, Dirleton is one of the prettiest villages in the area, with pantiled cottages, a 17th-century church, session house, old school and inns grouped round two wide, tree-lined greens.

Dirleton Castle (open daily: adm) is a 13th-century ruin overlooking the upper green from a rocky mound in the middle of the village. It was the last castle in the south of Scotland to resist Edward I and was demolished by General Monk, for Cromwell, in 1650. Surrounded by lawns, a garden and a 17th-century bowling green, it has a 17th-century doo'cot containing 1100 empty nests, a relic from when pigeon meat was a valuable supplement to the diet in the lean winter months. A coven of witches, possibly those of North Berwick, were imprisoned here before being half-strangled and publicly burnt at the stake on Dirleton Green.

Yellow Craig

Yellow Craig, a sandy beach studded with dunes and backed by woodland, is reached by a lane leading a mile (1.5km) seawards from the eastern edge of Dirleton. It has a caravan park, picnic sites and a nature trail. The small hillock rising from the trees was the model for Spyglass Hill in Robert Louis Stevenson's *Treasure Island*. The sandy bay, fringed with buckthorn and marram grass, overlooks Fidra Island, a lump of black basalt rock, eroded by wind and sea. There was a Celtic monastery on Fidra. Romanized in 1165, it was a popular place for pilgrimages and its ruins can still be seen. (Boat trips are available from North Berwick.)

Gullane

Gullane is a seaside golfing mecca about a mile west of Dirleton. Pronunciations vary, from Gillan and Gullan, to Goolan: Gillan was once considered 'posh', but Gullan and Goolan date from further back. Church land until the Reformation, it developed into a holiday centre for the wealthy genteel, with Muirfield among its golf courses and a sandy beach to occupy non-golfing members of the family. The Open Golf Championship is a great event at Muirfield.

St Andrew's Collegiate Church is said to have fallen into ruin in the 16th century when James VI/I objected to the minister smoking tobacco and transferred the parish 2 miles (3km) east to Dirleton.

Gullane Hill, to the west, was formed by wind-blown sand, a process that still continues. Sand has silted up Aberlady Bay on the west side of the hill and created a bird sanctuary and nature reserve, with over 200 recorded species of birds, including five species of tern. A footbridge leads from the roadside car park into the reserve. Many years ago, great sailing ships would have lain at anchor right up to the mouth of the river.

Luffness Castle (open to the public by appointment only: © 08757 218, free) overlooks Aberlady Bay. It dates from the 16th century, with a 13th-century keep built on the site of a Norse camp. You can still see the moat, curtain walls and towers. It was built by the Scottish-Norman family de Lindsay, one of whom was Regent of Scotland when Alexander III was a boy. He died on a Crusade, bequeathing land to the monk who carried his embalmed body home. The ruins of the monastery, built on the promised gift of land, are near the castle, with the tomb and effigy of the crusading laird.

Aberlady

Aberlady, no more than a straggling village on the southwest shore of the bay, was a thriving trading port until the Peffer Burn silted up. Pantiled cottages border the main street, with the Quill Gallery, inns and a mercat cross that lost its top in the Reformation. In the church, with 15th-century tower and vaulted stone basement, is part of an 8th-century Celtic cross with interwoven bird carvings. The original 'louping-on stane' at the gate was the mounting block.

Myreton Motor Museum (open daily: adm), signposted, a mile (1.5km) to the east, is a collection of vintage cars, old road signs, advertisements, petrol-pumps, cycles, motorcycles, military vehicles and memorabilia from early motoring days.

Gosford Sands, less than a mile beyond Aberlady to the southwest, overlook the Firth of Forth, cut by a network of tracks and picnic sites, backed by wind-sculpted trees. This long, rock-strewn beach can be scruffy but ideal if you want to stretch your legs or exercise the dog before reaching the suburbs of Edinburgh.

Port Seton

Seton Collegiate Church (open daily except Tues afternoons and Wed: adm) is just beyond Gosford Bay on the coast road. Built on the site of an earlier church, it was established as collegiate in 1492 and you can still see the ruins of the domestic buildings. In the church are effigies of the fifth Lord Seton and his wife: he was killed at Flodden in 1513; she built the transept and spire. Seton House, next to the church, has a collection of peacocks.

Seton Castle (private), an 18th-century building adjacent to the church, stands on the site of Seton Palace. This was frequently visited by Mary, Queen of Scots, the Setons having been loyal supporters of her cause. She came here with Darnley after Rizzio's murder and also the next year, with Bothwell, after Darnley's murder, when she took part in an archery contest, adding another nail to the coffin that was being built for her by her critics. The daughter of the house, Mary Seton, was one of the Queen's Four Marys.

Seton Sands, nearby, is a holiday park with permanent caravans and facilities for those who prefer holidays crammed with entertainment.

Prestonpans

Prestonpans straggles along the coast 2 miles (3km) to the east, forming an almost continuous waterside township with Port Seton, Cockenzie and Longniddry. It took its name from the open-air salt pans in which 12th-century monks from Newbattle Abbey used local coal to boil sea-water from the Firth to extract the salt. It would be easy to drive through this uninspiring sprawl without discovering its treasures, but the name Prestonpans will draw Jacobites like a magnet.

Go first to Meadowmill, between Prestonpans and Tranent. Looking from the viewpoint across grassland that now covers old colliery workings, it is hard to believe you are on the front line of the Battle of Prestonpans, when Prince Charles Edward Stuart defeated General Cope in a fifteen-minute dawn battle in September 1745. Cope established his army with Preston, Cockenzie and Port Seton behind them, a deep ditch and a boggy marsh in front and the ten-foot wall of Preston House protecting their western flank. With local knowledge, and in spite of disagreement among his staff officers, the Prince's army slipped in from the east as the sun rose, three men at a time down a narrow track, and overwhelmed the enemy by the ferocity and speed of their surprise attack, hacking their way through the Hanoverian lines with broadsword and dirk. The Hanoverians fled 'eskaped like rabets,' as the Prince later reported to his father. The outcome so boosted the Prince's morale that he believed they were invincible. The battle was the inspiration for the song 'Hey Johnnie Cope are you wauking yet?' A cairn in a field beside the A1 commemorates the battle.

Off the coast road in Prestonpans, in the heart of the village, **Preston Tower** was built by the Hamiltons in the 15th century. Originally about 50 feet (15m) high, it was burnt down by the English in 1544, quickly repaired, burnt down by Cromwell in 1650, and rebuilt again, this time with a two-storey addition on top, making it unique in Scotland. It is now the central feature of a new housing development, together with a boundary wall and a 17th-century lean-to doo'cot.

The 17th-century **mercat cross** is nearby, the only complete and unaltered cross of its kind in Scotland. It has a unicorn-crowned shaft rising from a circular base with pilasters and niches, and a turnpike stair to a platform from which public proclamations were read. Perhaps the town crier hurried here in 1745 to inform the townspeople of the victory of the Stuart prince just down the road.

Prestongrange Mining Museum (open Easter–Sept: free), on the western outskirts of Prestonpans is on a former colliery site and covers 800 years of mining history. Outside, you can see an 1874 Cornish Beam Pumping Engine with its five-storey engine house. The former power house is an exhibition hall full of mining artefacts. Special 'steam days' are held on the first Sunday of each month from April to September.

Musselburgh

Musselburgh, 9 miles (14.5km) beyond Aberlady, is the next sizeable town southwest along the coast, at the mouth of the River Esk whose tidal flats were once carpeted with mussel beds. The Romans had a fort here, to supply their camp at Inveresk, and 5000-year-old Bronze Age relics have been excavated locally.

On the direct route to Edinburgh, Musselburgh was often sacked by invading English armies. In 1332, Robert the Bruce's nephew, Thomas Randolph, Earl of Moray and Regent of Scotland, fell ill and was given sanctuary from the English by the citizens of Musselburgh, until he died. The town was called The Honest Toun thereafter and 'Honesty' remains its motto. **Honest Toun** celebrations are held every summer, with plenty of pageantry and entertainment.

From its beginnings, golf was played on **Musselburgh Links,** now more familiar as a racecourse, the Royal Musselburgh Golf Club having moved along the river to Prestongrange. James VI/I was an enthusiastic player and James IV is believed to have played here also. Cromwell stationed troops on the links in 1650, after his victory at Dunbar, while he 'sorted out' the district. The links are also the site for an annual shooting contest by the Queen's Bodyguard for Scotland, the Royal Company of Archers.

Fisherrow is Musselburgh's old harbour with terraces of fisher cottages round the harbour-basin on the waterfront. On the quay is a wooden cabin, painted bright red. Inside, Mr Clark sells smoked salmon, done in a cupboard just inside the door; it is the most succulent in Scotland and among the cheapest.

The Tolbooth, at the east end of Musselburgh High Street near the mercat cross, was once the town prison. Its unusual 16th-century spire was built from material taken from the chapel of Our Lady of Loretto, nearby, when the Reformation decreed its demolition. The chapel, founded by a hermit, Thomas Douchtie, in 1533, became a healing centre for the sick, much as Lourdes is today. When its stones were recycled for secular use the Pope was so outraged he excommunicated the Honest Toun for 200 years. Today a boys' public school stands on the lands of Loretto.

The Battle of Pinkie was fought southeast of the town in 1547, one of Henry VIII's victories during his 'Rough Wooing'.

Pinkie House (open to the public Tues afternoons during the summer and Christmas terms: free), opposite Loretto, is part of the school, an early 17th-century building with later additions. The painted gallery on the first floor, long and wide, has an arched timber ceiling painted in tempera by Italian artists.

Inveresk Lodge Gardens (open all year except Sat: adm) are a mile (1.5km) south of Musselburgh in Inveresk. This garden of a 17th-century house (private) is run by the National Trust for Scotland and specializes in plants suitable for small gardens.

Just south of Inveresk is **Carberry Hill**, scene of the battle that resulted in Mary, Queen of Scots' surrender and capture. Mary, aged 25, proud to the last, prepared to watch the chivalric encounters that were to decide the issue. No one of suitable rank among the rebel nobles stepped forward to take up Bothwell's challenge. There was no fight and Mary decided her surrender and the promise of a safe conduct for Bothwell were the best solution. There, at Queen's Mount, on Carberry Hill, watched by those of her army who had not melted away, she embraced her new husband whose child she was carrying, and watched him ride off. She never saw him again.

The Open Arms Hotel, Dirleton, ✆ 062 085 241, is an unexpected treasure in a smallish village, family-run for the last 40 years. Dating from 1685, it is on the edge of the green overlooking the castle. Comfortable and peaceful, with open log fires, it has long been acclaimed for its food. People drive out from Edinburgh to eat here. **Greywalls**, a Lutyens-designed country house overlooking Muirfield at Gullane, ✆ 0620 842144, is luxurious. Open from mid-April to November, it is one of the best hotels in Scotland. A few years ago, King Hussein and Queen Noor of Jordan ate at Greywalls and were so impressed by the food they pinched the chef: the replacement is just as good.

moderate

In Dunbar, **The Craig En Gelt Hotel**, Marine Road, ✆ 0368 62287, overlooking the harbour and ruins of Dunbar Castle, offers golf packages. **Point Garry Hotel**, West Bay Road, North Berwick, ✆ 0620 2380, is a comfortable, family-run hotel and has good golf packages. North Berwick is packed with homely guest houses, such as **Craigview** (inexpensive) ✆ 0620 2257, overlooking the sea.

Eating Out

La Potinière, Gullane, ✆ 0620 843214, is housed in what looks like a restored bus shelter on the main road. Proprietors David and Hilary Brown serve lunch on Sunday, Monday, Tuesday and Thursday, and dinner on Friday and Saturday—six meals a week and you must book, though it's worth trying for a last-minute cancellation. There is no choice: Hilary cooks a set French country-style meal each day of a quality that is outstanding as well as being remarkably cheap. The wine list was runner-up in the 'Best in Britain' awards, and is not expensive.

The Coast West of Edinburgh: Cramond to Bo'ness

This stretch of coast is rich in large country houses linked by attractive walks along the shore, giving way to the industrial sprawl around Grangemouth to the west.

Cramond

Cramond, on the western fringe of Edinburgh, is an 18th-century village at the mouth of the River Almond as it flows into the Firth of Forth. Cramond means fort-on-the-river. The fort was Roman, built in about AD 142 to guard the harbour. Its foundations can still be seen by the church, with an illustrated plan. (In the summer, free conducted walks round the village start from the kirk at 3pm every Sunday.)

The Goodman of Ballengeich

To the south, beside an older Cramond Brig than the present 17th-century bridge, James V was violently attacked. The king was given to wandering about dressed as a humble farmer, calling himself the Goodman of Ballengeich. He was thus disguised when he was attacked by robbers, or, some say, by the family of a peasant girl to whom he was making love. He was rescued by a local man, Jock Howieson. The king rewarded him with a gift of land on condition that Howieson and his descendants should wash the hands and feet of all new sovereigns on their first visit to Scotland. The present Queen upheld the tradition in 1952.

Dalmeny

Dalmeny, about 3 miles (4.5km) west of Cramond, is a group of cottages round a green, tucked away below the A90 some distance from Dalmeny House. The 12th-century **church**, dedicated to St Cuthbert, must be one of the finest gems of Norman architecture in Scotland. Its receding arches draw your eye towards a simple altar and east window. In the pulpit is a carved misericord, possibly unique, on which the weary preacher could surreptitiously sit between exhortations.

Dalmeny House is a good mile northeast of the village, on the Forth (open 1 May–29 Sept every afternoon except Fri and Sat: adm). This splendid example of Romantic-Gothic was built in 1815 for the Earl of Rosebery, whose family has lived here for more than 300 years. Although it isn't old in terms of history, it is a splendid mansion with a Gothic hammerbeamed hall, vaulted corridors and classical main rooms. There are 18th-century French furniture, tapestries and porcelain and a unique collection of Napoleonic memorabilia. Some of the paintings are very fine, especially the portraits. Queen Victoria stayed here with Prince Albert in 1842 and commented on the beauty of the setting—you can see why—and the 'excellent modern comforts' of the house, which might have had something to do with the plumbing. From the grounds you can walk along the shore to Cramond or South Queensferry.

South Queensferry

South Queensferry is 9 miles (14.5km) west of Edinburgh, where the Firth of Forth narrows to little more than a mile (1.5km). In the 11th century, Queen Margaret of Scotland established a free ferry here, to carry pilgrims to visit the holy shrines at Dunfermline and St Andrews. She built two hospices for the weary pilgrims, one on each bank. The ferry service continued (though latterly not free) until the opening of the road bridge in 1964, linking North Queensferry and South Queensferry. The four-span rail bridge, built between 1883 and 1890, was a tremendous engineering feat. Over a mile (1.5km) long, with the railway 157 feet (48m) above the water, its painted surface would cover 135 acres.

Naval ships come as far up as the dockyard at Rosyth, and great oil tankers lie at anchor, waiting to take on oil from the artificial island just east of the rail bridge. This is the terminal of the pipeline from the North Sea oil fields.

Stretching away on either side are private estates with houses open to the public, farmland and woods with views across the water to the hills of Fife. The Bury Man Festival is an annual summer carnival, held in the second week of August, with parades and entertainment. The 16th-century **Hawes Inn** stands on the site of the southern hospice, facing the old ferry ramp. Its view across the river is blinkered by the two bridges—a very different aspect from the days of Sir Walter Scott, who was often here and mentioned it in *The Antiquary*. In Robert Louis Stevenson's *Kidnapped*, David Balfour met Captain Hoseason at the Hawes Inn, in a bedroom ' heated like an oven by a great fire of coal', the captain having been 'carbonadoed in the tropic seas'.

The Queensferry Museum (open Thurs and Fri afternoons, May–Sept), in Burgh Chambers, has local history exhibits, including the building of the rail bridge.

Maid of the Forth sails from Hawes Pier to **Inchcolm Island** (see Fife, p.287), throughout the summer; ℭ 031 331 1454. At **Port Edgar**, west of the road bridge, there is a yacht marina in the former naval station, *HMS Lochinvar*. They have a launching ramp, races and regattas, water skiing, and lessons in sailing and wind-surfing.

Hopetoun House

Hopetoun House (open daily, April–Oct: adm) is 2 miles (3km) west of Queensferry along the shore. It is one of Scotland's most magnificent mansions, built for and still lived in by the Hope family. Originally completed between 1699 and 1704 by the architect Sir William Bruce (who rebuilt Holyrood) for the first Earl of Hopetoun, it was rebuilt and enlarged by William Adam and his sons Robert and John between 1721 and 1754. To appreciate fully its classical beauty, go to the end of the avenue and look back at the house, a perfectly proportioned sweep of inspired architecture. Among its furnishings and treasures are paintings attributed to Van Dyck, Titian, Rubens and Rembrandt, some hung on walls lined with silk and damask. The gardens were modelled on those at Versailles and landscaped to give views across the Forth to the Lomond Hills. Now almost all reduced to lawns, the Versailles pattern can only be seen from aerial photographs. There are a deer park, rare St Kilda sheep and a nature trail, as well as walks along the river. The stable block has an exhibition called 'Horse and Man in Lowland Scotland'. When exhausted, go to the licensed restaurant in the tapestry room and indulge in smoked salmon, Aberdeen Angus beef, or the 'Hopetoun Delight' dessert—all home cooking. The Antique Dealers' Fair is held at Hopetoun in September, a chance to pick up a bargain. For special arrangements for disabled people, ℭ 031 331 2451.

House of the Binns

The House of the Binns, a couple of miles (3km) west along the river from Hopetoun, is temporarily closed for restoration. When it re-opens, don't miss it. The curious name stems from *ben*, the Scottish word for 'hill'. The house, dating from 1630 with

19th-century Gothic embellishments, stands above parkland with views across the Forth. The moulded ceilings are very fine, and the rooms are beautifully furnished.

The most intriguing aspect of a visit to the Binns is the memorabilia of the notorious Tam Dalyell (pronounced Dee-el) who raised the Royal Scots Greys here in 1681 and whose father built the house. Stories about General Tam, whose mortal remains were popularly believed to have been removed from the family vault at Abercorn, nearby, and carried to a far warmer resting place by the Devil himself, are as spine-chilling as they are apocryphal. Known to his troops as the 'Bluidy Muscovite', he was alleged to hold flagellation parties, to munch wine glasses and to have conversations with the Devil—stories richly embroidered by his Covenanting enemies. In the house is a heavy carved table that was recovered from a muddy pond where it had lain for 200 years, having, it is said, been hurled there by the Devil, a bad loser in a game of cards with Tam. Among the relics of this legendary man are his sword, his Bible and the comb with which he groomed his beard, having sworn after the execution of Charles I never to cut a hair of his head until the restoration of the monarchy. His descendant, also Tam Dalyell, is a Labour MP.

Blackness Castle

Blackness Castle (open daily, except Thur and Fri afternoons, Oct–Mar: adm) is a mile or so north of the House of the Binns. The castle juts into the Firth of Forth, its northern walls pointed like the prow of a massive battleship, lapped on three sides by the river. Its original date is unknown. The present tower was built in the 15th century when it was one of Scotland's most important fortresses. Besieged by Cromwell, it has in its time been a royal castle, a prison for Covenanters, a powder magazine and a youth hostel. When Scotland and England were joined by the Acts of Union in 1707, Blackness was one of the four fortresses to be maintained at full military strength. If you look out across the water through the gun-slits in the curtain wall, you can almost hear the roar of cannon fire and smell the acrid tang of spent gunpowder.

The riverside village of **Blackness**, just along from the castle, was a medieval seaport, with wharves and warehouses, teeming with all the noise and smell and colour of a busy port which supplied the Royal Burgh of Linlithgow.

Bo'ness

Bo'ness or Borrowstownness, a couple of miles (3km) further west, is of historic rather than scenic interest. The **Antonine Wall** started a mile to the east, at Bridgeness. This was built by the Romans in AD 142 between the Forth and the Clyde in an abortive attempt to protect the south from the barbarians in the north (see 'History'). Bo'ness is also the home of the **Scottish Railway Preservation Society**, where steam enthusiasts can visit the Bo'ness and Kinneil Railway and take steam train rides at weekends and on certain weekdays in the summer.

Kinneil Museum

Kinneil Museum (open April–Sept, Mon–Sat: free) next to Kinneil House, a mile (1.5km) west of Bo'ness, is in converted 17th-century stables. They have Bo'ness pottery and cast-iron work, an exhibition of the estate's history going back 2000 years and an excavated fortlet from the Antonine Wall. Don't miss the bothy (hut) at the back where James Watt built his first steam engine while trying to solve the problem of flooding in a nearby mine in 1765.

Where to Stay

moderate

For history and character, go to **Hawes Inn**, South Queensferry, © 031 331 1990. A traditional inn, it serves pub food as well as *haute cuisine* and if you can get one of the few bedrooms, you lie awake listening to the hushed voices of Queen Margaret's pilgrims, and the tramp of sailors' feet. You may even catch an echo of David Balfour's voice yelling for his uncle Ebenezer from the rails of the brig *Covenant*, as it carries him off to sea. At Bo'ness, **Richmond Park Hotel** has good views over the firth to the Fife hills. It is comfortable if somewhat lacking in character.

The Hinterland: Linlithgow to Haddington

There is plenty of interest, both historical and aesthetic, on the way back eastwards, skirting the southern outskirts of Edinburgh. Don't be put off by built-up areas, they often conceal things worth seeing.

Linlithgow and Environs

Linlithgow, 3 miles (4.5km) south of Bo'ness, lies in an oasis of rural tranquillity, surrounded by rounded hills and remote farming communities untouched by the ugly sprawl of industrial and mining development just out of sight beyond the horizon. There was a Pictish settlement here before the Romans came and the first royal palace was recorded in the 12th century. Edward I had his headquarters in the town in 1301 and David II built a royal manor, destroyed by fire along with the town in 1424. The following year work began on the present palace. Since then the town has seen much of Scotland's history. In June, they celebrate the Riding of the Marches, with a parade, bands, decorated floats, flutes and drums, and plenty of fun.

Linlithgow Palace

The palace (open daily: adm) is one of the country's most poignant ruins. Only pigeons now inhabit the shell that stands on a slope of grass overlooking its own loch. Pinkish-ochre walls rise to five storeys, supported by flying buttresses: a roofless square with many of its rooms so well preserved that only a little imagination is needed to see how they must have been. Through its gateway in 1513, James IV rode out, against the advice of his lords, to lead his gallant army to tragic defeat at Flodden. The elaborate fountain in the quadrangle is said to have run with wine when James V gave it to Mary of Guise as a wedding present in 1538. Four years later, their daughter was born in one of the upper chambers, ill-fated Mary who was proclaimed Queen of Scots within a week of her birth. Over-enthusiastic fuelling of domestic fires, possibly with bedding straw, by General Hawley's troops who were garrisoned there on the night of 31 January 1746, reduced the palace to a smouldering shell. The swans on the loch add a royal touch: it is said they flew away when the Roundheads arrived and returned the day Charles II was crowned at Scone in 1649. Perhaps the best view of the palace is at night, as you drive past on the M9, from where it looks almost ethereal, floodlit against the dark sky.

St Michael's Church is so close to the palace that from a distance it seems to be part of it. As well as providing a place of worship for many of Scotland's monarchs, this large pre-Reformation church has had to endure much harsh treatment since its consecration in 1242. It was rebuilt after the fire of 1424; John Knox's followers despoiled it; Cromwell's soldiers stabled their horses in the aisle and left shot-holes in the walls. While praying for guidance and victory before Flodden, James IV saw a ghost which stood by the altar and warned him of his coming defeat. The original stone crown on the tower collapsed in 1820 and was replaced by the present astonishing laminated wood-and-aluminium 'crown of thorns' in 1964—an unfortunate flight of fancy.

Cockleroy Hill

Cockleroy Hill is on the right, along a country lane due south of Linlithgow, signposted to Beecraigs Country Park. It is an easy 15-minute stroll through dense pines and up a gentle slope of turf and vivid

green moss. Some say the name is derived from 'cuckold le roi', and hint at an indiscretion by Mary of Guise, getting her own back for the philanderings of her husband, James V. Others, more prosaic, say the name stems from the Gaelic *cochull ruadh*, meaning red hood. The keenness of your eyes is the only limit to the horizon from here. A view indicator points out 36 landmarks, including Goat Fell, 66 miles away on Arran. You can see the ramparts of a Pictish hill fort beyond the indicator: their look-outs would have been able to give good warning of attack.

Torphichen Preceptory

Torphichen Preceptory (open daily in summer, closed in winter: free), 2 miles (3km) further south, was founded as the community of the Scottish Order of the Knights of

St John of Jerusalem, in 1153. The 15th-century tower and vaulted transepts are all that remain, together with the nave, which was rebuilt in the 17th century, and is now the parish kirk. It stands on the outskirts of the village, among lawns backed by bracken-covered hills and is a good example of fortified church architecture. A folding green-baize table, in one of the box pews in the kirk, hinted at a less than spiritual attitude among past parishioners. One of the tombstones in the rather spooky churchyard is thought to be pre-Christian, and there are several with ancient primitive carvings.

Cairnpapple

Cairnpapple is less than a mile (1.5km) south again, in the Bathgate Hills. A bleak summit aptly known as 'windy ways', it has panoramic views, coast to coast, from the Bass Rock to Goat Fell. Follow the Historic Scotland signs to a parking bay from where a short climb over turf leads to a lofty site that was used for ritual and burial, from possibly 2500 BC until the 1st century. An underground **cist**, or tomb (open daily, except Mon mornings and Fri, Oct–March: adm), has been reconstructed. It is an eerie feeling, on that windswept plateau, trying to picture those ancient ceremonies and those 4500-year-old tragedies and tears. (When the cist is shut you can get the key from the curator of the preceptory in Torphichen.)

Beecraigs Country Park

Beecraigs Country Park (open all year: free) is also in the Bathgate Hills, between Linlithgow and Bathgate, covering 657 acres. There are: woodland walks, a deer farm, a trout farm, water sports on the lake, fly fishing, archery, a keep-trim course, orienteering, rock climbing and exhibitions in the park centre. For further information, © 0506 844516.

Where to Stay

expensive

Houston House at Uphall just off the A89, © 0506 853831, is a 16th-century fortified tower where Mary, Queen of Scots' advocate once lived. It has a pleasant garden, and excellent food with a good wine list is served in a panelled dining room.

inexpensive

Belsyde Farm, Linlithgow, © 0506 842098, is a late 18th-century house on a sheep and cattle farm beside the Union Canal with views over the Forth to the Ochils. It has the Duke of Hamilton's crest on one of the walls to give grandeur (he didn't live here; he just owned it). A family could do a lot worse than one of the **Craigs Holiday Lodges** at Williamcraigs, Linlithgow, © 0506 845025. These are fully equipped A-frame chalets, on a wooded hillside with panoramic views over the Forth Valley. You get linen and a colour television.

Champany's, Champany Corner, ✆ 050683 4532, is just off the M9, and surely the best steak house in Britain. Don't expect instant service here: lobsters glare out from a bubbling tank; cuts of raw meat, hung to full maturity, are laid out for inspection; whole salmon, fresh from the river, gleam on a slab; mouthwatering vegetables tempt from a huge wicker basket. Soaked in a house marinade, the steaks are seared on charcoal: the combination of method, marinade and maturity make them food fit for the gods. No one could begrudge a penny of the cost.

The Pentland Hills, Moorfoots and Esk Valley

The Pentland Hills run southwest from Edinburgh, sprawling across a width of 4 to 5 miles (6.5–8km); the high moorland is carpeted with heather, bracken and deer-hair grass and laced with reservoirs and streams. There are dozens of good walks, some along the old cattle-drove routes south. The highest peak is Scald Law, 1898 feet (584m). The Moorfoots run more or less parallel to the east, equally lovely with attractive villages at their feet. The North Esk rises in the Pentlands, the South Esk in the Moorfoots: they tumble out of their separate hills and rush into a turbulent marriage beyond Dalkeith and enter the sea as one.

Malleny House Garden

Malleny House Garden (open daily: adm), in Balerno, about seven miles (11km) south-west of Edinburgh off the A70, is lapped by the Water of Leith. Although the 17th-century house is not open to the public, it is a perfect focal point for the formal garden, with its rare shrub roses, clipped yews, rhododendrons and many shrubs and plants. The saddle-backed dovecote behind the house has not been inhabited since 1961 when its residents perished from a surfeit of treated grain.

Hillend Dry Ski Slope

Hillend Dry Ski Slope (open all year), on the northern slope of the Pentlands, is the largest of its kind in Europe. You can hire equipment and instruction.

Castlelaw

Castlelaw Iron Age Fort (open at all times) is signed off the west side of the A702 and easily reached by a short climb through gorse scrub from the road. There is a souterrain, or earth-house, with a stone passage and chamber, surrounded by three ramparts, occupied in the second century by Romans. Visit Castlelaw at dawn and walk to the top of Woodhouselee Hill, beyond. The sun, rising over the Moorfoot Hills, bathes the land in a pinkish light, with mist still clinging to the valley, well worth the early rise.

Flotterstone Inn is just south of Castlelaw on the A702. Here you can sit in the garden in summer beside the Glencorse Burn. (At the inn there is a good selection of dishes on the menu at reasonable prices.)

From here you can walk up beside the burn for about a mile (1.5km) to the **Glencorse Reservoir**, a pine-fringed stretch of water reflecting the surrounding hills. Like most of the reservoirs in the Pentlands, it is stocked with brown and rainbow trout, and day permits are available for both bank and boat fishing. The exposed mud shore and receding water-line too often indicate a shortage of rainfall. The water covers the remains of the Chapel of St Katherine in the Hopes, drowned when the valley was flooded to make the reservoir. In the 13th century Sir William St Clair of Roslin had a bet with Robert the Bruce. He wagered his head against this Glencorse valley, that his hounds would kill a certain deer that had eluded all huntsmen before it reached the Glencorse Burn. The deer was brought down at the burn, St Clair won his land and built the chapel on the site in thanksgiving. (He was later killed, with James Douglas, on the way to the Holy Land with Bruce's heart in 1330—see Dunfermline, p.285).

Penicuik

The Edinburgh Crystal Glass Factory, in Penicuik (pronounced Pennycook), run conducted tours showing the process of glassmaking: blowing, cutting, engraving, etc. There is a small charge for tours and no children under eight are allowed. The tours run Mon–Fri; the shop and restaurant are open daily.

The Penicuik to Bonnyrigg Walkway

The railway that used to link Penicuik with Bonnyrigg has been transformed into a 5-mile (8km) walk, following the course of the River North Esk, through **Roslin Glen**. Part of the wooded valley of the North Esk is preserved as a countryside park. You pass the remains of what was once Scotland's biggest **gunpowder mill**, supplying munitions for the Napoleonic Wars as well as for the First and Second World Wars.

Glencorse Kirk

Built in 1665, a mile (1.5km) northeast of Penicuik, Glencorse Kirk is roofless except for the tower, which was a 19th-century addition. In his youth, Robert Louis Stevenson was a fairly regular attender, having walked over the Pentlands from Swanston. In a letter from the South Seas, he wrote to the local minister and novelist, S. R. Crockett, one of the Kailyard School of writers: 'Go there and say a prayer for me. See that it is a sunny day; I would like it to be a Sunday. Stand on the right bank just where the road goes down in to the water, and shut your eyes; and if I don't appear to you . . .'

Roslin

Roslin, or Rosslyn, is 3 miles (4.5km) east of Castlelaw, in the lee of the Pentlands. A fairy-tale castle rises from trees near an historic chapel. To see it from the outside, park by the chapel and walk round the graveyard and over a narrow footbridge (once a drawbridge) that dizzyingly spans the North Esk, far below. The castle stands high over Roslin Glen, with dripping dungeons, an ancient yew tree and legends of buried treasure. Dating from 1304, when the Lantern Tower was built, it was the home of the St Clair family who came to England with William the Conqueror and were lured north by offers of land from

Malcolm Canmore. Sir William St Clair, third Earl of Orkney, lived here in sumptuous state in the 15th century, ate off gold plate, waited on by dozens of lords and ladies, and minted his own coins. When his wife, Elizabeth, went visiting, her mounted escort numbered two hundred. The castle was burnt and bombarded many times. In 1447, one of the women of the household scrambled under a bed to help a whelping bitch. Her candle set the bedding on fire and the old part of the castle was gutted. The castle suffered badly in the 16th century, when Hertford was obeying his king's order to 'put all to fire and sword' in Scotland. Part of the castle has been restored and can be rented, for eight people. Contact The Landmark Trust, Shottesbrooke, Maidenhead, Berkshire, © 0628 825925.

Rosslyn Chapel (open daily, 1 April–31 Oct: adm) was the creation of the flamboyant Sir William St Clair, in the 15th century. Worried, perhaps, that he might have used his great wealth too self-indulgently, he decided towards the end of his life that he'd better atone for some of his extravagances before going on to meet his Maker. He therefore started building a church. The St Clairs are hereditary Grand Master Masons, and the church was to be the world's High Temple of Masonry. Dedicated to St Matthew and founded in 1446, it was designed to be an enormous cruciform collegiate church but was never finished. When William died in 1484, enthusiasm for the project dwindled and all that was completed was the present chapel, a chancel and part of the transept, with a vault below. A number of St Clairs are buried in the vault, some, it is said, still in armour. The interior is so richly carved that you get visual indigestion. Nearly every inch has been decorated with men and animals, birds and foliage, flowers and insects: there are the Seven Cardinal Virtues, the Seven Deadly Sins, the Dance of Death and a lot more besides, all created by the finest craftsmen of the day.

Your eye will be drawn inevitably to the famous **Apprentice Pillar** on the south side of the Lady Chapel. The pillar's carving is so delicate that it makes the rest seem almost crude. It was named by Sir Walter Scott, after a fictional account of the apprentice who carved it being killed by his master who was jealous of the quality of the apprentice's work.

Roslin Inn, now the curator's house, beside the chapel, dates from 1662 and has had many illustrious visitors including Boswell, Johnson, Burns, Scott, the Wordsworths and Edward VII, who engraved a memorial to his visit on a window in 1859 when he was Prince of Wales. Next door there is a gift shop and café, and it is here that you get tickets for the chapel. Not far to the west, in the Pentlands, the Battle of Rullion Green took place in 1666, when troops under General Tam Dalyell, Commander of the King's Army in Scotland, defeated an uprising of Covenanters. Dalyell permitted appalling reprisals and his name became synonomous with terror. He also appropriated several of the forfeited estates.

Howgate

The Howgate Inn, not open to the public, a couple of miles (3km) south of Roslin, was another inn with literary associations: Walter Scott, Allan Ramsay, Dr John Brown, Henry Mackenzie and Robert Louis Stevenson were among its better known customers. Dr John

Brown wrote his memorable story *Rab and His Friends* about the dog who goes to Edinburgh every day with the Howgate carriers. (The carrier and his wife are buried in the churchyard of St Mungo's in Penicuik.)

Temple

Temple is a hamlet about four miles (6km) east of Howgate as the crow flies—an attractive 6-mile (10km) drive. In a tranquil churchyard, on a hillside beside a cascading burn, is the roofless ruin of a 14th-century church. It stands on the site of one built by the Knights Templar, the soldier-monks of the Crusades who had headquarters here until the Pope decided they were becoming too powerful and suppressed them in 1312.

Dalkeith

Dalkeith, 6 miles (10km) north of Temple and 6 miles (10km) southeast of Edinburgh on the A68, has a wide, cobbled main street, embraced by the North Esk and South Esk before they unite further north for their final sprint to the sea. In spite of being the junction of several main roads, it has a stately feeling about it, enhanced perhaps by its palace and the historic castles that surround it.

In **Dalkeith Park** (open daily, Easter–end Oct: adm) you can roam along the river among the trees. There is a 'tunnel walk', a woodland adventure play area, an 18th-century bridge and a ruined orangery. Although the palace is not open to the public it makes a splendid background to the park. Seat of the Scotts of Buccleuch since the 12th century, it is a large, reddish, neoclassical mansion. Designed in the 18th century by Sir John Vanburgh around an older castle, it has a recessed centre and two projecting wings, modelled on the Dutch Loo Palace. Here, in 1572, when the palace was known as the Lion's Den, the notorious James Douglas, Earl of Morton, lay on his sick-bed and held the council which plotted to bring Mary, Queen of Scots, to trial. George IV stayed here in 1822, during his state visit to Scotland, as did Queen Victoria, in 1842, when she remarked in her diary that she had 'tasted oatmeal porridge, which I think very good'.

The Collegiate Church of St Nicholas, dating from the 12th century and much restored, is on the north side of Dalkeith High Street. In the roofless ruin of the 14th-century choir and apse, a double tomb is believed to contain the remains of the first Earl Morton and his wife, Johan, daughter of James I. It was here, in 1445, that Aeneas Silvius, a papal diplomat, later Pope Pius II, was astonished to see 'black stones' being given to the poor as alms. Much travelled as he was, the Italian had never seen coal before.

Dalkeith Arts Centre (open daily, except Tues and Sun: free) has art exhibitions and musical recitals. **The Edinburgh Butterfly and Insect World** (open March–Oct daily: adm) is on the A7 2 miles (3km) north of Dalkeith. In exotic rainforest, landscaped with tropical plants, waterfalls and lily ponds, butterflies from all over the world fly freely around. There are displays of insects, a tearoom, garden centre, tropical fish shop, playground and picnic area.

Newbattle Abbey (conducted tours on written application to the Warden) lies a mile (1.5km) southeast of Dalkeith and can be clearly seen from the gate. It was founded for the Cistercians in the 12th century: after the Reformation it became the family seat of the Kerrs, later Marquesses of Lothian, who gave it to the nation as an adult education centre. In its heyday it was frequently visited by royalty: a murdered mistress of David II was buried here; James IV met his 14-year-old bride, Margaret Tudor, here; James V stayed here and George IV came, on his Scottish bonanza. The monks of Newbattle were among the first to work the local coal-mines.

Lady Victoria Colliery, Newtongrange

Just south of Dalkeith, Lady Victoria Colliery was built by the Lothian Coal Company in 1890 and pioneered many techniques in the mechanization of coal cutting and haulage. Converted into a **Mining Museum** (open daily Easter–Sept, 11am–4pm: adm), its award-winning displays bring to life what it must have been like for the people who worked and lived here. The interiors of the pit village are interesting and evocative. Look out for the miner, pale and exhausted, slumped in front of the fire in his kitchen after his shift in the mine, a blanket round his shoulders, his long-johns drying on a rail. There is a licensed Victorian tea-room.

Vogrie Country Park

A couple of miles (3km) east of Newtongrange, on Tyne Water, the Vogrie Country Park (open daily: free) has wooded glens and gardens round a great mansion and a nine-hole golf course. Vogrie House, built in 1876, contains an interpretative centre showing the park's history. In the grounds are a variety of gardens, including the Garden of Peace and Friendship where foreign visitors can plant trees as a token of friendship. Lime in the soil encourages wild thyme and quaking grass. The Rhododendron Walk, leading to the house, is glorious in the spring when the rhododendrons and azaleas are in bloom on a sea of daffodils. There is a pond, waterfall and rockery at the end, in front of the house. There is a Tree Trail, as well as nature trails with roe deer and even badgers. Over 70 species of birds have been recorded: look for dippers, bobbing up and down on the stones on the river bank.

Arniston House, Gorebridge

Arniston is a mansion built in 1726 by William Adam, for Robert Dundas, later Lord President of the Court of Session. (Open Tues, and the 1st Sun of the month, June–Sept, 2pm–5pm, or by apt: adm.) Walter Scott was a frequent guest and recorded in his diary in 1828: 'I am always happy in finding myself in the old Oak Room at Arniston where I have drank many a merry bottle . . .' Home-baked teas now replace the merry bottles and there is clay pigeon shooting.

Borthwick Castle

Borthwick Castle is 5 miles (8km) south of Dalkeith in a hamlet in the Moorfoot Hills, just off the A7. More than 500 years old, and the largest complete twin-towered keep in

Scotland (sadly somewhat over-restored), it is now a private hotel where guests dine in a stone-vaulted great hall with minstrels' gallery and hooded fireplace, and can sleep in the bedchambers once occupied by Mary, Queen of Scots and Bothwell. The ill-fated couple came here a month after their marriage. Insurgents surrounded them, and Bothwell escaped through the postern gate, followed later by Mary, disguised as a man. It is said that prisoners were invited to jump the 13-foot (4m) gap between the two towers at a height of 80 feet (24m). If they succeeded, they were allowed to go free. There is an information centre beside the lodge at the gate.

A right of way links Borthwick to Crichton Castle, an easy hour's walk.

Crichton Castle

Crichton Castle (open daily except weekends, Oct–March: adm) stands within sight and signalling distance of Borthwick, 2 miles (3km) to the northeast on a grassy plateau, high and isolated above a steep valley. Now a ruin, this was Bothwell's seat and it is said he kept his divorced wife here after his marriage to Mary. This, however, does not tie in with the belief that Mary came here for refuge after she escaped from Borthwick, on her way to meet up with Bothwell and run to Dunbar. The castle dates from the 14th century, and in the courtyard you can see a delightful memento of Bothwell's nephew, Francis Stewart, Earl of Bothwell, the half-mad demonist. He travelled widely in Italy in the 16th century and brought back the idea for this Italianate piazza. Its walls are of a classical diamond design over pillars, making a remarkable contrast to the sturdy structure of the rest of the castle. Mary came here as a guest of Bothwell, when she was newly arrived in Scotland, to dance at the wedding of his sister to her half-brother. The chapel-like ruin beyond is a fortified stable.

Crichton Collegiate Church, half a mile north, has been in continuous use since it was built in 1449 and has marvellous barrel vaulting.

Soutra Aisle

From Crichton, go east on the back road for a mile and a half (2.5km) to the A68 and then 3 miles (4.5km) or so southwest to Soutra. The B6368 climbs into the hills from here, taking you to Soutra Aisle, a small stone building with a mossy roof, so simple you might pass it off as a byre. In 1164, Malcolm IV founded a large hospice here, ideally sited far from the slums and sewers of the towns. Recent discoveries show that the medicine they practised was remarkably advanced, especially in the use of herbal remedies, which they even used as a form of anaesthetic. The hospice functioned for about 600 years. It incorporated the parish church in the 16th century and a service is held there once a year.

Haddington

Haddington is 12 miles (19km) northeast of Dalkeith, peacefully spread along the banks of the River Tyne. This compact town was extensively restored by an enterprising town council a few years ago, with a lot of help from local inhabitants: the results are outstanding. The wedge-shaped market square is divided at one end by the fine

William Adam **townhouse** whose church-like steeple was added by Gillespie Graham in 1831, and has a clock that still strikes the curfew at 10pm and 7am. Bright colour-washed houses front the main streets, with quaint wynds and courtyards leading off, affording vistas through into another, older way of life. Flood water from the river has been known to reach the steps of the mercat cross.

Over 130 buildings in Haddington are listed as of special architectural or historic interest, and an illustrated booklet, *A Walk Round Haddington*, is sold locally. There is also an architectural trail map, on the wall of the townhouse.

The medieval **Church of St Mary** is one of Haddington's greatest treasures. Built by the river in the 14th century on the site of at least two previous churches, the chancel and transepts were roofless for 400 years after the Reformation until it was restored to its full glory in 1973. Concerts are often performed here, honoured by such musicians as Yehudi Menuhin and Louis Kentner. The size of the church gives an idea of the early prosperity of this area. John Knox, who was born nearby in 1505, worshipped in St Mary's. A plain slab on the floor has a moving inscription on it by Thomas Carlyle, to his wife Jane Welsh, daughter of a Haddington doctor. She is buried in the churchyard, having left instructions that she did not wish to be buried with her husband with whom she shared a tempestuous though loving relationship.

Haddington House, 1680, in Sidegate, is the headquarters and library of the Lamp of Lothian Trust, responsible for much of the restoration of the church and the cultural life of the town. Its restored 17th-century garden (with roses, herbs and a paved sunken garden) is reached from Pleached Alley.

The Poldrate Corn Mill is a three-storey 18th-century mill beside the Tyne at Victoria Bridge. Its undershot water-wheel and cottages were also restored by the Lamp of Lothian Trust and it is now a community and arts centre. East of the river is the Nungate: malefactors were hanged from the hump-backed bridge, a gruesome thought as you look at the attractive river scene. The bridge led to the now vanished Abbey of Haddington, once known as the *Lucerna Laudoniae*, the 'Lamp of Lothian', for its reputation as a lamp of spirituality and learning, until the Reformation.

Traprain Law

Traprain Law dominates the plain east of Haddington, a massive whale-backed hump, part of a volcanic seam that includes North Berwick Law and the Bass Rock. Traprain, 734 feet (226m) high, was the capital of the North British Votadini tribe, overlooking the 'Scottish Sea' whence invasion frequently threatened. The people lived on the fertile lands below, in times of danger retiring to the summit, where you can still see the remains of a fort. Traces of their occupation on the lower slopes include standing stones and souterrains. In 1919 a hoard of 4th-century Christian and pagan treasure, possibly buried by pirates, was excavated from the top of Traprain. It is now in the Museum of Antiquities, in Edinburgh. The collection includes 160 silver-gilt bowls, goblets and clasps. Conservationists have managed to arrest stone-quarrying operations at the east end of the law and it is hoped the ugly gouged-out wedge will eventually be restored.

Hailes Castle, an open monument, is below Traprain on the northern side. The extensive ruin dates from the 13th century and was once a feudal stronghold. Built by the Hepburns, later Earls of Bothwell, and demolished by Cromwell, it was strategically sited on what was then the main north–south highway and charged extortionate tolls from passing travellers. The ruin stands beside a fast-flowing burn on a grassy bank carpeted with snowdrops and daffodils in spring. You can still see the water gate, bakehouse and vaulted pit prison into which prisoners were lowered and left to perish. The 29-year-old lover of the wife of one of the lairds was incarcerated here and his spirit is said to linger on, begging for a Christian burial.

Lennoxlove House

Lennoxlove House (open Wed, Sat and Sun afternoons, 1 May–30 Sept, or by arrangement, ✆ 062082 3720: adm) is a mile (1.5km) south of Haddington on the B6369. Home of the Duke of Hamilton, it stands in woodland, overlooking the Lammermuirs. The 15th-century keep has parapet gargoyles, bartizans and a watchtower penthouse. In the keep and 17th- and 18th-century house are paintings by Raeburn, Van Dyck, Janssens, Lely, Augustus John and de Lazlo, as well as porcelain and furniture. Look for the death mask of Mary, Queen of Scots, and her silver casket in which were found the letters (possibly forged) incriminating her in the murder of Darnley. The house got its name from the 17th-century Duchess of Lennox, Frances Teresa Stuart, a favourite of Charles II and possibly the model for the original Britannia on the pre-decimal coinage.

Preston Mill

Preston Mill (open daily, 1 April–31 Oct and weekends in Nov: adm) lies about 5 miles (8km) northeast of Haddington on the outskirts of East Linton. This delightful mill, restored by the National Trust for Scotland, stands in a picture-postcard setting, on a green beside the Tyne, where muscovy ducks and mallards bask in the shade of apple trees. It is probably the only mill of its kind in working order. Built of warm red sandstone and pantiles, it has a polygonal kiln with a ventilator, a working water-wheel and wooden machinery. Next door there is a small museum in an outbuilding.

Athelstaneford

Athelstaneford is a hamlet on a whinstone ridge a few miles north of Haddington. Immediately noticeable is the St Andrew's Cross flying from a flagpole high above a brass mural in the kirkyard. The mural is engraved with a scene from a Dark Ages battle between an invading Northumbrian army and the combined forces of the Picts and Scots. Legend states that the temporarily allied kings, normally at loggerheads, prayed for victory and were answered by seeing a saltire—the diagonal cross of St Andrew (diagonal at St Andrew's request because he did not wish to emulate Christ)—etched in cloud against a blue sky. When they then won their battle, the two kings agreed to make the saltire the national flag of their united kingdoms, with St Andrew as their patron saint; a resolution that was to be broken many times before it became reality. The head of the defeated Athelstane was stuck on a spike on Inch Garvie, an island near the Forth Bridge.

Stenton

Stenton, 6 miles (10km) east of Haddington, just off the A1, is a well-preserved village with a reputation for being one of the last places to have burnt witches, a practice for which it was notorious. A tron (tall timber weighing scales, used for measuring wool at the wool fairs) stands on one of the two tiny greens. Red sandstone cottages with pantiled roofs surround the greens, one with its original outside stairway. The old joiner's house lies below, with a picturesque courtyard, and beside it stands a farm with a wheelhouse. Near the school is the Smiddy and the Oak Inn, incorporating a picture gallery with frequently changing exhibitions by contemporary artists. Here, you can sit and enjoy an excellent light lunch (home-made soups, vol-au-vents, pâtés, fish creams and cheese washed down with wine) surrounded by the paintings.

The 16th-century **Rood Well** was once a popular place for pilgrims. It's easy to miss, on the right as you enter the village from the A1, in a hollow carpeted with St John's Wort. Nearby, the ruins of the old kirk, with crow-stepped tower and dovecote, lie in the shadow of the tall pinnacles of the present church.

Pressmennan Glen

Pressmennan Glen, a long, wooded hanging valley, is a mile (1.5km) south of Stenton, reached by forking left at Stenton school. Bennet's Burn was dammed in 1819 to form this artificial loch, a deep, dark snake of water, haunt of wildfowl and trout. There is a forest trail that takes about two hours.

Where to Stay

expensive

If you want to spoil yourself, you will be torn between two castles with an almost equal claim on your delight and your pocket. One is **Borthwick Castle**, Gorebridge, © 0875 20514, see above. Every stone drips with history, and you can lie in bed listening to the wind moaning, and picture Mary and Bothwell, so recently married, enjoying one of their few moments of happiness together.

Slightly cheaper, **Dalhousie Castle Hotel** at Bonnyrigg, © 0875 20153, is a massive keep, 800 years old, not quite so romantic but every bit as impressive with turrets and battlements and a great round tower. You eat in the dungeons and the food is sublime—don't think about the ghastly tortures that went on down here. In the wine cellar, marks on the walls were made by prisoners who were hung upside down to die. There are ghosts, of course, including a walled-up Grey Lady, but the canny manageress won't say where in case honeymooners are frightened away. Four-poster beds in some of the rooms, a spring well (under the bridal suite), and a crypt are some of the features of this excellent establishment. Clay pigeon shooting, croquet, riding and archery are all available.

Johnstounburn House in Humbie, ✆ 087533 696, is a very high class, elegant 17th-century country house at the foot of the Lammermuirs surrounded by 40 acres of park and gardens. It's comfortable and the food is excellent. Nice, but on the main A68, **The Stair Arms Hotel** at Pathhead, ✆ 0875 3202 77, is also comfortable and has reasonable food. **Brown's Hotel** in West Road on the outskirts of Haddington, ✆ 062082 2254, is comfortable. It's an elegant 19th-century townhouse with a nice garden and a good reputation for food.

inexpensive

You could do a lot worse than the **Laird and Dog Hotel** at Lasswade, ✆ 031 663 9219. A small family hotel, it has a cosy atmosphere and is comfortable.

Eating Out

If you don't fancy any of the above, for something a bit different, try **Bridge Inn**, Ratho, ✆ 031 333 1320, on the canal, with a canal-boat restaurant, cruises and dancing.

The Lammermuirs

South and east of Haddington, deep valleys cut into the rounded summits of the high moorland of the Lammermuir Hills. In summer, sheep graze among wine-red heather, whins and cascading burns; skylarks sing and wild thyme scents the air. In winter the roads are often blocked with snow and tractors go out from remote farmsteads to feed the sheep.

Garvald

Garvald, 3 miles (4.5km) south of Traprain Law, is a small redstone village nestling in a fold of the hills beside the fast flowing Papana Water. Behind a grille on the church wall and below a sundial dated 1633, you can see a metal neck-collar (the 'jougs') the height of a small man, where they tethered petty criminals for punishment.

Nunraw lies in trees above the village to the southeast, a 15th-century tower house with later additions. This massive red pile, founded as a nunnery in the 12th century and abandoned during the Reformation, was bought by Irish Cistercians in 1946. It was their monastery while they built their new abbey. Now, the monks in white and black habits welcome all visitors who come here looking for God. The new abbey, **Sancta Maria**, is further up the hill on the right, a starkly simple, pale stone building, high on the hillside. In the long plain church, the many clear-glass windows look out over the moors. When the wind moans outside and the clouds race across the sky, it is perhaps easy to feel closer to the God people come here to seek.

Gifford

Gifford, 4½ miles (7km) south of Haddington, is a 17th-century village straggling round a wide main street. The entrance to Yester House (private), at the end of an avenue, is a graceful wrought-iron and gilded arch between redstone gatehouses with columned pillars topped by urns. On the estate there is the **Goblin Ha'**, a mighty underground hall with a high vaulted roof. According to tradition, this was built in the 13th century by Sir Hugo Gifford, who was known to be a wizard. Sir Walter Scott could not resist putting such a romantic place into 'Marmion' ('Of lofty roof and ample size, beneath the castle deep it lies').

In **Gifford Kirk** the 'laird's loft' was a withdrawing room, with a fireplace for the pampered laird and his family. There is an illustrated history of local buildings on a wall in the main street.

Whiteadder Reservoir lies in a bowl of the Lammermuirs just inside the Lothian border 8 miles (13km) to the southeast. There is a sheltered picnic site below the dam surrounded by clumps of trees and a choice of good walks up into the hills.

Oldhamstocks

Oldhamstocks, eight miles (13km) northeast of the reservoir, on a plateau above a valley, has its cottages clustered round a wide green with a pump and cross. The name comes from the Saxon for 'old settlement'. As in Gifford, there is an illustrated board in the middle of the village giving the history of local buildings.

The **Watch Tower**, 1824, in the kirkyard was used to watch over the graves in order to protect them from the lucrative practice of body-snatching. The 15th-century chancel of the kirk has a stone-slabbed roof. Don't miss the proclamation hanging in the porch, granting the village 'two frie fares yeirlie . . .' and '. . . a werklie mercat for buying and selling of horse nolt, sheip meil, malt and all sort of grane, cloath, linnings, etc'. What an easy life our ancestors had, before spelling was standardized!

Where to Stay and Eating Out

moderate

Tweeddale Arms Hotel in Gifford, ℗ 062081 240, is a Georgian listed building beside the Reformation church. It combines an 18th-century atmosphere with modern comforts and the food is good.

inexpensive

Also in Gifford, **Goblin Ha' Hotel**, ℗ 062 081 244, is an old-fashioned place known for its friendly staff. The cooking is country-style with bar suppers and special Sunday lunches, and they have a beer garden and boule court.

Apart from these two, you would be advised to try one of the hotels in the previous sections, none of which are far away and some of which are worth driving a long way to stay in.

Edinburgh

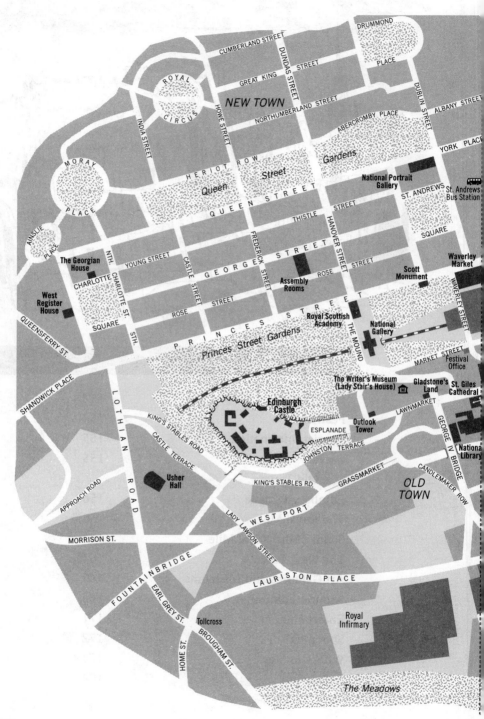

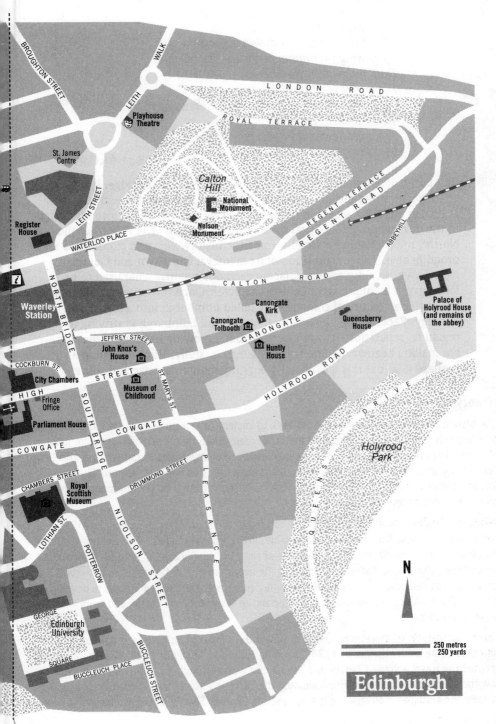

Edinburgh

Beautiful city of Edinburgh!
Where the tourist can drown his sorrow
By viewing your monuments and statues fine
During the lovely summer-time.
I'm sure it will his spirits cheer
As Sir Walter Scott's monument he draws near,
That stands in East Prince's Street
Amongst flowery gardens, fine and neat . . .

William McGonagall

Edinburgh is dominated by a castle built high on a craggy ridge. Its strategic, elevated position, guarding the route to the north, with the river at its feet and easy access to the south, made it an obvious choice for capital in the days when defence was paramount. Known as 'The Athens of the North', the capital has a violent, romantic history, versatile culture and a proud people. The juxtaposition of its medieval Old Town and Georgian New Town, so close together, facing each other across what used to be a loch, give it a unique architectural character. Once the cultural capital of the north, a century of complacency lulled Edinburgh into a dangerous lethargy. Recently, Glasgow stole that title and Edinburgh is striving to regain its reputation. It won't be easy, but a growing band of enthusiasts are making headway. Some say Edinburgh is 'stuffy, stuck-up, pompous'. Perhaps it is: but it is a lively city, bursting with enterprise and spirit.

History

The unwritten history of Edinburgh goes back to ancient British tribes who existed in clusters of wooden huts on the rocky slopes of the castle crag, choosing the windy heights for greater security. Excavations on the castle rock revealed Roman artefacts dating from the first centuries after Christ, when the Romans were busy trying to conquer Britain. They built a fort at Cramond, west of the town, and a naval harbour from which the Emperor Severus embarked on his northern campaigns.

When the Angles of Northumbria invaded Lothian in the Dark Ages, their King Edwin built a fortress on the rock, Dun Eadain, meaning literally 'Fortress-on-a-hill'. This became Edwin's Burgh and more excavation revealed traces of their occupation. Small communities settled around the castle walls, tradesmen supplying the needs of those in the garrison, but it was not until the 11th century, in the reign of Malcolm Canmore, that Edinburgh began to develop as a town. Queen Margaret persuaded her husband to move into the castle, and from then on building flourished.

Queen Margaret's youngest son, David I, moved the capital to Edinburgh from Dunfermline when he came to the throne in 1124, founding Holyrood Abbey in 1128. Robert the Bruce granted the town a Royal Charter in 1329. A city wall was built in 1436. The 16th century saw the building of a palace at Holyrood, and the hasty erection of the Flodden Wall, in 1513, to stem the anticipated advance of the conquering English. Shortly after this, the city suffered a dreadful battering from Henry VIII's 'Rough Wooing'. Mary, Queen of Scots spent most of her short reign based in Edinburgh, riding out from its walls on frequent excursions. When her son James VI inherited the English throne in 1603, he moved his court down to London, only returning once to his native land.

For a while, then, Edinburgh retreated into the shadows, with brief leaps into the daylight, such as when the National Covenant was signed at Greyfriars in 1638, and when Cromwell occupied the city in 1650. The Act of Union in 1707 pushed it still further into oblivion until Prince Charles Edward Stuart marched into the town in 1745 and captured Holyrood Palace and the hearts of the townspeople for five unreal weeks of feasting and triumph, before his march south.

From the death-throes of the Jacobite rebellion, peace finally emerged and with it came the Scottish Enlightenment, that glorious explosion of culture and science that was born in Edinburgh and spread its tentacles throughout the world (see 'History'). Walter Scott was largely responsible for the triumphal visit to Edinburgh of the Hanoverian King George IV, in 1822, who marched about resplendent in tartan and, some say, flesh-coloured tights. This was the first royal visit for more than 100 years, discounting that of Prince Charles.

In the middle of the 19th century, Queen Victoria and Prince Albert discovered what the Queen called 'my dear, beloved Scotland' and the country suddenly became socially acceptable to southerners.

Old Town and New Town

One of the best legacies of the Enlightenment is Edinburgh's New Town, built in the 18th century. Before this, Edinburgh consisted of a warren of ancient buildings in the shadow of the castle rock; tall tenements, stacked together for want of space, teemed with people, vermin and disease. At the northern foot of the rock lay Nor' Loch, a stinking pond of effluent. Both Dr Johnson and Sydney Smith commented on the filth and smell of Edinburgh's streets. In 1767, the city fathers held a competition for a design to improve the town. The winner was 23-year-old James Craig, with his plan for a spacious town, north of the castle. Building began at once, and continued well into the 19th century when the Nor' Loch was drained and turned into gardens. Edinburgh New Town is a masterpiece: elegant crescents, squares and gardens, lined with Georgian buildings, many recently cleaned to reveal their former pure stone. This stone cleaning has become highly controversial because experts now suspect that the process damages the stone. Only from the air is it possible to appreciate the symmetry of the New Town's formal design (described by some contemporary conservatives as 'windy parallelograms').

Edinburgh gained its affectionate sobriquet, 'Auld Reekie', in the days when *reek* (smoke), from the *lums* (chimneys) of the Old Town, lay over the city like a pall. The university, founded in 1582, attracts students from all over the world. Twice host to the Commonwealth Games, Edinburgh's sporting facilities are second to none. Murrayfield is a powerful magnet for rugby enthusiasts: the Murrayfield Roar can be heard from miles away on big match days. The stones of the city are honed by a pervasive east wind: they say you can always spot a native of Edinburgh—when he rounds a corner anywhere in the world, his hand will fly instinctively to clutch at his hat.

The Edinburgh Festival

The Edinburgh International Festival of Music and Drama, born in 1947, was conceived out of a desire to shake off the drabness of the post-war years. Its fathers were the Lord Provost, Sir John Falconer, Harry Harvey Wood of the British Council, and Rudolf Bing, the first artistic director. In that first year performers included: the Glyndebourne Opera Company, the Hallé Orchestra, the Vienna State Orchestra, the Old Vic Theatre Company, the Sadler's Wells Ballet Company, and many more.

The Festival takes a theme each year and many of the performances and exhibitions relate to this. For three weeks in August and September, the city goes a little mad. Accommodation is booked for months ahead and people dash about in a frenzy, trying to cram as much as possible into the time.

The Fringe started at the same time and has mushroomed to such an extent that it is now the world's largest arts festival, with more than 500 performances each day, by some 450 companies, sharing about 150 stages. Every spare inch is used: redundant kirks, halls, back rooms, basements, attics, schools, pavements. Students and drama companies come from all over to perform anything from monologues, poetry readings, street shows and acrobatics to full-scale drama and opera. Shows are staged all day and most of the night. It is impossible to see them all and escalating prices are making the punters more selective. Tom Stoppard, Rowan Atkinson and Billy Connolly are among the many stars who were first launched through the Fringe.

The Military Tattoo usually starts a week before the Festival and runs for three weeks. It takes place on the castle esplanade every night except Sunday, with some matinees, and is one of the most popular attractions. Lasting an hour and a half, against the backdrop of the floodlit castle, it is a pageant of military display, with massed bands, pipes and drums, dancers, precision drills and tableaux. Each year there is something different, as well as the set favourites, and you can never be sure whether the climax is going to be a Bulgarian belly-dancer or a parade of Indian elephants. The Tattoo always ends with a lone piper, floodlit on the battlements, his haunting music reaching out across the dark to echo in your heart for ever.

The Edinburgh International Film Festival coincides with the first two weeks of the main Festival with over 70 new feature films, documentaries, shorts, etc. There are discussions and conferences and it is attended by some of the world's leading film-makers.

The Edinburgh Book Festival is a biennial event (odd years) in August, a great literary bonanza spread through seven pavilions specially erected in Charlotte Square Gardens.

McEwan's Edinburgh International Jazz Festival presents top performers and bands from all over the world, with 80 hours of jazz daily throughout the city during the main Festival.

The Edinburgh International Folk Festival is a 10-day event in March with concerts, ceilidhs, cabarets and other events. During the festival there are lectures and tuition on piping, playing the harp, fiddle, guitar and other traditional instruments.

Edinburgh Tourist Information Centre, 3 Princes Street, ☎ 031 557 1700.

Tourist Desk, Edinburgh Airport, ☎ 031 333 2167.

Edinburgh International Festival Box Office, 21 Market Street, ☎ 031 226 4001.

Fringe Office and Society, 8 High Street, ☎ 031 226 5257.

Tattoo Office, Market Street, ☎ 031 225 1188.

Getting to Edinburgh

by air

A shuttle service operates between Edinburgh and London Heathrow. Booked two weeks in advance, a return fare costs from £107. Edinburgh Airport is 8 miles (13km) from the city centre, with frequent coach connections to Waverley Bridge and a fleet of taxis.

by train

Waverley Station, in the middle of the town, is linked by frequent inter-city trains to London Kings Cross in as little as four hours, as well as all other main towns and cities in Britain. British Rail offer a range of tickets which vary from month to month and are well worth asking about. The cheapest, Superapex, costs only £29 return.

by coach

A number of coach companies operate day and night between Edinburgh and London, taking about six hours, with an hour's stop on the way. This is the cheapest way to travel and not uncomfortable. A mid-week return costs about £24.

Getting around Edinburgh

Edinburgh is notorious for its abundance of traffic wardens and feet are unquestionably the best form of conveyance in the compact city centre. There are plenty of taxis and a good public bus service, with buses to all areas and maps displayed so you can plot your route. There are also conducted tours from Waverley Bridge, by the station, throughout the day from 9.30am—an excellent way to orientate yourself before a more detailed exploration. Several different companies run walking tours of the city; popular themes are spooks, witches and crime—better than you might expect.

City Sights

If your stay is limited, don't try to see the whole city: you won't manage to and you won't enjoy what you do see. If you only have one day, for instance, your best bet is to confine your sightseeing to the Royal Mile. Start at the castle, which takes a good two hours, and then wander down the Royal Mile towards Holyrood, lunching at one of the many places on the way and looking in at some of the dozens of tourist attractions you pass. Finish up at Holyrood Palace and Abbey. By now, you feet will be more than ready to go back to your hotel to freshen up before hitting the night-spots. If, however, you still have any energy left, climb Arthur's Seat (822 feet—253m) from the Holyrood car park, for a panorama of the city. (It doesn't take long and you can drive most of the way if you want to cheat.)

If you have two days, you should explore the New Town on the second day, including a couple of the art galleries or museums, with perhaps an hour or so browsing among the shops. If you have three days you should certainly visit the National Gallery, or the Modern Art Gallery: half a day at one of these is excellently counterbalanced by spending the other half in the Royal Botanic Gardens.

The Old Town

Edinburgh Castle

The history of the castle is the history of the city and its position makes it the focus of attention. Allow at least two hours, more if possible, and try to go on a reasonably clear day to get full advantage of the views. The green uniformed castle guides, many of them ex-servicemen, are a fund of knowledge as they lead you upwards on the rough, cobbled pathways. If you prefer to be independent (and you will miss many good anecdotes if you dispense with a guide), the following itinerary covers the main attractions.

The Esplanade, below the castle gate, slopes surprisingly steeply upwards: it is here, during the Festival, that the popular Military Tattoo is staged. Most Wednesday and Saturday evenings in May and June, the ancient, stirring ceremony of Beating the Retreat is performed on the Esplanade, with pipes and drums.

Beyond the entrance to the Esplanade, **The Witches Well**, on the right, is near where over 300 witches were burned, between 1479 and 1722.

At the top of the Esplanade a drawbridge crosses a dry moat through a massive gateway, flanked by statues of Robert the Bruce and William Wallace. Ahead, the path slopes up to the right, towards the **Portcullis Gate**, which dates from 1574. Just before this, up on the left, is a memorial stone to Sir William Kirkcaldy of Grange, a colourful, 16th-century character who helped murder the notorious Cardinal Beaton (see St Andrews, p.296) and was a leader of the Lords of the Congregation in the Reformation. Kirkcaldy was an accessory to the murder of Rizzio, Mary, Queen of Scots' secretary. Later, he received her surrender at Carberry Hill and was mainly responsible for her final defeat at the Battle of Langside. After her imprisonment in England, he changed his loyalties and held Edinburgh Castle in her cause until he was forced to surrender, and was hanged.

Above the Portcullis Gate is **Constable's Tower**, later known as Argyll's Tower because the Marquess of Argyll was held in the dungeon here before his execution in 1661. The mixed construction of the steep path, a seam of cobbles between smooth stones, allowed grip for the horses and free-running tracks for the vehicles they pulled. The path snakes up past the Argyll Battery, to the tourist administration area with a souvenir shop. Beyond this is the **Regimental Museum** of the Royal Scots, Britain's oldest infantry regiment, with regimental trophies, uniforms, flags, weapons, documents, pictures and other memorabilia.

Pontius Pilate's Bodyguard

The Royal Scots are known as Pontius Pilate's Bodyguard: there was a dispute with some French officers about which was the oldest regiment. 'We were on duty at the Crucifixion' declared the French. 'Had we been,' retorted the colonel of the Royal Scots (then called Le Regiment de Douglas), 'we should not have been asleep on duty.'

Saint Margaret's Chapel, at King's Bastion, is Norman and one of the oldest roofed buildings in Scotland. It is thought to have been built by Margaret after she moved to the castle in 1076, though some believe it may have been built in her memory by her son, David I. Although often restored, this simple chapel must look much the same now as it did when it was built. Weddings and christenings are sometimes held here.

Beside the chapel, on King's Bastion, is **Mons Meg**, a mighty 15th-century cannon about whose history people disagree. Some say she was forged in Mons, in Belgium; others will tell you she was hastily cobbled together by a local blacksmith and his family to help James II when he took Threave Castle in 1455 and finally subdued the Black Douglases. This story has some credence as the land given to the blacksmith as a reward was called Mollance, or Mons, and his wife's name was Meg. Whatever the true story, Mons Meg was taken to the Tower of London in 1754, but returned to its present home at the insistence of Sir Walter Scott.

Crown Square is signed to the right, off the path up to King's Bastion. The buildings round the square are: the Scottish National War Memorial, the Crown Room, Queen Mary's Apartments, the Old Parliament or Banqueting Hall and the Scottish United Services Museum.

The Scottish National War Memorial, on the right, is dignified and poignant. Designed by Sir Robert Lorimer and opened in 1927, it contains a Gallery of Honour, divided into recesses, each containing a roll of Scottish soldiers, sailors and airmen who gave their lives for their country. Stained glass windows, by Douglas Strachan, depict war as part of human destiny and carved reliefs illustrate all the services. There is a shrine opposite the entrance, built out of the rock, embodying the freedom these brave people bought with their lives.

The Crown Room in the 15th-century Old Palace is further round on the east side of the square and has imaginative tableaux to pass the time while queuing to get in. The regalia in the glass case have their origins in medieval times and are thus older than the English Crown Jewels in London, which are almost all post-Restoration (Cromwell having destroyed the earlier ones). The crown, made of Scottish gold, decorated with 94 pearls, 10 diamonds and many other precious stones, is said to have been used by Robert the Bruce in 1306. (It was set on his head by a brave woman, Isobel of Fife, Countess of Buchan, acting for her brother whose hereditary right it was to crown the king, but who was too frightened to do so. This lion-hearted woman was captured by the English and hung up in a cage from a wall in Berwick, as a punishment.) The crown was remodelled for James V in 1540 and was last used when Charles II was crowned at Scone in 1651. The glittering Sword of State was given to James IV by Pope Julius II. During the Civil War, the Scottish Regalia were hidden for safety (see Dunnottar Castle, Grampian, p.353). After the Act of Union in 1707, they were packed away in a chest and forgotten for a hundred years, until along came that tireless patriot, Sir Walter Scott. He organized a search and the regalia were discovered, in the same room in which they are now displayed.

Queen Mary's Apartments are also in the Old Palace, with the cupboard of a room in which Mary gave birth to James VI in 1566. An intriguing mystery hangs over that accouchement and it doesn't take a lot of imagination to picture what could have happened in this airless little room, where the young queen endured her labour pains so long ago. In 1830, a tiny oak coffin was discovered, behind panelling in a recess in the room, containing the remains of an infant, wrapped in silk, with a 'J' worked into the shroud. No one will ever know the story behind this relic: it was re-interred, carrying its secret with it, leaving our minds seething with speculation. It is worth remembering that it was crucial, for Scotland's security, that the queen gave birth to a live son. Mary had suffered some nasty shocks during her pregnancy, including witnessing the murder of her secretary, Rizzio. The room in which she laboured was so small that her loyal women could easily have blocked the view of the bed from the carousing nobles next door, gathered to witness the birth. It has been remarked that portraits of James VI show a definite similarity to portraits of John, second Earl of Mar, whose mother looked after the infant king after his birth.

The 15th-century **Banqueting Hall**, once the Old Parliament Hall, on the south side of Crown Square, extensively rebuilt by James IV, is a vast chamber with a high open-timber roof and displays of weapons on the walls. It is still used for social gatherings on ceremonial occasions. In 1440, this was the setting for the infamous 'Black Dinner'. The Black Douglases were becoming too powerful for the liking of those who ruled Scotland on behalf of the 8-year-old King James II. They summoned 14-year-old William, Earl of Douglas, and his younger brother, to attend a banquet in the presence of the boy-king in this room. Legend has it that a black bull's head was brought in, signifying a death sentence. The two young Douglases were arrested and summarily executed on trumped-up charges of treason.

In one of the dungeons below the Banqueting Hall, the ninth Earl of Argyll was held before his execution in 1685. He was a staunch Protestant who supported Monmouth's rebellion against James VII/II, but he was defeated and executed. French prisoners were also imprisoned here during the Napoleonic wars. On the west and east side of Crown Square, the **Scottish United Services Museum** covers the history, dress, weapons and equipment of all three services. On the way out, look over the northern and southern walls of the Esplanade: to the north lie Princes Street, the New Town, Leith and the Firth of Forth backed by the grey-blue hills of Fife; to the south, the Pentlands, Moorfoots and Lammermuirs and, on a clear day, the distant shape of Ben Lomond to the west.

A walk down the Royal Mile from the castle to Holyrood could take days if you explore everything.There are plenty of coffee shops, restaurants and wine bars for refreshment along the way.

The Royal Mile offers cameo glimpses into the past. From the 11th century onwards it was a warren of close-packed houses, struggling upwards, shouldering each other for light and air, a maze of wynds, yards and twisting stairways: a steaming, stinking, cauldron of humanity. During the 18th and 19th centuries, when the rich crossed the putrid Nor' Loch and began to build the New Town, the Old Town became the poor quarter, with many families to each tenement, huddled together in overcrowded squalor. These houses are now being restored and re-inhabited by the middle classes: a social reversal seen in cities the world over. All the way along, closes with intriguing names open off either side.

Castle Hill leads down the Royal Mile from the Esplanade. From here, Castle Wynd Steps on the right descend to the Grassmarket (see below). At the top is **Cannonball House**, so called from the ball embedded in its western gable, which is said to have been fired from the castle towards Holyrood during its occupation by Prince Charles in 1745.

The Scottish Whisky Heritage Centre, also here (open daily: adm), is a series of tableaux with life-like models, sounds and smells, progressing from the illicit stills, smuggling and evasion of the Redcoats, through to the laird with his decanter. An audio-visual show explains (in seven languages) the process of whisky making and blending.

Outlook Tower is opposite, on the left (open daily: adm). From here you can look at the city through a camera obscura, a contraption of mirrors giving an intriguing, reflected view. There are also view-finders and telescopes round the roof, and exhibitions.

The Assembly Hall of the General Assembly of the Church of Scotland is next to the Outlook Tower, past Semple's Close. It is not always open to the public. The Assembly Hall is primarily the meeting place for the annual General Assembly, the nearest Scotland has to a parliament at present. It is on the site of a palace where Mary of Guise, lived in the 16th century. Plays are staged in this magnificent hall during the Edinburgh Festival.

Castle Street runs into **Lawnmarket**. Not far down on the left is **Gladstone's Land** (open daily 1 April–31 Oct; weekends in Nov: adm). Dating from 1617, with its original arcaded front, this is a typical house of its period, expanding upwards to six storeys. Originally the home of a wealthy burgess, Thomas Gledstanes, it is furnished in the style of the time with painted ceilings.

Lady Stair's House, now **The Writers' Museum** (open daily except Sun: free) is behind Gladstone's Land. Dating from the early 17th century, it contains relics of those three literary giants: Burns, Scott and Stevenson. Lady Stair was a leading hostess of Edinburgh society in the 18th century.

Brodie's Close, opposite Lady Stair's House, was the home of the model for Robert Louis Stevenson's character, Dr Jekyll. Deacon Brodie was a respectable citizen by day and a notorious thief by night. He was hanged in 1788, on a drop he designed himself. He also made furniture, including a linen press owned by Robert Louis Stevenson.

On the corner of Lawnmarket and **George IV Bridge**, three brass studs in the road mark the site of the last public execution, in 1864. It is city tradition to spit on the heart-shaped stones in front of Parliament Square, a little further down. These, called the **Heart of Midlothian**, mark the site of the old city jail, demolished in 1817. It was here, in 1650, that the head of gallant Montrose was displayed on a pike.

St Giles Cathedral lies within **Parliament Square**, which covers the old churchyard. John Knox is buried somewhere here, near his statue behind the cathedral. Everyone must form their own impression of St Giles. For some, its unadorned Presbyterian gloom banishes all trace of the God whose house it claims to be. Correctly, it is the High Kirk of St Giles, and it is odd that a church that was once the centre of anti-Episcopal rioting, where clergy were physically assaulted for trying to retain Episcopalian ritual, is still referred to as a cathedral—a word that means the seat of the bishop. A church is thought to have stood here as early as the 9th century, but the present Gothic building dates from the 15th century. It has been much restored, not always to advantage, and contains many relics and monuments. Near the entrance to the side chapel, a tablet marks the spot where Jenny Geddes flung her stool at the dean, striking a blow for the Covenanters in the 17th century.

The Regimental Colours of the Scottish regiments hang above the nave—historic banners embroidered with the battle honours of the regiments. The Colours are treated with respect and honour: people stand up and men salute, when they are paraded.

The Chapel of the Thistle (adm) was designed by Robert Lorimer in 1911. Tiny and ornate, in honour of The Most Ancient and Most Noble Order of the Thistle, it is deliciously out of place among these dark, forbidding walls.

Parliament House (open all year, Tues–Fri: free) is just behind St Giles. Now the Scottish Law Courts, it was the home of the Scottish Parliament until after the Union in 1707. The Great Hall has a hammerbeam roof and stained glass. A Greek façade, added in 1808, hides the original front, but you can see how it once looked from George IV Bridge, round the corner.

In the High Street leading on from Lawnmarket, 17th-century **Tron Church**, a little way down past St Giles and no longer used as a church, is so called because of the *tron*, or weighing beam, that stood nearby. The tron checked the weights used by the merchants: those found using under-weight measures were nailed to the tron by their ears. Many locals have hazy recollections of storming up the Mound at Hogmanay, just before midnight, and staggering down the High Street to touch the tron, in salute to the New Year. The church is now used as a regional art gallery.

John Knox's House (open daily except Sun: adm) is on the left-hand corner where the High Street narrows before Netherbow Port. It dates from 1490 and still has an outside stair. Restoration revealed its original walls, fireplaces and painted ceilings. John Knox is believed to have lived here from 1561 to 1572 and it is thought he died in one of the upstairs rooms. Inside are relics of his life, with pictures of Edinburgh in the past. Somehow, his dynamic personality is stamped into the soul of the building. It is easy to dismiss him as a dark, melancholy fanatic, breathing fire and everlasting damnation, but there was much more to him than that. Knox served time as a galley slave before he made his name as a reformer. He had a sharp wit, a shrewd worldliness and more: at the age of 51, he took as his second wife a girl of 16 who gave him three daughters.

The Museum of Childhood, opposite John Knox's House (open daily except Sun: free), displays nursery memorabilia, including toys, games, books and medicines.

After Netherbow Port, High Street becomes **Canongate**—the road up which the canons, or clerics, walked from Holyrood Abbey through Netherbow Gate into the walled town. Canongate was once the smart residential quarter of the aristocracy.

Canongate Tolbooth, 1591 (open daily except Sun: free), contains the **People's Story Museum**, depicting ordinary people's lives in Edinburgh from the late 18th century to the present.

The Brass Rubbing Centre is in Chalmers Close (open daily except Sun, and including Sun during the Festival: free entry, charge for each rubbing). A collection of replicas moulded from Pictish Stones, rare Scottish brasses and medieval church brasses available for amateur brass rubbers, with experts on hand to instruct and supply materials. A shop sells ready-made rubbings, kits, booklets, etc.

Canongate Church, beside the Tolbooth, was built in 1688 for the congregation that James VII ousted from Holyrood Abbey. Opposite, 16th-century **Huntly House** (open daily except on Sun: free) is a museum showing Edinburgh life through the centuries.

The 17th-century **Queensberry House** is further down on the right. As you pass, spare a thought for the kitchen boy who used to turn the spit here. While the second Duke of Queensberry was busy accepting a bribe to help push through the Act of Union in 1707, his oldest son and heir, a homicidal lunatic, was equally busy roasting the kitchen boy on his spit. He was caught, but not before he had begun to eat his victim. The house is now a hospital.

Holyrood Abbey

The history of Holyrood Abbey, at the foot of the Royal Mile, runs in tandem with that of the castle. It was founded in 1128 by David I on the spot where, tradition has it, he was saved by a miracle from being gored to death by a wild stag. The name Holy Rood (or Cross) is said to come from a fragment of the True Cross, brought to Scotland by Queen Margaret in the 11th century and incorporated into the abbey by her son David. If this is true, the holy relic did not survive (perhaps it was taken by Edward I when he stole the Stone of Destiny from Scone). Only a shell now, with a soaring Norman arch, the abbey is a beautiful silhouette against the evening sky.

James II was born and crowned here in the 15th century and he and his two successors were married in the church, as was Mary, Queen of Scots (to Darnley in 1565). Several monarchs were buried at Holyrood and Charles I was crowned here as well as in London.

Holyrood Palace

Holyrood Palace, or the Palace of Holyroodhouse, is the Queen's official residence in Edinburgh (open daily, closed during Royal and State visits: adm). Built during the reign of James IV, around 1500, it took a severe bashing, with the abbey, during the 'Rough Wooing' in 1544. Mary, Queen of Scots came here, a high-spirited, sensual widow of 19, fresh from the French court, accustomed to French ways. Here she received Knox, and was berated by him for attending Mass in her chapel. Here, in 1565, she married dissolute Darnley, four years her junior, a vicious youth who suspected her of infidelity with her Italian secretary, Rizzio, and helped to murder him in front of her when she was six months pregnant. Finally, it was here that Mary married Bothwell, a squalid, hole-in-the-corner business that brought a swift end to her reign.

Of happier memory were the five weeks in 1745, when Charles Edward Stuart, the Young Pretender, held court at Holyrood: riding out to review his troops, spreading his magnetic charm at the magnificent Court levees in the evening, the darling of Edinburgh society and focus of all female eyes.

In the 150-foot (46m) long **picture gallery** is one of Scotland's best practical jokes. The gallery holds 89 of the original 111 portraits of Scottish monarchs, commissioned by the government in 1684 and completed in two years by a Dutchman called James de Wet. Many of the portraits are of fictitious characters and many of them, as Walter Scott commented when he saw them, 'lived several centuries before the invention of oil paints'. De Wet was paid £120 per annum for this daunting commission of monarchs 'in large, royall postures' and had to provide his own materials. One can only guess at the feelings of the official who received and hung these astonishing portrayals at a rate of more than one a week.

The turreted lodge on the edge of the palace grounds, on the left approaching from Canongate, is **Queen Mary's Bath-house**. Some say she bathed here in white wine. True or not, she was liable to catch pneumonia, returning to her apartments through the cold Edinburgh wind.

South of The Royal Mile

The Grassmarket lies at the foot of Castle Wynd Steps, or down Victoria Street, off George IV Bridge just before the Central Library. Victoria Street has an excellent print shop and antique, clothes and bric-a-brac shops. The Grassmarket, a long, wide rectangle, was the scene of several ignoble events. The cross in a railed enclosure at the foot of Victoria Street marks the site of the gallows where more than 100 Covenanters were hanged in the 17th century for refusing to give up their right to worship God in their own way. Another of the Grassmarket's victims was Captain Porteous. In 1736, a crowd became restless after an unpopular execution, just up the hill in the Lawnmarket. Porteous ordered the Guard to fire. Some people were killed and Porteous was tried for murder and acquitted. The angry mob dragged him from the Tolbooth Jail and administered their own justice, hanging him from a dyer's pole in the Grassmarket.

Part of the **Flodden Wall** can still be seen at the top of the steps in the Vennel (*vennel* meaning 'alley') from the southwest corner of the Grassmarket up to Heriot Place. This wall was hastily built to protect the city after the defeat at Flodden in 1513, when the victorious English army seemed too close for comfort.

A quick strengthener in the 17th-century **White Hart Inn** might encourage you to finish your tour of the Old Town. Both Burns and Wordsworth stayed here. **The National Library of Scotland**, on George IV Bridge, opposite the Central Library, was founded in 1682 and is one of the four largest libraries in Britain. As well as enjoying the right to claim a copy of every book published in the British Isles, the library owns a collection of illuminated manuscripts and documents relating to Scottish history, including the last letter Mary, Queen of Scots wrote to her cousin Elizabeth on the eve of her execution. There is also the written order that set in motion the Massacre of Glencoe in 1692.

Greyfriars Bobby

On down George IV Bridge, opposite the entrance to Chambers Street, is the statue of a Skye terrier, Greyfriars Bobby, who watched over his master's grave at Greyfriars for 14 years, from 1858. He was fed by local people and granted Edinburgh citizenship in order to save him from being destroyed as a stray dog.

Set back beyond Greyfriars Bobby, across Candlemaker Row, **Greyfriars Kirk** is another of the Old Town antiquities. The adoption and signing of the National Covenant took place here in 1638—that 'great marriage day of this nation with God', as Lord Warriston called it. In fact it led to even greater bitterness, hatred and bloodshed than before. Ironically, 1400 Covenanters were imprisoned in the kirkyard in 1679. The grave-yard contains some important gravestones.

The Royal Museum of Scotland (open daily: free) is less than five minutes' walk round the corner into Chambers Street, a Victorian building with a soaring glass interior and a range of exhibits so diverse you could wander happily for days. Collections include art, archaeology, ethnology, natural history, technology and social history, covering the whole world. A large extension is in the process of being built.

The University Old College, dating from 1789, in South Bridge, beyond the museum, is of both aesthetic and morbid interest. It is Robert Adam's largest work in the city and contains examples of his distinctive interiors. The upper library was designed in 1830 by William Playfair. The building stands partly on ground that belonged to Kirk o' Field, where Darnley met his nasty end.

The Talbot Rice Art Centre, also here (open daily except Sun: free), contains an old master gallery and an exhibition gallery. The Torrie Collection, with important paintings and bronzes, some of which date from the 16th century, came to the Talbot Rice from Sir James Erskine of Torrie. The exhibitions are mainly of contemporary art.

The New Town

Princes Street is unique: which other city's main street has shops on one side of the road only and gardens backed by a cliff-top castle on the other? When the town planners built the New Town, they drained the stinking Nor' Loch, in the 19th century, and agreed to leave the south side of Princes Street open, with no buildings—the effect is breath-taking. Coming down any of the side streets into Princes Street from the north, you see the silhouette of the roofs and spires of the Royal Mile on the ridge above, a frieze of architecture leading dramatically up to the castle. Seen at sunrise, this view is memorable. Unbelievably, in the 1960s a scheme was nearly approved to develop the south side of the street with the same sort of buildings as you see on the north. It was only squashed because professionals who lived nearby in the New Town had influence to wield. Had the scheme been allowed, it would have ruined Edinburgh's most famous, unique feature. There was controversy when Waverley Station, a fine building, was built, because of its position.

The shops are uninspiring, mainly chain stores, and the wide pavement is usually jammed with shoppers. After a couple of hours of ruinous shopping, cross the road and relax in Princes Street Gardens—in the summer, anyway. Terraced lawns and flowerbeds shaded by old trees make a haven from the exhausting jostle of the shops. Tame grey squirrels beg for scraps and fat pigeons strut fearlessly at your feet. From spring onwards you can join the Edinburgh office workers lying on the grass like holidaymakers on a beach at lunchtime; or sit in the open-air café in the piazza, serenaded by music from the bandstand. Also in the gardens is the **Floral Clock**, a horticultural showpiece.

The Scott Monument, at the eastern end of the gardens, will be familiar from photographs. Its 287 steps (open Mon–Sat: adm) lead to a panoramic view of the city. This very Victorian monument, erected in 1840, seems entirely suitable and just the sort Sir Walter might have designed for himself. He and his dog Maida look out from under a great canopy, set with niches containing 64 of his characters.

Waverley Shopping Centre lies beyond the Scott Monument, above Waverley Station, and contains the main tourist information centre. Recently created over the roofs of Waverley Station, it is an indoor shopping precinct, on several levels, light and airy with a fountain and pool in the middle and bistro-style cafés around. Apart from the shops and waggon-stalls, this is a colourful, cheerful place for a rest and a snack, often with live entertainment near the fountain in summer.

Calton Hill rises beyond the east end of Princes Street. A well-known landmark on the Edinburgh skyline, with its semi-Parthenon at the top, built as a war memorial for the Napoleonic Wars and left unfinished when funds ran out. There are marvellous views from the 102-foot (31m) **Nelson Monument** at the top, erected 1815 (open daily except Sun: adm). The buildings of the old Royal Observatory are open, too, on application to the custodian. (The present observatory is on Blackford Hill, due south, where there is a visitor centre (open daily: adm) where you can learn about the work of astronomers all over the world.)

George Street runs parallel to Princes Street along the ridge to the north, with some of the city's best shops and vistas down the intersections towards the Firth of Forth and across to the hills of Fife. **St Andrew's Square** lies at the east end of George Street, a mixture of old and new buildings, dignified but somehow lacking the character of other squares in the New Town. The coach station is in the northeast corner, with a taxi rank just outside.

Charlotte Square, at the west end of George Street, is a distillation of all the elegant charm of the New Town. Robert Adam designed it but died before it was finished: it is accepted as one of his masterpieces and renowned throughout Europe. The elegance of the buildings is outstanding, even when the square is full of cars.

The Georgian House (open daily, April–Oct: adm) is on the north side of the square. Furnished in its original, late 18th-century style, it gives a picture of the domestic and social conditions of a wealthy family in those days. It is the headquarters for the National Trust for Scotland.

The curious inverted cones on the houses in the square are link extinguishers—used by link boys who were employed to escort people home in the dark with flaming torches. They plunged the torch into the cone to extinguish it, saving the pitch for the next customer. These can be seen in other places but it is unusual to find a whole square with them.

Beyond Charlotte Square to the north, there are a number of other fine crescents and squares. The Moray Estate was developed by James Gillespie Graham in 1823. The grand curves of Moray Place, Ainslie Place, Randolph Crescent and many more, surrounding attractive gardens and linked by well-proportioned streets, contrast with Craig's grid pattern in the first New Town development. Most of the buildings are still private houses and flats and there has been little ugly modern development. Many of the streets have retained their cobbles, making the New Town a noisy place to live.

Art Galleries and Museums

Edinburgh's art galleries would take weeks to explore thoroughly. If there is only time to explore one, it ought to be the National Gallery, described by the art historian Sir John Pope-Hennessy as 'the finest small gallery in the world'.

The National Gallery of Scotland (open daily: free except for special loan exhibitions) stands at the foot of the Mound, across a piazza—a favourite haunt of buskers. The gallery, a neo-Grecian building designed by William Henry Playfair, was built in the middle of the 19th century. The first stone was laid by Prince Albert in 1850; a wing was added in 1978 and the end of the 1980s marked a complete refurbishment. The Director of National Galleries of Scotland, Timothy Clifford, restored the gallery to Playfair's original conception, with the paintings crowded together (some say too much so) on walls whose colours are carefully chosen to fit the theme of each room. The result is stunning: burgundy walls in the main rooms are a striking foil for gilt frames and intensify the colours of the paintings. Clifford follows his contention that the gallery should provide a variety of vistas, as in an 18th-century landscape garden: sublime, contemplative, unexpected, diverting and even witty. Picture hanging is an art form in itself and he has demonstrated this most effectively.

Among the gallery's Scottish paintings are works by William McTaggart; portraits by Allan Ramsay; ebullient works by David Wilkie, whose 'social history' pictures sum up the life of ordinary people in the 18th and 19th centuries. There are several of Raeburn's portraits, including a self-portrait.

Downstairs, there is a library, a print room and a prints and drawings gallery. Every January, 38 watercolours by Turner are displayed—the Vaughan Bequest—a collection whose colours are so delicate they are only allowed into the light for one month each year. (They can be seen at other times by request in advance.)

In the main part of the gallery, on two floors, there is a large collection of European and British paintings. Poussin's *Seven Sacraments* are on their own for silent contemplation, in Room 5, off Room 4 where the rest of the Poussins hang, in a setting meant to be an evocation of the Poussin interiors. The marble floor is newly laid, the walls drab and dimly lit. The colours in the paintings are so rich and deep they are almost indigestible and the faces glow with life. One of the most spectacular vistas in the gallery is that from Room 8, down the enfilade of wine-red galleries, to the largest canvas in Scotland, *Alexander III King of Scots Saved from the Fury of a Stag by the Intrepid Intervention of Colin Fitzgerald,* by Benjamin West.

A poignant story is attached to the portrait *The Hon Mrs Graham* by Gainsborough. In 1774, at the age of 17, Mary Cathcart married Thomas Graham. The couple adored each other, continuing to exchange passionate love letters until Mary died at the age of only 34. Thomas was so heartbroken he couldn't bear to look at this portrait, painted within the first year of marriage when she was still half a child. She glances uncertainly from beneath her plumed hat, dressed in a magnificent gown, giving the impression that she wishes the artist would hurry up so she can change into something more comfortable and curl up with a book. Thomas hid the painting away and it was forgotten until his heir inherited the property, found the portrait locked away in London, and gave it to Scotland on the proviso that it should never leave the country again.

The gallery runs excellent free public lectures on individual paintings on Fridays at 12.45pm.

The Royal Scottish Academy of painting, sculpture and architecture (open daily during exhibitions: adm) is beside the National Gallery, facing on to the Mound. It was founded in 1826 to promote fine arts in Scotland and holds two main exhibitions a year: the Annual Exhibition, in the summer, and the Festival Exhibition. These vary enormously and cover all aspects of fine art.

The City Art Centre (open daily: free, except for special exhibitions) is tucked away behind Waverley Station. It houses the city's art collection, including many Scottish works, and holds a number of exhibitions from all over the world. There is a café next door.

The Scottish National Portrait Gallery (open daily: free, except for special exhibitions) is at the east end of Queen Street, and includes the Queen Street Café. From this building, opened in 1899, statues of illustrious Scots stare down at the street from Gothic niches in the façade, each carefully vetted for authenticity before erection between 1889 and 1906: John Knox, looking rather benign, Mary, Queen of Scots, William Wallace, Robert the Bruce and many more. Inside, an arcaded floor-to-roof hall with an upper gallery is decorated with murals and friezes depicting Scottish history, and these alone deserve hours of study. Painted by William Hole and commissioned in 1897, they display a remarkable talent. A processional frieze of Scottish characters over the centuries, all dated and named against a richly gilded background, is remarkable. No one has been left out: Caledonia, Scotland personified, sits as the alpha and omega, with Stone Age Man on one side and Thomas Carlyle on the other. The procession is endless.

As for the portraits themselves, it has to be said that the Scots are good subjects for portraits: they seem to have particularly strong faces. The scope in this gallery is vast and presents a history lesson, sewn together by many of Scotland's most famous people, painted by the leading artists of their times: Darnley, aged nine, by Hans Eworth, looking as if butter wouldn't melt in his mouth; his wife Mary, by an unknown artist, carrying all the sadness of her life in her enigmatic face; James VI/I, her son, by John de Critz, weak faced and dour; the gruesome *Execution of Charles I*, artist unknown, with intricate detail and rich, gleaming colour. Paintings by Lely include one of John Maitland, Duke of Lauderdale, portraying the gross coarseness of an unprincipled Secretary of State who dominated Scotland after the Restoration. There are also temporary exhibitions. On Wednesdays at 12.45pm the gallery runs free lectures on some of its works.

Much of the collection will be rehoused in Glasgow in a few years' time if plans to build a new National Gallery of Scottish Art in Kelvingrove go ahead.

The Museum of Antiquities (open daily: free except for special exhibitions) is incorporated the Portrait Gallery. Relics from Scotland's history go back to the first settlers: excavated artefacts from Stone Age man; early Christian carved stones and crosses; pagan carvings; implements; pottery, and many other artefacts. Perhaps the most fascinating exhibit in the museum is the treasure dug up from Traprain Law in 1919: 4th-century Christian and pagan silver-gilt bowls, goblets, jewellery, clasps, etc., possibly buried by pirates.

The Scottish Gallery of Modern Art (open daily: free except for some loan exhibitions), in Belford Road northwest of Princes Street, was opened in 1984 in a neo-classical building, designed by William Burn in the 1820s as a school for fatherless children at the bequest of John Watson. It stands back from a green sward dotted with trees and sculptures, some by Henry Moore.

When the plan to form a separate gallery for modern art was finally executed, the trustees of the National Galleries of Scotland allocated a large proportion of their total purchase grant to the new gallery to allow it to catch up with the others. Thus significant examples of many of the great 20th-century movements were acquired before escalating prices made this prohibitive. It owns paintings and sculpture by key artists of all nationalities and has also gained a number of important works through bequests and gifts. Altogether the gallery owns some 3000 paintings, sculptures, drawings and prints, its greatest strengths being in works of German Expressionism, Surrealism and French art. There are two floors of galleries, with a licensed café in the basement and a shop. On Mondays at 12.45pm the gallery runs free lectures on some of its paintings.

Cathedrals

Among Edinburgh's many churches of all denominations, there are two cathedrals, excluding St Giles. **St Mary's Episcopal Cathedral** of 1879, in Palmerston Place west of Princes Street, has a central spire visible from all over the city. The cathedral's Music School is in the grounds of the late 17th-century Easter Coats House nearby. As well as services, the cathedral holds public concerts throughout the year.

St Mary's Catholic Cathedral is round the corner from York Place at the east end of Queen Street. Its all-male choir has been acclaimed as being among the best in the land, 'because they sing not as trained professionals, but with their hearts'. At the start of a High Mass the choir processes into the church, their voices swelling and deepening as they move forward filling the building with glorious sound.

Around Edinburgh

Holyrood Park and Surrounds

Holyrood Park stretches south and east of the palace. The steep hill rising abruptly to the south of the palace car park is Arthur's Seat, less of a slog than it looks. The easiest way up is from Dunsappie Loch to the east. The name has no connection with legendary King Arthur; it might relate to Prince Arthur of Strathclyde, but it is more likely to be a corruption of *Ard Thor*—Gaelic for 'height of Thor'. Views from the top make the climb worthwhile. On the eve of May Day, crowds head up the slopes of Arthur's Seat, like colonies of ants. It is traditional to greet the dawn of May Day from the top, and most years there are well over 2000 people there, including pipers, morris dancers, ministers of the Church and people in evening dress. **Salisbury Crags**, the rocky peaks west of Arthur's Seat, are part of the park. There are also three lochs, **Duddingston Loch** in the southeast being a bird sanctuary preserving a surprising variety of bird life so close to the city. The village of Duddingston, to the east of the loch, was the encampment for Prince Charles's army for six weeks in 1745 while he reigned in Holyrood Palace.

Meadowbank (open daily), northeast of Holyrood Park, is a huge leisure centre, which has twice been the venue for the Commonwealth Games.

Restalrig Church, just east of Meadowbank, was destroyed in 1560 by John Knox and his followers. They branded it 'a monument of idolatry' and pulled it apart. It was later restored. The small hexagonal chapel beside it, with a lovely groined roof resting on a central pillar, was the chapel of a college founded by James III in 1478. When it was restored in the 20th century, the new floor was split open by a spring of water, believed to be one that used to cure eye diseases. The original chapel that stood over the spring was called St Triduana. There was in fact no saint of that name, which comes instead from a three-day fast practised by the old Celtic Church.

The Royal Botanic Gardens

The Botanic Gardens (open all year: free) north of the city between Inverleith Row and Inverleith Terrace deserve frequent visits to appreciate their ever-changing beauty. The herbaceous borders are spectacular, backed by a gigantic beech hedge. There are glasshouses and pavilions full of exotic vegetation, steamy-hot and lush as a tropical jungle. The rock garden is huge, full of rare alpine plants, rising in miniature mountains from the water garden and sweeping lawns. There is none of that prim 'keep-off-the-grass' feeling in these gardens: they are beautifully kept but informal. In summer students lie on the lawns, studying and relaxing.

Warriston Cemetery

Not many people would think of seeking an hour or two of peace among the dead, but this can be done in Warriston Cemetery. Just to the east of the Botanic Gardens follow the Water of Leith northwards, across Inverleith Row and along Warriston Road towards the crematorium. The cemetery was bought by a property speculator who then found that some of the graves were too recent to allow excavation. It is now a secret garden, tended just enough to clear the paths but not so much as to spoil its wild character, with forgotten graves overhung by trailing creepers, shaded by fine trees. You can wander in dappled sunlight, pausing to read inscriptions, brushing aside a swathe of Old Man's Beard to examine a draped urn or a marble angel. There is no feeling of bereavement. Don't, however, go through the tunnel that leads under the road into an olderpart of the cemetery: there is an evil presence there, so tangible one almost receives a physical shock.

Leith

Leith, to the northeast, is the historic port of Edinburgh. Formerly an area of high unemployment and destitution, it is now becoming fashionable, as gentrification proceeds apace. A number of wine bars, pubs and restaurants stand along the waterfront, some with outside tables from which you can watch maritime activity in the port. The English used to batter Leith during their many campaigns against Edinburgh. Mary, Queen of Scots landed here when she came back from France to take up her crown in 1561. One can't help wondering what a mixture of feelings—of hope, excitement and anxiety—raced through her mind as she received her first taste of Scottish hospitality. Two years before, her mother Mary de Guise-Lorraine had her headquarters here—probably in Water Street—during her struggles with the Lords of the Congregation.

Charles I played golf on **Leith Links** and it was while he was playing here in 1641 that he was stopped, mid-putt, and told the news of the Irish Rebellion. Cromwell built a fort in Leith, which the Jacobites captured in 1715. George IV landed in the port in 1822, on his celebrated visit to Edinburgh organized by Sir Walter Scott.

Andrew Lamb's House, in Burgess Street, is owned by the National Trust for Scotland. This four-storey building with a projecting staircase tower was built as a house and warehouse combined, and is now an old people's day centre. It was here that Mary was entertained on her arrival in 1561 by Andrew Lamb, one of the rich merchants of Leith.

Trinity House in Kirkgate, Leith, was founded as an almshouse in 1555, rebuilt in Victorian times and contains four portraits by Raeburn, which can be seen on request. The much-restored **Church of St Mary**, nearly opposite, was built in the 15th century.

Dean Village

Northwest of the city centre, the main road north crosses the Dean Bridge, giving no hint of the Dean Village in the valley below. There was a grain-milling community here for 800 years, straggling along the Water of Leith. The old buildings have been restored and converted into flats and houses. You can walk for miles along this waterway, a peaceful haven close to the heart of a busy city.

Lauriston Castle

Lauriston Castle (open daily except Fri, April–Oct; weekends, Nov–March: adm) is further to the northwest, off Cramond Road South, overlooking the river in the suburb of Davidson's Mains. The original 16th-century tower was extended and is now a fine house which contains good paintings, furniture, tapestry and 'Blue John Ware'.

Edinburgh Zoo

The zoo (open daily: adm), at Corstorphine, going west out of Edinburgh on the A8, is one of the biggest in Britain. The perimeter fence runs halfway up Corstorphine Hill and it is worth climbing the hill in the early morning to watch the sun flooding in over the Lothian Plain. Suddenly, close by, the harsh roar of an African beast bellows out to greet the dawn.

Craigmillar Castle

Craigmillar Castle (open daily except Fri: adm) is 3½ miles (5.5km) southwest of the city centre on the A68—a route through open countryside in the days when Mary, Queen of Scots used to ride out with her court. The ruins of the castle stand high above a straggle of modern buildings that threaten to overwhelm it from all sides, yet fail to diminish its splendour. These well-preserved walls, dating from the 14th century, have witnessed some of the darker moments of Scotland's history. In 1475 James III imprisoned his brother, John, Earl of Mar, in the keep, accusing him of 'conspiracy'. Later, Mar died from 'overzealous bloodletting'.

Craigmillar was Mary's favourite country retreat. The village nearby was known as Little France when the overflow from her court took lodgings there. It was here in 1566, at the Craigmillar Conference, that Mary was urged by her lords (including Bothwell) to divorce Darnley. She was torn by the conflict between her strict Catholic upbringing, her repugnance for her dissolute husband and her growing passion for Bothwell. She lay in her chamber, sobbing: 'Would that I had died, that time in Jedburgh'.

The banqueting hall on the first floor is served by four stairways and it is easy to imagine it with hanging tapestries, straw on the flagged floor, blazing logs in the vast open hearth and a minstrel in the gallery below the barrel-vaulted ceiling. There are views from the roof across to Arthur's Seat, the Firth of Forth with the hills of Fife beyond, and the soft contours of the smoke-grey Pentlands on the southwestern horizon. The two ancient yew trees in the courtyard are relics from the days when they were believed to ward off evil spirits (a more prosaic explanation for their presence being that their wood was needed for making bows).

Entertainment and Nightlife

An information centre with ticket service is at 31/2 Waverley Bridge, just beside the station. They advise on theatre and concert ticket availability, information about events in Edinburgh and coach tours around the area, and sell tickets.

There are top-class concerts, opera, drama, ballet, variety shows, etc. in Edinburgh's theatres and the latest films in the cinemas. A new opera house, in Nicolson Street, should be open by the 1994 Festival.

theatres

Kings Theatre, Leven Street, ✆ 031 229 1201. Restored to its original Georgian splendour.

Netherbow, High Street, ✆ 031 556 9579. A multi-arts centre with a variety of shows and exhibitions.

Playhouse, at the top of Leith Walk, ✆ 031 557 2590. Family entertainment, pop concerts and the main opera house.

Queen's Hall, Clerk Street, ✆ 031 668 2019. Home of Scottish Chamber Orchestra and Scottish Ensemble and important jazz centre.

Royal Lyceum Theatre, Grindlay Street, near the Usher Hall, ✆ 031 229 9697. Recently extensively restored, one of Scotland's largest repertory companies

Theatre Workshop, 34 Hamilton Place, ✆ 031 226 5425.

Traverse Theatre, Cambridge Street, ✆ 031 228 1404. An acclaimed experimental theatre, moved to a new building.

Usher Hall, Lothian Road, ✆ 031 228 1155.

cinemas

Cameo, Home Street, ✆ 031 228 4141. Recently much improved.

Dominion, Newbattle Terrace, ✆ 031 447 2660/8450.

Edinburgh Filmhouse, Lothian Road, ✆ 031 228 2688. All the good films you missed, or long to see again, as well as new ones.

MGM, Lothian Road, ✆ 031 229 3030/031 228 1638. Several screens showing new films.

Odeon Film Centre, Clerk Street, ✆ 031 667 7331/2. Same as above.

UCI, Craig Park, ✆ 0800 88 89 55. A 12-screen multiplex.

UCI, New Craighall, ✆ 031 669 0777. Multi-screen.

Princes Street and the rather more up-market **George Street**, together with their connecting streets and the whole area between them, are the main shopping areas in the city centre. **Jenners**, in Princes Street, is the 'Harrods' of Edinburgh: if you can't get what you want anywhere else they usually have it. There are any number of tweed, tartan and wool shops, including the **Tartan Gift Shop**, 96 Princes Street.

Rose Street and its lanes, running parallel to Princes Street and George Street, are lively, humming with bars, restaurants, hot-food take aways and boutiques. Rose Street used to be the 'Red Light' district and had more pubs than any other street in Britain. Many of the shops here are 'fun' places, with gimmicky knick-knacks and craft work. Les Cadeaux, 121 Rose Street, sells a good range of china, crystal and gifts and run a tax-free mailing service to the USA.

The **St James Centre**, at the east end of Princes Street, is an indoor shopping complex. **Waverley Shopping Centre** is attractive, with lots of specialist shops and representatives of larger stores located elsewhere.

Hamilton and Inches, 87 George Street which was recently refurbished, is an old-established shop selling antique and modern silver and jewellery, Highland accessories, watches, clocks, crystal and china.

There are plenty of gift shops in and just off **the Royal Mile**, as well as antique shops, bars and restaurants.

The **Grassmarket** and the area around it is good shopping territory. There is a well-stocked print shop, already mentioned, in Victoria Street with framed and unframed prints of almost anywhere in Scotland at reasonable prices. There are second-hand bookshops here and several antique shops worth browsing in. There are also clothes and accessory shops, gift shops and smart interior decorating shops as well as good eating and drinking places.

Droopy and Brown, 37–39 Frederick Street, have a reputation for their own design of clothes.

Stockbridge, down by the Water of Leith on the edge of the New Town, has a village community atmosphere and several good shops, particularly for food.

St Stephen Street, at the bottom of northwest Circus Place, is lined with antique and junk shops. Some are smart and expensive, some a delightful clutter of cast-offs— clothes, boxes of old 78 rpm records, glass jars full of buttons, stuffed birds. On the corner of St Stephen Street, **Galloways** is an antique shop that also does high-class interior decoration.

Herbys, at 66 Raeburn Place further down, is a licensed delicatessen and take-away with everything anyone could want for an impromptu picnic: mouth watering cheeses, pâtés, cold-cuts, home-made bread, etc.

The **James Pringle Woollen Mill** in Bangor Road has tartans, tweeds and knitwear. They also have a 'trace your clan' computer.

The choice is enormous and you should consult the Edinburgh and Scotland Information Centre. Book well ahead during the summer and especially during the Festival. The following hotels are in the city centre, an easy walk or short taxi ride from the station

expensive

The Balmoral, at the east end of Princes Street, ✆ 031 556 2414, will be better known to many as the North British Hotel, from the days when it was the doyen of Edinburgh's hotels, the stage for elegant balls and smart receptions attended by Scotland's aristocracy. It suffered a grim decline but a recent facelift has restored it to the top rank.

Caledonian Hotel, at the west end of Princes Street, ✆ 031 225 2433, has a long-established reputation for comfort and impeccable standards; there are several bars and restaurants, including the elegant Pompadour Restaurant.

Edinburgh Sheraton, at the bottom of Lothian Road, ✆ 031 229 9131, is only a few years old and recently refurbished. It stands back behind fountains and a paved garden and is well up to the standard of all Sheraton hotels.

The George Hotel, at the east end of George Street, ✆ 031 225 1251, has long been one of Edinburgh's top hotels, with a high-class reputation.

Howard Hotel, 32–36 Great King Street, ✆ 031 557 3500, is a completely refurbished hotel in Georgian New Town, highly commended.

Roxburghe Hotel, Charlotte Square, ✆ 031 225 3921, is a comfortable, old-established hotel with excellent service and food, overlooking Edinburgh's loveliest square.

moderate

Braid Hills hotel, 134 Braid Road, ✆ 031 447 8888, is a Gothic building with good views of the castle and surrounding countryside and offers golf and tennis.

The Carlton Highland Hotel on the North Bridge, ✆ 031 556 7277, is a turreted baronial pile, very much at the hub of the city, with a sports and leisure centre underneath and very un-baronial decor inside.

Commodore Hotel, West Marine Drive, ✆ 031 336 1700, stands in parklands on the outskirts of the city overlooking the Forth.

Ellersly Country House Hotel, 4 Ellersly Road, ✆ 031 313 2543, is an Edwardian house in a walled garden with excellent food.

Old Waverley Hotel, 43 Princes Street, ✆ 031 556 4648, is opposite Waverley Station.

Prestonfield House, Priestfield Road, ✆ 031 668 3346, is a unique 17th-century country house in lovely grounds—see Eating Out.

Scandic Crown Hotel, 80 High Street, ✆ 031 557 9797, was recently built as a mock medieval tower amidst some controversy. It is very comfortable.

Thistle Hotel, 59 Manor Place, ✆ 031 225 6144, is a friendly establishment in the west end, not far from the centre.

inexpensive

Osbourne Hotel, 53/9 York Place, ✆ 031 556 5577, is a comfortable townhouse hotel within a few minutes' walk of Princes Street.

Maitland Hotel, 33 Shandwick Place, ✆ 031 229 1467, is a Georgian house near the centre in the west end, once owned by the Earl of Maitland. It offers a variety of package holidays which include dinner, B&B, and visits to many parts of the city.

Eating Out

There are masses of restaurants, cafés and wine bars, tucked away down steps, in narrow wynds and courtyards or on the main streets where you can eat very well. When the sun shines you can even sit at tables in the street, though the licensing laws are such that it is not always possible to drink alcohol at pavement tables. The following are a few suggestions—and it is always wise to book.

expensive

L'Auberge, 56 St Mary Street, ✆ 031 556 5888. Elegant, stylish restaurant serving the best Scottish produce, imaginatively and skilfully Frenchified. Try the terrine of venison.

Howard Hotel, 36 Great King Street, ✆ 031 557 3500, serves classical Scottish dishes in its original Georgian dining room: try the kipper and whisky mousse, poacher's broth, and Flummery Drambuie.

Merchants Restaurant, Merchant Street, ✆ 031 225 4009. Small, friendly atmosphere in converted tartan warehouse.

Pompadour Restaurant, Caledonian Hotel, ✆ 031 225 2433: remembering Scotland's Auld Alliance with France, this restaurant is decorated in the style of Louis XV's famous mistress, Madame de Pompadour, its bar overlooking the castle. Somehow, the Pompadour embodies Edinburgh's golden age, with subtle colours and delicate murals to soothe the digestion. As long as you don't mind having to put on a jacket and tie, and don't mind music while you eat, you won't be disappointed.

Prestonfield House, Priestfield Road, ✆ 031 668 3346, is a 17th-century house in attractive grounds where peacocks strut and highland cattle graze. Excellent food in a country house atmosphere.

The Witchery, 352 Castlehill, ✆ 031 225 5613, is not for the timid. It has ghoulish decor to emphasize its original purpose as a haunt for witches—and good food. For those who like organized spookery, walking tours set out from the Witchery at various times, with costumed guides and simulated ghoulery.

moderate

Alp Horn Restaurant, 167 Rose Street, ✆ 031 225 4787, combines a genuine Swiss atmosphere with good service.

Café Royal Oyster Bar, 17a West Register Street, ✆ 031 556 4124. If you saw the film *Chariots of Fire*, you will recognize this 1830s restaurant with its dark gleaming wood and reflecting glass.

Black Bo's, 57–61 Blackfriars Street, just off the Royal Mile, ✆ 031 557 6136. Unpretentious and imaginative with good vegetarian food.

City Café, 19 Blair Street, ✆ 031 220 0125: trendy US-style soda bar. Stark but stylish.

Kalpna, 2–3 St Patrick's Square, ✆ 031 667 9890. Vegetarian Indian food.

L'Etoile, 8a Grindlay Street (by Lyceum Theatre), ✆ 031 229 5405. Excellent French food, in friendly, casual atmosphere.

Le Marché Noir, in Eyre Place, ✆ 031 558 1608, splendid French provincial food and atmosphere: nouvelle cuisine but not precious. Excellent set menus, limited *à la carte*.

Martin's Restaurant, 72 Rose Street North Lane, ✆ 031 225 3106. This personally run, intimate restaurant, aptly described as 'a country restaurant in the city', is among the best in Edinburgh serving first-class food. No smoking in the dining room and a cheese board that defies description for freshness and imagination. Martin will give the history of each cheese. Highly recommended.

Negociants, 45 Lothian Street, ✆ 031 225 6313, has a predominantly Far Eastern menu.

Patisserie Florentin, 8–10 Giles Street, ✆ 031 225 6267. Best croissants in town.

Ristorante Ravello, 86 Morningside Road, ✆ 031 449 9724, is old-established with a first-class menu.

Tinelli Ristorante, 139 Easter Road, ✆ 031 652 1932 (opposite the entrance to Hibernian FC's stadium), is straight out of Italy. Highly recommended for food, bistro decor, service and atmosphere. Follow the advice of Paolo when choosing from the menu.

On the waterfront at Leith there are several good seafood restaurants with a 'waterfront' atmosphere, tables outside and excellent fish dishes. Try **Skippers Bistro,** 1a Dock Place, ✆ 031 554 1018. A nice Bohemian atmosphere and friendly staff. The menu, chalked up on a blackboard, is changed twice a day: mouth-watering smoked salmon roulade and scallops. **The Shore**, 3 The Shore, ✆ 031 553 5080, has lots of character. **The Waterfront**, 1 Dock Place, ✆ 031 554 7127, is an attractive wine bar overlooking the water—it was once the waiting room for steamboat passengers.

inexpensive

Bannermans, 55 Niddy Street, off Cowgate, ✆ 031 556 3254: built in the 1770s as a shellfish warehouse, then a dwelling, and later a tavern called 'The Bucket of Blood', Bannermans has managed to retain its original tavern atmosphere, with plenty of bare wooden surfaces: you almost expect to see rushes on the floor. It has traditional Scottish folk music, live, on Sundays, Tuesdays and Wednesdays, and serves Excellent soup and homely food. Highly recommended for atmosphere.

Chez Jules, 1 Craigs Close, 29 Cockburn Street, © 031 225 7007, and 61 Frederick Street, © 031 225 7983. Offshoots of the Pierre Victoire chain—excellent value and very French.

Engine Shed Café, 19 St Leonards Lane, © 031 662 0040, is a popular students' lunch spot with a friendly atmosphere and home-cooked food.

Ferri's Restaurant, 1 Antigua Street, © 031 556 5592, has a happy Italian atmosphere (genuine). It's good for children and extremely reasonable.

Fruitmarket Gallery Café, 29 Market Street, © 031 225 2383, is a stylish place in the recently refurbished Fruitmarket Gallery.

Henderson's Salad Table, 94 Hanover Street, © 031 225 2131, popular self-service vegetarian restaurant.

Keepers Restaurant, 13b Dundas Street, © 031 556 5707. Candlelit pre-theatre dinners in a friendly 'bistro' atmosphere.

La Bagatelle, 22 Brougham Place, © 031 229 0869. Small, intimate, French atmosphere.

Le Sept, Old Fishmarket Close, © 031 225 5428, is a cheerful bistro serving good-value French food.

Madogs, 38 George Street, © 031 225 3408. American-inspired cocktail bar specializing in exotic cocktails. It is known for its hamburgers but there is a wide alternative choice.

Pierre Victoire, 10 Victoria Street, © 031 225 1721, 8 Union Street, © 031 557 8451, 38–40 Grassmarket, © 031 226 2442, 5 Dock Place, Leith, © 031 555 6178: an Edinburgh institution, these restaurants offer very good value, and are crammed with atmosphere—and people, so you must book. Their vegetarian offshoot, **Pierre Lapin**, is at 32 West Nicholson Street, © 031 668 4332.

out of town

The true gourmet should forget all the above and go out of town. There are three restaurants within easy motoring distance that have been classed among the top ten in Britain—some go further and rank them the top three.

La Potinière is 15 or so miles (24km) east along the coast at Gullane, © 0620 843214 (see Lothian, p.131).

The Peat Inn, © 033484 206, is further away, near Cupar, in Fife (see p.304).

Champany's, Champany Corner, Linlithgow, © 050683 4532, is less than 15 miles (24km) from the city centre, a whisker off the M9, and surely the best steak house in Britain (see Lothian, p.138).

Strathclyde: Excluding Glasgow

Dumbarton Rock

Strath means 'broad valley' but Strathclyde is much more than just the valley of the Clyde. Glasgow lies at its heart, astride the river and surrounded by a straggle of satellite towns, not beautiful but vibrant with character. To the south, a string of seaside resorts line the sandy coast—Glasgow's playground—backed by farmland. The eastern boundary cuts through Loch Lomond, an over-popular beauty spot. Argyll, to the west, is completely different. Remote and wild, its serpentine sea lochs eat into the land to form long peninsulas and narrow isthmuses, like a misshapen lobster claw. Moor, hill and forest are fringed by miles of beaches, with many islands lying off the coast, like stray pieces of a jig-saw.

The ancient Dalriada Scots from Ireland settled in Argyll and formed their powerful kingdom. Here, Columba landed to spread the Christianity Saint Ninian had introduced at Whithorn, more than one and a half centuries earlier. Welsh Celts moved up and occupied the land south of the Clyde. As well as dozens of prehistoric burial mounds, stones and cairns, Strathclyde's coast is punctuated with the remains of fortresses and watch-towers, built to defend the land from invasion by sea. South of the Clyde is rich in Covenanting history and there is a Covenanting Trail, visiting a number of the places associated with those turbulent times.

Strathclyde's economy has risen and fallen with Glasgow's. Since the decline of shipbuilding and its related industries, diversification into electronics and the silicon chip has brought a new prosperity to Clydeside towns. In rural Argyll fishing, farming and tourism are the main occupations.

Most of the towns have a summer festival or civic week, with decorated streets and an excuse for plenty of entertainment and music.

Ayrshire is Burns country and a nostalgic Burns Heritage Trail takes in all the landmarks in the poet's life. (For details, write to Land o' Burns Centre, Alloway, Ayr.)

Tourist Information

Tourist Information Centre, 35–39 St Vincent Place, Glasgow, ✆ 041 227 4880.
Ayr Tourist Information Centre, 39 Sandgate, Ayr, ✆ 0292 284196.
Ayrshire Tourist Board, Suite 1005 Prestwick Airport, Prestwick, ✆ 0290 79000.
Clyde Valley Tourist Board, Horsemarket, Ladyacre Road, Lanark, ✆ 0555 2544.
Dunoon and Cowal Tourist Board, 7 Alexandra Parade, Dunoon, ✆ 0369 3785.

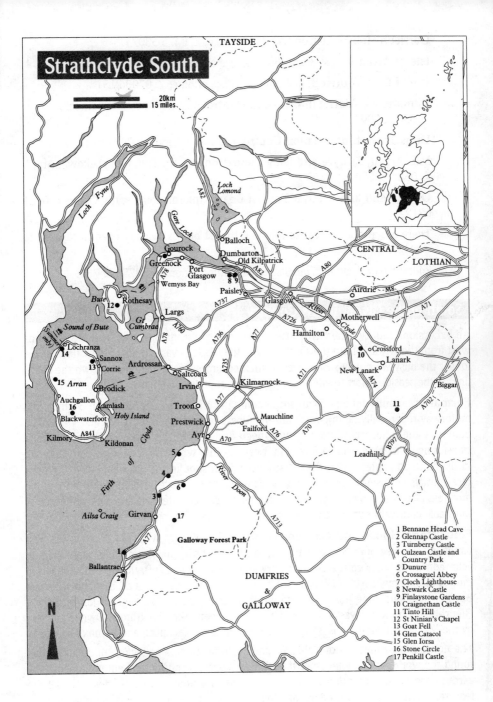

Strathclyde South

20km
15 miles

TAYSIDE

CENTRAL

LOTHIAN

Loch Lomond

Loch Fyne

Gare Loch

Balloch

Gourock
Greenock
Port Glasgow
Wemyss Bay

Dumbarton
Old Kilpatrick

8 9

Paisley

Glasgow

River Clyde

Airdrie M8

Bute
12
Rothesay

Largs

Gt Cumbrae

Sound of Bute

Lochranza
14

Sannox
13 Corrie

Ardrossan

Saltcoats

Motherwell

Hamilton

Crossford
10
Lanark

New Lanark

Irvine

Kilmarnock

15 Arran

Auchgallon
16

Brodick

Lamlash

Blackwaterfoot Holy Island

Troon

Prestwick

Mauchline

Failford

Biggar

11

Kilmory

A841

Kildonan

Ayr

A70

Leadhills

Firth

of

Clyde

5

4

6

3

River Doom

Ailsa Craig

Girvan

17

Galloway Forest Park

1

Ballantrae

2

DUMFRIES

&

GALLOWAY

N

1 Bennane Head Cave
2 Glennap Castle
3 Turnberry Castle
4 Culzean Castle and
  Country Park
5 Dunure
6 Crossaguel Abbey
7 Cloch Lighthouse
8 Newark Castle
9 Finlaystone Gardens
10 Craignethan Castle
11 Tinto Hill
12 St Ninian's Chapel
13 Goat Fell
14 Glen Catacol
15 Glen Iorsa
16 Stone Circle
17 Penkill Castle

Garrison House, Millport, Isle of Cumbrae, ✆ 0475 530741.

Isle of Arran Tourist Board, Brodick, Isle of Arran, ✆ 0770 2140/2401.

Isle of Bute Tourist Board, Rothesay, Isle of Bute, ✆ 0700 2151.

Kilmarnock Tourist Information Centre, 62 Bank Street, Kilmarnock, ✆ 0563 39090.

Largs Tourist Information Centre, Esplanade, Largs, ✆ 0475 673765.

Mid-Argyll, Kintyre and Islay Tourist Board, The Pier, Campbeltown, Argyll, ✆ 0586 52056.

Oban, Mull and District Tourist Board, Information Centre, Oban, ✆ 0631 63122.

There are also a number of seasonal tourist offices, usually open from April to October.

24-hour *What's on for Tourists* recorded information, ✆ 0475 686786.

South of the Clyde: Burns Country

All excursions south of the Clyde are an easy day-trip from Glasgow. The M8/A8 runs west from the city and hugs the south bank of the Clyde, a vast mudflat at low tide and no longer the busy waterway it once was. It then becomes the A78 and runs down the coast, linking the seaside resort towns that are the playgrounds of Glasgow.

Formakin, about a mile (1.5km) south along the B789 just after junction 31 from the motorway (open daily: adm), was built by Robert Lorimer between 1903 and 1911. The buildings and landscaped grounds have been designed in the Arts and Crafts style. He transformed a meal mill and a few farm dwellings into what you see today. You can walk in the restored gardens, visit the restaurant and gift shop in the old stable block and see rare animals on display in the old pigsty. Those with keen eyes should look out for stone monkeys clambering over ridges on the roof and a carved datestone above the entrance to the stable courtyard saying 1694, accompanied by DL—Damned Lie.

Finlaystone House and Gardens are about 20 minutes west of Glasgow just past Langbank. (House open Sun afternoons, April–Aug, or by appointment: garden open all year: adm.) Dating from the 14th century and extended in 1760, the house belonged to the Cunninghams, Earls of Glencairn, for five centuries. The 14th Earl befriended Robert Burns who spent some time here and wrote a stirring poem, 'Lament for James, Earl of Glencairn'. John Knox was another of Finlaystone's better-known visitors. Owned and run by the Macmillan family, it is now a centre for the Clan Macmillan and home of its chief.

The house has exhibitions of Celtic art and Victoriana and a collection of dolls from all round the world, and is sometimes the stage for concerts and musical entertainment. The gardens are outstanding and as varied as rooms in a house. A leaflet describes all the features, including a laurel hedge on a bank, cut once a year by a Flymo on water-skis. Landscaped in the 1830s and still being developed, its many 'rooms' open off sweeping lawns with magnificent views across the Firth of Clyde to the hills beyond. Look out for the ingenious Celtic Paving, near the bog garden and folly. This was laid in 1984 by the present chief's wife as an alternative to a maze. Its six circles and semi-circles form a continuous line, adapted from a one-inch design in the *Book of Kells*. The **John Knox Tree** behind the house (moved 40 yards from round the corner in 1900 because the lady of the house complained it made the drawing room too dark for her to sew in) is a yew, said to have been where Knox held the first reformed Communion in the West of Scotland in 1556. As well as the formal gardens there are woodland walks, a ranger service, pick-your-own strawberries and raspberries, a tea room and visitor centre, a play area and orienteering.

Port Glasgow, Greenock and Gourock form a more or less continuous urban sprawl along the south bank of the Clyde. Once the hub of the mighty Clydeside shipbuilding industry, these towns were hit hardest by the Depression and for many years were a gloomy spectacle of dying shipyards and dole queues. But the tenacious spirit that is part of the Clydeside character is revitalizing the area; buildings are being cleaned up, enterprising new developments are replacing the skeletons of the shipyards and a keen eye can pick out some fine architecture amongst the dreary tenements. Within a stone's throw inland, narrow lanes run through miles of unspoiled moor, dotted with gorse and heather and small villages.

Port Glasgow was built in the 17th century, the nearest deep-water port to the city.

Newark Castle (open daily: adm), east of the town, dates from the 16th century, with a 15th-century tower, and is said to be one of the best examples of a Scottish mansion house of this period. A solid, fortified pile, on a green sward overlooking the river, it is still almost intact with courtyard, hall and a large number of chambers. In the days when it was a Maxwell stronghold, with none of the surrounding scars of industry, it was strategically placed with commanding views of the river.

Also in Port Glasgow, there is a replica of the 25-tonne *Comet*, the first commercial steamship in Europe, an elegant craft built by John Wood in 1812. It had a three horse-power engine and dashed along at about six knots.

Greenock

Merging with Port Glasgow's western suburbs, Greenock boasts some splendid Victorian architecture including the Municipal Buildings with a 245-foot (75m) tower, and a Classical-style Custom House. The stained-glass windows in Old West Kirk, on the Esplanade, include work by pre-Raphaelites Burne-Jones, Rossetti and Morris. This was the first church to be built after the Reformation, in 1591, and the first Presbyterian church to be acknowledged by Parliament. It was moved here from its original site in 1920 to make room for development.

The Maclean Museum and Art Gallery in Union Street, Greenock (open daily except Sun: free), has exhibits of local and natural history, including model ships and information about James Watt who was born and educated in the town. The art gallery has work by Guthrie, another native of Greenock.

Captain Kidd

Captain William Kidd was born in Greenock in 1645 to a Covenanting minister. He went to sea as a boy privateer and earned a reputation for bravery, for which he received a reward of £150 from New York City. In 1696 he was given a ship with 30 guns and sent off to fight the French and capture pirates. A year later he got to Madagascar, the pirates' main headquarters, and, finding plunder more lucrative than government service, became a pirate himself. He was hanged in England in 1701.

Burns fans should go up Nelson Street to the cemetery, to see **The Tomb of Highland Mary** (see Topics), moved here when Old West Kirk was rebuilt. The original Burns Club was founded in Greenock in 1802.

On Lyle Hill, above Greenock, the huge granite **Cross of Lorraine**—with its two transversals rising from a gigantic anchor—is the Free French Memorial. During the Second World War, Greenock was a Free French Naval Base and this is the memorial to the sailors who died in the Battle of the Atlantic.

Gourock, merging with Greenock, is on the shoulder where the Clyde swings round from the east to flow out to sea. Half resort, half port, Gourock is the home of Caledonian MacBrayne, who run most of the west coast ferries, several of which depart from here. It is also a yachting centre. Gourock Highland Games are held in May.

Granny Kempock's Stone, on Kempock Point, beside the A78 overlooking the Firth, is a 6-foot (2m) high block of grey stone, dating from prehistoric times, thought to have been part of a Druid temple. Superstitious fishermen believed Granny Kempock commanded the sea. They laid offerings before her and walked round her seven times, begging for fair weather and good fishing. Newly married couples embraced her and asked for children. Today she is railed off, to prevent such familiarity.

Cloch Lighthouse, built in 1797, is an imposing white landmark, on rocky Cloch Point just west of the town, greeted with relief by homecoming sailors during wartime and by fishermen after a stormy night at sea.

Inverkip, a couple of miles (3km) south on the A78, has one of the biggest marinas in these parts, well supplied with chandlers and shore facilities. Skippers of bigger yachts should beware of the narrow, shallow entrance at low tide. A small back road east out of Inverkip leads up to **Cornalees Bridge** in the open moorland of **Clyde-Muirshiel Regional Park.** A nature trail here follows the aqueducts that used to supply the coastal towns with drinking water and power for the mills.

Cunninghame is the area from Skelmorlie to south of Irvine, including Arran and the Cumbraes.

Wemyss Bay is so called from the caves (weems) here, where Stone Age nomads may have lived while making foraging expeditions from Ireland. There is a splendid Victorian station from which you can get ferries to Bute.

Largs is easily the nicest of the Clyde resorts, with a history that adds stature to its bustling streets. Tucked in on a shelf below rolling moorland, with views across the Firth to Great Cumbrae and Bute, Largs was the theatre for a crucial, though rather ineffectual battle in the 13th century. Old King Haakon of Norway, determined to dominate the Western Isles and worried that Alexander III had the same intention, launched his fleet from Kirkwall in Orkney in July 1263. The weather was appalling. The fleet battled round Cape Wrath and down the Minch as far as Skye, suffering much damage. In Skye they were joined by Magnus, King of Man, and a few others. Into the teeth of southwesterly gales they struggled on, past the Inner Hebrides and round the Mull of Kintyre. They were well into the Clyde by the end of September when they were caught by a gale which tore Haakon's ships from their moorings and drove them on to the Ayrshire coast at Largs. The sailors waded ashore to meet Alexander's army. There was a confusion of arrows and horses and then the Scots withdrew and allowed the Vikings to wade back to their ships and sail away. History doesn't relate *how* they managed to get those cumbersome long-boats off a lee-shore, nor *why* the Scots, with such a strategic advantage, allowed them to, but the outcome was conclusive. Haakon lost interest and died, and his successor, Erik, sold the Western Isles for less than £3000 in 1266 and married Alexander's daughter Margaret. A phallic obelisk, known as the Pencil, on Bowen Craig, south of the town, celebrates the battle, and every September hundreds of Scandinavians come to Largs to join in the Viking Festival.

The **Largs Historical Society Museum**, in Kirkgate House, Manse Court (open June–Sept, afternoons daily: donation box), reconstructs the battle, and has exhibits of local history.

The Christian Heritage Museum, in a Benedictine Monastery at 5 Mackerston Place (open daily, Apr–Sept: adm), tells the history of Christian monasticism in Britain and southwest Scotland, with some fine vestments and displays as well as a café in the refectory, and a shop.

The town is packed with 'entertainment' for all ages. There are a couple of golf courses, a National Sports Training Centre, a big swimming pool—and the sea. Three times a week the last sea-going paddle steamer, *Waverley*, sails from the pier to other resorts on the Clyde. Largs is the port for Great Cumbrae Island (p.217).

The Largs Yacht Haven south of the town has berths for over 500 yachts and offers all marina facilities including chandlers, sea-school, diving equipment, provisions, sales, charter and repairs.

Kelburn Country Centre, on the A78 between Largs and Fairlie, offers a good day out for the family. Kelburn has been the home of the Boyle family, Earls of Glasgow since 1703, for 800 years and Kelburn Castle, dating from the 13th century with many later additions, is the home of the present Earl. (Open noon–4pm, July and Aug, or by appt, © 0475 568685: adm). The grounds (open daily: adm) feature wild woodland, dramatic waterfalls and gorges, pools and grottos with wild flowers, ferns, rare trees and shrubs, and a walled garden called The Plaisance, full of rare plants. There is a licensed café, a lampoon-type Cartoon Exhibition depicting the history of the Boyle family, and a museum with New Zealand exhibitions. Other attractions include a Commando Assault Course built by the Royal Marines, for adults; an Adventure Course and Stockade, for younger Tarzans; and a Ranger Service offering advice, guided walks, talks and slide shows. There is also an animals' and pets' corner, a riding centre and pony trekking.

Muirshiel Country Park covers 9 miles (14.5km) of high roadless moorland northeast of Largs. At **Lochwinnoch** there is a boating and fishing loch, with nature trails, picnic sites and four information centres.

The A78 runs through **Fairlie** and **West Kilbride**, to **Ardrossan** and **Saltcoats**, a string of unremarkable resort towns, some of which contain interesting museums and visitor centres. The museum in West Kilbride, for instance, has costumes and a large collection of Ayrshire lace and embroidery, (open Tue, and Thur–Sat: free). Ardrossan is the port for the island of Arran (p.218). Saltcoats was an important producer of salt in the days of James V. **North Ayrshire Museum**, at Kirkgate, Saltcoats is in a late 18th-century church and gives various aspects of life in this area.

At **Kilwinning**, 3 miles (4.5km) east of Saltcoats, 17th-century **Dalgarven Mill** is a working museum, with displays of artefacts of the period and live models in authentic costume. At **Kilwinning Abbey**, founded in the mid-12th century, and now derelict, an annual archery competition for the Papingo Trophy has been taking place for 600 years, the oldest such event in the world. Kilwinning claims to be the first centre in Scotland of freemasonry, that secret society for men, supposed to be based on brotherly love, faith and charity. It was introduced by the stonemasons working on the abbey.

Eglinton Country Park, south of Kilwinning, is landscaped with gardens, picnic sites, a visitor centre and walks, centred on the ruins of **Eglinton Castle**. Here, in 1839, below the 100-foot (30m) tower, built in 1796 and now derelict, a romantic attempt was made to re-establish ancient chivalric ceremonies. The Eglinton Tournament was a whimsical Victorian longing for 'the good old days': a jousting tournament, performed amidst much back-slapping and frolicking. Napoleon III took part as one of the knights, practising, no doubt, for his next abortive attempt at the French throne the following year. In his novel *Endymion* Disraeli borrows from this event.

Irvine, 3 miles (4.5km) south of Kilwinning, is Scotland's only coastal New Town. Under its modern façade, its history goes back a long way. William Wallace was deserted by his followers here in 1297, when they signed a treaty with the English. Marymass is a week-long festival held every August, which culminates with a procession past the castle and the crowning of a queen. At Marymass there is a horse race alleged to be the longest in the world. There is also a three-day Harbour Festival in July.

The Scottish Maritime Museum (open daily, April–Oct: adm) is in Irvine harbour, once one of Glasgow's main ports, and includes working boats, a puffer, sailing boats and lifeboats. There is a collection of documents, artefacts, photographs and small craft, all illustrating Scotland's sea-going heritage. There is also a tenement house, showing the 'room and kitchen' of a typical shipyard worker's dwelling at the turn of the century, complete with range, utensils and drying laundry.

Glasgow Vennel (lane), the historic core of Irvine, was the main road to Glasgow until the end of the 17th century. Derelict and facing demolition in the 1970s, it was rescued and designated a conservation area in 1974. Its 18th- and 19th-century buildings are now restored and in use on an attractive cobbled street.

Glasgow Vennel Museum, 4 and 10 Glasgow Vennel (open daily except Wed and Sun, June–Sept: free), includes Burn's Lodgings at No. 4 with a reconstruction of his attic room, and the thatched Heckling Shop where he worked. Heckling was a well-paid but unpleasant job, involving separating the fibres of the flax plant from the stalk. It was back-breaking, dirty and smelly and 22-year-old Burns loathed it, working from 10 to 12 hours a day, drawing the bundles of flax through the heckles. He suffered bad bouts of depression and it was during this time that he wrote 'Winter, A Dirge' and 'Prayer under the pressure of Violent Anguish':

> *. . . Sure Thou, Almighty, canst not act*
> *From cruelty or wrath!*
> *O, free my weary eyes from tears,*
> *Or close them fast in death!*

Fortunately the Almighty chose an alternative escape: on New Year's Eve, 1781, during a drunken party in the Heckling Shop, Burns' aunt, Mrs Peacock, knocked over a candle which ignited the bundles of dry flax and demolished the shop. Burns remarked with glee: 'The shop burnt to ashes and left me like a true poet, not worth a sixpence'.

There is also an art gallery in the the Vennel with local and international exhibitions.Irvine has splendid facilities for gregarious visitors, including a seaside park and a Magnum Leisure Centre, with swimming pools, water-chutes, an ice rink, squash courts, theatre, cinema, restaurants, bars and cafés.

Kilmarnock

Kilmarnock is about 8 miles (13km) inland, east of Irvine, the centre of industry in this area, with whisky as its most important product. The Johnnie Walker Distillery is world famous—the contents of its bottles certainly are—and they run tours of the premises on weekdays from April to October, except Friday afternoon, Easter week and Kilmarnock Fair Fortnight. The company was founded in 1820 when an Ayrshire man, John Walker, gave up farming and bought a grocery, wine and spirit business in Kilmarnock. Other industries include BMK, the carpet company, whose clients include the Houses of Parliament in London and the Disneyland Hotel in California. There are tours of the mill by special arrangement only.

Kilmarnock has a carnival in May, Burns Day in June, a horse show in July and a Festival of Leisure, in August.

The Burns Monument Museum, in Kay Park, is a red-sandstone tower, recently renovated. Burns was closely associated with the town and his first collection of poems, *The Kilmarnock Poems*, was produced here by John Wilson in 1786, a slim, 35-page volume containing 44 poems. Its success was immediate, rescuing the impoverished poet from emigration to Jamaica.

Kay Park has a boating pond, children's play area, crazy golf and an assault course. The Kilmarnock Bowling Club next door is the oldest in Britain, having just celebrated its 250th anniversary. Robert Burns and his friends used to bowl here, pausing frequently to quench their 'drouth' at the Kay Park Tavern, still there today.

The Dick Institute (open daily except Sun: free), in Elmbank Avenue, has geological and archaeological exhibits and family archives, as well as an art gallery. It is the finest library in Ayrshire and the headquarters for the International Burns Federation.

Dean Castle and Country Park (open daily: free) is in a wooded hollow in Dean Road, off Glasgow Road. The 14th-century fortified keep with a 15th-century palace (adm) contains collections of armour, weapons, old musical instruments and tapestries. There is a banqueting hall, old kitchens, a minstrel's gallery, and a gloomy dungeon.

A number of different events are held in the castle, including ancient warfare demonstrations, a jazz festival and fireworks in November.

The 200-acre country park is always open. As well as formal gardens, there are nature trails, a visitor centre, picnic sites, a Burns Garden, a riding centre and a ranger service. Tours of the park cover bird life, ecology, geology and industrial heritage. A garden is being cultivated by groups of disabled people. There is a children's corner and a deer park.

The Galleon Centre is an indoor leisure complex with swimming pools, ice rink, bowling hall, squash and badminton courts, a curling rink, sauna, fitness room, bar, crêche and lots more.

East of Kilmarnock, **Newmilns** and **Darvel** are renowned for their lace and woollen industries, and in **Stewarton**, to the north, traditional Scottish bonnets are made. Some of the mills have shops.

Dunlop is 3 miles (4.5km) north of Stewarton. Dunlop cheese was first made here in the 17th century, from milk from Dunlop cows—now internationally famous as Ayrshires. When the Milk Marketing Board tried to export Dunlop Cheese to England their customers, influenced by the name, complained it tasted rubbery: it is now called Scottish Cheddar and sells well.

On the way back to the coast from Kilmarnock on the A759, the rugged ruin of 13th-century **Dundonald Castle** is about 3 miles (4.5km) southwest of the outskirts, not open to the public but viewable from the road. Dundonald was inhabited by the Fitzalans, Lord High Stewards, from whom the Stewart line descended. Robert II, the first Stewart king, died here in 1390, as did his son Robert III in 1406.

On the coast again, **Troon**, about 5 miles (8km) south of Irvine, is another seaside resort with sandy beaches and good golf courses. *Troone* means 'nose', referring to the craggy hook of land thrusting out into the sea with a lighthouse on the end. Lady Island, 3 miles (5km) off the point, is a bird sanctuary.

Prestwick was chosen as the site for an international airport because of its reputation for being fog-free. **Bruce's Well** is in a railed enclosure surrounded by lawn and flowers in a residential area behind St Ninian's Church, south of the town and signposted from the Ayr Road. Here, Robert the Bruce, probably in the early stages of the skin disease that killed him, is said to have struck at the ground with his lance in desperation because he was exhausted and parched with thirst. Water gushed from the ground and he was revived.

Ayr and Alloway

Ayr, merging with Prestwick, is the main holiday centre on this coast and seems almost to sparkle with friendliness. It is a spacious town bordering a long sweep of sandy beach, with wide roads and villas set far apart in pleasant gardens. In spring it is a riot of pink and red blossom, carpeted with bluebells and daffodils. There are two theatres, good shops, three golf courses, fishing, and a famous racecourse. There was a settlement here as far back as the 8th century. Early in his struggles for Scotland, Robert the Bruce burnt down 'The Barns of Ayr' (a temporary barracks) with 500 of Edward I's troops inside.

For many, Ayr is of supreme importance as the capital of Burns country. Robert Burns was born on 25 January 1759, in the village of Alloway, now a suburb of Ayr to the south. Although he only lived there for seven years, the atmosphere in Alloway is electric with his presence and it would be difficult to go there and not catch mild Burns fever. Straggling round the River Doon, a cluster of buildings and monuments to the poet echo with his salty humour.

The Burns Heritage Trail, organized by the Scottish Tourist Board, visits all the places of importance relating to Burns' life and work. It is fun to follow the trail with a copy of his poems and a brief summary of his life: *Poems and Songs of Robert Burns* (Fontana), edited and introduced by James Barke is excellent. You can get a copy at **The Land o' Burns Centre**, in Alloway, a first-class visitor centre and the best place from which to start this nostalgic pilgrimage. As well as a book and gift shop, and café, they have an audio-visual show (adm) giving an introduction to the poet's life. Burns is frequently misunderstood; many of his admirers tend to deify him and miss the full flavour of his personality (see Topics).

Burns Cottage and Museum (open daily, except Sun, Nov–March: adm) is a few minutes' walk to the right from the Land o' Burns Centre. The simple white thatched cottage is the 'auld clay biggin' built by the poet's father, William and the place where he was born. Family and animals shared the same roof in this long, low building—a practice that helped to warm the living quarters in winter, if also to make them rather smelly. The museum, adjoining the cottage, contains Burns memorabilia including the family Bible and many original manuscripts. A recent addition is a Burns' Interpretation Gallery, with theme music.

> *. . . And, wow! Tam saw an unco sight!*
> *Warlocks and witches in a dance:*
> *Nae cotillion, brent new frae France,*
> *But hornpipes, jigs, strathspeys, and reels,*
> *Put life and mettle in their heels.*

Alloway Kirk is across the road from the Land o' Burns Centre, scene of Tam o' Shanter's witches' orgy. Tam was making his way home after a monumental bender with his 'trusty, drouthy crony—Souter Johnnie'. Built in 1510, the kirk is a shell now, but you can peep in and see the very *winnock-bunker* 'window seat' where Old Nick sat, in the guise of a shaggy dog 'black and grim and large' and the tombs from which the dead held up lights to illuminate the witches' wild dance. Perhaps the poet was somewhat inebriated himself, when he came here one moonlit night and let the setting work on his imagination. The grave of William Burns, Robert's simple, devout father who died of overwork, lies in the shadow of the walls.

Burns Monument on the left past the kirk, overlooking the River Doon, is a fanciful Grecian-style temple on an Egyptian base, built in 1823. Fluted columns support a round, domed roof surmounted by an urn held up by three dolphins—symbols of Apollo, patron of the Muses. Inside, a simple chamber displays such treasures as Jean Armour's wedding ring, and Highland Mary's bible with a lock of her hair. Books, papers, pictures and documents, including a photocopy of an original manuscript, fill this small museum. A selection of Burns' work includes translations into Russian, made as early as 1800, and Esperanto. The gardens are full of unusual shrubs and trees: tulip trees, rare heathers, cultivated thistles and many more. In a pavilion—the Statue House—life-sized statues of such familiar characters as Tam o' Shanter and Souter Johnnie sit in perpetual companionship, brought in from their original site in the garden, where weather threatened erosion of their soft-stone bodies.

Brig o' Doon, beyond the monument on the right, is a 13th-century, single arched bridge, soaring to a graceful peak, duplicated in reflection to form a frame for river scenery. This is the bridge over which Tam o' Shanter escaped on his Maggie, leaving the witches to their 'hornpipes, jigs, strathspeys and reels' in the kirk.

The Auld Kirk in Ayr is down a wynd off the High Street, on the banks of the river Ayr, and is where Burns was baptized. Through Kirk Port, look for the morbid 'mort-safes' dating from 1655, which were put over freshly filled graves to discourage body-snatchers. Cromwell supplied the funds to build this church, having used the old one as part of a fort he built in Ayr, of which little now remains.

The Auld Brig dates from the 13th century and was Ayr's only bridge until a new one was built in 1788 and replaced in 1877. Burns wrote a poem in which he watched the pretentious new bridge being built, through the contemptuous eyes of the old bridge, prophesying, with uncanny prescience, that the new bridge would not stand the test of time. 'I'll be a brig when ye're a shapeless cairn'. Sure enough, the new bridge had to be replaced after a flood in the 19th century.

Loudoun Hall (open in the summer or by arrangement, ✆ 0292 282109: free) is in Boat Vennel, Ayr, one of the few places around here that has nothing to do with Burns. Among the oldest surviving examples of townhouse architecture in the country, it was built for a rich merchant, in the late 15th century. It was restored, having been condemned as a slum and threatened with a demolition order, and is now a culture centre.

Heading for Mauchline on the B743, turn off to **Tarbolton** after about 6 miles (10km). Burns lived here between the ages of 18 and 24. He joined the local dancing class 'to brush up my manners'. He also helped form the Bachelors Club, a debating society, in a 17th-century thatched house now owned by the National Trust for Scotland (open daily, noon–5pm, 1 April–31 Oct). He was initiated into freemasonry here in 1781.

A somewhat incongruous pillar with a ball on top, in a field in **Failford** just outside Mauchline, is Highland Mary's Monument. Burns is said to have met Mary Campbell on this spot for the last time before she died.

Mauchline, 11 miles (17.5km) northeast of Ayr on the B743, is an important step on the Burns Heritage Trail. A cul-de-sac in the centre of this unremarkable main road town leads to **Burns House Museum** (open daily, Mon–Sat, afternoons; Sun, Easter–Sept: adm). Burns installed his mistress Jean Armour upstairs in this red stone cottage and lived with her for a few months before and after their marriage in 1788. She gave birth to twins, for the second time, a week after they moved in. Furnished in the style of the period it contains many relics of the poet. It was in the kirk above the cottage (open 2–4pm, June–Aug,) that Burns was forced to sit on the 'cutty stool' or stool of repentance, a humiliating punishment inflicted by the Elders of the Kirk because of his 'irregular marriage' with Jean. (It is said he refused to sit and stood defiantly beside the stool.) Four of his children are buried in the kirkyard and a board shows the graves of many of his contemporaries who feature in his poems: Poosie Nansie, Tootie and the Bleth'rin Bitch. **Poosie Nansie's Tavern**, an ale shop and lodging house in Burns' day, is opposite the kirk. The tower on the northern edge of the town is another Burns Monument, erected in his memory in 1895 and recently renovated. There is a tourist information centre on the ground floor (open weekdays, ✆ 0290 551916), an audio-visual display, 'Mauchline in the Time of Burns,' on the first floor, and 'Local Industries Past and Present' above. Good views from the roof are aided by telescopes.

Andrew Kay and Co, Victorian Works (not open to the public), is one of the only curling stone factories in the world. Burns and his brother Gilbert farmed at **Mossgiel**, to the northwest, without much success, from 1784–8.

It is a short walk to **Ballochmyle Viaduct**, a unique structure over the River Ayr. In one curving arch of massive sandstone blocks, it spans 181 feet (55.6m) across the river and is the largest and highest masonry arch railway bridge in Britain. A path along the north side of the river runs through a red sandstone gorge. Bronze Age cup-and-ring markings can be seen on the sandstone a few yards from the path, discovered in 1987.

Anyone interested in James Boswell, Dr Johnson's admirer and biographer, should go to **Auchinleck Boswell Museum**, 5 miles (8km) southeast of Mauchline on the A76.

Formerly a Celtic cell and later a chapel, the museum adjoins the Boswell family mausoleum, and is the burial place of five generations of Boswells, including James. Boswell and Johnson set off from here on their celebrated tour of the Highlands in 1773. (For entry and guided tour, ring 0292 420931/420757 in advance: donations welcome.)

Dunure (always accessible: free) is a gaunt ruin on the edge of the cliff about 4 miles (6km) southwest of Alloway back on the coast road, the A719. Once one of the strongholds of the Kennedy family who ruled Ayrshire and considered themselves above the law, it has a conical dovecote, jagged walls, and a carpark in its precinct. Mary, Queen of Scots came here in 1563, when she toured her kingdom accompanied by a cavalcade of courtiers. It is said that in 1570 the Earl of Cassillis, Chief of the Kennedys, 'roasted' Allan Stewart, Commendator of nearby Crossraguel, in an attempt to persuade him to hand over the abbey lands. This gruesome event took place in the black vault, and so that 'rost suld not burne, but that it might rost in soppe, they spared not flambing with oyle'.

Going south from Dunure on the A719, watch out for **Electric Brae**, an optical illusion that makes your car appear to be going downhill when it is in fact going up.

Culzean Castle and Country Park (castle open daily, 1st April–31 Oct: park open all year: adm) overlooks Culzean Bay less than 4 miles (6km) south of Dunure and is the most visited of all National Trust for Scotland's properties. Pronounced 'Culain', the castle was built on top of the cliff in 1777 by Robert Adam, incorporating an ancient tower that was one of the Kennedy strongholds guarding the coast. Built with an eye to grandeur rather than defence, this sumptuous mansion is full of architectural marvels. There is the Round Drawing Room with a specially woven carpet, an Oval Staircase under a great glass dome, and a profusion of Adam mouldings that make you feel you are encased in Wedgwood china. When Culzean was given over to the National Trust for Scotland in 1945, it was with the condition that an apartment be set aside for anyone whom Scotland might wish to honour. The first tenant for life was General Eisenhower.

The country park was created in 1969, the first in Scotland, with a visitor centre in the Adam farm buildings. An audio-visual show gives information about Culzean and there are exhibitions, a shop and a restaurant. The terraced gardens, with castellated walls enclosing a sunken fountain, are crammed with rare shrubs, palm trees, swathes of riotous colour and wafts of heady scent. There is a camellia house and orangery. The 565-acre grounds include a swan pond, aviary and deer park.

Maybole, a couple of miles east on the A77, has a tolbooth with a 17th-century tower and an important castle in the town centre, now used as offices, once stronghold of the Earls of Cassillis.

Crossraguel Abbey (open daily except Thurs and Fri, Oct–March: adm) is just to the south on the A77. Founded in 1244, it resisted the dissolution of the monasteries until, in 1592, the Reformation took its toll. It is a scattered ruin, giving a good idea of monastic life in those days. The 16th-century turreted gatehouse is particularly well preserved.

Dolphin fountain / Culzean

Kirkoswald is another step on the Burns Trail, 2 miles (3km) on towards the coast on the same road. Burns went to school here and bewailed 'a charming filette who lived next door to the school and overset my Trigonometry and set me off on a tangent from the sphere of my studies.' The poet learnt to drink here with John Davidson, the village cobbler, immortalized as 'Souter Johnnie', in the poem 'Tam o' Shanter'. Tam was Douglas Graham of Shanter Farm, nearby. **Souter Johnnie's Cottage**, owned by the National Trust for Scotland (open daily, April–Sept: adm), was Davidson's home, a thatched cottage with a cobbler's workshop and Burns memorabilia. Life-sized statues of the Souter, Tam, the innkeeper and his wife are in the restored ale-house in the cottage garden. Both Davidson and Graham are buried in the churchyard.

Turnberry is about 3 miles (4.5km) south of Culzean. The castle is a scrap of a ruin on a cliff-top by the lighthouse, which stands on what was the castle's courtyard. Some people claim that Turnberry, rather than Lochmaben, was the birthplace of King Robert the Bruce, and if this is so, he grew up with glorious views to inspire him. The castle was brought into the Bruce family by his mother, Margaret, and Robert's supporters used to meet here, to plot his accession to the throne.

Turnberry is internationally known as a golf centre, with two excellent courses and a huge hotel. It is incredible, looking at the velvet sward today, to think that these golf courses were surfaced with tarmac and used as an airfield during the war, while the hotel was requisitioned as a hospital.

Girvan

About 6 miles (10km) south of Turnberry, is a typical Ayrshire resort, with good sandy beaches, golf courses, a harbour where pleasure-boats mingle with fishing trawlers, and easy access to the Galloway Forest Park to the east and south (see Dumfries and Galloway, p.118). They have a Folk Festival in May, a Civic Week in June, and an Easter Cycle Race. **Knockcushan** is a public garden with an aviary, above the harbour. There used to be a hill fort here, and a stone commemorates the granting of a charter by Robert the Bruce, who administered justice from this hill.

Penkill Castle, 4 miles (6km) east of Girvan on the B734, an imposing 15th-century castle, was the home of the artist and poet William Bell Scott, 1811–90, and a favourite haunt of his fellow Pre-Raphaelites, including William Morris and Dante Gabriel Rossetti, who wrote some of his poems here. The last owner recently auctioned off the whole place including its very fine furniture and contents.

Ailsa Craig

Boats run from Girvan to Ailsa Craig, the 1114-foot (343m) high volcanic lump rearing from the sea, 10 miles (16km) due west and known as Paddy's Milestone because it lies halfway between Glasgow and Belfast. At low tide you can walk its 2 mile (3km) circumference. From the top there are lovely, if rather windy, views over to Arran, Kintyre and the mainland. Ailsa Craig comes from the Gaelic for fairy rock, an incongruous name for the place where miscreant monks were sent to cool off, and where persecuted Catholics took refuge during the Reformation. It is now a bird sanctuary, with gannets and puffins among its avian population: the guano smells quite powerful on a warm day. A special granite used for making curling stones is quarried here.

Carleton Castle (always accessible: free), 5 miles (8km) south of Girvan, was one of the watchtowers built by the Kennedys to defend the coast. A ballad tells of Sir John Cathcart of Carleton, who lived in the castle and pushed seven rich wives over the cliff. When it came to Mary Cullean, his eighth wife, he noticed she was wearing a sumptuous dress. He ordered her to remove it; coyly, she asked him to hide his eyes. When he obliged, she gave him a shove and over he went.

Bennane Head, a few miles further south, gives views as far as Turnberry, Ailsa Craig, the Mull of Kintyre and sometimes even Ireland. On the shore below lies ghastly **Sawney Bean's Cave**. Access is extremely difficult and only the very sure-footed should attempt to visit this macabre spot, the alleged hide-out of Sawney Bean. In the 16th century it is said that a number of wealthy travellers, known to have passed through this area, vanished without trace. Local gossip led the authorities to this cave where they discovered Sawney Bean and his large, incestuously bred family, with an enormous quantity of human bones. Sawney and his ghoulish tribe had been living off the flesh, and the gold, of their unfortunate victims for years. Some accounts of the discovery of the cave describe a gruesome array of 'joints' pickled in brine or hanging from the roof like hams in a farm-house kitchen. Sawney Bean and his family were taken to Edinburgh and executed.

Ballantrae, 3 miles (4.5km) south, was immortalized by Robert Louis Stevenson and twice tricked by literature. Burns wrote a song about the Stinchar valley, which carried the River Stinchar into the sea at Ballantrae, but fastidious editors changed it to: 'Beyond yon hill where Lugar flows', depriving Ballantrae of its rightful acclaim. Then Stevenson was attracted to the name of the place, and used it for his novel *The Master of Ballantrae*, but set the story further south in the Stewartry of Kirkcudbright.

Carrick Forest starts 8 miles (13km) due east of Girvan. Wild, hilly, country, studded with lochs and forests, offers a respite from holiday crowds and fruit machines. **Loch Doon**, on the eastern edge of the forest, marks the border with Dumfries and Galloway. The castle on the southwest shore once stood on an island in the loch. When the Hydroelectric Board raised the level of the water, the ruined castle was dismantled and re-built on its present site. It used to be called Balliol Castle and was owned by King John Balliol.

Paisley

West of Glasgow on the A737, Paisley's suburbs merge with those of the city. This historic town gave its name to an internationally acclaimed design of shawl. Soldiers returning from India at the end of the 18th century brought with them the shawls they had bought in Kashmir. The people of the town adapted these and created the distinctive Paisley design, based on segments of pine cones, which were Kashmiri in origin. The town has its annual festival in May.

Paisley Abbey was founded in 1171 for Cluniac monks and was almost completely destroyed by Edward I. Rebuilt after Bannockburn, its tower collapsed in 1553, wrecking the nave, and it remained in this state for many years. The present restoration, which includes work by Robert Lorimer, is the parish church, a dignified building, austere but serene. **The Barochan Cross** in the abbey is a weathered 10th-century Celtic cross that once stood on a hillock overlooking Port Glasgow. The tombs of several of the Bruces are in the choir, under a stone-vaulted ceiling, and there is a chapel dedicated to St Mirin, a 6th-century saint who was adopted as Paisley's patron saint.

Paisley Museum and Art Gallery (open daily except Sun: free) has a display of at least 500 Paisley shawls with their looms and design patterns. The **Sma' Shot Cottages**, in George Place (open daily May–Sept: free), are traditional 19th-century millworkers' two-storey houses with iron stairways, displaying social conditions in Victorian times. **Coats Observatory** in Oakshaw Street (open daily except Sundays: free) has had a continuous tradition of astronomical observation and meteorological recording since it was built in 1882. The **Lagoon Leisure Centre** has all kinds of swimming attractions.

The Clyde Valley

The A724/72 south from Glasgow follows the Clyde Valley, once renowned for orchards cultivated by the Romans. Although overshadowed by suburban development, there is plenty to see and do.

Coatbridge, not far east of Glasgow, has much to offer. **Summerlee Heritage Trust** (open daily: free) is a major industrial heritage museum, advertised as 'Scotland's noisiest museum'. It contains working trams, steam and belt-driven engines, iron works, a walk-in coal-mine and reconstructed miners' cottages.

The Time Capsule, Monklands, in Coatbridge (open daily: adm), is a leisure centre designed round a swimming pool and ice rink. Themes span a million years with prehistoric monsters, a swamp, volcano, frozen loch, River of Life, waterfall and much else.

Drumpellier Country Park, Monklands, is 500 acres of heath, wood and moor around two lochs. There is a sub-tropical Butterfly House (open daily, April–Oct: adm) with a collection of brilliantly coloured butterflies living naturally among exotic hot-house plants.

About 3 miles (4.5km) east of Coatbridge, **The Weavers' Cottages Museum**, at Wellwynd, Airdrie (open daily except Wed and Sun: adm), is good for social history. Airdrie used to be a prosperous handloom weaving town and the museum occupies two weavers' cottages dating from 1780, illustrating the old 'but 'n' ben': the but for living and the ben for working. The museum's 'but 'n' ben's are rather sanitized versions of the originals when there was no indoor plumbing: waste was chucked outside and rats and bugs thrived.

Bothwell Castle, 7 miles (11km) southeast of the city on the A74 (open daily except Thurs afternoons and Fri, Oct–March: adm), is an impressive red sandstone castle on the banks of the Clyde, once the largest and finest stone castle in Scotland. Dating from the

13th century and rebuilt in the 15th century, it was a stronghold of the powerful Black Douglases.

The David Livingstone Centre, beyond Bothwell, at Blantyre (open daily: adm), was the birthplace of the famous explorer and missionary in 1813. (He died in 1873, looking for the source of the Nile.) The 'single-end' tenement where he was born, and the cotton mill where he worked, give details of his life and the social conditions of the day. There is an Africa Pavilion, built in the shape of a cluster of rural African huts, illustrating African life today.

Hamilton

Hamilton, the former county town of Lanarkshire, is a commercial and administrative centre. Originally called Cadzow, it was here that St Mungo converted King Rederech of Strathclyde to Christianity in 568. David I made the town a Royal Barony in the 12th century and this was superseded by a charter from James II, changing the name to Hamilton in recognition of the great landowning family in the area. In 1570 the town was sacked as reprisal for the Hamiltons' loyalty to Mary, Queen of Scots. Between 1770 and 1870 the population rose by 800 per cent, due to cotton and coal. By 1880, more than half Scotland's coal was produced in this area.

Hamilton Museum in Muir Street (open Mon–Sat: free) dates from the 17th century and was once the Hamilton Arms Coaching Inn. It houses a transport museum, the 18th-century Assembly Room with original plasterwork, a musicians' gallery and a Victorian kitchen. Other displays are devoted to natural history, local industry and history. **The Cameronians Regimental Museum**, in Mote Hill off Muir Street (open daily except Thurs and Sun: free), displays uniforms, medals, banners and documents of this famous Covenanting regiment, now disbanded.

Alexander, 10th Duke of Hamilton, known as Il Magnifico, built the domed **Hamilton Mausoleum** in Strathclyde Park behind the museum, very prominent from the A74. In 1852, he had his ancestors removed from the graveyard of the old Collegiate Church and placed in the mausoleum. He installed an Egyptian sarcophagus on a marble pillar for himself but was worried that it would be too small to contain him. The story is told of his testy order, as he lay dying, to 'double me up; double me up', and it is even said that his feet had to be amputated to get him into the coffin. (The bodies were moved in 1921.) The chapel was never used as a place of worship, owing to a disconcerting echo, lasting 15 seconds. The park has a 200-acre loch, used for watersports, nature trails and a Roman bathhouse.

Calderglen Country Park, near East Kilbride, five miles (8km) west of Hamilton, has gardens and a children's zoo.

About 7 miles (11km) southeast along the A726, **Strathaven Castle** dates from the 15th century and was once home of the Earls of Douglas and later the Dukes of Hamilton. **John Hastie Museum** (open Easter–Nov: free) in Strathaven Park has local history displays and relics from Covenanting times.

Chatelherault

Situated beyond the southern outskirts of Hamilton on the A74 , this hunting lodge (open daily: adm) was built by William Adam in 1732 for the Duke of Hamilton, who also had the title Duke of Chatelherault. The buildings include gardeners' and keepers' bothies, stables, kennels, banqueting hall, the Duke's apartments and kitchens (the headkeeper had the use of the Duke's apartments when he was away). The mansion and part of the 18th-century park around Hamilton Palace, now demolished, were sold to the Scottish Office to help pay death duties. The gardens are being restored to their former grandeur. It is said the oaks in the park were planted by David I. The visitor centre illustrates the 18th-century characters who helped build Chatelherault. The banqueting hall and kitchens are available for hire for weddings, concerts, conferences, etc.

Craignethan Castle

Craignethan Castle (open daily: adm) is about 9 miles (14.5km) southeast of Hamilton on the A72, at Crossford, reached across a green plateau where shaggy cattle roam among gnarled thorn trees. The castle materializes abruptly, on a spur between the deeply eroded beds of the Water of Nethan and the Craignethan Burn. This 16th-century stronghold was destroyed after Mary, Queen of Scots was hounded from her throne—the Hamilton family who owned it had been loyal supporters of her cause. The well-preserved ruin has a keep, passages, basement and well, round an open courtyard. In 1962, excavations unearthed a rare 'caponier'. Buried for nearly 400 years, this dank, stone-roofed vault was built across the floor of a dry moat to protect 'handgunners' defending the castle. It contained bones of cattle, sheep, rabbits and chickens from the hasty meals of those 16th-century gunners.

Although he denied it, Craignethan is believed to have been the inspiration for Tillietudlem Castle, in Walter Scott's novel, *Old Mortality*, home of the heroine Edith. A nearby halt on the long-disused branch railway was called Tillietudlem, in its honour.

Lanark

Lanark is less than 14 miles (22km) southeast of Hamilton, just after the junction of the A72/73, on a plateau above the upper reaches of the Clyde. Seen from afar it still looks like the compact, walled city it once was. The agricultural market centre for the area, it could be just another main-road town, with the A72 carrying heavy traffic through its centre. A closer look invites further exploration.

The main street is so broad that a long central flower bed, studded with chain-linked pillars, divides it into a dual carriageway. It slopes between cheerfully painted houses and shop fronts to the 18th-century parish church standing like a bulwark at the bottom. Don't let impatient drivers behind you prevent you from stopping here to inspect the statue of William Wallace in a canopied niche in the face of the colour-washed church tower. It is an endearing statue: a huge, genial, Father Christmas-like figure who seems embarrassed by his bare, fat knees. He certainly doesn't look like the man who roused the Scots to rebellion in 1297. The statue was presented to the town in 1822 by its sculptor, Robert Forrest, who, it is said, was self-taught. This is easy to believe. William Wallace lived in

Lanark, and when the English murdered his wife (or mistress) Marion Bradfute, it was here that he struck the first blow for Scottish independence. Every June Lanark celebrates Lanimer Day, which coincides with the Riding of the Marches.

New Lanark

It would be easy to dash through Lanark and miss New Lanark, a delightful backwater a mile (1.5km) to the south. Stop at the top, as the narrow road takes a final hairpin bend before descending into New Lanark, and admire the view down over the village to the distant Falls of Clyde. A mist of spray rises from the trees above a glint of foaming water and if the sun is shining and it happens to be autumn, there are few more breath-catching views in this part of Scotland. New Lanark was built in 1784 as a model cotton manufacturing village by a rich industrialist, David Dale and his partner Richard Arkwright. Dale's son-in-law, Robert Owen, became manager of the estate in 1800 and instituted some radical innovations, including the founding of the first infant school in Britain. Owen's reforms for better working conditions and 'villages of unity' were the forerunners of today's co-operative societies.

Today, New Lanark is a monument to those days of reform. (Visitors centre open daily: adm.) The old workers' houses have been brought back to life, austere but not ugly, uncluttered by architectural adornment, rising tall and plain from the street, some with outside stairways, overlooking the river. They are now much in demand as middle-class homes. The bell that summoned the people to work or to pray still hangs high in its belfry. There are exhibitions illustrating the social history of this classic industrial village. Particularly popular is the **Annie McLeod Experience**, in which the spirit of the 10-year-old mill girl takes you on a tour of the past with excellent special effects. There is also a reconstructed village shop and the Edinburgh Woollen Mill's largest store in Scotland.

Falls of Clyde Nature Reserve can be reached on foot from the far end of New Lanark. A fenced path follows the Clyde a couple of miles upstream past the Falls of Corra Linn to those of Bonnington Linn. The river tumbles over black slabs of granite, overhung by pines, oaks and birches, spray rising like smoke. This stretch of the river, known as the Falls of Clyde and beloved of many artists, runs through Corehouse Nature Reserve. On the way is **Wallace's Tower**, or Corra Castle, too dangerous to enter but stirring to the imagination. It clings to a rock pinnacle high above Corra Linn, its walls rising directly from the edge of the sheer cliff. Although this reach of the Clyde is harnessed to serve the hydro-electric power stations and is thus robbed of much of its splendour, enough water remains to provide salmon with access to their spawning grounds up-river and to give dramatic effects as it pours over gigantic layered slabs of granite. Corra Linn drops 86 feet (22m) in a series of steps, to a dark still lagoon below, set in an amphitheatre of rock, and hung with damp vegetation and precariously rooted trees. **Bonnington Linn** is about a mile further on, with two branches of the river descending round a rock island.

Leadhills

Leadhills is 18 miles (29km) due south of Lanark as the crow flies. A pink road straggles over humpbacked bridges between drystone walls with views across farmland and smooth-turfed hills. Forest and pasture create a patchwork, green and brown and sepia, dotted with rural cottages, rising to desolate moor and peat bogs where the farms are linked by single telephone wires. High on this moorland, Leadhills is second only to nearby Wanlockhead (p.115), as Scotland's highest village. In the small, windswept cemetery above the village lie the remains of John Taylor who died at the age of 137, having worked for more than 100 years in the lead mills.

Allan Ramsay, the 17th-century poet, was born here, surrounded by hills alive with the ghosts of Covenanters who used their shelter for holding conventicles.

Biggar

Biggar, 10 miles (16km) southeast of Lanark on the A72, close to the Borders Region, is a typical lowland market town, the main road running through its centre widening to form a market place. **Cadgers Brig** at the bottom of the town is the bridge where William Wallace is said to have crossed the burn dressed as a *cadger* (pedlar), on a spying mission. The bridge is more likely to have been named after the cadgers who crossed it on market days. Biggar has several good museums.

Moat Park Heritage Centre, in the town centre (open daily: adm), is in a former church, adapted to show the history of the Upper Clyde and Tweed Valleys, from the days of volcanoes and glaciers to the present. Among a collection of embroidery is the largest known patchwork quilt from the mid-19th century.

The Gladstone Court Museum (open daily, Easter–31 Oct: adm) is a reproduction of a Victorian street complete with grocer, photographer, dressmaker, bank, school, library, ironmonger, chemist, china merchant, etc.

Greenhill Covenanters House at Burn Braes (open Easter, and daily, mid-May–mid-Oct: adm), is a 17th-century farmhouse with strong Covenanting connections. It contains furniture and relics from those times, as well as a collection of dolls, rare breeds of animals and poultry and an audio-visual programme.

Biggar also has the oldest surviving rural gasworks in Britain, built in 1839 and now a museum, open in July and August. **Biggar Puppet Theatre** (open daily except Tues, March–mid-Jan: adm) is a miniature Victorian puppet theatre. There are guided tours, an exhibition, tearoom and outdoor Victorian games.

Tinto Hill, 2320 feet (714m), 6 miles (9km) southwest of Biggar, west of the A73, dominates the landscape for miles. It is a long but not arduous climb through scree and heather and the views from the top are terrific. Keen eyes on a clear day will see 18 counties plus peaks in Cumberland, the tip of Ireland, the Bass Rock, Ailsa Craig, Arran and Jura. Tinto is wrapped in legend: William Wallace camped on the hill with his army in the 13th century, and there is a depression in a boulder at the top called, somewhat doubtfully, **Wallace's Thumbmark**. Tinto is derived from the Gaelic *teinteach* (place of fire) hinting that it may have been one of the sites for the Beltane fire rites, sometimes connected with human sacrifice.

expensive

Gleddoch House Hotel, Langbank, ℂ 047 554 711, is a converted family mansion in 250 acres overlooking the Clyde and Loch Lomond Hills and is without doubt the pick of the bunch. It contains many of the original furnishings and pictures which give it the atmosphere of a private country house. Guests automatically become members of The Gleddoch Club, with free use of the 18-hole golf course, squash courts, snooker room and sauna. There is also riding. The food is renowned, the service excellent, and dogs are allowed in the bedrooms.

Manor Park Hotel, Skelmorlie, ℂ 0475 520832, stands on a hill overlooking magnificent views of gardens, hills and sea lochs on the Clyde coast. It is comfortable, the food and service are good and there are even peacocks in the grounds.

Chapeltoun House Hotel at Stewarton, 3 miles (4.5km) off the A77 on the B769, ℂ 0560 82696, was built in 1900 as a family house. There are 20 acres of garden with views across Ayrshire countryside. Friendly, efficient staff and excellent food and wine.

Golfers have to say a prayer to their bank manager and go to **Turnberry Hotel**, ℂ 0655 31000 (single B&B a mere £165). This vast golfing mecca on the coast has everything the punter could want.

Modest in comparison, **Montgreenan Mansion House Hotel**, Kilwinning, ℂ 0294 57733, is a country house in 45 acres near a championship golf course. For those who like to know exactly what they are going to, the **Hospitality Inn** at Irvine, ℂ 0294 74272, is predictable. Ultra-modern outside, the interior has arches and rattan, palms and bold carpets and a stifling heating system. Some of the suites open on to a tropical lagoon with lush jungle, rocks, waterfalls, bridges and hot air.

inexpensive

Elderslie Hotel, John Street, Largs, ℂ 0475 086460, looks across to Cumbrae and Arran, and is nicely old fashioned. Also with a good atmosphere, **Burns Monument Hotel**, Alloway, ℂ 0292 42466, is by the River Doon, opposite Burns Monument, its floodlit garden running back to the Brig o' Doon. **Finlayson Arms Hotel**, Coylton, ℂ 0292 570298, is a country pub/hotel. **Kings Arms Hotel**, Dalrymple Street, in the middle of Girvan, ℂ 0465 3322, is where John Keats wrote 'A Tribute to Ailsa Craig' in the summer of 1818, three years before his death. Other bargains include **Jolly Shepherd Hotel**, Barr, near Girvan, ℂ 0465 86 233, a friendly place with five bedrooms. **Kings Arms**, also in Barr, ℂ 046 586 230, is much the same, a small, unpretentious, whitewashed inn. Burns fans should go to **Poosie Nansies Inn**, in Mauchline, ℂ 0290 50316. Echoing with memories, if not with mod cons, it is dirt cheap. Also in Mauchline, **Loudoun Arms**, ℂ 0290 51011, is another bargain: generous breakfasts are served by an easy-going Irish host in an upstairs room full of Burns murals.

In south Strathkelvin, just across the Clyde, there are mainly uninspiring dormitory towns. But the region does include the Campsie Fells with attractive villages, a few parks and gardens, a scrap of the Antonine Wall on Bar Hill at Twechar, and the Forth and Clyde Canal. Take the Erskine Toll Bridge over the river, off the M8, a magnificent sweep of modern engineering replacing a tiny cable-ferry.

The Heatherbank Museum of Social Work (open all year by appointment, ✆ 041 956 2687: free) is about 4 miles (6km) northeast of the bridge on the A809. It is the only museum of its kind in the world, with over 2500 slides of life in the 19th and early 20th centuries and a 5000-volume reference library.

Some say St Patrick was born at **Kilpatrick** a couple of miles west of the Erskine Bridge— a claim made by many other places on this coast down as far as Cumbria. Certainly he was captured near here in the 4th century and deported to Ireland as a slave. The Kilpatrick Hills to the north are attractive moorland with rivers and reservoirs.

Dumbarton

Dumbarton is an industrial town, about 3 miles (4.5km) west of the Erskine Bridge. Whisky has taken over in importance from the shipbuilding that once flourished on the waterfront. The famous clipper *Cutty Sark* was built in Dumbarton in 1869, named after the 'short shirts' seen by Tam o' Shanter when he watched the witches' orgy.

Dumbarton Castle (open daily: adm) stands high in a cleft in Dumbarton Rock over-looking the Clyde, a lump of volcanic basalt, site of a fortress since prehistoric times. The name is derived from Dun Bretane (Hill of the Britons). From about the 5th century, this fortress rock was the centre of the kingdom of Strathclyde. It was a royal castle in the Middle Ages, later a barracks and is now a museum. Mary, Queen of Scots sailed to France from here in 1548, aged five.

A wall protects the front, shaped like the prow of a ship, with turret and guns. Up the steps, Wallace's Gatehouse is where William Wallace was imprisoned before being taken to his trial and barbaric execution in London in 1305. It was Sir John Monteith, Governor of Dumbarton Castle at the time, who finally betrayed Wallace, that brave rebel who struck such a memorable blow for Scottish independence.

The town of Dumbarton is modern, but there are a few old buildings , particularly 'Greit House', built in 1623, once the home of the Duke of Argyll and the tower arch of the collegiate church of St Mary, founded by the Duchess of Albany in 1454.

The Scottish Maritime Museum's **Denny Experiment Tank** is in Castle Street (open all year, Mon–Sat: adm), it is the oldest surviving experimental tank in the world, showing how wax and wooden scale models were used to test for such things as stability and resistance. It was the first tank of its kind, and was built in 1882 by William Denny and used for over 100 years.

Oh, ye'll take the high road,
An' I'll take the low road,
An' I'll be in Scotland afore ye,
But me an' my true love will never meet again
On the bonnie, bonnie banks o' Loch Lomond.

The song 'Loch Lomond' was composed in Carlisle jail by Donald MacDonald of Keppoch, a Jacobite awaiting a trial that ended in brutal death after Culloden. The English were capricious in their distribution of justice: some prisoners were arbitrarily sent to the gallows, others were set free and told to walk home. MacDonald, fairly sure of his fate, wrote that his spirit would get back to Scotland on the low road of death faster than his living companions on the high road.

There is a choice of two routes north from Dumbarton, one being West Loch Lomondside on the A82. (The boundary with Central Region goes up the middle of the loch.) A new road gives views across the loch with its islands and anchorages, to the hills on the far side. This is particularly beautiful in the early morning when there is little traffic and mist clings to the glassy water as the sun rises over Ben Lomond. Bluebells carpet the ground under oak woods. The loch is 24 miles (38.5km) from north to south, its southern end as much as 5 miles (8km) wide, narrowing to a long, thin neck in the north. The largest inland loch in Scotland, Loch Lomond is one of the most beautiful, though being so accessible it is also one of the most popular.

Balloch, at the south end of the loch, is a holiday resort with a marina. **Balloch Castle Country Park** (open daily: free; visitor centre open Easter–Sept) is 200 acres of woodland, park and gardens on the shore of Loch Lomond). You can drive up the east side of the loch as far as Balmaha from where you can climb Ben Lomond.

Luss on the west side is a popular village with a kilt shop. All this part of the country is owned by the Colquhoun family, whose former home Rossdhu is being converted into a country club with golf courses.

A number of cruise boats operate on the loch. The small islands scattered over the south end are steeped in history. **Inch Cailleach** (Island of the Old Women) was the burial place of the fierce MacGregor clan. It belongs to Scottish Natural Heritage and has trails and woodland paths. Ruined **Lennox Castle**, on Inch Murrin (Isle of Spears), was where the Duchess of Albany retired, after James I slaughtered her husband, sons and father in 1425 (not without cause, see History, pp.35–6).

There are plenty of places to launch small boats and a number of boats for hire from the many marinas, holiday parks and water-sport centres lining the shore.

Helensburgh

The other route north from Dumbarton is the A814 via Helensburgh and Loch Long. This route is narrow and twisting in some parts, clinging to the water most of the way and keeping company with the railway.

Helensburgh, at the mouth of the Gare Loch, 8 miles (13km) northwest of Dumbarton, is a resort built on a grid of wide streets, the town sloping up from the Clyde. Ferries cross the river to Gourock and pleasure cruises run from the pier. This is sailing territory, the water usually speckled with craft of all sizes. There are good shops, plenty of places to stay and lovely views across the Clyde. Helensburgh was the birthplace of John Logie Baird, one of the inventors of television.

The Hill House, overlooking the Clyde in Upper Colquhoun Street (open daily: adm), was designed by Charles Rennie Mackintosh (see pp.249–50) for the publisher W. W. Blackie in 1902 and is his finest domestic work, demonstrating his flair for simplicity of line. Owned by the National Trust for Scotland, its gardens are being restored to Mackintosh's original design and an audio-visual programme describes his life.

Glen Fruin, within easy walking distance of Helensburgh, is surrounded by beauty and solitude, serenaded by the clatter of streams flowing down from the hills. Climb **Ben Chaorach** and look down into the glen. You may hear the echo of war cries and pleadings for mercy. In 1603 there was a battle between the Colquhouns (pronounced Ka'hoon) and the MacGregors, arising from boundary disputes and accusations of cattle pilfering. The MacGregors slew not only the Colquhoun men, and their families who had been shut away in a barn for safety, but also a party of schoolboys who had been taken to watch the fun. The clan was proscribed in punishment.

Rhu, a mile (1.5km) west of Helensburgh, is another boating mecca, with woodland and lovely shrubs at **Glenarn Gardens** (open Mar–June: adm).

The two routes meet at Tarbet where the A82 goes north past the hulk of **Ben Vorlich** into Central Region. The Strathclyde route goes west to the Cowal Peninsula, through Glen Croe on the A83.

Where to Stay

expensive

Buchanan Highland Hotel in Drymen, © 0360 60588, is an excellent place with good food.

moderate

Ardlui Hotel, © 03014 243, is a small country hotel on the northern tip of Loch Lomond, with moorings. It is a delightful, friendly place. **The Inverbeg Inn** at Luss, © 0436 86678, also overlooks Loch Lomond and runs a fleet of self-drive motor cruisers, with sleeping accommodation for from two to 12 people. Prices on request. **Rosslea Hall Hotel**, Rhu, © 0436 820684, overlooks the Gare Loch and the Firth of Clyde. It has good food and wine, pony trekking from the hotel and a free dram on arrival. **Duck Bay Hotel and Marina** on Loch Lomond, © 0389 52789, is a lively spot for boating people. **Salmon Leap Inn** in Drymen, dating from 1759, is a lively place with good bar meals.

inexpensive

Tarbet Hotel, © 03012 228, is a Scottish baronial-style mansion overlooking Loch Lomond, with a comfortable modern interior, friendly staff and reasonable food. What it lacks in elegance is made up for by the position. The **Lomond Youth Club** on Loch Lomond is a particularly grand youth hostel.

The Cowal Peninsula

The Cowal Peninsula attracts many climbers, sailors and holidaymakers in the summer. The drive west from Tarbet through Glen Croe on the A83 is spectacular. The distinctive shape of **The Cobbler**, 2891 feet (890m), looms to the north of the road as it twists and climbs up the shoulder of **Beinn Ime** to **The Rest and Be Thankful**—which speaks for itself. The views from the car park here are worth stopping for. A stone commemorates the completion of this military road in 1750, part of a network constructed to try to keep order in the Highlands after the Jacobite risings. Known as the **Arrochar Alps**, the hills round here offer excellent climbing for experts. Apart from The Cobbler and Beinn Ime, there are Beinn Narnain, Ben Vane and Ben Vorlich marching away to the northeast—all 'Munros' over 3000 feet (923m).

The Cowal Peninsula stretches to the south, part of Argyll's misshapen lobster claw, washed on either side by Loch Long and Loch Fyne. **Carrick Castle** is a 14th-century ruin on a promontory in fjord-like Loch Goil. The Glen Mhoir approach down the B828 from The Rest and Be Thankful is dramatic, the road dropping from 1000 feet (308m) to sea level in 3 miles (4.5km). This was where the Argylls kept their documents and their prisoners. A remote enough place in those days, the great shell of the keep is still impressive, even with its rash of water-sport enthusiasts nearby. The road ends here but you can just see where the loch joins up with Loch Long, to the southeast. The area within the triangle formed by The Rest and Be Thankful, Loch Long and Loch Goil is known as **Argyll's Bowling Green**. A more unlikely name would be hard to find. Measuring 8 miles by 4, (13 by 6.5km), it includes 10 major summits and is only accessible on foot. Fantastic views can be had from the tops of the hill; a jigsaw of moor and hill, each irregular piece linked by a gleaming sliver of water.

The motorist must retrack to where the road branches, 3 miles (4.5km) north of Lochgoilhead.

The award-winning **European Sheep and Wool Centre**, at Lochgoilhead (open daily, Apr–Oct: adm), is the first of its kind in Europe. There are 19 different breeds of sheep, demonstrations of shearing and a shepherd and his dog working the sheep (three shows daily, at 11am, 1pm and 3pm: Sat by prior arrangement only). There is a shop and a coffee shop. Adjacent is **Drimsynie Leisure Complex**, with a heated swimming pool, jacuzzi, sauna, 9-hole golf course and a restaurant. In the winter (Nov–Mar), Drimsynie is converted into a four-lane **curling rink**.

The B839 then runs northwest through **Hell's Glen**, a steep hanging valley overlooking Loch Fyne at its far end.

Loch Fyne is renowned for sea fishing and oysters. A string of villages line the loch: Cairndow, St Catherines and Strachur. Much of this area is covered by the Argyll Forest Park.

From Strachur, the A815 runs south down forest-fringed Loch Eck. Branch left at the Whistlefield Hotel and take the long way round, down Glen Finart—more lovely views— to **Ardentinny**, a picturesque village with a sandy beach on Loch Long. The road hugs the shore to Strone Point and back northwest along Holy Loch. The loch is said to have been so named when a ship, carrying earth from the Holy Land intended as foundations for Glasgow Cathedral, foundered in a storm as it tried to get round the corner into the sheltered Clyde and finished up in this appendix of the river.

Younger Botanic Garden (open daily, April–Oct: adm) is barely 2 miles (3km) north of the head of the loch. In May and June the gardens blaze with yellow, orange, flame and crimson azaleas, and rhododendrons ranging from white to deep maroon. There is a splendid avenue of sequoias (giant Californian Wellingtonias).

Dunoon and Around

Dunoon is 5 miles (8km) south of the junction with the A815 and is the chief resort on the Cowal Peninsula. It was just a village until early in the 19th century, when rich merchants built villas and developed it into a resort. The long, low sprawl of the town, washed by the Firth of Clyde, is backed by a crescent of blue-green tree-covered hills. Two ferry companies operate a service across the Clyde between Gourock and Dunoon—a 20-minute crossing. Dunoon is an ideal holiday centre on the threshold of some of the finest walking and climbing country. It is also at the heart of idyllic sailing water. For those who prefer to let someone else take the helm, there are cruises on the Firth of Clyde in the summer.

The Cowal Highland Gathering is one of the town's highlights, on the last Friday and Saturday in August. Over 150 pipe bands compete, drawing huge crowds. It also stages World Highland Dancing Championships.

Dunoon Castle, of which only a trace remains, dates from the 13th century. It was built on the site of an earlier fort, with a colourful history that kept it bouncing back and forth between English and Scottish hands like so many of the strongholds of Scotland. Edward I took it; Robert the Bruce re-took it; then Edward Balliol, who was ousted by Robert II. In 1471 the Earls of Argyll were made Honorary Keepers by James III, on condition they paid the Crown a fee of a red rose, whenever demanded. When Queen Elizabeth II visited Dunoon in 1958, she was presented with a red rose without having to demand it.

An attractive drive south from Dunoon takes you to Toward Point with a lighthouse on the tip. The track beyond goes only halfway up the east side of Loch Striven.

Lazaretto Point, north of Dunoon on the A815, beyond Hunter's Quay, was the quarantine station for servicemen fighting in the Napoleonic Wars.

To explore the rest of the peninsula take the B836 west from the head of Holy Loch to the head of Loch Striven and on to the A886. Here turn left and take the new road down the east side of Loch Riddon to Colintraive, with views across to Tighnabruaich and the Kyles of Bute. A car ferry runs from Colintraive to Bute (see pp.221–3). The new road then peters out but it is possible to get on down to Strone Point and some way up the west shore of Loch Striven.

Back up to the head of Loch Riddon on the A886, take the A8003 down the west side, high above the Kyles of Bute with views in all directions. **Tighnabruaich** (house on the hill) and **Kames** are two popular resorts looking across the Kyles to Bute. A B road runs on down to Ardlamont Point, the most southern tip of the Cowal Peninsula, rising to 205 feet (63m). The waters of Loch Fyne, Kyles of Bute, Sound of Bute and Kilbrannan Sound meet at the foot of the headland.

From Ardlamont, go north about 4 miles (6km) to Millhouse and then west a couple of miles to **Portavadie**. With deep water off-shore, this area was chosen as an oil-platform construction site and £14 million was spent on ground preparation. An enormous dry dock was built. But no one seemed to want any oil-platforms and the place stood unused. Eventually, the sea-wall was breached, the dock flooded and the £14 million washed away.

Back to Millhouse, take the B8000 north, through Kilfinan, a hamlet where the hotel has 16th-century vaults and the church stands on a Celtic site. **Otter Ferry**, 3 miles (4.5km) to the north, takes its name from the Gaelic *oitir* (a sandbank): yachtsmen beware. The sandbank sticks out more than a mile into Loch Fyne, prominent at low tide but easy to trip up on when submerged by the flood tide. The Norsemen who fought in the Battle of Glendaruel in 1100 beached their longships side by side on the sand bar, clambered ashore and marched over the pass into Glendaruel 5 miles (8km) to the east. They were slaughtered by the Scots, who threw their bodies into the river: *ruel* is a corruption of the Gaelic for 'blood flowed'.

Where to Stay and Eating Out

expensive

Creggans Inn, Strachur, on the shores of Loch Fyne, ✆ 0369 86 279 is well known for excellence in both food and ambience. They have a very good bar here.

moderate

Ardfillayne Hotel, West Bay, Dunoon, ✆ 0369 2267, looks over the Firth of Clyde and has a good reputation for service, comfort and food. **Hafton Country Club, Hotel and Lodges**, Hunter's Quay, ✆ 0369 6205, is an excellent base for a family holiday, with both baronial-style hotel accommodation and self-catering chalets. Prices include club membership for all the facilities of this lochside complex: swimming pool, snooker and games room, video cinema and video games, table tennis, tennis, putting. For an extra fee, golfers get unlimited play over Cowal Golf Course.

Ardentinny Hotel, © 0369 81 209/275, is on Loch Long, surrounded by rhododendrons. Boats can be hired from the hotel and package holidays include free ferry tickets, and entry to the Younger Botanic Garden and Inveraray Castle. The food is first class.

Kilfinan Hotel is an old coaching inn in a rural hamlet near Loch Fyne. Whitewashed, with 16th-century vaults, it has excellent food and log fires. Among the many hotels overlooking the scenic Kyles of Bute, try **Kames Hotel**, © 0700 811489, on the seafront in Kames. It is comfortable, serves reasonable food and has a friendly atmosphere.

inexpensive

In Dunoon, **Esplanade Hotel**, © 0369 4070, overlooks the traffic-free West Bay Promenade, a few minutes' walk from the pier. This is a jovial hotel for the gregarious. **Abbeyhill Hotel,** Dhailling Road, © 0369 2204, has a good view overlooking East Bay Promenade. It is comfortable and well run. **Rosscairn Hotel**, Hunter Street, © 0369 4344, is in a quiet, residential area next to the 18-hole Cowal Golf Club, and offers free golf in March, April and October. **Drimsynie House Hotel and Leisure Complex**, Lochgoilhead, © 03013 247/284, is a Victorian mansion, with mock battlements and turrets. It stands in wooded grounds overlooking Loch Goil with a 9-hole golf course, heated swimming pool and jacuzzi, good food and a pool room.

Mid-Argyll: Knapdale and Kintyre

This is walking country where spectacular views unfold at every turn and the best places are inaccessible except on foot.

Loch Fyne, a long narrow arm of the sea, washes the western shore of the Cowal Peninsula. It seems to eat its way into the Highland landscape—a mixture of hill and forest, in some parts rising steeply from the water, in others rolling back in sweeps of farmland. At the head of the loch, near Cairndow, look for the long, white-washed 'Loch Fyne Oyster Bar'—a really excellent restaurant in an old farm building. A shop sells fresh and smoked sea food including oysters from the local oyster beds, mussels, salmon and scampi; also fresh and smoked venison, special cheeses, home-baked bread, sauces, etc. It isn't cheap but it's well worth a visit, even if just for the seafood chowder.

At the head of Loch Shira, an appendix off the northwest corner of Loch Fyne, a track leads north up remote Glen Shira to a ruined cottage where Rob Roy hid for some time during one of his adventures.

Inveraray

Inveraray stands on the northwest shore of Loch Fyne, a pretty 18th-century town with a gracious air. It is curiously un-Scottish, built in a T-plan with the road north passing through an archway and the parish church on a mound, dividing the Main Street. Inveraray was once a small fishing village, always a domain of the Campbells of Argyll. It was sacked by Montrose in 1644. The present town was the creation of the third Duke of Argyll, in 1743, employing Roger Morris and William Adam, both of whom died before the work was finished. John Adam, son of William, completed the job with the help of Robert Mylne.

Inveraray Castle (open daily except Fri, Easter–mid-Oct; open Fri also, July–Aug: adm) was built on the site of a 15th-century fortress, but the present castle dates from 1770, when the town was being built. The castle is a square pile with round towers topped by conical roofs at the four corners, added in 1878. Designed by Roger Morris, with help from William Morris who was Clerk of Works, and decorated by Robert Mylne, the castle may have been based on a sketch by Vanbrugh and is imposing rather than beautiful. The grounds are on the site of the original village, demolished when the castle was built.

A bad fire in 1975 destroyed the roof and top floor but these have been rebuilt. Magnificently decorated rooms provide perfect settings for paintings, tapestries, Oriental and European porcelain, 18th-century furniture and many other treasures. Among the paintings are portraits by Kneller, Raeburn, Hoppner, Gainsborough, Batoni, and Ramsay. The grounds, with old trees framing vistas over Loch Fyne, are reminiscent of an 18th-century painting. A folly overlooks Inveraray from a steep, wooded hilltop.

Inveraray Bell Tower, in the Episcopalian church (open daily, early May–late Sept: adm), was established in this century by the 10th Duke of Argyll, its peal of 10 bells being rung in memory of the Campbells who died in the First World War. The 126-foot (39m) granite tower gives views over Loch Fyne and Inveraray though it is rather an eyesore within the context of the rest of this elegant town.

Inveraray Jail (open daily: adm), in Church Square, comprises the Old Prison with ghastly cells where men, women, children and lunatics were crammed, complete with sound effects and smells; the New Prison (19th-century), with improved conditions; the courtroom as it was in 1825 when men were deported to Australia for minor crimes; and many exhibitions, including one on Crime and Punishment with details of medieval punishment—hanging, branding, tongue-boring and burning. You can also see the open-air cages called airing yards where prisoners took exercise. There is a souvenir shop.

Argyll Wildlife Park, 2 miles (3km) south of Inveraray (open daily: adm), is a 60-acre site with European wildfowl, a large owl collection and such unlikely residents as wallabies, which hop about the forest tracks. Wildcats, badgers, Highland foxes, deer, wild goats, soay sheep and many other species can be seen.

Auchindrain Museum (open daily, Easter–30 Sept; closed Sat, June, July and Aug: adm), 6 miles (9.5km) south of Inveraray, is an old West Highland township with

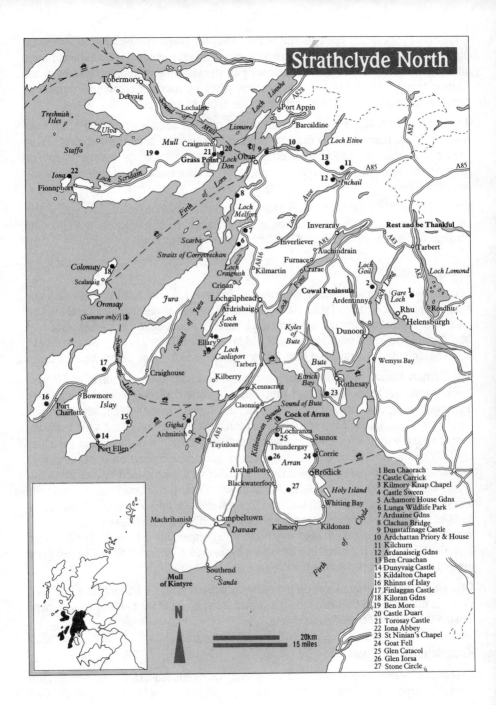

Strathclyde North

Tobermory
Dervaig
Lochaline
Treshnish Isles
Ulva
Staffa
Mull
Craignure
19
21
20
Grass Point
Loch Don
Oban
22
Iona
Loch Scridain
Fionnphort
8
Loch Melfort
7
6
Scarba
Straits of Corryvreckan
Colonsay
18
Scalasaig
Oronsay
(Summer only)
Jura
Crinan
Lochgilphead
Ardrishaig
Loch Sween
Ellary
3
17
Craighouse
Loch Caolisport
Tarbert
Kilberry
Kennacraig
16
Port Charlotte
Bowmore
Islay
15
5
Gigha
Ardminish
14
Port Ellen
Tayinloan
Claonaig
Sound of Bute
Cock of Arran
25
Lochranza
Sannox
Thundergay
26
24
Corrie
Arran
Auchgallon
Brodick
Blackwaterfoot
27
Holy Island
Whiting Bay
Machrihanish
Campbeltown
Davaar
Kilmory
Kildonan
Mull of Kintyre
Southend
Sanda

Port Appin
Barcaldine
Lismore
Loch Etive
10
13
11
A85
12
Inchail
Loch Awe
Loch Fyne
Inveraray
Rest and be Thankful
Inverliever
Auchindrain
Tarbert
Furnace
Crarae
Loch Goil
Loch Long
Loch Lomond
Kilmartin
Cowal Peninsula
2
Gare Loch
1
Ardentinny
Rhu
Rosdhu
Helensburgh
Kyles of Bute
Dunoon
Bute
Wemyss Bay
Etrick Bay
Rothesay
23

N

20km
15 miles

1 Ben Chaorach
2 Castle Carrick
3 Kilmory Knap Chapel
4 Castle Sween
5 Achamore House Gdns
6 Lunga Wildlife Park
7 Arduaine Gdns
8 Clachan Bridge
9 Dunstaffnage Castle
10 Ardchattan Priory & House
11 Kilchurn
12 Ardanaiseig Gdns
13 Ben Cruachan
14 Dunyvaig Castle
15 Kildalton Chapel
16 Rhinns of Islay
17 Finlaggan Castle
18 Kiloran Gdns
19 Ben More
20 Castle Duart
21 Torosay Castle
22 Iona Abbey
23 St Ninian's Chapel
24 Goat Fell
25 Glen Catacol
26 Glen Iorsa
27 Stone Circle

18th- and 19th-century cottages and outbuildings furnished in their original styles. On display are parlours, kitchens with box beds, byres, barns, a smiddy, and all the old utensils. There are demonstrations of the runrig or strip-farming methods prevalent in the Highlands until the end of the 18th century, when villages had communal tenancy of farmland and paid their rent jointly, in this case to the Argylls.

The name of **Furnace**, a couple of miles further on, is an unhappy reminder of the troubled times that reigned during the 18th century. It is so called from the charcoal-burning smelting furnace, established here to utilize trees felled by order of the Hanoverian government, so that rebel Highlanders still clinging to the Jacobite cause would have less cover in which to hide.

Crarae Woodland Garden (open daily: adm), 3 miles (4.5km) south, has azaleas and rhododendrons in season. Walks cross and re-cross a burn as it cascades over falls and through a gorge among a variety of conifers, hardwoods and shrubs.

Lochgilphead

Lochgilphead, 24 miles (38km) southwest of Inveraray, at the head of Loch Gilp and another appendix off Loch Fyne, is a holiday resort as well as the shopping centre for the area, with good shops around the wide main street that was once the market place. The Mid Argyll Show takes place in Lochgilphead in August. **Kilmory**, once a country house, is the headquarters of Argyll and Bute District Council and the grounds are a public park.

The **Crinan Canal** cuts through from Ardrishaig on Loch Gilp to Crinan on the west coast. It was built at the end of the 18th century, and stretches for 9 miles (14.5km), with 15 locks, through the top of the Kintyre Peninsula. It was designed to cut out the treacherous waters around the Mull of Kintyre that inhibited trade between the west coast and Glasgow, and was much used at first by commercial puffers, fishing boats and passenger craft. With the decline of the herring industry and the introduction of rail and road networks, it lost most of its commercial traffic and is now mainly used by pleasure boats, saving the sailor 130 miles (208km). Going down the canal in a small boat is a peaceful way of passing a fine day, though you have to work the lock gates yourself, straining at the handles that wind up the sluices in the massive wooden gates, and leaning on the great timber arms that swing them open when the water either side is level. In 1847, Queen Victoria sailed down the canal in a decorated barge drawn by horses ridden by postilions dressed in scarlet, on her way to the Western Isles.

Crinan is a hamlet around a sheltered harbour, popular with sailors, with the tidal gate between the canal and the open sea. The Crinan Hotel is one of the best in Scotland, overlooking the island-speckled Sound of Jura.

Knapdale

Knapdale is nearly an island. It runs south from Lochgilphead like a clenched fist, just managing to hang on to the long arm of Kintyre. This part of the west coast, on the Gulf Stream, is unbelievably lush in the summer. Autumn is glorious; a wonderful range of colours shades the hills. So too is spring, when rhododendrons and azaleas are in bloom against the soft new green and the sparkle of water. Perhaps the best time of all, though, is November, when a light dusting of snow covers the last autumn leaves, and the water shows steel-grey against the hills etched in white. It is possible to drive right round the coast from Lochgilphead and across the middle from Inverneil to Achahoish. Along the coast each mile opens up a fresh view to the islands of Jura and Islay in the west, or down through layers of hills to distant lochs and the sea.

The Ormsary Estate on the west coast of Knapdale runs historic holidays, garden holidays and drawing and painting holidays. Each is carefully planned with every attention to comfort, ease and interest. You are transported to places of historic interest or to gardens with an informed guide, the accommodation is first class—both self-catering and full board—and the situation is glorious. The drawing and painting holiday is suitable for beginners and the more experienced. For details, contact Ormsary Estate Holidays, PO Box 7, Lochgilphead, Argyll PA31 8JH, © 08803 222.

Travelling clockwise from Lochgilphead, **Kilberry**, in the southwest corner of Knapdale on the B8024, has a collection of 9th- and 10th-century stones and some from the Middle Ages, gathered up from the surrounding area and housed under cover in a steading, just north of the hamlet, signposted **Kilberry Stones** from the road. Marion Campbell, the archaeologist who collected the stones, lived in Kilberry Castle, a brooding pile which has belonged to the Campbells of Kilberry for centuries.

St Columba's Cave, 12 miles (19km) northwest of Kilberry on the western shore of Loch Caolisport (pronounced Killisport) near Ellary, is an enchanted spot, almost tangibly spiritual. There is an altar on the right with two crosses carved above, a smaller cave, reached by steps, traces of dwellings outside the cave and the ruin of a chapel. As its name indicates, tradition associates this cave with the saint's mission in Scotland. Excavations in the 19th century unearthed evidence that there was a settlement here as far back as 8000 BC, making St Columba comparatively modern.

Unfortunately, there is a private road with a locked gate and it is not possible to go on round the peninsula. You must backtrack via Lochgilphead to explore Loch Sween.

Castle Sween guards the entrance to Loch Sween from the eastern shore. Now alas surrounded by a caravan site, some say it is the oldest stone castle on the Scottish mainland. Dating from the 11th century, it is a great sprawl of a ruin, Norman in style, with buttresses. You can see the old ovens, the well and the original drain and rubbish-chute in the wall of the round tower, down which everything, including sewage, was indiscriminately cast.

The castle was a stronghold of the MacSweens in the 12th and 13th centuries but they lost their lands when they sided with the English in the 14th century. Robert the Bruce besieged it and installed the McNeills of Argyll to maintain it, one of whom married a MacMillan. Thus, Knapdale became MacMillan territory. The castle was destroyed in 1647 by Royalists, fighting the cause of Charles I.

The 13th-century **Kilmory Knap Chapel**, on the southern tip of the peninsula north of

Loch Caolisport, contains sculpted stones and **MacMillan's Cross**, elaborately carved in the 15th century, possibly by monks from the monastery at Kilberry.

Kintyre

An isthmus between East and West Loch Tarbert, straddled by the village of Tarbert, joins Kintyre to Knapdale. Here, in the 11th century, Malcolm Canmore struck a bargain with the Norwegian King Magnus Barelegs who was harrassing him. He told Magnus he could claim any western island he could get to by boat with his rudder down. Magnus had his Vikings tow him across the isthmus— and claimed Kintyre as his.

A road circles most of the coast of the peninsula, passing through villages and hamlets, most of which cater for summer visitors. The landscape is similar to that of Knapdale, cut by wooded valleys rising to hilly moorland. The east and west routes meet at **Campbeltown** at the head of Campbeltown Loch, a haven for boats in a westerly gale, and subject of that hopeful song: 'O Campbeltown Loch I wish you were whisky'. It is a holiday town and boating centre, and was once an important herring port, with 33 distilleries, of which two remain open. Although less than 40 miles (64km) from Glasgow as the crow flies, Campbeltown is about 135 miles (216km) by road.

Flora Macdonald sailed to North Carolina from Campbeltown in 1774, emigrating with her family nearly 30 years after her brave actions helped save the life of Prince Charles Edward Stuart. William McTaggart, that great painter of Scottish life and scenery, was born in the town in 1835.

Campbeltown Museum (open daily except Wed and Sun: free) in Hall Street has a demonstration of how vitrified forts were formed.

Davaar Island is a lump of rock with a cave in it at the mouth of the loch, accessible at low tide along a shingle spit on the southern shore. Here in 1887 a man called Archibald Mackinnon secretly painted a picture of the Crucifixion on the rock, inspired by a dream. It is a moving picture after the style of El Greco, lit by a shaft of light that streams into the large cave through an aperture. In 1934, when the artist was 80, he returned to the cave and restored the painting.

Machrihanish, 6 miles (9.5km) west of Campbeltown and fully exposed to the fury of Atlantic gales, is a holiday village with a hotel, golf course, camp site and sandy beaches, as well as an airport.

Mull of Kintyre

Southend, tucked round the corner to the east of the Mull of Kintyre, is another holiday village. There is a golf course and sandy beaches with dunes covered in marram grass, which offer shelter from the wind. Nothing remains today of **Dunaverty Castle**, which once stood above vicious rocks here, shrouded in uncomfortable memories. Three hundred of Montrose's men, fighting the cause of Charles I, were besieged there by the merciless Covenanter General, David Leslie. The Royalists, mostly Irish mercenaries, were forced by thirst to surrender and shamelessly massacred.

Keil, just west of Southend, has a flat rock traditionally regarded as the place where St Columba first landed in Scotland. Keen eyes will spot footprints burnt into the rock where he stood, turning his back on the land that had outlawed him.

From Southend you can hire a boat and go to **Sanda Island**, about 2 miles (3km), where Robert the Bruce hid in 1306 on his way back from Rathlin Island.

The **Mull of Kintyre**, the southern tip of the peninsula, is a rocky extremity with a lighthouse and sheer cliffs. You must walk the final 1½ miles (2.5km) or so to the point. Only 13 miles (21km) from Ireland, it is impressive in westerly gales. The Mull of Kintyre was the subject of a popular song by Paul McCartney, who bought a house close by.

Where to Stay

expensive

Crinan Hotel, ✆ 054683 261, already mentioned, is worth it. It is supplied daily by fishing boats that unload a short distance from the kitchen, and its food is renowned. The views across the water to the islands are marvellous, especially at sunset. Open mid-March to end October.

moderate

Lochgair Hotel, ✆ 0546 86333, near Lochgilphead and the loch, is comfortable. **Stonefield Castle Hotel**, Tarbert, ✆ 0880820 836, overlooks Loch Fyne, with moorings, fine gardens, summer swimming pool, good food and service. **Columba Hotel**, Tarbert, ✆ 0880820 808, has a sauna, gym and solarium.

See Knapdale above for **Ormsary Estate Holidays**, ✆08803 222, for historic, garden and painting and drawing holidays in marvellous accommodation in a glorious setting.

inexpensive

In Inveraray, **The Great Inn**, ✆ 0499 2466, overlooks Loch Shira and Loch Fyne, close to the castle entrance. Open April to October, this is a family hotel without too many frills. In the middle of the town, **George Hotel**, ✆ 0499 2111, is the most attractive hotel/inn in Inveraray with open fires, panelling, a good atmosphere, nice bar and excellent food. **Fernpoint Hotel**, ✆ 0499 2170, is highly recommended with lovely views. **Stag Hotel**, Lochgilphead, ✆ 0546 602496, in the town centre, has friendly, easy-going staff and comfortable rooms. **The Argyll Hotel**, ✆ 0546 602221, also in Lochgilphead, is old. **Tarbert Hotel**, ✆ 0880820 264, is right on the harbour in this sailing centre, popular for *après* sailing.

In Campbeltown, **Royal Hotel,** Main Street, ✆ 0586 552017, overlooks Cambeltown Loch from the harbour. It is lively. **White Hart Hotel**, ✆ 0586 552440/553356, is a family hotel on a busy corner in the Main Street.

See above for **The Loch Fyne Oyster Bar**. Also good are: **The Smiddy** off Lorne Street in Lochgilphead, where they serve delicious wholefood-type meals at reasonable prices, and **Tayvallich Inn**, an excellent bar and restaurant on the shores of Loch Sween where the seafood is particularly good.

Lorne and Oban

The new A816 runs up the west coast from Lochgilphead to Oban. It flirts with the sea, dipping and rising, pulling away and swooping back again with magnificent views.

Four miles (6.5km) northwest of Lochgilphead is all that is left of **Dunadd Fort**, capital of the kingdom of Dalriada from the 6th to the 9th centuries, a powerful political centre. It was the headquarters of early missionaries, including St Columba, until Kenneth MacAlpine moved the capital to Pictland. A rocky hillock above a meandering river is all that remains, and, if you search carefully, a rock with carvings of a boar, some Ogham inscriptions . . . and a footprint. Historians believe this was the place where kings were crowned and that St Columba crowned Aidan here in 574, using the disputed Stone of Destiny as the throne (see Topics). The footprint is indisputable and only the most prosaic could resist the urge to stand in it and imagine those ancient ceremonies on this lofty site.

From Dunadd to **Kilmartin** is about 3 miles (4.5km) and packed with well-labelled prehistoric standing stones and burial cairns dating from the Stone Age and Bronze Age. Some of the cists have been reconstructed and you can go inside and see the carvings on the walls. There are also carved stones erected on plinths in the old church at Kilmartin.

Carnasserie Castle, 9 miles (14.5km) north of Lochgilphead, is the ruined home of John Carswell, first Protestant Bishop of the Isles, who in 1597 translated Knox's liturgy into Gaelic. It was the first Gaelic book ever to be published.

Lunga Wildlife Park, on the Ardfern Peninsula, north of Loch Craignish, has indigenous animals and there is experimental white fish farming in the loch.

Arduaine Gardens, just north on Loch Melfort (open daily: adm), has sub-tropical plants as well as magnolias, rhododendrons and azaleas, a water garden and rock garden and many rare trees and shrubs.

Seil is a hook of land west of Loch Melfort—an island joined to the mainland by the much-photographed hump-backed Clachan Bridge, celebrated as 'the only bridge over the Atlantic'. From this bridge a narrow road twists down to Easdale, scarred by old slate-quarry workings, flooded out in a terrible storm and no longer operating. Rows of traditional slate-workers cottages add atmosphere. There is a large souvenir shop/art gallery manned by a tartan-clad artist. Part of *Whisky Galore* was filmed here, many years ago, transforming the township into a stage set.

Oban, 37 miles (59km) north of Lochgilphead, is unmistakably a holiday resort in summer, when the streets seethe with visitors and traffic. The town rises steeply from a crescent-shaped bay, its main street fronting on to the harbour. High above stands **McCaig's Tower**, a large circular folly with pillars, built in 1897 by a banker, McCaig, to give work to the unemployed and create a museum and observation tower as a memorial to his family. It was never finished.

The Catholic See of Argyll and the Western Isles has its well-attended cathedral, St Columba's, in Oban, overlooking the harbour. Although this area is predominantly Protestant, there are still communities which were left untouched by the Reformation.

The harbour is a busy boat terminal. MacBrayne's steamers ply between Mull and the Inner and Outer Hebrides, and smaller ferries, fishing boats and pleasure craft create an ever-changing scene. The quays are thronged with cars, people and freight. The town is fringed by hotels and neat villas offering bed and breakfast. Cafés and restaurants are packed and there is a fairly lively night life offering a choice between discos, public *céilidhs*, or family fun shows.

Oban Distillery in Stafford Street, © 0631 62110, is open to visitors on weekdays: ring for an appointment.

World in Miniature, on North Pier (open daily: adm), is a display of miniature rooms, furniture, dioramas, etc, all scaled at one inch to one foot.

Among the many entertainments, the Argyllshire Gathering in August is a great Highland occasion, with lots of piping and dancing and traditional games. In September the Oban Gala Day and Street Fair is a colourful carnival, especially when the sun shines.

Oban Rare Breeds Animal Park is a couple of miles (3km) on past the golf course, with unusual breeds of sheep, cattle, goats, pigs, poultry, ducks, deer, etc. It also has a pets' corner, nature trails, tea-room and shop.

Ganavan Sands, just north of Oban, is a good place to relax if you enjoy company—it tends to become densely populated in good weather. It has a restaurant, bar, coffee shop, car park, play area, putting, donkey rides, watersports and a launching slip.

Oban is a base for sub-aqua divers, with air supplies in the town and good underwater terrain. The Sound of Mull is littered with wrecks and the waters offer a wealth of marine life and cliff scenery. It is also ideal for sailing, with some fairly challenging, breathtakingly beautiful stretches, especially south through the Firth of Lorne to the Sound of Jura, past the infamous Corryvreckan whirlpool (see p.227).

Lismore Island

From Oban, a car ferry (taking an hour) runs 6 miles (9.5km) north to Lismore Island in Loch Linnhe. There is also a passenger ferry from Port Appin. This long sliver of rock, overlaid with loam and heather, was the seat of the diocese of Argyll from 1200 to 1507, in the days before Luther stirred up the beginnings of the Reformation. Traces of the miniature cathedral that was once here are incorporated into the parish church, built in 1749. The bishop's dwelling, the 13th-century **Achadun Castle**, is at the southwest end of the island, now a ruin. The overgrown, jagged ruin of **Coeffin Castle**, in the northwest, also dates from the 13th century. The remains of **Broch of Tirefour** stands on the northeast coast, overlooking the mainland.

Bachuil House (open by arrangement, ✆ Lismore 256: free) is on the island and contains the Bachuil Mor, or pastoral staff of St Moluag, the man who converted the island to Christianity in the 6th century. Moluag and Columba are said to have been rivals, the one being a Pict, the other a Celt.

North Argyll and Appin

Dunstaffnage Castle (open daily except Thurs afternoon and Fri, Oct–March: adm) is 4 miles (6km) north of Oban on a rocky promontory guarding the entrance to Loch Etive. A splendid ruin, it seems to grow out of the rock. Parts of it stand over 60 feet (18.5m) high, its massive walls more than 10 feet (3m) thick. Flora Macdonald was held prisoner here for a few days after helping Prince Charles in 1746. Tradition holds that the Stone of Destiny came here from Dunadd, staying until Kenneth Macalpine moved it to Scone in an attempt to draw together his kingdom of Picts and Scots (see Topics).

The coast road north from Oban and Dunstaffnage crosses the crooked finger of Loch Etive at Connel, where sea and loch are in constant turmoil trying to pour in and out through a bottleneck. It loops round Loch Creran, clinging to the coast in places with more good views. This northern tip of Strathclyde is rugged, mountainous hinterland laced with rivers and cascading burns, cut by Loch Etive.

About a mile (1.5km) north of the Connel Bridge, a minor road to the right runs 5 miles (8km) out to the northern shore of Loch Etive and **Ardchattan Priory** (always accessible: free) founded in 1230. This was the meeting place of Robert the Bruce's Parliament, in 1308, one of the last to be held in Gaelic. Among the remains of the priory, burned by Cromwell's soldiers, some carved stones can still be seen. The gardens of **Ardchattan House** (open April–November: free) are next door.

Bonawe has an impressive iron ore smelter, of great importance during the Napoleonic Wars, well looked after by Historic Scotland.

Port Appin is an attractive little place with a pier and lovely views to the islands. There is a craft shop and an excellent bar/fish restaurant in what was the old ferry house—an excellent place to stop off for lunch.

Castle Stalker (open by appointment, March–Sept: adm, ✆ Upper Warlingham 2768), dating from 1500, has a magnificent setting on an islet at the mouth of Loch Laich. Keep an eye out for seals round here; they bask on the rocks in large numbers, flopping down into the water if disturbed, to pop up and stare balefully at intruders with great velvety eyes (see Ballachulish, p.409, for the Appin Murder.)

The A828 goes on north up Loch Linnhe and crosses into the Highland Region.

The A85 east from Connel to Loch Awe is an attractive drive with views of Loch Etive, through the Pass of Brander below the looming bulk of **Ben Cruachan** (3695 feet— 1137m). **The Hollow Mountain**, 6 miles (9.5km) beyond Taynuilt, is a great cavern hewn out of Ben Cruachan to accommodate an underground power house (open daily March–Oct: adm). Electric buses run through the tunnel and there is a visitor centre. This glistening subterranean empire is not for the claustrophobic.

Anyone with the time and energy to climb Ben Cruachan will get some of the best views in Scotland from its summit.

Loch Awe is a 23-mile (37km) long serpent of water with thickly wooded shores, many islands, and more than its share of midges clinging to the dense vegetation. The huge Victorian building you see from the road is the **Loch Awe Hotel**, fairly hideous inside and out but with wonderful views from its terrace. **St Conan's Church** on the north shore of the loch is charming with unusual architecture made up of all sorts of bits and pieces.

Kilchurn Castle, on a commanding site at the north end of the loch, dates from 1440. It belonged to the Campbells of Breadalbane until it was taken over by Hanoverian troops in 1746, with the consent of the anti-Jacobite Campbells. The gale that destroyed the Tay Rail Bridge also demolished one of Kilchurn's turrets.

When the level of the loch is low, traces of several *crannogs* can be seen—man-made islands where early settlers built dwellings for protection against attack. Some of the islands were used as clan burial grounds, especially **Inchail**, where there is a ruined chapel dating from the 13th century and several graves of the Macarthur Clan.

There are good walks either side of the loch. On the west side there is an information centre at **Inverliever**.

Ardanaiseig Gardens (open 31 March–31 Oct: adm) are at the north end of the loch, east of the B845. They contain rhododendrons, azaleas, rare shrubs and trees and good views across the loch to Ben Cruachan. There is a hotel with a restaurant, open for coffee, lunch and tea.

White Corries Chairlift (open daily in summer and weekends, Jan–April: adm) is north of Tyndrum on the A82, almost on the border with the Highland Region. The lift climbs 2100 feet (646m) into the hills with glorious views over Rannoch Moor and into Glencoe.

Where to Stay and Eating Out

expensive

South of Oban, **Knipoch Hotel**, Kilninver, near Oban, © 08526 251, is open all year except January. It looks across Loch Feochan to a sunset behind the Hills of Lorne. Knipoch stands on the burial route along which the Kings of the Scots (including Macbeth and Duncan) were carried from Scone Palace to Iona. With award-winning food, it caters for 'the more discriminating traveller'.

In Oban, **The Manor House**, Gallanach Road, ℂ 0631 63053, on Oban Bay, was built by the Duke of Argyll in 1780 as his Oban retreat and later used as a dower house. It has marvellous views, is comfortable and serves good Scottish and French food, expecially seafood. The following are all similar—comfortable, old-fashioned seaside-resort hotels, overlooking the harbour, giving value for money and serving wholesome, if predictable, food: **Alexandra Hotel**, ℂ 0631 62381; **Columba Hotel**, ℂ 0631 62183 and, slightly more lively, **Great Western Hotel**, ℂ 0631 63101.

Loch Melfort Hotel, Arduaine, ℂ 08522 233, only open April–Oct, has established a reputation for good service, comfort and excellent food. Yachtsmen of the yellow-boot variety tend to stop off here for a civilized evening out, swapping Force Nine stories in the Chart Room Bar. The main house, built in 1900, gazes out across an island-speckled sea. The six bedrooms are done up like guest rooms in a country house. An adjoining Cedar Wing, long and low, has 20 rooms, each with its own bathroom, balcony and picture window, facing south across the water.

Isle of Eriska at Ledaig, ℂ 063172 371, is a Scottish baronial pile, built in 1884, connected to the mainland by a bridge. Its proprietors, Robin and Sheena Buchanan-Smith, have created a comfortable private-house atmosphere, with log fires and an excellent kitchen. **Invercreran Country House Hotel**, Glen Creran, near Appin, ℂ 063173 414/456, in a sheltered glen surrounded by hills, is a well-run, comfortable hotel, with an excellent dining room. **Ardsheal House**, Kentallen of Appin, Appin, ℂ 063174 227, stands on a peninsula with views over Loch Linnhe to the Morvern hills. Open from April to November, Ardsheal was built in 1760 in 900 acres of woods, meadows and beach. Oak panelling, open fires and antiques give it a country house atmosphere and the food is excellent. **Airds Hotel**, Port Appin, ℂ 063173 236, overlooking Loch Linnhe, Lismore and Shuna and Morvern hills, is very comfortable, with good food and friendly staff. It is open from March to January with special winter reductions.

Ardanaiseig, Kilchrenan, ℂ 08663 333, stands beneath Ben Cruachan on the shores of Loch Awe, in a garden of rhododendrons and azaleas. It was built in 1834 to designs by William Burn and has a 'country house' atmosphere. It has been the family home of the proprietors since 1964. The food is excellent, and the accommodation very comfortable.

In Oban, try the **Caledonian Hotel**, ℂ 0631 63133 and **Argyll Hotel**, ℂ 0631 62353. There are dozens more.

North of Oban, **Falls of Lora Hotel** at Connel, ℂ 063171, overlooks Loch Etive, 5 miles (8km) from Oban. Another of the old-fashioned style hotels, they give good service.

Cuilfail Hotel, Kilmelford, ✆ 08522 274, is an attractive old coaching inn, serving excellent food. **Lorne Inn**, at Ardfern, further south, ✆ 08525 284, is an unpretentious, family-run inn, not over-endowed with mod cons.

Ford Hotel, Ford, ✆ 054681 273, just north of Kilmartin, is good value, as is **Tigh-an-Truish**, Clachan Bridge, ✆ 08523 242.

For very special bed and breakfast, try Mrs McAuslan, Cornaig, Kilmartin, ✆ 05465 224.

Eating Out

For a good bistro-type restaurant, go to **The Cairn Restaurant** at Kilmartin.

The Strathclyde Islands

Cumbrae

Great Cumbrae is so close to the Ayrshire mainland that it hardly counts as an island.

Getting There

It takes just seven minutes to reach in the roll-on, roll-off ferry that runs every 15 minutes from Largs.

Tourist Information

All year, **Largs**, ✆ 0475 673765.

Tourist Information Centre, **Millport**, ✆ 0475 530753, April–Oct.

Less than 4 miles (6km) in length and 2 (3km) in width, the island has a 12-mile (19km) coastal road round it and is ideal for bicycling.

Millport straggles around a wide bay looking south across the Tan to Little Cumbrae. A great many people go to Cumbrae in the summer, so don't expect to 'get away from it all'. The beaches are packed on a fine day.

There is a National Water Sports Centre on the island and these waters are excellent for sub-aqua diving.

Although Cumbrae is not ideal for the recluse, it has some interesting rock formations and good plant and animal life. The earliest village was at **Kirkton** about half a mile from the old pier in Millport, where the chapel was dedicated to St Columba in 1330 and replaced in 1612. The 'Cathedral of the Isles' in Millport is the smallest cathedral in Britain, designed by the important Victorian architect William Butterfield.

The **Museum** (open Tues and Sat in season: free) shows the history of Millport and Cumbrae over the centuries. Boats run from Millport to Little Cumbrae. The ruined castle there was a residence of Robert II in the 14th century.

There are a few hotels, guest houses and bed and breakfasts in Millport, but the standard is not high. The **Royal George Hotel**, © 0475 530301, overlooking the bay, is probably the best bet, or **Millerston Hotel**, West Bay Road, © 0475 530480, which is only open April to October.

Arran

The miracle of Arran is that it has clung to its character despite the thousands of holiday-makers attracted every year by its beauty. It is slightly larger than the Isle of Wight, about 20 miles (32km) from north to south, 9 miles (14.5km) across and 56 miles (90km) in circumference. Although hotels, guest houses and chalet settlements ring the island, it is possible to roam inland for miles, and feel totally remote.

Arran was inhabited way back before the dawn of recorded history, as its ancient stones and burial cairns prove. Since then its lovely landscape and mild climate have been put to many uses. The Irish Scots came over and settled in the early 6th century, making Arran part of the Kingdom of Dalriada. The Vikings held it for a time, until they were ousted by Somerled, Lord of the Isles, who was possibly of Norse descent himself. In the 18th century sportsmen established deer here, overrunning the crofts and driving out many of the tenant farmers.

There is so much to do here it would be easier to list what is not available. Sea sports include: swimming, sailing, windsurfing, water skiing, sub-aqua diving and fishing. Land sports include: golf, riding, pony trekking, tennis, squash, bowling, and of course, walking and climbing. Time spent birdwatching will reward you with sightings of rare species and the flora and fauna of the island are diverse.

A holiday atmosphere prevails on the ferry from Ardrossan to Brodick on Arran. For an hour crowds jostle for tables in the bar and lounges. If it is raining at Brodick don't worry; Arran usually manages to show a smiling face for at least some of the day.

Getting there

The car ferry from Ardrossan, with train link from Glasgow, takes about an hour. April–Oct: Claonaig, Kintyre–Lochranza takes half an hour. Further information: Caledonian MacBrayne Ltd, Ferry Terminal, Gourock, Renfrewshire, © 0475 33755 (enquiries)/34531 (reservations).

Tourist Information

The Pier, **Brodick**, © 0770 2140/2401.

Brodick

Brodick is a large resort-village with plenty of hotels, guest houses, and bed and breakfast places. It spreads around Brodick Bay overlooked by Brodick Castle.

Brodick Castle (open Mon, Wed, Sat, April and first half Oct; daily May–Sept: grounds open all year: adm) belongs to the National Trust for Scotland. The home of the Dukes of Hamilton, it was built in the 13th century on the site of a Viking fortress. Much of the treasures on display were brought to the castle by Susan Euphemia Beckford, who married the 10th Duke in 1810. She inherited them from her father William Beckford, the reclusive, eccentric collector of fine art, who built Fonthill Abbey in Wiltshire, and wrote *Vathek*. The guidebook to the castle gives details of all the silver, porcelain, paintings and furnishings. The castle is a tall, stately building of red sandstone, facing the sea and surrounded by a range of hills dominated by Goat Fell. The gardens are a surprise—the fabulous colours and pungent scents are exotic enough to to have been part of the rich oriental settings in *Vathek* itself.

The **Isle of Arran Heritage Museum** (open Easter–Oct, Mon–Sat: adm) occupies an 18th-century croft-farm on the edge of Brodick. The smithy, cottage and stable block illustrate changing conditions from the far past to the turn of the century. Rooms in the cottage show nostalgic Victoriana, complete with black kettle on the hob and iron bedstead under the eaves.

The road round the island only loses the sea in a couple of places, while the String Road cuts through the middle from Brodick to Blackwaterfoot. Another road cuts through Glen Scorrodale from Lamlash to Lagg Inn.

Goat Fell, 2866 ft, north of Brodick, dominates Arran. It is best attacked on a clear day; there are several ways up and the views from the top make it all worth while. There won't be any goats— 'Goatfell' comes from *Gaoith Bheinn*, windy mountain, but you might see golden eagles gliding on air currents in a corrie below.

Corrie is a about 6 miles (9.5km) north of Brodick. Its white cottages, trim colourful gardens, harbour, quay and beach have made it a favourite with artists.

Walk up into the glens that cut into the hinterland like spokes of a wheel. There are two at **Sannox**—delightful, secret places away from the road, with heather, lichens, mosses and alpine willow, and many rare wild flowers. The **Fallen Rocks**, beyond Sannox, are thought to be the relics of a landslip in the Palaeozoic Age which sent these massive boulders—some as big as houses—tumbling to the beach. This is a popular place for rock climbers. Sannox has a nine-hole golf course. **North Sannox Farm Park** (open Mon–Sat: adm) has small and pet animals, including chipmunks, and play areas for children.

Lochranza, possibly from Loch of the *chaoruinn* (rowan), lies two miles (3km) southwest of the northern headland, Cock of Arran. The 13th/14th-century Lochranza Castle (open daily: free) is a romantic ruin on the tidal flats, backed by hills. The castle is L-plan, three storeys high with a pit prison in the vaulted basement. It is said to have been a staging post for Robert the Bruce in 1307, when he returned from his famous encounter with the spider of Rathlin Island. Seen against a flaming sunset, this roofless shell is stunning. Lochranza has a nine-hole golf course.

Heading south from Lochranza down the west side of the island, the road clings to the sea with hills tumbling down almost to the beach. Steep-sided **Glen Catacol** runs inland up into the hills through beech, oak and larch, chestnut and fir, and vivid green ferns. **Thundergay**, 5 miles (8km) south of Lochranza, gets its strange name from *Tor-na-Gaoith* (hill-of-the-wind). Two miles (3km) further south, **Pirnmill** is derived from the bobbin mill that was here in the days when linen was an important industry in the island. The mill has now been converted into holiday flats. **Glen Iorsa** runs northeast through marshy bog land, hemmed in by barren hills. It is a great tract of lonely, waterlogged moor, lying below frowning crags cut by steep ravines and lochans.

The southwest quarter of Arran is rich in prehistoric remains. These include **Auchagallon Stone Circle**, 15 red sandstone blocks which once encircled a cairn; the **Farm Road Stone Circle**, close by (within range of the nine-hole Machrie golf course), the **Machrie Standing Stones**, slim, primeval monoliths whose mysterious purpose is still unknown, and the **Kilmory Cairns**, at Lagg Inn.

King's Caves at Drumadoon, Blackwaterfoot, are where Robert the Bruce is said to have sheltered when returning to free Scotland from the stranglehold of English domination. Legend brings the 3rd-century warrior-poet Fingal (Fionn) MacCumhail here, father of Ossian and leader of the Feinn, who feature in the old sagas. There are rock carvings of typical Pictish hunting scenes and animals in the caves.

A lovely 10-mile (16km) walk takes you up **Glen Scorrodale** from **Sliddery** and along Sliddery Water to Lamlash Bay.

Kildonan, 6 miles (9.5km) east of Sliddery, is a sprawling farming village with two hotels and a sandy beach. There are views from here of Pladda Island Lighthouse and Ailsa Craig, which rises like an iceberg 13 miles (21km) out to sea. Look for a large colony of Atlantic grey seals along the shore towards Bennan Head to the west. Unafraid and curious, they come quite close to the shore to inspect passers-by. The mysterious carcass of a large sea-creature, discovered here in 1981, baffled experts for some time until it was identified, with great disappointment, as a gigantic basking shark. Before the headland, a winding path used by smugglers in the 18th century hugs the cliffs and leads to the road above. **South Bank Farm Park**(open Easter–Oct: adm) has sheep dog demonstrations and rare breeds of farm animals and deer.

Whiting Bay, 5 miles (8km) north of Kildonan, is a popular holiday village. Here, shops and hotels jostle with holiday cottages along the waterfront. There are also craft shops which specialize in leather, pottery and wood carving. A jewellery workshop, signposted at the north end of the village, sells locally made silver and gold jewellery. For evening entertainment, **Nags Bistro** has live music and a disco in the summer. There is an 18-hole golf course with fine views across the Firth of Clyde to the Ayrshire hills. **Glen Ashdale Falls** are signposted from the south end of the village, up a steep, wooded glen to where crystal water cascades down on to glistening rocks. **The Giant's Graves** (signposted) are a stone circle traditionally associated with Fionn MacCumhail.

Lamlash completes the circular tour of the island, 3 miles (4.5km) south of Brodick on Lamlash Bay, which is almost blocked at the mouth by Holy Island. This wonderfully safe anchorage, now a yachtsman's haven, has given shelter to many an important traveller. King Haakon and his fleet took refuge here after they had been defeated in the Battle of Largs in 1263, and in 1548 the ship carrying five-year-old Mary, Queen of Scots to France from Dumbarton sheltered here. Lamlash has annual sea angling competitions, renowned throughout Scotland.

Holy Island, with St Molio's Cave, is not at present open to the public. It is the home of a Buddhist community.

Take home one of Arran's unique blends of mustard, locally made and sold at **Arran Provisions**, The Old Mill, Lamlash. The range is enormous. They also do delicious jams, jellies, sauces, and chutneys. Another local speciality is Arran cheese—a Dunlop cheese made at The Creamery in Kilmory.

Where to Stay

moderate

Auchrannie Hotel, Brodick, ✆ 0770 2234/5, is a 19th-century mansion, five minutes from beach and golf course. Excellent food is served in a conservatory-style restaurant. **Douglas Hotel**, Brodick, ✆ 0770 2155, on the sea front, has live entertainment, dancing, sauna and a beauty salon. **Kinloch Hotel**, overlooking the sea at Blackwaterfoot, ✆ 077086 444, is a comfortable modern eyesore with good food, indoor swimming pool, solarium, sauna and squash court. Not for the recluse.

inexpensive

Arran Hotel, on the sea front in Brodick, ✆ 0770 2265, welcomes children at reduced prices and has a nice garden. Open March to October. **Invercloy Hotel**, Brodick, ✆ 0770 2225, is opposite a safe sandy beach and has balconies in front and a friendly atmosphere.

Lagg Hotel, Kilmory, ✆ 077087 255, is an 18th-century coaching inn set in 10 acres of attractive woodland by the Lagg Burn. The food is first rate.

Eating Out

For an evening out, try **Wishing Well Restaurant**, Lagg, ✆ 0770 87255, in converted stables. Seafood is a speciality, with lobster when available.

Bute

Bute is a holiday island, attracting many people in the summer, including Glaswegians who like to take a trip 'doon the watter'. Rothesay is a town of bright lights and tourist traps, a little run-down at present but great efforts are being made to revive it. There are plenty of hidden corners if you are prepared to walk to some of the less accessible beaches and coves, especially in the northwest. The **Kyles of Bute** are the very beautiful narrow straits separating the island from the mainland in the northwest and northeast. Sailors exploring the coast will find a number of secret bays populated only by seals and sea birds. Mountstuart (not open to the public), an incredible Gothic mansion, is the main home of the Bute family who own the island as well as much else in Britain and have been revered patrons of the arts for generations. They are Scotland's premier Catholic aristocratic family and are responsible for some very important architecture in Britain.

Throughout the season the island plays host to many events, including a Jazz Festival in May, a Folk Festival in July and Bute Highland Games in August. There are also angling competitions and a bowling tournament; three golf courses, tennis, riding, good fishing and every sort of water sport in wonderfully clear water. Nature lovers will appreciate the walking and birdwatching. During the summer there is plenty of organized jollity to while away the evenings and pleasure cruises for the day time.

Getting there

There is a roll-on, roll-off car ferry from Wemyss Bay, which is an hour's drive or train journey from Glasgow. There are frequent sailings daily, lasting half an hour. The roll-on, roll-off car ferry from Colintraive, Argyll, also has frequent sailings daily; the crossing takes 5 minutes. For further information, contact Caledonian MacBrayne, The Ferry Terminal, Gourock, Renfrewshire, © 0475 33755, or 0700 502707.

Tourist Information

15 Victoria Street, **Rothesay**, © 0700 502151, open all year.

Rothesay is the hub of Bute, a town humming with activity and tourist attractions.

Rothesay Castle (open daily except Thurs mornings and Fri, Oct–March: adm) was built in 1098 in the days when Norsemen dominated the islands. It reverted to Scotland after the Battle of Largs, in 1263. Added to over the centuries, it is an impressive fortress with high curtain walls and drum towers enclosing a circular courtyard. King Robert the Bruce captured it in 1313 and it was his great-great-grandson who was first created Duke of Rothesay, a title held by the present Prince Charles. The castle was used as a headquarters when both James IV and James V tried, with little success, to subdue the arrogant rule of the Lords of the Isles. Cromwell battered it badly during the Civil War and it was burned by Argyll in 1685 during the Monmouth Rebellion; it then lay in ruins until restoration began in the 19th century.

The **Bute Museum** is behind the castle (open every day except Sun during April and May; daily June–Sept; Tues–Sat afternoons, Oct–March: adm). There are displays of Bute's geology, ancient history, maritime traditions, culture and natural history.

Winter Garden Visitors' Centre in Victoria Street, in a restored 1920s seaside theatre, contains a heritage centre, cinema and bistro. **Rothesay Pavilion** is a multi-purpose entertainment centre with fun-filled family shows.

Ardencraig Gardens, (open daily May–Sept: free), south of Rothesay, supply plants for the whole island. As well as demonstration gardens and fish ponds, there are aviaries with exotic foreign birds. Fuchsias add a vivid splash of colour.

Canada Hill, above the town in the lower middle part of the island, is an easy walk and gives panoramic views of the Firth of Clyde, Argyll and Arran.

St Blane's Chapel, on the southern toe of Bute, is a 12th-century ruin with a Norman arch, built on the site of a monastery founded by St Blane in the 6th century.

St Ninian's Chapel, halfway up the west coast, on a point by a glorious sandy bay is another early settlement.

Ettrick Bay, further north, has a sandy beach.

Where to Stay

inexpensive

Guildford Court, Watergate, Rothesay, ✆ 0700 3770, is a listed building overlooking the harbour with both hotel accommodation and self-catering suites. **Kingarth Hotel**, at the south end of the island, ✆ 070083 662, is comfortable and friendly with a bowling green, near a golf course. **Bayview Hotel**, 22 Mountstuart Road, Rothesay, ✆ 0700 2339, is a Victorian house on Craigmore Shore, 10 minutes from the pier with views of Rothesay Bay. **Royal Hotel**, Albert Place, Rothesay, ✆ 0700 3044, overlooks the yacht marina, a short distance from the ferry terminus. Cabaret every night during the season. Private loch fishing arranged and special terms for golfers can be arranged. **Glenburn Hotel**, Glenburn Road, Rothesay, ✆ 0700 2500, stands in six acres overlooking the water. It's a busy place, next door to a heated swimming pool and a golf course, and the food isn't too bad.

Ardencraig, ✆ 0700 4550, has seven cheap self-catering chalets high above the Firth of Clyde, each with one public room and two bedrooms which sleep six.

Gigha

(Pronounced with hard g, 'Ge'a'.)

Gigha is Norse for god, and indeed this is an earthly Garden of Eden, 6 miles (9.5km) long and never more than 1½ miles (2.5km) wide, warmed by the Gulf Stream, with frost almost unknown.

Getting There

Six ferries a day (four on Sundays) run to Gigha from Tayinloan, halfway up the west side of Kintyre. (Fewer in winter.)

For further information contact Caledonian MacBrayne, ✆ 0475 33755.

West Highland and Islands Tourist Board, The Pier, **Campbeltown**, ✆ 0586 552056.

Gigha has been on the market several times recently. Islands like this suffer from being bought and sold by rich businessmen who see them as toys.

Perhaps the most celebrated of Gigha's residents is Seumas McSporran, a sturdy figure past his half century with a genial smile almost as wide as his face. He has lived on the island for all but two years of his life and holds some 14 or 15 jobs. 'I have to consult a list to get up to date with them.' They include: sub-postmaster, postman, registrar, Pearl Assurance agent, special constable, fireman, ambulance driver, taxi driver, and undertaker. He and his wife run the general store and he has a uniform or outfit to go with each job.

Achamore House Gardens (open daily Apr–Oct, 10am–6pm: adm) contain a riot of sub-tropical plants and shrubs, all thriving in the mild westerly climate. The gardens were developed by Sir James Horlick, who bought the island in 1944. A lucky combination of the acidic soil, the warm air of the Gulf Stream and Sir James' milk-drink-derived fortune created this paradise of rhododendrons, camellias, and azaleas. There are carpets of bulbs and many exotic blooms to give a vivid foreground to lovely views.

The ruined church at Kilchattan dates from the 13th century. There is a golf course, a visitor centre, a hotel and a Boathouse Bar.

moderate

Gigha Hotel, ✆ 05835 275, would be a perfect honeymoon retreat on this paradise island. Almost ranch-style, and not a bit grand, it has good local food and lovely views.

Gigha Enterprises have a house and two self-catering cottages, ✆ 05835 254; quite pricey.

inexpensive

Down the scale a bit, but also full of character, **Post Office House**, ✆ 05835 251, has four bedrooms, one public bathroom and a great atmosphere.

Islay

(Pronounced Eyela.)

Islay, the most southerly of the Inner Hebrides, is some 14 miles (22km) off Kintyre, about 25 miles (40km) from north to south and 20 (32km) across at the widest point. Farmland rises to moor transversed by burns; rugged coastline gives way to open sweeps of beach. A favourite holiday island for birdwatchers, naturalists, photographers and artists, it also has much to interest archaeologists; the island has been inhabited since Neolithic times.

Excellent trout and salmon fishing can be found on the rivers Duich and Sorn, and on well-stocked lochs such as Gorm, Torrabus and Ballygrant. Boats can be hired locally for sea-angling, too. Warmed by the Gulf Stream, so they say, miles of sandy beaches offer swimming and sunbathing. The surf is sometimes good. Machrie 18-hole golf course is well known.

Perhaps best known for its distinctive peaty malt whisky, Islay has eight distilleries which scent the air with the pungent smell of smouldering peat. Now and then islanders tangle with conservationists who insist that the special Duich Moss peat, essential for the flavour of Islay whisky, should be preserved for rare Greenland white-fronted geese. At a stormy meeting not so long ago the islanders, furious at Green interference, argued that whisky was more vital to their survival than 'any bloody goose'. The distilleries welcome visitors.

Getting There

Ferries run to both Port Ellen and Askaig from Kennacraig in northwest Kintyre, taking just over two hours.

Loganair fly from Glasgow to the island's airport at Glenegadale. Flights take half an hour.

A local bus service links most of the island communities with extra runs in the summer. There are day tours of beauty spots and places of interest.

Tourist Information

West Highlands and Islands Tourist Board, The Pier, **Campbeltown,** ℗ 0586 552056.

Tourist Information Centre, **Bowmore,** ℗ 049681 254.

Port Ellen is the ferry arrival point at the south of the island. Port Ellen Distillery, built in 1815, dominates the skyline overlooking Leodamus Bay. Closed during the slump of the 1930s, it was then modernized. It was closed briefly again in 1983 due to a 'Whisky Lake'.

The 14th-century **Dunyvaig Castle** is an impressive ruin on a cliff, 3½ miles (5.5km) east of Port Ellen. It was the stronghold of the Macdonalds of Islay in the days when the Lords of the Isles considered themselves to be separate from the authority of the Crown. **Kildalton Cross** beside ruined Kildalton Chapel 7 miles (11km) further north along this road, is an important survival of Celtic art. It is a 9th-century Celtic cross carved from a single block of blue stone and inscribed with early Christian symbols. Similar to one in Iona Abbey, it is one of the finest in the country. There is a hotel here. **Claggain Bay** beyond the chapel is sandy with rocky pools, backed by Beinn Bheigeir (1612 feet— 496m), the highest hill in Islay.

The rugged **Oa Peninsula**, 5 miles (8km) southwest of Port Ellen, was a haunt of smugglers and illicit whisky distillers, who made cunning use of its sheer cliffs honeycombed with caves. One road crosses it but most of the peninsula is only accessible on foot.

Machrie, north of Oa, has an 18-hole golf course on the machair, and borders the sandy crescent of Laggan Bay.

Bowmore, 14 miles (22km) or so north of Port Ellen, was the old capital and administrative centre of the island. It was seat of the Islay Parliament, a sort of feudal court. The village was built by Daniel Campbell the Younger in 1768, on the site of monastic lands and was one of the earliest of Scotland's planned villages introduced by wealthy 'improvers' in the 18th century. The village is crowned by an intriguing, round church, Italian in design. Its shape deprives the devil of any corners in which to lurk.

Bowmore Distillery, established in 1779, claims to be the oldest legal distillery on Islay and is still privately owned.

Brigend is a hamlet among woods at the head of Loch Indaal with good beaches and a hotel. **Islay Woollen Mill** is an old working mill where you can watch tweed being woven and buy the products.

The Rhinns of Islay sticks out from the west side of the island like a great hammer-head. Here there are more wonderful walks and views. Bruichladdich Distillery overlooks Loch Indaal and produces an excellent 10-year-old single malt.

The award-winning **Museum of Islay Life** is in a converted church in **Port Charlotte**, on the southeast shore of the Rhinns (open daily Easter–Oct; Sun afternoons, Nov, Jan–March; closed Dec: adm). Exhibits cover the history of the island, with traditional craft work and tools, a maritime section and domestic artefacts. A lapidarium, below the museum, displays an important collection of carved stones dating from the 16th century.

There is a wildfowl sanctuary at **Ellister** south of Port Charlotte, and an RSPB reserve at **Loch Gruinart** to the north. **Portnahaven** is the southwest tip of Islay, with the green shores of Ireland only spitting distance away.

Ruined **Finlaggan Castle** stands on an islet in Loch Finlaggan, just off the road from Bowmore to Port Askaig. This was the main stronghold of the Macdonalds, Lords of the Isles. The 14 chiefs of the Lordship were summoned to council meetings here, to confer with their overlord. They came from all over the Kingdom of the Isles, many in coracles, accompanied by members of their clans. They were proud men, settling their disputes and problems independently of the Scottish Parliament, often with great wisdom and justice and often with bloodshed.

Port Askaig is the other ferry terminal, and boats run from here to the Isle of Jura. The views across the narrow Sound of Islay to the Paps of Jura are glorious. There is a hotel and a roadless hinterland to the north.

Where to Stay

moderate

Bridgend Hotel, © 049681 212, not only has a private bathroom for each of its 10 bedrooms, but three extra, public ones as well. It has a pretty garden, good food and is open all year.

inexpensive

Port Askaig Hotel, ℂ 049684 245, open all year, looks over the harbour, and is attractive and cosy, with three public bathrooms between nine bedrooms. **Lochside Hotel**, Bowmore, ℂ 049681 265/244, overlooks Loch Indaal, and is old-fashioned, friendly, and ideal for birdwatching. Open all year, with two public bathrooms to seven bedrooms.

Jura

Just off the northeast coast of Islay, Jura has very little tourist accommodation and is far less frequented though more beautiful. Wild and rugged, it is famous for its deer, which are keenly stalked by the owners and guests of the sporting estates of which the island is comprised. Over 20 miles (32km) long and sparsely populated, it has a small village, Craighouse, a distillery and a hotel. Silver and white sandy beaches give way to rugged shingle which teems with wildfowl. Loch Tarbert almost cuts the island in two from the west. The three Paps of Jura rear up at the south end of the island—the highest is 2576 feet (793m). A single-track road runs south from the ferry, and then some way up the east coast. Most of the island is only accessible on foot. The west coast—private land—has some amazing caves, some of which have been adapted for temporary use by shepherds.

Getting There

A car ferry runs frequently from Port Askaig on Islay to Feolin. It is a 10-minute crossing (there are fewer ferries on Sundays).

Tourist Information

West Highlands and Islands Tourist Board, The Pier, **Campbeltown**, ℂ 0586 552056.

Craighouse, the only village, has the island's single hotel, **The Jura**. They will arrange riding, fishing, sea-angling, boating, shooting and water skiing.

The **Corryvreckan Whirlpool** in the strait between Jura and Scarba is notorious to west-coast sailors and can be both lion and lamb. In the right conditions of tide and weather, its mighty maw has been known to suck down whole boats, roaring like an express train. But at slack tide, it can be approached by sea, its satin-smooth water ruffled by tiny eddies that pull gently at the boat without harm.

Seven miles (11km) beyond Ardlussa, on a rough track, lies **Barnhill**, the white farmhouse where George Orwell lived, and wrote *1984*, struggling against the consumption that killed him.

Jura House Garden and Grounds (open all year: adm) at the southern end of the island were laid out around the middle of the last century to exploit the natural features and beauty of the area. There is a lovely walled garden and walks.

inexpensive

Jura Hotel, Craighouse, ✆ 049682 243, has a relaxed atmosphere in a lovely setting, with good food. It gets very booked up. There is a self-catering house at Craighouse, sleeping five: c/o Mrs Mary Keith, Keills, Craighouse, Isle of Jura, Argyll PA60 7XG, ✆ 049682 214; open April–Oct. Another, a bit more expensive, sleeps six: c/o Mr Renwick, 5 Kelvin Drive, Glasgow, ✆ 041 946 4361. A third **Ardfarnal**, sleeps nine: c/o Mr A. Fairman, 83 James Street, Helensburgh, Dunbartonshire, ✆ 0436 75760.

Colonsay and Oronsay

These two tiny islands, joined at low tide, lie 10 miles (16km) west of Jura, 25 miles (40km) from the mainland. To the west, the only thing between here and Canada is **Du Hirteach Lighthouse**. The landscape is made up of craggy hills, woods and a rocky coastline broken by silver sands. Their names are derived from the Saints Columba and Oran who landed here on their way to Scotland from Ireland. Legend holds that when Columba discovered he could still see the shore of the land from which he had been exiled, he pressed on to Iona; whether from repugnance or sadness is not related. It is also said that he banished snakes from the two islands, as he did on Iona.

Both islands have a high average of sunshine. Over 500 species of wild flowers can be found, including rare purple orchids, sea samphire and marsh helleborine. Bluebells and primroses bloom in the woods, wild irises flower in damp corners, harebells nod on the sand dunes and purple thrift clings to the rocks. Eucalyptus, palm trees and rare shrubs flourish in the mild climate. There are also over 150 different bird species.

Getting There

The car ferry from Oban, three times a week, takes 2½ hours, and in summer, from Kennacraig via Islay, about the same time.

Tourist Information

Tourist Information Centre, **Oban**, Argyll, ✆ 0631 63122.

Colonsay House Gardens (open daily: free) have sub-tropical shrubs and plants, rhododendrons, embothriums, magnolias and palm trees.

Wild goats roam the island, reputedly descended from survivors of a Spanish Armada wreck in 1588. Otters can be seen occasionally and there are lots of grey seals. **Balnahard** is a beach with hundreds of cowrie shells in the coves. When the wind is in the west, **Kiloran Bay** in the northwest offers safe surfing in huge Atlantic rollers. **The Strand** is a beach a mile (1.5km) wide in the south of the island festooned with mussels on the rocks, and prawns in the pools. For about three hours at low tide, the Strand becomes a causeway to Oronsay, an enchanted island populated by sheep and serenaded by skylarks.

St Oran's Chapel, on Oronsay, is a ruined 14th-century priory, named after St Columba's faithful companion. Although the cloisters have collapsed this is a splendid ruin with gravestones carved with boats and warriors and hunting scenes. A tall, carved Celtic cross stands at the entrance. Excavations revealed that Oronsay was inhabited in the Middle Stone Age. Certainly Norsemen lived here, long before the present chapel was built by Columban monks.

Where to Stay

moderate

Isle of Colonsay Hotel, ✆ 09512 316, is highly recommended, informal, and serves good food. It also has three self-catering chalets, each with two bedrooms and one public room.

inexpensive

There are three bed and breakfast places: **Baleromindobh Farm**, ✆ 09512 305, a farm house with three bedrooms: **Seaview**, ✆ 09512 315, a working croft with three bedrooms; and **Garvard**, ✆ 09512 343, a farmhouse with three bedrooms. There are also a number of cottages to let on Colonsay and flats in Colonsay House.

Mull

Mull, 'isle-of-the-cool-high-bends', is the largest of the Inner Hebrides and merits a whole book to itself. It is shaped like a caricature of the British Isles, its southwestern peninsula kicking frivolously upwards. Encircled by 300 miles (480km) of rugged coastline, it is deeply cut by lochs with many wooded hillsides and secret corners, easily reached by coastal roads. The western seaboard is sprinkled with islands: **Inch Kenneth**, **Ulva**, **Staffa** and, further west, the **Treshnish Isles** with **Coll** and **Tiree** beyond. There are plenty of boat trips to the islands and some of the hotels charter their own boats. In addition, local men will take you fishing or sightseeing. The whole coast is a sailor's paradise. Around the head of Loch Na Keal about halfway down the west coast, there are steep cliffs fringed by sandy inlets. The hinterland is a mass of hills, dominated by **Ben More**, 3169 feet (975m), in the west.

Johnson and Boswell came to Mull during their tour of the Hebrides. Johnson lamented the lack of trees, attributing this to idleness, but applauded the French wine he was given.

There are more red deer on Mull than people: over 3000 roam the island and the smaller fallow deer can be seen in the woods around Gruline and Salen. There are also polecats, weasels, stoats, mink, feral ferrets and otters. Wild white goats can be seen from Grass Point down to the Ross of Mull.

Unlike some other islands, the depopulation of 150 years has been reversed in Mull. With fishing, farming, tourism and building to employ them, fewer young people are seeking the bright lights of the mainland and there are a number of incomers who prefer insular peace and beauty to the materialistic scramble of the cities.

There is a Drama Festival in March, a Music Festival in April, Tobermory Highland Games in July, and also Children's Highland Games. West Highland Yachting Week takes place in early August, Salen Show, which includes a dogshow, is in August and there is a car rally in October.

Getting There

Car ferries run frequently from Oban to Craignure in just under an hour; Oban–Tobermory takes about two hours and Lochaline–Fishnish, a quarter of an hour. There is also a car ferry from Kilchoan to Tobermory, taking half an hour. You can get 'Multi-stop' ferry tickets, much cheaper, if you want to visit several places.

Further information: Caledonian MacBrayne, ✆ 0475 34531, or 0631 62285.

There is an airfield on the island to which charter flights can be arranged from Glasgow. Most roads are single-track with passing places.

island cruises

Inter-island cruises in high-speed charter boats, to Staffa, Treshnish, Coll, Eigg, Muck, can be booked from Richard and Judy Fairbairns, Dervaig, ✆ 06884 223. Or try Turus Mara, ✆ 06884 242/0631/63122. You need to go prepared: take a good picnic and weatherproof clothing as conditions change quickly, and seasick pills—the slow Atlantic swell can be disastrous for uneasy stomachs. You might see whales and dolphins.

The boat from Oban passes **Lady Rock**, an islet off Lismore Lighthouse at the head of Loch Linnhe. In the 16th century, a Maclean of Lochbuie, disenchanted by his wife, tethered her to this rock. Passing fishermen took pity and released her and she fled to her father, Campbell of Inveraray. This irate chief invited Maclean to stay on the pretext of commiserating with him on the death of his wife. At the end of dinner, the 'deceased' wife confronted her husband, and her relatives set on him with broadswords.

Tourist Information

Oban, Mull and District, Oban, Argyll PA34 4AN, ✆ 0631 63122.

Tourist Information Centre, **Tobermory**, Isle of Mull, ✆ 0688 2182.

fishing

Wet- or dry-fly trout fishing is available in Mishnish Lochs, Loch Tor and Loch Frisa. Licences, tackle and bait can be obtained from Brown's Ironmongers in

Tobermory High Street or the National Forestry Commission's office at the south end of Loch Frisa. You can also hire rods and boats.

Tobermory

Having stopped off at Craignure, the ferry sails up the Sound of Mull to Tobermory —the Well of St Mary—the 'capital' of Mull. Founded as a fishing village in 1789 on the site of an earlier Christian settlement, it has one of the most sheltered harbours in Scotland, tucked round behind a headland. The village clusters round the anchorage. Terraced houses, colour-washed in strong reds, pinks, yellows, blues, ochres, rise from the harbour up a steep, wooded bank. Yachstmen and fishermen jostle for mooring space.

The **Mull and Iona Museum** (open weekdays, May–Sept: adm) is in a converted church in the Main Street, with exhibitions of the island's history. In the bay beyond the harbour lies the wreck of a galleon, the *Florencia*, part of the Spanish Armada, which is still a focus of attention for treasure seekers today. The ship sought shelter here in a storm in 1588. Always hospitable, the islanders treated the Spaniards with courtesy, restocking their stores and entertaining them in grand style. But Scotsmen are thrifty as well as hospitable and when rumour came that the *Florencia* was about to depart without having paid its dues, a local man, Donald Maclean, went aboard to remonstrate. He was locked up in the ship's cell, but managed to escape. In retaliation he blew up the ship, together with the hoard of gold and treasure it was alleged to have been carrying. So far, only a few coins and cannon have been discovered, but the search continues. Divers should note, however, that the wreck is protected and it is forbidden to dive in its area.

Tobermory has a nine-hole golf course, on the northern tip of the island, owned by the Western Isles Hotel. Spectacular views down the Sound of Mull are apt to distract the players.

Going west on the B8073, look for three small, linked lochs where there is trout fishing. Snake Pass, beyond the last loch, is said to be the home of many adders. This is also the start of a good walk to Loch Frisa.

On the steep hill down into **Dervaig** there is a cemetery at Kilmore, with some of the oldest gravestones on Mull. Filmgoers may recognise this as one of the sets for *Where Eight Bells Toll*. **Mull Little Theatre**, in Dervaig, 6 miles (9.5km) from Tobermory, is in the Guinness Book of Records as the smallest professional theatre in Britain, with 37 seats. Six times a week in the summer, two or more actors from visiting professional companies stage really excellent productions, which should be booked well in advance: ✆ 06884 245. In the winter there are amateur productions. A restaurant and guest house serves dinner before and after the show. Lunch is also served before matinées. Meals should be booked, ✆ 06884 345.

The Old Byre Heritage Centre, a mile (1.5km) beyond Dervaig (open daily, Easter–mid-Oct: adm) is a crofting museum with tableaux showing life at the time of the Highland Clearances with the family and animals round the central fire, busy about their daily lives. A half-hour audio-visual programme illustrates further what life was like.

The west coast road gives views out to the scattering of islands that create such wonderful seascapes, especially when seen against a setting sun. There are good sandy beaches and it is usually possible to find shelter on one of them.

Boats run from Dervaig or Ulva to the **Treshnish Isles** and to **Staffa**, when the weather is fair. A new landing stage on Staffa makes access easier in rough weather and some cruises allow you an hour ashore. You can go into **Fingal's Cave** by boat or walk round the side on a platform. This huge cathedral-like cavern is made up of columns of basalt, some hexagonal, truncated at different levels like organ pipes and of similar construction to Ireland's Giants Causeway. The formation inspired Mendelssohn in 1829 to write the *Hebrides* overture.

Cruises which include **Lunga** in the Treshnish Isles, are especially good during the nesting season. You are advised not to linger too long over the puffins at the start of your tour because they are so bewitching you may never see the rest of the island. They sit scratching, chatting and popping in and out of their burrows, an arm's length from you. There are also kittiwakes, razorbills, shags and guillemots and lots of black rabbits.

The island of Ulva will be familiar to anyone who knows the poem 'Lord Ullin's Daughter', which tells the tale of 'The Chief of Ulva's Isle' and his lover, fleeing her father's wrath and drowning in the ferry, crossing to the island. Lord Ullin stood helpless on the shore, while:

> The waters wild went o'er his child,
> And he was left lamenting.

A couple of miles before the Ulva Ferry look for the Eas Forss, a waterfall that cascades over the cliff into a pool and then under a rock, arching into the sea.

The walks and views all down the west coast are good. Much of the coastline is columned basalt with sandy bays and rock coves, with seals, guillemots, oystercatchers and herons in the rock pools. Wild flowers are abundant: orchids, bright pink thrift, yellow irises.

Where the road turns south, before cutting back inland across the Ardmeanach peninsula, you can look out across the entrance to Loch na Keal to Inch Kenneth. This was the burial place of many Scottish kings and was visited by Johnson and Boswell in 1773, as guests of Sir Allan Maclean and his two daughters. Unity Mitford took refuge here with her family after her unfortunate association with Hitler and the Nazis. To the right, **Tragedy Rock** is a huge boulder which crashed onto the cottage of a young local couple on the first night of their married life, 200 years ago, killing them both.

The Ardmeanach Peninsula is owned by the National Trust for Scotland. At Burgh on the southern tip, aptly named The Wilderness, there is a fossilized tree 50 million years old embedded in the shore.

The Ross of Mull is the southwest headland, with softer scenery. **Erraid**, the tidal islet off the southwest tip of the Ross, was once home to Robert Louis Stevenson, and it was here that David Balfour swam ashore from the wreck of the brig *Covenant*, in *Kidnapped*. **Uisken** on the south side, reached by a road from Bunessan, is a lovely beach with lonely crofts, mostly ruined—another village abandoned in the Clearances.

Isle of Mull Wine Co at Bunessan welcomes visitors and will arrange tastings by appointment, ✆ 06817 403. They make the Isle of Mull Vermouth, and The Mull Riveter, a blend of their own vermouth and bitters with vodka. Children will enjoy a visit to the **Angora Rabbit Farm** at Ardtun near Bunessan, where they can see how their clipped coats are made into wool. Further east at Pennyghael, take the road south to Carsaig, a lovely spot where salmon fishermen still work. The amazing Carcaig Arches is a famous geological freak—a natural, jagged archway through the rock.

The A849 goes inland back towards the east coast from the head of Loch Scridain. At Ardura a road turns south to Loch Buie, a lovely drive down past Loch Spelve and Loch Uisg. Moy Castle, at the end, now a ruin, was the ancestral home of the MacLaines of Lochbuie. If you take the track on round the coast for 3 miles (4.5km) you come to **Lord Lovat's Cave**.

Duart Castle (winner of the Castle of the Year award in 1988: open daily, May–Sept: adm), is 15 miles (24km) east of the head of Loch Scridain across great tracts of moor and hill. It is an impressive fortress on a headland guarding the approach to the Sound of Mull. It dates from the 13th century, and was the home of the Chiefs of Maclean, until it was confiscated after the Jacobite rising in 1745. It was bought back and restored in 1912 by Sir Fitzroy Maclean, who was then the chief. He was a gallant Hussar Colonel who had ridden with the Light Brigade in the Crimea and died at the age of 100, affectionately known as Old Man A Hundred. As well as the keep, visitors can see the cell where prisoners from the Spanish galleon *Florencia* were held after it had been sunk in Tobermory, in 1588, by Donald Maclean. There are relics of the Maclean family in the main hall, with many of the gifts presented to the late Chief—who was among many other things, Chief Scout and Lord Chamberlain—during his world tours. There is also an exhibition of scouting throughout the Commonwealth, in the old staff rooms at the top of the castle.

Just south of Duart, the road to **Grass Point**, on Lochdon, was the old drovers' road for cattle and sheep from the outer isles, bound for mainland markets. It was also the landing point for pilgrims going to Iona. The seal on one of the rocks round the bay is of rather a different species to those living in the waters round Mull. It was the handiwork of the eminent sculptor, poet and writer, the late Lionel Leslie. First cousin of Winston Churchill, he and his wife Barbara came to live in the old Drover's Inn, after the last war, building it up from a ruin with their own hands. Boatloads of visitors came over from Oban in the summer to have tea, buy local crafts and listen to the sculptor's stories. Even in his mid-eighties his wit was as sharp as the stone he could no longer see to carve. There are also bas reliefs of a deer, an eagle, fighting swans and horses on the walls of a roofless byre beside the house, in lasting memory of a great artist. The house has been done up as a holiday home.

Torosay Castle (open daily, late April–mid-Oct: adm) is a mile (1.5km) south of Craignure near Duart. This 19th-century Scottish baronial building, with all the embellishments so beloved by the Victorians, was designed by David Bryce. The 11 acres of terraced Italian-style gardens with a statue walk and water garden were laid out by Robert Lorimer. The house contains magnificent paintings of wildlife by Thorburn, Landseer and Peter

Scott, and family portraits by Poynter, de Lazlo, Sargent and Carlos Sancha. There are also hunting trophies, a library and an archive room with photographs and scrapbooks going back over 100 years. In the high season boats run from Oban direct to Torosay. A **miniature railway** runs from Craignure Pier, a mile and a half, to the castle, the only passenger train service in the Hebrides.

The roofless, ruined church by the cemetery at **Salen** is unlikely to be restored. A wicked Maclean of Duart was buried here many years ago and the consequence was the roof blew off. Three times they put it back and three times it blew away, unable to settle over the remains of such a villain. Sadly, the first-century statue of the Virgin Mary that used to be in this church has been stolen.

Iona

Getting There

The passenger ferry from Fionnphort, on Mull, to Iona, takes five minutes. There is also a Sacred Isles Cruise, on certain days in the summer, sailing from Oban, via Staffa, to Iona. They allow two and a half hours on Iona before the return journey.

No one can visit Mull without making a pilgrimage to the 'cradle of Christianity', though, in fact, St Ninian was spreading the word for nearly 150 years before St Columba founded his church on Iona in 563. The island is beautiful; white cockle-shell sand and vivid green slopes, slashed with rust-red granite and painted with wild flowers.

The powerful Irish saint, of royal descent, outlawed from his own land, came here with a few followers and set about converting the heathen Picts of Scotland to the Celtic Christianity of his homeland. Many Scots, Irish and Norse kings were buried on Iona including Macbeth and Duncan.

In 1938, George Macleod, a saintly Presbyterian Socialist, who renounced an inherited title but accepted one bestowed by the State, settled a new community on the island. Its purpose was to restore the ancient stones and create the present abbey and its domestic building. When Johnson and Boswell came here in 1773, the abbey was a complete ruin. Johnson was deeply moved by the atmosphere: 'That man is little to be envied . . . whose piety would not grow warmer among the ruins of Iona.' Today he may not have been so impressed. Opinions differ about this historic abbey: for some, the sanctity of the stark, unadorned interior has been erased by stalls selling postcards, souvenirs and booklets. They complain that the sightseers, slung about with cameras, are seldom inspired to kneel and say a prayer, and unfriendly ferrymen have been known to ram visiting boats which innocently trespass on ferry berths. But even if it does not, at first sight, feel like the house of God, Iona is special because St Columba was here, all those years ago. If you scratch below the rather worldly exterior, you will find informal services, taken by the warden and his wife, at which visitors are welcomed to share in the community worship. Visiting preachers and members of the community take part and everyone is encouraged to meet up afterwards for tea and coffee. There is a well-stocked bookshop.

Anyone feeling a tug of disappointment at the museum-like feeling of this sacred spot should climb the small hill, **Dun I**, to the north of the abbey. Look down on the buildings, the boats around the pier, the trails of people in bright anoraks and strap-hung impedimenta chattering, munching and scattering litter. Stay very quiet and listen: you may catch a faint echo of ironic laughter, and feel a gentle Celtic presence beside you. St Columba was known to have a well developed sense of humour.

Look out for **Iona Scottish Crafts** by the nunnery where they sell everything from jewellery and pottery to knitwear—very reasonable.

Where to Stay

expensive

Druimnacroish Country House Hotel, Dervaig, ✆ 06884 274/212, has what its name implies: a country-house atmosphere and excellent service; *céilidhs* often erupt when locals visit the bar. In conjunction with the Mull Little Theatre, they serve excellent dinners, by arrangement, before the plays begin. **Tiroran House**, ✆ 06815 232, is another place specializing in a small country-house atmosphere with candlelit dinners. The food is renowned.

moderate

Western Isles Hotel, Tobermory, ✆ 0688 2012, stands high above the harbour, open March to October. It is an old-fashioned, comfortable hotel. **Ardfenaig House**, Bunessan, ✆ 06817 210, is a small, country-house hotel, peaceful and remote, open May to September, with good food. **Isle of Mull Hotel**, Craignure, ✆ 06802 351, is a Benidorm-style monstrosity with 60 bedrooms.

inexpensive

Tobermory Hotel, ✆ 0688 2091, is right on the waterfront, and full of character. **Craignure Inn**, ✆ 06802 305, is the original drovers' inn, once scene of pungent activity, now more genteel with cars rather than beasts parked outside. It has four bedrooms and one public bathroom—which was more than the drovers got. **Quinish House** is a guesthouse in Dervaig, ✆ 06884 223, family run and comfortable. **Glenforsa Hotel** near the airport at Salen, ✆ 06803 377, is a log-cabin hotel with an easy, relaxed atmosphere.

Artists should head for **Inniemore**, at Pennyghael, ✆ 06814 201, a guesthouse-painting-school for promising amateurs, with first-class tuition. Prices on application.

On Iona, The Abbey, ✆ 06817 404, offers full board from March to December: visitors are expected to take part in the day to day activities of the community. There are also week-long courses: details from the joint wardens, Philip and Alison Newall. It's very cheap and pretty spartan, with 23 rooms, four bathrooms and monkish food (no licence). **Argyll Hotel**, ✆ 06817 334, on the shore looking back towards Mull, is open April to October. **St Columba Hotel**, ✆ 06817 304, is a modern, rather utilitarian place with 27 bedrooms and not much soul.

Eating Out

For an evening out, try **The Puffer Aground**, in Salen, © Aros 389. The food is good and you should book.

Coll and Tiree

Coll and Tiree, less than 11 miles (17.5km) off the northwest tip of Mull, are low islands which look barren from the sea but are charming, with green fields surrcunded by an almost continuous string of deserted white beaches, where you may see many sea birds, seals and even otters. Sturdy cottages have rounded, thatched or tar-felted roofs to withstand the winter gales.

Getting Around

You can hire cars which meet you at the ferry, very reasonably.

Coll

Coll is fish-shaped, about 13 miles long and 3 miles ((5km) wide. Sandy beaches, azure water, rocky coves, backed by machair strewn with wild flowers in spring, make this another away-from-it-all paradise. The record of sunshine is good (usually tempered by a persistent wind).

Two standing stones at Totronald, called *Na Sgeulachan* (the Tellers of Tales), are thought to be part of a pagan temple, and traces of prehistoric forts and duns scatter the island. Adamnan, Saint Columba's biographer, mentions it in his *Vita Sancti Columbae*. During the Norse occupation of the islands, Coll was the headquarters of Earl Gilli, brother-in-law of Sigurd, Ruler of the Orkneys and Hebrides in 1000. By the end of 13th century it belonged to the MacDougalls of Lorne, from whom it was taken by Robert the Bruce because they opposed him. It passed to a second son of the Macleans of Duart in the early 1400s and remained in their keeping until 1856, when Hugh Maclean, last laird of Coll, was forced to sell his estates to pay for his extravagant life style. John Stewart of Glenbuckie, factor to the Duke of Argyll, bought it and his ruthlessly efficient farming methods resulted in mass emigration to Canada and Australia by the unfortunate crofters who could no longer afford his inflated rents (see 'Topics: Highland Clearances'). Traces of their abandoned croft houses can be seen at the northern end of the island. The resident population is now about 130, with quite a few incomers and holiday-home owners. Coll has attracted a number of *literati* and features now and then in glossy magazines. Coll is known for its trout-filled lochs. Sea fishing is also good and local fishermen will take visitors out in their boats. Walking, bicycling, swimming, birdwatching, botany and relaxation are the chief occupations for visitors. There is a nine-hole golf course at **Arinagour**. This village has the main concentration of population, a trim place which lies round the western shore of Loch Eatharna, with twee cottages and gardens..

The economy depends mainly on farming, commercial fishing and tourism. A recent innovation is a small factory in Arinagour where a range of herbal skin-care products are made.

Breachacha Castle, recently restored and private, dates from the 15th-century, ✆ 08793 444/353.

Getting There

Boats run from Oban, four times a week in summer and three times in winter, and take three hours. Boats also run from Tobermory, taking two hours. For details, contact Caledonian MacBrayne, ✆ 0631 62285.

Tourist Information

Tourist Information Centre, **Oban**, ✆ 0631 63122.

Where to Stay

inexpensive

Isle of Coll Hotel, ✆ 08793 334, at the head of Arinagour Bay overlooking the Treshnish Islands, has six bedrooms and a Hebridean atmosphere. Also in Arinagour, with a restricted drink licence, **Tigh-na-Mara Guest House**, ✆ 08793 354, is a modern house overlooking the bay with eight bedrooms. Self-catering places include: one chalet and three flats in Arinagour, c/o Janet Driver, Arinagour, Isle of Coll, ✆ 08793 373; and a house, a bungalow and a bothy, c/o Mrs Stewart, Estate Office, Isle of Coll, ✆ 08793 339.

Tiree

Tiree, southwest of Coll, is about 12 miles (19km) long, 7 (11km) at its widest, dwindling to less than 1 mile (1.5km) at its narrowest. Its name comes from *Tir Eth* (Land of Corn), dating from the days when it supplied corn to Iona. It is so low and flat that it has the Gaelic nickname *Tir fo Thuinn* (Land Below the Waves). It used to be famous for its snipe before much of the ground was drained. The highest hill, **Ben Hynish**, is a 480-foot (148m) pimple. It shares with Coll a reputation for glorious beaches, abundant wild flowers and birds, as well as a high average of sunshine. This, with its magnificent Atlantic rollers, has earned it the title 'Hawaii of the North'. Windsurfers come from all over Britain to compete in Tiree where conditions are first rate. During championship weeks, world-class windsurfing can be watched. Tiree also has a phenomenal population of hares.

A standing stone near **Balinoe** is thought to have been part of a Druid temple. Many of the island names are Norse in origin, dating from the 400 years of Norse occupation from about 890 to 1266. Among the many ancient remains scattered over Tiree is **Dun Mor Broch** on **Vaul Bay** on the north coast. A well-preserved ruin, it is one of the tall, hollow towers probably built for refuge from Norse and other invaders. It is 30 feet (9m) in diameter, its walls as much as 13 feet (4m) thick.

Gott Bay is a 3½-mile (5.5km) crescent of sand, backed by rich machair carpeted with wild flowers. **Hynish** has a small dry dock, flooded by an elaborate system of fresh water from springs. **Skerryvore Museum**, in the old signal tower at Hynish, tells the story of the construction of the Skerryvore Lighthouse, visible at the end of a telescope, built by the father of Robert Louis Stevenson. There is a young people's outdoor training centre based in the lighthouse cottages. On the north shore of **Balephetrish**, another good beach, *Clac á Choire* (Stone of the Corrie) is a large granite boulder perched on a rocky base, a relic from the Ice Age. Decorated with intriguing prehistoric carvings, it is known locally as the Ringing Stone because of the metallic note it produces when struck. It is said that when *Clac á Choire* shatters, Tiree will sink below the waves.

Views are marvellous all round the coast, especially those to the Treshnish Islands to the east with the aircraft-carrier-shaped *Bac Mor* (The Dutchman's Cap). One of the best places to see the birdlife is under the sheer cliffs below Carnan Mor in the south. Look for the distinctive 'greenstone' on the beaches, found also in Iona. Tiree has a nine-hole golf course.

Getting There

Loganair fly twice daily from Glasgow to Tiree, ✆ 041 889 3181.

The car ferry from Oban to Tiree usually calls at Coll on the way, a four-hour journey in all. Boats also run from Tobermory. Further information: Caledonian MacBrayne, ✆ 0631 62285.

Tourist Information

Tourist Information Centre, **Oban**, ✆ 0631 63122.

Where to Stay

inexpensive

Scarinish Hotel, ✆ 08792 308, stands on the sea, with 11 rooms, one with private bathroom and two public bathrooms between the other 10. Good Highland hospitality. **Tiree Lodge Hotel**, ✆ 08792 353/368, also overlooking the sea, has 12 bedrooms, seven with private bathrooms plus two public ones, and the same easy atmosphere. **Balephetrish Guest House**, ✆ 08792 549, is a pebble-dash croft house, overlooking Balephetrish Bay, with four bedrooms and one bathroom. **The Glassery Guest House**, with a restaurant, is at Sandaig on the west coast, ✆ 08792 684.

Glasgow Necropolis

Glasgow

Beautiful city of Glasgow, with your streets so neat and clean,
Your stately mansions, and beautiful Green!
Likewise your beautiful bridges across the River Clyde,
And on your bonnie banks I would like to reside . . .

William McGonagall

Glasgow was once the ugly, boisterous, working-class hub of redundant industrial Scotland. Because of the flourishing Clydeside shipyards and all the associated heavy industry that grew up after the Industrial Revolution, Glasgow was particularly badly hit by the Depression of the 1930s. Unemployment brought hardship to seething warrens of slum tenements. But now, the 'Gorbals Image' (brilliantly encapsulated in *No Mean City*, by A. McArthur, written in the 1950s) has disappeared. Glasgow is a punchy, 20th-century city, humming with enterprise and vitality.

Edinburgh, with its Festival, its gracious Georgian buildings, its historic past and its genteel Morningside ladies, was for many years lulled into a complacent acceptance of its role as cultural centre of Scotland. That complacency has been exploded: Glasgow celebrated its reign as Cultural Capital of Europe in 1990, only the sixth city to be nominated, succeeding Athens, Florence, Amsterdam, Berlin and Paris. Poor Edinburgh: quietly, almost stealthily, that dirty, slum-infested tramp that was 'Glesca' had moved up and surged into the lead. Only Glaswegians themselves are unsurprised.

History

When Edinburgh consisted of a cluster of huts round a wooden fort, St Mungo was busy in Glasgow, establishing a church from which the present cathedral grew, on a site that had already been consecrated by St Ninian, two centuries before in the 4th century. So, although it cannot boast a saga of royal dramas, its recorded history goes back to the dawn of Christianity and relates to the fortunes of the church from that time.

Assuming that legend is born from fragments of fact, a Pictish princess, possibly the daughter of King Loth, was banished from her father's court at Traprain Law in Lothian in the 6th century because of her liaison with an undesirable suitor. She was cast adrift in a coracle on the Firth of Forth, and landed at Culross in Fife. St Serf (or Servanus) took her in and cherished her during the birth of her son, Kentigern. St Serf baptized mother and babe and brought the child up, giving him the affectionate nickname of Mungo (or Munchu), the Latin-Welsh endearment for 'dearest friend'. Mungo became a missionary: in fulfilment of a prophecy, he took the bones of a holy man, Fergus, and carried them until God told him to stop. Glasgow Cathedral now stands on that spot, and the bones of Fergus are interred there. The town that grew up around the church was called *Glas Cau*

(Gaelic for 'the dear green place') and in the mild, dampish climate that prevails, the land would certainly have been very green and fertile. Indeed, aerial photographs show a surprising amount of grass even now—over 70 parks in all.

Glasgow's coat of arms incorporates a salmon, a ring, a tree, a bird and a bell, all of which are related to the patron saint. Mungo saved the honour, and the life, of a queen by arranging for a ring that she had given her lover to be found in a salmon in the river, and returned to her to be shown to her suspicious husband. The tree is a branch that burned miraculously, enabling Mungo to rekindle the monastery fire that he had been entrusted to keep alight. The bird was a robin, a favourite of St Serf's, killed by accident and brought back to life by Mungo. The bell was one given to Mungo on his ordination and taken everywhere with him.

Glasgow's self-confident motto, 'Let Glasgow Flourish', stems from the more cautious invocation that was inscribed on the 16th-century bell on the Tron Church: 'Let Glasgow Flourish Through the Preaching of the Word and Praising Thy Name'.

The city saw moments of secular history: William Wallace defeated the English in a battle in 1300, over what is now the upper end of the High Street. The university was founded in 1451 by Bishop Turnbull, only 40 years after St Andrews. Mary, Queen of Scots' final bid for power after her escape from Leven Castle, in 1568, took place at Langside, near Queen's Park. She watched the battle from her horse, at Castle Knowe, riding forward into the mêlée to encourage her troops, who were, even so, soon defeated. Cromwell came to Glasgow in 1650, and heard himself denounced as a 'sectary and blasphemer' by the Rector of the University, Zachary Boyd, in a two-hour sermon. Cromwell took this public humiliation with rare humour, inviting Boyd to dinner and making him sit through three hours of prayer. Prince Charles Edward Stuart lodged in the town on his way to Culloden, in 1745.

Separated from America by the Atlantic Ocean, Glasgow merchants grew rich on the import of tobacco and sugar after the Union of Parliaments in 1707. The Clyde, once a shallow salmon river, was deepened by dredgers and the city flourished as a major port, developing into the world's leading shipbuilding centre. Times of recession always hit hardest at areas of heavy industry, however, and Glasgow's docks are no longer the hives of activity that they were: Clydeside no longer reverberates to the ceaseless clang, clatter and fizzle of thriving shipyards and the Clyde is no longer a busy waterway. But Glasgow has shaken itself free of dependence on heavy industry and diversified its economy so successfully that it is now a centre of modern technology, covering almost every form of manufacture.

Modern Glasgow: Renaissance

Glasgow offers as much top-class entertainment as anywhere in the country. Home of the Royal Scottish Opera, one of Scotland's most prestigious possessions, as well as the Scottish National Orchestra and Scottish Ballet, Glasgow also has the Burrell Collection, attracting art lovers from all over the world. There are top-class art galleries and museums, most of which are free and there is soon to be a new national art gallery. There are two universities.

The three-week Mayfest, only a few years old, is the second-largest arts festival in the UK, next to Edinburgh. There are Folk and Jazz Festivals in June and July and the World Pipe Band Championships in August, all attracting huge crowds. The Centre for Contemporary Arts is the best in Scotland, stimulating international interest. It mounts major art seasons with international themes—Polish in 1988, Soviet in 1989. Glasgow was recently said to rival Milan and Barcelona as one of the design capitals of the world.

Because the river flows through the heart of Glasgow, it is very much the main artery of the city, flanked by greens and quays, spanned by a network of bridges. A redevelopment programme has transformed the old docklands so that it is now possible to take a 'scenic' walk from Glasgow Green to Finnieston without danger of being hoisted on a crane. Glasgow Green, the oldest public park in Britain, was the common grazing ground for the medieval city.

From any elevation on a clear day, the horizon is smudged by distant hills: to the north, beyond the modest Kilpatrick Hills and Campsie Fells, the great humps of Ben Lomond, Ben Venue and Ben Ledi; the hills of Strathclyde in the west; the Lowther Hills to the south and the Pentlands to the east.

Architecturally, Glasgow is a curate's egg. Some of Britain's finest Victorian buildings are jostled by some of the 20th-century's worst examples of architectural sacrilege, mostly high-rise. The efficient motorway network, taking traffic through the heart of the city, has improved communications beyond belief but heartrending acts of vandalism were committed to build it. The M8 effectively cuts the city centre in two, dividing the commercial side from what is now the West End and university. Many of the older buildings have been cleaned recently: streets that used to be blackened by pollution have been restored to the warm glow of biscuit and red sandstone.

On the whole, the suburbs are a nightmare: an almost surreal jungle of ugly monsters marching away in all directions, built in a misguided attempt to depopulate the slums. In time, as people move back into the now tenable inner city, these travesties of architecture may be replaced.

All this is incidental to Glasgow's magic: the history, the monuments, the blossoming culture in every field of fine art are like facets in a diamond. In the earlier chapter on Edinburgh, there are long lists of things to see; a great parade of attractions and amusements: compared with that, this chapter may seem disappointingly bare and lacking in specific descriptions. Glasgow is not easily revealed on paper: its magic lies not in its tangible, visible, material assets, but in its soul. It is an elusive magic: a will o' the wisp vitality; a vibrant atmosphere; a bewitching character only discovered by experience.

This magic is to be found in the streets of the city; in the bars and cafés; down on the waterfront; in the markets and shops. It is found in conversation with the people of Glasgow.

If comparisons must be made, and perhaps this is inevitable with two major cities so close to each other, Glasgow is to Edinburgh what New York is to Washington. The Glaswegian is to the Scottish music hall what the Cockney is to the English, and as in all parodies, there is some truth in these images, but only in self-mocking overstatement. The Glaswegian is unique: a blend of the Irish who came over in their starving hundreds during the potato famine, and the deposed Highlanders, driven from their crofts by sheep farmers. He has the lyrical, romantic charm of the former and the gentle courtesy of the latter, combined with the Celtic wit and sensitivity of both. He adds to this endearing mixture a shrewd, worldly cockiness that stems from his independent spirit and courage.

Glasgow is like any strong personality: on first acquaintance one feels daunted and nervous and perhaps a little shy. But perseverance will uncover a warm character under the awe-inspiring façade and it soon becomes a 'dear, familiar friend'. Walk down to the river and stand on one of the bridges at night. The lights and reflections transform the work-a-day city into a fairy-tale kingdom of ethereal beauty.

It has to be said that Glasgow's climate, mild and moist, includes a higher than average rainfall that makes possession of an umbrella almost mandatory.

The logo that announced the city's explosive rebirth in the early 1980s, was a beaming yellow 'Mr Happy', with the words: 'Glasgow's miles better'. If this was a *double entendre*, it summed up the ebullient spirit of Scotland's most warm-hearted of cities. A new logo, 'Glasgow's Alive', sums up its awareness of Europe, people, business, the environment, visitors and culture.

Festivals

Glasgow has more than its share of annual festivals and it would not be surprising to see some of these move into the front line over the next few years, given the enthusiasm and enterprise mushrooming in the city's cultural pastures.

The Mayfest, now well established, and second only to Edinburgh as an arts festival, attracts international companies with first-class reputations. Drama, music, ballet, opera and art—all flood the theatres and halls and galleries for three weeks in May, incorporating various side-shoots of a 'fringe' character.

RSNO Proms are performed for two weeks in June, at Glasgow Royal Concert Hall.

The Flower Festival in Glasgow Cathedral is at the beginning of June—a celebration of nature in an ideal setting.

During the **Folk Festival** and **Jazz Festival**, in June and July, the city vibrates with folk music and jazz, indoors and out, played by groups from all over the world, especially Scandinavia and northern Europe. Ceilidhs and musical gatherings go on far into the night.

Greater Glasgow Tourist Board and Convention Bureau, 35/39 St Vincent Place (off George Square), © 041 204 4400. As well as an information centre, this is a Bureau de Change, with booking facilities for accommodation—both local and national— theatres, concerts, etc., as well as coach and tour tickets.

Scottish Tourist Guides Association, 3 Myrtle Avenue, Lenzie, © 041 776 1052, for information on guided tours throughout the country.

Mayfest Central Office, 18 Albion Street, Glasgow, © 041 552 8000.

Getting There

by air

Glasgow Airport, Scotland's transatlantic airport, in Renfrew, © 041 887 1111, is 15 minutes from the city centre. Regular scheduled flights are operated by United Airways from Washington, Northwest Airlines from Boston, American Airlines from Chicago, Air Canada from Toronto and Halifax, and British Airways from New York. There are also regular flights from London and other UK cities, and cities throughout Europe. Prestwick Airport, © 0292 79822, with transatlantic and international flights, is an hour away.

by rail

There is a high-speed rail link with London, taking about 5 hours, with sleeping cars, as well as direct or connected links with all other major towns in UK. British Rail do special packages, frequently changing and worth asking about. Central and Queen Street Stations, © 041 204 2844: 24-hour service.

by road

There are direct motorway links with all major UK cities. A number of inter-city coaches operate between Glasgow, London and other main towns. This is the cheapest form of public transport and not uncomfortable. Anderston Bus Station, © 041 248 7432. Buchanan Bus Station, © 041 332 9191.

Getting Around

Buses run frequently in and around the city as well as a large number of taxis. There is also an underground railway, 'The Subway', circling the city from Hillhead, north of Kelvingrove Park, round as far as Buchanan Street to the east, across the river to Shields and Kinning Park in the south and back round to Govan in the west before re-crossing the river to Partick. Because of the excellent motorway network, it is meant to be possible to get from the city centre to, for instance, the Burrell, way out in the suburbs, in a matter of minutes. Extensive roadworks on the M8 cause horrific traffic jams at present. A one-way system makes driving in the heart of the city remarkably un-fraught. The Tourist Office will give information about guided coach tours in the city and to other parts of Scotland.

There are also Clyde Cruises in the world's last ocean-going paddle steamer, *Waverley*, during the summer.

Discovering Glasgow

Don't try and cram all Glasgow into one day: if that is all the time you have, take a guided coach tour to orientate yourself in the morning, spend the afternoon at the Burrell Collection and Pollok House and sample one of the dozens of entertainments on offer in the evening. If history and culture are paramount, go to the cathedral, the St Mungo Museum of Religious Life and Art, and Provand's Lordship in the morning, or to the Museum and Art Gallery, and Hunterian Museum, at Kelvingrove Park.

Two days would allow you to do all the above, and in three days you could take in a cruise on the Clyde and find time to wander through the older parts of the city.

Glasgow Cathedral

Glasgow Cathedral (open daily: free) is on the site of the church built by St Mungo, and Glasgow grew up around it. It is the city's parish church, less than a mile (1.5km) east of the centre. There are still traces of the original stone building, dedicated in the presence of King David I in 1136 and rebuilt after a fire in 1197 in the lower church. The crypt, choir and tower were built in 1233, the rest being added at various stages in the succeeding years. During the destruction of church embellishment, in the Reformation, the last Catholic Archbishop, James Beaton, stripped Glasgow Cathedral of its finery and carried the treasures off to France, together with the archives, for safe-keeping. Tragically, in the later turmoil of the French Revolution, these were lost and have never been found. In 1578, when the iconoclasts of the Reformation threatened to destroy the cathedral entirely, the city's trade guilds intervened, and, miraculously, managed to prevent them: thus, today the cathedral is one of the finest examples of pre-Reformation Gothic architecture in Scotland. Although austere, like most Scottish churches, it is still very impressive.

St Mungo was buried here in 603. His tomb stands under a fan-vaulted ceiling among a forest of pillars in the Lower Church. In 1451, the Pope decreed that it was as meritorious to make a pilgrimage to Glasgow Cathedral as to Rome, and many thousands of pilgrims made their way here in medieval times. Look for the rood-screen with fire-and-brimstone carvings of the Seven Deadly Sins on its corbels.

The cathedral stands on a grassy slope embedded with horizontal gravestones, backed by the Necropolis, on a hill behind. This gives a sky-line of elaborate monuments, overshadowed by a Doric column from which John Knox keeps a stern eye on the city.

The new **St Mungo Museum of Religious Life and Art** (open daily: free) next to the

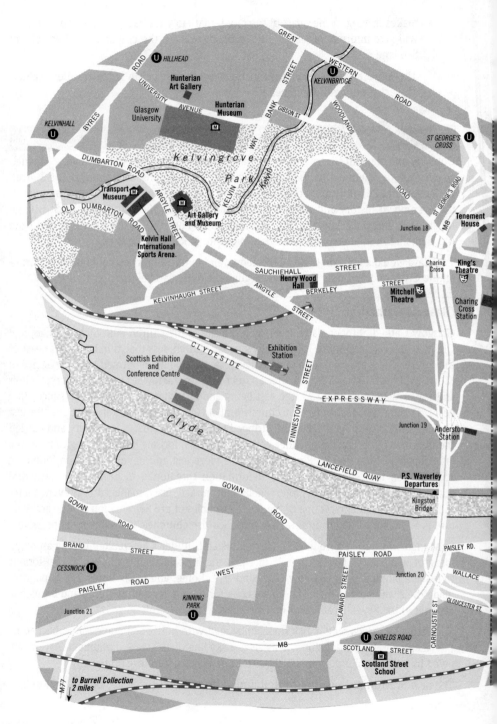

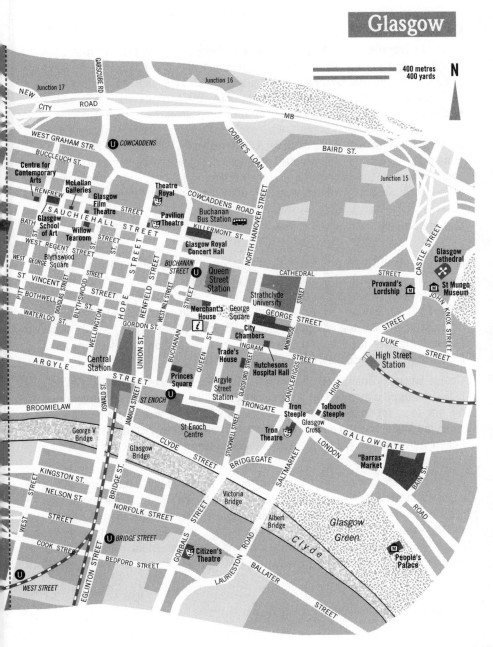

Glasgow

400 metres
400 yards

N

Junction 17
NEW CITY ROAD
Junction 16
M8
Junction 15
BAIRD ST.

GARSCUBE RD.
DOBBIE'S LOAN

WEST GRAHAM STR.
BUCCLEUCH ST.
Centre for Contemporary Arts
RENFREW
McLellan Galleries
Glasgow Film Theatre STREET
Theatre Royal
Pavilion Theatre
COWCADDENS ROAD
Cowcaddens
Buchanan Bus Station
NORTH HANOVER STREET
Junction 15

SAUCHIEHALL STREET
Glasgow School of Art
BATH STREET
Willow Tearoom
KILLERMONT ST.
Glasgow Royal Concert Hall

WEST REGENT STREET
WEST GEORGE STREET
Blythswood Square
ST VINCENT STREET
PITT
BOTHWELLS
DOUGLAS STREET
BLYTHSWOOD ST.
HOPE STREET
RENFIELD STREET
WEST NILE STREET
BUCHANAN STREET
Queen Street Station

BUCHANAN STREET

Merchant's House
George Square
Strathclyde University
CATHEDRAL STREET
Provand's Lordship
Glasgow Cathedral
St Mungo Museum
CASTLE STREET
JOHN KNOX STREET

WATERLOO ST.
GORDON ST.
City Chambers
GEORGE STREET
DUKE STREET

ARGYLE STREET
WELLINGTON ST.
UNION ST.
Central Station
Trade's House
INGRAM STREET
Hutchesons Hospital Hall
GLASSFORD STREET
MONTROSE STREET
HIGH STREET
High Street Station

OSWALD ST.
JAMAICA STREET
Princes Square
QUEEN ST.
Argyle Street Station
CANDLERIGGS
TRONGATE
Tron Steeple
Tolbooth Steeple
GALLOWGATE
BAIN ST.

BROOMIELAW
George V Bridge
St Enoch
St Enoch Centre
STOCKWELL STREET
Tron Theatre
Glasgow Cross
LONDON ROAD
"Barras" Market

KINGSTON ST.
BRIDGE ST.
Glasgow Bridge
CLYDE STREET
BRIDGEGATE
SALTMARKET
Glasgow Green

NELSON ST.
NORFOLK STREET
Victoria Bridge
Clyde

WEST STREET
EGLINTON STREET
COOK STREET
Bridge Street
GORBALS STREET
Citizen's Theatre
Albert Bridge
LAURIESTON ROAD
People's Palace

BEDFORD STREET
BALLATER STREET

cathedral precintc, the first museum of religion in the world and well worth a visit. The three galleries include an Art Gallery, Religious Life Gallery and Scottish Gallery and there is a Buddhist Zen Garden. Salvador Dali's *Christ of St John of the Cross* is here.

Provand's Lordship

Provand's Lordship (open daily: free), in Castle Street, opposite the cathedral, dates from 1471 and is Glasgow's only other pre-Reformation building of interest. Built as a priest's house and well preserved, it is a museum with 17th- and 18th-century furniture, tapestry and pictures, as well as the key of Leven Castle in Tayside, where Mary was imprisoned. She may have stayed in this house when she came to Glasgow in 1567 to visit her husband Darnley, who was sick with some disfiguring disease diagnosed as anything from smallpox to syphilis. Whatever it was, she took him back to Edinburgh—and murder. Provand's Lordship is the oldest house in the city, visited by both James II and James IV during their reigns in the 15th and 16th centuries. Mysteriously, among its exhibits is an early 20th-century sweetie shop.

George Square

George Square is at the heart of the city, barely a quarter of an hour's stroll from the cathedral, along Castle Street and George Street. There is something continental about the square on a sunny day, like the main piazza of a Mediterranean town, where crowds gather to pass the time. Visitors in shirt sleeves, slung about with cameras, linger among the trees and statues. The Square is a popular venue for demonstrations and the odd pop concert and other public events. At Christmas people bring their families to see the very special decorations, old fashioned and attractive with lit-up candles, swinging bells, angels, etc.

George Square is dominated by a statue of Sir Walter Scott on an 80-foot (24.5m) high column (first intended for a statue of George III). This mighty monument was the first to be set up in honour of Sir Walter, in 1837. He was barely 10 years old when the square was laid out in 1781. He towers over Queen Victoria, Prince Albert, Robert Burns, James Watt, and many others, wearing his plaid across the wrong shoulder as was his custom.

The Italian Renaissance City Chambers, topped by a wedding cake concoction of cupolas and a soaring tower, forms the eastern side of the square. A free guided tour of its interior (© 041 221 9600) includes a loggia, a great staircase, marble columns, soaring vaulted ceilings and a banqueting hall. It only lacks a gilded potentate, attended by bowing courtiers, stepping out from behind one of the columns to hold an audience in the Council Chamber.

The Museum and Art Gallery (open daily: free) occupies a vast red-sandstone building on the western side of Kelvingrove Park about 1½ miles (2.5km) west of the city centre. Ranking among Britain's best, this place needs several leisurely visits to be properly appreciated. Built as recently as 1901, it has a solid, Victorian feeling about it. An enormous central hall soars to the full height of the building, used sometimes for organ recitals and special exhibitions.

The museum has archaeological collections, including a reconstruction of the Antonine Wall, and some Bronze Age cists with their contents. There are also displays of armour, ethnological exhibits, natural history and social history. The engineering collection is so big that it is not possible to display everything: people with a special interest must ask at the enquiry desk.

The art gallery claims to have one of the finest collections owned by any city, beautifully displayed in upper galleries leading off the balcony that encircles the central hall. On the balcony there are sculptures (including works by Rodin and Epstein), ceramics, silver, jewellery, and furniture displays (including work by Charles Rennie Mackintosh, the Glasgow-born architect who had a considerable influence on European design in the late 19th and early 20th centuries).

Artists include Delacroix, Rubens, Rembrandt, Corot, Millet, Manet, Degas, Raeburn, Allan Ramsay, Reynolds, Hogarth, Whistler and Turner. There are lots of Impressionists and post-Impressionists, a Glasgow gallery, and a gallery for recent and contemporary paintings.

Kelvingrove Park is an ideal setting for the Museum and Art Gallery. It has an academic atmosphere, with the River Kelvin flowing through its 85 acres. It was twice used for international exhibitions at the turn of the century as well as for the Scottish National Exhibition in 1911. Concerts are performed several times a week in the summer, in the amphitheatre on the river bank. Strolling among the trees, lying on the grass, listening to the music—it is hard to believe one is close to the heart of this vibrant city. In winter, at dawn, the frost sharpens the skeleton trees and breath hits the cold air like smoke. The sun comes up over the roof tops, painting the walls of the university on its hill a fiery pink and you want to fling out your arms and shout with joy. Usually, however, you don't, because by that time the first joggers are emerging, as well as the man with his road-sweeping equipment.

Glasgow University was founded in 1451, with just a few classes in the cathedral crypt. It then moved to the High Street, south of the Cathedral Square, and was finally moved to Kelvingrove in 1870 where it now caters for more than 10,000 students.

The Hunterian Museum and Hunterian Art Gallery (open daily except Sundays: free) are in Hillhead Street, running north from the university and part of it. William Hunter was a student at Glasgow University in the 1730s. Having risen to fame and fortune as a physician, he left his collections of coins, paintings, prints, books, manuscripts, zoological, mineral and medical specimens to the university. The Hunterian Museum opened in 1807, Scotland's first public museum, and, since 1980, the Hunterian Art Gallery has been housed separately.

The museum has, as well as the world-famous Hunter Coin Cabinet, excellent geological, archaeological and ethnographical collections among its many exhibits. The art gallery's collection of work by Whistler, the contents of his studio at his death in 1903, is rivalled only by the collection in Washington's Freer Gallery. These paintings were inherited by Rosalind Birnie Philip, his sister-in-law, in whom he had instilled a determination that the English should not get their hands on work by a man whose genius they had failed to acknowledge. Rosalind gave a number of the paintings during her lifetime, on condition they should never leave the university. She bequeathed the remainder on her death in 1958. The present collection is made up of 80 paintings, over 100 pastels and several hundred watercolours, drawings and prints. Many of the works are unfinished.

The Hunterian Art Gallery houses the largest and most comprehensive print collection in Scotland, as well as paintings by Rembrandt, Chardin, Stubbs, Pissarro, Ramsay, Reynolds, Sisley and many more. Sculptures include work by Rodin, in the courtyard. It also boasts a comprehensive collection of work by Charles Rennie Mackintosh (1868–1928). One of Glasgow's talented sons, this architect and designer was a leading exponent of 'The Glasgow Style', which influenced the modern movement and had strong affinities with the Continental 'Art Nouveau', highly influential throughout Europe though less so in Britain. There is a reconstruction of No.6 Florentine Terrace nearby, now demolished, where he lived from 1906 to 1914. The rooms show all the decorations, alterations and improvements done to the original house by Mackintosh, together with some from his previous home at 120 Mains Street. For anyone who admires his austere approach to architecture and design, his clean, stark lines and manipulation of space and light, this is the finest existing example of his innovative flair and brilliance.

Glasgow is proud of her son Charles Rennie Mackintosh and he has left his stamp all over the city. The Mackintosh memorabilia and tourism has been somewhat overdone, however, with pseudo-Mackintosh lettering and furniture wherever you go.

The Glasgow School of Art, (open weekdays when the school is open and by arrangement, ✆ 041 332 9797), in Renfrew Street, is said to be one of Mackintosh's most outstanding creations. He designed it in 1896 and each façade of the building reflects a facet of his imaginative style. Members of staff will conduct tours at set times.

The Willow Tea Room, 217 Sauchiehall Street, is another memorial to Charles Rennie Mackintosh. Restored to his original design, it is furnished with chairs and tables of his design and they serve light lunches and tea, between 9.30am and 5pm.

The Headquarters of the Charles Rennie Mackintosh Society (open Tues, Thurs, Fri and Sat: free) is in the former Queen's Cross Church, at 870 Garscube Road, north of the Willow Tea Room. Built in 1897 Art Nouveau-Gothic style, the only church Mackintosh designed, it has an information centre, reference library and book stall.

The Centre for Contemporary Arts (open Tues–Sat: free), 346–354 Sauchiehall Street, is in a Grecian building that caused a stir when it was designed by Alexander Thomson in 1865. Thomson was Glasgow's, perhaps Scotland's, most important architect, only recently recognized by a growing public. This is Scotland's largest contemporary arts centre; a dynamic example of how the city has exploded into the forefront of the arts scene. Founded in 1975, it contains galleries, a studio theatre, a bookshop, café and bar. It holds an average of 30 exhibitions a year, and these exhibitions tour internationally as well as nationally. Programmes include drama, dance, music, readings, talks, films and festivals. The centre demonstrates effectively just how much Glasgow has reinterpreted its sobriquet of 'No mean city'.

McLellan Galleries, 270 Sauchiehall Street, © 041 331 1854, has recently been done up and has exciting visiting exhibitions.

The Regimental Museum of the Royal Highland Fusiliers (open weekdays: free) is at 518 Sauchiehall Street, with uniforms, pictures, medals, documents, photographs, trophies, and memorabilia, going back over the 300 years of the regiment's history.

The Tenement House (open daily 1 April–31 Oct, and otherwise at weekends: adm) at 145 Buccleuch Street, a few blocks north of Sauchiehall Street, is a first-floor apartment in a red-sandstone tenement built in 1892, restored to give an insight into the living conditions of the working-class family who lived here for half a century. There are two rooms, as well as kitchen and bathroom, with the original kitchen range, period furniture and fittings. Although authentic, it is perhaps a little too clean and neat. It is not difficult to visualize what was more likely the reality—the overworked mother, standing over her 'jaw-box' sink, admonishing her brood of children, anxiously awaiting the tipsy return of her man on payday.

The People's Palace (open daily: free) is on the eastern side of Glasgow Green, half an hour's easy walk southeast of George Square, so called because it was built in 1898 as a cultural centre for the people in the East End of Glasgow. It is a museum devoted to the story of the city from 1175 to the present, including the growth of trades and industry, trade unions, labour movements, women's suffrage, entertainment and sport. Among its exhibits are a purse and a ring that belonged to Mary, Queen of Scots; a bible that belonged to the notorious Archbishop Beaton, an organ built by James Watt and portraits of many famous Glaswegians. There is a café, shop and an exotic winter garden, with tropical plants and birds.

Glasgow has a number of museums of specialist interest. From the People's Palace, cross the river and go southwest to Albert Drive.

The Museum of Transport (open daily: free) is in the Kelvin Hall, in Argyle Street, across from Kelvingrove Park. It is one of the most renowned of its kind. Most forms of transport are represented, from bicycles and motor cycles and a painted, carved caravan, to six railway engines, some of which are 100 years old. There are trams, horse-drawn vehicles, commercial vehicles and cars. The Clyde room is a shipping gallery with models. Old photographs show many of the exhibits in use. Incorporated into the museum is a reconstruction of a 1930s street, with shops, a cinema, cars and delivery bikes and an underground station.

Scotland Street School (open weekdays: free), on the south side of the river, is a wonderful piece of architecture by Charles Rennie Mackintosh, particularly impressive when seen lit up at night from the M8. Each classroom is done as a reproduction of a different period of schooling—Victorian, wartime, etc. Recent complaints that cuts in the education budget will hamper the chances of modern schoolchildren are reduced to laughable proportions when you see the facilities and equipment that were responsible for the education of some of Scotland's leading industrialists, economists, doctors, historians, artists, writers, and academics. Well worth a visit.

Haggs Castle (open daily: free) is at 100 St Andrew's Drive, a mile (1.5km) to the west of the Museum of Transport. Built in 1585, and much restored, Haggs Castle was opened in 1976 as a museum for children, although only the snootiest of adults could fail to be fascinated by some of the exhibits. There is a reconstructed Victorian nursery, an 18th-century cottage interior and period gardens. Children are encouraged to use the workshops for museum-based activities such as spinning, weaving, candle-making and other crafts.

The Burrell Collection

Open daily, free, the Burrell Collection is 3 miles (4.5km) southwest of the city, in Pollok Country Park, signposted off the main roads and motorways, and served by a good bus service. Buses 21, 23, 45, 48A and 57 run from the centre, and 34, 89 and 90 across the south of the city.

Opened in 1983, the Burrell is Glasgow's greatest treasure, attracting thousands of visitors from all over the world. The collection was given to Glasgow by the wealthy industrialist Sir William Burrell (1861–1958) in 1944. Sir William joined his father's shipbuilding firm at the age of 15 and even then he had begun to collect paintings, against the wishes of his father who would have preferred him to spend his money on more 'manly' pursuits. By the time he was 96, he had some 8000 objects, an average of two acquisitions a week. He was a careful collector, canny in his haggling, sometimes missing an important piece because he refused to pay inflated prices.

In 1971, a two-stage architectural competition was staged with an almost impossible brief: to design, not an institution, but a home in scale and in sympathy with the collection and the environment of the park. Had there not been a postal strike, causing the entry deadline to be extended, the winning design by Barry Gasson would not have been submitted in time. The building has won prestigious architectural awards. From the big car park it is all sharp angles, glass, red sandstone and wood, designed to give the best possible light and perspective to the treasures inside, making full use of the reflection of the trees and grounds of Pollok beyond the windows. Opulent courtyards and arcades create the illusion of being out of doors.

The breadth of Burrell's taste is astonishing. He was a traditionalist, with no time for the avant-garde, but within that scope his eye was caught by anything: prehistoric artefacts, oriental art, stained glass, porcelain, silver, paintings, sculpture, carpets, crystal, and tapestries. The beauty and diversity of the collection gathered by one man dazzles the senses. Ideally, it should be taken in several bites to avoid aesthetic indigestion.

Reconstructions of the dining room, hall and drawing room of Hutton Castle, the Burrell's home on the Whiteadder near Berwick-on-Tweed, are incorporated into the building. Medieval stone and oak fireplaces and chimneypieces, antique furniture, tapestries, Eastern carpets, stained glass and the original soft furnishings, are all displayed with splendid effect.

There are objects from the ancient civiizations of Egypt, Iraq and Iran, Greece, the eastern Mediterranean and Italy. Among these can be seen: stone reliefs, bronzes, alabaster figures, an almost life-sized terracotta lion's head, amphora, Greek earthenware vases, mosaics.

Almost a quarter of the collection is oriental. Chinese ceramics include polychrome figures from the Tang Dynasty (AD 618–907); porcelain from 14th-century Yuan and 15th-century Ming dynasties; every sort of domestic ware and bright ceramic roof tiles with elaborate figures on them, to ward off evil spirits. Chinese bronzes include a 'champion vase': two cylinders joined by an eagle with outspread wings standing on a bear's head, probably awarded in archery contests. Chinese jades include jewellery, vessels, animals, fruit, and figures. There are Japanese prints, ceramics from the Near East, and Near Eastern carpets.

From medieval Europe, there is a 12th-century limestone portal from a church in Montron, in France, looking entirely right in its ultra-modern setting, as does the magnificent 16th-century sandstone portal from Hornby Castle. Medieval church art and sculpture are also well represented.

Burrell looked on his medieval tapestries as being the most valuable part of his collection. Most were originally woven for churches and private houses and displayed as status symbols by ecclesiastics and nobles alike. The colours of some are still so rich it is hard to believe they were stitched over 500 years ago. Look for the 15th-century *Ferret Hunt* and *Hercules Initiating the Olympic Games*.

Another relic of the Middle Ages is stained glass, and not all of it comes from churches. There are vignettes of everyday life, including a jolly man warming his bare toes before a roaring fire and an industrious Dutchman making roof tiles.

Among decorative arts, the Burrell Collection includes exquisite porcelain, silver, gilt, glass, 'treen' (made of wood), needlework, furniture, armour and weapons.

Sir William Burrell started his collection with paintings and was still buying them two years before he died, 80 years later. As with the rest of his treasures, he seems to have had an astonishingly catholic taste, ranging from Degas and Cézanne to Bellini and Hans Memling, whose *Annunciation* is so rich in colour and yet so simple in conception. Some of the paintings are disappointingly hung and lit and not easy to appreciate. There are a number of Impressionists and an assortment of prints and drawings.

Among the sculpture in the collection is Rodin's *The Thinker*, a bronze from one of the many casts of this best known of his works, in the original size. (The Thinker was meant to be Dante, pondering the fate of mankind, crowning Rodin's magnum opus, *The Gates of Hell*.)

Pollok House (open daily: free) is in the same grounds as the Burrell Collection—a much older-established show-piece now often neglected in favour of its magnificent neighbour. This is a pity. It was built in 1750, given to Glasgow in 1966 by the Maxwell Macdonald family, including the 361 acres of garden and parkland and contains one of the finest collections of Spanish paintings to be found anywhere in Britain. These were acquired by Sir William Stirling Maxwell when Spanish art was neglected and under-rated and range from 16th-century Cosida, across the whole field of Spanish painting, including El Greco, Murillo and Goya. There are also many works by other European masters, 18th- and 19th-century furniture, silver, ceramics and crystal. Look for the unusual astronomical clock, just like a standard grandfather clock until closer inspection reveals a face set with complicated dials. It is a lovely house in a fine setting and should certainly not be missed.

Pollok Park includes a Demonstration Garden, displaying all aspects of landscape gardening.

Outdoor Attractions

Glasgow Zoo (open daily: adm) is in Calderpark, 6 miles (9.5km) southeast of the city, on the A74, with all the animals you expect to see in a zoo.

The **Fossil Grove** (open daily: free), in Victoria Park west of Kelvingrove, is unusual. In 1887, workmen, cutting a path across an old quarry, revealed a fragment of a 230-million-year-old forest. The weird stumps and roots were formed by the setting of mud within the bark of the trees, which, compressed for millions of years, became the coal that fired the Clydeside furnaces in the 20th century. The stresses and worries of yesterday and tomorrow seem trivial, seen in the perspective of this relic.

The **Botanic Gardens** (open daily: free) are in Great Western Road, north of Kelvingrove. They cover 42 acres with flowers, trees, shrubs and a famous collection of orchids. The Kibble Palace, a Victorian glass pavilion, houses a luscious collection of tree ferns, and plants from the temperate zones of the world.

'**The Barras**' (Barrows) (open every weekend) at Gallowgate, north of Glasgow Green, is Glasgow's flea-market. Over 800 traders sell anything you want from stalls, barrows and shops along Gallowgate. This is a light-hearted place to idle away a sunny day. A good-humoured, jostling crowd fingers the bargains: beaten copper pots, leatherwork, straw mats, wicker baskets, silks and batiks, cottons and man-made fibres, polished wood and plastic urns. One could be serenaded by a busker; touched for a fiver by a conscience-stabbing down-and-out, or have one's wallet slid dexterously from a pocket or bag as one haggles over the price of a strip of foam rubber. For more information, go to 244 Gallowgate, or © 041 552 7258.

Top-class drama, music, ballet, variety shows, etc. can be found in Glasgow's theatres and cinemas.

Citizens Theatre, Gorbals Street, ✆ 041 429 0022/8177. Glasgow's repertory theatre, opened in 1878 as a music hall, with main auditorium and two studio theatres.

City Hall, Candleriggs, ✆ 041 552 5961. A versatile stage where you can see anything from the Scottish Chamber Orchestra to *céilidhs*.

Glasgow Royal Concert Hall, ✆ 041 332 3123. Specially designed by Sir Leslie Martin and opened by the Princess Royal in 1990, this modern complex has a 2500-seat hall, two good restaurants, conference and exhibition facilities. Leading international orchestras perform classical music and jazz here, as well as the Glasgow-based Royal Scottish National Orchestra, BBC Scottish Symphony Orchestra and City of Glasgow Philharmonic.

Glasgow Theatre Club, Tron Theatre, 38 Parnie Street, ✆ 041 552 5961. Actors and musicians meet in a club atmosphere.

Henry Wood Hall, Claremont Street, ✆ 041 221 4952. In what was Trinity Church, this classical concert hall is the administrative home of the Royal Scottish National Orchestra.

Kings Theatre, Bath Street, ✆ 041 552 5961. Drama, family entertainment, shows, musical and amateur shows.

Mitchell Theatre, Granville Street, ✆ 041 221 3198. Meetings, lectures and amateur dramatics.

Pavilion Theatre, Renfield Street, ✆ 041 332 1846. Family entertainment, variety, pop, rock, and pantomimes.

Theatre Royal, Hope Street, ✆ 041 331 1234. Home of Scottish Opera and frequent host to the Scottish Ballet, Scottish Theatre Company, National Theatre, Ballet Rambert and other international companies.

Tramway Theatre, Albert Drive, ✆ 041 423 7527.

cinemas

Odeon Film Centre, Renfield Street, ✆ 041 332 8701. Nine screens.

MGM Film Centre, Sauchiehall Street, ✆ 041 332 9513. Five screens.

Glasgow Film Theatre, Rose Street, ✆ 041 332 6535. Two screens.

Shopping

Glasgow's main shopping area radiates from George Square with branches of most leading chain stores. Don't miss a visit to the 'Barras' market, in Gallowgate, every weekend.

Princes Square, 48 Buchanan Street, is a luxury specialist shopping area, and the **St Enoch Centre**, 55 St Enoch Square, has over 50 stores under one huge glass roof.

For tweeds, tartans and woollen things, try **The Edinburgh Woollen Mill**, 72 Nelson Mandela Place, or **R. G. Lawrie Ltd**, 10 Buchanan Street, or **Pitochry Knitwear Company**, 130 Buchanan Street, or **Hector Russell Kiltmaker**, 85 Renfield Street.

Italian Centre, John Street, has designer shops such as Versace and Emporio Armani, which was one of the first designer label stores to open in Glasgow and helped to put the Italian Centre on the map. There are restaurants, cafés and a central courtyard with a fountain. For trendy clothes, try **Ichi Ni San** in Bell Street. For designer originals, go to **Cruise Clothes** in Renfield Street. **Flip**, in Queen Street, specialize in American-style clothes. There are lots of leather shops at the eastern end of Argyle Street. The **Warehouse**, 61–5 Glassford Street, is a designer superstore, reasonably priced considering some of the names on the lables.

Paddy's Market, Shipbank Lane, is Glasgow's repository for second-hand clothes. The City Council tried to close it down because it didn't suit Glasgow's new image but there was such an outcry they couldn't. In the past, Irish immigrants sold their possessions here in order to subsist.

Where to Stay

The following is a small selection of the many available, within an easy walk or short taxi ride from the main stations.

expensive

One Devonshire Gardens, Great Western Road, © 041 339 2001/334 9494, is definitely the best, comparable to a smart London hotel.

Forte Crest Glasgow, Bothwell Street, © 041 248 2656. A large (248 rooms *en suite*), ultra-modern, but friendly 4-star hotel that won the 1986 Hotel of the Year Award. Good food and very central.

Copthorne Hotel, George Square (formerly The Diplomat), © 041 332 6711, is an elegant, listed, 18th-century hotel, recently refurbished, incorporating the house in which Sir William Burrell grew up. International cuisine with a reasonable table d'hôte dinner or à la carte is served either in the conservatory or in the Window on the Square Restaurant.

The Carrick, 377–83 Argyle Street, © 041 248 2355, is another 4-star modern building in the city centre with all comforts and a friendly staff.

Buchanan Hotel, 185 Buchanan Street, © 041 332 7284, is an old-fashioned Victorian hotel with friendly personal service. The Buonasera is their Italian restaurant, serving Italian and continental food.

Kelvin Park Lorne Hotel, 923 Sauchiehall Street, ✆ 041 334 4891, recently renovated, has a friendly relaxed atmosphere. Their Butlers Restaurant has been designed in manor-house style and the food is good at a reasonable price. Newbery's Bar is decorated in the style of Charles Rennie Mackintosh and honeymoon couples get a special deal.

You might also try: **Glasgow Marriot**, Argyle Street, ✆ 041 226 5577, **Hospitality Inn and Convention Centre,** 36 Cambridge Street, ✆ 041 332 3311, and a number of **Stakis Hotels, The Devonshire Hotel**, ✆ 041 339 7878, **Glasgow Hilton**, ✆ 041 204 5555 and **Moat House International**, ✆ 041 2212022.

moderate

Babbity Bowster Hotel, Blackfriars Street, ✆ 041 552 5055, is small and friendly with an old-style tavern atmosphere. They burn peat on the fires and have a nice bar/restaurant on the ground floor.

Kirklee Hotel, 11 Kensington Gate, ✆ 041 334 5555/339 3828, is in Glasgow West, quieter and comfortable.

Central Hotel, Gordon Street, ✆ 041 221 9680, is a massive Victorian building in the city centre, with a warm welcome. The food is very reasonable; there is a carvery buffet and you can 'eat Scottish'.

inexpensive

Burnbank Hotel, 67–85 West Princes Street, ✆ 041 332 4400. All modern conveniences in splendidly Victorian surroundings. The staff are friendly and the food reasonable, with a full Scottish breakfast.

Arfon Hotel, 969 Sauchiehall Street, ✆ 041 334 7802, is in a terrace in the centre and good value.

Coach House Hotel, 14 Hyndland Road, ✆ 041 357 2186/339 6153, is also good value.

Eating Out

expensive

The Buttery, 652 Argyle Street, ✆ 041 221 8188, serves good food in the style and environment of a Victorian gentleman's club.

Poachers Restaurant, Ruthven Lane, Byres Road, ✆ 041 339 0932. Small, privately owned restaurant in a 1870 farmhouse, serving fresh Scottish produce cooked to order: prime meat, fish, shellfish and game.

Rogano, 11 Exchange Place, ✆ 041 248 4050. Dating from 1876, the Rogano was remodelled in 1935, when the *Queen Mary* was being built on the Clyde, in classic art deco style. It is now renowned for its atmosphere and excellent seafood.

(It has a cheaper **Café Rogano** downstairs where the food is just as good.)

moderate

See Café Rogano, *above*.

Cantina del Rey, King's Court, Osborne Street/King Street, ✆ 041 552 4044, serves exclusively Mexican food.

Di Maggio's, Royal Exchange Square, ✆ 041 248 2111. Delicious and unusual pizzas and pastas. You can get a set meal in the basement for under a fiver.

The Colonial India Restaurant, 25 High Street, ✆ 041 552 1923. In the merchant part of old Glasgow, the Colonial features in the *Good Food Guide* and uses only fresh ingredients, mostly local: fillet of beef, shellfish, chanterelles from Fort William.

Hospitality Inn, 36 Cambridge Street, ✆ 041 332 3311. Garden café restaurant in American style, or elegant Prince of Wales cocktail bar and restaurant.

Forte Crest Hotel, see above. Good Scottish food in Jules' Bar—American-style cocktail bar and grill.

Butlers Restaurant, Kelvin Park Lorne Hotel, see above. Traditional manor house decor and excellent food.

Ubiquitous Chip, 12 Ashton Lane, ✆ 041 334 5007. Plants, a waterfall, batiks and murals, in a lively cobbled courtyard restaurant. Original and traditional recipes using the best Scottish ingredients.

inexpensive

Baby Grand, 3 Elm Bank Gardens, Charing Cross, ✆ 041 248 4942. Likened to a New York café, Baby Grand specializes in fish dishes, accompanied by the baby grand, whose mood varies depending on the pianist: jazz, soul, blues, requests.

Joe's Garage, Bank Street, ✆ 041 339 5407, has good pizzas and pastas and unusual starters.

Pierre Victoire Millar Street, ✆ 041 221 7565, and Byres Road, tel041 339 2544 serve authentic French food in informal surroundings.

Nico's Sauchiehall Street, ✆ 041 332 5736, serve good continental food.

Entresol Restaurant, Central Hotel, see above. The menu includes haggis and trimmings, fillet of sole Bressay, whisky cream crowdie.

Ewington Hotel, 132 Queens Drive, ✆ 041 423 1152. West-coast fresh seafood, Aberdeen Angus beef and home-made soups such as delicious Cullen Skink.

Good drinking places include the bar in The Babbity Bowster (see above); John Street Jam, John Street; The Scotia, Stockwell Street; Tron Cafe Bar, Trongate; Cottiers, Hyndland Road; Uisge Beatha, Woodlands Road and Whistler's Mother, Byres Road.

Central

Central lies at the heart of Scotland, with Stirling rearing up on a crag like a sentinel towards the east. Part of it is a densely populated industrial sprawl and part is flat and dreary, but there are many beauty spots and the long view is of hills all around and the promise of Highland scenery beyond. Small and compact, this area offers an astonishing variety of scenery, some of it lovely, but because it is so close to Edinburgh and Glasgow it attracts many holidaymakers. The Trossachs, a subtle combination of loch, wooded slopes and crag backed by green and russet hills, are a magnet for tourists.

Within the protection of these hills, with no sea coast, the climate is gentle and often hot. Lush vegetation carpets the glens, vivid green ferns and mosses, with great slabs of forest, hardwood and conifer, climbing the shoulders of the hills and giving a glorious display in autumn. Further north is rugged moorland.

History

This was Pictland, home to those mysterious aboriginal settlers, indigenous long before the Irish Scots, the Angles and the Welsh began to push north, followed by the Romans, who built the Antonine Wall in AD140. Hadrian's Wall, further south, had been built ten years previously but was not proving to be strong enough to deter the ferocious northerners. This new wall was built by Roman legionaries in a somewhat futile attempt to push the barbarians back and cut them off. It stretched 37 miles (59km), from Old Kilpatrick on the Clyde to Bridgeness on the Forth and you can see some of its best-preserved sections around Falkirk. If possible, go first to the Royal Museum of Scotland in Edinburgh or the Hunterian Museum in Glasgow, where there are excellent descriptions of how it was constructed as well as many relics. In spite of the enormous effort that went into the building of it, the wall was abandoned by the Romans after less than 25 years, and the Picts were left to their own devices.

Christianity crept in from the west, spread first by St Ninian's missionaries in the 4th century and then by those of St Columba in the 6th. The Picts were canny about change: you will find sacred stones carved with a combination of Christian and pagan symbols to appease any of their old gods who might be jealous. In the 9th century, when Kenneth Macalpine drew the Picts and Scots together, the Picts began to lose their identity as a dominant race and gradually faded from existence before their history could be recorded.

Stirling reflects the subsequent history of this central hub of Scotland: in 1297 William Wallace kindled the fire of rebellion against English suppression at Stirling Bridge, and Robert the Bruce refuelled the blaze in 1314 by defeating Edward II at Bannockburn. Stirling became a favourite royal residence as well as an important fortress, guarding one of the gateways to the highlands. Prince Charles Edward Stuart wasted valuable time and resources laying siege to the castle in January 1746 but failed to capture it.

Today, the region draws its wealth from the industrial belt in the southeast, from a thriving tourist trade, agriculture on the flat lands below the hills, and from sheep on the moors.

While you aren't likely to get the nose-to-tail traffic so familiar near popular resorts in England, you can expect frustration on twisting single-carriageway roads, when dozens of impatient drivers get trapped behind slow-moving, impassable caravans.

Tourist Information

The head office is at Tourist Information Centre, Dumbarton Road, **Stirling**, © 0786 475019, open all year round. The smaller centres, usually open April–Oct, are at **Falkirk**: The Steeple, High Street, © 0324 620244, open all year; **Aberfoyle**: © 08772 352; **Airth**: Pine 'n Oak, Kincardine Bridge Road, © 0324 683422; **Callander**: Rob Roy & Trossachs Visitor Centre, Ancaster Square, © 0877 30342; **Drymen**: © 0360 60068; **Dunblane**: Stirling Road, © 0786 824428; **Killin**: Main Street, © 0567 820254; **Stirling**: 41 Dumbarton Road, © 0786 475019; **Tillicoultry**: Clock Mill, © 0259 752176; **Tyndrum**: Car Park, © 08384 246.

Falkirk, the Hillfoots and Stirling

The southern part of Central Region around Falkirk is dominated by Stirling, on its cone of volcanic rock in the distance. Although not attractive, it contains unexpected treasures and a wealth of history. Beyond, where the Ochils guard the way north, fringed by the towns and villages of the Hillfoots, lie glens whose fast-flowing rivers once powered woollen mills supplied by sheep in the hills. In spite of its proximity to the industrial belt, this area has a peaceful, unspoilt charm.

Falkirk

Falkirk, deep in the heart of industrial Scotland, does not, on first acquaintance, tempt one to linger; but there is much history behind its modern face and it should not be passed by too quickly. A pedestrian precinct within the High Street has made the town centre very much more attractive, and an enterprising council has plans for a number of other schemes that should revitalize the whole place. This is where the best-preserved sections of the Antonine Wall can be seen.

Falkirk was once one of the cattle drovers' main trysting places—it's hard to picture the scene now in the busy streets. Two battles were fought here; one in 1298, when William Wallace was defeated by Edward I, and one in 1746, when Prince Charles Edward Stuart, retreating north, turned to defeat the government forces who pursued him. His victory was partly due to the cowardice of the Hanoverian troops, many of whom, when confronted by the ferocity of the charging Highlanders, threw down their arms and fled.

Falkirk Museum in Orchard Street, behind the main car park, is small but extremely interesting (open daily, except Sun: free). Here you will find the history of the area, including a good section on the Antonine Wall, and details of the two battles. Prince Charles lodged in **Callendar House**, in Callendar Park, surrounded by woodland. The house is a huge pile in French chateau style and was empty and at risk. It is in the process of restoration for public use and makes a good centrepiece for the park, where you can walk and play golf.

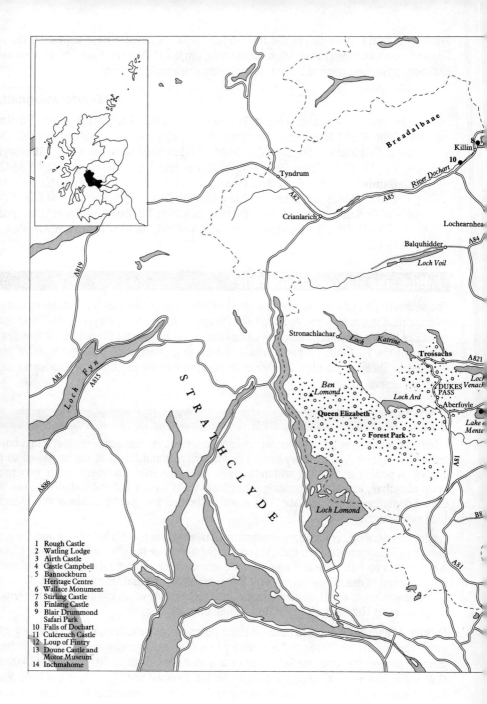

1 Rough Castle
2 Watling Lodge
3 Airth Castle
4 Castle Campbell
5 Bannockburn
  Heritage Centre
6 Wallace Monument
7 Stirling Castle
8 Finlarig Castle
9 Blair Drummond
  Safari Park
10 Falls of Dochart
11 Culcreuch Castle
12 Loup of Fintry
13 Doune Castle and
   Motor Museum
14 Inchmahome

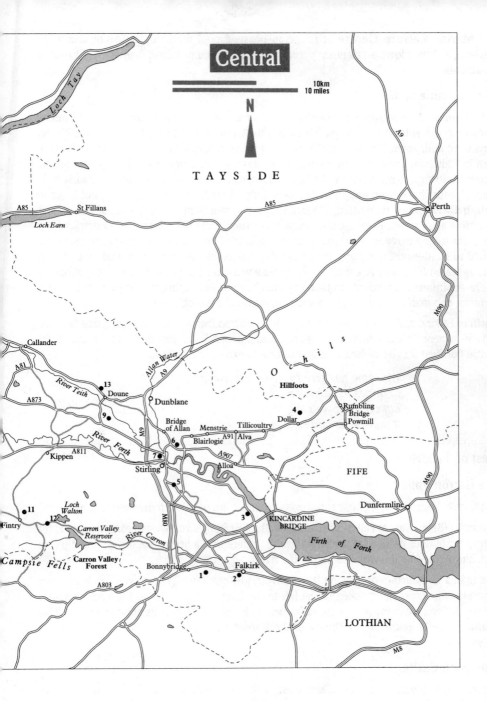

The **Marina Leisure Centre** at Camelon boasts a pool with tropical decor and wave machine, a chute (down an elephant's trunk), saunas, solarium, squash courts, multi-gym and restaurants.

The Antonine Wall

The Antonine Wall was an earth rampart consisting of a ditch, with a military road running along its south side and the displaced earth thrown up to create a wall on the north side. Forts were built about 2 miles (3km) apart along its 37-mile (59km) length. A part of it can be seen in Callendar Park Housing Estate, to the east, and another at Watling Lodge, on the western outskirts of the town by the canal. Here, just by the road, you can see clearly how the wall must have been and there is a description board. To get the best idea of it, go to **Rough Castle**, well signposted, 1½ miles (2.5km) from Bonnybridge, west of Falkirk and accessible at all times. Even the slag heaps that overshadow the plateau fail to detract from the queer feeling that you get, standing there thinking of those unfortunate legionaries, accustomed to gentler postings, condemned to this bleak place, menaced by a wild race of men who appeared from nowhere with blood-curdling war cries and primitive but lethal weapons. There are information boards to help the imagination, explaining where there was a fort, barracks, commander's house, granary, headquarters and a bathhouse.

North of Falkirk, and now closed, are the famous Carron Ironworks, a massive place founded in 1759, where Britain's cannons were once made. Robert Burns paid a visit to the works and was so horrified that he dashed off a quick verse to express his feelings:

> We came na' here to view your works
> In hopes to be mair wise,
> But only lest we gang to hell
> It may be no surprise!

West of Falkirk

The Carron Valley

The Carron Valley is surprisingly rural, even though it lies so close to the industrial belt.

Five miles (8km) west of Falkirk, at Dunipace, the B818 takes you westwards along the River Carron for 6 miles (9.5km) to the reservoir. Just before this, a bridge reaches an island picnic spot, surrounded by the white tumult of the river.

Less than a mile further on beyond the reservoir, just past Loch Walton, you can leave your car and walk across the bracken to the left to the Loup of Fintry. Here, the Endrick Water tumbles in long creaming falls to the valley below, filling the air with its noise and spray. **The Campsie Fells** guard the southwest of the Carron Valley, offering easy climbs with fine views.

Culcreuch Castle

Culcreuch, at Fintry, 3 miles (4.5km) west of the falls, was built by the Galbraith clan in 1296. The Galbraiths lived here until their chief, Robert, had to flee to Ireland after a scandal in 1630. The castle has had various owners since then and is now a well-preserved mansion run as an hotel, with the old keep incorporated. There is parkland, a walled garden, pinetum and loch.

North of Falkirk to the Hillfoots

The Pineapple

Instead of going straight up to Stirling on the motorway, take the A905 4 miles (6km) north of Falkirk, past the road to **Kincardine Bridge**. Past the Airth Castle Hotel turn off left on B9124. Not far along the road, a clear sign directs you to The Pineapple (always accessible on the outside: free), an amazing garden folly, built as a retreat on the Dunmore estate in 1761 and now owned by the National Trust for Scotland. This is a relic from when the privileged classes could indulge their fancies with the help of a large labour force. A double wall surrounds a 14-acre garden, the space between the walls being for the circulation of hot air from furnaces. On top of the north wall is a vast stone pineapple, 45 feet (14m) high, whose interior forms the domed roof of a circular chamber below. Pineapples were grown here in 1761, under hothouse conditions in the buildings flanking this centrepiece, with an army of stokers beavering away to feed the fires that provided the necessary heat. The buildings are now converted to a holiday home which you can rent through the Landmark Trust (✆ 0628 825920).

Rumbling Bridge

Go back past Airth Castle Hotel to the roundabout and cross Kincardine Bridge, taking the A977 north for 9 miles (14.5km). Turn off left after Powmill to Rumbling Bridge. It would be all too easy to cross the River Devon at Rumbling Bridge and completely miss the significance of its name, so narrow and steep is the gorge as you cross the bridge by car. There is a car park just beyond the hotel on the right. A gate by the bridge gives access to steps, from where you can see this breathtaking chasm, 120 feet (37m) deep and so narrow in places that you could shake hands with someone on the far side, if you were both acrobats.

The gorge was formed from the fast-moving water from melting ice sheets at the end of the last Ice Age, about 10,000 years ago. From an observation point, well fenced, you can see how the present bridge, built in 1816, spans the older one, built in 1713, with a queer, leap-frog effect. The lower bridge is an alarmingly narrow stone span lacking any sort of parapet, and this was once the main highway.

A securely fenced path, built by Sappers, winds along the river from the bridge. Trees cling tenaciously to the steep limestone rock face of the gorge, as well as vivid green ferns, mosses, liverworts and trailing vines, with the river rumbling over the rocks far below.

A short distance up from the bridge is **Maceachin's Cave**, a truly romantic spot where an escaping Jacobite, Hector Maceachin, hid after Culloden in 1746, having escaped from Castle Campbell (see below). He was hidden by the daughter of the local laird, Hannah Haig. How could they not have fallen in love in this wonderful setting? They did: and were married. You can walk a short distance up to Devil's Mill, where the thumping of the water on the boulders sounds like a mill grinding; it is so called because it didn't even stop for the Sabbath. Downstream from the bridge you get to **Cauldron Linn**, a double waterfall, impressive after rain.

Castle Campbell

Castle Campbell (open daily, Apr–Sept; closed Thurs afternoons and Fri, Oct–March: adm) is 3 miles (4.5km) west of Rumbling Bridge and a mile (1.5km) north of Dollar. Visitors should use a map and look out for the Historic Scotland signs, for the castle is not well signposted.

Try to go on a fine day, preferably in autumn. The reasonably agile can park at the bottom, instead of driving up the rough track to the car park, and take the footpath up the burn, through steep, mossy, wooded banks; a secret place overhung with ferns where you must watch where you walk. The path crosses narrow foot bridges, offering sudden glimpses of cascading water through rocky ravines. Ahead, high up and apparently inaccessible, the castle soars in lofty isolation on a spur above the wooded ravines of the Burn of Care and the Burn of Sorrow, backed by a crescent of bracken-covered hills, which are copper-coloured in autumn.

Enigmatically, the castle was once called *The Gloume* (Gloom), yet even with the dismal names of the two burns, it is the least gloomy of any place in the world. Seen in sunlight, with the trees at their autumnal best, it is much more a castle of enchantment.

The present castle dates from the 15th century, built on the site of an earlier fortress and acquired in marriage by the Campbells of Argyll, who changed its forbidding name by Act of Parliament in 1489. John Knox preached here in 1556, on the grassy slope now called Knox's Pulpit. Montrose's army tried (and failed) to take the castle in 1645. (Some of his troops, of the Maclean Clan, having a private feud with the Campbells, wanted an excuse to burn it.) General Monk was also here, nine years later, and his troops made a better job of destruction.

A vaulted 'pend' leads into the courtyard and a substantial amount of the ruin is intact. In the tower is the great hall with the entrance to the pit prison, on the right of the fireplace. From the roof there are views down across Dollar Glen and up into the hills.

The Hillfoots

The Hillfoots villages, strung out westwards from Rumbling Bridge under the Ochils, provide a scenic **Mill Heritage Trail**, tracing the history of the development of wool production in this area. The villages of **Dollar**, **Tillicoultry**, **Alva** and **Menstrie** grew up at the foot of the Ochils, above the marshy bog of the plain, in the 16th century. The good grazing of the hills and the pure, soft water of the burns that ran down to feed the River Devon, were ideal for the foundation of what was to become a world-famous woollen industry, with easy access to the markets in Stirling, Edinburgh, Glasgow and Perth. As you follow the Mill Heritage Trail westwards from Dollar to Stirling, take time off to walk up any of the glens that run north into the Ochils, where the burns that used to drive the mills cascade downwards. The hills beyond are haunted by the ghosts of Covenanters who took refuge here.

Dollar is best known for its Academy, one of Scotland's leading schools, once called MacNabb's School. John MacNabb, who died at the beginning of the 19th century, was a local boy who made a fortune at sea and returned to his native land to share his wealth. The village straddles the tree-lined River Devon, with stone cottages whose gardens shout with colour in the summer. You can see Castle Campbell, high on its crag, floodlit at night—a most impressive sight. Dollar's milling tradition was the least developed in the Hillfoots villages, possibly because the local landowners were reluctant to encourage industry so close to the prestigious MacNabb's School. **Brunt Mill**, by the burn above the village, was built in 1820 and now belongs to the Academy.

Tillicoultry, less than 3 miles (4.5km) to the west, at the heart of the Mill Trail, has the **Clock Mill Heritage Centre** with all the information you could want: looms, workshops and an audio-visual show. There is also a tourist information centre. This village was producing cloth in Mary, Queen of Scots' day and their coarse, hand-woven cloth became known nationally as Tillicoultry Serge. Don't miss a visit to **Paton's Mill** in Lower Mill Street, where you can buy Glen Gordon knitwear from the mill shop. **Sterling Mill**, built in 1846 and used as a barracks in the First World War, was later a paper mill. Now a furniture warehouse, it has a picture gallery, gift shop, garden centre and restaurant.

Alloa, 4½ miles (7km) southwest of Tillycoultry, has a fine medieval tower in the process of extensive restoration for public use. This was once a stronghold of the Earls of Mar. Mary, Queen of Scots stayed here as a child, as did her son James and his son Henry. Mary returned here when she was married to Darnley.

Alva, a couple of miles or so further west, is dominated by the massive six-storey Strude Mill, built in 1827 when the cottage-based woollen industry was being taken over by factories. If you walk up Alva Glen you see traces of a complex water system of pipes, weirs and overflow channels, once used to feed the waterwheel of the mill. There are several mill shops to visit in Alva. **Inverallan Hand Knitters** in Shavelhaugh Loan are the largest hand-knitting company in Europe, employing about 2000 knitters who work in their own homes. Their patterns go back to AD 830 and are found in the Book of Kells.

Menstrie, a couple of miles west of Alva, is another of the Hillfoots villages with a milling tradition. **Menstrie Castle** (open by appointment with the NTS Perth Office, ✆ 0738 31296: adm) is a 16th-century tower house. It has been rather over-enthusiastically restored and rises from the middle of a housing development like a toy fort on the nursery floor amidst a clutter that should have been tidied away. It contains a Nova Scotia Exhibition Room, run by the National Trust for Scotland in honour of Sir William Alexander, who was born here. He was sent off to found a Scots colony in Canada in 1621, as a reward for his services to the Crown. He was an indifferent poet and an unpopular Secretary of State for Scotland, and one thing he would never have permitted is the building of a modern housing estate on his doorstep.

Still going west towards Stirling on the A91, about 1½ miles (2.5km) beyond Menstrie, look for a concealed entrance signed 'The Square'. This leads to the tiny village of **Blairlogie**, a delightful huddle of pretty old houses and a whitewashed church, built along narrow, winding streets on a ledge below the Ochils among orchards and colourful gardens. Blairlogie is one of the first of the Hillfoots communities. It grew up around the castle, a sturdy little fortress on a shelf above the village, not open to the public.

Stirling

Stirling, backed by the Ochils, beckons to you from whichever way you approach. It rises abruptly from the flat plains: a fortress-crowned rock with a grey town clinging to its steep sides—a colourful but blood-stained history book. Because of its strategic position, guarding the route north, this was a fortress town since earliest times; bitterly fought over, bravely defended. Seven battlefields, including Bannockburn, lie within its shadow. Stuart monarchs held court here. In 1746, Prince Charles wasted precious time and equipment besieging it. The history of the town is encapsulated in the castle.

Stirling has flung itself into tourism with wholehearted gusto. (Some of this gusto, unfortunately, has allowed insensitive development to spoil parts of it, particularly around the station.) It is the ideal centre for a holiday, if you like plenty of organized fun. For the entire summer the town is ablaze with colour and excitement, humming with every sort of entertainment, exhibition and event, decorated with flowers and banners. There is **Stirling Tartan Festival Fortnight** in July, a celebration of all things Scottish, with dancing, ceilidhs, concerts and guided walks. **The Top of the Town**, centred on Broad Street, the heart of the Old Town and former market place, is vibrant with medieval street stalls, period costumes and buskers. There is an **Orientation Centre** opposite the castle esplanade, where you can find out exactly what is on offer. During the summer, an antique open-topped bus links the Old Town with the commercial centre.

Stirling Castle

Stirling Castle (open daily: adm) stands aloof above all the summer frivolity at its feet. Run by Historic Scotland, the castle has a visitor centre in the car park, run by Loch Lomond, Stirling & Trossachs Tourist Board with an excellent film of introduction.

Legend credits King Arthur with having taken the castle from the Saxons, adding a touch of romance to a stronghold that seems otherwise too solid for the chivalric wisps of Arthurian tales. What is certain is that Alexander I died here; Henry II took it as part-payment for the release of William the Lion after the Battle of Alnwick; and that same William died here in 1214. In those days it would have been built of timber, superseded by masonry in the 13th century. Continual alteration and restoration have resulted in the castle seen today, most of it 15th- and 16th-century with Renaissance architecture added by James IV and James V.

One of the castle's many memorials to its history is the **Douglas Room** where in 1452 James II summoned the eighth Earl of Douglas, whom he suspected of disloyalty, stabbed him to death and threw his body out of the window at the end of the passage. Tradition held that a skeleton, found in the garden in 1797, was that of Douglas. You can't help feeling sorry for the frantic king, trying to heave the gory remains through the window.

In **The Chapel Royal**, nine-month-old Mary was crowned Queen of Scots, surrounded by scheming nobles and a miasma of conflicting loyalties and ambitions. Mary lived in the castle until she was taken to France at the age of five. The chapel was rebuilt by her son, James VI/I, and is now the Memorial Hall for the Argyll and Sutherland Highlanders, whose head-quarters are in the castle. In the recently expanded **Argyll and Sutherland Highlanders Museum**, there is a good collection of regimental memorabilia with some 15 Victoria Crosses won by members of this famous regiment.

In the **Lions' Den**, outside the palace, James III and James IV both kept lions. Catching and shipping them must have presented a terrible problem for whoever had the job of supplying them.

Floodlit at night, the castle is transformed into a fairy-tale setting, visible from miles away. Various stirring events take place periodically on the esplanade: Beating the Retreat, solo piping, massed pipe bands, all enhanced by the historic setting.

The Old Town

The old part of Stirling town is clustered up the hill to the castle: Spittal Street leads up to St John's Street and Broad Street, which converge at the top to form Castlewynd. A number of historic buildings line the steep, narrow streets, including the **Church of the Holy Rude**, built uphill with the choir elevated, where Mary of Guise was made Regent for Mary, and where James VI/I was crowned. **Mar's Wark**, at the top of Broad Street, is the remains of a palace that was started in 1570 by the Earl of Mar but never finished; it was mostly destroyed during the Jacobite rising in 1746.

Below the Old Town, the **Thistle Centre** is a covered shopping precinct. **Rainbow Slides Leisure Centre** (open daily: adm), in Goosecroft Road, has over 200 metres of translucent water tubes, filled with lighting and sound effects, down which you swoosh, in breathtaking spirals. There is also a pool, solarium, sauna, steam room and café.

Smith Art Gallery and Museum in Dumbarton Road (open daily except Mon: free) was founded in 1874. Extensive redevelopment recently won it the Scottish Museum of the Year Award. It provides an excellent introduction to the history of Stirling, and a constantly changing programme of exhibitions, demonstrations and lectures.

Around Stirling

Bannockburn Heritage Centre

> *Sir Robert the Bruce at Bannockburn*
> *Beat the English in every wheel and turn,*
> *And made them fly in great dismay*
> *From off the field without delay . . .*

from 'The Battle of Bannockburn', by William McGonagall

A visit to Bannockburn is more of an historical pilgrimage than a search for scenic beauty. From Stirling follow the signs for **Bannockburn Heritage Centre** (open daily, April–Oct:

adm), not for Bannockburn. The Battle of Bannockburn took place in 1314, over an area that is now mostly housing, less than 2 miles (3km) from Stirling.

The heritage centre is on higher ground, to the southwest, at Borestone Brae, where Bruce is said to have set up his standard on the evening before the battle. You can see fragments of the 'bored-stone' with its socket hole, in the visitor centre where an audio-visual theatre gives a history of the battle.

If you walk through the hedge from the car park, you come to the imposing **Robert the Bruce Memorial Statue**. Bruce was that great general who won his battle mounted on a pony, a golden circlet on his helmet to identify himself, armed only with a battle-axe. He instructed his men to dig man-traps all over the plain, disguised with branches, and to scatter iron spikes, or calthrops, over the field. Before the battle, Bruce's army knelt to receive a blessing from a friar who walked among them with a crucifix in his hands. Edward mistook the situation and thought they were begging for mercy. 'They are,' he was told, 'but from God, my liege, not from us. Yonder men will win the day or die upon the field.'

The National Wallace Monument

A visit to Stirling is not complete without going to see the Wallace Monument (open daily, April–Oct: adm). It is almost as much of a landmark as the castle, 1½ miles (2.5km) northeast of the town on top of 300-foot tall (92m) Abbey Craig. It is a Victorian monster of a tower, 220 feet (66m) high with a mighty bronze statue of Wallace set in its wall above the door.

It is a steep, zig-zagging climb from the car park but there are seats where you can rest. Recently refurbished, the five floors contain a 'battle tent' with the talking head of Wallace, his sword and the story of the Battle of Stirling Bridge in 1297, which he is said to have directed from the top of Abbey Craig. There is a Hall of Heroes with marble busts of some of Scotland's heroes. Don't be daunted if you can't recognize them all: there is an audio-visual presentation which fills you in on each of them. There is a 360° diorama of the surrounding landscape with the history described and you can climb to a parapet below the crown of the monument for dizzying views across the Carse of Forth to the castle on its rocky eminence above Stirling town. From here you can see seven battlefields, each of which played an important part in Scotland's history: Cambuskeneth, Stirling Bridge, Falkirk (two battles), Bannockburn, Sauchieburn and Sheriffmuir. There is a shop and café, woodland walks and a picnic area.

Bridge of Allan

A couple of miles (3km) north of Stirling, Bridge of Allan was a spa town in Victorian times, visited by fashionable people from near and far. The **Museum Hall** is a fine piece of architecture lying derelict in the centre of the town. Essential repairs have recently been carried out and it is hoped that it will be restored soon, though whether for public use or for private dwellings is not yet known. There are some pleasant riverside walks, to remind you of Burns' 'Banks of Allan Water'. The University of Stirling is southeast of the town in the grounds of Airthrey Castle, designed by Robert Adam and used by the university. The Strathallan Highland Games take place here in August.

Dunblane

Dunblane, 4 miles (6km) north of Stirling and by-passed by the A9, is a small town built around its ancient cathedral in the valley of the Allan Water. A narrow main street leads up to the cathedral close, with some fine old buildings around it.

The **Queen Victoria School**, on the northern outskirts of the town, is a State-endowed boarding school for the sons of servicemen, run on military lines, where the boys receive both a good education and a firm discipline not always found in fee-paying public schools.

The Doune and Dunblane Agricultural Show is in July.

Dunblane Cathedral (open daily: free) was founded in 600 by St Blane of Bute, grandson of King Aidan of Dalriada, and still has parts of the old Celtic church in its red sandstone walls. Most of the present cathedral was commissioned by Bishop Clement in the mid-13th century. The roof was stripped after the Reformation but it was restored in 1892 and is now the parish church. This Gothic building has an oval window that you can only see from outside, decorated with carved leaves and flowers and called the Ruskin Window because John Ruskin praised it. After a visit to the cathedral, he said: 'I know not anything so perfect in its simplicity, and so beautiful, as far as it reaches, in all the Gothic with which I am acquainted.'

Three poignant stone slabs in the cathedral are memorials to Margaret Drummond and her two sisters, all poisoned in 1502 by scheming nobles. James IV was in love with Margaret. (Some go further and say he was secretly married to her.) Politicians desired a union with England, and Margaret Drummond was a threat to this plan. Why her luckless sisters had to be eliminated as well remains a mystery—perhaps they all ate from the same dish. Within a year of this awful crime, James married 14-year-old Margaret Tudor and found himself the brother-in-law of bellicose Henry VIII.

The Cathedral Museum and **Library** (open daily in the summer except Sun, with a donation box) is in the cathedral close. The museum was the Dean's House, built 1624, and displays local history.

Blair Drummond Safari Park

Blair Drummond Safari Park (open daily, mid-March–Oct: adm) is on the River Teith 7 miles (11km) to the southwest. This is one of Scotland's more enthusiastic attempts to cater for whole families on holiday. Here you can see lions, giraffes, tigers, hippopotami, etc., or take a boat-trip on the lake and see a chimp island, or take a 'Flying Fox' cable slide across the lake. This is a bonanza for children, with aquatic mammal shows, a pets' corner, adventure playground, a 3D 'Cinema 180', an 'Astraglide', picnic areas, shops, amusement arcades, restaurants and a bar for exhausted parents. The house, which is a school for handicapped children, is not open to the public.

Doune

Doune, 3 miles (4.5km) west of Dunblane, is a small, winding village with wooded hills rising in folds to the north. In the 17th and 18th centuries, this was an important pistol-making town, with three factories to support the industry, and the drove road linking Highlands and Lowlands for carrying the pistols to market. The coat of arms has crossed pistols on it.

Stand in the attractive, triangular market square and try to picture the scene when it was a 17th-century sheep and cattle market, to which people flocked from miles away. There would have been ramshackle stalls selling broth and ale; a press of wild-looking men from the hills, herding their beasts; smoke from fires and the smell of animals and the unwashed. It was a living, seething scene, full of bawdy jokes and raucous laughter, with underlying tension and sharp eyes on the watch for trouble between Covenanters and soldiers.

Doune Castle

Doune Castle (open daily, Apr–Sept; closed Thur and Fri p.m, Oct–March: adm) is one of Scotland's best-preserved medieval castle ruins. Built in the 14th century by Robert, Duke of Albany and his son, Murdoch, it was annexed by the Crown after the wholesale execution of the Albany family by James I. James IV gave it to his Queen, Margaret Tudor, who in turn passed it to her second husband, Henry Stuart, Lord Methven. Later it passed to the Earls of Moray who still own it; the Bonnie Earl of Moray, in the ballad, who came 'soondin' through the toon', lived here. The gatehouse is a self-contained complex complete with its own water supply in case of siege. Built round a large courtyard, it is protected by two rivers and a deep moat. A long, vaulted passage leads into the courtyard with a vaulted chamber on the right where Prince Charles put the prisoners he took at the Battle of Falkirk, having captured the castle.

The **Lord's Hall** on the first floor of the main tower has two magnificent fireplaces side-by-side and a window from the steward's room beyond the thick wall. Picture it when it was filled with smoke from the two blazing fires, with rushes on the floor, dogs squabbling over bones, and a throng of people jostling for attention from the nobles at the high table. The gardens were created in the early 19th century by the tenth Earl of Moray. They include a walled garden, a pinetum, shrubs and woodland walks through the glen.

The Bridge in Doune was apparently built by Robert Spittal, in 1535. Spittal was tailor to the wife of James IV. (He also founded Spittal's Hospital in Stirling, so the queen must have paid him well.) Spittal is said to have come to the ferry that preceded the bridge and been refused passage because he had no money on him. He built the bridge to spite the unfortunate ferryman.

Doune Motor Museum

The Doune Motor Museum (open daily, April–Oct: adm) contains Lord Moray's collection of vintage cars, mostly in working order. The collection includes Hispano Suiza, Bentley, Jaguar, Aston Martin, Lagonda, and the second oldest Rolls Royce in the world. There is a tarmac track, about a mile long, for racing hill climbs: during hill climb weekends the Motor Museum and café are open only to people attending the climb. A number of other events take place here throughout the summer including car rallies and radio-controlled aeroplane rallies.

expensive

North of Stirling, **Cromlix House**, Dunblane, ✆ 0786 822125 is a typical Victorian country house, exuding an air of self-satisfaction that might have something to do with an impressive collection of awards and stars. It is undeniably comfortable, though the food, like the curate's egg, is good in parts.

moderate

Culcreuch Castle at Fintry, ✆ 036086 228, will satisfy anyone looking for antiquity and history (see above). This 14th-century castle is log-fire cosy, without too many frills, in 1600 acres of parkland. A very different sort of atmosphere greets you at **Airth Castle Hotel** near Kincardine, ✆ 0324 83411. The castle's history goes back to the early 14th century, but conversion to hotel has somehow robbed it of any feeling of history, and though it is extremely comfortable, it is too restored and modconnish to keep you on the watch for ghosts. Even in the Dungeon Bar and restaurant, you are too aware of the self-conscious decor to pick up any echoes of the screams and moans of the wretched prisoners.

In Stirling, **Golden Lion** in King Street, ✆ 0786 75351, won't let you down if it's dependability you are after. The decor is a bit glitzy but the food is good. **Park Lodge Hotel**, 32 Park Terrace, ✆ 0786 74862, is a treat. Partly Victorian, partly Georgian, this charming town mansion overlooks the park and castle, in nice gardens. Some of the rooms are replicas of period rooms, with antique furniture and drapes, old paintings, ornaments and there is a four-poster bed. The food is haute cuisine and there is a good wine cellar.

Stirling Arms Hotel, Dunblane, ✆ 0786 822156, is a 17th-century coaching inn on the banks of the Allan Water. Its Oak Room Restaurant will give you a good meal. **Stakis Dunblane Hydro Hotel**, ✆ 0786 822551, is large, modern, comfortable and convenient. It has an indoor swimming pool, a whirlpool spa and sauna, all-weather tennis, crazy golf, an adventure playground and a gymnasium.

The Trossachs

Callander

Once beyond Doune, you begin to feel the lure of the Highlands. Callander, 8 miles (13km) from Doune and a good holiday centre for this area, is a sturdy town to the east of the Trossachs, overshadowed by Ben Ledi. The town was rebuilt to its present wide design by military architects in the wake of Prince Charles, perhaps because it is easier for rebels to hold a town if the streets are narrow and houses close together. Television addicts might experience a sense of *déjà vu* here, for this was Dr Finlay's *Tannochbrae*. It also features in *The Country Diary of an Edwardian Lady*. From here you are within easy reach of the Trossachs and invigorating walks up through wooded glens onto the moors, with streams and rivers rushing down to fill Loch Lubnaig and the River Teith. Walk up to the Bracklinn Falls and remind yourself that Sir Walter Scott once rode his horse across here for a bet: or to the Falls of Leny and watch out for the water sprites, dancing in the spray-mist. In the summer, Callander is the stage for a variety of entertainments such as organized ceilidhs, open-air pipe-band concerts and Highland dancing, as well as wild-life slide shows. Callander International Highland Games are in August.

Rob Roy & Trossachs Visitor Centre, in Ancaster Square (open daily, March–Dec), tells the life of the Highland folk hero. There's traditional entertainment on summer evenings.

There is no one particular thing to see in and around the Trossachs. The scenery is attractive if you have not already been spoiled by the Highlands. Because it is easily accessible from the densely populated industrial towns to the south, it has become popular and perhaps over-rated. Preferably explored outside the tourist season, this area is best appreciated on foot. Even in the high season, most sightseers prefer to stay within sight of their cars and few are on the prowl before ten o'clock in the morning. Avoid weekends. You have only to make an early start and get away from the roads to shake off the feeling of claustrophobia that can attack when there are too many people. Autumn and early spring are the best time in this land of forested ravines and gullies.

Although people tend to refer to the whole of the area between Callander and Lochearnhead on the east, and Loch Lomond on the west, as the Trossachs, in fact the Trossachs proper is only the gorge that runs from Loch Achray to Loch Katrine, a rugged pass barely a mile (1.5km) long. Locals will give you two meanings for this strange name: 'bristly country' or 'the crossing place'; no one is sure which is correct. Thick woods often obscure the view, but now and then you get a hint of the magic that enchanted Sir Walter Scott. The road twists and climbs through gorse and bracken and very green moor, past rhododendrons, with plenty of footpaths leading off.

Loch Katrine

Loch Katrine, 9 miles (14.5km) west of Callander, is the setting for Walter Scott's 'Lady of the Lake'. Ellen's Isle is named after the heroine of the poem. From 1 May to 28 September you can take a 45-minute trip in the Victorian steamer *Sir Walter Scott* and cruise along the length of the loch from Trossachs Pier to Stronachlachar. As you watch the passing shore, picture fair Ellen being wooed by the mysterious James FitzJames, who bore a remarkable resemblance to King James V, the monarch who enjoyed roaming the countryside disguised as the Goodman of Ballengiech. A prosaic guide will tell you that this loch is also Glasgow's water supply. Because of this, there is a large notice at the pier forbidding you to swim, paddle, picnic, fish, camp, light fires, or throw coins in the loch: though why anyone should feel the urge to throw their money into a loch is a mystery.

There is a café at the pier and souvenir shops.

Aberfoyle

Aberfoyle guards the southern approach to the Trossachs and is a lively holiday centre. The road north, 'Duke's Pass', is too densely wooded to give more than a glimpse of the lochs below. Walter Scott made his first notes for *Rob Roy* in the dining-room of the village manse.

The Scottish Wool Centre (open daily: adm) in Aberfoyle, displays the history of sheep in Scotland over 2000 years and the story of wool, with films, sheepdog demonstrations, spinning and weaving, a children's farm, shop and restaurant.

Queen Elizabeth Forest Park Visitor Centre is a modern stone building just before you come down into Aberfoyle, with an ornamental lake and walks. In the lodge, displays illustrate the wild-life and vegetation of the park and there is a shop and café.

You can walk right through the park to the eastern side of Loch Lomond. A single track road runs south from Rowardennan and you can climb Ben Lomond from here (3192 feet—982m), for a bird's-eye view. For those who like organized sightseeing, the 45,000-acre park includes a forest car trail, and a cycle-way.

Inchmahome Priory

Before going on north from Callander, take the A81 6 miles (9.5km) southwest to Lake of Menteith and take the ferry to Inchmahome Priory, a semi-roofed ruin on the largest island of three on the lake. (The weather dictates the running of the ferry, for which you pay, and the priory is open daily April–Sept: free.)

Founded for Augustinians in 1238, the priory was a refuge for Mary, Queen of Scots for a short while before she was sent off to France to grow up out of range of Henry VIII's 'Rough Wooing'. It is nice to think of the little girl, in the garden now called Queen Mary's Bower, playing hide-and-seek, perhaps, with the indulgent monks.

A surprising number of pilgrims come here to see the grave of Robert Cunninghame Graham, the 'rebel laird' of the estate, who died in Buenos Aires in 1936 aged 84. This flamboyant character travelled extensively in South America, Spain and Morocco; married a Chilian poetess; was imprisoned for 'illegal assembly' in 1887 (a Socialist demo in Trafalgar Square); was elected first president of the Scottish Labour Party in 1888 and wrote many travel books, essays and short stories. He was a close friend of both Joseph Conrad and W. H. Hudson.

The Farmlife Centre (open daily, May–Oct: adm) at Dunaverig Farm, 2 miles (3km) west of Thornhill, has traditional farm buildings with old farm implements, machinery and memorabilia, farm animals, an adventure playground, nature trails, a craft shop and tearoom.

Balquhidder

> *A famous man is Robin Hood,*
> *The English ballad-singer's joy!*
> *And Scotland has a thief as good,*
> *An outlaw of as daring mood;*
> *She has her brave Rob Roy . . .*

from 'Rob Roy's Grave', by William Wordsworth

Another popular literary association in this area is at Balquhidder, on Loch Voil, north of the Trossachs, 10 miles (16km) or so north of Callander, and just west of the A84. This is where **Rob Roy** lived, died and is buried. This colourful, Robin Hood-like character, much romanticized by Scott, lived between 1671 and 1734, son of Macgregor of Glengyle. Rob Roy started life peacefully enough as a herdsman. But the Macgregors had been outlawed for their blood-thirsty habits and life was hard. He took to cattle rustling and smuggling, robbing the rich to pay the poor, and legends of his daring escapades and narrow escapes around Loch Katrine make good reading, even if, in reality, he was no doubt a rogue and a menace to his neighbours. He died uncharacteristically in his bed and was buried in Balquhidder churchyard. You can't miss the grave: the Clan Gregor have been unable to resist the temptation to 'do it up'.

Stronvar House (see Where to Stay, below) has a Bygones Museum and Balquhidder Visitor Centre (open daily March-Oct: adm) with a collection of memorabilia.

Lochearnhead

Fourteen miles (22.5km) north of Callander on the A84, you come to Lochearnhead, on the western corner of Loch Earn. There are several good hotels here and a boating and water-skiing centre. The loch runs 7 miles (11km) east to St Fillans (see 'Tayside', p.338), a ribbon of water sheltered by hills and an ideal place for a holiday.

Where to Stay

expensive

Probably your best bet is **Roman Camp Hotel** in Callander, ✆ 0877 30003. In 20 acres of garden beside the River Teith, on which you can fish, this hotel dates from 1625 and was a hunting lodge of the Dukes of Perth. It's only open from mid-March to mid-November. It's comfortable and the food is good.

moderate

The Lake Hotel, Port of Menteith, ✆ 08775 258, stands right on Scotland's only lake, looking across to Inchmahome. They've retained much of the art deco furniture and decor and provide good food. The **Stronvar Country Hotel** in Balquhidder, ✆ 08774 688, has four-poster beds in a laird's mansion with crow-stepped gables overlooking Loch Voil. With only five bedrooms, this hotel is peaceful. There is a Bygones Museum and Visitor Centre in the house.

Bridgend House Hotel, in Bridge Street, Callander, ✆ 0877 30130, faces the road with a mock-Tudor face and has good views, four-poster beds and tries hard with its garden.

Forest Hills Hotel in Kinlochard, near Aberfoyle, ✆ 08777 277, is a big country-house hotel with a multi-million-pound leisure centre, including a swimming pool, set in 20 acres of informal gardens overlooking Loch Ard. It also has luxury self-catering apartments.

inexpensive

Victorian **Brook Linn**, in Callander, ✆ 0877 30103, has spectacular views from a two-acre garden. It is only open from March to November and the food isn't bad.

In Lochearnhead, **Clachan Cottage Hotel**, ✆ 05673 229, is a charming old white cottagey building overlooking Loch Earn, with lovely views. What it may lack in sophistication is made up for in atmosphere.

For an exceptional bed and breakfast, in a charming house with a warm, friendly welcome, try Mrs Duke, Norrieston, Thornhill, ✆ 0786 85 234.

Breadalbane

Called after the Earls of Breadalbane (emphasis on the middle syllable) who used to own most of it, the land north of the Trossachs is your overture to the Highlands. In the days before the clan system was abolished, many bitter battles were fought for supremacy over these hills and moors. Campbells, MacNabs, Macgregors and MacLarens contested every inch, committing ghastly atrocities to wreak revenge on each other. You are likely to find a different sort of tourist here: more energetic, striding out with knapsack and climbing boots. It is rugged territory, where you may see roe deer and golden eagles, tumbling rivers, spectacular falls, and dark lochs. For botanists there are masses of wild flowers and unusual plants. Cut by the glens of the rivers Dochart and Lochay, and veined by the network of burns that pour out of the hills to feed them, this is walking and climbing country, backed by the massive hills of Strathclyde to the northwest.

Killin

Killin is about 7 miles (11km) north of Lochearnhead, a couple of miles off the A85, on the A827. This attractive village with hotels, shops and eating places has an almost alpine feel to it, especially when there is snow on the hills. It sits astride an old bridge, under which the Falls of Dochart carry the River Dochart in a tumble of falls and rapids, swirling down through the village into Loch Tay, long and deep between two ranges of hills (see p.336 for the Ben Lawers Visitor Centre, on the north side of Loch Tay).

On **Inchbuie**, the lower of two islets below the old bridge in Killin, is the burial ground of the MacNabs, an aggressive clan who ruled the district until they emigrated to Canada in the 19th century, forever at loggerheads with the neighbouring clans of Neish and Gregor. The tourist information centre has the key to the burial ground.

Finlarig Castle, hidden among trees on a primrose-carpeted mound, half a mile (1km) north of Killin past the cemetery, is a dangerous ruin now. It was the seat of the sinister sounding Black Duncan of the Cowl, a fierce Campbell chief. All that remains is a stark keep and a separate building with a coat of arms on it, possible a chapel. Close to the tower, you can still see a gruesome 'beheading-pit'. It is said that it was the privilege of the gentry to be beheaded, while the common people were hanged from a tree. Beyond the ruin are two 20th-century graves with simple Celtic crosses: Sir Gavin Campbell, Marquess of Breadalbane, and his wife of 50 years, Lady Alma.

Crianlarich

From Killin the A85 goes about 11 miles (17.5km) west to Crianlarich, tucked in among the moors, about 13 miles (21km) southwest of Killin. Isolated but by no means deserted, it has the somewhat incongruously urban-sounding title of 'railway-junction'. This is where the railway lines from Oban and Fort William join up on their progress south. (The West Highland Line, from Glasgow to Mallaig, takes you through such glorious scenery that it is worth travelling on it for the journey itself.)

There are usually a number of people striding around Crianlarich in climbing boots and knapsacks: the 90-mile (144km) West Highland Way passes by on its way from Milngavie (pronounced Mull-guy) to Fort William and this is a favourite staging post.

Three road-routes also meet in Crianlarich: south to Loch Lomond, northwest to Oban and Fort William, or northeast to Pitlochry.

Tyndrum

Five miles (8km) north, on the A82, brings you to Tyndrum, nestling in a glacial valley, gateway to the Highlands. This is another junction of three roads: south, north and west, where the cattle drovers used to meet up on their way to markets at Falkirk and Crieff. Some years ago Tyndrum gained a 'gold rush' status: extensive gold mining in the area led to the speculation that this was about to become an important gold centre in Britain and some rather hideous hotels were built. The gold fever seems to have died down now, but the hotels remain. Tyndrum is now a place to stop off *en route* to the western Highlands and for walkers and climbers. There are walks in all directions and several hills rising to heights above 3000 feet (923m).

Where to Stay

moderate

Ardeonaig Hotel, near Killin, ✆ 05672 400, is a drovers' inn, dating from 1680, on the south side of Loch Tay. Its standards have improved since the drovers used to come here. **Morenish Lodge Hotel** also near Killin, ✆ 05672 258, is a former shooting lodge with panoramic views over Loch Tay, and private fishing rights. Open from April to October, this is a friendly, cosy place.

inexpensive

Clachaig Hotel, Killin, ✆ 05672 270, overlooking the bridge, is good value. The bedrooms are all en-suite, and there's a cosy bar-restaurant, the Salmon Lie, in a converted smithy, with stone walls, a big log stove and reasonable food.

In Crianlarich, try **Portnellan House**, ✆ 08383 284, a 19th-century shooting lodge overlooking Loch Dochart, with clay-pigeon shooting and free fishing. As well as the hotel, which only has three bedrooms, there are also 17 rooms in chalets on the surrounding hillside. **Invervey Hotel**, Tyndrum, ✆ 08384 219, is a friendly, family-run hotel.

the market place Culross

Fife

Fife sticks out between the Firth of Forth and the Firth of Tay, thrusting its nose into the North Sea like the head of an aggressive Scottie dog, with the M90 as its collar, Dunfermline as its name-tag and St Andrews as its beady eyes. Bordered thus on three sides by water it has a disproportionate coastline for its size. Industrial towns in the south give way to fishing villages around the East Neuk, strung out along miles of sandy beaches. Filmgoers may recognize the sands around St Andrews as those used for the running scenes in *Chariots of Fire*. The Tay supports the remnants of the salmon netting industry and has abundant wildlife. With humps like Largo Law and the Lomond Hills on the western boundary with Tayside, Fife is broken and the slightest elevation gives you a feeling of open spaces and vast skies with sweeping views inland over a landscape of farmland broken by clumps of trees. A network of rivers, lochs and reservoirs provides agricultural irrigation and some fishing. Because of the lack of height, you won't find dramatic scenery, but Fife has an elusive charm, tied up in its history and its coast.

With the sea so close, Fife takes its share of battering when the wind is in the east, but it has a higher average of sunshine and less rainfall than most of the rest of Britain. Seaside holidays are bracing.

Abernethy, just over the border in Tayside, was once a Pictish capital, whose overspill left many prehistoric sites to be excavated in the whole area. Once known as the Kingdom of Fife, two of its towns go back to the dawn of history: Dunfermline was the capital in the 11th century, and some say St Andrews received the shipwrecked remains of that saint in the 4th century. Geographically isolated, Fife used to be a place people went to, but not through, until the Tay Road Bridge was opened in 1966. When the new regional divisions were planned in 1975, the Kingdom of Fife was to be split horizontally, one half to become part of Tayside and the other, part of Lothian. But the planners reckoned without the people of Fife, who had no intention of being annihilated and who protested so violently that their kingdom remained intact.

Coal-mining and heavy and light industry in the southwest corner give way to agriculture in the fertile hinterland. Fishing is still a way of life for some. Tourism, especially round the coast, plays an important part in the economy, including, as everyone knows, golf.

Tourist Information

The following are open all year: **St Andrews and North-East Fife Tourist Board**: 78 South Street, St Andrews, © 0334 72021; **Burntisland**: 4 Kirkgate, © 0592 872667; **Glenrothes**: Glenrothes Tourist Association, © 0592 754954; **Inverkeithing**: Forth Road Bridge, © 0383 417759; **Kirkcaldy**: Information

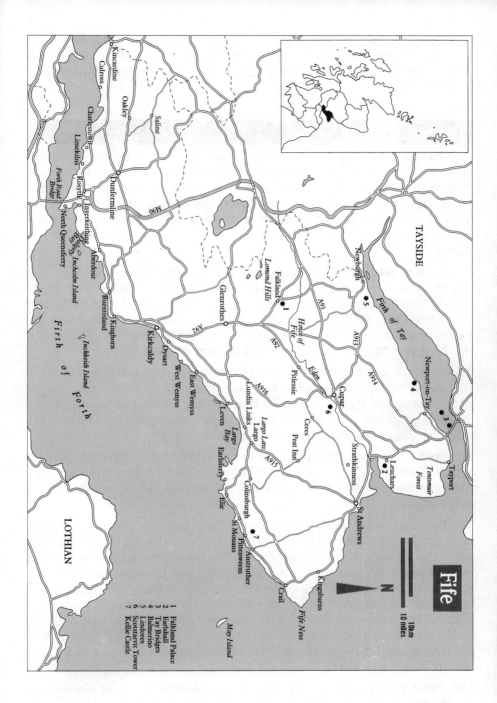

Fife

N

10km
10 miles

1 Falkland Palace
2 Earlshall
3 Tay Bridges
4 Balmerino
5 Lindores
6 Scoonie Tower
7 Kellie Castle

TAYSIDE

LOTHIAN

Firth of Forth

Firth of Tay

Centre, Esplanade, ℂ 0592 267775; **Leven**: South Street, ℂ 03334 29464. The Centre, **Dunfermline**: ℂ 0383 720999, is open Easter–end Sept, and there is also an information centre at the Museum and Heritage Centre, **Crail**: ℂ 0333 50869.

The South Coast

The south coast of Fife is the northern shore of the Firth of Forth, a string of industrial towns and villages whose people have toiled in coal mines and dockyards, factories and fishing boats. (The holiday resorts that serve these towns are popular in the summer; on a hot day their beaches can be as overcrowded as those of the Costa Brava.) Among the sprawl of utility buildings that must support such communities, there lurk hidden gems.

Culross

Going anti-clockwise round the coast, the first stop will be at Culross (pronounced Coo-rus). This miniature town on the shore of the Firth of Forth has been restored by the National Trust for Scotland over the past 50 years. A showpiece Royal Burgh of the 16th and 17th centuries, it looks almost exactly as it must have done in those days though, like most museums, it can never restore the smell and teeming, boisterous splurge of life as it was. But it gives the imagination an accurate framework on which to build.

Culross was once one of the largest ports in Scotland, comparable in importance to Liverpool. It traded in coal, iron, fish, hand-loom weaving, and salt, extracted from sea water in salt pans heated by local coal. The combination of the Industrial Revolution and a bad storm that silted up the port severely damaged the economy, and the town became a backwater until the National Trust moved in, in 1932.

Historically, Culross was the site of a 5th- or 6th-century religious foundation presided over by St Serf (or Servanus), and St Kentigern was born here (see Glasgow, p.240). Leave your car on the outskirts of the old part and explore the steep, narrow, cobbled streets on foot.

The Palace (open daily: adm) was built in 1597 by a prosperous merchant, Sir George Bruce, overlooking the river which in those days came much closer to the town. Standing within a walled court, with crow-stepped gables, decorated dormer windows and pantiled roofs, its garden rising steeply behind with terraced walks, the whole complex is most attractive. Bruce, trading local salt for valuable glass, cheated James VI of window tax by incorporating half-shutters of wood into the windows. You won't find a better example of a Scottish laird's house anywhere else. Bruce's private counting house, through an iron door, is stone-vaulted, fireproof and has safes sunk into the walls. The painted ceiling, with allegorical figures, Latin texts and 'improving' admonishments, is on the second floor and is one of the best in Scotland.

The Town House, or **Tolbooth** (open daily, 1 May–30 Sept or by arrangement, ℂ 0383 880359: adm), built in 1626, is on the right of the palace. It has a double outside stair and was restored, with the tower being added, in 1783. The National Trust for Scotland has its headquarters here and you can see an audio-visual show in the visitor centre, telling the history of the town and showing how it was rescued from decay. You can see the iron house, or prison, on the ground floor, the council room with a painted ceiling and the debtors' room. The 'high tolbooth' or turret was apparently used for witch-spotting. The tron, or public weighing scales, stood outside the tolbooth, where traders' measures could be checked against the standard weights to curb cheating.

The Study (open all year by arrangement and weekends in April, June, July, Aug and Oct, *©* Newmills 880359: adm) is an L-plan, late 16th-century house with a turnpike stair and a small room at the top of its tower, which gave it its name. It is reached by climbing steep, narrow streets, cobbled and paved, behind the Town House until you get to a tiny asymmetrical market place with a reconstructed mercat cross. Inside the house is a small museum with furniture, pottery, pewter of the period and maps illustrating the early town.

The Little Houses of Culross, which are privately occupied, can all be enjoyed from the outside. They are good examples of the domestic architecture of the relatively humble working-class people of those days, in apparently random positions against each other, straggling up the narrow streets.

Culross Abbey (open daily: free) was founded in 1215 for Cistercian monks on the site of St Serf's church. The present parish church, dating from 1300, was rebuilt in 1633 from the original choir and central tower. Inside is a spectacular alabaster monument in memory of Sir George Bruce who built the palace.

East from Culross, just along the shore, is the ruin of **St Mungo's Chapel** (always accessible, free). Built in 1513, it commemorated the spot where a Pictish princess, after escaping the wrath of her family, landed and gave birth to St Kentigern, affectionately known as Mungo (see Glasgow, p.240). Across the Forth the flaming stacks of the refinery at Grangemouth on the far shore are strangely ethereal when seen through the haze they create, or in the half-light, against a darkening sky, reflected in the water.

Undulating farmland reaches inland, with narrow lanes and sudden splendid views. Along the shore you pass through picturesque harbours and villages such as **Charlestown**, 6 miles (9.5km) east of Culross. This 18th-century village surrounds a green on a wooded plateau above the Forth. Charlestown Harbour, a small haven that dries out at low tide, was built by the 18th-century laird, the 5th Earl of Elgin, for sailing ships bringing iron ore and carrying away locally quarried lime. This is Bruce country, for the Earls of Elgin trace their descent from King Robert. It was the 7th Earl who 'acquired' the ancient Greek marble sculptures, mostly a frieze from the Parthenon (now called the Elgin Marbles), and sold them to the British Museum in 1816 for £35,000. (The Parthenon was being used by the Turks, who were then occupying Athens, for target practice.) These marbles continue to be a bone of contention between Britain and Greece. Just before the Second World War they were cleaned, emerging so pristine from this laundering that the public were outraged and the Assistant Keeper in the Department of Greek and Roman Antiquities was most unfairly forced to resign.

Limekilns, a mile (1.5km) east of Charlestown, is an old-world village whose pretty cottages were lived in by the seamen who worked the ships out of Charlestown. Although those days are gone now, there is a great feeling of community here in the riverside settlement.

Oakley, a few miles inland, northwest of Limekilns, is a mining village built to house workers in the Comrie Colliery. Many of the miners came from declining areas in the west to create a strongly Catholic community. The church, endowed by the Catholic laird, Captain Smith-Sligo, in 1958, has some beautiful stained glass, and woodwork carved by a local craftsman.

Dunfermline

Dunfermline is 2 miles (3km) inland, about 7 miles (11km) east of Culross, and was once the capital of Scotland. Hub of the southwest corner of Fife, it is dominated by the abbey and palace that stand above the town like sentinels. The town falls away from this crowning glory, an endearing mixture of Scottish Baronial, modern industrial and ancient ruins. Dunfermline means 'fort-by-the-crooked-pool' after a fort that stood in what is now Pittencrief Park, sloping down from the abbey to the southwest.

King Malcolm Canmore lived in Dunfermline in the middle of the 11th century. He was an unremarkable, blood-thirsty, perhaps rather boorish man, until along came saintly Margaret, an English princess, fleeing with her brother from the Norman Conquest. She married Malcolm in 1067 and set about anglicizing Scotland, both culturally and ecclesiastically. Edward I held court here during his campaigns against the Scots at the end of the 13th century; Charles II agreed to accept the Covenant while staying in Dunfermline in 1651.

The town is probably best known today as the birthplace of Andrew Carnegie (1835–1919), the son of a linen weaver, who went to America and made a fortune in steel. One of the best-known philanthropists of the modern world, he used his millions for the benefit of mankind in numerous ways. To his home town alone, he gave the Pittencrief Park, public baths, a library and an annual Festival of Music and Art. Dunfermline has a Civic Week in June, an excuse for all sorts of festivities, parades and entertainment.

Dunfermline must be lodged in many minds as the subject for the ballad about Sir Patrick Spens. Sir Patrick was dispatched on a mission by his king who 'sat in Dumfermline toune, drinking the blude-red wine'. Poor Sir Patrick put out in a storm, against his better judgement, and drowned, 'half owre, half owre to Aberdour, wi' the Scots lords at his feit'. According to Sir Walter Scott, Spens' voyage was to collect the Maid of Norway in 1290, but that cannot have been so because the Maid was not collected until the king was dead.

The Abbey (open daily: free) is reached by steps from a terraced car park. The church, much restored, stands adjacent to the ruined monastery buildings and palace, which are linked to each other by a pend. It is hard to believe, when you look at these remains, that in the 13th century they were said to be 'big enough to hold two sovereigns with their retinues, at the same time, without inconvenience to one another'. There was a Culdee

Chapel on the site where Malcolm Canmore, a widower, married Margaret. Two years later, the queen, horrified by the lax ways of the Celtic Church, began to build a new church to be administered in the English manner to which she was accustomed. When she endowed the Benedictine priory, she set up a shrine, with a relic of the True Cross, and encouraged pilgrims to come from miles away to venerate it.

The present church stands on the foundations of Margaret's church, some of which you can see through iron grilles in the floor. Frequently sacked and burned over the centuries, today's building is a jigsaw of different tastes and styles, the nave dating from 1128 and the massive buttresses from the 16th century. In 1818, workmen unearthed a vault with a stone coffin in it, containing a skeleton wrapped in thin sheets of lead. Shreds of cloth-of-gold clung to the bones and the breastbone had been sawn through, almost conclusively proving that this was the coffin of Robert the Bruce. Bruce died in 1329 having begged Sir James Douglas to carry his heart to Palestine and bury it in Jerusalem. (He had always intended to make a pilgrimage to the Holy Land in atonement for murdering his rival for the throne, Red Comyn.) Douglas set off with the heart but was killed in Spain in battle with the Moors. The heart was retrieved from the battlefield, returned to Scotland and buried in Melrose Abbey, where it is today. Bruce's remains were re-interred; a brass plate, set in Italian porphyry, under the pulpit, marks the spot. To celebrate this historic find, an over-enthusiastic architect designed the vast inscription that you cannot fail to notice, written in stone-fretwork round the top of the square tower: 'King Robert the Bruce'.

Malcolm Canmore and Queen Margaret died within a few days of each other in 1093, and their shrine is against the outside wall of the present abbey, where the Lady Chapel once stood. The abbey succeeded Iona as the burial place for Scottish kings.

The ruined **Palace** (open daily: free), still magnificent, especially against an evening sky, was built when Margaret and Malcolm married. You can imagine the queen, walking up each day from Malcolm's Tower, now a ruin in Pittencrief Park below, to inspect the progress of her new home. Although she would have chosen to have been a nun rather than a queen, Margaret loved fine clothes and exotic furnishings and no doubt her palace was very splendid. It provided an admirable setting for her task of 'refining' the rough, Celtic ways of her husband's court.

Pittencrieff Glen is reached through a gate opposite the west door of the abbey. When Andrew Carnegie was a boy, before he emigrated to Pennsylvania to make his fortune, he was forbidden entrance to the privately owned park. He never forgot this and when he returned with his millions, he bought it and gave it to the people of Dunfermline so that 'no wee child should ever feel locked oot of it, as I was'. So anyone can now roam among shrubs and flowers and trees, along the steep-sided, wooded glen, where birds sing and a burn tumbles down over its rocky bed and no child is ever 'locked oot'. It is a beautiful place, and Queen Margaret, known for her generosity to the poor, would have heartily approved.

Pittencrieff House (open daily except Tues, May–Oct: free) was built in 1610. It, too, was bought by Carnegie and makes a good focal point in the park. Inside there are displays of local history, costumes and an art gallery.

The Carnegie Museum (open daily: free) is in Moodie Street. This small cottage was Carnegie's birthplace.The rooms are furnished as they were in his lifetime, and the millionaire himself, remarkably life-like in waxen effigy, sits at his desk in his study, looking rather stern, perhaps planning where to bestow his next gift.

Dunfermline Museum (open daily except Sun: free) is at Viewfield. This Victorian villa has displays concentrating on local history, including the weaving and linen industries, both of which enriched the town in the past.

Rosyth

Rosyth is 3 miles (4.5km) south of Dunfermline, on the shore of the Forth. Its dockyard, now privatized, has played an important part in British naval history over the years. At one time it was the only naval dockyard where the entire fleet could anchor at any state of the tide.

St Margaret's Hope is east of the dockyard, near the foot of the Forth Road Bridge. Tradition has it that it was at this rocky promontory that Queen Margaret landed for the first time in Scotland. Perched on a terrace on the point is the house of the admiral who commands the navy in Scotland. In the recent past, another admiral lived on Castland Hill, across the marsh opposite, and the two old salts communicated by hoisting witty signal flags on their respective flagpoles—an essential part of any naval establishment.

North Queensferry

North Queensferry, a mile (1.5km) southeast of Rosyth, was originally the northern terminal of the ferry established by Queen Margaret to carry pilgrims to Dunfermline. It remained a ferry terminal until the road bridge was opened in 1964, and is now a backwater with a big yacht marina.

In **Deep Sea World** (open daily: adm), you go through an aquarium in an underwater, transparent viewing tunnel and literally come face to face with the fish. An extraordinary experience. There is also an audio-visual theatre, shop and café.

Inverkeithing

It is worth stopping off in Inverkeithing, a stone's throw north of Queensferry. It is an older place than you might think at first glance—granted a Royal Charter in 1165.

Behind the busy central square in the High Street, the 14th-century **Greyfriars Hospice**, restored as a community centre, has a small museum (open all year Wed–Sun: free), crammed with items of local interest—religious, military, industrial and domestic history.

Dalgety Bay

Keeping to the shore road, a couple of miles (3km) east of Inverkeithing, you come to Dalgety Bay, now fringed by a sprawling residential development, but haunted by ghosts.

Donibristle House, stands on the site of the house where, in 1592, 'the Bonnie Earl of Moray' was murdered by an avenging Huntly on the order of the king. There are many versions of the murder story, one being that there was a tunnel from the house down which the unfortunate earl tried to flee, but because his hair had been set alight by his enemies he acted as a living torch for his pursuers. The house has been restored as part of a housing development.

St Bridget's Church, further along the shore of Dalgety Bay, is an unexpected little ruin right beside the water, its mossy banks dotted with tumbled headstones. It was dedicated in 1244; the eastern part of the church is the oldest. It was a two-storey kirk with a burial vault and laird's loft.

Aberdour

Aberdour, only 5 miles (8km) east of the Forth Road Bridge, is a popular resort, known for its silver sands. There is plenty here for a family holiday: golf, water sports, a sailing centre and a little harbour. The picturesque town has a cluster of medieval buildings above it, overlooking the sea. These include St Fillan's Church, the castle and dovecote.

St Fillan's Church is part Norman, part 16th-century, like a miniature cathedral, with a leper-squint in the west wall and an atmosphere of peace and timelessness.

Aberdour Castle (open daily except Thurs mornings and Fri: adm) stands close by on 14th-century foundations and still has its original tower. It was added to in succeeding centuries, and is an imposing, rather gloomy place, but it adds majesty to the overall scene. The circular **Dovecote** is part of the castle complex.

Inchcolm

A boat runs from Hawkcraig Point, in Aberdour, © 0383 830665, to the small island of Inchcolm, across Mortimer's Deep, the watery grave of poor Sir Patrick Spens (see p.284), or a boat runs from the pier at South Queensferry.

Inchcolm is a perfect place to visit on a fine day, the boat trip making it more special. There are usually a few private boats at anchor in the harbour, with much good-natured 'giving-way' to the official cruise boats. On calm days the water is often ruffled by the wakes of powerboats and waterskiers.

The Abbey of St Columba (open daily, weather permitting, except Wed afternoon and Thurs in winter: adm) is just next door to the landing jetty, overlooking a small rocky bay. It was founded in 1123 for Augustinian monks by Alexander I. A Columban monk-hermit who lived on the island saved the king when his boat foundered on the rocky shore; building the abbey was the King's act of gratitude. There is a rough cell at the northwest corner which could have been the hermit's. Although it was often sacked by the English and desecrated during the Reformation, the abbey has been restored and looks a little too new, but the monastic buildings are the best you will find in Scotland. You can see the 13th-century octagonal chapter house with stone roof, and a 14th-century cloister with chambers above.

Burntisland

Burntisland, 3 miles (4.5km) east of Aberdour, once famous for shipbuilding, is now more popular as a holiday resort, its boatyards closed down. The town climbs from the water and on a fine day in summer the beach resembles that of any Mediterranean resort, with scant room to lay a lilo.

The octagonal **Church of St Columba** was the first to be built in Scotland after the Reformation. It was copied from a church in Amsterdam and has a central pulpit and galleries reached by outside stairs. The tower, added in 1749, is joined to the corners of the church by great flying arches. The General Assembly of the Church of Scotland was held here in 1601, when, in the presence of James VI, it was proposed that there should be a new translation of the Bible, the Authorized Version, published in 1611.

Agricola is said to have used the natural harbour for his fleet in about AD 83—it's strange to think of those Roman galleys at anchor where fibre-glass pleasure boats are now moored.

Rossend Castle is a 15th-century tower house that was saved from demolition and recently restored. Now it is one of Burntisland's treasures. It is used as offices but can be seen from the outside. It was here that an ardent French poet, Chastelard, hid himself in Mary, Queen of Scots' bedroom in 1563, a crazy escapade that cost him his life. He was executed in St Andrews and died reciting poetry and crying 'adieu, thou most beautiful and most cruel Princess in the world'. It is tempting to speculate whether perhaps the lively, 21-year-old widow had led him on, lonely for the French manners she had grown up with.

Kinghorn

At Kinghorn, a couple of miles (3km) further along the coast, you will see a Victorian monument beside the road in the shape of a Celtic cross. This is where Alexander III was thrown from his horse and killed, an event which altered the course of Scottish history. The king had been sitting in council with his lords in Edinburgh. They had eaten well and washed down their meal with plenty of wine. He set off to return to his wife of six months, Jolande, whom he had married in a desperate attempt to get himself an heir. There was a violent storm but he insisted on being taken across the Forth at Queensferry. On the far side, he refused to shelter till daybreak but set off, galloping eastwards towards Pettycur where his queen awaited him. His horse stumbled on the edge of the cliff at Kinghorn and that was the end of the King, thus fulfilling a prophecy made at his wedding feast in Jedburgh. The country was plunged into many years of bitter conflict and power struggles. Kinghorn is now a holiday resort, with a sandy beach, good hotels, a golf course and campsites.

Inchkeith

You need to hire a boat to go out to the island of Inchkeith, southeast of Burntisland. Its strategic position in the Firth of Forth has made it an important defensive stronghold over many centuries, ever since Mary de Guise-Lorraine (mother of Mary, Queen of Scots, invited her French compatriots to fortify and occupy the island to defend Scotland's shores from English invasion. The island was used in the last two World Wars, to defend Rosyth dockyard and the rail bridge. It is now occupied only by the lighthouse keepers and by thousands of seagulls.

The story is told of an experiment that was tried by James IV. He wanted to see what language a child would speak if it had no example to follow. He sent two infants to the island with a totally dumb woman as their nurse. Some say that the children grew up speaking excellent Hebrew, others that they emerged from the experiment speaking fluent Gaelic.

Kirkcaldy

Once known as 'the Lang Toun', Kirkcaldy (pronounced Kirkoddy) stretches along the coast 3 miles (4.5km) north of Kinghorn. It is a busy seaport, industrial centre, holiday resort, and Fife's main shopping town, with 4 miles (6km) of seafront and an esplanade whose retaining wall was built in the early 1920s in an effort to relieve unemployment as much as to hold back the pounding sea.

Linen, weaving and textiles were the town's first occupations, until a weaver of sailcloth, Michael Nairn, turned his talents to the invention of linoleum, which erupted into a major industry. It is said that at the height of the linoleum boom you could smell Kirkcaldy from many miles away. With the development of synthetic fibres and more sophisticated floor coverings, the town's industry has diversified tremendously. Among Kirkcaldy's famous sons are the architects Robert and James Adam, and Adam Smith, a brilliant scholar and philosopher who wrote, among other learned works, *Inquiry into the Nature and Causes of the Wealth of Nations* in 1776.

Every April, the Esplanade is closed for five days for **The Links Market,** the largest and oldest fair in Britain. A great gala of events is presented with plenty of music, colour, pomp and ceremony. The Esplanade also boasts a modern indoor swimming centre with sauna and fitness rooms to help you sweat off an over-indulgent holiday.

If you explore the heart of Kirkcaldy you will find more than just a modern town full of good shops and busy streets. In the older parts you can come upon delightful little wynds and courtyards and old houses with pantiled roofs and crow-stepped gables, as for example in the eastern suburb of **Dysart**.

Dysart is full of character, with a picturesque harbour below the ancient battlement tower of St Serf's Church. In the old days, Dutch traders in tall-masted sailing ships came here to barter, exchanging cart-wheels, kegs and pipes for local coal, salt, beer and cured fish.

Kirkcaldy Museum and Art Gallery (open daily: free) is in the War Memorial Gardens, next to the station. They have a good archaeological collection with 300-million-year-old fossils as well as local social history, natural history and industry. The art gallery has work by many Scottish artists. A whole room has been devoted to William McTaggart, that great master who captured simple everyday life and familiar scenes so well. Other artists include Peploe, Lowry, Sickert and Raeburn. There are also displays of the local Wemyss Ware pottery.

The McDouall Stuart Museum (open every afternoon, June–Aug: free) is an award-winning museum in Fitzroy Street, Dysart, in a building restored by the National Trust for Scotland. The house, which has a lintel dated 1575, was the birthplace of John McDouall Stuart, the first man to cross Australia from south to north through the central desert in 1866. The museum tells you all about Stuart and his fascinating, and often hair-raising, expeditions, including his encounters with Aborigines and Australian wildlife.

Kirkcaldy has several parks: **Beveridge Park** with flower gardens and a boating lake; **Dunniker Park**, to the northwest, with a nature trail and golf course, shaded by cedar trees; and **Ravenscraig Park**, along the shore beyond Dysart.

Ravenscraig Castle

Ravenscraig (open daily: adm) towers dramatically above Ravenscraig Park, on a rocky promontory overlooking the river. This substantial ruin dates from 1460 when James II intended it as a dower house for his wife. He lost interest in it when she died. James III gave it to the Earl of Orkney in exchange for Kirkwall Castle, which he had long coveted, and it was finally demolished for Cromwell in 1651 by General Monk. It was the first castle in Britain to be designed for defence by and against cannon shot and you can still see the wide gun loops in the massively thick walls. The views over the Forth made Ravenscraig a splendid vantage point against invasion. Sir Walter Scott called it Ravenshough, in his poem 'Rosabelle'. Near the castle, the steps that lead from the high-rise flats in Nether Road down to the beach should number 39, and are said to have inspired John Buchan, though he moved his 39 steps several hundred miles south.

West and East Wemyss

West Wemyss is 1½ miles (2.5km), and East Wemyss 3 miles (4.5km) east of Dysart. They are so called from the many 'weems', or caves, in this bit of the coast. People have sheltered in these caves for thousands of years and the graffiti they left behind them is fascinating, possibly dating back to the Bronze Age (2500 BC). Owing to erosion they are not at the moment safe to explore, but a campaign to Save Wemyss' Caves is under way. The villages are characterized by their colliers' cottages, some of which are in dire need of rescue.

The ruin just east of East Wemyss is called **Macduff's Castle**, and was once the stronghold of the Thanes of Fife.

Leven

Leven, 3 miles (4.5km) up the coast from the castle, on Largo Bay, is another holiday centre with a good beach and plenty of holiday facilities, including golf and fishing. It is hard to believe that the harbour was once a busy port, used to ship in provisions to the Royal Palace of Falkland. It silted up and is now a car park and swimming pool complex.

In Silverburn Estate, east of Leven near the beach, you can walk in the woods and gardens and observe the wildlife, including, if you are lucky, red squirrels. There are paddocks where the Silverburn Shetland ponies graze if they are not pulling carts in the park and in spring there are usually foals to see, as well as pygmy goats from Africa and pot-bellied pigs from Vietnam.

Lethem Glen, on the northern outskirts of Leven, is another nature centre, with displays and information about wildlife, with a 45-minute nature trail and a pets' corner for young children.

Lundin Links, also on Largo Bay, is yet another family holiday resort. It has a sandy beach, sea fishing and golf. The standing stones just to the west are thought to have been part of a Druid temple.

Glenrothes

Five miles (8km) inland from either Kirkcaldy or Leven, Glenrothes is for the gregarious holidaymaker who enjoys masses of organized, modern entertainment. It is the sort of place you would not be surprised to find in America. The town is new and unbeautiful: the entertainments cover all tastes from indoor swimming, bowling, snooker, skating and curling, to outdoor gliding, parachuting, hang-gliding and golf. Glenrothes is not for the recluse.

Where to Stay and Eating Out

moderate

If you prefer modern comfort and convenience to antiquity, the brand-new **Queensferry Lodge Hotel** in North Queensferry, © 0383 413685, is undoubtedly the place for you. With panoramic views of the River Forth, not only will you get all the mod cons you'd expect in a new hotel, but also a tourist information, craft and interpretation centre. Probably the most elegant of the hotels in this area is **Rescobie House** at Leslie, north of Glenrothes, © 0592 742143. Secluded and creeper-clad, in four acres of lovely garden and grounds, this is a peaceful place to stay. It feels like a home, with sporting prints on the walls, antique furniture and log fires. A good base for golfing.

inexpensive

The Old Toll Tavern in St Leonards Street, Dunfermline, © 0383 721489, was once what its name implies, so if you like antiquity you might do worse. For cosiness try **Grey Craig House** at Saline near Dunfermline, © 0383 852334. The house is old and attractive, more like a home than a hotel. It only has three bedrooms.

Hawkcraig House, Aberdour, © 0383 860335, is a gem—the old ferryman's house at Hawkcraig Point, on the water's edge overlooking the harbour and Inchcolm Island. Open from February to mid-December, it only has two bedrooms so book well in advance. You can lean out of the window and watch the seals and birds. They don't have a licence but you are encouraged to bring your own wine and the home-cooked food is excellent. No credit cards. **Forth View Hotel**, also on the water at Hawkcraig Point, Aberdour, © 0380 860478, has gorgeous views near Silver Sands Beach and the golf course. It is only open from April to October and the food isn't at all bad.

Inchview Hotel in Kinghorn, © 0592 872239, is a listed Georgian building over-looking Pettycur Bay. Not wildly exciting but they do golf packages.

East Neuk

Neuk is a Scots word meaning 'corner', and that is exactly what this small wedge of land is, jutting off the eastern edge of Fife from Largo Bay to St Andrews, coming to a point at Fife Ness. This is a genteel holiday centre, where you are more likely to stumble on quaint pantiled cottages with neat, bright gardens than on fun-parks. On a nice day, tour the fishing villages that ring the East Neuk, each with its own character. In medieval Scotland there was much sea-trade with Europe and Scandinavia. Scottish wool, coal, leather and cured fish were exchanged for timber and manufactured goods. As well as goods, however, fashions were exchanged: crow-stepped gables, for instance, are of Flemish origin. When trade declined, fishing took over, particularly for herring, and was at its height in the last century. Now these little ports are less busy: built round picturesque harbours, crow-stepped houses rise in steep terraces, joined by twisting cobbled streets and wynds. The very names of these villages suggest stoic Scots dependability with no frills and flounces: Pittenweem, Anstruther, Crail, names to be reckoned with. The beaches are gorgeous and less populated than those further south, the hinterland is pleasant farmland, and St Andrews provides history and culture.

Largo

Largo, at the head of Largo Bay, 3 miles (4.5km) northeast of Leven, was once an important fishing centre. It is now mainly residential and popular in summer with its golden crescent of sand.

The real Robinson Crusoe

Look out for the statue of Alexander Selkirk, who was born in Lower Largo in 1676. Selkirk was a wild young man who ran away to sea, quarrelled with his captain and was dumped, at his own request, on the uninhabited island of Juan Fernandez, where he existed for five years until he was rescued. He and his story were immortalized by Daniel Defoe, in his novel *Robinson Crusoe*.

While you are here, climb the volcanic cone of Largo Law, where an ancient chief is said to have been buried, dressed in silver armour. There are good views of Fife from the top.

Colinsburgh

Colinsburgh, inland, 4 miles (6km) east of Largo, was built by Colin, third Earl of Balcarres, in the 18th century. An ardent Jacobite, he built the village for his soldiers when he realized that the Stuart cause was hopeless.

Elie and Earlsferry

Elie and Earlsferry, at the eastern end of Largo Bay, 6 miles (9.5km) from Largo, are more or less one place. Both are popular resorts with lovely sandy beaches where, if you look carefully, you may find garnets in the sand. **The Ship Inn**, in Elie, has good pub meals—book first. Earlsferry is the place where Macduff, Earl of Fife, is believed to have hidden from Macbeth in the 11th century in a cave at Kincraig Point, before being ferried to Dunbar. **The Elie Fair** is in July.

St Monans

St Monans, 3 miles (4.5km) northeast, has a cluster of charming old houses reaching down to the sea. When the wind is in the southeast, the spray rises over the churchyard wall to wash the gravestones in the cemetery of a small fishermen's church that stands on the edge of the water. The foundations of this church date from 1362 when David II dedicated it to St Monans, or Mirren, an Irish missionary, in gratitude for a miraculous recovery from an arrow wound. The unusual T shape of the church is because the nave was never built.

The town rises steeply from a double harbour, an attractive network of narrow, twisting streets and restored old houses. **Miller's Yard** was established in 1747. Although it ceased boatbuilding in 1993, a number of employees still do boat repairs.

Pittenweem

Pittenweem, meaning 'place-of-the-cave', a mile (1.5km) up the coast, is the home port of the fishing-fleets of the East Neuk, with a thriving fish market and an arts festival in August. It is an attractive town, its old harbour often crammed with fishing boats, its quays stacked with fish boxes and gear. It is well worth getting up early in the morning to see the fish market in full fling—a mass of activity, sound, smell and vitality.

The National Trust for Scotland has done tremendous work on several of the buildings in the town. These include **Kellie Lodging**, a tower that juts into the High Street, and **The Gyles**, a group of 16th- and 17th-century houses by the harbour. You can see the remains of a priory in the grounds of the Episcopal Church, founded in 1114, whose Augustinian monks established a shrine in St Fillans Cave, where services are still occasionally held.

Kellie Castle

Kellie Castle (open Easter weekend; daily 1 May–30 Sept; weekends, April and Oct; grounds open daily all year: adm) is 3 miles (4.5km) inland on the B9171. Kellie dates from the 14th century, an impressive pile of mainly 16th- and 17th-century domestic architecture, in landscaped gardens. It was rescued from decay in 1875 by Professor James Lorimer, whose son, the famous architect Robert Lorimer, designed the walled garden, the garden house, walled doo'cot and some internal decoration, and whose grandson, the sculptor Hew Lorimer, is the resident custodian. It has some splendid plaster work and painted panelling.

Anstruther

Anstruther, a mile (1.5km) up the coast from Pittenweem and contracted to 'Anst'er' by locals, was once an important fishing centre but is now better known as a holiday resort. It has, however, hung on to its link with its fishing past.

The Scottish Fisheries Museum and Aquarium (open daily: adm), at the head of the harbour, gives a unique insight into the life and work of a fishing community, with interiors of a typical fisherman's home—complete with wife, baby and cradle.

You can also see over the **North Carr Lightship**, in the harbour, which did 43 years' service off Fife Ness. Picture what life must have been like for the seven-man crew in those cramped quarters for weeks on end, particularly in bad weather. There is also a Fife fishing boat on display.

East Neuk Outdoors, in Anstruther, runs activity holidays with abseiling, archery, boardsailing, canoeing, climbing, coastal walks, cycling, bird-watching, historic tours and special activities for children. They have a playgroup for 2–5 year olds (✆ 0333 311929).

There are guided historical walks round Anstruther from the end of June to the end of September, and there is a Holiday Fair week in July. Boats run from here to the Isle of May, weather permitting: ✆ 0333 310103.

The Isle of May

Boats run from Anstruther and Crail to the Isle of May, the largest of the four islands that command the entrance to the Firth of Forth, and once of vital strategic importance. The island, 1 mile (1.5km) long and about a quarter of a mile (0.4km) in width, has an intriguing history stretching back into the dark ages and embroidered with legend, all told in *The Story of the May Island*, published by Largo Field Studies Society, in Upper Largo. 'The May' became a National Nature Reserve in 1956, since when the seabird population has increased dramatically. Look for the puffins with their unreal-looking striped beaks, living in burrows in the turf, and the incredible camouflage of nesting eider ducks, which manage to stay totally motionless within only a few feet of the path. Other birds include guillemots, razorbills and kittiwakes. You are more than likely to see seals here, too.

The remains of a beacon in the middle of the island are from the first Scottish lighthouse, built in 1636. The tower was at least twice the height of today's and it had a huge brazier on top that burned coal at the rate of between one to four tonnes a night, depending on the wind. It needed stoking every 20 minutes, was invisible upwind and was easily confused with the lights of the saltpans along the mainland shores. In a storm in 1792, sulphurous fumes from the cinders of the beacon killed the lighthouse keeper and his family, seven in all, as they slept. The present lighthouse was built by Robert Louis Stevenson, grandfather of the writer, in 1816.

Crail

Crail, three miles (4.5km) beyond Anstruther, is another well-restored fishing town with one of the prettiest harbours in Fife. (The Harbourmaster, Roger Banks, is an acclaimed artist and paints exquisite cameos of natural history. He has several books to his name.) Crail was made a Royal Burgh in 1310 and was granted the right to trade on the Sabbath. (This can't have pleased John Knox when he came preaching here some 200 years later.) Picturesque colour-washed houses and cobbled streets lead down to the harbour and its crow-stepped customs house: a lovely place to sit on the harbour wall, the sun on your face, and listen to the sounds of the water slapping at the stones. Crail Festival Week is in July.

The Church of St Mary is a 12th-century church. The large blue stone at its gate is said to have been hurled there by the Devil, from the Isle of May, 5 miles (8km) out to sea. You can see an 8th-century Pictish cross slab in the church, and in Victoria Gardens the early Christian **Sauchope Stone**. The restored **Tolbooth** dates from the early 16th century, and at 62 Marketgate you can explore the **Crail Museum and Heritage Centre** (open for two weeks around Easter and daily, June–Sept: adm) and learn much of the history of this ancient town. There is a tourist information centre in the museum, too, © 0333 50869.

Kingsbarns

From Crail, the coast road turns northwest towards St Andrews and you lose the sea for a while. You come first to Kingsbarns, 3 miles (4.5km) from Crail, whose name will tell you that this is good farmland. There is a nice story attached to the original owners of **Pitmillie**, just north of the village. In the 11th century, before Malcolm Canmore was king, he asked a stranger for the loan of 'a few pennies'. 'Not a few: mony pennies', came the munificent reply. King Malcolm did not forget. When he came into power he granted his benefactor the lands at Kingsbarns and the family became known as 'Moneypenny'.

St Andrews

St Andrews, 10 miles (16km) beyond Crail, unfolds below you: its ghosts beckon irresistibly. Many of the stones used to build the older houses came from the ruined cathedral on the eastern edge of the town, towards which the three main streets lead. Scotland's oldest university, founded in 1411, is now the living heart of the town whose medieval spirit is kept young in many ways. For instance, you might be lucky and see the Sunday parade of students processing from the chapel in the scarlet medieval gowns that were introduced so that they could be spotted easily when entering brothels. (Divinity students wear black gowns: presumably they were above suspicion.)

Andrew, brother of Simon Peter and the first disciple to be called by Jesus, was 'the most gentle of the Apostles'. Among his many converts was the wife of the Roman Governor of Patrae. The governor was so furious and jealous of his wife's conversion that he had Andrew crucified. (Andrew asked to be tied to an X-shaped cross so that he should not appear to be emulating Christ.) According to legend, St Rule, who was custodian of the Saint's remains in Patrae, some time between the 4th and 8th centuries, had a vision of an angel who ordered him to take five of Andrew's bones, sail to the western edge of the world and build a city in his honour. Rule set off and was shipwrecked on the rocks just to the west of today's harbour. He hurried ashore and enshrined the sacred relics on the headland where the ruins of the 12th-century cathedral now stand. The shrine became a place of worship for Christian pilgrims from far and wide and a special ferry was kept on the River Forth to transport them. St Andrew became Scotland's patron saint and the city where his sacred relics lay enshrined became the ecclesiastical capital of Scotland.

In spring, the **Kate Kennedy Pageant** takes over, with 60 to 70 students parading the streets in costume. Kate, the niece of one of the founders of the university, was so beautiful that all the students were in love with her. The pageant is all-male: Kate is played by a first-year student, and all the others are members of the elite Kate Kennedy Club, dressed as famous Scottish figures, past and present.

The Lammas Fair, in August, is Scotland's oldest surviving medieval market, with showmen from all over Britain setting up stalls and booths in the streets—a bright, colourful carnival that lasts for two days. There are also the bi-annual St Andrews Festival, the Festival of Food and Wine in March, St Andrews Highland Games in July, and great celebrations for St Andrews Day on 30 November. On top of all this there are the golf championships: the Annual Golf Week in April and the Dunhill Nations Cup in October.

St Andrew's Cathedral (open daily: adm), founded in 1160, was once the largest cathedral in Scotland. Medieval pilgrims came in their thousands to pray at one of its 31 altars. It is strange to stand in front of the remains of the high altar and recall that Robert the Bruce stood here at the consecration of the cathedral in 1318, 160 years after the building began. Here too stood James V and Mary of Guise-Lorraine at the ceremony of their marriage. In 1559, that zealous reformer John Knox preached some stirring sermons on the 'cleansing of the temple' and roused his congregations to such hysteria that they stripped the cathedral of its glorious embellishments and riches, leaving it to decay into ruin. Even as a ruin it is magnificent. A great twin-towered façade soars towards the sky, surrounded by neat green turf, graves, the foundations of the priory, a few massive walls and a Norman arch.

The **Cathedral Museum** is full of interesting relics including a unique sarcophagus. **St Rule's Tower** is also within the precinct: a gaunt chaperone. Here the holy relics were kept until the cathedral was completed. If you feel energetic you can climb the 158 steps inside the tower and see wonderful views of the town and out to sea. **The Pends**, now roofless, was the vaulted gatehouse entrance to the cathedral precinct. Dating from the 14th century, it is said that it will collapse when the wisest man in Christendom walks through the arch. The prophecy doesn't include women so the Pends still stands.

St Andrew's Castle (open daily: adm) is northwest of the cathedral on a rocky headland overhanging the sea beyond a deep moat. Now a ruin, it was built as the Bishop's Palace at the end of the 12th century and it witnessed some extremely nasty incidents in the blood-stained history of the Scottish Church. George Wishart, the ardent Protestant reformer, was burned at the stake in front of the castle in 1545 and tradition tells of the notorious Catholic Cardinal Beaton, lying on velvet cushions inside the castle, watching his death throes. Whether this is true or not, Beaton paid for Wishart's life with his own. A worldly, immoral man, the Cardinal did not hesitate to plead for mercy on account of his priestly status two months later, when he was stabbed to death by a party of avenging Reformers. His body was hung over the battlements and then slung into the 'bottle dungeon', a fearsome rock pit, where it was preserved in salt until its discovery more than a year later. After the murder, the Reformers held the castle against a siege, having been joined by John Knox and others, before they were all captured and sent off to serve time as galley slaves. Knox was a close friend of Wishart: it was to be 14 years before he returned to stir the reforming pot again.

The castle fell into ruin in the 17th century but you can still see the bottle dungeon. A large number of the Reformers were imprisoned in this hell-hole: it is hard to believe that many can have survived. Beaton's apartments are thought to have been in the tower to the southwest.

One of the features of the castle is the mine and counter mine, tunnelled through the rock during the siege that followed Beaton's murder in 1546–7. The besiegers started their tunnel but were frustrated by the defenders who tried to intercept them. Uncertainty about who was where led to abandonment. The galleries were later useful as secret tunnels in those days of intrigue.

The Church of St Salvator is among St Andrews' many fine university buildings. In North Street, it was founded as the University Chapel by Bishop Kennedy in 1450, uncle of the beautiful Kate who is fêted in the April pageant. The Bishop's tomb is in the church, along with a magnificent mace from his time, which is still carried on ceremonial occasions. The pulpit was the one John Knox preached from, carried here from the parish church; he thumped out his message on that very wood.

Patrick Hamilton, the proto-martyr of the Reformation, was burned for his Lutheran heresy in front of St Salvator's College in 1528. Archbishop James Beaton, uncle of the notorious Cardinal, was mainly responsible for his persecution. Above the site of his death you can see an impression of his face engraved in the stone wall, said to have been left there when his soul flew out of the flames as he died.

The Royal and Ancient Golf Club makes history pale into insignificance for golfers. Known to the cognoscenti as the R and A, this world-famous establishment determines the rules of the game, although it is by no means Scotland's oldest club. The club house is open to members only. The autumn Golf Meeting, at the end of September, is the main event of the year, and when you see the preparations beforehand (the tents and booths and marquees) you would imagine an army was preparing for a major battle. It is at this meeting that the Captain for the Year plays himself into office, watched by thousands of anxious eyes, in case he should miss that important ball. Of the four courses, 'The Old' is the most famous.

The **British Golf Museum** (open daily, May–Oct; Thurs–Mon/Tues, the rest of the year: adm), opposite the R and A, is a must for golfers—everything you didn't know about the history of golf and a lot more besides.

St Leonard's College, founded in 1512 and no longer extant, was on the present site of St Leonard's Girls' School, beyond Abbey Street (known to its inmates as The Prison).

Many ardent reformers, including John Knox it is thought, studied at the college, and the term 'to have drunk at St Leonard's Well' was coined from those times, meaning to have listened to the Protestant doctrine. The library of St Leonard's School is in Queen Mary's House, in South Street, where Mary is believed to have stayed, in 1563, taking a holiday with her ladies from the burdens of State affairs. While she was there she planted a thorn tree that still flourishes in the quadrangle of St Mary's College.

The Byre Theatre, which you get to through the attractive South Court, stages productions throughout the year and began its life in a cowshed of the Old Abbey Street Dairy Farm, hence its name. Another place to visit is the **Crawford Centre for the Arts**, which has a changing programme of art exhibitions, professional theatre and music performances in its drama studio and galleries.

West Port at the end of South Street, built in 1589, was the main entrance to the old city. It gives a good idea of what it must have been like in the days when a town could literally shut its gates and defend itself from within.

In North Street, there is the **St Andrews Preservation Trust** in a 17th-century building, where you can learn more about all the treasures in this ancient city.

Don't miss the picturesque **harbour**. The main pier was rebuilt in the 17th century with stones from the ruined cathedral and castle.

St Andrews Sea Life Centre (open daily: adm) is a good place to occupy children.

Around St Andrews

Craigtoun Country Park

Craigtoun Country Park, 2 miles (3km) south of St Andrews, is 50 acres of parkland surrounding Mount Melville House, now a hospital, and open to the public all year. The park has an Italian garden, a Dutch village surrounded by an ornamental lake built in 1918, a Rio Grande Miniature Railway, putting, bowling, trampolines, shops, a licensed restaurant and a picnic area. There are nature walks and a ranger service, too. They run a Country Fair in May.

Leuchars

The railway line to St Andrews was closed some years ago and Leuchars, 5½ miles (9km) northwest, is now the station that serves the town. In the village of Leuchars you could easily miss one of the best relics of Norman architecture in Scotland. Only an apse and chancel remain, incorporated into the parish church, with an arcaded exterior to the apse. If you look carefully you can see the axe-marks of the ancient masons on the blind arches and pilasters. It is a pity that the modern church is so plain, but perhaps its dullness offsets the triumph of the Norman part.

The peace of this part of Fife is often interrupted by low flying planes working from the RAF base nearby.

Earlshall Castle

A mile (1.5km) east of Leuchars, Earlshall Castle (open Easter and June–3rd Sunday in Sept: adm) was built in 1546 by Sir William Bruce. It is a massive fortress, with thick walls and musket loops, set among fanciful topiary—the yew topiary represents chess men—and beautiful, peaceful gardens. Robert Lorimer was responsible for the renovation of the castle and gardens at the turn of the century. Mary, Queen of Scots stayed here only 15 years after it was built, and you can see her bedroom. In the long gallery the ceiling is painted with the arms of Scotland's leading families interspersed with mythological beasts. Hanging from the walls are over 100 broadswords. Lots of historic memorabilia to see here and the guides will tell you strange tales of mysterious red shoes and the footsteps of the Bloody Bruce who can be heard on the stairs now and then. They stage special exhibitions in the Rod and Gun Room, and in the Museum Room you can see letters dating back 200 years and bagpipes that were played at Waterloo.

Where to Stay and Eating Out

expensive

In St Andrews, the **St Andrews Old Course Hotel**, ✆ 0334 74371, is very swish, with free use of spa facilities.

moderate

The Craw's Nest in Anstruther, ✆ 0333 310691, was built as a manse in 1703 and has been extended considerably since those days. The extra size makes it a bit impersonal but it is comfortable. **The Smuggler's Inn,** also in Anstruther, ✆ 0333 310506, is a bit cheaper, overlooks the harbour and is full of atmosphere. You eat well here, in great comfort with cosy log fires, and as you lie awake you hear the tramp of the excisemen outside your window and the whisper of the smugglers as they hide their booty. **Old Manor Hotel**, at Lundin Links, St Andrews, ✆ 0333 320368, overlooks the golf course and the sea, and the food is excellent.

Rufflets Country House Hotel in Strathkinness Low Road, St Andrews, ✆ 0334 72594, is a real treat, in 10 acres of award-winning gardens, with superb food, and quiet, friendly service. It has been owned and personally managed by the same family for more than 35 years which probably accounts for its high standards. **Rusacks**, at 16 Pilmour Links, St Andrews, ✆ 0334 74321, is a little cheaper: very luxurious and prestigious.

inexpensive

Golfers could do worse than **Lundin Links Hotel**, ✆ 0333 320207, a mock-Tudor house with an air of solemn respectability. Surrounded by golf courses and close to the beach, it offers special golfing breaks.

If you want to be flexible and self-supporting, **Kincaple Lodges**, St Andrews, © 0334 85217, are nine pinewood chalets among trees, three miles (4.5km) west of St Andrews. They provide linen, electric blankets and televisions. There are tennis courts, play areas and a babysitting service.

The Ship Inn, at Elie, already mentioned, is a popular eating place and has summer barbecues in the garden, by the beach. **The Grange Inn**, Grange Road, St Andrews, is a good pub/restaurant.

South of the Tay

The north coast of Fife is less developed than that of the East Neuk and has more of an estuary feeling, with views of the river over the mudflats and a rich bird life. Inland it is all farms and towns and villages with sturdy names like Auchtermuchty and Strathmiglo— pronounced Strathmigla. Falkland, with its splendid palace, lies at the heart of this area which has several other interesting ruins as well.

Tentsmuir Forest

Going north towards the Tay you come to the Tentsmuir Forest a couple of miles (3km) northeast of Leuchars. Pines grow right down to the broad, sandy beach, providing shade for summer picnics. Keep your eyes skinned for deer, and families of seals sunning themselves on the sands, as well as lots of different birds.

Tayport and Newport-on-Tay

Tayport and Newport-on-Tay, 5½ miles (9km) north of Leuchars, are holiday resorts on the southern shores of the Firth of Tay. Both claim to have had the oldest ferry in Scotland and it seems likely that boats might have run from both places since earliest times when they were crude settlements. Neolithic remains have been excavated on this northeastern corner of Fife.

The Tay Rail Bridge

> *So the train mov'd slowly along the Bridge of Tay,*
> *Until it was about midway,*
> *Then the central girders with a crash gave way,*
> *And down went the train and passengers into the Tay!*
> *The Storm Fiend did loudly bray,*
> *Because ninety lives had been taken away,*
> *On the last Sabbath day of 1879,*
> *Which will be remember'd for a very long time.*

The southern approach to the Tay Rail Bridge is a short distance west of the one that collapsed in a gale on 28 December 1879, sending a train and about 100 passengers into the water, a disaster that shocked the world and still brings a shiver of horror to hearts today. Stumps of the piers of the original bridge can still be seen on the north side. Anyone who has not read the account of the disaster as told by that astonishing poet William McGonagall should do so at the first possible opportunity.

The new rail bridge, built only a few years later, is a graceful construction curving across the river like a 2-mile (3km) memorial to the disaster. The road bridge, 2 miles downstream, is a toll bridge.

McGonagall was fascinated by the Tay and wrote several other of his epic verses in its honour. There was one about a monster whale that came to 'devour the small fishes in the silvery Tay' and one to the railway bridge before it collapsed, and even an address to the New Tay Bridge. In fact, no traveller in Scotland should set out without a copy of the poetic gems of William McGonagall, poet and tragedian.

Balmerino Abbey

Balmerino Abbey (always accessible: free) is a ruin 3 miles (4.5km) west of the rail bridge on a hill overlooking the river. It was founded for Cistercians in the 13th century by Alexander II, whose mother is buried here. It was mostly destroyed by the English in 1547, during the 'Rough Wooing' and a later attempt to restore it was foiled by the Reformation. The last Lord Balmerino was a brave old man, beheaded as a Jacobite in 1746. Seen against a stormy sky, it is a poignant shell, with just the entrance to the chapter house and the roofless sacristy standing among farm buildings.

Lindores Abbey

The scattered remains of Lindores Abbey (always accessible: free) are 8 miles (13km) southwest, just before Newburgh, and also overlooking the Firth of Tay. This abbey was an important religious community until it was secularized in 1600. The main entrance arch and part of the west tower still stand in jagged isolation, all that remain of a place that witnessed the savage burning of exquisitely illuminated mass books and manuscripts by John Knox. Lindores was founded in the 12th century for Benedictines and numbered among its many pilgrims several Scottish monarchs.

Newburgh

Newburgh, 13 miles (21km) southwest of Newport, almost on the border with Tayside, is a Royal Burgh with a pretty little harbour. On the hill to the south of the town you can see the remains of Macduff's Cross, the legendary place of sanctuary for any Macduff who had committed a murder in hot blood. To achieve pardon, the murderer had to touch the cross, wash himself nine times at Ninewells nearby, and forfeit nine cows, each to be tied to the cross.

Laing Museum (open daily, 16 March–15 Oct; Wed, Thurs and Sun for the rest of the year: adm) has exhibitions of fossil fish discovered in Dura Den, a feature on Scottish emigration, and Victorian displays including a reconstructed Victorian study.

Falkland

Falkland, 9 miles (14.5km) south of Newburgh, is an ancient town, clinging to the lower slopes of the Lomond Hills, looking across the Howe of Fife. The rich farmland that you see now was once a forest full of deer and wild boar. Many of the 17th- to 19th-century buildings have been restored, making it a delightful place to wander about in, especially on a fine day when the sun plays tricks with the old stones, dappled with light and shade.

Falkland Palace (open daily Easter–30 Sept and weekends in Oct: adm) was built in the 15th and 16th centuries as a hunting lodge for the Stuarts. Much of it has been restored, giving an example of early Renaissance architecture—compact and ornate, its massive walls and barred windows a reminder that even hunting lodges had to be fortified. The south wing is the best preserved, with an elaborate façade, mullioned windows and a gate house flanked by round towers.

It was in an earlier castle on this site, in 1402, that the heir to the throne, the Duke of Rothesay, was starved to death by the ambitious and greedy Duke of Albany. Falkland was annexed by the Crown when James I eliminated the powerful Albany family by the simple, if somewhat drastic, method of murdering all their menfolk. The elegance of the architecture was enhanced by French masons employed by James IV and then by his son James V. James V came to Falkland in 1542, after his defeat at Solway Moss. He died here, a broken man, having just heard of the birth of his daughter, Mary. He prophesied on his death bed that his infant daughter would be the last of the Stuarts to rule Scotland.

The palace was restored from complete ruin by the Hereditary Keeper, the third Marquess of Bute, in 1887 and he also rescued the gardens and many of the houses in the town. The original Royal Tennis Court, 1539, is still in use as one of Britain's few 'royal' or 'real' tennis courts. Perhaps Queen Mary had a game here. She certainly played golf and is known to have come often to Falkland on hunting expeditions.

Wander along the High Street, beyond the palace gates, through the Market Square, and up the Maspie Burn on to East Lomond Law. From here, the landscape is all rolling hills and rounded hillocks, and attractive villages with stone cottages and pantiled roofs. This is the Howe of Fife, 'howe' meaning sheltered place.

Cupar

Cupar, 10 miles (16km) northeast of Falkland, heading back to St Andrews, was once the administrative centre of Fife and is still the headquarters for North East Fife District Council. It has elegant 18th-century houses built of mellow, honey-coloured stone. In 1276, Alexander III held an Assembly of the Three Estates in Cupar, made up of the Church, the burghers, and the aristocracy. It was this that inspired Sir David Lindsay, who lived nearby, to write *Ane Pleasant Satyre of the Thrie Estaitis*, holding them up to ridicule. The play has recently been revived, in a greatly shortened form, and is aired now and then during the Edinburgh Festival. Cupar has a Gala Week in June.

The Scottish Deer Centre (open daily: adm) is 3 miles (4.5km) west of Cupar on the A91. Children will enjoy seeing deer at close quarters and even touching them, and there is lots to see and do in the visitor centre in the Georgian courtyard, which has a restaurant. Outside there is a farm walk, nature trail and falconry centre.

Hill of Tarvit

Hill of Tarvit (open Easter; weekends only April and Oct; afternoons daily 28 April–30 Sept: adm) is a mansion 2 miles (3km) south of Cupar. Dating from 1696 and splendidly remodelled by Robert Lorimer in 1906, the house has a nice lived-in feeling. The collection of treasures inside includes tapestries, porcelain, paintings, and 18th-century English and French furniture. There is also an Edwardian laundry where you can almost see steam from the boiling sheets in the copper and feel the ache of the women's tired muscles at the end of the day. The gardens are laid out in French style with box hedges and yews: there is a woodland walk and a hilltop 'toposcope'. The view of the house from the garden, with a double flight of steps leading up to the terrace, is lovely.

Scotstarvit Tower opposite Hill of Tarvit (open daily: free) is a five-storey, 16th-century tower house with battlements and turrets. It was the home of John Scott, a 16th- and 17th-century scholar and mapmaker in the days when new routes were opening up all round the globe.

Pitlessie

Pitlessie, 4 miles (6km) southwest of Cupar, will be familiar to fans of David Wilkie, from his famous painting 'Pitlessie Fair'. The artist was born at Cults Manse nearby in 1785 and many of his paintings of everyday life were set locally, so you find yourself looking round for one of his jovial, bucolic peasants. Sadly, the manse was destroyed by fire in 1926, together with a wealth of wall paintings done by Wilkie in his youth.

Ceres

Ceres is 4 miles (6km) east of Pitlessie. Pantiled cottages surround a green on which annual games are still held, dating from victory celebrations after Bannockburn in 1314.

The Fife Folk Museum (open afternoons daily except Tues, April–Oct: adm) is spread between a restored 17th-century tolbooth weigh house, two cottages and out of doors. This award-winning museum has collections of the domestic and agricultural tools and equipment in daily use before the invention of electricity and the petrol engine. Don't miss the dungeons in the tolbooth. There are also two nature trails from the village, planned by the Scottish Wildlife Trust, of botanical and geological interest.

Peat Inn, 3 miles (4.5km) to the southeast, is a hamlet that takes its name from its inn. It is well worth a detour to this inn, where you can eat as good a meal as you could hope for anywhere in the country.

Magus Muir is 3 miles (4.5km) north of Peat Inn and just south of Strathkinness. This grisly spot is where a party of Covenanters butchered Archbishop Sharp in 1679, in the presence of his daughter. Sharp's attempts to restore Episcopacy to Scotland had not been entirely straightforward and he had won for himself universal detestation. This was hardly surprising, when you remember that he went, as a Presbyterian, to plead the Covenanters' cause with Charles II and returned as the consecrated Bishop of St Andrews.

Old Dairsie, about three miles (4.5km) west of Magus Muir, has a bridge over the River Eden that was built by Archbishop Beaton in 1522. **Dairsie Castle**, in the process of restoration, lies above the river, where David II spent part of his youth. The Kirk of Dairsie, St Mary's, was built in 1621 by Archbishop Spottiswood in an attempt to bring the English church to Scotland. It is a mixture of Gothic and classical, with an octagonal belfry, in a peaceful graveyard. Dura Den is a wooded gorge south of the bridge, where a large number of fossils have been found. These fossils gave vital clues to the formation of land and life here, over many millions of years. Beside the Ceres Burn that cuts the gorge are the ruins of several linen and jute mills, once an important part of Fife economy.

Where to Stay

expensive

Fernie Castle Hotel, near Letham, ✆ 033 781381, is a must for castle addicts. Built in 1510 in 30 acres of park and woods, this is a prince among castles, with a round tower and a prize-winning French chef. Well placed for golfers, it's well worth the price.

If you prefer self-catering, you could do a lot worse than **The Weaver's House**, Auchtermuchty, ✆ 0337 28496, a very well-set-up cottage for six people.

moderate

Sandford Country House Hotel near Wormit, Newport-on-Tay, ✆ 0382 541802, is built round three sides of a courtyard garden with narrow passages leading to comfortable bedrooms. It does special golf packages and the food is good.

In Falkland, try the **Covenanter Hotel**, ✆ 0337 57224, with only three bedrooms.

inexpensive

A little different is **Redlands Country Lodge** near Ladybank, ✆ 0337 31091, in lovely gardens surrounded by open country, with separate pine log-cabin bedrooms, self-contained and comfortable. The food is excellent and they'll arrange golf, fishing, shooting, wildfowling and pony-trekking.

Eating Out

People travel a long way to eat in the 18th-century **Peat Inn**, ✆ 033 484206, at the junction of the B940/941 in the village of that name. This is a true French auberge, complete with Michelin star, modelled on the proprietors' favourite establishment in Vonnas, France, with decor and ambience to match. The food is accurately aimed at discerning taste buds, the wine list is excellent and the service unbeatable.

the figure of Prudence at Edzell Castle, Angus

Tayside

The sun shines kindly on Tayside and the east wind hones its coast. In winter the peaks glisten with snow; in summer the hills and moors are bruised with purple heather. Birch, conifer and hardwood trees shade the glens, giving a blaze of metallic colours in autumn: bronze, gold, copper, rust.

Once the centre of the Pictish kingdom, Tayside's hill forts and stone circles are haunted by the ghosts of the Picts. The Romans came and went in the 1st/2nd centuries. They built sophisticated fortifications but failed to subdue the Picts, who reigned supreme, with their own kings and culture. They gradually absorbed Christianity as it crept in from the west and left carved stones to prove it. The Vikings swooped in from the sea, but were beaten off. In the middle of the 9th century, Kenneth Macalpine united Dalriada in the west with Pictland, and Scone, just north of Perth, became the capital until the middle of the 15th century, with nearby Dunkeld an important ecclesiastical centre. In the turbulent 17th century, many battles—political, religious and territorial—were fought in the narrow passes that linked north and south. The Battle of Killiecrankie, in 1689, was perhaps the best known, when the Highlanders almost annihilated the Government's army. Control of several of Tayside's castles was hotly disputed half a century later, during the final Jacobite rebellion.

Agriculture and fishing have been the main sources of income for these rural people, with little industrialization except around Dundee. Whisky distilling plays an important part in the economy and tourism is growing fast, backed up by the revival of old crafts.

Among the many local events to look out for are the Bull Sales in Perth, in February and October. Whether you are interested in cattle farming or not, this wonderful assembly of bucolics has faces as rich in character as any in a David Wilkie painting. Farmers come from far and wide and pay astronomic prices for the finest bulls in the land.

Highland Games are held in a number of places, including Blair Atholl in May, Dundee and Arbroath in July, Perth and Birnam in August and Pitlochry in September. In May, the renowned Perth Festival of Arts is held and Pitlochry's Annual Summer Festival runs from May to October with plays, concerts and Fringe events. A traditional Scottish Folk Festival is held for three days every April in Glenfarg, drawing artists from all over the country. International Fly Fishing Championships are often held on Loch Leven in autumn.

Many people hurry through Tayside, blind to its attractions in their rush to get to the Highlands proper. They miss a great deal. Approaching through Kinross in the south, the main routes into Perthshire and Angus radiate from Perth, following the river valleys like the wavering legs of a giant spider. That is how this guide will cover the region.

Tourist Information

The following tourist information centres are open all the year: **Auchterarder**: 90 High Street, ✆ 0764 63450; **Blairgowrie**: 26 Wellmeadow, ✆ 0250 2960/3701; **Crieff**: High Street, ✆ 0764 2578; **Dundee**: 4 City Square, ✆ 0382 27723; **Perth**: 45 High Street, ✆ 0738 38353; **Pitlochry**: 27 Atholl Road, ✆ 0796 2215/2751. There are also several centres which open seasonally, generally from Easter to the end of September or October.

Kinross-shire

Scotland's second-smallest county, Kinross-shire, is dominated by Loch Leven within a semi-circle of hills. You come in from the south on the M90, with the loch stretching away to your right, and a tantalizing thickening of the skyline ahead, beckoning you towards the Highlands. If you aren't concentrating, the motorway will whisk you through it and away past Perth before you can blink.

Kinross

The market town of **Kinross** lies at the heart of farming country. The tolbooth dates from the early 17th century, later repaired and decorated by Robert Adam whose descendants still live at Blairadam House, nearby. The thriving woollen industry goes back many years to when wool and linen were hand-spun in the cottages. Kinross is the only place where cashmere is spun in Britain. The goat hair is imported, but there are plans among Scottish farmers to establish Scottish goat farms which, it is thought, could be an important addition to the economy. In the 17th century, Kinross was famous for making cutlery, until Sheffield stole the market in the 19th century.

The Butterfly Farm at Turfhills, Kinross (open daily, April–Oct: adm) is an amazing jungle paradise where you can see literally hundreds of colourful butterflies and moths in a tropical setting. They also have an aviary, a childrens' farm, a gift shop and a tea house.

At **The Scottish Centre for Falconry**, also at Turfhills (open daily, March–Dec: adm) falcons and other birds of prey give flying demonstrations and there are exhibitions and information about all aspects of falconry.

Loch Leven

Loch Leven is by no means Scotland's most beautiful stretch of water but it has an irresistible fascination. It is renowned in the fishing world for its unique pink trout and international fishing competitions are held here frequently. As a nature reserve, it gives refuge to a large variety of migratory wildfowl: pink-foot and greylag geese and many

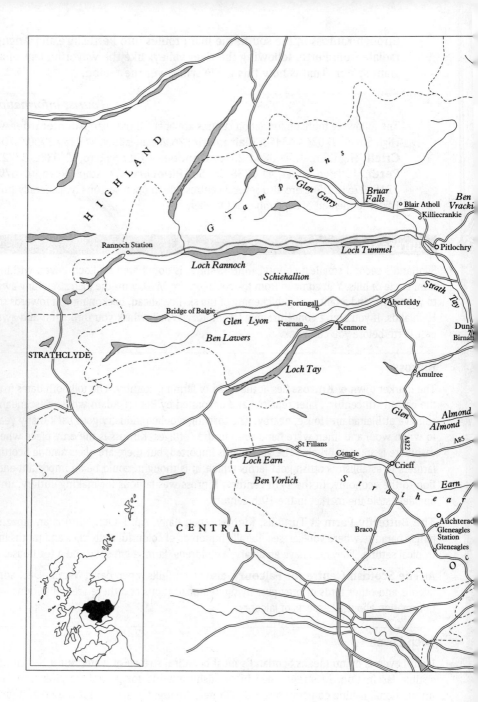

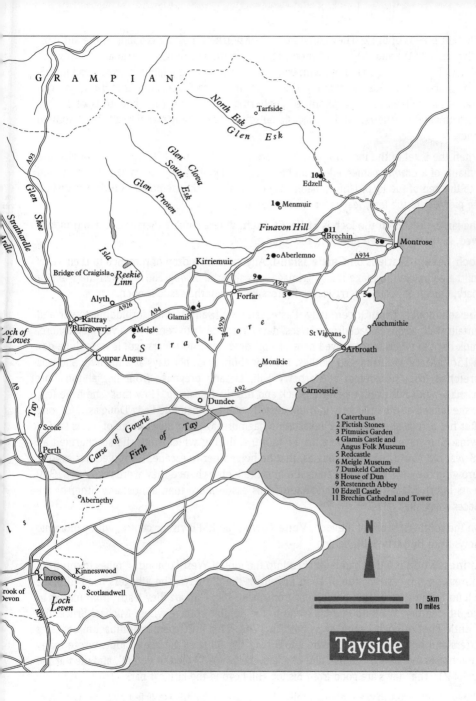

Tarfside

North Esk

Glen Esk

GRAMPIAN

Glen Clova

South Esk

Glen Prosen

10● Edzell

1● Menmuir

Finavon Hill

11● Brechin

8● Montrose

Strathardle

Ardle

Glen Shee

Isla

Kirriemuir

2●○ Aberlemno

A934

Bridge of Craigisla

Reekie Linn

9●

A932

Alyth

A926

A94

Forfar

3●

5●

Rattray
Blairgowrie

Glamis

4●

A929

Strathmore

Auchmithie

Loch of
e Lowes

Meigle
6●

St Vigeans○

Coupar Angus

Monikie

Arbroath

Tay

A9

A92

Carnoustie

Scone

Dundee

Carse of Gowrie

Firth of Tay

Perth

Abernethy

1 Caterthuns
2 Pictish Stones
3 Pitmuies Garden
4 Glamis Castle and
  Angus Folk Museum
5 Redcastle
6 Meigle Museum
7 Dunkeld Cathedral
8 House of Dun
9 Restenneth Abbey
10 Edzell Castle
11 Brechin Cathedral and Tower

N

Kinross
Kinnesswood

rook of
Devon

Scotlandwell

Loch
Leven

5km
10 miles

Tayside

different breeds of duck. They come from their northern nesting grounds in the autumn, between 10,000 and 20,000 of them, and graze the surrounding farmland during the winter. The haunting sound of them, coming in on the evening flight in arrowhead formation, is one of the most poignant in the world. In the early morning or at dusk, you can hear a marvellous low symphony of chattering birds: little runs and trills of sound; murmurs and mutterings and an occasional squawk as a fussy mother calls her family to order.

When the level of the loch dropped by more than 4 feet in a 19th-century drought, the remains of a *crannog* emerged—a prehistoric lake-dwelling built on wooden piles driven into the bed of the loch. Unfortunately the elements quickly demolished it: it was just off the pier where the ferry leaves for Castle Island.

The largest island on the loch is **St Serf's Inch**, where Culdee (Servants of God) monks lived, in the now-ruined priory, in the 8th century.

Loch Leven Castle is on **Castle Island**. Anyone with a drop of romance in their veins will be compelled to make this pilgrimage, crossing the olive green water in the wake of Mary, Queen of Scots. A ferry leaves Kinross Pier when the castle is open.

The solid-looking ruin (open daily, Easter—end Sept: adm), with forbidding tower and curtain wall, against a backdrop of trees, dates from the 14th century. As you step ashore, think back to when Mary arrived here as a prisoner, over 400 years ago. It was a June day in 1567. Mary was in ragged clothes, her hair shorn from her days as a fugitive. She was wretched from her defeat at Carberry Hill, already pregnant from her all-too-short marriage with Bothwell; exhausted, sick and utterly despairing. How must she have felt, as she landed at the little jetty into the custody of unsympathetic Lady Douglas? Not long after her arrival she suffered a devastating haemorrhage and miscarriage of—it is said— twins. She stayed in the castle for 11 months, during which time she so charmed an 18-year-old youth, William Douglas, that he helped her to escape. He rowed her ashore, throwing the keys of the locked castle into the loch (whence they were recovered, 300 years later). Mary's elusive spirit haunts this castle more than almost any other of the places she visited.

On the southern shore of the loch, **Vane Farm** is an RSPB visitor centre, with panoramic views from **Benarty Hill**, behind.

Kinnesswood is a tiny hamlet tucked into the foot of West Lomond, 4 miles (6km) from Kinross on the eastern side of Loch Leven. In the old days, the villagers used to make vellum from calf skin, and parchment from sheep skin—an art they learnt from monks in the 8th century. Walk up Puddin Wynd to the humble cottage where Michael Bruce, the 'Gentle Poet of Loch Leven', was born in 1746. This little memorial museum contains letters and books of the poet who could read the Bible at the age of four, wrote many paraphrases familiar to Scottish churchgoers, including 'O God of Bethel', and died at the age of 21. The views are good from Bishop Hill beyond the kirk car park.

The well at **Scotlandwell**, about a mile (1.5km) to the southeast, is fed by a spring of very clear, pure water that bubbles up through the sand and is reputed to cure leprosy.

Burleigh Castle, in the care of Historic Scotland, is a mile (1.5km) north of the loch and dates from 1500. It was the seat of the Balfours of Burleigh who were visited here several times by James VI.

At **Crook of Devon**, (where some wag added 'Twinned with the Thief of Baghdad' to the road sign), 6 miles (9.5km) west of Kinross on the A977, there is a fish farm where you can feed the fish with pelleted food or try to fish them out of the tanks. They sell delicious fresh and smoked trout. The pub has excellent food.

Abernethy

Strictly speaking, Abernethy is in Perthshire, not Kinross, but it is *en route* to Perth from the south. You should take exit 9 from the motorway, 11 miles (17.5km) north of Kinross, and go 4 miles (6.5km) east on the A913.

It would be easy to dismiss Abernethy as 'just another village' but that would be a mistake. The Romans certainly sailed this far up the Tay and left the remains of a fort just to the south. More important, however, Abernethy was once a mighty Pictish kingdom. The 74-foot (23m), tapering tower, whose lower part dates from the 9th century, is one of only two such on the mainland of Scotland, the other being in Brechin. When Abernethy was the centre of the Celtic Church, this tower provided the clergy with an almost impregnable refuge, as well.as an excellent look-out in times of threatened invasion. The upper part dates from the 11th century, with a 7th-century stone, set into the base, carved with Pictish symbols. Also set into the wall is the 'jougs', an iron neck collar by which malefactors were chained for punishment. The design of these towers came over from Ireland with the missionary priests.

It was here in Abernethy, below the Ochil Hills, that Malcolm Canmore was forced to kneel and pay token homage to William the Conqueror in 1071. William had come north, conducting such a brilliant campaign against Scotland that Malcolm's humiliating capitulation seemed the only way to prevent the country being devastated. Perhaps he only intended to acknowledge William as his overlord in connection with his English estates. Whatever his motive, he allowed his son by his first marriage, Duncan, to be taken as a hostage to England, and his submission was to create centuries of unrest in both countries.

Where to Stay

moderate

In Cleish, at the foot of the hills, there is **Nivingston House Country Hotel and Restaurant**, © 0577 850216, a Victorian mansion in 12 acres of landscaped gardens with terrific views. Log fires and candle-lit dinners cooked by a gold-medallist chef make this a nice place to stay. The food is delicious, especially if you go for unusual sauces. It is at the top end of the moderate price bracket. **Duchally House Hotel**, Auchterarder, © 0764 63071, in 28 acres of landscaped gardens and woodland, has good food and sporting packages.

If it's atmosphere and history you want, try **Lomond Country Inn** in Kinnesswood, © 0592 84 253. The food isn't bad. There is a lovely view across Loch Leven from the dining room and fishing permits are available. **Bein Inn** in Glenfarg, © 057 73216, is an old country inn, with public rooms full of character and a reasonable restaurant. **Kirklands Hotel** in Kinross, © 0577 863313, is another old coaching inn, recently done up.

Eating Out

Gourmets should try **Croftbank House Hotel and Restaurant** in Station Road, Kinross, © 0577 863819. People come a long way to eat the food prepared by the chef-patron, who recently won the Scottish 'Chef of the Year' award. There are four bedrooms only in this Victorian house, so it is more of a restaurant than a hotel. Bed and breakfast is cheap so you can afford to splash out on dinner. **The Grouse and Claret**, at Heatheryford, junction 6, M90, © 0577 864212, has a reputation for good game and fish dishes and the dining room overlooks the loch.

Perth

Anyone visiting Perth for the first time should have Walter Scott's *The Fair Maid of Perth* as a companion. The city is 17 miles (27km) north of Kinross and as you come down into it from the motorway, you get a fine view of the town, spread out below, round the Tay. This view, 'new' since the building of the motorway, is in fact the old one, extolled by Scott in the first few pages of introduction to *The Fair Maid*. Two wide green parks, North and South Inch, unfold on either side, with a collage of spires reaching for the sky.

Perth was the first place where it was easy to bridge the river. It was a thriving port in the old days and is now an important livestock market at the centre of a productive agricultural area. Its fine setting earned Perth the title 'The Fair City' in the past, and a recent transformation has done much to restore it to that status. In the days before conservation became fashionable, many of its old buildings were replaced by utilitarian monsters that are little short of architectural vandalism, but now, with traffic-free shopping streets and award-winning floral displays, Perth is once again an attractive town. If you poke around you will find traces of the past and there are some very fine late-Georgian terraces, especially round the Inches, and nice vistas of the river. When a new Marks and Spencer store was being built in the High Street some time ago, the remains of a medieval market were unearthed, resulting in a valuable stay of execution. A new by-pass has considerably eased traffic congestion in the town centre.

Traces of an old city wall indicate that there was a Roman camp here, although Perth doesn't appear in the records until the 12th century. A devastating flood destroyed Old

Perth in 1210 and William the Lion granted a Royal Charter to the town that was built in its place the same year. It was the capital of Scotland for a while, until the middle of the 15th century.

The Battle of the Clans

Among the city's more colourful events was the Battle of the Clans, so graphically woven by Scott into the convoluted plot of *The Fair Maid*. This was a contest between the Clans Chattan and Quhele (pronounced Kay), to establish who should take precedence in battle—a hotly disputed honour in those swashbuckling days. Thirty men from each side were to fight in a tournament on the North Inch, watched by King Robert III, his wife and court. One of the Clan Chattan lost his nerve at the last moment and fled. The rule was that the two sides must be matched man-for-man, so a blacksmith, small and bandylegged, offered to stand in for the price of half a French crown. All but one of the Quhele Clan were slaughtered. Among the survivors of the Chattans was the blacksmith, who had done more than anyone else to secure victory (he is Scott's Henry, who wins the hand of virginal Catharine).

The highly dubious drama of the Gowrie Conspiracy took place in 1600, in the now demolished Gowrie House. According to James VI, the Earl of Gowrie and his brother, Alexander Ruthven, lured him to an upstairs room in the house and tried to tie him up. He shouted for his lords through an open window was rescued, while Gowrie and Ruthven were killed in the flurry. The whole affair was shrouded in mystery and speculation, with hints of homosexual motives mingled with hints that the king set the thing up in order to get rid of the brothers, whose ruthless political ambition was notorious.

Perth Art Gallery and Museum (open daily except Sundays: free), in George Street, has local history displays and an exhibition showing the growth of the whisky industry which plays an important part in the economy of the area.

St John's Church (open daily) was restored in 1923, with a War Memorial Chapel designed by Robert Lorimer. It dates from the 15th century and is on the site of a church built in the 12th century. Edward III is said to have killed his brother, the Earl of Cornwall, in that earlier church in 1335. John Knox preached one of his iconoclastic sermons in St John's in 1559, urging his followers to purge the churches of idolatry; this sermon led to the destruction of many of the churches and monasteries in the area and helped to fuel the Reformation. This church alone had at least 40 richly decorated altars, dedicated to saints. A few of the sacred treasures rescued from the purgers include the 16th-century German Cellini Cup, given to Mary of Guise-Lorraine by the Pope, 17th-century chalices and a 16th-century baptismal basin.

The Fair Maid's House (open daily except Sun: free, gallery shut in Jan) is behind Charlotte Street, in North Port, and was the home of virtuous Catharine Glover, The Fair Maid of Perth. One of the oldest buildings in the town, it holds a series of month-long exhibitions of contemporary Scottish crafts and paintings. Perhaps a little over-restored, it is nevertheless an intriguing place. There is a craft shop.

Blackfriars Street, nearby, was the site of the long-vanished Blackfriars Monastery, where James I was murdered in 1437. The story of Catherine Douglas, Catherine 'Bar-Lass', who supposedly tried to bar the door to the murderers by using her arm as a bolt, is a 16th-century invention.

Balhousie Castle, a 15th-century Scottish Baronial castle beyond Rose Terrace on the west side of North Inch, has been restored. Former home of the Earls of Kinnoull, it is the Regimental Headquarters of the Black Watch and contains its **Regimental Museum** (open weekdays, and Sun in summer: free). The Black Watch was raised in 1739 to help the government pacify the rebellious Highlanders. There is a comprehensive display of the history of this famous regiment, with uniforms, weapons, pictures, documents, photographs and trophies, all recording its many honours and triumphs.

Dewars Whisky Plant dominates the western suburbs of Perth. Free conducted tours during the week demonstrate how Scotland's most popular export finds its way into the bottles.

The Perth Leisure Pool has the reputation of being the best in Scotland, with more than 700,000 visitors a year.

Kinnoull Hill rises 729 feet (224m) above the town, barely a mile (1.5km) to the east. An easy climb gives a bird's eye view of the geological 'Highland Line' that divides the Highlands from the Lowlands.

Fairways Heavy Horse Centre is at Kinfauns, about 2 miles (3km) east of Perth on the A85, between the Tay and Kinnoull Hill. Here, you can see great Clydesdales and shire horses and their foals, ride in waggons, or watch video shows of horses and farriers at work.

Elcho Castle (always accessible) is a ruin 4 miles (6.5km) east of Perth. This is one of the more interesting of the later Scottish castles, having been both defensive and yet incorporating palace-like comforts. The square tower with a crow-stepped gable dates from the 15th century. The huge kitchen has a fireplace as big as a small room and there are traces of fine.plasterwork in the hall on the first floor. The bedrooms above had en-suite garderobes. James III granted the lands of Elcho to John de Wemyss in 1468. A subsequent Sir John de Wemyss became the first Earl of Wemyss under Charles I but sided with the Parliamentarians in the Civil War.

Scone Palace

Scone Palace (open daily, Easter–Oct, or by arrangement, © 0738 52300: adm) is 2 miles (3km) north of Perth on the A93. Pronounced 'Scoon', the palace is a 19th-century restoration of 16th-century and earlier buildings, with battlements, a toy fort façade and the original gateway. In 1297, Edward I stole the Stone of Scone and took it to London (see 'Topics').

The abbey and palace that stood here in the 16th century were destroyed by John Knox's followers, after he had denounced 'idolatry' in his sermon from St John's in 1559.

The palace contains French furniture, including Marie Antoinette's writing desk; 16th-century needlework, including bed hangings embroidered by Mary, Queen of Scots; porcelain; 17th- and 18th-century ivories; 18th-century clocks. The walls are lined with Lyons silk. There is a coffee shop serving home-baked food, a gift shop and gardens with a playground and pinetum.

Where to Stay

expensive

If luxury is what you seek, particularly if you are a golfer, **The Murrayshall Hotel** at Scone, ✆ 0738 51171, will suit you. This country-house hotel stands in 300 acres of parkland with an 18-hole, par 73 golf course. It has a multiple-award-winning chef, and provides tennis, croquet and bowls, and, if you book ahead, shooting, fishing and riding.

moderate

Ballathie House Hotel at Kinclaven, 10 miles (16km) north of Perth, ✆ 025 083 268, is an overgrown shooting lodge in its own estate overlooking the Tay; open from early March to mid-January. It has four-poster or canopied beds, ancestral furniture and paintings, *haute cuisine*, croquet, tennis, putting, trout and salmon fishing, shooting and all mod cons. (The shooting and fishing must be booked ahead.) It even has its own helipad for tycoons. Prices vary seasonally and can verge on the expensive.

The Royal George, Tay Street, Perth, ✆ 0738 24455, got its Royal appendage from a visit paid by Queen Victoria in 1848. It is a Trust House of the good old-fashioned style, in the moderate to expensive price bracket, right on the river. **The Station Hotel**, Leonard Street, ✆ 0738 24141, is one of Perth's dowagers—comfortable and reasonably priced with four crowns. Modern **Isle of Skye Hotel**, Dundee Road, ✆ 0738 24471, is popular.

inexpensive

Salutation Hotel, 34 South Street, Perth, ✆ 0738 30066, was established in 1699 and was Prince Charles's headquarters for a while. Considerably more comfortable today, the hotel has the largest Adam-style window in Scotland in its dining room. Modernization has obliterated all trace of the past, but you can see the Prince's ops room, now a meeting room.

If you are an outward-bounder and like a cheap, organized holiday, try **Kinfauns Castle,** a couple of miles east of Perth on the A85, ✆ 0738 20777, but don't expect to be pampered. Another baronial pile with battlements, in 40 acres of woodland, Kinfauns is owned by the Countrywide Holiday Association. They lay on walking and outdoor holidays, with group-leaders and a host and hostess who arrange your evening entertainment.

✕ **Timothy's**, 24 St John's Street, Perth, © 0738 26641, is a cheap, informal restaurant, half-Scottish and half-Danish, and you'll eat well.

Angus and Perthshire: East of the A9

Angus covers most of that part of Tayside that lies to the east of the A9, north of the Firth of Tay. The coastal plain consists of gently rolling farmland in the Carse of Gowrie, running back up into the Sidlaw Hills where winter can linger into spring, and from whose southern slopes you can get magnificent views across the firth of Tay to northern Fife. The coast is rugged red sandstone with sandy bays. The rest of the land east of the A9 is Perthshire, and here you are in the Highlands with all the wonderful range of scenery they contain. Perth is the hub from which all the following routes lead.

Dundee

> *'Twas in the month of December, and in the year 1883,*
> *That a monster whale came to Dundee,*
> *Resolved for a few days to sport and play,*
> *And devour the small fishes in the silvery Tay.*

from 'The Famous Tay Whale', by William McGonagall

Dundee, fourth-largest town in Scotland and administrative headquarters for Tayside, is 22 miles (35km) northeast of Perth on the Firth of Tay.

Although the history of the town goes way back, there is little to show for it architecturally: what was not destroyed by the English and by the Reformation, the Dundonians replaced, in the name of modernization and progress. The architectural vandalism of the 1950s and 1960s, however, is now being replaced by more dignified modern developments.

Traces of Bronze Age settlements have been found locally, and a number of Pictish stones underline the importance of this area in the Dark Ages. 'The Law', with the remains of a Roman hill fort on top, is the highest point of the city, just north of the centre—an excellent place from which to get a bird's-eye view.

Kenneth Macalpine used Dundee as his headquarters in 834, when he was campaigning for the union of Picts and Scots. William the Lion granted it a Royal Charter in 1190. William Wallace went to school in Dundee (which claims, in competition with Lanark, that it was here he tangled with authority and was outlawed). It was the first town in Scotland to adopt the reformed religion and it took George Wishart as its paragon, suffering badly as a result, when he was burned at the stake in 1546. Hereford pounded the town for Henry VIII during the 'Rough Wooing'; Montrose stormed it in 1645 during the Civil War and General Monk occupied it in 1651. In 1689, James VII raised his standard on The Law, after William and Mary had been declared King and Queen of Scotland.

Fickle in their loyalties, the Dundonians swung between the Jacobite and the Hanoverian causes, conferring the Freedom of the Burgh on Butcher Cumberland after his victory at Culloden.

In 1889, Queen Victoria granted Dundee a charter confirming all previous charters given since the 12th century, one of which, from Charles I, allowed rights over revenues earned from the river—including salmon fishing. She also made it a city and a county in its own right so that, strictly speaking, it is not part of Angus.

When the great surge of energy swept through Scotland during the Scottish Enlightenment period, Dundee earned its popular alliteration as the town of **Jam, Jute and Journalism**. Towards the end of the 18th century, Mr Keiller, a local grocer, bought a bargain crate of oranges, down at the docks. They proved too bitter to sell, so frugal Mrs Keiller boiled them up with sugar and water and made delicious orange jam. This caught on, and in 1797 the Keillers opened their famous jam business. There are various explanations for the name marmalade. One is that it comes from *marmelo* (quince); another, accepting that Mrs Keiller was not the first to make orange jam, that when it was made for Mary, Queen of Scots, she announced that it was good for *ma malade*. The original white stone jars in which Keiller's Marmalade was sold are collectors' pieces.

The jute industry, helped by whale oil from a flourishing whaling fleet, blossomed in the early 19th century, introduced by people from Angus who settled in Calcutta. Dundee became a 'boom-town', with factories and tenements shooting up like mushrooms. This prosperity lasted for 100 years until India learned to develop her raw jute and materials became scarce. Until as late as the 1950s, up to 7000 people were employed at the jute mills and there are many who remember the flood of people pouring out of the mill gates at five o'clock. Some of the old mills have been restored: one, opposite the police station, a handsome, mid-19th-century building, has been converted into a number of small workshops. A little jute is still worked but the industry has diversified in recent years and includes oil-related enterprises. Whaling remained an important industry for many years, with large numbers of boats going out from Dundee, as far as the Arctic.

One of the by-products of the jute boom was the arrival in Dundee of many hundreds of Catholic Highlanders and Irish, dispossessed by the potato famine and land clearance, flocking to find work in the jute mills. As a result, the city today is about one-third Catholic, an unusually high proportion for the east of Scotland.

Journalism, the third of Dundee's Js, is the great Thomson and Leng empire. This autocratic publishing firm, which has no truck with unions or Catholics, is renowned for its wholesome, unsalacious publications, which include the *Sunday Post*, *People's Friend*, the *Dandy* and the *Beano* and dozens more. Until 1992, the *Dundee Courier* was the last reputable daily newspaper to have no news on the front page.

Dundee cake, a rich, dark, fruit cake with sliced almonds on top, finds its way on to tea tables all over the world.

Dundee University was founded in 1883 and incorporated with that of St Andrews in 1889, but became independent again in 1967.

In spite of its ancient history, Dundee is a modern city catering for modern tastes, bursting with young enterprise rather than inherited culture. Among the city's imaginative innovations is its Public Art. In 1982, artists sponsored by the Manpower Services Commission and the Scottish Development Agency went on to the streets with their paints and tools and got to work. The result is a stimulating trail of open-air sculpture, ceramics, murals, mosaics and every sort of graphic and plastic art. Start at the corner of Nethergate and Marketgait, outside the Angus Thistle Hotel, and wander. You'll trip over examples wherever you go. It is a remarkable achievement.

The Dundee Highland Games are in July. Other summer entertainments include Dundee Water Festival which encompasses a number of events both on and off the water, and jazz and folk festivals which spill out of the theatres into the city's pubs and clubs.

Dundee has three city churches under one roof, just west of City Square, forming a large, cruciform building surrounded on three sides by a pedestrian shopping precinct. **The Old Steeple**, or St Mary's Tower, Dundee's oldest surviving building, is 15th-century, the only part that remains of the pre-Reformation church that stood here since the 12th century.

The Howf (burial ground or meeting-place) is northwest of the square. It was once the orchard of the Greyfriars Monastery, founded in the 13th century. Mary, Queen of Scots gave the land to the city and it became a cemetery. You can still see a number of old gravestones with curious inscriptions.

McManus Galleries (open daily, except Sun: free), a Victorian Gothic building in Albert Square, north of City Square, is the Central Museum and Art Gallery. Exhibitions cover local history, archaeology, and a guide to the development of the town. The art gallery contains work by Flemish, Dutch, French and British artists with some lovely Scottish paintings and frequent modern exhibitions.

The Barrack Street Museum (open daily, except Sun: free), further west, along Meadowside, concentrates on natural history and develops themes such as the relationship between nature and art. There are displays of exotic wildlife and geology and the skeleton of the Tay Whale.

If you have salt in your veins, HM Frigate *Unicorn* is in Victoria Dock (open daily: adm), a 46-gun wooden warship, launched at Chatham in 1824. She is the oldest British-built ship still afloat and the fourth-oldest ship afloat in the world, a unique survivor from the transitional period between wooden sailing ships and iron steamships. She was never fully rigged and never engaged in enemy action: for some years she was a prison hulk.

Discovery, on Discovery Quay (open daily: adm) is the research ship used by Captain Scott for the first of his two expeditions to the Antarctic at the beginning of the century. Built in Dundee and now returned home, it has been equipped to jog sluggish imaginations, with smells and sounds and life-sized models.

Dens Road Market is a good, lively place for collectors of bric-a-brac.

On top of **Balgay Hill** northwest of City Square, **Mills Observatory** (open daily except Sun: free) has telescopes, displays on astronomy and space exploration, a lecture room and a small planetarium. There is an audio-visual programme, and an astronomer in residence. Even without the telescopes, the view from up here is good.

Camperdown Park further northwest, one of Dundee's 28 parks and gardens, was opened by the present Queen in 1946, when she was still Princess Elizabeth. It consists of about 400 acres of wooded parkland and garden with rare trees, a golf course, tennis courts, and a children's zoo. Camperdown House, the mansion in the middle, was designed by William Burn in 1828 and contains a restaurant. **Clatto Country Park**, in Dalmahoy Drive off the A972, is a reservoir area with 24 acres of water sheltered by woods; it is popular for windsurfing and sailing, and you can hire equipment. **Dundee University Botanic Gardens** (open daily except Sun: adm), off Riverside Drive, has an award-winning visitor centre and landscaped gardens with native and exotic plants, both outside and in tropical and temperate pavilions.

Claypotts Castle (open daily 1 April–30 Sept: adm) jumps out at you from a nightmare housing development just off the busy junction of the A92 and B978. One of the few castles in Scotland to remain unaltered since it was built in the 16th century, Claypotts is a four-storied Z-plan tower house with two round towers, crow-stepped gables, tiny windows, massive stonework and parapet walks. Incongruous as the setting now is, the castle somehow manages to retain a certain dignity, shrugging off the clutter of modern suburbia that sprawls at its feet. It belonged to the Grahams of Claverhouse and was given to the Douglas family after the famous 'Bonnie Dundee', Earl of Claverhouse, was killed at the Battle of Killiecrankie. Keep an eye out for the ghost that haunts its chambers, the vengeful spirit of a favoured maid servant who was unfairly deposed by a jealous rival.

Broughty Ferry, dominated by its castle, is on the coast road 4 miles (6.5km) to the east. Although the fishing fleet has long vanished, a number of fisher cottages remain, in the narrow wynds and courtyards off Fisher Street, steeped in the seafaring history of the community. It is easy to imagine the old fishermen, mending their nets on the shore by their boats, drawn up above the tide. The village still mourns the tragic loss of its lifeboat *Mona* in 1959, with her crew of eight brave men, stranded and capsized on nearby Budden Sands in one of the ferocious gales that sweep this coast. The beach stretches away to the east in a long, sandy crescent.

> *Ancient Castle of Broughty Ferry*
> *With walls as strong as Londonderry;*
> *Near by the sea-shore,*
> *Where oft is heard and has been heard the cannon's roar*
> *In the present day and days of yore,*
> *Loudly echoing from shore to shore.*

> from 'Broughty Ferry', by William McGonagall

Broughty Castle (open daily, April–Sept: adm) stands on a rocky promontory, towering over a tiny harbour that dries out at low tide. Built in the 15th century on the site of a Pictish fort, it had a commanding position guarding the entrance to the firth, from which to levy tolls from ships wanting to come up the river. The Gray family who owned the castle also controlled the ferry linking Broughty with Fife. The fourth Lord Gray sided with the English during the 'Rough Wooing' and allowed English troops to occupy this strategic stronghold for three years until the French managed to recapture it for the Scots in 1550. Extensively restored in 1860, it is now a museum devoted mainly to the whaling industry that once flourished along this coast and to the ecology of the Tay.

Two miles (3km) inland from Broughty Ferry, Historic Scotland signs point to **Ardestie**, on the A92, and **Carlungie**, a mile (1.5km) to the north, two well-preserved souterrains. These underground earthhouses, once covered by stone roofs, have chambers and passages which were the byres and silos of Pictish farmers in the 1st/2nd centuries. It is thought they did not live in these souterrains, but nothing is certain about the Picts and they may have used them as places of refuge. At **Monikie**, 5 miles (8km) north of Broughty Ferry on the archaeological detour, there is a country park round the reservoir, with walks, boating and picnic sites. You get splendid views from up here, down over fertile farmland to the distant coast where the constantly shifting sandbanks have claimed many ships over the centuries. The trees on the ridge above are sculpted into curious wedge shapes by the strong prevailing wind.

Where to Stay

expensive

The Stakis Earl Grey Hotel on the waterfront in Earl Grey Place, Dundee, © 0382 29271, has every possible convenience including a leisure club with swimming pool, sauna and whirlpool. They do packages.

A very different atmosphere awaits you at **The Old Mansion House Hotel** at Auchterhouse, 7 miles (11km) north of Dundee, © 082 626 366/7. This is a 16th-century baronial home in 10 acres of gardens and woodland. There is an outdoor heated swimming pool, squash court, croquet and tennis. The food is worth travelling for.

moderate

The Angus Thistle Hotel, 101 Marketgait, Dundee, © 0382 26874, is modern, soulless and antiseptic, but it is comfortable and convenient and the food won't choke you. If you want to indulge yourself, you can have an expensive 'executive' suite with four-poster bed and whirlpool bath.

Eating Out

If you want to eat out, **Mains Castle** at Caird Park, Dundee, © 0382 456797, gives 'Jacobite Nights' with a four-course banquet in 15th-century trappings, with jolly Scottish entertainment all evening and dancing. (Hermits, stick to your cells.)

✗ **Raffles,** 18 Perth Road, Dundee, ✆ 0382 26344, is a popular restaurant near the university with reasonable food. **Fat Sam's Night Club, Discotheque Diner** is at 31 South Ward Road, Dundee, ✆ 0382 26836 and runs special events such as Fat Sam's Cocktail Night with half-price drinks all night. Take your ear-plugs.

Carnoustie

Back on the coast road, Carnoustie, 10 miles (16km) east of Dundee, is a holiday resort and golf centre, with a championship course. Right on the sea, the town is a popular place in summer with its own musical society, plenty of holiday activities and a conference centre which seats 500 people. Campers will find an attractive caravan site among trees in the grounds of Carnoustie House.

Arbroath

Arbroath is 17 miles (27km) northeast of Dundee. The massive ruin of the red sandstone abbey rises from the heart of the town, surrounded by lawns and flower-beds, the hub of a holiday resort and fishing centre. The Declaration of Independence was signed in the abbey in 1320 after Robert the Bruce's victory at Bannockburn, establishing Scotland's independence from England.

Perhaps Arbroath is best known now as the home of the 'smokie'—haddock, smoked over wood-chip fires in the backyards of the fishertown between the harbour and the abbey. Many of the cottages display signs, indicating that they sell the freshly smoked fish, and anyone who has not tried an Arbroath smokie should do so. One of the nicest ways to eat them is cold, with brown bread and butter and plenty of lemon juice and black pepper.

Arbroath Highland Games and a Donkey Derby are in July, the Flower Show is in August and there is a Festival of Highland Dancing in September.

Arbroath Abbey (open daily: adm) was founded by William the Lion in 1178 and dedicated to Thomas à Becket who had recently been murdered in Canterbury Cathedral. You can see William's tomb in the sacristy. The abbey managed to survive the Reformation until 1606, when it was made a temporal lordship. Its final decay was due to neglect rather than vandalism or deliberate destruction. Parts of the ruin date from the 13th century, including the gable of the south transept and the west façade with its tower and entrance. They used to put lamps in the round window high above the south transept, as a landmark for ships at sea. The abbot's house is now the **Museum** with displays illustrating the domestic life of the religious community and a collection of Scottish medieval art.

Signal Tower (open daily except Sundays: free) is a museum with exhibitions of local interest. It was originally built in 1813 as the signalling station for the Bell Rock Lighthouse and its displays include fishing, the flax industry, archaeology and natural history. There is an **art gallery** in the library, which has works by Brueghel as well as a good variety of Scottish paintings.

From **Whiting Ness**, north of the wide promenade, you can walk for miles along the clifftop, with the sea pounding restlessly at the redstone rocks below, honeycombed with caves and deep inlets. Wild flowers cling to the steep slopes: thrift, vetch and sea grasses. The lonely cry of curlews with long, curved beaks and the shrill 'kubik-kubik' of black and white oystercatchers with vivid orange beaks can be heard over the booming sea. From the narrow path you get views over a sea dotted with trawlers, tankers, coasters and small boats. If the visibility is good you should be able to see the **Bell Rock Lighthouse**, 12 miles (19km) out to the east and familiar to anyone who knows Southey's 'Ballad of the Inchcape Rock'. The Abbot of Arbroath fixed a warning bell on the hazardous rock to warn off mariners. Sir Ralph the Rover, a notorious pirate with a grudge against the abbot, cut the bell adrift. Later, sailing home in a fog, the pirate was wrecked on the rock.

The cliff path takes you to **Auchmithie**, 3 miles (4.5km) to the north. Referred to as Musselcraig, in Walter Scott's *The Antiquary*, it is an ancient, picturesque village believed to have been the fishing centre in the old days. In the 18th century, fishermen carried on a flourishing lobster trade with London and it was here that the smokie industry was born. It is built on a rocky ridge above a tiny harbour with a flat chequerboard of farmland stretching away inland. The caves along this coast were much used by smugglers in the 18th century.

St Vigeans

As you come out of Arbroath going north on the A92, take the road signposted to St Vigeans, on the left. After less than a mile, park at the railway bridge and cross the Brothock Burn by footbridge to discover this gem of a hamlet, nestling out of sight below modern housing developments. A small red sandstone church is perched on top of a steep mound, 40 feet (12m) high, like an upturned basin, neatly kept and studded with gravestones. Extensive restoration conceals the 12th-century origins of the kirk, but you can find traces inside.

A row of red sandstone cottages with stone-slabbed roofs forms a semi-circle at the foot of the mound and in one of these is the **St Vigeans Museum** (open daily: free). The museum contains a well-displayed and comprehensively explained collection of Pictish and Celtic stones. The **Drosten Stone** has an inscription in the Pictish language, suggesting that the Picts were more literate than is often supposed. Even if archaeology bores you stiff, you will be intrigued by the intricate carvings on these ancient stones, and read the descriptions: they quickly become more than 'just a few more old stones'.

Redcastle (always accessible) is 7 miles (11km) up the coast. A 15th-century ruin jutting out on a cliff high above the sea, it dominates the sandy crescent of Lunan Bay below. To reach it you have to climb up a short, steepish path through trees and whins. The castle was built on the site of an old fort, to protect the coast from Danish pirates, and William the Lion lived here while he was building Arbroath Abbey. It witnessed several battles and was partly demolished during one that sprang from a feud between its occupant and her divorced husband.

Montrose

Beautiful town of Montrose, I will now commence my lay,
And I will write in praise of thee without dismay,
And in spite of all your foes,
I will venture to call thee Bonnie Montrose.

from 'Montrose', by William McGonagall

Montrose, 14 miles (22km) north of Arbroath, not far from the Grampian border, is almost on an island. It has sea to the east, the River South Esk to the south, and a wide tidal basin to the west. There is a spacious feeling about the town, the middle section of its High Street being as wide as a market square. You can still see a few of the houses that were built gable-end on to the street, leading through to narrow closes and secret courtyards. Records tell of a Danish invasion of Montrose in 980.

The castle that once guarded the town was taken over by Edward I in 1296 and destroyed by William Wallace a year later. It was from here that Sir James Douglas embarked, carrying the heart of Robert the Bruce, on its abortive pilgrimage to the Holy Land. James Graham, the brave Marquis of Montrose, was born in Old Montrose on the south side of the tidal basin in 1612. In 1715, the first of the Jacobite Rebellions ended ignominiously in Montrose when the Old Pretender set sail back to France from here.

A tenth of the world's population of pink-footed geese migrate to Montrose's tidal basin every November from their Arctic breeding grounds. This great wildfowl sanctuary is a marvellous place in winter, when you can hear the ceaseless grumble and chatter of the birds as they feed on the mud flats and the haunting sound they make as they circle in from the sky. It is remarkable to find such a wild haven so close to the town with its docks and shipping, its sturdy buildings and oil-related prosperity.

A profitable slave trade flourished briefly in Montrose and smuggling was a thriving activity in the 18th century. Because of its out-of-the-way situation, and a shortage of customs officers, the strongly Jacobite population had no conscience about defrauding a Hanoverian government of its income from excise duty. The words *Mare Ditat* (the sea enriches) are aptly inscribed on the Montrose coat of arms. The undulating countryside has several good golf courses. In July the town holds its Rose Queen Ceremony and in August a Flower Show and Highland Games.

The House of Dun, 3 miles (4.5km) west of Montrose (open daily in summer: adm), is a modest-sized Palladian house overlooking Montrose Basin. Owned by the National Trust for Scotland, it was designed by William Adam in 1730 for David Erskine, Lord Dun. One of his descendants married Augusta, the natural daughter of William IV and Mrs Jordan, who created the lovely garden. It has flamboyant plasterwork in the saloon and much of the original furniture, found hidden away when the house was resurrected. Outside, there are woodland walks and exhibitions in the courtyard, including bothies containing a keeper's room and a gardener's potting shed and weaving displays.

moderate

Park Hotel, John Street, Montrose, ☎ 0674 73415, is probably your best bet.

Near Arbroath, **Letham Grange Hotel** at Colliston, ☎ 024189 373, has four crowns. **Auchmithie Hotel** at Auchmithie, ☎ 0241 73010 is cheaper, has three crowns and overlooks the harbour.

inexpensive

The Pipers Private Hotel & Licensed Restaurant, Union Place, Montrose, ☎ 0674 72298, is friendly with good Scottish food.

Brechin

Returning to Perth on the inland route, Brechin is 9 miles (14.5km) west of Montrose, sprawled up a steep bank above the South Esk in fertile Strathmore.

You can get a good picture of the local history in a small museum in the library.

The Cathedral and Tower (always open: free) are the focal points of this ancient town. These red sandstone buildings are perched above the town's twisting wynds, little court-yards and houses built gable-end on to the road. The tapering tower, restored in 1960, is one of only two such towers in mainland Scotland, the other being in Abernethy. (It is a curious coincidence that Malcolm Canmore was forced to acknowledge the sovereignty of William the Conqueror in 1072 at Abernethy, and the weak John Balliol was forced to renounce his crown to Edward I in 1296 near Brechin, as if the two round towers have survived as monuments to two unhappy events.) Dating from 990, the tower's door is 6 feet (1.8m) above the ground, giving the inhabitants greater security. The feet of the cruci-fied Christ, carved on the lintel, are uncrossed, indicating an Irish influence in the design. (There are 76 of these towers in Ireland today.)

Now a parish church, the cathedral dates from the 13th century and was restored in 1900. The Pictish stones inside have interesting carvings on them and you can also see a 16th-century font and 17th-century pewter and silver.

Maison Dieu, off Market Street, is a single wall with a pointed, arched door, three narrow windows and a piscina—all that remains of an almshouse, hospice and chapel founded in 1256.

Edzell

Six miles (9.5km) north of Brechin on the B966, Edzell, in the valley of the North Esk, is one of the places visited by Queen Victoria, with a memorial arch to show for it.

Edzell Castle (open daily: adm) is a 16th-century ruin forming a red backdrop to the Pleasance, a walled garden designed by David Lindsay, Lord Edzell, in 1604. Even if your taste runs to gardens that overflow and burgeon, all soft lines and merging shapes, you cannot but be impressed by this immaculate formal garden. It is modelled on the gardens at Nuremburg and the flower-filled recesses in the walls are intricate heraldic emblems, concealing gun loops. A beautifully kept box hedge, bordering rose beds, has been clipped to spell out the somewhat phlegmatic Lindsay family motto: *Dum spiro spero* ('While I breathe I hope'). The foundations of a bath house were excavated in the corner of the garden in 1855, revealing a bath and a dressing and reclining room with a fireplace.

Mary, Queen of Scots held a council in the castle in 1562 and it was garrisoned by Cromwell's troops in 1651. A grisly story is told of a curse put on the Earl's family at Edzell by a gypsy, after they had ordered her two dumb sons to be hanged for poaching. Lady Crawford died the same day and her husband was torn apart by wolves a year later.

The Caterthuns are 6 miles (9.5km) southwest of Edzell, at **Menmuir**. These are two Iron Age hill forts on a ridge, the higher one having spilled its masonry down the hill to mix with the lower. The original enclosing wall must have been as much as 40 feet (12m) thick. If you follow the wooded valley of West Water from here up into the hills towards Loch Lee, you are following in the footsteps of Macbeth, as he fled from his defeat at Dunsinane.

Before you go on towards Forfar, you should explore **Glen Esk** running north into the Grampians, carved by the North Esk and its tributaries. **Glenesk Folk Museum** (open Easter weekend; daily, June–Sept: adm) is 10 miles (16km) northwest of Edzell at Tarfside. Once a shooting lodge, it contains exhibits that give a picture of what life was like in this area from about 1800 onwards. All the Angus glens, such as Glen Isla and Glen Clova, are lovely.

Finavon Castle (always open: free) is 6 miles (9.5km) southwest of Brechin on the A94. This jagged ruin is overgrown by nettles and scrub. It doesn't look much of a place now, until you look up at the 86-foot (26m) tower and think of the day when the notorious Earl Beardie Crawford hanged his minstrel from a hook somewhere at the top. This he did because the wretched minstrel had foretold Earl Beardie's defeat at the Battle of Brechin in 1452. The history of the Lindsay family is full of bloodcurdling stories, and it is for these that the ruin is memorable, rather than for its appearance.

Finavon Hill

Take the little back road that climbs and twists 2 miles (3km) southeast from Finavon, up over the hills through rugged scenery of dry stone walls and moorland, where black-faced sheep graze the turf between patches of bracken and gorse. As you come down the far side of the ridge, Finavon Hill is on your left. It is a short climb to one of the finest vitrified Iron Age hill forts in the land, in a shallow depression at the top. Its shape and turf-covered ramparts are easily seen, and there is a central spring, or well. Excavations in the 1930s revealed evidence of metal working, pot making, and weaving on this lofty summit with its glorious views up Strathmore to the Mearns and west to Blairgowrie. It is strange to think of those tough Picts busy up here, striving to exist on the hill top, keen-eyed and ever alert for danger.

Aberlemno

If you are interested in the early settlers, go on down the back road from Finavon to the B9134 and turn left a few hundred yards to **Aberlemno**. This tiny hamlet has four remarkable Pictish stones. Three stand beside the road. The finest, however, is in the churchyard. The carvings on this stone, 7 feet (2m) high, are amazingly clear: a Celtic cross on one side, flanked by intertwined creatures, and a stirring battle scene on the other, all with intricate detail. This stone is believed to mark the grave of a Pictish king, Feradach. The little kirk is simple and charming. Inside, an 18th-century Bible has dates printed at the top of each page: the date of Genesis is set at 4004 BC.

Pitmuies Garden, off the A932 to Forfar (open all year: adm), is an outstanding garden, round an 18th-century house, with masses of spring bulbs, roses, herbaceous borders and many shrubs. There is a waterside walk and fine old trees. Look out for Guthrie Castle (private), close by on the main road. The entrance was built about 150 years ago to disguise a bridge on the old railway.

Restenneth Priory

Restenneth Priory (always open: free) is 5 miles (8km) southwest of Aberlemno, just before you get to Forfar on the B9134. It stands surrounded by gently sloping meadows and scattered trees, rising from a bowl of marshy ground. It was once on a peninsula jutting into a loch which was drained in the 18th century.

In AD 710, Nechan, High King of the Picts, was baptized here by St Boniface. Nechan used Northumbrian masons to build a church in Romanesque style, possibly to celebrate his victory over the King of Northumbria at the Battle of Nechtansmere. In the 13th century, Augustinian monks built a priory on the same site, incorporating the original tower. It is a tranquil place, the old stones rising from green sward. You can almost hear the voices of those far-off monks, chanting plainsong, as you stand in the ruined choir. An infant son of Robert the Bruce is believed to have been buried here.

Forfar

Just southwest of Restenneth, the busy town of Forfar has little left to see of its history. Once a thriving jute and linen milling centre, it now produces synthetic textiles, as well as tartans and tweeds. The **town and county hall** is early 19th century, designed by William Playfair, with a splendid council chamber in which you can see paintings by Raeburn, Romney, Hoppner and Opie. The town centre is attractive, with cobbled streets and warm sandstone buildings swirling round an island on which the town hall stands. Just round the corner in West High Street is the **Meffan Institute** (open daily except Sun: free) which houses, as well as the library, a small museum of local interest, in which you can see the dreadful **Forfar Bridle**. This is a metal collar, hinged to clip round the neck, with a prong in front to gag the unfortunate women who wore it while being burned at the stake as witches in the 17th century. Forfar Loch, west of the town, is a so-called pleasure park, with picnic areas around an uninspiring small stretch of water.

From Forfar, you have a choice of two main routes back to Perth.

Forfar to Perth via Glamis

Glamis

The southern route, on the A94, takes you first to Glamis (pronounced *Glahms*), about 6 miles (9.5km) southwest, a hamlet in a wooded hollow just off the main road.

Glamis Castle (open daily, April–Oct or by appointment, © 030784 242: adm) is approached down a wide tree-lined avenue and is so familiar from photographs that the reality is almost an anti-climax. From the top of the avenue the pink-grey castle stands out against the distant hills, all angles, towers, wings, turrets and heraldic embellishments. It is grand rather than beautiful.

Queen Elizabeth, the Queen Mother, spent much of her childhood at Glamis and her daughter Princess Margaret was born here. Don't rush a visit to this history-steeped castle; take it slowly and absorb the atmosphere under the tourist-wooing gloss. It's well worth getting the excellent guide book.

The land was granted to the Lyon family, Earls of Strathmore, by King Robert II in 1372, and it was their descendants who became Earls of Glamis, Kinghorne and Strathmore. Glamis has the reputation for being the most haunted castle in Scotland and many are the spine-chilling tales that have been born from its stones. No one dares to enter the sealed crypt where huge red-bearded Beardie Crawford played cards with the Devil on the Sabbath; no one can account for the window that looks out from a chamber that does not exist on an upper floor.

The present castle dates mostly from the 17th century with bits of the older building incorporated, including King Malcolm's room where Malcolm II is said to have died. The oldest part is Duncan's Hall, traditionally the setting for Shakespeare's Macbeth.

There are formal 19th-century Italian gardens and extensive parkland. A licensed restaurant sells light lunches and teas and there is a gift shop, a gallery shop selling paintings by Scottish artists, a garden shop and a playground.

The Angus Folk Museum (open Easter weekend; daily, 1 May–30 Sept: adm) is in Kirkwynd in the village beyond the castle, past the Strathmore Arms and a thatched cottage that is a rare sight among the pantiles and slates in this area. In the care of the National Trust for Scotland, the museum is in a terrace of picturesque early 19th-century cottages, meticulously restored in 1957, with stone-slabbed roofs and flagged floors. There are over 1000 things to see, including a kitchen from 1807 with all the original fittings and furnishings, and a collection of agricultural tools and equipment. The museum gives a picture of how country people lived, up to 200 years ago. There is even a Victorian manse parlour.

The Glamis Stone is in the garden of today's manse, opposite the museum, visible from the road. This 9-foot (3m) high stone has intricate Pictish carvings. It is also called King Malcolm's Stone, from the belief that Malcolm II was buried here in 1034, having died in the castle. In fact, the stone is of an earlier date, possibly 9th century.

If ancient stones are what you enjoy, you will find plenty more nearby including **St Orland's**, or the **Crossans Stone**, standing 7 feet (2m) tall in a field by the railway 2 miles (3km) to the north. This slender, repaired stone has carvings showing men in a boat.

Meigle

Meigle, nearly 7 miles (11km) southwest of Glamis, is the legendary burial place for King Arthur's poor faithless Guinevere. It also has a remarkable collection of early Christian Pictish stones. **Meigle Museum** (open daily except Sun: adm), in the old school, contains about 30 stones, from the 6th to the 10th centuries, almost all found in or near the old churchyard. The carvings disprove any idea that the Picts were half-naked savages. Instead, they show elaborate clothing, weapons and equipment and an unquestionably civilized culture. The large stone in the centre is thought to be Queen Guinevere's gravestone and portrays *Daniel in the Lion's Den*, possibly symbolizing Guinevere being torn apart by wild beasts. Beautifully displayed, with a descriptive leaflet, these stones stir the imagination.

Coupar Angus

Coupar Angus, about 5 miles (8km) southwest of Meigle, is in the Tay valley and is a good centre from which to tour this area. It is a market town, very typical of the area and so called to distinguish it from Cupar Fife.

Only the gatehouse remains of a once flourishing Cistercian abbey, beside the Dundee Road. It was built about 1164 by Malcolm IV and destroyed in 1559. The parish church stands on the site of the old monks' chapel and you can still see the remains of the original piers from the nave. From Coupar Angus it is about 12 miles (19km) back to Perth, passing Perth Aerodrome.

Forfar to Perth via Blairgowrie

Kirriemuir

If you take the northern route back to Perth from Forfar on the A926, Kirriemuir is 6 miles (9.5km) to the west, on a hillside with a straggle of narrow streets lined by picturesque houses. This jute manufacturing town is where J. M. Barrie was born. He renamed it 'Thrums' in the series of novels he wrote based on small-town life in Scotland. The house where Barrie was born, 9 Brechin Road, is maintained by the National Trust for Scotland as a museum called **Barrie's Birthplace** (open Easter weekend; daily, 1 May–30 Sept: adm). It contains a nostalgic collection of manuscripts, letters, personal possessions and mementoes of the writer who belonged to that group known as 'The Kailyard School' at the end of the 19th century. These Kailyard writers exploited a sentimental, ᵣ image of life in Scotland that brought them a certain amount of contempt from ᵣ critics. Their naivety was blown by George Douglas, in *The House with Green Shutters* which, according to J.B. Priestley, 'let the east wind into this cosy chamber of fiction'. However much people may despise whimsicality, no one can deny the talent of the man who created Peter Pan, Mary Rose, Dear Brutus and the Admirable Crichton. James Barrie was made a Freeman of Kirriemuir and was buried in the churchyard in 1937.

A **Camera Obscura** in the Barrie Pavilion above the town gives a panoramic view of Strathmore by an ingenious method of reflection.

You should make time to go north from Kirriemuir to explore some of the glens that stretch back into the Grampians—Glen Clova, Glen Prosen, Glen Isla; each with a mass of tributary glens like the veins of a feather, with tumbling rivers and tranquil lochs, hidden away among the hills.

Reekie Linn

It is worth making a detour from Kirriemuir to see Reekie Linn. It is about 9 miles (14.5km) due west and if you've got a good map, the back roads are very attractive. Park at the Bridge of Craigisla and take the footpath through the wood. Reekie Linn is a dramatic waterfall haunted by water sprites and kelpies. The River Isla, constricted by narrow rock cliffs, pours into a deep gorge in a single cascade, the spray rising like smoke, stirring the dark waters of the river into tumult. The path takes you to a spur jutting out level with the top of the falls. If you suffer from vertigo you should go along to the right and see them from further off.

Barry Hill is beside the road about 3 miles (4.5km) south of the falls, just short of Alyth. It is a short, steep climb through whins and bracken, over turf honeycombed by rabbits. On top are the ruins of a large Pictish fort in a shallow depression. The oblong shape is very clear with round turrets and ramparts. Romance clings to these stones. If you believe the Scottish versions of the Arthurian legends, Queen Guinevere was imprisoned in this fort by King Arthur because of her love affair with a Pictish prince. If this was true, the captive queen had glorious views to comfort her.

Alyth, below the hill, is a pleasant little milling town bisected by the Alyth Burn.

Blairgowrie

Blairgowrie, 5 miles (8km) southwest of Alyth, beside fast-flowing Ericht Water, is a popular tourist centre all the year round, much favoured by golfers. Old mills still stand along the river, some derelict, some converted into dwellings and at least one open to the public. In summer there are the Highlands to explore and in winter you can ski at Glenshee. The fertile soil produces abundant raspberry crops. This is magic walking country: fast-flowing rivers slice through steep mountain glens, with sudden glimpses of snow-capped peaks, massing on the horizon.

While you are in this area, visit Mrs MacDonald in Rattray. You can't miss the shop, which outside. Switzerland means cheese and chocolate, and Mrs MacDonald ...st of both.

...is north from Blairgowrie into the Grampian region and is one of Scotland's main skiing centres. Its challenging pistes are often icy and demanding. Weather conditions can be extreme, roads sometimes becoming impassable in snow (see p.23). For skiing information, ring the Glenshee Information Officer, Blairgowrie, © 0250 5509.

From spring to autumn, the A93 to Braemar—Britain's highest main road—is a spectacular route and in the summer you can take the chairlift up to the top of Cairnwell mountain for panoramic views and invigorating walks. **Strathardle** forks off west of Glen Shee from the **Bridge of Cally** where the River Ardle and Black Water converge: another good launching pad for climbers and walkers.

From Blairgowrie, it is about 16 miles (26km) back to Perth on the A93.

Birnam

> Be lion-mettled, proud, and take no care
> Who chafes, who frets, or where conspirers are:
> Macbeth shall never vanquish'd be until
> Great Birnam wood to high Dunsinane Hill
> Shall come against him.

> William Shakespeare, *Macbeth*, Act 4, scene 1.

Birnam, about 14 miles (22km) north of Perth, bypassed by the A9, is a village familiar to all lovers of Shakespeare. From Birnam Hill you can see Dunsinnan, or Dunsinane, 12 miles (19km) to the southeast—opinions and tastes dictate the spelling. Macbeth, in his castle on 'Dunsinane Hill', confidently believed the witches' prophecy that he was immortal until 'Birnam Forest come to Dunsinane'. Meanwhile, Malcolm was busy instructing his soldiers to camouflage themselves with branches from the trees in Birnam Wood and march on Dunsinane. There are remains of a fort on Dunsinnan Hill, thought to be Macbeth's. Some of the trees in Birnam Wood are thought to date from the original forest.

Dunkeld

Fifteen miles (24km) north of Perth, just off the A9 route, Dunkeld is an old cathedral town on the banks of the Tay, sheltered by wooded hills and much favoured by fishermen. Its history goes back to when it was a refuge for Pictish kings. Being close to the ancient capital of Scone, Dunkeld became a stronghold of Columban monks who founded an abbey here in 729, having been driven from Iona by Norsemen. They enshrined holy relics of St Columba in their abbey. The saint himself is believed to have come to Dunkeld in the 6th century and to have founded some sort of religious establishment with the help of St Mungo. There is a St Colms Well nearby.

Dunkeld suffered badly during the Covenanting Wars and it was here that the Cameronians, extreme Covenanters, held the town against a troop of Highlanders in 1689. Triumphant after Killiecrankie, the Highlanders stormed the town, whereupon the Cameronians set fire to most of its buildings, driving the Highlanders out and securing eventual supremacy for William and Mary.

Dunkeld Cathedral (open daily: free) is a substantial ruin beside the River Tay. The choir has been restored and is the parish church. The nave and great northwest tower date from the 15th century. The original medieval cathedral, which took two centuries to build, was only entire for about 60 years before the Reformers reduced it to a roofless ruin. Ironically, it contains the rather splendid tomb and effigy of the Wolf of Badenoch, who was a keen destroyer of churches, including Elgin Cathedral.

The Little Houses, lining Cathedral Street, were built after the destruction of the town in 1689 and were saved from demolition by the National Trust for Scotland in 1950. Well restored and privately occupied, they form a delightful approach to the cathedral and give the old part of the town a unique character.

The Dunkeld Smokehouse at Springfields sells excellent smoked products and will also smoke any of the fish you may have been lucky enough to catch.

Loch of the Lowes

A couple of miles northeast of Dunkeld, Loch of the Lowes is a nature reserve, where you can watch ospreys from a hide. These large brown and white sea-eagles, cousins to the falcon, are common in America, where they nest on every navigation mark in the estuaries. Here, they are a rare, protected species, though their numbers are increasing slightly now that their nesting sites are so fiercely protected.

Pitlochry

Pitlochry, 13 miles (21km) north of Dunkeld on the A9, is in the middle of Scotland, cradled by hills, with Ben Vrackie (2759 feet—849m) looming to the north. With above-average hours of sunshine and below-average rainfall, this has been a popular holiday town since Queen Victoria, staying at Blair Atholl, declared it to be one of the finest resorts in Europe. This royal stamp of approval resulted in many fine houses and mansions being built in the area, with spas that are now hotels. Today, it is hard to believe it was once a remote hamlet. There were no roads north of Dunkeld until General Wade built his network of military roads after the Jacobite uprisings, linking the trouble-spots in the Highlands. In spite of its popularity—it gets very crowded in the summer and caters well for its tourists—it manages to retain a leisurely, strolling atmosphere, a perfect centre from which to explore the Highlands. The rivers Tummel and Garry converge from their valleys into Loch Faskally, 2 miles (3km) to the north, and hurry through the town to join the Tay at Ballinluig to the south. The main street is cheerful with its bright façades, hotels and shops, distilleries and, not far off the road, hydroelectric development. Pitlochry runs a summer school in July with a host of activities ranging from pottery to clay pigeon shooting. There is also a Gala Day in July.

The Pitlochry Festival Theatre was founded in 1951. Its lively summer programme includes drama, concerts and foyer events and you can also see exhibitions of Scottish art.

The Hydroelectric Dam and Fish Ladder, open all year, has an observation chamber from which to see the ingenious method of ensuring the salmon cycle is not broken. Thousands of salmon are 'lifted' annually and you can watch them through glass walls. Sometimes you can see sealice clinging to the fish, showing that they have come fresh from the sea. There is also a **Visitor Centre and Exhibition**, with a description of all the activities throughout the country and in the Loch Tummel group in particular. Few can deny that the hydroelectric schemes often enhance rather than spoil the Highland scenery.

Blair Atholl Distillery, on the southern edge of Pitlochry, has a visitor centre (open daily, Easter–Oct; daily except Sun for the rest of the year: free). There are conducted tours with a free dram, audio-visual shows, a coffee shop, a bar with snacks and a shop selling whisky.

Edradour Distillery (open daily, Easter–31 Oct: free) is the smallest in Scotland, hidden in the hills, less than 3 miles (4.5km) east of Pitlochry. It was founded in 1825 by a group of local farmers, a small complex of white-washed buildings under neat grey slate roofs, tucked into a hollow beside the Edradour Burn. Here, after a conducted tour of the distillery, virtually unchanged since Victorian times, you get your free dram in a cosy barn before a peat and log fire.

Walking in this area is endlessly rewarding; every path you choose reveals fresh beauty and unexpected views. There are waterfalls and gorges, festooned with lush ferns; woods and hills; rivers running fast over shallow rocky beds.

Pass of Killiecrankie

Six thousand Veterans practised in War's game,
Tried Men, at Killicranky were arrayed
Against an equal Host that wore the Plaid,
Shepherds and Herdsmen.—Like a whirlwind came
The Highlanders, the slaughter spread like flame;

from a sonnet by William Wordsworth

The road north from Pitlochry climbs along the upper slope of the Pass of Killiecrankie, a recently opened section of road that cost a great deal of money and took considerable skill to engineer. It clings precariously to the densely wooded gorge where, far below, the River Garry cuts its way through to join up with the Tummel. At the far end of the pass about 3 miles (4.5km) from Pitlochry, there is a National Trust for Scotland **Visitor Centre** (open daily from 1 May to 31 Oct: free) with a pictorial description of the history of the Battle of Killiecrankie. Graham of Claverhouse, 'Bonnie Dundee' and his brave Jacobite Highlanders charged the British Army under General Mackay in 1689, in an attempt to depose William of Orange and restore James VII/II to the throne. The British were almost annihilated by the wild Highlanders, but Claverhouse was mortally wounded and his death, leaving his army leaderless, ensured the subsequent victory of the government troops three weeks later at Dunkeld.

You can walk down to the river from the visitor centre, past the terrifying **Soldier's Leap**, an 18-foot (5.5m) jump across the gorge, said to have been made by one of Mackay's soldiers, escaping from the Highlanders. Queen Victoria walked along this path and noted its great beauty in her diary in 1844.

Blair Atholl

Three miles (4.5km) north of Killiecrankie, the new road bypasses the village of Blair Atholl giving a good view of **Blair Castle** from across the river. This white, turreted baronial castle (open daily, Easter–mid-Oct: adm) is the home of the Duke of Atholl, dating from 1269 though much Victorianized. It has seen many royal visitors: Mary, Queen of Scots stayed here; Prince Charles accepted hospitality here on his march south in 1745; Cumberland garrisoned his troops here the following year, during which time the Duke of Atholl's brother, Lord George Murray, inflicted severe damage on the castle in his attempts to win it back; Claverhouse stayed here before the Battle of Killiecrankie and it was here that his body lay after the battle.

Queen Victoria visited the castle in 1844 and granted the Duke of Atholl the privilege of being the only British subject allowed to retain a private army, the Atholl Highlanders.

The interior gives a good idea of what castle life was like in the old days. The rooms are numbered and there is a guide book. Look for the Tapestry Room, hung with rich tapestries and containing a sumptuous four-poster bed topped by two vases of ostrich feathers. The Old Scots Room is furnished in the style of a simple cottage living room, complete with box bed, cradle and spinning wheel. There is much to see, from arms and armour, to Jacobite relics, china, toys, furniture, lace, paintings (including portraits by Lely, Ramsay and Raeburn) and even a natural history museum. There is a licensed self-service restaurant and, if you want to impress your friends, there is a separate dining room for private parties of up to 50 people. If you really want to splash out, you can also use the ballroom for up to 200 people, a truly noble setting for a knees-up, its panelled walls hung with a forest of antlers under a timber-ribbed roof with plenty of ancestral portraits to add distinction. In the grounds there is a large caravan park.

Beyond Blair Atholl is good walking and climbing country, over moor and scree, with lovely views. A nice walk is that to **The Bruar Falls**, well signed about 3 miles (4.5km) to the west: you can park by the road. A short walk takes you up to the falls, where the River Bruar cascades down through rocky chasms and over great gleaming slabs of granite. Robert Burns came up here when he was a guest of the Duke of Atholl. He was so disgusted by the treeless moorland that then surrounded the falls that he dashed off a poem: 'The Humble Petition of Bruar Water', and dispatched it to the Duke.

> *Would then my noble master please,*
> *To grant my highest wishes,*
> *He'll shade the bank wi' towering trees,*
> *And bonie spreading bushes.*

This plea, as you can see, found its mark and inspired the fourth Duke of Atholl to plant the trees now growing there. Walk on beyond the falls up the path for another mile or so, through birches and rhododendrons. A bridge then takes you over the stream and down the other side, making a round trip of about 2½ miles (4km). You can get a good pub lunch in the hotel down by the car park.

Where to Stay and Eating Out

expensive

If you want modern comfort, **Stakis Dunkeld House**, ✆ 03502 771, won't let you down. It stands in 280 acres on the Tay at Dunkeld and provides just about everything you could ask for except simplicity. Indoors there is a swimming pool, sauna, spa bath, steam room, solarium and multi-gym. If you've any energy left, there are tennis courts, croquet, salmon and trout fishing and mixed game shooting. Hermits and stoics, beware.

moderate

Kinloch House Hotel, near Blairgowrie, ✆ 025084 237, is highly recommended with four crowns. It is a typical Scottish country house with oak-panelled hall, gallery, antique furniture and paintings, in 20 acres of wooded grounds. The food is first class and has won an award. Moderate to expensive, its rates vary seasonally. Shooting, fishing and golf can be arranged.

Altamount House, Coupar Angus Road, Blairgowrie, ✆ 0250 3512, is a Georgian manor house with four crowns in 6 acres of ground. It shuts from early January to mid-February. **Castleton House Hotel** by Glamis, ✆ 030 784 340, in 11 acres of garden and woodland, was built in 1902 within a 13th-century moat. The food is good.

Pitlochry Hydro, ✆ 0796 2666, is a great stone building above the town overlooking the Tummel Valley. Moderate to expensive, it has an indoor swimming pool, jacuzzi, sauna, solarium and gymnasium. **Fisher's Hotel**, Atholl Road, Pitlochry, ✆ 0796 472000, is large and comfortable. **Killiecrankie Hotel and Restaurant**, ✆ 0796 3220, once a dower house, is attractive in pleasant grounds close to the Soldier's Leap. The staff tend to wear kilts and the food is excellent. It's only open from February to November.

Dalmunzie House Hotel, Glenshee, ✆ 025 085 224, is known as 'the Hotel in the Hills'. It is a vast Highland mansion in 6000 acres with a nine-hole golf course, tennis courts and fishing. Shooting and stalking can be arranged. Comfortable, with log fires and good Scottish cooking, it is only 5 miles (8km) from the ski slopes.

Bridge of Cally Hotel, ℂ 0250 886231, has three crowns.

Perthshire: West of the A9

Lochs Tummel and Rannoch

If you take the B8019 west from Pitlochry, you should start humming Harry Lauder's famous song 'The Road to the Isles': 'by Tummel and Loch Rannoch and Lochaber I will go . . .' The drive out to Rannoch Station, on the northern side of lochs Tummel and Rannoch to where the road ends and back along the south side, is a round trip of about 65 miles (104km). The scenery is beautiful, dominated by the great cone of **Schiehallion** in the south, with a kaleidoscope of vistas through the trees and the wasteland of Rannoch Moor stretching away to the west. Loch Tummel is less dramatic than Loch Rannoch, its gentler scenery reshaped by the hydroelectric development.

Queen's View, 2 miles (3km) up from the dam, was so called before Queen Victoria visited it in 1866. Perhaps Mary, Queen of Scots also stood on the promontory and looked down to the water, glinting in the sunlight, far below.

The **Loch Tummel Forest Centre** (open daily April–Sept: donation box) is at the south-east corner of the loch. Here you can learn about the geography and ecology of the area and how to find the Black Wood, south of Loch Rannoch, with part of the remains of the old Caledonian Forest.

Harry Lauder must have taken to the moors when he was 'walking with his crummock to the isles' because the road ends at Rannoch Station.

Five miles (8km) south of Pitlochry, the A827 takes you 10 miles (16km) west to Aberfeldy, and then out through Strath Tay to Loch Tay, a memorable drive especially in late summer, winding through small villages, with the river shaded by overhanging trees, backed by the hills beyond.

Aberfeldy

Let Fortune's gifts at random flee,
They ne'er shall draw a wish frae me,
Supremely blest wi' love and thee
In the birks of Aberfeldy.

'The Birks of Aberfeldie', by Robert Burns

Aberfeldy is a pleasant little town on the Urlar Burn at its confluence with the River Tay. Robert Burns' poem refers to the silver birches beside the burn. The bridge over the Tay was built by General Wade in 1733 and is said to be the best of the many he was responsible for during his arduous task of trying to link up all the remote trouble-spots in the Highlands during the Jacobite uprisings. The dramatic **Falls of Moness** are just a short stroll south of the town.

The **Black Watch Monument**, a kilted soldier, is at the south end of the bridge, erected in 1887 to commemorate the raising of the Black Watch by General Wade in 1739.

The Oatmeal Mill (open Mon–Fri: adm) in Mill Street shows the process of milling raw grain into oatmeal, and you can buy the finished products. **Aberfeldy Distillery** runs free tours and tastings from April to October.

Castle Menzies (pronounced Mingies) (open daily, 1 April–30 Sept: adm), a mile (1.5km) west of Aberfeldy, is a 16th-century, Z-plan fortified tower house, with carved gables over its dormers. In the process of restoration after centuries of neglect, it belongs to the Clan Menzies Society and houses their Clan Museum.

Loch Tay, 5 miles (8km) west of Aberfeldy, is a long, dark snake of water under the brooding hulk of Ben Lawers, Perthshire's highest hill, 3984 feet (1226m) high. All types of water sports take place on the loch, though keen fishermen might wish otherwise.

Ben Lawers is well worth climbing on a clear day if you are fit—allow about 3 hours. At the top you can see from the Atlantic to the North Sea. There are masses of mountain flowers and birds. Look out for the great brown buzzard, sailing lazily on broad wings, or the kestrel, hovering on pointed wings, long tail fanned out. Listen for the distinctive whirring of red grouse, and their 'go-bak, go-bak-bak-bak-bak', the mournful, liquid song of the golden plover, the lonely cry of the curlew and the silly cuckoo call. Needless to say, there is a visitor centre, for those who like their wildlife in consumer packages, off the A827 six miles (9.5km) northeast of Killin. Run by the National Trust for Scotland, who care for the southern slopes of the hill, it is a particularly dismal place where they dish up the inevitable booklets, information sheets and audio-visual programmes together with instructions about what to wear and take if you climb the hill. (For which they can be forgiven: the Mountain Rescue people are frequently called out to risk their lives rescuing idiots who would do better to confine their outdoor activities to their gardens).

Kenmore, at the head of the loch, was built for estate workers of Taymouth Castle in 1760 by the fourth Earl of Breadalbane and is now a conservation village. The gigantic castle is empty, in a magnificent designed landscape, and has a golf course in its grounds. You can hire boats here for fishing on the loch.

If you can't climb Ben Lawers, you can drive round it—about 25 miles (40km) in all. Leave the A827 at Fearnan on Loch Tay and take the back road along Glen Lyon, Scotland's longest glen, to **Bridge of Balgie**, and then drive south through the hills, back to the loch past the NTS visitor centre. You can complete the circle on the main road along the loch back to Fearnan, but the nicest way to see Loch Tay by car is on the minor road that hugs the southern shore.

At **Fortingall**, 2 miles (3km) to the northwest as the crow flies, the yew tree in the churchyard is said to be over 3000 years old—Europe's oldest living object. This delightful little village has a single street of cottages, some thatched and rather English in character, and an intriguing legend. Some say that Pontius Pilate was born here, son of a Roman officer who had been sent on a peace mission to the Picts in Dun Geal, a fort on the steep, rocky hill behind the village. True or not, it adds romance to an already enchanted spot. You should try to abandon your car in this area: it is marvellous walking and climbing territory.

From Kenmore, take the narrow back road through **Glen Quaich** to **Amulree**, 9 miles (14.5km) south of Aberfeldy. This was an important junction of the old drove roads, where drovers broke their lonely journeys to exchange news and banter.

The Sma' Glen

The Sma' Glen is the moorland valley through which the A822 descends from Amulree to Crieff. It follows the River Almond as it thunders down over rapids and falls, with hills rising steeply to about 2000 feet (615m) on either side. You can see salmon leaping in September and October; the best place for this is the Buchanty Spout, in Glenalmond on the B8063, just off the A822.

After Newton, look out on the left of the road for **Ossian's Stone**, which is said to mark the grave of Ossian, the legendary Gaelic hero and bard who spent many years in fairyland until he was baptized by St Patrick. The stone was in fact moved to its present position by General Wade's road-builders, when it blocked the path of one of their roads. Traces of a prehistoric burial, found when they lifted the stone, were given a reburial in a secret place by local Highlanders who were convinced that they were indeed the remains of the poet. Wordsworth thought so too:

> In this still place, remote from men,
> Sleeps Ossian, in the narrow glen.

Crieff

Crieff, about 12 miles (19km) south of Amulree, is a Highland holiday town, built on a steep hill facing south over the valley of the River Earn. The town is dominated by the Knock of Crieff, 911 feet (280m) high in the north, a woodland area with footpaths and good views from the top.

Nothing much is old in the town today. It was sacked and destroyed by Highlanders during the Jacobite rebellion. Later, a bleaching and tanning industry brought prosperity to its people. It became a spa town in the 19th century and you get echoes of Victorian splendour as you look at the Crieff Hydro Hotel, above the town, with its glass domes and pavilions.

Glenturret Distillery (open daily, March–Dec; weekdays, Jan–Feb: adm) is the oldest in Scotland. Conducted tours show all stages of whisky distilling. The tour includes a taste, and a visit to the award-winning **Visitors' Heritage Centre** with an audio-visual show, exhibitions, a whisky museum and retail shop.

Stuart Crystal (open daily: free), in Muthill Road, is a crystal factory where you can see glass being engraved. There is an audio-visual show, shop and café.

Crieff Visitor Centre (open daily) has factory tours showing Thistle pottery and Perthshire paperweights being made. There is a video presentation, showroom, restaurant and plant centre.

Bookworms should slip off to **Innerpeffray Library**, 4 miles (6.5km) southeast of the town (closed Thurs: adm). This is the oldest public library in Scotland, founded in 1690 by Archbishop Hay Drummond, in the attic of the chapel next door, and moved here in the middle of the 18th century. Among the collection of old and antiquarian books, mostly religious or classical, is the Bible printed in 1508 and carried by Montrose when he was finally defeated at the Battle of Carbisdale in 1650. If you are good on scripture, look out for the *Treacle Bible*, so called because 'Is there no balm in Gilead?' is translated as 'Is there no treacle . . ?'.

Comrie

Comrie, 6 miles (9.5km) west of Crieff along the River Earn, is an attractive conservation village. At midnight on Hogmanay, the unique Flambeaux Procession takes place, with villagers parading round in a torchlit procession, followed by much revelry. This custom has its roots in the ancient pagan fire-festivals, held to drive off evil spirits for the coming year.

Because it lies on the Highland Line—the geological fault that divides Highland and Lowland Scotland—more seismological tremors have been recorded here than anywhere else in Britain. Shocks were especially common during the 19th century: in recent years tremors have never done more than rattle the village teacups.

Earthquake House was built in 1874 to house one of the earliest seismometers in the world. They have a model of the original instrument as well as a modern one, in use, and a chart recorder.

The Tartans Museum (open daily: adm, but check, © 0764 670779) is the world head-quarters of the Scottish Tartans Society, the leading authority on tartan and Highland dress. They have over 1300 tartans on display as well as comprehensive information, a library, weaving demonstrations and a garden that shows which plants produce what dyes. You can look up your own name and discover which tartan you are entitled to wear.

Drummond Fish Farm (open daily: adm) is a working fish farm where you can catch your own supper.

Just north of Comrie, and a pleasant walk, **Deil's Cauldron** is an impressive waterfall carrying the River Lednock down to meet the River Earn.

Fowlis Wester is a hamlet, 5 miles (8km) east of Crieff. Here, 13th-century St Beans Church has a leper squint, an 8th-century Pictish stone and a fine lychgate—the roofed gateway to the churchyard where coffins could await the arrival of the priest, sheltered from the elements.

St Fillans, on Loch Earn 6 miles (9.5km) further west, is a popular holiday resort for anyone who enjoys sailing, waterskiing and windsurfing. It is also a good centre for walking and climbing.

Drummond Castle Gardens

Two miles (3km) south of Crieff, Drummond Castle Gardens (open every May–Sept: adm) are approached down a mile-long avenue. The sundial is dated there are flowers and shrubs in a formal Italian setting, against the backdrop of Founded in 1491, this was the setting for a terrible murder in 1502. Margaret Drummond and her sisters were poisoned, to prevent James IV from making Margaret his queen. Cromwell did his best to destroy the castle and it was deliberately damaged in 1745 by its owner, the Duchess of Perth, to prevent Hanoverian troops from capturing it.

Muthill

Muthill is a conservation village 3 miles (4.5km) south of Crieff, with late 18th- and early 19th-century houses delightfully unspoiled. Muthill (pronounced Mew-thill) is derived from Moot-Hill (hill of meeting). **Muthill Folk Museum** (open April–Sept: adm) has exhibits illustrating past domestic life in the village. Also in Muthill are the ruins of a once-important 15th-century church with its 12th-century Norman tower.

A couple of miles to the east of Muthill, **Tullibardine Chapel** is one of the very few of its kind that has not been altered. Cruciform, built of red sandstone, it was founded as a collegiate church in 1445 by Sir David Murray, whose arms and those of his wife can be seen on the inside west wall. Since the Reformation it has been used as a burial vault for the Drummond Earls of Perth.

Gleneagles Hotel

About 6 miles (9.5km) south of Muthill and a mile (1.5km) or so west of the village and station, Gleneagles Hotel is Scotland's premier golfing mecca, whose internationally famous courses lie along the edge of the Muir of Ochill, looking towards the Ochil Hills and Glen Devon—see below.

Braco

Ardoch Roman Camp is at Braco, about 4 miles (6.5km) west of Gleneagles Hotel. Grass-covered earthworks are all that remain of a Roman fort, dating from the 2nd century. It was once big enough to house as many as 40,000 men. You can still see the shape of it—a great rectangle with ditches and ramparts. Here, in wooden dwellings, the Romans tried to subdue the barbaric tribes who swooped down on them from the hills and glens and forests. The old Roman road runs north of Muthill and then east towards Perth, and an overgrown arch beside the bridge over the River Knaik is all that remains of the Roman bridge.

Auchterarder is 8 to 10 miles (13 to 16km) southeast of Crieff depending on which road you take, tucked in under the northern slopes of the Ochil Hills. This is another holiday centre, with a golf course, good fishing and walks.

expensive

Gleneagles Hotel, Auchterarder, ✆ 076 46 2231, is Scotland's only 5-star hotel. Prices and details on application (comfort doesn't come cheap). If you get fed up with the sauna, the solarium, the jacuzzi, the gymnasium, the shooting, the fishing, the snooker, the swimming, the squash, the bowling, the croquet and the tennis, you can always fall back on a round of golf. The 5-star rating embraces the chef as well as everything else. Don't look at the right-hand side of the menu: who wants to toy with an omelette in a place like this?

moderate

Drummond Arms Hotel, on Loch Earn in St Fillans, ✆ 0764 685212, is quiet and unspoiled, with a friendly staff and relaxed atmosphere. **Four Seasons Hotel**, St Fillans, ✆ 076485 333, is more expensive and has an excellent reputation for food. **Kenmore Hotel**, ✆ 08873 205, is Scotland's oldest inn, established in 1572, with its own salmon fishing and rights over all Loch Tay. It has a good atmosphere and a golf course on the estate. **Loch Rannoch Hotel**, ✆ 088 22 201, in 250 acres beside the loch, has pretty well every sort of facility to offer: indoor pool, jacuzzi, sauna, solarium, steam bath, squash, tennis, sailing, windsurfing, canoeing, dry-ski slope, snooker, bicycles, fishing plus live entertainment and Highland Evenings.

Crieff Hydro, ✆ 0764 655555, beams down on the town from the hill like a very respectable dowager, with its splendid glass pavilion in front. It provides an indoor swimming pool, riding, tennis, free golf, sailing, windsurfing and waterskiing. In the evenings activities include dancing, films, discos and competitions, if you are the sort of person who likes to be organized.

inexpensive

Achray House Hotel in peaceful St Fillans, ✆ 0764 685231, is cosy, right on Loch Earn, with excellent food. Their high reputation is endorsed by the fact that people go back.

the Aberdeen Angus with Angus

Grampian

Grampian, better known as the shires of Kincardine, Aberdeen, Banff and Moray, is that shoulder of Scotland that juts out into the North Sea below the neck of Caithness and Sutherland. The name Grampian has a forbidding and stark ring to it, but in fact the region is lovely. It is a fertile land veined with rivers, half-girt by sea and backed by mountains. Routes, along the coast and inland following the straths and glens of famous rivers, radiate from Aberdeen like the ribs of an outspread fan. From the Cairngorms and Grampians in the west, a series of ravines and waterfalls, wooded glens and heathery straths carry the River Dee through forest and moorland to the east coast. Further north the River Don makes more gentle progress to the sea, and north again, the Spey completes its journey through very attractive country to join the sea at Tugnet.

Moors give way to undulating farmland that forms a wide coastal plain, patchworked with neat fields. The coast road links a chain of fishing towns and villages with sheltered harbours offering refuge from the wild North Sea. The coastline is both rugged and gentle—gaunt rock cliffs interspersed with long sweeps of clean sand.

History

Many prehistoric remains tell of early settlement on the fertile plains, but the region doesn't feature much in history books until Kenneth Macalpine united its Picts with the Dalriada Scots in the 9th century. One of the Comyns, who came over with William the Conqueror, made his way north, married the daughter of a local chief and rapidly gained supremacy in the area. The Comyns, Earls of Buchan, were as much of a threat to Robert the Bruce's ambition to rule Scotland as the English. In 1307 he came north and crushed them in a couple of decisive battles.

With the Comyns effectively subdued, the Gordon family clambered to power. They ruled the land like despots for about 250 years, becoming Earls of Huntly and too big for their boots. Being so far from the seat of government their dominance didn't seem threatening until Mary, Queen of Scots came to the throne in 1561. Sir John Gordon, third son of the 4th Earl of Huntly, was then rash enough to boast of his aspirations to be consort to the widowed queen. Mary raged north with an army to curb such impertinence. Having hanged the Huntly Governor of Inverness Castle for refusing to admit her, she stormed into Aberdeen and disposed of the 4th Earl and Sir John (see p.348). From then on, except for an occasional rumble of rebellion, the city of Aberdeen was loyal to the Crown and disinclined to rally to the Jacobite standard.

In the middle of the 19th century, Prince Albert and Queen Victoria discovered Scotland and built Balmoral. From then on, a stampede of tartan-clad southerners over-ran Deeside and its environs, enthusing over the scenic splendours. They tiptoed after the deer, slaughtered the game and hooked the fish, integrating with the landed families. They built or refurbished a series of baronial mansions and castles to enhance their status. Balmoral is still the holiday home of the British Royal Family and even today the struggle for royal recognition goes on.

The oil boom of the 1970s brought great prosperity to Grampian, whose wealth had relied previously on farming, fishing, granite, textiles and paper. Land prices soared; property speculators thrived. But now that the oil in the established offshore oilfields is past its peak, many of the jobs that went with its exploitation will suffer. A number of upwardly mobile incomers have taken advantage of plummeting land prices and Grampian is gradually changing hands, though a number of the old landed families remain. To wring a living from vast estates, some are forced to supplement farming revenues by opening their castles and stately homes to the public and also by squeezing fortunes out of trigger-happy sportsmen and fishermen.

Grampian is the home of the Gordon Highlanders, raised in 1794 by the Duke of Gordon to fight the Napoleonic Wars. They wear the Gordon tartan and it is said that the Duchess of Gordon helped in a recruiting drive by giving a kiss and a silver shilling to each volunteer. (She was well over 40 and described as 'well run'.) The Gordons are fiercely resisting plans to amalgamate them with the Queen's Own Highlanders.

From June to September the tartan-tinged air vibrates with the skirl of pipes and the thud of the caber, as towns stage exuberant Highland Games. These unique Scottish gatherings, dating from the 11th century when Malcolm Canmore held contests to find the best soldiers for his struggles against the Normans, are usually well supplied with beer tents and sideshows. The most popular is probably the Braemar Highland Gathering in September because of the presence of the Royal Family: others include Aberdeen, Drumtochty, Grange, and Burghead in June; Forres, Elgin, Dufftown, Tomintoul, Stonehaven and Strathavon in July; Aboyne, Aberlour, Strathspey, Ballater and the Lonach, in August. A large number of other entertainments take place throughout the region during the summer months.

 One of Grampian's attractions is the 70-mile (112km) **Malt Whisky Trail** that takes in conducted tours of eight distilleries where some of the best-known malts are produced. It would be churlish to say 'if you've seen one, you've seen the lot': it is an attractive drive and you don't have to go over them all. (But each one beckons with a free dram.)

There is also a Castle Trail, a Victorian Heritage Trail and a Coastal Trail, all excellent.

Tourist Information

There are a number of tourist information centres throughout Grampian.

The following are open all year: **Aberdeen**: St Nicholas House, ✆ 0224 632727; **Banchory**: Bridge Street, ✆ 03302 2000; **Banff**: Collie Lodge, ✆ 0261 812789/812319; **Braemar**: The Mews, ✆ 03397 41600; **Elgin**: 17 High Street, ✆ 0343 542666/543388.

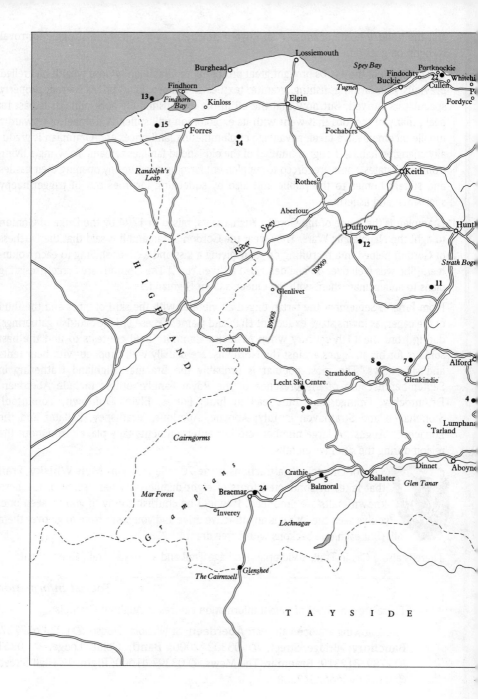

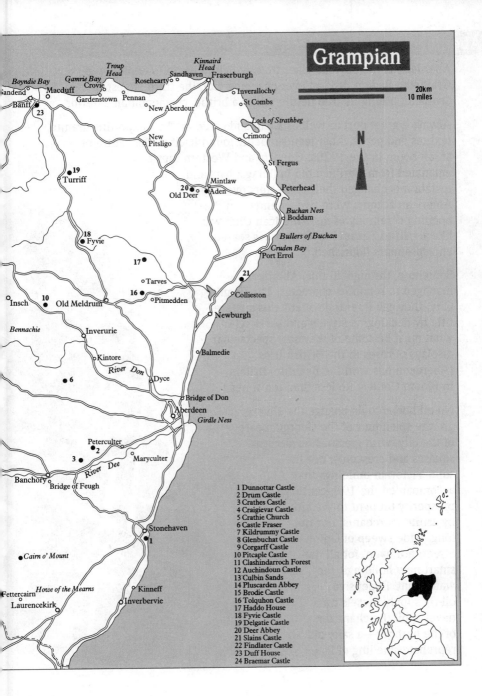

Grampian

20km
10 miles

N

Boyndie Bay
Sandend
Macduff
Banff
23
Gamrie Bay
Crovie
Gardenstown
Pennan
Troup Head
Rosehearty
Sandhaven
Kinnaird Head
Fraserburgh
Inverallochy
St Combs
New Aberdour
Loch of Strathbeg
Crimond
New Pitsligo
St Fergus
Turriff
19
Mintlaw
Old Deer
20
Aden
Peterhead
Buchan Ness
Boddam
Bullers of Buchan
Fyvie
18
Cruden Bay
Port Errol
17
Tarves
21
16
Pitmedden
Collieston
Insch
Old Meldrum
10
Newburgh
Bennachie
Inverurie
Kintore
River Don
Dyce
Balmedie
6
Bridge of Don
Aberdeen
Girdle Ness
Peterculter
2
3
Maryculter
River Dee
Banchory
Bridge of Feugh
Cairn o' Mount
Stonehaven
1
Fettercairn
Howe of the Mearns
Laurencekirk
Kinneff
Inverbervie

1 Dunnottar Castle
2 Drum Castle
3 Crathes Castle
4 Craigievar Castle
5 Crathie Church
6 Castle Fraser
7 Kildrummy Castle
8 Glenbuchat Castle
9 Corgarff Castle
10 Pitcaple Castle
11 Clashindarroch Forest
12 Auchindoun Castle
13 Culbin Sands
14 Pluscarden Abbey
15 Brodie Castle
16 Tolquhon Castle
17 Haddo House
18 Fyvie Castle
19 Delgatie Castle
20 Deer Abbey
21 Slains Castle
22 Findlater Castle
23 Duff House
24 Braemar Castle

345

Aberdeen is the obvious place from which to begin to explore the Grampian Region. It is an ever-changing city, the third largest in Scotland, hiding its true nature under a brittle, cosmopolitan exterior.

Always a great port as well as a fish and cattle market, exporting granite, textiles and paper, Aberdeen suddenly found itself in the centre of an oil boom in the 1970s. Country and Western music emanated from dignified old buildings; bars and restaurants changed their characters overnight; American accents were two-a-penny and the opening ceremony of the American Club was like a visit to Texas. Property prices soared: entrepreneurs flourished.

Somehow, through all this, Aberdeen managed to retain its character. The Granite City, they call it, and it softens this austere title by decking its streets and parks with what must be some of the most spectacular displays of roses in the British Isles. (Aberdeen has won the Beautiful Britain in Bloom Contest no less than ten times.)

No oil boom could change the silvery-granite splendour of the Georgian part of the city, with gracious terraces, squares and crescents; nor the solid Victorian buildings that accompanied the 19th-century prosperity brought to the city by astute merchants; nor the long, wide sweep of Union Street; nor even, for all the smart new buildings, the waterfront. Expensive oil-rig supply vessels can never spoil the character of the harbour—a salty old reprobate smelling of fish.

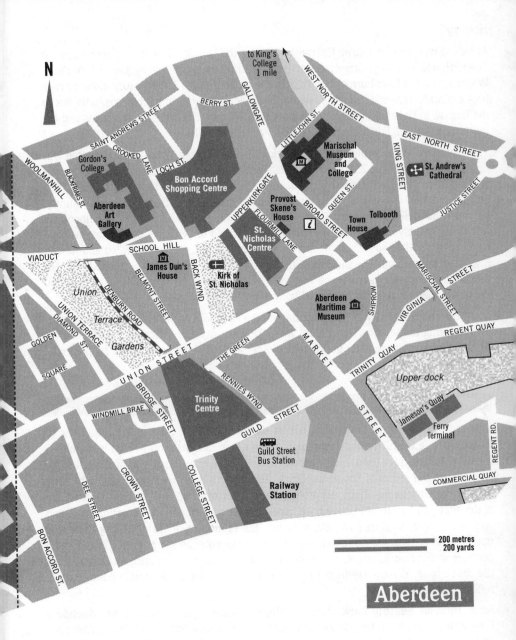

History

Aberdeen was granted a Royal Charter by William the Lion in 1179, now preserved in the Town House in Union Street, endorsing an earlier one granted by David I. William Wallace is said to have burned 100 ships in the harbour in the 13th century. Robert Bruce held a council here in 1308. As a reward for the loyal support of the citizens, who forced the English to surrender their hold on the castle, he gave the city its coat of arms and the motto *Bon Accord*. Edward III burned down Aberdeen in 1336.

The Gordon clan, incomers from Berwickshire and Lothian, who had dominated this northeastern corner for 250 years, over-reached themselves in their ambition for power and began to eye the throne. Mary, Queen of Scots was forced by her Protestant half-brother, Moray, to come north in an attempt to quell them. The Countess of Huntly, however, had been promised by a local witch that the Earl would be in the Tolbooth in Aberdeen, entirely unwounded after any battle he cared to fight. She begged her husband to stand up to Mary so he summoned his army and fought. He was defeated and he and his son were captured. The shock brought on a massive heart attack which killed him. His unwounded body was taken to the Tolbooth. Mary executed Sir John Gordon and ordered the posthumous trial of the embalmed body of his father for treason.

Montrose sacked the city in 1644, fighting for the cause of Charles I. General Monk occupied it during in the mid-17th century when he was Governor of Scotland for Cromwell. Although nominally Jacobite, the citizens of Aberdeen were not enthusiastic supporters of the cause.

Old Aberdeen

This area, north of the city centre, is best explored on foot. Start at the little **Brig o' Balgownie**, a Gothic bridge spanning the River Don near its mouth. This is the oldest medieval bridge in Scotland, built by Richard the Mason, affectionately known as Dick the Cement, on the orders of Robert the Bruce. There was a time, some years ago, when the unrestricted discharge of effluent from mills and factories up the river so polluted the water that you had to hold your nose here. Stricter control and conservation have had their effect and the Don flows cleaner now, the salmon once again making their way upstream to spawn. On the north side of the bridge you can see a terrace of old stone cottages with colourful gardens: the one nearest to the bridge was once an ale-house on the drove road. Walk away from the bridge and look back at the simple pointed arch, reflected in the water.

Stroll through **Seaton Park**, Old Aberdeen, to twin-spired, fortified **St Machar's Cathedral** (open daily: free) in the Chanonry. It is the oldest granite building in Aberdeen and the only granite cathedral in the world. Founded in 1157, St Machar's stands on a promontory overlooking the Don, taking its name from the saint who founded a Celtic church here in the 6th century. A 14th-century red sandstone arch is all that remains of an older building, in contrast to the simple dignity of the later granite. Look for the oak heraldic ceiling, added in 1520, with 48 heraldic shields.

Old Aberdeen grew up round the cathedral, an independent burgh with its own council and charter. Today, cobbled streets and charming old houses, some of which date back to 1500, give an air of tranquillity undisturbed by the roar of the modern city beyond. Near the cathedral, **Cruickshank Botanic Gardens** (open daily May–Sept; weekdays in winter: free) belong to the university, with extensive collections of shrubs, herbaceous and Alpine plants, and a rock and water garden.

King's College, in the High Street (open daily except Sun: free), stands on a green sward with a distinctive 'crowned' tower and buttressed walls. This was Aberdeen's first university, founded in 1495, in the reign of James IV. Its chapel, first Catholic, then Protestant, is now interdenominational. The tomb of its founder, Bishop William Elphinstone, is a magnificent sarcophagus outside the chapel, supported by figures of the Seven Virtues. **Kings College Visitor Centre** (open daily except Sun in winter: adm), in the former University Library, tells the story of 500 years of the university and its students.

Marischal College (pronounced Marshal), Broad Street, in the city centre, was founded in 1593 as a Protestant rival to King's, the two colleges being united to form Aberdeen University in 1860. The present building is an edifice of soaring pinnacles, a neo-Gothic granite fantasy, glittering with mica, its roots in the 19th century with some of the older parts incorporated. The granite façade was added in 1906. Award-winning **Marischal Museum** (open daily except Sat: free) has local, classical, Egyptian and Chinese antiquities and illustrates evolving cultures of the world.

Provost Skene's House (open daily except Sun: free) is opposite the college. Now a museum, this well-restored building dates from 1545. It was named after one of its owners, Sir George Skene, who was Provost of Aberdeen in 1676 and responsible for extensive renovation of the house. Butcher Cumberland lodged here from February until April 1746, on his way to defeat Prince Charles at Culloden. In those days the house formed two dwellings, both of which suffered considerable losses from the misbehaviour of the Duke and his officers. They made free with the stocks of provisions: coals, candles, ales and other liquors in the cellars. They milked the cow, spoiled the bed and table linen and robbed their landlady of her hoard of precious sugar. It is a fascinating museum with some of the original decoration. The Painted Gallery, known as the Chapel, on the second floor of the west wing, revealed traces of religious paintings in 17th-century style, showing that medieval ideas and imagery persisted in this northeastern corner of Scotland far into the Reformation period. On the top floor, exhibits illustrate the history and domestic life of Aberdeen over the ages. There is a coffee shop in the original kitchen.

The Tolbooth, on the corner of Broad Street and Castle Street, was built in 1627. Its ancient town jail with original cells was the stage for the death of the 4th Earl of Huntly after his wife's witch had misleadingly promised him immunity from battle scars.

From the Tolbooth, go up Union Street to **Kirk of St Nicholas**, beyond the shopping precinct a few blocks along on the right. The old parish church (open daily) stands among trees in a peaceful churchyard, bordered by Upperkirkgate and Back Wynd. Its 48-bell carillon rings out across the roar of the city. Founded in the 12th century and split into two at the Reformation, the present building dates from 1752. In the east part of the church, the little stone-vaulted crypt-chapel, St Mary's, dates from the 14th century. Witches were imprisoned down here in the 17th century, and you can see the rings to which they were chained. More prosaically, the chapel has also been used as a plumber's workshop and an early Victorian soup-kitchen. The **Oil Industry Chapel** is in the church.

Aberdeen Art Gallery and Museum (open daily: free) is also in Schoolhill. Among the many things to see here are 20th-century British paintings and sculptures, Raeburn portraits, works by Zoffany, Romney, Reynolds, Augustus John and Ben Nicholson, and an important collection of Scottish domestic silver and glass. There are also regular exhibitions, music, dance, poetry readings and films, a reference library, gallery shop, print room and café.

James Dun's House (open daily except Sun: free) is almost opposite, in what was the Georgian home of James Dun, former master and rector of Aberdeen Grammar School. There are a variety of exhibitions and audio-visual shows.

His Majesty's Theatre, a little further on in Rosemount Viaduct, was built in 1906. Recently refurbished, it is the town's main theatre, seating 1500 people. Its programmes include ballet, opera and concerts.

The Maritime Museum (open daily except Sun: free) is in Provost Ross's House, Shiprow, north of Trinity Quay and the Upper Dock. Overlooking the harbour, it is one of the oldest houses in the town and a fine example of early Scottish domestic architecture. Displays include Aberdeen's maritime heritage of fishing, shipbuilding and trade and models of offshore oil installations.

Aberdeen Harbour is a conglomeration of seafaring life: fine old buildings line the waterfront where fishing boats are packed into the inner basins, some old and rusty, some so sophisticated that they need an electronic genius to operate them. If you want to see another face of Aberdeen, get up early one weekday morning and visit the **fish market** before the sales start at 7.30am. The action starts at around 4.30am and the earlier you go, the more impressive it is. (There are no official tours of the fish market.) As one of Britain's major fishing ports, Aberdeen exports hundreds of tonnes of fish daily. The boats dock in the cold pre-dawn and box after box of fish is unloaded and stacked in open-sided warehouses. Fat gulls squabble over the fish. Fishermen, with faces as resilient as the granite of the city, toil at the final stages of their demanding job, their rich, salty humour warming the often bitterly cold air. Then the auction begins, in an unintelligible language of grunts, yells, mutterings and gestures.

Satrosphere (open daily except Tue: adm) is a marvellous science and technology centre where you can find out about such subjects as prisms, light, lasers etc., and you are encouraged to take part in do-it-yourself experiments. This is a discovery place for all ages, whether science is your thing or not.

The Gordon Highlanders Regimental Museum (open Tues and Thurs and one Sun a month: free) in Viewfield Road, southwest of the city centre, displays the uniforms, pictures, medals, letters and documents, weapons and memorabilia of this famous, locally recruited regiment. The Gordons fought with distinction all over the world and are now fighting amalgamation with the Queen's Own Highlanders.

Duthie Park Winter Gardens, south of the city on the banks of the Dee, were recently hailed as Scotland's top tourist attraction. The glasshouse extension makes them the largest glassed gardens in Europe. They include a Japanese Garden, the biggest collection of cacti in Britain, birds, fish, and turtles. Sit under a palm tree in mid-winter and picture yourself in some tropical paradise. Outside, in **Duthie Park,** there is a play area, boating pond, Victorian bandstand and a Rose Mound, which brings on a severe attack of gardener's elbow as you contemplate the pruning season.

Footde, known locally in the inimitable Aberdonian accent as 'Fittie', is a fishing village at the mouth of the Dee. The early 19th-century houses were designed by the fisherfolk themselves. Come here in an easterly gale and watch the sea breaking high over the harbour walls.

Another place from which to watch the changing moods of the sea is **Girdleness Lighthouse** in Walker Park, the grassy headland that juts eastwards from the other side of the harbour. You get a bird's-eye view of the harbour and the city from here.

A sandy beach stretches 2 miles (3km) northwards from the harbour, backed by dunes matted with marram grass and fringed by golf courses, an amusement park, and the Beach Leisure Centre, with everything from wave machines, water cannons and jet streams to aerobics, keep-fit training and ball games. It is open daily from 8.30am to 10.30pm and has a crèche, café and bar. The Linx Ice Arena is incorporated, a full size rink for skating, curling, dance, hocky and disco. Bathing in the North Sea is only for the hardy: watch out for undercurrents.

Festivals

Regular festivals include: Scottish Connection, a festival celebrating all things Scottish, in March/April; Scottish Fiddle Orchestra Concert and Granite City Car Rally in April; a Marathon Road Race in May; Aberdeen Highland Games and the Bon Accord Carnival Parade and Aberdeen Festival in June; an International Football Festival in July; Clydesdale Horse Show, Summer Flower Show, and the International Youth Festival in August; Aberdeen Alternative Music Festival in October; Christmas Shopping Festival in November/December and finally, St Nicholas Festival in December.

Where to Stay

expensive

Altens Skean Dhu Hotel, Souter Head Road, © 0224 877000, is comfortable and has a heated outdoor swimming pool. **Copthorne Hotel**, Huntly Street, ✆ 0224 630404, is a city-centre hotel off Union Street and near the Catholic Cathedral. The decor is fanciful, with fluted columns and dribbling fountains, and it has a good restaurant called **Poachers**.

Ardoe House, South Deeside Road, Blairs, ✆ 0224 867355, on the outskirts of Aberdeen, is a baronial-style mansion overlooking the Dee Valley. It's expensive, elegant and comfortable and the food is excellent.

moderate

Atholl Hotel in Kings Gate, ✆ 0224 323505, is a typical Aberdeen granite town house in the west end; no frills but respectable. Golfing, fishing and shooting can be arranged, and also distillery tours. You can even have secretarial services.

Caledonian Thistle Hotel, overlooking Union Terrace Gardens in the city centre, ✆ 0224 640233, is moderate to expensive, with modern fittings, good food and not much character. There are in-house movies, tea/coffee-making facilities in the bedrooms, sun-beds and a sauna room. **Imperial Hotel**, Stirling Street, ✆ 0224 589101, is also central and has an imposing frontage that makes you think of top hats and carriages. They give good service and the food's not bad. **Stakis Tree Tops Hotel** in Springfield Road, ✆ 0224 313377, is in wooded landscaped grounds, 10 minutes from the city centre; it's moderate to expensive depending on what sort of room you take. The hotel has all the Stakis extras, like a swimming pool and leisure complex, and excellent food in a split-level Regency-style restaurant.

If you want something less overpowering, **Palm Court Hotel**, 81 Seafield Road, ✆ 0224 310351, is cosy and friendly in a quiet residential area.

Eating Out

Try **Mr G's**, 74 Chapel Street, ✆ 0224 242112. This is a wine bar and restaurant where the food is excellent and there is a friendly atmosphere. **Gerards**, 50 Chapel Street, ✆ 0224 639500, has an outstanding chef: you eat in a garden room with a glass roof. **Atlantis Seafood**, 16 Bon Accord Crescent, ✆ 0224 591403, do good, fresh sea-food and **Poldinos**, 7 Little Belmont Street, ✆ 0224 647777, do excellent pizzas. Otherwise, ask around for the current 'in' eating place: fashions change fast.

The Coast South of Aberdeen

The A92 south from Aberdeen takes you along the coast with the North Sea stretching away to the horizon, always busy with shipping. When the wind is in the east, big seas pound the beaches and cliffs, sending up great plumes of spray.

Stonehaven

Stonehaven is a holiday resort town, as sturdy as its name implies, 14 miles (22km) south of Aberdeen, crouched around a bay below red sandstone cliffs. The sheltered harbour is used mainly by pleasure boats now. Stonehaven has a heated open-air swimming pool, a golf course, boating and windsurfing, fishing and sea-angling, and an indoor leisure centre with swimming pool.

Tolbooth Museum (open daily except Tues, June–Sept: free) is a 16th-century building on the quay by the north pier, displaying local history and archaeology, with a special emphasis on fishing. The building was a storehouse of the Earls Marischal, later used as a prison. In 1748–9, three Episcopal priests were imprisoned here, for their insistence in following the old religion. During their incarceration, women came from all over the county, smuggling babies in creels on their backs, to hold them up to the barred windows so that the priests could baptize them.

Every New Year's Eve the town celebrates a 'Swinging the Fireballs' ceremony, going back to pagan times when fireballs were swung through the streets to ward off evil spirits.

Dunnottar Castle (open daily except closed weekends in winter: adm) is about 2 miles (3km) south of Stonehaven, just off the A92. This spectacular ruined fortress stands high on a rocky promontory towering 160 feet (49m) above the boiling sea, protected to landward by a deep natural cleft. It has been written: 'Dunnottar speaks with an audible voice; every cave has a record, every turret a tongue.' A Pictish fort stood here in the Dark Ages, and one of the earliest Christian chapels. The fort was replaced by a primitive castle in the 13th century. William Wallace stormed the English garrison in 1297, burning down the church where they had taken refuge, but failing to take the castle. Dunnottar was a stronghold of the Earls Marischal of Scotland from the 14th century. The extensive ruins include a great square tower and the chapel, built by Sir William Keith in 1392, and a gatehouse, built in 1575, said to be the strongest in Scotland. In 1645, the 7th Earl Marischal, a stubborn Covenanter, withstood a siege by Montrose, who took his revenge by laying waste to Stonehaven and the surrounding lands. His actions are recorded by a chronicler as having left the country 'utterlie spoilzeit plunderit and undone'.

During the Civil War, the Scottish Regalia were brought to Dunnottar for safety. The castle was besieged in 1652, but the governor refused to surrender until the Regalia had been smuggled out in the apron of the local minister's wife, Mrs Grainger, and in a bundle of flax carried by her servant. They were hidden in the kirk at Kinneff and kept safe until the Restoration of the Monarchy.

In 1685, 167 Covenanters were imprisoned at Dunnottar in such awful conditions that you can almost sense the horror now, looking at the 'Whigs Vault' where many of them were confined: 'ankle deep in mire, with one window to the sea, they had not the least accommodation for sitting, leaning or lying and were perfectly stifled for want of air and no access to ease nature'. Some tried to escape through the window that overlooks the sea, but were recaptured and cruelly tortured. Many died. It was a chapter in the history of the castle that seems to overshadow it, even now adding a gloomy touch to the very well-preserved ruins.

The castle was used as the setting for Zeffirelli's film *Hamlet.*

Dunnottar's history is further commemorated in the 18th-century kirk at **Kinneff** (usually open). Kinneff is 7 miles (11km) to the south, just off the A92. Parts of the old kirk are incorporated into the current building and include those parts in which the Scottish Regalia were hidden for nine years by the Rev. James Grainger. The hiding place was under the flagstone below the pulpit. You can see memorials to Grainger, his wife, and to Sir George Ogilvy, Governor of Dunnottar Castle at the time.

Fowlsheugh is an RSPB reserve, signed off the A92, 3 miles (4.5km) south of Stonehaven. Always open but best in spring and summer, this is home to one of the largest seabird colonies in Scotland.

Inverbervie

Inverbervie is a milling town just to the south on the banks of Bervie Water. Here, at Craig David on the north shore, David II and his wife, Johanna, were driven ashore by a storm while returning from nine years' exile in France in 1341. King's Step is the rock where David is said to have stepped ashore. He granted the town a Royal Charter the following year. There is also a memorial to Hercules Linton, the man who designed the famous clipper *Cutty Sark.* Today, this wild, rugged coastline offers little refuge from the ferocious storms that often rage in from the North Sea. The villagers take what shelter they can from harbours built into the cliffs.

Arbuthnott House and Gardens are 3 miles (4.5km) inland from Inverbervie (open by arrangement, © Inverbervie 361226: adm). The house has a 17th-century Renaissance façade, with 18th-century additions, and there is an extensive 17th-century formal garden, attractively terraced with a pretty 18th-century stone bridge. A tower on the site of the house was the home of the Arbuthnott family in 1206. The chancel of the village church dates from 1242.

The sheltered area to the west of here is called Howe of the Mearns, with forest trails and picnic sites. (Howe is a wide plain, surrounded by hills, or a shallow depression.)

Glenbervie, just off the A94, is 6 miles (9.5km) southwest of Stonehaven. It was the home of the ancestors of Robert Burns and you can see the family tombstone and a cairn in memory of the poet, whose father it was that emigrated west to Ayr.

The Grassic Gibbon Centre at Arbuthnott (open daily, April–Oct: adm) is a memorial to Lewis Grassic Gibbon (James Leslie Mitchell), the writer whose powerful Scottish prose in his trilogy *A Scots Quair* brings to life the Mearns at the beginning of the century. He spent his childhood here and used recognizable local settings in his books.

From here you can make a quick detour inland through Laurencekirk to Fettercairn where you can tour the Fettercairn Distillery. Go on to Fasque almost on the border with Tayside, often missed by tourists hurrying north on the main road.

Fasque

Just to the north of **Fettercairn**, with its turreted arch into the village commemorating a visit by Queen Victoria and Prince Albert in 1861, Fasque is down a side road to the left. This delightful, rambling mansion is for Victoriana addicts. (Open every afternoon except Fri, May–Sept: adm). The house, built in 1809, was the home of the Gladstones, including one of Britain's best-known prime ministers, W. E. Gladstone—he who chewed each mouthful a hundred times to aid digestion. He spent his honeymoon here before moving to Wales. Fasque, still owned by the family, has managed to preserve all the marvellous relics of Victorian times without becoming like a museum. Nothing seems to have changed for a hundred years. The kitchens are a joy and you can see portraits of all the family servants. A slightly ramshackle air hangs over the whole fascinating place and there is a splendid deer park.

While you are here, go a few miles north on the B974—a glorious drive over bald, rolling hills—and climb Cairn o' Mount for fantastic views.

Where to Stay

moderate

You shouldn't go far wrong at **Heugh Hotel**, Westfield Road, Stonehaven, © 0569 62379. A turreted granite baronial mansion, with lots of oak panelling and nice grounds, it won't raise your blood pressure with excitement but you'll eat well and be comfortable.

inexpensive

The best thing about the **Marine Hotel**, Shorehead, Stonehaven, © 0569 62155, is that it is right on the waterfront in the harbour. The staff are friendly and they cater for children.

If you want something a bit different but aren't much good at planning, try **Hiking and Biking Scotland**, Bogfur, Inverurie, © 0467 21312. From April to November, they lay on walking and cycling holidays, guided or independent, using guest-house accommodation or country hotels, with comprehensive information packs. Their routes take in the Castle Trail and the Whisky Trail, as well as mountain and island tours.

Royal Deeside

The River Dee is born high in the Cairngorms, to the west. It boils down through steep-sided ravines, thunders over precipices gathering myriad tributaries from corries in the surrounding hills, foams through the deer forests of Mar, ripples at a suitably majestic pace past Balmoral Castle and finally meets the North Sea in Aberdeen.

You can enjoy Deeside all through the year: perhaps it is best of all in autumn when the rich blaze of colour is unforgettable. In winter the landscape becomes a dramatic sweep of snow-covered hills and torrents of ice: a skier's delight, with the Glenshee Ski Centre, with 25 miles (40km) of runs, and the Lecht Ski Centre. In summer, with a good map and sensible equipment, you could spend a whole holiday exploring the hills and valleys of the Cairngorms and Grampians.

Peterculter and Maryculter

Leaving Aberdeen on the A93, to follow the Dee west, you pass Peterculter and Maryculter (pronounced kooter), 7 miles (11km) from the city and once a Roman camp. William the Lion granted the lands to the Knight's Templar—the powerful soldier-monks of the Crusades—who built a chapel to St Mary, in the late 12th century. Its ruins can still be seen in Templars' Park on the south bank of the river. The highly coloured statue of Rob Roy standing above the Leuchar's Burn has no historic significance. It was originally a ship's figurehead and has been replaced twice since it was erected.

Children and adults will enjoy **Story Book Glen**, off South Deeside Road in Maryculter (open daily, 1 March–31 Oct and at weekends for the rest of the year: adm). A host of familiar characters await introduction, ingeniously arranged among flowers, streams and waterfalls.

Drum Castle (open daily 1 May–30 Sept; weekends in April and Oct; grounds open all year: adm) is about 3 miles (4.5km) to the west, signposted off the A93, and is one of the three oldest tower houses in Scotland. A massive granite tower, built towards the end of the 13th century, adjoins a mansion built in 1619. Robert the Bruce gave Drum to his standard bearer, William de Irwin, in 1324, and it remained in the possession of the family until the late Mr H. Q. Forbes Irvine left it to the National Trust for Scotland in 1975. It contains antique furniture, silver, portraits, family treasures and relics. The grounds are lovely, with an oak wood, rare trees and shrubs, sweeping lawns, woodland nature trails, and a café.

Crathes Castle and Gardens

Crathes is 5 miles (8km) beyond Drum, signposted off the A93. (The castle, visitor centre, shop and restaurant are open at Easter, at weekends in April and Oct, and daily 1 May–30 Sept; the grounds are open all year: adm). Although Crathes is familiar to many people from picture books, postcards, calendars and chocolate boxes, it is still a pleasant surprise when seen in reality. The Burnett family had been granted lands north of the Dee by Robert Bruce early in the 14th century, and it was Alexander Burnett who, in 1552, decided to move from his stronghold on an island in the Loch of Leys nearby, and build a modern house, in keeping with his status as laird. The castle took many years to complete and is one of the best examples of Scottish domestic architecture as it developed from the previously necessary fortified dwellings—a style that was to die out within 60 years. When a Victorian extension, overlooking the upper garden, was burnt down in 1966, it was agreed to restore the castle to its present, original proportions. The interior is just as it was, with painted decorations on the beams and woodwork, allegorical designs, proverbs and biblical texts. You can also see some of the original furnishings, among some of the many treasures that are on show. The little ivory hunting horn in the main hall symbolizes the Burnetts' right of tenure over part of the Royal Forest, given them by Robert the Bruce.

The Green Lady

Crathes has its ghosts, notably the Green Lady, who, dressed in green and carrying a baby in her arms, haunts certain rooms. A baby's skeleton was unearthed under the hearthstone in the Green Lady's room during the 19th century, and the story is told of a young girl, under the laird's protection, giving birth to a baby, fathered by one of the servants. Mother and infant died, under mysterious circumstances.

The gardens are a delight in every season of the year and you could happily pass days enjoying them. They consist of a series of small, interlinked gardens, each with its own motif and character, a profusion of colours, scents and blended textures. There are also nature trails in the grounds.

Banchory

Banchory, about 3 miles (4.5km) beyond Crathes, is a pleasant, sheltered town on the Dee. It rises in layers of terraced streets, backed by the **Hill o' Fare**, 1545 feet (475m), to the north, and rolling hills to the south. You catch an air of genteel respectability as you stroll among its antique shops and high-class boutiques.

The brand-new **Banchory Museum** in Bridge Street (open daily, April–Oct: free) tells the history of the area. In the 5th century, St Ternan, a local man and follower of St Ninian, established a monastery where the churchyard now is, and you can still see traces of its medieval successor. Incorporated into the walls of the manse, carved wheel-crosses date from this early Christian period. Palaeolithic flints, excavated nearby, suggest a very early settlement. There is a golf course by the river and the salmon fishing is renowned. Walk to the south of the town, where the Dee is joined by the Feugh, at **Bridge of Feugh**. The footbridge above the rapids is a good place from which to watch the salmon leaping up the ledges to get to their spawning grounds. There are forest and riverside walks as well as energetic hill climbs.

Aboyne

Aboyne, 13 miles (21km) to the west, is famous for its annual Highland Games. They takes place every August on the large green, with all the traditional activities such as tossing the caber, putting the weight, piping and dancing. Aboyne is a good base from which to explore this part of Deeside and there are some excellent walks in the area. Follow the Water of Tanar, southwest of the town, through Glen Tanar, in whose woods you can see remnants of the old Caledonian Forest. Tanar oak was much used in the building of ships, being floated down the Dee to Aberdeen, in the 19th century. **The Braeloine Visitor Centre** (open daily April–Sept: donation box) is 5 miles (8km) up the glen, with all the usual educational information on local wildlife, farming, and forestry, as well as advice on where to walk. There are several tracks leading south, over the hills, one of which, Fir Mounth, is thought to be the route taken by Macbeth as he fled from the castle at Dunsinane to his death at Lumphanan.

Lumphanan is 5 miles (8km) northeast of Aboyne. The **Peel Ring** is a medieval motte with wall, earthworks and ditches and is believed to be where Macbeth fought his final battle against Malcolm Canmore in 1057. Macbeth's Cairn, in a circle of trees on the hillside, marks the spot where he is said to have died, crying: 'Lay on Macduff; and damn'd be him that first cries "Hold enough!" ' (Actually, Shakespeare sets the death scene at Dunsinane.)

Tarland

Tarland, less than 5 miles (8km) northwest of Aboyne, is an old-world village set round a square and is the centre of the MacRobert Trust—a huge complex of farming and charitable foundations. Walk a short way to the east, beyond the golf course to the well-preserved souterrain, **Culsh Earth House** (open daily: free), by Culsh Farmhouse. Its roofing slabs are intact over a large chamber. Another prehistoric feature is **Tomnaverie Stone Circle**, on a rocky hillock a mile (1.5km) to the southeast, unexcavated and recumbent, probably dating from 1800 BC.

From Tarland, drive round Scar Hill on the B9119 and back to the A93 at **Dinnet**. The **National Nature Reserve** here covers heathland, scrub and birchwood, with old oaks and fenland.

Ballater

Ballater, 11 miles (17.5km) west of Aboyne on the A93, used to be the end of the line for the Royal Train, before the railway was closed. It's a popular holiday centre in the summer, in wooded moorland where you can roam for miles, discovering fresh enchantment at every turn.

The town developed in the late 18th century after an old woman discovered the healing powers of the spring water at the foot of Pannanich Hill. Her discovery was exploited by an ex-Jacobite, Francis Farquharson of Monaltrie, 20 years after his exile and near-execution, following Culloden. This enterprising entrepreneur built an inn at the hamlet of Cobbletown of Dalmuchie and developed it into a spa, which quickly became fashionable. After Queen Victoria fell in love with Scotland and came to Balmoral, the whole area developed into the prosperous place it is today.

The views from **Ballater Golf Course**, sweeping away to the hills, must be distracting enough to kill concentration on the game. Ballater Highland Games are in August in Monaltrie Park, with all the traditional events, both athletic and musical, and a Hill Race to Craig Cailleach, south of the bridge. Victoria Week is in August.

There are some sizeable hills to climb, with panoramic views, and always the sound of rushing water and the song of skylarks and linnets.

Balmoral (grounds and paintings in ballroom open daily except Sun, in May, June and July: adm), 7 miles (11km) west, is another of those places so familiar from photographs that its reality is almost an anti-climax. Queen Victoria lost her heart to 'this dear Paradise', and she and Prince Albert bought the estate and the old castle in 1852, for £31,000. The old building, however, was too small for the royal household, and Prince Albert commissioned the building of the present granite mansion in 1853, a Scottish baronial edifice designed by William Smith of Aberdeen. It is still the Royal Family's holiday home and it holds a place of great affection in most British hearts as being the place where their much-loved 'First Family' relax and enjoy the same sort of country pursuits as ordinary people.

Crathie Church, just north of the castle, was built in 1895 to replace a series of previous churches whose origins went back to the 9th century. It is attended by members of the Royal Family when they are on holiday.

Lochnagar towers over the Balmoral area, among 11 peaks over 3000 feet (923m) high: massive sentinels, reflected in the waters of Loch Muick to the south. This scenery inspired Byron to write:

> *England! thy beauties are tame and domestic*
> *To one who has roved o'er the mountains afar:*
> *Oh, for the crags that are wild and majestic!*
> *The steep frowning glories of dark Lochnagar.*

More recently, Lochnagar inspired another writer, the present Prince Charles, to write a delightful story, *The Old Man of Lochnagar*, to amuse his brothers during a cruise in the royal yacht.

Royal Lochnagar Distillery (open daily, Easter–Oct: free) was founded in 1845.

A good 8-mile (13km) walk starts at **Spittal of Glenmuick** northeast of Loch Muick and goes round the loch anti-clockwise to the southwest corner and then across to the Dubh (black) Loch, deep in a corrie among brooding cliffs. You are about 2000 feet (615m) up here, and ice lingers on the water well into summer. Watch out for golden eagles, soaring overhead on long, splay-tipped wings. Less rare than they used to be, they are still a protected species, hated by sheep farmers. Another bird of prey you might see up here, also protected, is the peregrine falcon, plummeting to earth, its long pointed wings and tail streamlined, diving on its prey at speeds of 112 miles per hour (180km/h). In autumn you might hear the roaring of rutting stags.

Braemar

Braemar, 9 miles (14.5km) southwest of Balmoral, is a very popular holiday centre surrounded by beautiful scenery.

Braemar Castle (open daily except Fri, May–mid Oct: adm) is a massive turreted fortress, built by the Earl of Mar in 1628. It was burnt by the Farquharsons in 1689 and garrisoned by the English after the Jacobite risings in 1715 and 1745 to protect the military road from Perth. The castle has barrel vaulted ceilings, a sinister pit prison, spiral stairways and gun loops. Look for the carved graffiti on the internal woodwork, left by off-duty soldiers in the 18th century.

The Invercauld Arms stands on the spot where the Earl of Mar raised the Jacobite standard in 1715 and a plaque in the hotel commemorates the occasion.

Braemar Royal Highland Gathering is held every year on the first Saturday in September, drawing upwards of 20,000 people. It includes all the traditional events, both athletic and musical, together with plenty of stalls and sideshows. The Royal Family attend the games, which might be why it is one of the biggest events of its kind in Scotland. The origins of these Highland Games are said to date from the 11th century, when Malcolm Canmore held contests to find the best soldiers for his struggles against the Normans.

Braemar Highland Heritage Centre(open daily: free) has audio-visual presentations and exhibitions giving the history of the area.

Linn of Dee

A tour of about 12 miles (19km) takes you west from Braemar through the wooded Dee Valley to the Linn of Dee. It is an attractive drive, which means it is also popular. The traffic can be tedious as the narrow road winds up through birches, with splendid views to the Cairngorms. Park at **Inverey** and walk the couple of miles on to the Linn of Dee. The narrow, rocky gorge is about 150 yards (138m) long and the river boils through this bottleneck in a tumultuous frenzy, filling the air with noise and a haze of spray. This lovely place is best appreciated early or late in the day.

Experienced walkers should try the famous **Lairig Ghru**, a testing walk from Linn of Dee over the Cairngorms to Aviemore.

Another walk from Inverey is south up the Ey Burn to **The Colonel's Bed**. The Colonel was John Farquharson of Inverey, a legendary character known as the Black Colonel, who used to ride his horse up sheer rock slopes and summon his servants by firing at a shield on the wall which rang like a bell when hit by a bullet. The Colonel's Bed is a ledge of rock in a gorge through which the Ey runs, where the Black Colonel hid after his castle had been burnt down by government troops following the Battle of Killiecrankie in 1689.

Where to Stay

expensive

Invery House, Banchory, ✆ 03302 4782, is a luxury country-house mansion by the River Feugh, where you could be forgiven for trying to remember who has invited you so you can thank them for having you to stay—until you get the bill. They'll arrange golf and salmon fishing for you and you'll eat like a king. **Raemoir House Hotel**, at Raemoir, near Banchory, ✆ 03302 4884, is an 18th-century mansion, converted from a private house in 1943. A number of the rooms have tapestried walls and antique furniture as well as all mod cons. They will arrange shooting, game fishing and stalking in season, and there is a tennis court and a mini nine-hole golf course in the grounds. There are also four self-catering apartments in the coachhouse. The food is first class.

Craigendarroch Hotel and Country Club, Ballater, ✆ 03397 55858, prides itself on its leisure facilities. It is comfortable, if a little soulless, standing in 29 acres of wooded hillside, overlooking the River Dee and Lochnagar. It has a 55-foot (17m) indoor swimming pool, a whirlpool bath, two saunas, two squash courts, snooker, games room, gymnasium, health and beauty treatment, and a dry ski slope. When you've worked up an appetite, there are three restaurants to choose from.

moderate

Banchory Lodge Hotel, Banchory, ✆ 03302 2545, is a Georgian house where the Water of Feugh flows into the Dee. Nice old-world hospitality and decent food makes this popular with the fishing fraternity. Closed in January. **Darroch Learg Hotel**, Ballater, ✆ 03397 55443, is worth a visit for the views alone. This granite country house is in five acres of garden with views across the golf course to Lochnagar. Closed in January.

inexpensive

Invercauld Arms Hotel, Ballater, ✆ 03397 55417, is a Victorian pile overlooking the Dee. It stands on the spot where the Earl of Mar raised the Jacobite standard in 1715 and displays a plaque commemorating the event. Some rooms overlook the river. The food isn't bad. Further down the scale, **Hazelhurst Lodge,** Aboyne, ✆ 03398 86921, is a really friendly little place, with only four bedrooms and excellent candlelit dinners.

For really good value, try **Netherley Guest House**, Ballater, ✆ 03397 55792. This pretty little house overlooks the green in the centre of the town

Aberdeen to Tomintoul

The A944 takes you west from Aberdeen through farm and moorland towards the hills. Less spectacular than Deeside, it is nevertheless attractive country with several prosperous private estates.

Castle Fraser

Castle Fraser (open every afternoon 1 May–30 Sept: adm; gardens and grounds open daily all year: donation) is about 15 miles (24km) from Aberdeen, to the north of the road. It is one of the most spectacular of the Castles of Mar, Z-plan, dating from the 16th century and incorporating an earlier castle. The Great Hall conjures dreams of feudal lairds: look for the eavesdropping device known as the 'Laird's Lug'. If you look closely at the great heraldic panel on the north side, you can see the inscription 'I Bel', left by one of the Bel family, who were important master masons, very active in Aberdeenshire. They may also have helped to build both Crathes and Craigievar. An exhibition, off the courtyard, tells the story of the Castles of Mar.

Alford

Montrose fought one of his victorious battles against the Covenanters in 1645 near Alford (pronounced Arford), 10 miles (16km) further west, on the ground between the village and the bridge over the Don. A sad story hangs over **Terpersie Castle**, recently rebuilt and lived in by its restorer, 4 miles (6.5km) northwest of Alford, and dating from 1561. The last owner, George Gordon, fought for Prince Charles at Culloden. He fled to the castle after the battle, to lie low until the worst of the reprisals were over. His young children, unaware of the threat, revealed that 'papa was at home' to his pursuers. He was captured in the castle and later executed.

Alford is on the Castle Trail and has a heritage centre in the old cattle mart (open daily, April–Sept: free). Also in the village is the **Grampian Transport Museum** (open daily April–Oct: adm); **Alford Valley Railway**, a narrow-gauge passenger railway which runs half-hour trips; and **Montgarrie Oatmeal Mill** (open Tues and Thurs, April–Oct: adm), a traditional, water-powered mill.

Kildrummy Castle

Kildrummy (open daily, April–Sept: adm) is a ruined courtyard castle 10 miles (16km) west of Alford, on the A97. Founded in the early 13th century, it is one of the most impressive and historic of the castles in this area. Edward I captured it and altered its design. Robert the Bruce sent his wife and children here when he went into exile on Rathlin Island in 1306. The story is told of a treacherous blacksmith who betrayed the fugitives to the English in return for their promise of 'as much gold as he could carry'. He set fire to the castle, whose inhabitants surrendered, receiving as his reward the molten gold, poured down his throat. The English executed Nigel Bruce, Robert's brother; the garrison was 'hangyt and drawyn' but Robert's intrepid wife, Elizabeth, escaped with her children and fled north to Tain. In 1404, Alexander Stewart, son of the Wolf of Badenoch, kidnapped the Countess of Mar, having killed her husband in order to widow her, and forcibly married her, to gain the title of Mar. The castle was destroyed because of the part it played in the 1715 rebellion.

It is an extensive ruin, with a broad ditch and curtain wall, round towers, a keep and gatehouse. The nearby gardens include a Japanese rock and water garden built in the quarry from which stone was taken for the castle, and a replica of Old Aberdeen's Brig o' Balgownie, spanning the stream among shrubs and alpines.

Two miles (3km) to the south, at **Glenkindie**, you can see a well-preserved earth house in a clump of trees, its short entrance passage leading to two chambers, under massive roof slabs. You need a torch for the inner chamber.

From Glenkindie, follow the course of the Don through the valley of Strathdon and up into the hills to the west for less than 3 miles (4.5km). **Glenbuchat Castle** stands by the road at Bridge of Buchat, and dates from the 16th-century. It was the seat of 'Old Glenbucket' (sic), a staunch Jacobite, who died in exile in France after Culloden.

Big Foot, at Heughhead, is an adventure holiday establishment, with climbing, canoeing, etc: ✆ 09756 51312.

Corgarff Castle

About a mile (1.5km) south, go right on the B973 for 8 miles (13km), through Strathdon to the A939: turn left to **Corgarff Castle** (open daily, April–Sept: adm; contact key keeper in winter, ✆ 097 54 206). It is a stark, 16th-century tower house, within a star-shaped wall with gun loops. One terrible day in 1571, the family of the laird, Alexander Forbes, was besieged here by supporters of the deposed Mary, Queen of Scots. In her husband's absence, Forbes' wife refused to surrender. Edom o' Gordon ordered that the castle be burned, and she died in the flames, with her entire family and household, 24 in all. Corgarff was used by Jacobites in both 1715 and 1745. In 1748, in the aftermath of Culloden, the Hanoverians converted it into a garrison post and barracks to guard the military road from Perth to Fort George. In the 19th century the castle was used by the Redcoats in their unpopular campaign against whisky smuggling. Recently reconstructed rooms are excellent.

This is skiing country, for hardy skiers who don't need too many sophisticated lifts and resorts. **The Lecht Road**, from Corgarff to Tomintoul, is part of the military road built by the Hanoverians after Culloden. It rises steeply from 1330 feet (409m) to 2100 feet (646m) within a distance of about 3 miles (4.5km). The wild moorland is frequently cut off by snow in winter, when fierce winds cause high drifts: remote farms and communities can be isolated for days.

Lecht Ski Centre is at the summit of the road, with several ski tows, a dry ski slope, ski school, ski hire and a café and crèche. A little further on is the **Glenmulliach Nordic Ski Centre** for cross-country skiers, with ski hire and tuition and miles of trails.

Lecht Mine, in the hills north of the Lecht Road near Well of Lecht, is where lead was mined between 1730 and 1737. The ore was taken on pack horses over the hills to Nethy Bridge where there was timber for smelting. Later it became a manganese ore mine but fell into disrepair when the price of ore fell.

Tomintoul

Tomintoul, 8 miles (13km) northwest of Corgarff, is second only to Dalwhinnie as the highest village in the Highlands, at 1150 feet (354m). Pronounced 'Tommin-towl', the name comes from the Gaelic *Tom-an-t-sabhal*, meaning 'hill of the barn'. The village lies along a gentle ridge flanked on one side by the River Avon (pronounced 'Arn'), famous for the clarity of its water, and on the other by Conglass Water. It is easy to drive through in a hurry and miss the attractions of this lofty, wild territory. Walkers will discover glens hidden in folds of the hills, with tumbling burns and tiny lochans, rich in bird, animal and plant life. The Tomintoul and Strathavon Highland Games are held on the third Saturday of July every year.

Tomintoul Museum (open daily from Easter to the end of Oct: free) is in an old baker's shop in the square and incorporates a tourist information centre. Displays include a reconstructed farm kitchen with all the old implements, a blacksmith's shop, a peat-cutting exhibition and information on wildlife, climate, landscape and geology.

Glenlivet, running north to the Spey, is not only at the heart of malt whisky country but also a settled farming area. In 1594, 1500 local men routed 10,000 Highlanders at the Battle of Glenlivet, and after the 1745 Rising army units were garrisoned in Glenlivet to maintain order and to try to stamp out the illicit distilling of whisky. Catholicism has remained strong here, especially in the secluded Braes of Glenlivet where, in the 18th century, the Seminary of Scalan was the only place in Scotland for young men to train for the priesthood. The college survived several attacks by Hanoverian soldiers and was finally moved to become Blairs College, near Aberdeen. The building at Scalen is being restored as a museum—a beautiful remote spot.

Tamnavulin Distillery (open daily except Sun, mid-March–end Oct: free) is about 5 miles (8km) north of Tomintoul on the B9008 and is one of the eight on the Malt Whisky Trail. It gives the usual tour, audio-visual show and free dram, and claims to be the most attractive and friendliest of them all. Opinions may differ on this, depending on how many free drams have already been tucked away, if you are doing the whole trail.

The Glenlivet Distillery Visitor Centre (open daily except Sun, Easter–end Oct: free) is a couple of miles north and also on the trail. It was founded as an illicit still in 1746 by a fugitive Jacobite after Culloden. (He changed his name from Gow to Smith because Gow, being the anglicized spelling of the Gaelic equivalent to Smith, was liable to arouse suspicion.) The distillery was subsequently made legal by his grandson. It offers the usual tours and a 10-minute audio-visual show called 'The Ballad of The Glenlivet'. There is a coffee shop and salad bar and a souvenir shop. Adults get their free dram but children under eight aren't allowed on the tours: either for safety or perhaps to protect them from the evils of the demon drink.

moderate

If you like a touch of class, **Kildrummy Castle Hotel**, by Alford, © 09756 71288, will suit you well. With all the style of a country mansion and the comforts of a modern first-class hotel, it stands in gardens and woods overlooking the castle from which it takes its name. It has a good restaurant and offers skiing, fishing and shooting packages.

The Glenavon Hotel, Tomintoul, © 0807 580218, is comfortable and has good food.

inexpensive

For impoverished skiers, **Allargue Arms Hotel**, Corgarff, by Strathdon, © 09754 210, is close to the Lecht slopes in gorgeous scenery. It is very friendly and relaxed. **Minmore House Hotel**, Tomintoul, © 0807 590378 is also good value and friendly.

If you want something different, try **Glenavon Hotel**, Tomintoul, © 0807 580218. They do adventure activity holidays, including hill-walking, rock-climbing, abseiling, canoeing, pony-trekking, gorge-walking and mountain-biking, all with instruction. Prices vary and they will tailor-make courses for you if you prefer.

Aberdeen to Elgin

The A96 is the main road from Aberdeen to Inverness, flanked by rich farmland and studded with ancient castles. Along the minor roads lie farming communities in pleasant, undulating scenery.

Kintore

About 10 miles (16km) from Aberdeen is the village of Kintore, a Royal Burgh since 1506. Its town hall, with outside stairs, was built in 1737. The church has a 16th-century tabernacle decorated with painted angels on a panel. A Pictish stone in the graveyard has both Christian and Pictish carvings—a good example of how careful those early Christians were not to offend any pagan gods that just might exist in spite of what the missionaries said. (The more prosaic explanation is that the converted Picts recycled the old stones after their conversion.)

Inverurie

Inverurie, 16 miles (25.5km) from Aberdeen, is surrounded by Pictish remains. The **Museum** (open daily except Wed and Sun: free) has an interesting permanent archaeological exhibition. It also stages three 'thematic' exhibitions each year. The **Bass** is a 60-foot-high (18.5m) motte, just outside the town, the site of a 12th-century castle. Mary,

Queen of Scots visited a castle on this site in 1562. Pictish stones in the cemetery have clear carvings on them. There is a tourist information centre in the town hall in the Market Place, open from May to September.

Brandsbutt Stone is 2 miles (3km) north of Inverurie, with clear Pictish symbols and Ogham inscriptions, dating from the 8th century. The **Harlaw Monument**, on the B9001 less than 5 miles (8km) north of Inverurie, is a red granite obelisk marking the site of a particularly bloody clan battle in 1411. The cause of this carnage was the Countess of Ross. She renounced her inheritance to become a nun, leaving two uncles to fight for it: Donald, Lord of the Isles and Buchan, son of Regent Albany. Donald was beaten, lost his claim to the title, and was forced to swear allegiance to the Crown at a time when the Lords of the Isles considered themselves to be kings. Not much further along the road, the **Loanhead Stone Circle** is a burial cairn marked by a ring of standing stones surrounding a mass of smaller ones.

Pitcaple Castle

Pitcaple Castle (open if convenient: © 04676 204) is on the A96, south of Loanhead, a 15th- to 16th-century Z-plan tower house with 19th-century additions including two round towers. It is still a family home. Mary, Queen of Scots came here in 1562 and danced on the lawn, as did her great-grandson, Charles II, in 1650. The tree under which these two monarchs danced was replaced with a red maple by Queen Mary in 1923. Also in 1650, Montrose was brought here, a prisoner, renounced by the king for whom he had fought, on his way to execution in Edinburgh.

A mile (1.5km) south of Pitcaple, the 9th-century **Maiden Stone** is thought to be one of the finest early Christian monuments. It is 10 feet (3m) high and has a Celtic cross and Pictish symbols.

Bennachie is the long, wooded ridge rising to 1733 feet (533m) to the south, with an Iron Age hill fort on **Mither Tap**, one of the peaks. From all around this part of Aberdeenshire, Bennachie dominates the skyline with its distinctively shaped top. Many claim it to be the site of the Battle of Mons Graupius, where Agricola penetrated the northeast and defeated the tribes in AD 83. Forestry Enterprise has developed signposted walks in this area for those who like to be guided.

The Picardy Stone, dating from the 7th or 8th century, is about 13 miles (21km) north-west of Inverurie on the B9002. Its Pictish symbols include a serpent, mirror and the mysterious 'spectacles' that are featured so often in those ancient carvings.

Leith Hall

Leith Hall (open every afternoon 1 May–30 Sept: adm; garden and grounds open all year: donation) is 4 miles (6.5km) west of the Picardy Stone, down an avenue. The earliest part of the house dates from 1650, a tower house with turrets and gables, with further wings added during the 18th and 19th centuries, around a central courtyard. In the exhibition room, you can see a writing case presented to Andrew Hay, the laird, by Prince Charles on the eve of Culloden, and the official pardon given to him after he had fought for the prince. Andrew Hay, known as 'The Gentle Jacobite', was a philanthropic man, 7ft 2in (2.2m) tall. The grounds include a zigzag herbaceous border, a rock garden, a pond walk with observation hide, a picnic area and a flock of Soay sheep. There are 18th-century stables and an ice house.

Eight miles (13km) north of Leith Hall, you pass through **Strath Bogie**, with **Clashindarroch Forest** to the west, cut by picturesque valleys.

Huntly

Huntly, 38 miles (61km) northwest of Aberdeen, is an 18th-century town on the plain, surrounded by hills, lapped by the rivers Deveron and Bogie.

Huntly Castle, once Strathbogie Castle (open daily: adm), is the ruin of a stately 17th-century palace in a wooded park above Deveron Water. It was the seat of the Marquesses of Huntly (the Gay Gordons), the most powerful family in this part of Scotland until the middle of the 16th century. The 12th-century fortress on the motte was owned by the Earl of Fife, a Gaelic Norman. Robert the Bruce convalesced here in 1307 after an illness. Just before the Battle of Bannockburn, the laird turned against Bruce. After the battle, his lands were forfeited and given to Sir Adam Gordon of Huntly, who had supported Bruce.

In those days the fortress was made of wood, which was gradually replaced by stone. It was finally destroyed during the Civil War of 1452, in the reign of James II. James IV was a frequent visitor, during an era when the Gordon Earls of Huntly were at the zenith of their power, and it was here that he witnessed the marriage between Catherine Gordon and Perkin Warbeck in 1496. Warbeck was a Flemish impostor, Pretender to the English throne, claiming to be Richard, Duke of York, the younger of the two 'princes in the tower'. It suited the Scottish king to encourage his claims, but Warbeck met his comeuppance in the Tower of London and was executed in 1499.

The rise and fall of the Gordons was reflected in the rise and fall of Huntly Castle, until the second Marquis of Huntly lost his head for supporting Charles I, having first been imprisoned in the castle. Don't miss the awful dungeons and the basement passage walls marked by the graffiti of the dungeon guards. The carved fireplaces and heraldic doorway are splendid.

Huntly Museum (open Tues–Sat: free), in the library in Main Square, gives a good grounding in local history, with temporary 'thematic' exhibitions throughout the year. **Glendronach Distillery** is open on weekdays for tours. **North East Falconry Centre**, at nearby Cairnie, flies eagles, owls and falcons daily (open April–Oct: free).

Dufftown

Dufftown, 10 miles (16km) west of Huntly, was founded in 1817 by James Duff, 4th Earl of Fife, to give employment after the Napoleonic Wars.

The Clock that Hanged MacPherson

The clock on the battlemented tower at the junction of the four main streets is known as 'the clock that hanged MacPherson'. MacPherson was an infamous freebooter who was condemned to death in Banff, to the north, in 1700 for robbing the rich and giving to the poor. A local petition for his reprieve was successful, but Lord Braco, the Sheriff of Banff, who loathed MacPherson, advanced the clock by an hour and hanged him before the reprieve arrived. The clock was subsequently removed from Banff and installed in this tower.

Dufftown is known as the capital of Scotland's malt whisky distilling, giving rise to an old couplet:

> *Rome was built on seven hills*
> *Dufftown stands on seven stills.*

Good barley, peat and the right sort of water are the three essential ingredients for whisky making and this area has them all. Whisky is more than just an industry in Scotland, it is part of its social history, with romantic tales of smugglers and illicit stills. The **Glenfiddich Distillery** is part of the Malt Whisky Trail (open weekdays all year and also at weekends May–mid-Oct; closed from Sat before Christmas to Sunday after New Year: free). It was founded by William Grant who bought second-hand equipment at a knock-down price in Cardhu, and produced the first bottling on Christmas Day, 1887. This is one of only two distilleries to have its own bottling plant. The audio-visual show is in six languages and you get your free dram at the end.

Dufftown Museum in the Clock Tower (open daily except Sun, May–Sept, and including Sun in July and Aug: free) has a collection of local photographs and information about Lord Mount Stephen who founded the Canadian Pacific Railway. The tourist information centre is here too.

Auchindoun Castle (plainly visible on a steep hill above the River Fiddich but unsafe and not open to the public), 2 miles (3km) southeast of Dufftown, is a massive three-storey keep, enclosed by prehistoric earthworks. It was built by Robert Cochran, who was one of the favourites of James III and was hanged by enraged barons in 1482. In 1689, a party of Jacobites gathered within these walls to hold a council of war after the death of their gallant leader, Graham of Claverhouse (Bonnie Dundee) at Killiecrankie.

Balvenie Castle

Some of the stones from Auchindoun were removed and used in the building of Balvenie Castle (open daily April–Sept: adm), a mile (1.5km) north of Dufftown, next to the Glenfiddich Distillery. Now a ruin, this was a 14th-century stronghold owned by the Comyns. Edward I was a visitor in 1304; Mary, Queen of Scots spent two nights here in 1562 while campaigning against the powerful Gordons; Montrose took refuge here in 1644; victorious Jacobites occupied the castle in 1689 after Killiecrankie, and Cumberland's troops occupied it in 1746.

Mortlach Parish Church (check opening times, ✆ 0340 20380), on the southern edge of the town, is one of the oldest places of Christian worship in Scotland, believed to have been founded in 566 by St Moluag, a contemporary of Columba. There are monsters, beasts and a horseman carved on the weathered Pictish cross in the graveyard and an earlier Pictish stone in the porch. Substantially reconstructed in 1876 and again in 1931, it still has traces of an earlier building. There is a leper squint in the north wall and the lancet windows date from the 13th century. The watchtower in the graveyard, now used as a power house, was originally used to keep watch for body-snatchers.

Speyside Cooperage Visitor Centre at Craigellachie, 4 miles (6.5km) north of Dufftown (open weekdays all year, and Sat from Easter to mid Oct), displays the cooper's craft over thousands of years and you can watch coopers at work.

A slight detour takes in three more distilleries on the Malt Whisky Trail. **Cardhu** (open weekdays all year and Sat from May to Sept: free), at Knockando, about 6 miles (9.5km) west of Craigellachie; **Tamdhu** (open weekdays, April–Oct and Sat from June to Sept: free), also at Knockando and **Glenfarclas** (open weekdays all year and Sat from June to Sept: free) at Ballindalloch, on the A95.

Ballindalloch Castle(open daily, Easter–Sept: adm), close to the distillery, is one of the few castles to be lived in continuously by its original family, the Macpherson-Grants, since 1546. The fortified 16th-century tower house is flanked by later additions down to Victorian times and some of the interior is impressive. Nice grounds, too.

The eighth distillery on the Malt Whisky Trail is **Glen Grant**, at Rothes, about 3 miles (4.5km) north of Craigellachie, (open weekdays Easter–Sept and Sat in July and August: free).

Keith

Keith is 11 miles (17.5km) northwest of Huntly, on the Isla, the hub of an area of rich farmland. The present town was developed in the late 18th and early 19th centuries but its history goes back to at least 700 when St Maelrubha of Applecross converted the inhabitants to Christianity. Scotland's post-Reformation saint St John Ogilvie was born in 1580 at Drumnakeith. He studied in Europe and returned to preach to his own people. He was hanged in 1615 for refusing to take the anti-Catholic oath of loyalty to the Crown. Beatified in 1929, he was canonized in 1976. There is a statue of him in the Roman Doric-style Catholic church. This building, partly copied from Santa Maria degli Angeli in Rome, comes as a surprise in an area that is not given to ornamentation of churches. It was built in 1830, helped by a donation from King Charles X of France, who took refuge in Scotland after he was exiled. He also gave the picture over the altar, *The Incredulity of St Thomas* by François Dubois. The stained-glass windows are by Father Ninian Sloane of Pluscarden Abbey. The imposing copper dome was added in 1915.

Keith has a Festival of Traditional Music and Song, the second weekend in June, and a major agricultural show in August.

Strathisla Distillery (open on weekdays, mid-May–mid-Sept: free) is nearby, on the Malt Whisky Trail, giving you another chance to watch the processes that produce Scotland's most popular export and to sample the result.

Fochabers

Fochabers, 8 miles (13km) northwest of Keith, on the Spey, is a good base from which to explore this area with riverside walks, excellent fishing and proximity to the Malt Whisky Trail. The village grew in the shadow of the walls of Gordon Castle, which provided employment for most of the people in the old days. It was moved to its present site in the 18th century to make room for extension of the castle. Part of the High Street is conserved and the buildings are much as they were when first built.

The Spey, with only 4 miles (6.5km) left in its race to the sea, runs slower now through shingle banks that threaten to close the mouth which has had to be dredged four times in this century, the most recent being in 1989. Salmon netting has been carried out for centuries from the spit at Tugnet, just down the river at Spey Bay, and this estuary region is rich in birds: kittiwakes, fulmars, cormorants, sandpipers swooping low over the water, curlews with their long curved beaks, tan-headed teal, black-collared ringed plovers, gannets, terns, shelduck, heron and osprey, to name but a few.

The northern section of the **Speyside Way** goes south from Spey Bay for 30 miles (48km) to Ballindalloch; from there, if you are still feeling energetic, it's only another 15 miles (24km) to Tomintoul. The walk begins at **Tugnet Ice House**, built in 1830 to store ice for packing the netted salmon and now a visitor centre with an exhibition on the salmon fishing industry, as well as information about local wildlife (open daily, June–Sept: free).

Fochabers Folk Museum in the High Street (open daily: adm) has the largest collection of horse-drawn vehicles in the north of Scotland and a mass of memorabilia from the days of service to the castle. There is a reconstructed village shop from the turn of the century, before the days of plastic wrappings and prepacked food.

Baxters Visitor Centre, a mile (1.5km) west of Fochabers, is well worth a visit (open weekdays, Jan–Dec; weekends during summer; check for tour days, © 0343 820393: free). George Baxter was a gardener at Gordon Castle 120 years ago. He opened a grocery shop in Fochabers and sold jam made by his wife, Margaret. From this simple beginning evolved a business that has been handed down through the family to the present, producing a wide range of food that can be bought all over the world. The Duke of Richmond and Gordon, Baxter's old boss, took a keen interest and personally measured out the site for the factory one Sunday on his way home from church. You can see a Victorian kitchen similar to the one where the first Mrs Baxter tried out new recipes, and the modern kitchen where they are still experimenting to create new products. There are guided tours, an audio-visual show, shops, and a restaurant. Outside there are landscaped gardens by the river.

Elgin

Elgin, 9 miles (14.5km) west of Fochabers on the banks of the River Lossie, is the administrative and commercial capital of Moray, a busy market for the prosperous farms of the region and a popular holiday centre. The ruined cathedral is one of Scotland's jewels. The town, at first sight sturdy and austerely granite, invites closer inspection. Wander through it and you will discover a number of fine old buildings, excellently proportioned with delightful embellishments, and intriguing glimpses into wynds and closes. Elgin is drenched in history and is an excellent centre for exploring the northwest corner of Grampian.

First mentioned in history books in 1190, Elgin was the northern limit of English King Edward I's progress through the country. The town was partly burned by the Wolf of Badenoch in 1390, and again in a struggle for power between the Douglases and Huntlys in 1452. James II of Scotland used Elgin as a royal residence in the 15th century and Prince Charles lodged at Thunderton House for 11 days before the Battle of Culloden.

The town's Highland Games are held in July and there is a Fiddlers' Rally in September.

Elgin Cathedral (open daily: adm) stands on grass beside the river, a soaring symphony of arches, towers and windows, fretted against the sky. It was founded in 1224 and damaged by fire in 1270. In 1390, the Wolf of Badenoch, the wild and vicious natural son of Robert II, having been excommunicated by the bishop, burned down both town and cathedral, which contained treasures and valuable documents and manuscripts, with his 'wyld, wykked Helandmen'. After many ups and downs, the cathedral was stripped of its lead in 1567, by order of the Privy Council, in order to raise funds for defence. This act of authorized sacrilege was rewarded by the sinking of the ship that carried the lead. In 1650, Cromwell's troops did their worst to what remained, tearing down a beautiful rood screen and smashing the tracery of the west window. In spite of all this, peace and sanctity cling to this mellow ruin.

Bishop's House is just northwest of the cathedral. Here you can see a wing of the Precentor's Manse, with a 16th-century coat of arms on the wall.

Elgin Museum (open Tues–Sat, June–Sept and by appointment in winter: adm) is in an Italian-style building in the High Street, and won the 1990 Scottish Museum of the Year award. There is a collection of old red sandstone, Permian and Triassic fossils. Other exhibits include Bronze Age relics and natural history displays.

Little Cross in the High Street, dating from 1733, replaced an earlier one erected in 1402. In the old days, this was the place of public punishment, with stocks and jougs.

Lady Hill, opposite the post office in the High Street, bears only scant remains of the castle which once stood here, occupied by Edward I in 1296. The column, 1839, and statue, 1855, were put up in memory of the 5th and last Duke of Gordon.

Moray Motor Museum (open daily, April–Oct: adm) is in an old converted mill in Bridge Street. The small collection of vintage cars and motorbikes includes a stately 1929 Rolls Royce Phantom I, a 1913 Douglas motorbike and a macho 1939 SS100, gleaming red.

Old Mills (open daily except Mon, May–Sept: adm), west of the town on the Lossie, is a working meal mill dating from 1793. You can watch the milling in progress and learn what it's all about in the Old Mills Visitor Centre.

Johnstons Cashmere Visitors Centre at Newmill, to the east of the town (open daily except Sun: free), has exhibitions, production demonstrations, a coffee shop and a mill shop.

The ruins of **Spynie Palace** are a couple of miles (3km) north of Elgin—there is access to a small car park from the Elgin–Lossiemouth Road. This was the castle of the Bishops of Moray in the 13th to 17th centuries. At one time the sea reached as far as the hillock on which the palace stands, with a good harbour and town. The sea then threw up a bar of sand and shingle across the mouth of the estuary, cutting off Spynie and turning the area into a loch surrounded by marshland. A canal was built by Thomas Telford in 1808, to drain the loch into the sea 5 miles (8km) north at Lossiemouth. Great floods in 1829 destroyed all the works and the loch grew again until the 1860s. The old palace saw much history. Mary, Queen of Scots stayed there in 1562 during her tour of the north, and it became a refuge for Covenanters in 1654, during Montrose's campaigns. James Ramsay MacDonald, Britain's first Labour Prime Minister, was buried in Spynie churchyard in 1937. (The church was moved to New Spynie, 4 miles (6.5km) to the west.)

Pluscarden Abbey

Pluscarden Abbey (always open: free) is signposted off the A96, about 5 miles (8km) southwest of Elgin, and is one of Grampian's jewels. Lying in a sheltered valley below a ridge of wooded hills, Pluscarden represents an act of faith that must be an inspiration to believer and non-believer alike and is spiritually uplifting. The original abbey was founded by Alexander II in 1230, for an order of white-habited monks, the Valliscaulians, whose mother house was in France. It suffered damage at the hands of Edward I of England in 1303, and far worse damage from the Wolf of Badenoch, during his revenge on the Bishop of Elgin in 1390. In 1454 it took in Benedictines from Urquhart Priory, probably for economic as well as political reasons. Just before the Reformation took off, a greedy, scheming prior, Alexander Dunbar, anticipating what was to come, managed to 'redistribute' priory funds and lands in favour of his family. He died in 1560 and by the end of that century the priory had passed into the authority of a lay commendator. The estate passed through various hands, gradually falling into disrepair and ruin.

In 1943 the Pluscarden lands were given to the Benedictine community of Prinknash Abbey, near Gloucester, a breakaway community from an Anglican order, whose proposals of doctrinal reform had caused some of its monks to rebel and become Roman Catholic. This order of converted Benedictines started rebuilding Pluscarden in 1948 and today you can see what they have achieved: a truly remarkable feat.

The choir and transepts are entire, as are the domestic buildings. The interior is a haven of timeless tranquillity, lit by a rich glow of colour from the modern stained-glass windows and overlaid by a lingering smell of incense. If you are lucky, you may hear, filtering through the walls from the Lady Chapel, the sound of the monks singing their daily office. You can go into the transept aisles, now a public chapel, and kneel at the south end to look through a wide squint into the Lady Chapel.

Monks, dressed in coarse white habits, busy about their work on the land, add a medieval touch to Pluscarden.

Coastal towns and villages beyond Elgin are mentioned in the final section of this chapter.

Where to Stay

expensive

The pick of the bunch on this route has to be **Leslie Castle** near Insch, © 0464 20869, especially if you fancy a touch of class and don't mind paying for it. This nicely restored 17th-century castle, with corner turrets and a truly ancestral feeling, will fill you with illusions of grandeur and you'll eat well. **Pittodrie House Hotel**, at Pitcaple, is a 15th-century pile overlooking farmland, furnished with antiques, tapestries and fine paintings. The food is cordon bleu and they have two squash courts, tennis court, billiards, croquet and clay pigeon shooting.

moderate

Delnashaugh Inn, Ballindalloch, © 0807 500255 is excellent value. **Rothes Glen Hotel**, Rothes, © 03403 254, is a castle-style Victorian mansion designed by William Smith who designed Balmoral, in 40 acres of attractive parkland grazed by Highland cattle. The food is good, especially the local beef and fish. **Thainstone House Hotel** in Inverurie, © 0467 21643, is a country house surrounded by meadows and woods, with a comfortable, easy-going atmosphere. There are only eight bedrooms and the food isn't at all bad.

Gordon Arms Hotel, in Fochabers High Street, © 0343 820508/9, is an old coaching inn on the A96 to Inverness, full of old-world atmosphere and an ideal stopping-off place for excellent food. **Mansion House Hotel**, The Haugh, Elgin, © 0343 48811, is a comfortable mock castle by the river where you will eat and sleep well and not feel cheated.

inexpensive

The Old Manse at Bridge of Marnoch, near Huntly, © 04665 873, is an attractive Georgian country guest-house in peaceful surroundings in the Deveron Valley. **Ugie House Hotel** in Church Road, Keith, © 05422 7671, is an unpretentious and dependable establishment.

The northeast shoulder of Grampian, well clear of the dramatic hills and spectacular glens further west, is mainly flattish farmland, studded with clumps of trees and a maze of burns and small rivers.

Pitmedden Garden and Museum

Pitmedden is best reached along the rural lanes to the east of the A947, 14 miles (22km) north of Aberdeen off the B999. The garden (open all year, daily: adm) was created by Sir Alexander Seton who inherited Pitmedden in 1667: it was restored by the National Trust for Scotland in 1952. July and August are the best months to see this re-creation of a formal 17th-century garden, split-level with an upper garden and terraces overlooking the Great Garden. Sir Alexander modelled three out of the four symmetrical parterres, bordered by box hedges, on floral designs first used in Holyrood in 1647, in honour of Charles I. The fourth depicts the Seton coat of arms. Pillared gates lead into the Great Garden, down a graceful twin stairway, with two ogee-roofed pavilions. There is a fountain in each garden and no less than 27 sundials, none of which is more than ten minutes off true time. Whether you admire formal gardens or not, you cannot fail to appreciate the splendour of this one. You can see Sir Alexander's bathhouse, in one of the two-storied pavilions, and a key to all the flowers in the garden. (The two 'thunder houses' are rare in Scotland.) In the other pavilion is an exhibition on the evolution of formal gardens.

The Museum of Farming Life (open daily 1 May–30 Sept: adm) has a collection of agricultural and domestic implements. You can walk around the 100-acre estate, through attractive woods and farmland, and there is the usual adventure playground, picnic area and visitor centre.

Tolquhon Castle

Tolquhon Castle (open daily: adm) is a roofless ruin, a mile (1.5km) northwest of Pitmedden. Once the seat of the Forbes family, a 16th-century quadrangular mansion was built on to an early 15th-century rectangular tower. The forbidding fortress exterior hides a domestic residential inner court. You can still see the kitchen, cellars and stairways, with the hall and laird's room (which has a private stair to the kitchen) on the first floor. An inscription on the gatehouse is an endearing trumpet blast from the laird who did so much to enlarge the original castle: 'Al this wark, excep the auld tour, was begun be William Forbes 15 Aprile 1584, and endit be him 20 October 1589'.

William Forbes' master mason was Thomas Leiper, of a renowned family of masons, and it was he who designed the elaborate Gothic tomb of William and his wife, Elizabeth Gordon, in the church at **Tarves** a couple of miles north. It is rich in Renaissance detail, with statuettes of the couple standing on either side.

Haddo House

Haddo (open daily 1 May–30 Sept: adm) is less than 4 miles (6.5km) north of Tarves. This fine Georgian mansion was built in 1732 by William Adam on the site of a former house, House of Kellie, home of the Gordons of Haddo, Lords of Aberdeen, for over 500 years and burned down by Covenanters. The present house stands in a park surrounded by lovely gardens, showing all William Adam's mastery of symmetrical design. It contains antique furniture, pictures and treasures in its elegant rooms. The stained-glass window in the chapel is by Burne-Jones.

Haddo has developed its own choral society, with a theatre, beside the house. This is one of Scotland's leading musical bodies with productions of opera and concerts starring international artists. (If you are interested, write to the Choral Secretary, Haddo House, Grampian. Seating is limited.)

Fyvie Castle

Fyvie is about 6 miles (9.5km) northwest of Haddo, and is off the A947 (open daily 1 May–30 Sept: adm). Dating from the 13th century, the castle has been described as the 'crowning glory of Scottish baronial architecture'. It stands on a mound above a bend in the River Ythan, approached up a long drive that skirts the lake among trees and rhododendrons. In the days when kings moved from house to house, William the Lion used to visit Fyvie. It passed through many hands over the centuries and its five towers represent its five dynasties of lairds: Prestons, Meldrums, Setons, Gordons and Leiths. The National Trust for Scotland acquired it from Sir Andrew Forbes-Leith in 1984. The splendid structure incorporates substantial remains of the medieval Fyvie. The square and round towers soar to a mass of corner turrets, conical roofs and corbels and inside there is an impressive wheel stair.

Alexander Forbes-Leith bought the estate in 1889. He used the fortune that he had made in the American steel industry to restore the castle, sweeping away much of the ugly additions that had been added over the years, and filling it with treasures that can still be seen there today. The paintings include some of the finest portraits you could ever hope to see, by Gainsborough, Romney, Opie, and Raeburn. The *pièce de résistance*, perhaps, is the 18th-century portrait of Colonel William Gordon, by Pompeo Batoni—a deliciously romantic study of a patrician colonel, standing in rich silken tartan, gazing somewhat disdainfully at a statue of Roma. Fyvie is a stately home not to be missed.

Gight Castle is a scant ivy-clad ruin to the east of Fyvie, by the River Ythan, reached by a footpath off the B9005. There isn't a signpost, but look for a turning by the scrapyard near Cottown. It dates from about 1560 and is associated with a particularly wild branch of the Gordon family, infamous for murders and suspiciously sudden deaths. Watch out for the Hagberry Pot, close to the castle—a bottomless pit reputed to be a direct route to Hell. The 13th Laird of Gight was Catherine Gordon who married 'Mad' Jack Byron. Their son was George Gordon, Lord Byron. Mad Jack, alas, was a compulsive gambler and gambled the castle away long before the birth of his talented son.

Towie Barclay Castle (open by appointment, © 088 84 347), 3 miles (4.5km) north of Fyvie, is an ancient stronghold of the Barclays dating from 1136, recently restored and the winner of a number of major European restoration awards. There is a formal walled garden in the grounds.

Turriff

Turriff, 8 miles (13km) north of Fyvie on the A947, stands at the confluence of the River Deveron and the Water of Idoch. It is a red sandstone town, first mentioned in the 6th century when the Gaelic poet Ossian described it as the capital of a Pictish prince, Lathmon. It is believed that St Congan founded a monastery near the village in the 8th century. The old church, now a ruin, at the end of Castle Street existed in the 11th century, and in 1179 Knights Templar—soldier monks of the crusades—were given land in Turriff to found their second Scottish base. The 20-foot (6m) mercat cross in Castle Street is 16th-century. The town is still remembered for 'The Trot of Turriff', when a party of Royalists defeated the Covenanters in the first skirmish of the Civil War, in 1639.

More recently and within living memory of a few, Turriff hit the national news in 1913, when a local farmer, Robert Paterson, refused to join Lloyd George's National Health Insurance Scheme. One of his cows was impounded and the sheriff officers tried to sell it in the town, to cover the National Insurance payments Paterson owed. There was a riot; the officers were chased out of town. Attempts to sell the cow in Aberdeen were also unsuccessful and finally Paterson's neighbours bought it and gave it back to him. The 'Turra Coo' was front-page news. The two-day annual Turriff Show in August is one of the largest agricultural events in Europe, attracting over 50,000 people each year.

Delgatie Castle (open by appointment only, © 0888 63479: adm) is 2 miles (3km) east of Turriff. This L-plan tower house, home of the Clan Hay, dates back to the 12th century, with later additions. Inside there are pictures, weapons, the widest turnpike stair in Scotland and 16th-century painted ceilings which are believed to caricature people who lived in the castle at the time. Mary, Queen of Scots stayed here for three days in 1562 and there is a portrait of her in the room she used. Part of the castle and stables have been converted into self-catering holiday flats.

Eden Castle, 7 miles (11km) north of Turriff, not open to the public but visible from the outside, is a ruin with a grisly legend attached to its 17th-century stones. The wife of a tenant on the estate asked the laird to control her wild son. He did so, by drowning the boy in the river, and the mother's subsequent curse caused the castle to fall down. All that remains now is the tower, inhabited by animals from a nearby farm.

Where to Stay

Fife Arms Hotel, Turrif, © 0888 63468, is very reasonable and comfortable. Otherwise, the hotels mentioned in the previous section, Aberdeen to Elgin, and those in the following, coastal route section, are the best ones to go for, unless you want to sample one of the self-catering flats mentioned under Delgatie Castle, above. The prices vary: © 0888 63479 for details.

Going north from Aberdeen on the coast road, you see another face of Grampian: miles of sandy beaches interspersed with rock cliffs, bordering an endless stretch of ocean to the east and north. Fishing towns and villages are strung out along the way, each with its legends of seafaring adventures and smuggling. *The Fringe of Gold* by Charles Maclean is a delightful collection of anecdotes and illustrations about these places. Inland lie prosperous farms and good fishing rivers. Golfers will find a number of courses, both coastal and inland.

Leaving Aberdeen on the A92, you go through **Bridge of Don**, past the barracks that were once the home of the Gordon Highlanders. Long, dune-backed beaches fringed by brambly golf courses, and an army firing range, stretch north for 6 miles (9.5km) to **Balmedie Country Park**. Further up, **Ythan Estuary** cuts into the dunes at **Newburgh** and from here to **Collieston** a vast nature reserve comprises heath, dunes, pasture and cliff: a haven for both ornithologist and botanist. Collieston is a picturesque village with a harbour, very similar to the villages in the East Neuk of Fife. T. E. Lawrence wrote much of *The Seven Pillars of Wisdom* here.

The sandy sweep of **Cruden Bay**, about 5 miles (8km) north of Collieston, is where the pipeline comes in from the Forties Oil Field, over 100 miles (160km) out in the North Sea. The name Cruden comes from *croju-dane*, meaning slaughter of the Danes. This refers to a bloody battle between Malcolm II and the Danes in 1012, led by Canute, later King of England. The Scots won and the Danes withdrew, undertaking to leave Scotland alone. Canute then turned his attention to England which he conquered four years later. Once a tiny fishing hamlet, Cruden Bay was to be a luxurious holiday resort at the end of the last century. The Great North of Scotland Railway built a huge 55-bedroom hotel with tennis courts, croquet lawns, bowling greens and a championship golf course. It was too isolated, however. The project failed and the hotel was demolished after the war.

Whinnyfold, the cliff-top village at the south of Cruden Bay, once had 24 fishing boats, despite not having a harbour. The boats were drawn up on the shingle beach and the fish laid out on the stones to dry. The jagged rocks off here—the Scours of Cruden—have claimed many wrecks. It is said that at a certain time of year the bodies of those who have perished during the previous 12 months come out of the sea to join their spirits in heaven or hell. (This legend inspired Bram Stoker to write *Mystery of the Sea*. It is said that Stoker was inspired by Slains when he wrote *Dracula* and used Cruden Bay for the setting when the vampire comes ashore to vampirize the unfortunate Lucy. He used to holiday in the area and finally retired to Whinnyfold.)

New Slains Castle

Walk north from Cruden Bay, a couple of miles (3km) along the cliffs, till you get to New Slains Castle (always accessible: free). This extensive ruin stands high above the sea, which rages at its feet in rough weather. It was built by the 9th Earl of Errol in 1598 to replace Old Slains Castle, further south, of which only a fragment remains. Old Slains was destroyed by James VI to punish Erroll for taking part in a revolt of Catholic nobles. 'New' Slains is a splendid, awe-inspiring ruin and its extremely dangerous situation makes it unsuitable for children to visit unaccompanied. It is amusing to walk among its massive, rather gloomy walls and recall Johnson and Boswell's visit in 1773. Johnson was most impressed by its position, writing: 'when the winds beat with violence it must enjoy all the terrifick grandeur of the the tempestuous ocean . . . the walls of one of the towers seem only a continuation of the perpendicular rock, the foot of which is beaten by the waves.' Boswell, always fastidious about his comforts, wrote: 'I had a most elegant room: but there was a fire in it which blazed; and the sea, to which my windows looked, roared; and the pillows were made of the feathers of some sea-fowl which had to me a disagreeable smell: so that by all these causes I was kept awake a good while.' Slains reached its zenith at the turn of the century when the 19th Earl, a philanthropic man, created what has been described as a mini welfare state in the district and played host to many writers, actors, musicians and singers of the day. As a result of crippling death duties, taxation and the 19th Earl's generosity, his heir was forced to sell the castle to an absentee landlord who allowed it to fall into disrepair.

Johnson and Boswell also visited the **Bullers of Buchan**, just north of Slains Castle. Here the sea has eroded a sheer 200-foot (60m) rock chasm, into which the water pounds through a natural archway. Bullers means 'boilers'. Johnson wrote of this: 'which no man can see with indifference, who has either sense of danger or delight in rarity'. Much to the horror of Boswell, Johnson insisted on exploring the cavern by boat, writing later: 'If I had any malice against a walking spirit, instead of laying him in the Red Sea, I would condemn him to reside in the Buller of Buchan'.

Buchan means 'the land at the bend in the ocean' and was the name of Scotland's most northeasterly corner where the North Sea meets the Moray Firth. **Boddam**, about 3 miles (4.5km) north of Slains, is an old fishing village on Buchan Ness, the most easterly point on the mainland. There is a pleasant 19th-century character in the older parts of Boddam, though it is hard to believe they once boasted 85 herring drifters and 13 curing yards. All the fishing boats now operate out of Peterhead.

Peterhead

Peterhead, originally called Peterugie, is a couple of miles (3km) north near the mouth of the River Ugie and is known locally as the 'Blue Toon'. It is the most easterly town on the Scottish mainland. The first harbour was built in 1593 and the town has always been linked with fishing, from early times when the first fishermen used lines to catch cod and ling. Whaling began in 1788 and Peterhead quickly became the leading whaling port in Britain, until herring fishing took over in 1818. By 1836, 260 boats fished out of Peterhead, rising to over 400 by the middle of the century. During this time extensive, deep-water harbours were built, so that when fishing boats grew larger and could no longer use the smaller ports, Peterhead flourished. Although herring fishing is dying fast, the town continues to prosper, with white fish as its main catch. It is now the largest white fish port in Europe with over 400 highly sophisticated boats. It was also ideally placed to cope with the influx of sea traffic during the oil-boom of the 1970s.

Peterhead was a popular spa town in the 17th, 18th and 19th centuries and the remains of a mineral well and some baths can still be seen by the lifeboat shed. Burns was one of the many people who took the waters here. Surrounded by sandy beaches, golf courses and dunes, it is the largest town in the northeast, after Aberdeen. Many of the houses are built of local pink granite.

The Harbour with its three main basins is an energetic place, with boats coming and going; vessels being refitted, repaired, repainted; chandlers and all the clutter of a seafaring port. The **Fishmarket**, as in Aberdeen, is a place to visit early in the morning when the boats are landing their catches in up to 14,000 boxes. Business starts at 8.30am except on Sundays, but you are best to go well before this to get the full flavour of this salty industry. Catches include whiting, haddock, sole, cod, mackerel and herring.

Town House, built in 1788, has a spire 125 feet (38.5m) high. The statue in front is of Field Marshal Keith, born in Peterhead, who became Frederick the Great of Prussia's most trusted general, killed in battle in 1758.

The Arbuthnot Museum and Art Gallery (open daily except on Sundays: free) is in Arbuthnot House. Displays include fishing, whaling and local history.

Deer Abbey (officially open Thurs–Sun, but the caretaker is usually there and will let people in) is 9 miles (14.5km) west of Peterhead. This insubstantial ruin was a Cistercian monastery founded in 1219 by Comyn, Earl of Buchan. It thrived until the late 16th century and you can see the ground plan quite clearly, though most of the masonry was taken away for other uses.

Aden Heritage Centre (pronounced 'Adden') is a mile (1.5km) west of Mintlaw, near Deer Abbey (open daily May–Sept and at weekends in April and Oct: adm). The semi-circular farm steading, recently restored from almost total dereliction, was inspired by the French wife of a former laird. Reconstructions show past and present farming life in this agricultural area—you can almost smell the oatcakes, cooking on the griddle. Audio-visual shows and exhibitions give further information on the life of estate staff at the turn of the century. There is a shop, a café, a picnic area and separate camp site. Aden stands in a country park around the consolidated ruin of the old mansion, with nature trails and all the trimmings, open all year.

Back to the coast, the villages along this northeast corner are unspoiled and soaked in seafaring history, their deserted sands a hermit's dream. Many of the original fisher cottages remain, sturdy and low, their gable-ends to the sea, to take the full force of winter storms. In some of the villages, the old tradition of painting the houses with oil paint to protect them from the weather has become a competitive attempt to produce the most striking colour.

Rattray is a wild, unfrequented area south of Loch of Strathbeg, about 6 miles (6.5km) north of Peterhead. Once a thriving fishing port and Royal Burgh, its records go back to the 12th century, to the days when the loch was open to the sea. In 1720, a great storm caused the dunes to shift, cutting off the loch and silting up the harbour. Today, all that remains is a ruined chapel, said to have been built in the 13th century in memory of the son of the Earl of Buchan who drowned in a well there, and the remains of a Comyn fortress in the process of excavation by Aberdeen University.

You will find no trace today of **Cox Haven,** or Cockshafen, a hamlet that existed in the 18th century round the Strathbeg Burn, somewhere north of Rattray. Thought to have been refugees from religious persecution in Holland, the people are believed to have held curious ritualistic ceremonies connected with 'fresh water' dolphins that were stranded in Loch of Strathbeg during the storm that cut it off from the sea. The community was completely wiped out during a cholera epidemic in the 19th century.

Loch of Strathbeg Nature Reserve covers 2300 acres including the loch, with over 180 different birds recorded, including such rarities as the Caspian tern with its black crown and heavy orange-red bill, the pied-billed grebe from North America—such a rare visitor to Scotland that only five have been seen since 1963—and the red-footed falcon with bright red patches round its eyes as well as its legs. There are two hides and entry to the reserve is by written permission only; write to The Warden, Loch of Strathbeg Nature Reserve, Crimonmogate, Fraserburgh.

Crimond, just west of the loch on the main road, has two claims to fame. Its clock shows 61 minutes to the hour—a slip of the clockmaker's hand—and the Crimond version of the 23rd Psalm was composed by Jessie Seymour Irvine, daughter of the local manse.

On the southern slopes of **Mormond**, the hill to the west of the main road and the highest point in this area, at 768 feet (236m), the glittering white quartzite horse and stag were cut out of the hill in the 18th century by a Captain Fraser, possibly as memorials. Fraser built the now ruined hunting lodge above the horse.

Cairnbulg and Inverallochy, one either side of the B9107 about 3 miles (4.5km) north of Loch of Strathbeg, are among the oldest coastal settlements in the area with their original fisher cottages. One of these, known as 'Maggie's Hoosie', was to be restored and fitted out to show life in a 19th-century fishing community but the Community Council are now debating whether this plan is feasible.

Fraserburgh

Across Fraserburgh Bay from Cairnbulg Point, Fraserburgh stands on the shoulder of Grampian at Kinnaird Head, a great slate rock thrusting into the North Sea and the Moray Firth. It is not a beautiful town but an unmistakable tang of the sea lurks in its bones, giving it great character, and its 3 miles (4.5km) of dune-backed beach has won international awards for cleanliness. Known locally as the Broch—Scots word for burgh—the town began as a village called Faithlie. The Frasers bought the lands of Faithlie in 1504 and began developing the town. The first harbour was built in 1546 and in the 1570s Sir Alexander Fraser built a castle on Kinnaird Head. At the peak of the herring boom, during the last 30 years of the 19th century, more than 1000 drifters would land their fish during the season which ran from July to September. Today the town is a major white fish port and the harbour is an increasingly busy commercial port.

Kinnaird Head Lighthouse is the oldest in Scotland and the original was built on to the castle in 1787. Admission by appointment: © 0346 28175. **The Wine Tower**, overlooking the cove beside the lighthouse, is thought to have originally been a chapel dating from the 16th century and then perhaps a watch tower. It is a strange building with three floors which have no connecting stairs. Six carved pendants attached to the arched room have been acclaimed as the finest examples of late 16th-century three-dimensional heraldry in Scotland. Access is by arrangement with the Tourist Board.

The **Mercat Cross** in Saltoun Square is dated 1736 but thought to have been carved around 1603, as it is the only one in Scotland to show the royal arms of both the old Kingdom of Scotland and the new United Kingdom. The carved **Moses Stone** inside the South Church, dated 1613, is all that remains of the University of Fraserburgh, a short-lived establishment that attracted many students for a brief time when there was a cholera epidemic in Aberdeen.

Rosehearty about 4 miles (6.5km) west of Fraserburgh, is one of the oldest ports in Scotland. A party of Danes is said to have been shipwrecked here early in the 14th century. They were absorbed by the crofting community whom they taught to fish, an industry that was to swell to vast proportions along this coast. In the mid-19th century, Rosehearty rivalled Fraserburgh as a fishing port but when the herring fishing declined, Fraserburgh's railway link and larger harbour drew the new steam drifters and Rosehearty's industry dwindled.

Pitsligo Castle (always accessible: free), half a mile (1km) to the south, was built by the Frasers in 1424 and is now a large and impressive ruin with 9-foot (3m) thick walls. Originally the square keep had three rooms, one on top of the other: a vaulted kitchen, a vaulted banqueting hall and at the top, a sleeping apartment with 24 beds. It was extended into a courtyard castle in the 1570s.

The last laird was Alexander Forbes, 4th and last Lord Pitsligo, a fervent Jacobite who was forced into hiding when his lands were forfeited after Culloden in 1746. He dressed in rags and hid in caves or in the houses of his tenants for 46 years until he died at the age of 84. He is remembered for his generosity to the poor. The castle was bought by one of his descendants, an American multi-millionaire, Malcolm Forbes, who is said to have plans for turning it into a heritage centre.

New Aberdour, a mile (1.5km) inland from Aberdour Bay, west of Rosehearty, was built in 1798 to succeed an earlier village on the bay. Saints Columba and Drostan are said to have landed here around AD 597 and founded a Celtic monastery at **Old Deer**, some 10 miles (16km) southeast as the crow flies. *The Book of Deer* came from here—one of the most precious literary relics of the Celtic church—a 9th-century Latin manuscript of parts of the New Testament, with Gaelic notes in the margin. It is now in the Fitzwilliam Library in Cambridge.) Ruined **Old Aberdour Church** stands above the Dour Burn on the road down to the bay. It was founded by the two saints and part of it is Norman. The old font is said to have held the miracle-working bones of St Drostan and the oldest readable gravestone is dated 1440.

The broad sweep of Aberdour Bay is popular with holidaymakers, with rock pools and caves. At low tide you can get away from the crowds by walking round the headlands to more deserted stretches of clean sand. Everyone has heard of Grace Darling, but not so many of Jane Whyte whose memorial can be seen on the ruin of a woollen mill, where she lived, on the bay. In 1884, this brave lass saved the lives of 15 men, shipwrecked when their steamer ran aground during a storm. She struggled through raging seas to carry a line out to the ship along which the seamen could escape.

Dundarag Castle is a ruin on the cliffs above Aberdour Bay to the northeast. Dun Dearg—Red Fort—was probably Pictish before it was turned into a monastery by St Drostan. It later became a Comyn stronghold and was destroyed by Robert the Bruce in 1308. Quickly refortified, it was as quickly re-demolished, this time in the 16th century by the English. It is now privately owned and can be visited with permission from the owner who lives in the gatehouse.

Rocky **Ceard's Cove**, west of Aberdour Bay, has a hermit's cave, where an anti-social retired sailor lived in the 1920s and 1930s.

Pennan, on the western side of Aberdour Bay, is a picturesque village on a ledge below high red sandstone cliffs with a pebbly beach running down to the sea. You have to be practically on top of the village before you see it. If it seems familiar to filmgoers, it was one of the settings for *Local Hero*, including the public telephone box from which the central character made his reports to his American boss. (Other settings were at Arisaig and Morar.) The smuggling of liquor and silk ran a close second to fishing as the main industry here, with lots of secret coves and caves in which to evade the exciseman.

Bronze Age **Fort Fiddes**, on a promontory above sandy **Cullykhan Bay**, west of Pennan, is said to be the earliest industrial site in Europe. Beads from the Rhine region are among the artefacts excavated from the ruins by archaeologists, suggesting that the inhabitants traded with the Continent as far back as 700 BC. It's an impressive site, overlooking the sheer face of Lion Head and the deep gash in the cliff called Hell's Lum (chimney).

Troup Head is a massive red sandstone headland beyond the bay, separating Pennan from **Crovie**, which is reached either by a narrow footpath along the bottom of the cliff or by a steep, zigzag road with a 1 in 5 gradient. It clings to the foot of the cliffs, its cottages with one gable-end practically in the sea and the other tucked into the cliff. There is only a narrow footpath between the cottages and the sea. This tiny village once had nearly 100 fishermen and over 60 boats. A tremendous gale in 1953 drove many of the villagers to seek a more sheltered home and Crovie was temporarily deserted.

Gardenstown, a mile (1.5km) to the west, is larger, built on the cliff that rises from Gamrie Bay in a series of narrow terraces. The road through the village descends steeply in a series of hair-raising bends dropping from roof level behind a house to run level with the door in front. The original Seatown is at the bottom with narrow footpaths and huddled, whitewashed cottages. This lower bit, severely threatened by the gale that depopulated Crovie, was saved by the newly built seawall.

There were no inland villages in Buchan before the 18th century. Between 1750 and 1850 local landowners built a succession of 'planned' villages, to house and employ displaced tenants during a period of 'enclosures' for estate improvement. These little inland villages have down-to-earth names: Auchnagatt, Longside, Maud, Mintlaw, Stuartfield, Cuminestown, Fetterangus, New Blyth, New Leeds, New Pitsligo, Strichen. Dotted over the hinterland, each of them retains a strong community spirit and many of the traditional trades continue to flourish.

Central Buchan Tourism Group publish a leaflet 'Walks Roon Aboot Buchan', giving 33 walks that take in places of interest on the way.

Macduff

Macduff is a fishing town about 6 miles (9.5km) west of Gardenstown, at the foot of the Hill of Doune beside the Deveron estuary. It developed as a spa when **The Well of Tarlair**, a mineral spring just east of the town, was found in 1770 to have healing properties. Health fanatics used to flock to drink the waters until the well dried up. (It was blown up by a mine in the last war and is now a derelict swimming-pool.) Macduff stands around a four-basin harbour, with a thriving fish market and a customs house. Next to the Doune Church there is an anchor, 13 feet (4m) long, weighing more than 3 tonnes. It is believed to be from an 18th-century sailing ship and was dragged up in a fishing net. It was placed here by the Town Cross to symbolize the town's long association with the sea. The Harbour Master organises tours of the harbour on Wednesday afternoons and Friday mornings in July and August. If you climb the hill to the 70-foot (21m) high octagonal War Memorial Tower, you get splendid views of the rugged coastline.

Banff

Banff, less than 2 miles (3km) west of Macduff, is an old county town looking across the Deveron Estuary and Banff Bay. From the 16th to the 18th century, the landed gentry built themselves elegant town houses in Banff, to retreat to during the winter months, when their castles became too cold and draughty. The town's history goes back to 1120 when it was one of the Hanseatic trading towns sending ships as far afield as the Mediterranean and the Baltic, carrying hides, wool, sheepskin and salted salmon. Smuggling was rife. Banff was an important herring fishing port, with 90 boats and an annual export of 30,000 barrels of herring, until the harbour silted up after a storm and caused the Deveron to change course. The fleet then moved across the bay to Macduff.

Duff House, beside the golf course, is due to reopen in 1995 after extensive renovation. The Duff family, later Earls of Fife, made a considerable fortune buying up land from impoverished lairds just before the Union in 1707. The house is among the finest works of Georgian Baroque architecture in Britain and could accurately be described as unique. Its original design included flanking pavilions, which were never built, hence its rather tall stark appearance. In its time, it has been a hotel, a hospital and a prisoner of war camp. It can be viewed from the outside, until it reopens, and you can walk in the park.

Banff Castle, now a municipal building, was designed by William Adam, built on the site of a medieval fortress of which the moat remains.

Banff Museum (open daily except Thurs, June–Sept: free) has a collection of armour, costumes, burial urns, silver and local natural history.

Plaques have been put up on many of Banff's finest old buildings and you can get a *Royal and Ancient Banff* booklet from the tourist information centre, giving details of a town walk. They also do a 'Walkman Tour of Banff', on tape. Every July there is a yacht race to or from (alternate years) Stavanger in Norway. Banff Golf Week is in September.

A 2-mile (3km) walk south along the river from Duff House takes you to **Bridge of Alvah**, a single-arched bridge built high across a gorge of the Deveron: not for vertigo sufferers.

Whitehills, just west of Banff, is the smallest village to retain its own fishing fleet and daily fishmarket. It is another place where the 19th-century cottages, built gable-end to the sea for protection from storms, are unchanged. In the *New Statistical Account of 1845*, the Rev A. Anderson wrote of a prosperous fishing village whose villagers were 'cleanly in their habits', so that 'fish cured by them has a superior reputation'. He also noted that the women of Whitehills were dominant over the men, claimed the entire proceeds of the white fish market, and were of a 'superior comeliness'.

Whitehills is built round **Knock Head**, said to be where grey rats first came ashore in Scotland from a wreck. There is a sandy beach to the east, at Boyndie Bay. **The Red Well**, near the shore past the caravan park, is a beehive-shaped house built by the Romans to protect a spring with a high iron content. At the spring and autumn equinox, the first rays of the sun, rising over Troup Head 10 miles (16km) away, illuminate the interior of the well while the surrounding area is still in complete darkness. It is thought the well must have been some sort of calendar.

Boyne Castle is a ruin in a wooded valley above the Burn of Boyne, not far to the west. It was built by the Ogilvy family in 1580 and in those days was a great complex with four corner towers, four storeys high. The Ogilvys lost their estate after Culloden and the castle eventually fell into ruin.

Portsoy is a fishing town, less than five miles (8km) west of Whitehills, built round a 17th-century harbour. Many of the 17th- and 18th-century buildings were restored in the 1960s, and a large part of the town is preserved as a conservation area. Among the buildings to look out for are **The Old Star Inn** dating from 1727, and **Soy House**, possibly built in 1690 and the oldest house in the town. Green and pink Portsoy marble was cut from a seam of serpentine which runs across the hills west of the harbour, and provided two chimney pieces for Louis XIV's palace at Versailles. The **Portsoy Marble Workshop and Pottery** (open daily except Sun: free) continues to make things out of the local marble and sell small samples in the form of paperweights and knick-knacks.

Fordyce, 3 miles (4.5km) southwest of Portsoy, nestles under Durn Hill. This cluster of cottages, among narrow streets, with a small late 16th-century tower and quaint church, has won many conservation awards.

Sandend, a couple of miles (3km) north on the coast, is a 19th-century fishing village much painted by artists and said to have the smallest harbour in Scotland. It stands on the western arm of Sandend Bay, one of the most popular beaches in the area.

Findlater Castle is a spectacular three-storey ruin built into a rock face beyond Sandend, its windows overlooking a sheer drop of 50 feet (15m) to the sea. Built as a fortress by the Ogilvys in 1455, it was unsuccessfully besieged by Mary, Queen of Scots when she was trying to subdue the powerful Gordons in 1562. Although easy to get to, the castle is highly dangerous and children should be tethered.

Cullen, about 3 miles (4.5km) further west, is tucked in under a steep hill overlooking Cullen Bay—a sweep of white sand on which are curious red sandstone rocks called the 'Three Kings of Cullen'. The small harbour, once busy with herring boats, is now mainly used for pleasure craft. One of the things you notice here is the series of railway viaducts which divide the sea town from the upper town. They were built in 1886 because the Countess of Seafield refused to allow the railway line to cross the grounds of Cullen House. The village specialized in smoked haddock and the local delicacy, 'Cullen Skink', is a fish stew based on smoked haddock. George Macdonald, a 19th-century Congregationalist minister who was rejected by his congregation and had to support his family of 11 by writing, set two of his novels in Cullen, *Malcolm* and *The Marquis of Lossie*. He is better known, however, for being the author of *The Princess and the Goblin*.

Portknockie, 3 miles (4.5km) west of Cullen, had to be built on the clifftop because there was no room between the water and the foot of the cliff, and has wonderful views across the firth to the hills of Sutherland and Caithness. Its harbour is the only one in the area that is accessible at lowest tides. An archaeological dig revealed the remains of an Iron Age fort on the promontory.

Findochty, a couple of miles (3km) further west, is a striking example of villages whose houses are painted in brightly coloured oil paints, vying with each other for effect. The old smugglers' route to Buckie ran along the edge of the Strathlene Golf Course and beach. In the old days, the pack ponies of the nightriders, with their hoofs muffled, would not have had the footbridges and steps.

Buckie

Buckie is another 2 miles (3km) on, taking the A942 round the coast, overlooking **Spey Bay**. This long town is an important fishing base with all the attendant maritime establishments: chandlers, boat builders, ice works, fish market and the largest scampi-processing factory in Scotland. It's a solid, unpretentious town with the fisher houses being typical of the area, some are restored, with external stone steps going up to what used to be the net loft on the upper floor.

Buckie Drifter, to be opened some time in 1994, will be a 'hands-on' experience of the fishing industry. The mouth of the River Spey is about 3 miles (4.5km) to the west. A footbridge crosses the river on the old railway viaduct and you can walk an invigorating 8 miles (13km) along the beach to Lossiemouth. Spey Bay is also the beginning—or end—of the Speyside Way, which goes south to Ballindalloch and Tomintoul, via Tugnet.

Lossiemouth

Lossiemouth is a popular resort with a pretty harbour and two good beaches. It is also a busy fishing port. It developed as the port for Elgin, 5 miles (8km) to the south, after sand and shingle silted up the previous port at Spynie. Ramsay MacDonald, Britain's first Labour Prime Minister, was born here in 1866 and his house is marked with a plaque. There is a reconstruction of his study in the **Lossiemouth Fisheries and Community Museum** (open daily except Sun, May–Sept: free), as well as exhibits relating to the fishing industry of the area.

This stretch of windswept coast has great sweeps of sand, rich in wildfowl. The peace is frequently shattered by low flying planes from RAF Lossiemouth.

Burghead

At Burghead, 7 miles (11km) west of Lossiemouth, there are traces of both Iron Age and Norse forts. In the Iron Age fort you can go down steps to what is called the 'Roman Well', probably an early Christian baptistry, fed by a natural spring. In common with many communities, Burghead re-enacts ancient ceremonies that were performed to scare away evil spirits. In a ceremony called 'Burning the Clavie', a lighted tar barrel is carried through the streets every 11 January—the old-style New Year's Eve—unless it falls on a Sunday when the ceremony takes place a day earlier.

Findhorn Bay

Findhorn is a village, 7 miles (11km) on along the coast, on the eastern arm of Findhorn Bay, a large expanse of tidal flats which dry out at low tide. If the name is familiar it may be because of the local sailing club's challenge for the America's Cup in 1991.

Findhorn Heritage Centre is in two salmon fishery huts by the Culbin Sands Hotel. One hut is a reconstructed salmon fisher's bothy and the other traces Findhorn's history.

In the huge caravan park, there is the Findhorn Foundation, an international community of some 200 members, founded in 1962, as a centre for 'spiritual and holistic education'. The inhabitants stroll about, smiling politely and somewhat vacantly, and you will need determination to get through their apparent unwillingness to communicate with strangers.

In the village of **Kinloss**, on the southern edge of Findhorn Bay, the small overgrown ruin of Kinloss Abbey was once an important Cistercian centre. It was founded by David I who was led there by a dove after he had lost his way in the forest.

Much of this coastline has changed dramatically over the years, as a result of the storms that batter it. **The Culbin Sands**, stretching away to the west of Findhorn Bay, were built up over the years by wind-blown sand until 1694, when a mighty storm finished the job, engulfing all the farmland and buildings in its path. The sands now cover 3600 acres of dunes and marram grass.

Forres

Forres, a scant 3 miles (4.5km) southwest of Kinloss, has a long history going back to before the mythical day when Shakespeare's Macbeth and Banquo met the witches on the blasted heath, on their way to the town to attend the court of King Duncan. The location of the heath is fairly flexible, including Macbeth's Hillock, 5 miles (8km) west, and Knock of Alves, 8 miles (13km) east. The town preserves its medieval layout with the main street widening to form the market place, linked to parallel streets by a series of narrow lanes. Forres has well-kept parks, especially Grant Park, at the foot of Cluny Hill, which is a riot of colour in summer, with amazing floral sculptures. The town won a certificate of commendation in the European 'Entente Florale', in 1990. **Nelson Tower**, on top of the hill, is a landmark for miles and is open to the public.

The Crimean Memorial Obelisk, at the west end of the High Street, stands on the site of Forres Castle, where King Duncan held his court. **The Falconer Museum** (opening times under review: free), also in the High Street, gives you an idea of the town's history. It has displays of natural and social history, fossils and archaeology and temporary exhibitions. **Witch's Stone** in Victoria Road is thought to date from Pictish times and to have been used as an altar to the Sun God. It marks the site where one of three barrels, containing three condemned witches, came to rest, having been rolled down Cluny Hill.

Sueno's Stone, on the northeastern outskirts of the town, is an outstanding example of a Pictish sculpted stone. It stands over 20 feet (6m) high, a slender sandstone shaft dating from the 9th or 10th century. It is clearly carved with a battle scene on one side, full of bodies and heads and weapons, round a broch, with a cross on the reverse side (probably a cenotaph commemorating a victory). Its once splendid setting, overlooking the Moray Firth, has been necessarily diminished by encasing the stone in a protective building, without which it was doomed to erosion.

Brodie Castle

Brodie (open daily, Easter–30 Sept; weekends in Oct: adm) is about 5 miles (8km) west of Forres. It was built on land given to the Brodies by Malcolm IV in 1160 and owned by them until the present day. Part of the existing building dates from the 17th century, rebuilt after the castle was destroyed in 1645. There are also 18th- and 19th-century additions. It is a pale cream-coloured building, with conical turrets and coats of arms on the outer walls, approached down a beech avenue. The castle contains French furniture, English, Continental and Chinese porcelain and paintings. There are woodland walks by a 4-acre loch, a picnic area, adventure playground, car park and shop.

Darnaway Farm Visitor Centre (open daily, May–Sept, but check, ✆ 03094 469: adm) offers the opportunity to see a working dairy farm on a large modern estate. Attractions include an exhibition, audio-visual show, guided walks and estate tours, including a visit to **Darnaway Castle**. Seat of the Earls of Moray, this has a magnificent 15th-century oak hammer-beam roof. Among the Stuart portraits there is one of the murdered 'Bonnie Earl'.

Randolph's Leap at Logie, 7½ miles (12km) south of Forres on the B9007, should be called Cumming's Leap. Robert the Bruce gave land belonging to the Cummings to Thomas Randolph, Earl of Moray. The Cummings raided Darnaway Castle in retaliation but were forced to flee. Alistair Cumming leapt across the narrow gap above this impressive gorge to evade pursuit.

Where to Stay

moderate

Saplinbrae House Hotel, Old Deer, ✆ 0771 23515, is a nice old country house in 400 acres, with shooting, fishing and pony trekking. The food is good.

Fife Lodge Hotel, Banff, ✆ 02612 2436, is an historic building overlooking the River Deveron and Duff House Gardens. The Lodge specializes in traditional cooking.

Tufted Duck, St Combs, Fraserburgh, ✆ 0346 582481, is friendly and comfortable, overlooks the sea and has four crowns and exceptional food. **Waterside Inn**, Fraserburgh Road, Peterhead, ✆ 0779 71121, is a large modern hotel with five crowns, a leisure club and swimming pool, and award-winning chefs.

inexpensive

Crown and Anchor Inn, in Findhorn, ✆ 0309 690243, is an 18th-century coaching inn on the bay—friendly, with free boats. **Royal Hotel,** Tytler Street, Forres, ✆ 0309 672617, is a comfortable Victorian town house retaining many of its original features, but plenty of mod cons as well. **Skerrybrae Hotel**, Lossiemouth, ✆ 0343 812040, is a typical seaside hotel, on the edge of the golf course, and near the sea, with splendid views.

The County Hotel, High Street, Banff, ✆ 02612 5353, is an elegant Georgian mansion overlooking Banff Bay.

It is hardly necessary to recommend **Pennan Inn**. People book far ahead and travel across oceans to stay in one of the six simple bedrooms here (although, actually, it is not *the* inn that featured in the film *Local Hero*, set in Pennan). The seafood is good.

Highlands

Behold her, single in the field,
Yon solitary Highland Lass!
Reaping and singing by herself;
Stop here, or gently pass!
Alone she cuts, and binds the grain,
And sings a melancholy strain;
O listen! for the Vale profound
Is overflowing with the sound.

from 'The Solitary Reaper', by William Wordsworth

When the new regional boundaries were drawn in 1975, Highland Region encompassed the northern two-thirds of Scotland but excluded Perthshire and Argyllshire, both of which belong to 'the Highlands' in their true sense.

Until relatively recently, when Jacobites made a bid for the English throne, the Highlands were so isolated geographically that few outsiders ventured into them. Communication between remote communities, cut off by mountain ranges and huge tracts of water, was arduous and almost entirely by water. The people turned westwards and across to the islands for their culture: to the east lay remoteness and barbarism. It was only after 1715 and the first Jacobite rising that General Wade's planned road system evolved and people like Dr Johnson were able to travel about and 'discover' this untapped source of purple prose.

The Battle of Culloden sparked off the death of the clan system and contributed to the mass exodus that took place over the succeeding century or so. All that remains are tumbled stones, where villages of crofters once squeezed a living from the poor soil, subsisting under the protection of their chief.

Agriculture, fishing and tourism are the main occupation of Highlanders. Main roads are excellent but it is often necessary to drive long distances to get round mountains and sea lochs. Many of the minor roads are single track, with passing bays, infuriating in the caravan season.

In the remoter parts, not much has changed in the last hundred years or so. There may be kit houses and new hotels with picture windows, pile carpets and bathrooms en suite, but the people who staff them are not very impressed by these modern trappings. In the vicinity there are probably a dozen derelict vehicles, discarded over the last 20 years. The surrounding countryside is littered with rusting beer cans and empty whisky bottles, and it would not be surprising to find a live sheep among the inhabitants of a cottage kitchen.

It was in the Highlands, particularly in the west, that you used to find the old bards and tellers of folk tales handed down orally over the centuries. These days you must go to the islands to find them. In those parts of the Highlands that were untouched by the Reformation, and by the banning of fun and gaiety by the stern Calvinists, you will find the best fiddlers and pipers.

Highland Games are a popular summer diversion throughout the region, usually less showy than the smart dress parades of Grampian. A piper practises a pibroch behind a shed, pacing with precise steps, while his rival faces a row of intent judges in the ring. Two little girls, in full Highland costume, perform the intricate steps of a sword dance on a wooden platform. A huge man with bulging biceps totters under the weight of a gigantic caber; another heaves a cannonball-weight across the grass, another a javelin. Young men hurl themselves up and over a high jump. There are side shows and stalls, hot dog stands, fish and chips, and always a well-attended beer tent. Sometimes these games were fairs, organized by clan chiefs, but they usually had a serious purpose: the chief would be talent-spotting for fit men for his army.

Look out for **sheep dog trials**, where these intelligent animals are put through their paces. There can be few things more stirring than to see a first-class pair of dogs working a flock of sheep, controlled by a minimum of monosyllabic or whistled commands. The Great Glen Sheepdog Trials, in Fort William in July, is one of the best of these, and there are often smaller trials at agricultural shows.

Tourist Information

Open all year:

Inverness, Loch Ness and Nairn Tourist Office, Castle Wynd, Inverness, ✆ 0463 234353.

Aviemore and Spey Valley Tourist Office, Main Road, Aviemore, Inverness-shire, ✆ 0479 810363.

Ross and Cromarty Tourist Office, North Kessock, Black Isle, Ross-shire, ✆ 046373 505.

Ross and Cromarty Tourist Office, Gairloch, Ross-shire, ✆ 0445 2130.

Sutherland Tourist Board, The Square, Dornoch, Sutherland, ✆ 0682 810 400.

Caithness Tourist Board, Whitechapel Road, Wick, Caithness, ✆ 0955 2596.

Fort William and Lochaber Tourist Board, Cameron Centre, Cameron Square, Fort William, ✆ 0397 3781.

There are also a number of seasonal information offices, usually open from Easter to the end of September or October.

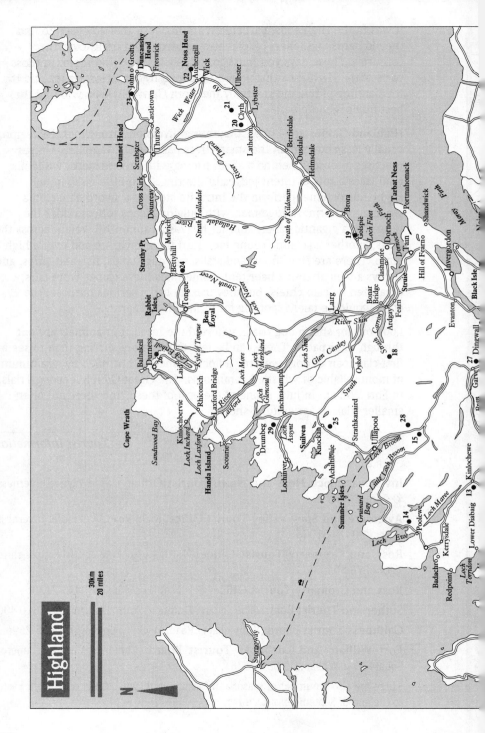

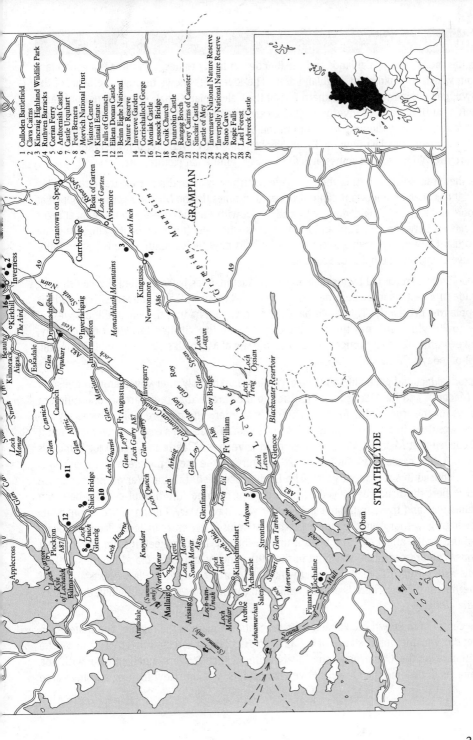

1 Culloden Battlefield
2 Clava Cairns
3 Kincraig Highland Wildlife Park
4 Ruthven Barracks
5 Corran Ferry
6 Ardtornish Castle
7 Castle Urquhart
8 Fort Bernera
9 Morvich National Trust
   Visitors Centre
10 Kintail Estate
11 Falls of Glomach
12 Eilean Donan Castle
13 Beinn Eighe National
   Nature Reserve
14 Inverewe Garden
15 Corrieshalloch Gorge
16 Moniak Castle
17 Kessock Bridge
18 Croik Church
19 Dunrobin Castle
20 Rangag Broch
21 Grey Cairns of Camster
22 Sinclair Castle
23 Castle of Mey
24 Invernaver National Nature Reserve
25 Inverpolly National Nature Reserve
26 Smoo Cave
27 Rogie Falls
28 Lael Forest
29 Ardvreck Castle

GRAMPIAN

STRATHCLYDE

Grantown on Spey
Boat of Garten
Loch Garten
Aviemore
Loch Inch
Carrbridge
Kingussie
Newtonmore
Monadhliath Mountains
Loch Laggan
Loch Ossian
Loch Treig
Blackwater Reservoir
Loch Swan
Roy Bridge
Ft Augustus
Invergarry
Glen Roy
Glen Garry
Glen Loy
Ft William
Glencoe
Loch Leven
Loch Eil
Glenfinnan
Loch Shiel
Ardgour
Strontian
Glen Tarbert
Loch Linnhe
Oban
Loch Sunart
Morvern
Lochaline
Funary
Mull
Sound
Ardnamurchan
Ardtoe
Acharacle
Kinlochmoidart
Salen
Loch Moidart
Loch nan Umah
South Morar
Loch Morar
Loch Nevis
Knoydart
North Morar
Mallaig
Arisaig
Armadale
Loch Hourn
Glenelg
Loch Duich
Plockton
Balmacara
Kyle of Lochalsh
Loch Carron
Applecross
Shiel Bridge
Loch Cluanie
Loch Quoich
Glen Garry
Loch Loyne
Glen Moriston
Glen Affric
Glen Cannich
Strath Glass
Cannich
Aigas
Eskadale
Beauly
Kilmorack
Kirkhill
The Aird
Inverfarigaig
Drumnadrochit
Inverness
Loch Ness
Inverness
Caledonian Canal
Loch Oich
Loch Garry
Glen Spean
Loch Arkaig

393

Inverness

As the capital of the Highlands and the junction of many routes, Inverness is a good place from which to explore the Highland area. The River Ness flows through the heart of the town, converging with the northern end of the Caledonian Canal. Although not outstandingly beautiful, parts of Inverness have a certain sturdy charm and the riverside is most attractive. Perhaps the best view is from the bridge below Bridge Street. Fishermen stand thigh-deep in the fast-flowing River Ness, flanked by well-proportioned houses and churches. When the sun shines, it is a curiously continental picture.

Its sheltered position beside the sea made Inverness a natural place for trade to develop and it has been an important centre from earliest times. In the Middle Ages it developed as a port and ship-building centre, with trade links with Europe. It was often the focal point of clashes between Highland and Island Chiefs who ruled their lands like kings, and the Scottish Crown, ever trying to subdue them. It is now the communications and administrative centre for the north of Scotland.

St Columba is recorded by his biographer, St Adamnan, as having visited the Pictish King Brude in a castle somewhere near the River Ness in AD 565 and converted him and his people to Christianity. This could have been on Craig Phadrig, the small hill just west of the town which still has the remains of a 4th-century vitrified fort. It is more likely, however, that Brude's stronghold stood on the site of Macbeth's castle on Auld Castle Hill, east of today's Castle Hill.

Historical fact and poetic fiction have become so inextricably interwoven around the story of Macbeth and his bloodstained journey to the throne that there are several different claims for the true setting for King Duncan's murder. The most reliable sources say the deed was done in a house near Elgin, in 1039, not in Macbeth's castle in Inverness, but it is believed that Malcolm Canmore destroyed **Inverness Castle** in revenge for Duncan's death. A new castle was built in the 12th century on the site of the present one, and was much abused in subsequent years. The English occupied it in the War of Independence and Robert the Bruce destroyed it. Its successor became the hub of conflict between Highlanders and those trying to subdue their wild ways. Mary, Queen of Scots hanged its rebellious governor from the ramparts when he refused her entry in 1562. Jacobites occupied it in 1715 and 1745 and blew it up in February 1746 to keep it from government hands. The present castle was built in the 19th century and looks brand new, its pinkish walls rising from the small hill exactly like a toy fort. It houses the law courts and local government offices. There is a small exhibition (open Easter–Oct: free) telling the history of the castle.

The centre of the town is compact, with the Station Square in the middle, dominated by a splendid war memorial statue of a Cameron Highlander, erected in 1893 to mark the centenary of the Camerons—the local regiment. (They were amalgamated with the Seaforths to become the Queen's Own Highlanders, who are now fighting a losing battle against amalgamation with the Gordon Highlanders.) There are some excellent shops in a hideous new indoor shopping complex.

Inverness stages a Folk Festival in March, Highland Games in July, a Festival Week and Cadet Tattoo in August. The Northern Meeting Piping Competition is in September, when the finest pipers of the day compete for prestigious awards.

Inverness Museum (open weekdays: free) in Castle Wynd, between the castle and the town hall, has displays of social and natural history, archaeology, the culture of the Highlands and Jacobite relics. There are often exhibitions, talks and slide shows.

St Andrew's Episcopal Cathedral is to the south. An imposing, pinkish building on the banks of the river, it was built between 1866 and 1874, with an octagonal chapter house and an elaborate interior.

Eden Court, beyond the cathedral, is a glass edifice built in 1976, incorporating the 19th-century house of Bishop Eden. It is an 800-seat multipurpose theatre, conference centre and art gallery, with an excellent restaurant. Ambitious programmes are laid on throughout the year: concerts, ballet, drama, the latest films and many art exhibitions.

Ness Islands, up-river away from Eden Court, form a public park spread over a series of small islands in the River Ness. They are linked by foot-bridges, with views down the river towards the town.

Tomnahurich—Hill of the Yews, sometimes called Hill of the Fairies—is the small, boat-shaped hillock to the southwest. Two wandering fiddlers, Thomas and Farquhar, were lured to Tomnahurich by the Fairy Queen, to play for a night's dancing. In the morning they found the town and its people strangely altered and everyone laughing at them. The 'night' had lasted a hundred years. They crept into a church for refuge—and crumbled into dust. Tomnahurich is now the town's cemetery, with many elaborate monuments clinging to the steep, wooded sides and a splendid viewing point from the top. Below lie the environs of Inverness, with neat villas, well-kept gardens and an air of respectability.

The northern entrance to the **Caledonian Canal** is in the western suburbs. It was constructed in the 19th century by Thomas Telford, and much used in the old days by boats wishing to avoid the long and often hazardous slog round the north coast. Still used by fishing boats, it now offers a perfect way for sailors to explore the Great Glen. Cabin cruisers can be hired from the marinas just down from the entrance, and passenger cruises operate in the summer.

The **Mill Shop** of Holm Woollen Mills (James Pringle), in the western suburbs of Inverness, is a good place to stock up on woollens, tweeds, kilts, rugs, etc. They also do factory tours.

The 19th-century **Cameron Barracks** stands on a ridge high above Millburn Road on the eastern edge of Inverness—a wise old sentinel guarding the town. From here, many a brave young Cameron Highlander walked out, newly trained, to give his life so that his Highland home should remain free.

The south side of the Moray Firth is flattish open farmland with views across to the Black Isle and the hills of Easter Ross.

Culloden

Taking the back roads, east of the A96, Culloden is about 5 miles (8km) east of Inverness. Start at the first-class new visitor centre on the edge of the battlefield (open daily, Easter–end Oct: adm for audio-visual show and cottage). The audio-visual show gives details of the battle, on 16 April 1746, when Prince Charles Edward Stuart and his 5000 exhausted, starving and ill-equipped Highlanders were defeated by the Duke of Cumberland, son of George II, and his 9000 well-trained and well-equipped men. During that battle 1200 Highlanders fell; many more were butchered by order of the Duke as they lay wounded. Accounts of the Prince's reaction to the failure of his dreams vary: some say he tried to rally his Highlanders; some that he had to be held back from galloping forward to a hero's death; others are less starry-eyed. Whatever is true, one thing is sure: he was led away and hidden by loyal Highlanders for five months, with a price of £30,000 on his head, until he returned to the Continent in a French frigate, to live out the rest of his life in wretched, debauched exile.

As well as exhibitions and displays, the visitor centre has a study room for school parties, with a library and Jacobite relics. In addition there is a coffee shop and restaurant and a very good bookshop with a comprehensive range of Scottish publications.

The old cottage, outside, is the only building to survive the battle. It was still inhabited at the beginning of the 20th century and is now a folk museum. It still has its old furnishings and domestic equipment; taped music and Gaelic add an authentic touch.

On the battlefield (always open: free), wooden plaques tell which clan fought where, and how the battle progressed. There are clan graves: communal burial sites with headstones bearing clan names, and a memorial cairn, erected in 1881. On the edge of the bleak battle site is the Well of the Dead where wounded Highlanders were slain as they drank water to revive themselves. A single stone bears

Highland Village

the inscription 'The English were buried here'. The flat stone beyond the visitor centre is called the Cumberland Stone, thought to have been the vantage point from which the Duke viewed the battle.

The Clava Cairns are signed, a mile (1.5km) east of Culloden. These form a remarkable Stone Age and Bronze Age burial site, possibly dating from 2000 BC. Three large burial cairns in a glade of beech trees take you back to the prehistoric rituals that would have accompanied the internment of those farmers and herdsmen so many years ago. Two of the cairns have passages leading into them; the third has curious stone strips radiating from it like the spokes of a wheel. Each is surrounded by a circle of standing stones, some inscribed with cup-and-ring symbols. Excavations revealed traces of cremated human bones, pottery and other remains: memorials of people who were alive nearly 4000 years ago.

Kilravock Castle (pronounced Kilrawk) is 5 miles (8km) northeast of Culloden, still keeping to the back roads (open Wed afternoons, April–Sept, or by appointment, © 06678 258; grounds open daily except Sun: adm). Dating from the 15th century, this castle has been preserved almost intact because the owners never had enough money to mess about with its original design. In 1190, a Norman called Rose came north, married into a local family and settled on these lands. Kilravock has been the home of the Rose chiefs ever since. Among its relics are two reminders of Culloden—a punch bowl and a pair of leather thigh boots. Rose of Kilravock entertained Prince Charles before the battle and offered punch from this bowl. He was not a Jacobite, but the Prince had ridden over to call on him and no true Highlander refuses hospitality. Shortly afterwards, Cumberland came blustering up, flushed with celebration of his 25th birthday: 'I hear, sir, you've been entertaining my cousin!' Rose explained and was excused. Cumberland, for some inexplicable reason, left his boots behind. These two relics are an ironic reflection of the two people associated with them: Prince Charles, merry and charismatic, who later drowned his failure in alcohol; Butcher Cumberland, brash, gross and cruel—very much a jackboot image. The gardens and grounds are lovely, especially in spring. Prince Charles walked here with his host and watched young trees being planted. He remarked on the contrast between this peaceful scene and the commotion that was going on all round, preparing for the battle. Some of the beautiful old trees today must be the ones that were being planted. (Kilravock is now a hotel: see 'Where to Stay', below.)

Cawdor

Cawdor (pronounced Cawder), 8 miles (13km) northeast of Culloden, is familiar to anyone who has read Shakespeare's *Macbeth*. Within moments of having been told by the witches he is to become Thane of Cawdor, Macbeth is told that the king has indeed bestowed the title on him. The fulfilment of this prophecy encourages him to bring about the final one, that he would be king, by murdering King Duncan.

Cawdor Castle (open daily 1 May–1 Oct: adm) dates from 1372, when the central tower was built. Domestic buildings were added in the 16th century and later remodelled. Protected by a gully on one side and a dry moat on the other, the castle, floodlit at night, has a walled garden, ablaze with colour in the summer. Entry is over a drawbridge, and it feels like a living home, rather than a museum, probably because the Cawdors still live here. It is easy to imagine it in medieval times, with its winding stairways and massive walls. Among the things to see are Flemish tapestries, paintings, weapons, household equipment and family heirlooms. Carbon dating has confirmed that the scrap of an ancient tree, railed off in the basement, is older than the castle, thus authenticating an old story. The original founder, Thane William, was granted a licence to build himself a fortress. He was told in a dream to load a donkey with panniers of gold and build a castle wherever it stopped. He obeyed and the donkey stopped for a rest in the shade of a thorn tree round which Thane William built his castle.

Outside there are nature trails, a nine-hole mini-golf course, putting green and picnic spots, as well as a licensed restaurant and souvenir shop.

In a conservation area, Cawdor village, straggling round the castle grounds, is not at all typical of Scotland: its peaceful cosiness matches that of the castle. The church is 17th-century, built in thanksgiving by the twelfth Lord Cawdor after he was saved from a shipwreck.

Cawdor Tavern, in the heart of the village, has a dark wood and velvet interior and is decorated by ornamental plates and hunting scenes, its atmosphere being almost that of an English pub. A bust of Shakespeare gazes benignly over the saloon where they serve good food.

Fort George

Fort George (open daily: adm) is about 8 miles (13km) northwest of Cawdor on the B9006, on a windswept promontory jutting out into the Moray Firth. It is the most unspoilt example of an artillery fort in Europe. Built between 1748 and 1769, to replace 'Old' Fort George in Inverness, destroyed by Prince Charles in 1746, it is a classic 18th-century fortress. The defences include the traditional outer works: ravelin, ditch, bastion and rampart, designed by William Skinnor who was in his day the leading expert on artillery fortification. The government contractor who built it was John Adam, oldest son of architect William Adam, and brother of Robert.

Passing through the forbidding fortifications, one is brought to a delighted standstill by the mellow pink sandstone garrison buildings, their impeccable 18th-century proportions mercifully unscarred by Victorian or later 'improvement'.

The fort was built to house a garrison large enough to overawe Jacobite support in the Highlands, but by the time it was completed the Jacobite threat was finally dead, so it has never had a history of conflict. It became a base where a long series of regiments were mustered and equipped and whence they embarked for service in America, the West Indies, the Middle East, India and South Africa. In 1881, when each British infantry regiment was allocated its own territorial recruiting area and home base, Fort George became the depot of the Seaforth Highlanders. Generations of Highland soldiers trained there for colonial service, for two World Wars and for modern Cold War campaigns.

The regiments of the garrison change over every two years, and they have the privilege of living in barracks that are the oldest in the world still occupied by a battalion of British infantry.

The **Regimental Museum of the Queen's Own Highlanders** (open daily except some Sat, April–Sept; weekdays, Oct–March: free, donations welcome) is in the fort. Formed in 1961 by the amalgamation of the Seaforth Highlanders and the Queen's Own Cameron Highlanders, they are the present-day descendants of the two historic regiments of the northern Highlands. In the building formerly used by the Lieutenant Governor, the Queen's Own Highlanders preserve a superb collection of uniforms, pictures, medals, weapons, colours, artefacts and treasures, representing nearly every major campaign fought by the British Army over the past 200 years. The splendour of red coat and tartan, the glitter of gilt plate and dirk, the glint of steel broadsword and bayonet, cannot fail to stir the imagination and make hearts beat a little faster. With its history, its atmosphere and its garrison, Fort George is unique as a 20th-century military base where the 18th century lives on.

Nairn

Nairn, not quite 9 miles (14.5km) east of Fort George, is a seaside holiday town, sometimes called the Brighton of the North. On the mouth of the River Nairn, it has sandy beaches along the Moray Firth, two golf courses and a reputation for a high average of sunshine. (In Victorian times, a Dr Grigor put Nairn on the map by recommending it to his patients as 'one of the healthiest spots in Britain'.) Imposing houses built by retired Victorian Empire-builders and trim villas with neat gardens give it an aura of old-fashioned gentility. The Nairn Highland Games are in August. There is a Holiday Week and a Vintage Car Rally in July. The Fairground Fortnight and the Farmers Show are also in August.

Originally called Invernairn, the old fishertown is a collection of restored cottages. **Nairn Fishertown Museum** (open afternoons except Sun, May–Sept: adm) is in Laing Hall, King Street. Here you can see photographs and articles relating to the Moray Firth and the herring fisheries during the steam drifter era. There are also displays of domestic life in a fishing community. (Nairn now has a yacht marina, but no longer any local fishing boats.)

The Little Theatre, also in Fishertown, is a small theatre with a repertory company who perform every Wednesday in the summer and there is a thriving Nairn Performing Arts Guild.

See Grampian for Brodie Castle (p.387) and Pluscarden Abbey (p.372), nearby, both well worth a visit during this tour from Inverness.

Where to Stay

expensive

Caledonian Hotel, Church Street, Inverness, © 0463 235181, is convenient, in the centre backing on to the river, but huge and soulless with cabaret most nights.

Culloden House Hotel, 4 miles (6.5km) east of Inverness, ℂ 0463 790461, is a Georgian mansion built round a Jacobean castle. Prince Charles made it his headquarters for two months before the Battle of Culloden, when it was the home of Duncan Forbes, the Lord President. (He and his officers managed to get through 60 hogsheads of the Lord President's claret—3150 imperial gallons—so perhaps the outcome of the battle was inevitable.) The hotel is luxurious, with an Adam dining room, four-poster and curtain-framed beds, ornate plasterwork and attractive grounds. The food is worth staying in for.

moderate

Drumossie Hotel, on the A9 to Perth, 3 miles (4.5km) out of town, ℂ 0463 236451, is modern, with views over the Moray Firth. The food isn't too bad. **Bunchrew House Hotel**, Bunchrew, ℂ 0463 234917, is a much better bet, though bordering on expensive. A 16th-century mansion in 15 acres of gardens on the shores of the Beauly Firth, about 5 miles (8km) west of Inverness, it has turrets and towers and tremendous atmosphere. There are only six bedrooms. **Dunain Park**, Inverness, ℂ 0463 230512, is a country house on the western outskirts, in six acres of lovely grounds. Comfortable and well-run, but bordering on the expensive.

Newton Hotel Nairn, ℂ 0667 53144, has five crowns and is well recommended as one of Nairn's best; friendly, quiet and with excellent food. **The Clifton Hotel**, also in Nairn, ℂ 0667 53119, is highly recommended as one of the best in all the good food guides. **Carnach Country House Hotel**, Inverness Road, Nairn, ℂ 0667 52094, is at the lower end of this price bracket, comfortable and peaceful, in eight acres overlooking the Moray Firth. Also overlooking the Firth, close to the golf course, at the top end of the bracket, **Golf View Hotel**, Nairn, ℂ 0667 52301, has tennis courts, outdoor swimming pool, sauna, games room and regular entertainment.

inexpensive

Glendruidh House, Old Edinburgh Road, Inverness, ℂ 0463 226499, is a delightful, family-run hotel overlooking the Moray Firth and the town. **Heathmount Hotel** in Heathmont, Inverness, ℂ 0463 235877, has a good reputation, a nice pub atmosphere and five comfortable bedrooms.

Kilravock Castle, Croy, ℂ 06678 258 (see above for description), is a great experience for anyone who is an abstemious Christian. Pronounced 'Kilrawk', this historic old castle is where Prince Charles dined before Culloden. It stands in peaceful grounds near the river and the emphasis is very much on God: grace before meals, Bible readings and comment at breakfast and dinner; no drink—though naughty guests have been known to smuggle bottles into their cells and smoke up the chimney. Country-house bedrooms in a wing of the castle are cheap, while historic rooms in the castle proper cost a few pounds more.

For a night out, go to **Culloden House**, ✆ 0463 790461, and don't look at the prices. (An Adam dining room adds to the occasion.) Or try **The Longhouse** in Nairn, which is expensive but has seriously good food.

Inverness to Kingussie

The Spey, Scotland's second-longest river, is born high in the hills above Loch Laggan, 40 miles (64km) south of Inverness, and cuts across the southeast corner of the Highland region. Beginning as a mere stream, it gathers momentum as it flows east and then north to the sea near Buckie in Grampian region, fed by many burns that drain from the hills on either side, turning it into a rushing tumult of water. Running between the great Cairngorms in the east and the Monadhliath Mountains to the west, the Spey is famous for astonishing natural beauty. In spring, fresh green shows through winter brown and snow still caps the mountains; in summer it is a patchwork of mulberry heather, emerald bracken, sparkling water and grey granite; in autumn, snow already dusts the hills making a backdrop to the splendour of the turning leaves; in winter, a white Alpine world dazzles and enchants. Leave the main roads and explore any of the minor roads and tracks.

Grantown-on-Spey

About 26 miles (41.5km) down the A9 from Inverness, branch left at Carrbridge on the A938. Grantown-on-Spey, 10 miles (16km) east and 6 miles (9.5km) south of the Grampian border, is one of Speyside's tourist centres, a Georgian town at the junction of several routes. On the banks of the River Spey and surrounded by trees, the town was founded in 1776 by Sir James Grant, one of the Highland's 'improving lairds'. With the development of skiing in the hills, this area is popular all the year round for holidays. The Grantown-on-Spey Highland Games are held in June.

The Loch Garten Nature Reserve, 8 miles (13km) south of Grantown-on-Spey, is known for its breeding ospreys. Americans, accustomed to seeing these 'fish-hawks' in countless numbers nesting in their rivers and estuaries, are amused by the security surrounding Scotland's few pairs, but it must be remembered that before the mid-1950s (when one pair set up their nest in a tree at Loch Garten) they had not been seen in Britain for almost 50 years. When an over-enthusiastic egg thief robbed this precious nest in 1958, precautions had to be taken. Now, it is not so unusual to see the slow, flapping flight of one of these brown and white birds, or hear its shrill, cheeping cry. The nature reserve has a lot more than ospreys for any one who will stand still and observe. Its bird life includes blackcock, capercaillie and crossbills, and among the animals are red squirrels and deer. In winter the haunting cry of geese and the eerie honk of whooper swans float across the waters of Loch Garten.

Boat of Garten, west of the loch, is so called after the ferry that operated here until a bridge was built in 1898. It is the home of the **Strathspey Steam Railway Association**, which has its own station and some remnants of the old Highland railway (closed in 1965). It was re-opened in 1978 and enthusiasts can travel to Aviemore in a steam train. There is a museum of railway memorabilia. While you are in the area, visit the Tomatin Distillery, Scotland's largest malt whisky distillery and the first to be acquired by the Japanese, in 1985, with guided tours and a free dram (open weekdays, Easter–Oct: Sat mornings, May–Sept: free). Tomatin is derived from a Gaelic word meaning 'the hill of the juniper bushes'—curious for a whisky distillery.)

Also nearby, award-winning **Speyside Heather**, 6 miles (9.5km) from Granton (open daily except Sun, Nov–March: free), grows over 300 different heathers: its visitor's centre will give advice on growing them at home.

Aviemore

Aviemore, about 14 miles (22.5km) southwest of Grantown-on-Spey, is a thriving tourist centre and dormitory for the Cairngorm ski resort, teeming with energetic holidaymakers. Dominated by the Cairngorms, with several peaks over 4000 feet (1230m), this area has some of Scotland's grandest scenery.

Aviemore has every sort of accommodation, cafés and restaurants, bistros and bars, gift shops, craft shops, souvenir stalls, amusement arcades and discos. It is just the place for gregarious people looking for action. Throughout the year the surrounding countryside is a kaleidoscope of anoraks and knapsacks, psychedelic skiing clothes, or shorts and tee-shirts. Within spitting distance of this hub of sporting activity lie heather-clad moors, mountains, valleys, tumbling burns and beautiful lochs.

The Aviemore Mountain Resort (open daily: adm for various attractions) offers a bewildering choice of activity. There is an ice rink and curling rink, theatre/cinema, ballroom, artificial ski slope, games room, squash courts, go-kart track, and children's outdoor amusements.

Rothiemurchus Visitor Centre, (open daily: adm) gives an insight into everyday life on a working Highland estate. **The Cairngorm Reindeer Centre** (open daily: adm), at Glenmore, has Britain's only herd of reindeer, living free on the slopes of the Cairngorms.

Loch Morlich, 5 miles (8km) to the east, is a water-sports centre for gregarious aquarians—camping and caravanning included, not for the recluse. **Kincraig Highland Wildlife Park** (open daily, March–Nov: adm) is 6 miles (9.5km) southwest of Aviemore. Animals which once roamed free over the Highlands live here in a natural setting: boar, wolves, bears, bison and many more. You drive through the park and must leave pets in the kennels provided. There are also aviaries with indigenous birds such as capercaillie, eagles and hawks, and an exhibition on man and fauna in the Highlands.

Loch Insh, a mile (1.5km) southeast of Kincraig, is formed by a widening of the river and is surrounded by blue hills and trees. **Loch Insh Watersports and Skiing Centre** offers courses in canoeing, wind surfing, sailing, swimming and skiing— all the ingredients necessary for an excellent action holiday.

The white 18th-century church on a rocky point at the northern end of the loch was built on a site said to have been used by Druids, and used continually for Christian worship since the 6th century. Inside is an 8th-century hand-bell, shaken to call the faithful to worship, before the days of bells in steeples. The **Rock Wood Ponds**, southeast of the loch, teem with wildlife.

The gaunt shell of **Ruthven Barracks** (pronounced 'Rivven') stands on a hillock east of the A9, five miles (8km) southwest of Kincraig, dramatically floodlit at night. On the site of a stronghold of the Wolf of Badenoch (notorious son of Robert II), it was built after the 1715 Jacobite uprising to discourage further rebellion and extended by General Wade in 1734. Prince Charles captured it from government troops during his ascendancy and it was here, after Culloden, that some 1500 surviving Jacobites assembled, awaiting their Prince. They waited in vain, until they received the message that the cause was dead and they must now fend for themselves. On the day after the battle, Lord George Murray sat down in the barracks and wrote a long, bitter letter to the Prince, resentfully listing all the blunders that had contributed to their defeat. Prince Charles never forgave him. Before disbanding to return to the homes they had so eagerly left, the loyal Highlanders, abandoned by their leader, blew Ruthven up to save it from the enemy.

Kingussie

Kingussie, a mile (1.5km) to the west and by-passed by the A9, is another popular holiday resort. Derived from the Gaelic *cinn giuthasich*, meaning 'at the head of the first', and pronounced 'King-yewsie', it has one main street, backed by lovely Highland scenery. The Badenoch and Strathspey Music Festival is held here in March.

The Highland Folk Museum (open daily, April–Oct; weekdays, Nov–March: adm) is a must for anyone interested in Highland life and folklore. It was founded in Iona in the 1930s and later moved here under the control of the universities of Glasgow, Edinburgh, St Andrews and Aberdeen. Beautifully arranged, both indoors and outside, it includes an authentic black-house from Lewis, built by someone who was bought up in one, a clack mill (named from its 'clacking' noise), and many exhibits of farming and domestic life, including a salmon smokehouse.

At Newtonmore, **Waltzing Waters**, (open daily except from 5 Jan to 20 Feb: adm) is an indoor 'water, light and music spectacular' that defies description: go and see it.

From Kingussie, south to the Tayside Border, the A9 runs through Glen Truim to Dalwhinnie, backed by hills, forest and moor, crossing the border through the Pass of Drumochter. Very isolated and unpopulated, this is not an area for running out of petrol on a winter's night.

The A86, west from Kingussie to Glen Roy and Spean Bridge, runs through glens flanked by steep hills, the road dipping and climbing beside Loch Laggan. Cars should be abandoned to walk up valleys into the hills, past secret lochans and hidden glens.

See also previous section.

Carrbridge Hotel, ✆ 047984 202, is an old-established, rambling, easy-going establishment. Also in Carrbridge, **Dalrachney Lodge Hotel**, ✆ 047984 252, has four crowns, and **Fairwinds Hotel**, ✆ 047984 240, has three crowns.

In Grantown-on-Spey, **Grant Arms** in the town centre, ✆ 0479 2526, is an old-fashioned grey pile. A bit cheaper, **Garth Hotel** in Castle Road, ✆ 0479 2836, is a white and black building just off the square, dating from the 17th century, in four acres of landscaped garden.

In Aviemore, **Stakis Badenoch**, ✆ 0479 810261, and **Stakis Four Seasons**, ✆ 0479 810681, offer comfort and all mod cons. **Stakis Coylumbridge Resort Hotel**, 3 miles (4.5km) out of Aviemore, is much the same. **Freedom Inn** in Aviemore Centre, ✆ 0479 810781, is modern, with a cheerful staff. **Red McGregor Hotel**, ✆ 0479 810256, on the main road in the village, is attractive and comfortable.

Muckrach Lodge Hotel, Dulnain Bridge, ✆ 047985 257, is an old family home in attractive grounds, with a good reputation for comfort and food.

Struan House, in the middle of Carrbridge, has log fires, tennis and a small dry ski slope and putting green. In the same village are **Feith Mhor Country House**, ✆ 047984 621, and **Cairn Hotel**, ✆ 047984 212. **Seafield Lodge Hotel,** in Woodside Avenue, Grantown-on-Spey, ✆ 0479 2152, is a fishing hotel and runs fishing courses.

Boat Hotel, Boat of Garten, ✆ 047983 258, is a country house near the loch with 6 miles (9.5km) of fishing on the Spey, and a good reputation for food.

In Kingussie, **Columba House Hotel**, Manse Road, ✆ 0540 661402, and **The Osprey Hotel**, ✆ 0540 661510, are both good value with no frills.

For local colour and good value, try **Tomatin Inn**, at Tomatin, ✆ 08082 291.

Craggan Mill Restaurant on the Grantown–Dulnain Bridge road, ✆ 0479 2288, is in a converted mill: the food is good and not too expensive.

Inverness to Glencoe via the Great Glen

Some 400 million years ago, the landmass of Scotland split apart along what is now the Great Glen, the fissure being eroded by glaciers in the Ice Age until the final retreat of the ice as recently as 10,000 years ago. The Caledonian Canal, a waterway through the glen, was surveyed by James Watt in 1773. Thomas Telford started work on construction in 1803, and completed it in 1821. Of its 60-mile (96km) length, 22 miles (35km) is true canal; the rest takes advantage of the natural lochs and rivers in the rift. The Great Glen, starting with Loch Ness, is spectacular and the best way to enjoy it is by boat. Caley Cruisers, Canal Road Inverness, ✆ 0463 236328, hire boats sleeping from four to eight. Passenger cruises include: Jacobite Cruises, ✆ 0463 233999 and Loch Ness Cruises (Drumnadrochit), ✆ 04562 395.

Loch Ness

Loch Ness is world famous, thanks to Nessie: it is also extremely beautiful. Long and narrow, its steep wooded banks form a wind-funnel, causing surprisingly rough seas at times. Depths of 900 feet (278m) have been recorded, deeper than much of the North Sea.

Feelings run high over Nessie—the Loch Ness Monster—known to the cognoscenti as *Nessiteras rhombopteryx*. Sceptics may scoff, but St Adamnan, not given to telling fibs, records a sighting of her in his biography of St Columba, when they were sailing up the loch to convert Inverness. Columba, it seems, had a calming effect on her when she threatened one of his monks, and she has never been troublesome again. Setting aside whisky-induced hallucinations, and wishful-thinking sightings, many eye-witness accounts of Nessie come from people whose honesty and integrity are beyond doubt. A 16th-century chronicle describes 'a terrible beast issuing out of the water early one morning about midsummer, knocking down trees and killing three men with its tail'. A monk who was organist in Westminster Cathedral saw her in 1973, and several of the monks at Fort Augustus Abbey have seen her. Thirty hotel guests saw two humps appear in an explosion of surf and cruise half a mile before sinking, in 1961. Bertram Mills was sufficiently convinced to offer £20,000 to have Nessie delivered alive to his circus. However logical one is, it is impossible to drive down Loch Ness without scanning the dark waters hopefully. Anyone who spends a night at anchor in a boat on the loch will find themselves starting up in the darkness, every time a ripple slaps the hull.

There are two roads down Loch Ness from Inverness: the A82 is the main road down the west side, with views of the loch and quite a lot of traffic in the summer. The B862/852 is much less frequented, very attractive, but with not so many views of the loch, some sections of it being inland.

The Loch Ness Monster Exhibition Centre is at **Drumnadrochit**, 15 miles (24km) down from Inverness on the A82, west-side route (open daily: adm). Here is all the information known about Nessie: documents, photographs, possible explanations, models, a sonar room, etc, all presented objectively—a study for sceptic and credulous alike. In summer there is also a tartan shop and a house of heraldry, where people can check up on their origins. There is a glass blower, too, and a Hollywood-style model of Nessie for family photographs.

Urquhart Castle (open daily: adm) is just beyond Drumnadrochit on the southern tip of Urquhart Bay, overlooking Loch Ness, with free off-road parking from where there is an overview of the whole layout. A jagged keep rises from crumbling walls against a backdrop of loch and hills beyond. This was once one of the largest castles in Scotland, dating from the 14th century. Built on the site of a vitrified fort, it was given to John Grant of Freuchie in 1509 by James IV. In 1692 it was blown up to save it from Jacobite hands. Romantics say that Nessie lives in a subterranean cave below the castle.

At **Balbeg**, about 4 miles (6.5km) on, is the memorial cairn to John Cobb who was killed in 1952, trying to break the world water speed record on Loch Ness's measured mile. The memorial is inscribed in Gaelic: 'Honour to the brave and to the humble'.

Fort Augustus

Fort Augustus, on the southern end of Loch Ness, is the halfway halt down the Great Glen, a popular tourist centre with an ancient history. There is a pre-Christian crannog, Cherry Island, just to the north in Loch Ness.

The town's original name was Kilcumein (burial place of Cumein who was one of St Columba's followers). After the Jacobite rising in 1715, barracks were built in the town to quell further rebellion and there are still traces of the old buildings behind the Lovat Arms Hotel. General Wade made his headquarters here in 1724, and in 1729 began the building of the fort beside the loch. It was named Augustus after William Augustus, Duke of Cumberland, at that time the fat, eight-year-old schoolboy son of George II, who was to go down in history as Butcher Cumberland. Jacobites took the fort in 1745 and held it until after Culloden. Lord Lovat bought the ruins and presented them to a Benedictine community in 1876, for the founding of an abbey which became a public school until it closed in 1993. Much of the old fort was incorporated into the ground floor. The Great Glen Gala is a lively occasion in Fort Augustus in July.

To complete a circular tour of Loch Ness, rather than go on down the Great Glen, take the B862 from Fort Augustus back up the east side, which is prettier and quieter. Part of the way is one of General Wade's military roads, built in anticipation of further Jacobite uprisings.

Just after Whitebridge, 10 miles (16km) from Fort Augustus, the road forks. The left fork goes to **Foyers**, where there are woodland walks and a spectacular waterfall. From Inverfarigaig, about 3 miles (4.5km) northeast of Foyers, back to Inverness, there are a number of excavated remains of burial chambers, forts and cairns, some in good condition, including a vitrified Iron Age fort, at **Ashie Moor**, west of Loch Duntelchaig.

Going on down the Great Glen from Fort Augustus, **Tobar nan Ceann** is the 'Well of the Heads' monument beside the road on the western shore of Loch Oich. An obelisk supports the bronze heads of seven men, held together by a dirk through their hair. Beyond, steps lead through a damp tunnel to a sinister well underneath. This is where Iain Lom MacDonell, poet of his clan, washed the severed heads of the murderers of his chief, Alasdair MacDonell, 12th Chief of Keppoch, in 1663. He presented the washed heads to MacDonell of Glengarry, who had refused to help him avenge the murder. It was the 15th

Chief MacDonell of Glengarry who erected the monument in the 19th century. Inscribed in English, Gaelic, French and Latin are the words: 'this ample and summary vengeance'.

Nearby, three days before the raising of the standard at Glenfinnan, two companies of government troops surrendered to a handful of Jacobite Macdonalds. They had heard a great din of pipes and noise and believed themselves to be in the midst of a mighty army. The two companies were from the Royal Scots, in garrison at Fort Augustus, ambushed at High Bridge and retreating with ignominious haste back to barracks: the engagement was commemorated by the pibroch 'The Rout of the Lowland Captain'.

A little further down, at **Laggan** between Loch Lochy and Loch Oich, there was a ferocious clan battle between the Frasers and the Macdonalds in 1544. It was called *Blàr-na-léine*—the Battle of the Shirts, because it was so hot: they all threw off their cumbersome plaids and fought in their shirts. Of the 1000 men engaged, only 12 survived. The casualties included the entire Fraser hierarchy, leaving Clan Fraser leaderless: fortunately, 80 of the gentlemen's wives had been left pregnant and each one produced a male heir.

Several routes meet at **Spean Bridge**, about 12 miles (19km) south down Loch Lochy. Just short of the village is the much-photographed **Commando Memorial** by Scott Sutherland, erected in 1952. A bronze group of commandos stand on a high promontory looking out over the view towards Ben Nevis and Lochaber, surrounded by the harsh terrain where they trained during the Second World War. The simplicity of the statue is dramatic.

Spean Bridge Woollen Mill is worth a visit for anyone who wants to buy traditional Scottish tweeds and woollens. The old station at Spean Bridge has been turned into an excellent restaurant.

Highbridge, 2 miles (3km) from Spean Bridge, is one of Wade's most remarkable bridges, completed in 1736. It crosses the gorge of the River Spean, 100 feet (31m) below.

Glen Roy is a slight detour from Roy Bridge, 3 miles (4.5km) east of Spean Bridge on the A86. At first it seems just another glen, with the River Roy tumbling down through wooded gorges to flatten out and meander at a more stately pace across the valley floor, bare hills rising on either side. Stop at the large observation car park some way along and look down the valley. A number of horizontal lines run across the hillside, quite high up, each line exactly matched by one on the opposite side of the valley. These 'parallel roads' are terraces left by the receding glacier that once filled the valley. They are geologically famous because of their clarity, and date from a late Ice Age build-up about 11,000 years ago. Glen Roy used to be well populated but like so many others in this area it is now virtually empty.

Several secret glens lie beyond the end of the track. Tucked away up in the hills, the source of the Roy, about 6 miles (9.5km) from the end of the road, is very close to the source of the Spey, gathering courage for its long trek to the sea.

Northwest of Spean Bridge, at Achnacarry, **The Clan Cameron Museum** (open afternoons, mid-April–mid-Oct: free) covers Clan Cameron, Lochaber, the Jacobite risings and the use of the estate for Commando training in World War II, and has a section on the Cameron Highlanders.

On the western route down the Great Glen (B8004), Strome is the site of Bonny Dundee's headquarters where he mustered the clans loyal to James VII before Killicrankie.

At **Erracht** close by, tucked away up a track, a cairn was unveiled in 1993 by Colonel Sir Donald Cameron of Lochiel, to commemorate Alan Cameron of Erracht, the founder of the 79th Highlanders, raised in 1793. Cameron was born in the little house above the cairn.

Continuing on down the Great Glen from Spean Bridge on the A82, **Inverlochy Castle** stands by the road about 8 miles (13km) to the southwest and is being restored by Historic Scotland as a consolidated ruin. Dating from the 13th century, it has a walled courtyard and round corner towers, one of which was the keep, and a water gate. The castle was once a stronghold of the Comyns and scene of several battles, including one in 1645 in which Montrose defeated a Covenanter army under Argyll with a loss of 1500 men. This was one of the greatest feats of arms in Scottish history. The first Argyll knew of Montrose's presence was the sound of the pibroch: *Sons of the dogs, come out and get flesh.* Legend tells of a Pictish settlement on this site, where King Archaius signed a treaty with Charlemagne in 790.

Fort William

Fort William is 10 miles (16km) southwest of Spean Bridge and is the southern gateway to the Caledonian Canal. It is a tourist resort, the epitome of a West Highland town, shopping centre for the whole of this area and hub of several routes. It lies in the lee of Ben Nevis, Britain's highest mountain, 4406 feet (1356m)—an ugly lump, with several routes to the top depending on expertise and physical fitness.

The fort for which the town was named was demolished in the 19th century to make way for the railway. It was first built by General Monk in 1655, an earth construction that proved to be of insufficient strength when put to the test by rebellious Highlanders later in the century. It was then rebuilt in stone, withstanding Jacobite attacks in 1715 and 1746. The town was named Maryburgh after the wife of King William III, before being named in honour of the king himself. It grew up around the railway and is Victorian and sturdy, with a cheerful holiday atmosphere. For Gaelic speakers its official name is still An Gearasdan—the Garrison

Steam trains run from Fort William to Mallaig from May to October, past many historic sites, through glorious scenery. Special trips linked with a visit to Skye are arranged every Sunday from the end of June to mid-September. It is essential to book in advance: ✆ 0397 703791.

Don't miss the **Great Glen Sheepdog Trials** at the end of June or beginning of July. The Highland Games are also in July and the Lochaber Agricultural Show is in August.

The West Highland Museum (open daily except Sun: adm), in Cameron Square, is crammed with interesting historical, natural history and folk exhibits. There is a crofter's kitchen, just as it was in the old days with all the original equipment, as well as agricultural implements. Montrose's helmet and many Jacobite relics are displayed. The most fascinating exhibit is the 'secret' portrait of the prince, used in the days when loyal Jacobites toasted 'the king across the water', a meaningless blur of paint until you view it from the right angle through a cylinder, when it is transformed into a recognizable portrait.

You can pass a sunny hour or so leaning over the rails beside the long ladder of locks that bring the Caledonian Canal down to the level of the sea. The locks are used by fishing boats and pleasure craft and the gates are hydraulically operated, the water boiling through sluices until the level is equal either side. Eight of the 11 locks that link Loch Linnhe with the canal are called **Neptune's Staircase**, a rise of 80 feet (24.5m) which presented Telford with an enormous problem when he built the canal. Loch Linnhe is always busy with pleasure boats in the summer.

There is a new skiing complex 4 miles (6.5km) north of Fort William on **Aonach Mor**, close to Ben Nevis. Nevis Range, the operators, anticipate more people using the gondola system lifts in the summer than in the winter.

A fast road runs along the east side of Loch Linnhe to the new Ballachulish (pronounced Balla-hoolish) Bridge, 13 miles (21km) to the south. The bridge spans a narrow constriction between lochs Linnhe and Leven, where not so long ago a small car ferry used to slither and slide on the fast current. Look out for the stark, stone memorial to James Stewart, with its bitter inscription, beside the road. Stewart was falsely hanged for the 'Appin Murder' in 1752, on which Robert Louis Stevenson based *Kidnapped* and its sequel, *Catriona*. The staunchly Jacobite Stewarts of Appin had to forfeit their lands after Culloden. The Crown factor, Colin Campbell of Glenure, known as the Red Fox, took delight in evicting Stewarts in favour of Campbells. He was assassinated during one of his forays and James Stewart was unjustly used as a scapegoat, tried before the Duke of Argyll at Inverary by a jury of 11 Campbells, found guilty and hanged. The rough stone on top of the monument came from his farm. A memorial cairn marks the site of the Red Fox's murder in the Wood of Lettermore, about a mile (1.5km) west of Ballachulish, near the road.

Ballachulish was the centre for Scotland's biggest slate quarry, still full of slate but no longer used because slate is now imported. Some of the slate workers' cottages have been converted into a teashop, craft shops, etcetera.

Glencoe

Glencoe is 4 miles (6.5km) to the east. This dramatic pass with raw peaks reaching up on either side is slashed by white scars of cascading water. In good weather, away from the road, Glencoe is staggeringly beautiful, with creaming burns and falls, glistening rocks and hidden lochs and glens. But when the weather closes in, there is an unmistakable aura of doom, enhanced by its well-known history. *Glen Coe* means 'Glen of Weeping', and many tears were shed on 13 February 1692. Macdonald of Glencoe, late with his oath of allegiance to King William III, provided the government with an excuse to get rid of his troublesome clan. It was an affair of the greatest possible dishonour. Campbell of Glenlyon billeted himself and 128 soldiers with the Macdonalds for several days, living as guests and accepting the generous hospitality that was such an integral part of Highland life. Glenlyon's company, acting on higher authority, rose one dawn and massacred their hosts as they slept. Tradition has it that the Glenlyon's piper, who was called MacKenzie, played to warn the Macdonalds. No one can drive through the glen now, 300 years later, and not glance up into the hills and remember that bitter morning and hear the cries of the women and children, and see the bloodstains in the snow. The Massacre Memorial, in the village of Glencoe, is a tall, slender cross—a poignant reminder of senseless slaughter.

Glencoe and North Lorne Folk Museum (open daily except Sun, May–Sept: adm) is in Glencoe village. It contains many Jacobite and historic exhibits, domestic implements, weapons, costumes, photographs, dolls and dolls' houses, tools, and much else, all housed in a group of thatched houses. **The National Trust for Scotland** has a visitor centre, 2 miles (3km) east of the village, full of information.

Clachaig, 2 miles (3km) east of Glencoe village, is a hotel/hostel which always seems to be peopled by cold, wet climbers sitting about looking miserable. Here a resident warden will advise about good walks and climbing in the glen. This is a centre for some of the most challenging mountaineering in the country, much of which is not suitable for amateurs. There is a chairlift and T-bars for skiers at the head of the glen, and good skiing on Meall a Bhuiridh, when conditions are right.

Loch Ossian is about 17 miles (27km) northeast of Glencoe as the crow flies, tucked into a valley surrounded by hills and inaccessible by road. There is a youth hostel and the train stops at Corrour Station, but the energetic should get out the map and attack it on foot. It is a lovely 10-mile (16km) tramp from Black Corries Lodge, over the shoulder of Stob na Cruaiche, round the eastern end of Blackwater Reservoir and along the course of the railway.

Beyond Glencoe, Rannoch Moor stretches away to the east, a vast swampy wasteland, unpopulated except by birds, bleak even in summer. Plans to extend the West Highland Line across this most desolate of moors in the last century, so it could link up with Perthshire, were abandoned after a group of top railway executives set out over the moor to survey it, got lost, had to spend the night out in the bog and nearly died of exposure.

Kinlochleven, at the head of Loch Leven, was a big iron ore smelter, founded to bring employment at the beginning of the century and now closed. Most of the houses were built for the workers.

Where to Stay and Eating Out

expensive

The grandest is the Victorian mansion, **Inverlochy Castle Hotel**, at Torlundy,

3 miles (4.5km) north of Fort William, ℂ 0397 702177. It is so exclusive it doesn't publish its prices.

Knockie Lodge Hotel, Whitebridge, ℂ 04563 276, in an old family house, set amidst remote scenery high above Loch Ness, is comfortable, with fishing.

moderate

Alexandra Hotel, Old Fort Parade, Fort William, ℂ 0397 702241, is old-fashioned, not wildly exciting but dependable.

Ballachulish House, ℂ 08552 266, is an 18th-century laird's house overlooking Loch Linnhe and the Morven Hills. It has a great atmosphere and you feel welcome as you walk through the door. **Ballachulish Hotel**, ℂ 08552 606, has a marvellous position overlooking the water and the food is excellent.

Corriegour Lodge Hotel, Loch Lochy, near Spean Bridge, ℂ 039781 685, has good views over the loch and reasonable food. Slightly more expensive, **Spean Bridge Hotel**, ℂ 039781 250, is old-fashioned, comfortable and jolly.

Glengarry Castle Hotel, at Invergarry, ℂ 08093 254, is a rather grim-looking pile but should suit those who hanker for ghosts. Not historic itself, it has in its grounds the ruins of Invergarry Castle, where the seven severed heads were presented to the chief of the MacDonells of Glengarry (see Tobar nan Ceann, p.406). The hotel is comfortable, in a lovely position overlooking Loch Oich. It is only open from April to October.

For Nessie-spotters, **Loch Ness Lodge Hotel** at Drumnadrochit, ℂ 04562 342, has a lot to offer. Perched above Loch Ness, the hotel is comfortable and friendly and includes a visitor centre with interesting exhibits of local history and culture and a 200-seat cinema with simultaneous translations in six languages.

Lovat Arms Hotel, Fort Augustus, ℂ 0320 6206, is comfortable, overlooking Loch Ness and the abbey. Good food.

inexpensive

Kings House Hotel in Glencoe, ℂ 08556 259, claims to be Scotland's oldest inn. Whether it is or not, it is cosy, in dramatic surroundings.

Roy Bridge Hotel, ℂ 039781 201, is at the entrance to Glen Roy, a pleasant, well-run hotel with passable food. **Invergarry Hotel**, ℂ 08093 206, is nice, cheap, and recently completely refurbished.

Another one for monster-spotters is **Drumnadrochit Hotel** at the Exhibition Centre, ℂ 04562 218. Surrounded by monsterabilia, this is slightly tawdry.

Lewiston Arms Hotel, near Drumnadrochit, ℂ 04562 225, is a charming, 200-year-old inn in a pretty garden. **Glenmoriston Arms Hotel**, ℂ 0320 51206, is a traditional Highland inn, with comfortable rooms, good food and a choice of 170 malt whiskies.

West of the Great Glen to Kyle of Lochalsh

There is a detour from Invermoriston or from Invergarry, 13 miles (21km) to the south, off the A82. The two roads join up and go west of the Great Glen to Kyle of Lochalsh, the stepping stone to the Isle of Skye. The A887 from Invermoriston goes 16 miles (25.5km) through Glen Moriston to meet the A87 from Invergarry. Some 12 miles (19km) from Invermoriston, look out for the cairn beside the road beyond Achlain. It is in memory of a brave man, Roderick Mackenzie, an Edinburgh lawyer, who had the dubious honour of being a Bonnie Prince Charlie look-alike. Hoping to deflect government troops from their quest for the Prince's head after Culloden, Mackenzie allowed himself to be captured. He lost his life for his gallantry and his head was presented to Butcher Cumberland in triumph at Fort Augustus.

The A87 is an excellent new road along the north side of Loch Garry, over high moorland with sweeping views. Five miles (8km) west of Invergarry, a narrow single-track road goes out to **Kinloch Hourn**, Loch of Hell. This, despite its name, is another glorious sea loch, snaking out towards the western isles, steep sided and treacherous for sailors in certain winds. The Glengarry Highland Games are held in July.

After the two roads join, the A87 runs north of Loch Cluanie, through mountain passes that are a patchwork of heather and scree, with rich wooded glens where the many rivers and burns cascade down from the surrounding hills. The Five Sisters of Kintail dominate Glen Shiel.

At **Shiel Bridge** on Loch Duich, 10 miles (16km) west of Cluanie, a narrow, twisting road branches left and climbs over the **Mam Ratagan Pass**. This was the route taken by the drovers bringing cattle and sheep from Skye, down to trysts at Falkirk and Crieff. It follows the course of the military road out to **Fort Bernera**, 8 miles (13km) west of Shiel Bridge. Johnson and Boswell travelled along this road in 1772, when soldiers were still working on it. The ruins of the Bernera Barracks are north of Glenelg, just before the ferry across to Kylerhea in Skye. They were built in 1722 and used until after 1790. Boswell eyed them as he shepherded an ill-humoured Dr Johnson towards what proved to be very poor lodgings: 'I looked at them wishfully, as soldiers have always everything in the best order.'

Glen Beg runs east off a narrow road 2 miles (3km) south of Glenelg. Here are two of the most splendid examples of the Iron Age brochs built to provide shelter and refuge for the chiefs and their people: **Dun Telve** and **Dun Troddan**. Their double walls are honey-combed with galleries, and pierced by a single small entrance, easily defended. At the end of the road a track leads to Dun Grugaig, an earlier fort, on the brink of a steep gorge.

Not far south of Glen Beg is Sandaig. The house where Gavin Maxwell lived with his otters was on the beach below Upper Sandaig—it was burnt to the ground. In his books, *Ring of Bright Water*, *The Rocks Remain*, etc., Maxwell miscalls the place Camusfeàrna (bay of the alders), in order to preserve its remoteness and isolation. There are many other, genuine Camusfeàrnas in Scotland, causing some confusion.

This rough road goes right on down to Arnisdale and Glen Corran on Loch Hourn, 10 miles (16km) or so to the south.

Back on the main road round Loch Duich, stop at Morvich, 2 miles (3km) beyond Shiel Bridge at the head of the loch. There is a National Trust for Scotland visitor centre here, with an audio-visual exhibition giving an excellent picture of the surrounding Kintail estate, with its many walks and climbs. They have details of the route out to the spectacular Falls of Glomach, 3 miles (4.5km) further on by road to the northeast and then about a 4-mile (6.5km) walk and climb. The 370-foot (114m) falls are among the highest in Britain, falling in two spectacular cascades over a projecting rock, into a breathtakingly deep chasm. The air is full of the sound of water and the sides of the gorge are hung with lush green ferns and foliage.

Eilean Donan Castle (open daily, Easter–Sept: adm) is 10 miles (16km) northwest of Shiel Bridge, one of the most photographed castles in Scotland and familiar to anyone who saw the film *Highlander*. Standing on a rocky island reached by a causeway, on the edge of Loch Duich, it was built in 1230, on the site of an ancient fort, and was the seat of the MacKenzies, Earls of Seaforth. What you see today is almost entirely Victorian—a loose 19th-century reinterpretation of a medieval castle, not entirely accurate. It was garrisoned by Spanish troops in 1719, supporting one of the Jacobite attempts to regain the throne for the Stuarts: in reprisal it was bombarded by English warships. It is open to the public and dedicated as a war memorial to the Clan Macrae, who held the castle as Constables to the Earls of Seaforth. Among other things are interesting Jacobite relics.

Kyle of Lochalsh is 7 miles (11km) west, terminus for the railway from Inverness and the ferry to Skye. This busy little holiday resort has several shops, a swimming pool and is usually full of a cheerful crowd of holidaymakers. Cars wait to catch the ferry to Kyleakin, a 24-hour service that takes only a few minutes. A new bridge across to Skye is planned. There are plenty of good walks round here.

Where to Stay

See also previous and following sections.

expensive

Lochalsh Hotel, © 0599 4204, stands right on the water at Kyle of Lochalsh, a huge hotel, worth every penny for position alone, but also for comfort and good food.

moderate

A lot cheaper and just as nice in a different way, **Balmacara Hotel** nearby, © 059986 283, looks across Loch Alsh. **Kintail Lodge Hotel**, Glenshiel, © 059981 226, has a nice atmosphere. **The Castle Inn**, Dornie, © 059985 205, has a reputation for being particularly kind and hospitable to weary travellers. The food is good, they offer trout fishing and you can hire their motor launch.

Loch Duich Hotel, Ardelve, Dornie, © 059985 213, is good value. **Cluanie Inn** Cluanie, Glenmoriston, © 0320 40238, is a welcome haven in a remote landscape and reasonable.

The Southwest Corner

The southwestern corner of the Highland Region is Jacobite country and still remains a very Catholic pocket of the mainland. It is an enchanted land, full of beauty as well as history. Cars should be abandoned whenever possible and sailors should put to sea.

The **Corran Ferry**, 9 miles (14.5km) southwest of Fort William, crosses Loch Linnhe at the Corran Narrows, a frequent service taking 5 minutes. Several districts occupy the peninsula to the west and south: Ardgour, Moidart, Sunart, Ardnamurchan, Morvern and Kingairloch. Rugged, mountainous and beautiful, deeply cut by lochs and glens, this is one of the most magical corners of Scotland.

The road south from Corran goes down Loch Linnhe, branching left after 7 miles (11km) to become the B8043. Keep on southwest through Morvern, cut by lush green glens alive with the sound of water and bird song. **Lochaline**, on the southern shore of the peninsula, means 'the beautiful loch'. It faces across the Sound of Mull to Fishnish Point, linked by a fairly frequent car ferry taking 15 minutes. Silica sand is mined at Lochaline, used for making optical glass.

There is no road to **Ardtornish Castle** on a point a couple of miles east of Lochaline. Built in 1340, it was for many years a stronghold of the Lords of the Isles. The ruined keep and ramparts are custodians of a stirring past when proud, independent chiefs ruled over this territory with a total disregard for the authority of the Crown.

Fiunary is 5 miles (8km) west of Lochaline along the coast, the home of George Macleod, the left-wing Presbyterian who re-established a community on Iona in 1938 and took the name Lord Macleod of Fiunary when he was made a life peer in 1967. There are lovely views across the sound from this road, which peters out after 8 or 9 miles (14km).

Strontian, north of Lochaline on the A884, is at the head of Loch Sunart. From Strontian Lead Mines, opened in 1722, came the discovery of the element strontium. These mines, manned by French prisoners of war, provided bullets for the Napoleonic Wars. There is a well-stocked yacht chandler here and an inn where groups of holidaymakers often create their own spontaneous ceilidhs in the summer months.

The Floating Church

It was just off Strontian, in Loch Sunart, that the 'Floating Church' was anchored in 1843, during the 'Disruption', when the Free Church broke away from the Church of Scotland. The local laird refused members of the breakaway church land on which to build their kirk, so they bought an old ship on the Clyde, fitted it up as a church and towed it to Loch Sunart; the congregation rowed out to worship in it.

Loch Sunart is a perfect, safe anchorage for boats. For sailors, there can be few more enjoyable experiences than to sail out of Loch Sunart early on a fine morning, the wind on your quarter, the sun on your back, watching the whole of the island-studded Minch open up ahead.

Halfway along the north shore of Loch Sunart, the B8007 is a cul-de-sac branching west to **Ardnamurchan**, a rugged, windlashed peninsula, familiar to west-coast yachtsmen as the most westerly point on the mainland of the British Isles. The ruin of **Mingary Castle**, about 16 miles (25.5km) along, was once the stronghold of the MacIans of Ardnamurchan. The castle stands on a rock cliff, its walls rising sheer with the cliff on the seaward side, guarding the entrance to Loch Sunart and to the Sound of Mull. James VI came to Mingary to receive the homage of the Lords of the Isles, and was disappointed by their lack of enthusiasm for his sovereignty. The castle was taken by Montrose's men in 1644 and garrisoned in 1745 by government soldiers, who built a barracks within the walls.

Ardnamurchan Point, about 22 miles (35km) from Salen, is wild, heather-clad rock with a lighthouse at its tip, at present closed to the public and a good 5-mile (8km) walk from the road. The lighthouse is a listed building. Although it was restored not so long ago when visited by the Queen, it is already at risk again. This dramatic headland takes the full force of westerly gales and can present quite a challenge to small boats, even in lighter winds.

Moidart, north from Salen, has a Jacobite legend in every glen, hill and loch. **Acharacle** (difficult to pronounce: the 'ch' is guttural) is a scattered village at the western end of **Loch Sheil**, 3 miles (4.5km) north of Salen. With plenty of kit houses, this is a very typical 20th-century Highland community. From here, **Ardtoe** is another 3 miles (4.5km) west on **Kentra Bay**. This sheltered, sandy haven has been turned into a vast seawater reserve for white fish farming. Ardtoe is a delightful place, popular with artists.

Castle Tioram

Just north of Acharacle, an unmarked lane to the left twists and turns out to the South ·Channel of Loch Moidart, and one of the most stirring, romantic ruins in Scotland. Castle Tioram, pronounced 'tiram' and meaning 'dry land' in Gaelic, stands high on a rocky promontory overlooking Eilean Shona, reached on foot by causeway at low tide. This 13th- to 14th-century castle was the seat of the Macdonalds of Clanranald. It was burnt in 1715 by the staunchly Jacobite chief, to prevent it from falling into government hands while he was away fighting at Sheriffmuir. The tower dates from 1600; the walls enclose an inner court yard, with several chambers.

In 1984 these ancient walls became the fine setting for a gathering of Clanranald Macdonalds from all over the world. They were entertained by their chief, in the roofless banqueting hall, roasting whole lambs in the old hearth, and for a few hours the castle lived again. The darkness was vibrant with pipe music and laughter. The next day an open-air Mass was celebrated in the courtyard to rededicate the Clanranald banner, said to have survived from Culloden.

It was at **Kinlochmoidart**, 5 miles (8km) north of Acharacle, that Prince Charles waited while the clans were rallied to his cause, and it was here that his charm won over the chiefs who were reluctant to take part in his rebellion. Seven oak trees here, (some replanted after a gale, are called the Seven Men of Moidart, in memory of the Prince's followers.

The road twists up through Moidart and follows the zigzag of **Loch Ailort** to its head. Here turn left on the A830 (another cul-de-sac) for about 6 miles (9.5km) to **Loch nan Uamh** (Loch of the Caves). Here, on 25 July 1745, Prince Charles landed from Eriskay, with only seven companions, at the start of his campaign to restore the crown to the Stuarts. A cairn, on a crag overlooking the loch beside the road, commemorates the event. A year later, broken and defeated, the Prince embarked from this same place, to return to France, effectively ending what became known as *Bliadhna Teàrlach* (Charles's Year). The knobbly hills of South Morar, to the northeast, mottled sepia-greyish, are rather gloomy but the view across to Eigg and Rum is splendid.

Arisaig, about 7 miles (11km) west of the cairn, has a sheltered anchorage and is a peaceful holiday village from which boat cruises run to the islands. Around the bay, where trawlers lie at anchor, attractive houses cling to the hillside. The prominent tower of the Catholic church was erected in memory of Alasdair MacMhaigstir Alasdair, one of the greatest of the Gaelic poets, who took the Jacobite side in 1745. The tower is a landmark for boats. Arisaig has its Highland Games in July.

Morar, about 7 miles (9.5km) north of Arisaig, stands on a sheltered bay with glorious silver sands. **Loch Morar** runs nine miles (14.5km) eastwards, the deepest inland loch in Europe at over 1000 feet (308m). North Morar, on its far shore, and Knoydart, beyond Loch Nevis to the north, are wild and roadless, accessible only by boat or on foot. Knoydart is in the process of being developed for holidaymakers, but time moves slowly in these parts.

Mallaig

Mallaig is about 10 or 11 miles (17km) north of Arisaig on the western tip of North Morar. The road to it from Fort William is one of the most scenic in Scotland and under heavy pressure, being the only route to the rail and ferry terminus. This bustling little fishing port is unspoilt, in spite of being a favourite for holidaymakers. The quays are a jumble of fish-curing sheds and all the clutter of fishing: stacks of creels and fish boxes, piles of netting and gear. If you want to take a box of kippers home with you, this is the place to buy them. Cruises run to many of the islands, and there is a steam train to Fort William. The Mallaig and Morar Highland Games are held in August and there is a **Marine Life Centre**, covering the fishing tradition.

Glenfinnan

From Mallaig it is necessary to back-track. Glenfinnan is 14 miles (22.5km) east of Lochailort. The road twists and is very steep, with lovely views, between banks of rhodo-dendrons, until it drops into Glenfinnan. A column, topped by a Highlander, rises from a marsky plain at the head of Loch Shiel, where three glens meet against a backdrop of layers of blue-grey hills. The Glenfinnan Monument, another milestone in *Bliadhna Teàrlach*, was erected in 1815 to commemorate the raising of Prince Charles's standard on 19 August 1745.

It is easier to recall the past if you turn your back on this Victorian folly, and look down the loch and up into the hills. This was where the Prince stood on that summer's day, so full of hope, surrounded by those of the clans who had already committed themselves to his cause, waiting to see if Cameron of Lochiel would join them, a man whose great influence would sway the decisions of other clans. This powerful chief had not been enthusiastic about the uprising, but he was a brave man and a loyal one. 'I'll share the fate of my Prince', he had said, and now, in the still afternoon, the waiting clans heard the skirl of pipes. They turned to watch Lochiel, at the head of 700 clansmen, marching down from the hills to join Prince Charles's cause. The well known 'March of the Cameron Men' was composed by Mary Maxwell Campbell, in 1829, to commemorate this event.

The excitement must have mounted to fever-pitch, for Lochiel's action quickly brought in other clans and later in the afternoon the great red and white silken banner was unfurled: the Prince's father was proclaimed King James III of Britain, with Prince Charles Edward his Regent.

Whatever misguided folly may have influenced this final Jacobite rising, no one with a shred of romance in their veins can stand here, remembering that day, and not feel staunchly Jacobite. However, many wise, clear-sighted chiefs remained neutral, without dishonour, and it was those men, ruled by their heads rather than their hearts, who did more for Scotland's subsequent survival than the impetuous Jacobites.

The Gothic-style Catholic church above Loch Shiel, with the hills behind, must be the most beautiful Catholic church in Scotland. It contains another monument to the Prince. The **Glenfinnan Viaduct** is an impressive landmark and a great engineering feat, carrying the railway westwards.

The **National Trust for Scotland Visitor Centre** (open daily, April–Oct: adm) is across the road from the monument. It provides excellent maps showing the progress of the Prince's army, and traces his wanderings after Culloden out to the islands and finally back to Loch nan Uamh.

The Glenfinnan Games are held every August on the nearest Saturday to the 19th.

The old station at Glenfinnan has a new railway interpretive centre, which, no doubt, will be wildly interesting for some.

What hotels lack in mod cons and sophistication in this area, they make up for in hospitality and courtesy.

expensive

Glenborrodale Castle, near Ardnamurchan, ✆ 09724 266, is a restored Victorian pile in 850 acres overlooking Mull and Loch Sunart. Open from May to October, it has a quirky Highland character, with unreliable plumbing in beautifully fitted-out bathrooms, and a half-size billiard table.

moderate

The Arisaig Hotel is a delightfully warm, friendly coaching inn, with glorious sea views and reasonable food. Another nice one is **Arisaig House**, highly recommended, with terraced gardens and views to sea, and with good food and wine.

Stage House Inn, Glenfinnan, ✆ 039783 246, is fairly sophisticated, on Loch Shiel. Open April to October, it has good food.

West Highland Hotel, Mallaig, ✆ 0687 2210, is a splendid family-owned hotel, overlooking the islands, oozing with hospitality. Open April to October.

inexpensive

Ardgour Hotel, ✆ 08555 225, is very good, and right on the water at Ardgour with glorious views.

Salen Hotel, Acharacle, ✆ 096785 661, has a friendly atmosphere and serves delicious salmon sandwiches for lunch. **Clanranald Hotel**, Acharacle, ✆ 096785 662, is a homely little hotel with not too many frills and masses of character. The six bedrooms share two bathrooms. Open from Easter to October.

Kilchoan House Hotel, near Ardnamurchan, ✆ 09723 200, is an attractive Highland lodge with one bathroom between eight bedrooms. The food is good.

Glenfinnan House Hotel, Glenfinnan, ✆ 039783 235, is a splendid old mansion overlooking the Glenfinnan Monument, with glorious views of Loch Shiel. Open April to October. You might get pipe music if you are lucky.

Morar Hotel, ✆ 0687 2346, is a good, family hotel, with very friendly staff, in a lovely position overlooking the Silver Sands of Morar. Open April to October.

Glenuig Inn, near Lochailort, ✆ 06877 219, is a dear little inn on a secluded bay with a sandy beach and freshwater trout lochs nearby. The food is first class, especially the seafood. Open April to October.

Kyle of Lochalsh to Inverness via the West Coast

The coastal route back to Inverness opens up more wonderful scenery. Take the narrow road to the left in Kyle of Lochalsh and follow the coast (and the railway) round for about 7 miles (9.5km) to **Plockton**. The views are across to Applecross and Torridon in the north and west to Skye. Plockton is an unexpected holiday village, its neat stone cottages all painted and trim, with velvet lawns and palm trees, lush shrubs, birches and pines, all grouped most attractively round a sheltered bay. Built in the 18th century as a fishing village, it is now unashamedly given over to up-market holidaymakers, with craft shops and pleasure boats, surrounded by picture-postcard scenery. This is an artist's haven. From Plockton the road follows the southern shore of Loch Carron, to the narrows at Stromeferry (no ferry now), and up to Strathcarron at the head of the loch.

It is interesting to reflect that there were virtually no roads in this area until General Wade's military roads were constructed in the first half of the 18th century. When the Highlands were so devastated by the potato famine in the middle of the 19th century, Destitution Committees were set up to send supplies of meal and provisions to the starving Highlanders. Some of the 'Destitution Funds' collected were used to build access roads to remote communities, making it easier to send help and providing work for the people. Some of these roads became known as 'Destitution Roads.'

Applecross Peninsula, round the head of Loch Carron and west from Lochcarron village, is another area of striking Highland scenery. Spectacular *Bealach-nam-Bo*, Pass of the Cattle, is a steep, narrow road across the southern end of the peninsula with hair-pin bends that make the adrenalin flow. The scenery is almost alpine, fringed by cliffs and rock spurs, dotted with glinting lochans and burns, with the distant hills of Skye ever present to the west. Cattle were driven over this pass from Applecross *en route* for the lucrative markets on the east coast. Records in 1794 tell of 3000 cattle leaving the district.

Don't miss the excellent **Carron Tweed Factory** at Lochcarron.

There is a sandy beach at Applecross, on the west coast of the peninsula, in a sheltered bay. An Irish monk, Maelrubha, founded a monastery north of the village, in 673. It became an important centre of Christianity until it was destroyed by Norsemen. A cul-de-sac runs to the south of the peninsula. It is possible to drive right round the north coast from Applecross beach, along the southern shore of Loch Torridon, Loch Shieldaig and Upper Loch Torridon to Torridon village.

The 26,000-acre **Torridon Estate** was acquired by the National Trust for Scotland in 1967. There is a visitor centre at the road junction at the head of Upper Loch Torridon, with an audio-visual presentation on the area. There is a deer museum and enclosures, a programme of guided walks and advice on where to go. The 750-million-year-old red sandstone mountains dominate the whole of this part of the region with their distinctive white quartzite peaks.

The Beinn Eighe National Nature Reserve is northeast of Torridon on the A896, and was the first in Britain established for the preservation and study of the remains of the

Caledonian Forest. The wildlife in the area includes deer, wild mountain goat, wild cat, pine marten, and eagles. For those who like leaflets and posters and illustrated information, there is a visitor centre at **Aultroy Cottage,** just northwest of **Kinlochewe**, with advice on walks, an illuminated model of the district and details about the work done on the reserve.

The drive west along the northern shore of Loch Torridon goes through scattered crofting townships, with sea views, backed by massive hills, as far as Lower Diabaig, about 8 miles (13km). A track goes further round the coast to a youth hostel. From here it is a lovely walk up the rocky coast to Redpoint.

The A832 goes northwest from Kinlochewe along the south shore of beautiful **Loch Maree**, dominated by **Slioch** on the opposite side. Loch Maree is 12 miles (19km) long, its name derived from St Maelrubha, the monk who founded the monastery at Applecross. He spent some time as a hermit on one of the islands on the loch and is, according to tradition, buried there.

About 8 miles (13km) along is the **Loch Maree Hotel**. Nothing seems to have changed here since Queen Victoria visited it in 1877 and stayed for six days. A rock on a bank in front of the hotel, inscribed in Gaelic, commemorates the queen's visit. This is a fishing hotel, with an impressive log of catches on the hall table. Some locals can still remember the day, in the mid-1920s, when a fishing party from the hotel ate sandwiches made from paste that had seen better days. Several of them died from botulism—others were dreadfully ill.

The A832 leaves Loch Maree soon after the hotel and goes west towards Gairloch. At **Kerrysdale**, about 10 miles (16km) beyond the hotel, the River Kerry dashes towards the sea, through mossy glades and silver birches, with a few gnarled oaks and feathery rowans. Carpeting the dappled turf are a profusion of wild flowers: lousewort, milkwort, primroses, bluebells, wood anemones, orchids, and many more.

Take the very minor cul-de-sac left from Kerrysdale, past the sheltered anchorage of **Shieldaig**, and the attractive bay at **Badachro**. This was once a large fishing station where curers bought herring, cod, ling, etc., from local fishermen. Now the community life is centred on a tiny, friendly shop-cum-post office. The road, which was built with money from the Destitution Fund, goes on to **Redpoint**. Heather-carpeted moorland runs down to rocky cliffs and crescents of red-gold sand. The views are across to South Rona and Raasay, with the island of Skye beyond. An otter swims in the sea and builds its cone of fish-remains on the turf. Wheatears, ringed plovers, linnets and skylarks fill the air with song. Colonies of seabirds mass on the rocks: cormorants, shags, gulls, terns, fulmars, gannets. An old man with piercing blue eyes sits on a rock, sucking his pipe: 'You could never be bored, here', he says: 'If you run out of things to do, you can just watch the weather.'

Back at Kerrysdale, turn left to **Gairloch**, a well-developed holiday resort with excellent sandy beaches and several hotels. The hub of this community seems to be the Wild Cat Stores, purveyors of fresh milk, fresh baps and local chat. Opposite is the award-winning

Gairloch Heritage Museum (open daily, Easter–Sept: adm), easy to miss and well worth a visit. In only a few rooms one can learn a great deal about life in the western Highlands. The exhibits range from Pictish stones and relics to Victoriana. There is a portable pulpit for outdoor preachers of the Free Church; an old ice-making machine; stuffed birds and wild animals; an illicit still; spinning wheels with the various wools and natural dyes; a wash house; a school room, with Gaelic on the blackboard; a village store; and a fisherman and his gear. The highlight is the replica of the inside of a croft house. This is imaginatively set up with press buttons to illuminate it, set the spinning wheel in motion, and animate the old woman in front of the peat fire. She sings a haunting Gaelic lullaby to the baby, rocking in a cradle. An annex contains interesting history displays and old photographs of the area.

Poolewe is 7 or 8 miles (12–13km) northeast of Gairloch. Stop on the bridge to watch the mighty force of water from Loch Maree, thrusting its way out into Loch Ewe, forming the pool that gave the place its name.

Inverewe Garden (open daily: adm) at Inverewe, half a mile from Poolewe, is famous to horticulturists all over the world. It was created by Osgood MacKenzie, a Victorian who had spent much of his early life on the Continent. Son of the Laird of Gairloch, he was given the estate at the head of Loch Ewe in 1862: a peninsula of red Torridonian sandstone, pocked by peat-hags and bare of vegetation except for heather, crowberry and dwarf willows. It is hard to believe, now, what this enterprising man achieved from such unpromising beginnings in an era when there were few roads and soil was carried in wicker creels. He planted an outer windbreak of Corsican and Scots pine, behind deer- and rabbit-proof fences. Plants were introduced from all over the world. Now, there are some 2500 species, in 50 acres of woodland, covering a steep hillside that juts into the loch, sheltered by hills behind. This exotic, sub-tropical paradise lies only a little to the south of the latitude that runs through Cape Farewell, in Greenland. The proximity of the Gulf Stream is responsible for making this garden so fertile. Palm trees, rock gardens, peat-banks, ornamental ponds, all display a profusion of blooms from Japan, Chile, South Africa, the Pacific, and many other places.

An attractive cul-de-sac drive down the west side of Loch Ewe goes as far as **Cove**. Cove Cave is so deep and sheltered it was once used as a place of worship.

Gruinard Bay, about 11 miles (17.5km) north of Poolewe, has sandy beaches surrounded by hills, and views out to the Summer Isles. It is a magnificent spot, with a campsite right on the beach at **Mellon Udrigle**. Gruinard Island, in the bay, was infected with anthrax during the last war and was forbidden territory for years. It is now decontaminated, and has been restored to its original owner.

Sand

A small sign beside the road, not far east of **Laide** on the bay, points the way down a cliff path to two caves. The largest was a meeting place for hundreds of years and was used as a church for Presbyterians, as late as 1843. The smaller cave was lived in by an old woman and her girl companion in 1885. Families evicted from their crofts during the Clearances used to take shelter here. It is a magic place: at the entrance to the larger cave, with its protective wall in front, it is intriguing to picture it when perhaps several families were huddled together inside, with what they had saved of their possessions and livestock. The fire would be burning, children and dogs playing, and people making do with whatever fish and game they had managed to catch. Picture it when the wind blew in from the north, rolling the great boulders on the shore. Picture it too, in summer, with thrift and honeysuckle growing down the rocks, and the sea as calm and clear as a Pacific lagoon.

The A832 skirts Little Loch Broom (stop and look at the spectacular **Ardessie Falls** about two-thirds of the way along), and cuts across the moors. The part of the road from Dundonnell, by Feithean, to Braemore Junction, was built with funds raised during the potato famine and so is called the 'Destitution Road'. The name is misleading: it's lovely.

Braemore Junction is where the A832 meets the A835 to Ullapool, about 28 miles (45km) from Gruinard. It is also at the confluence of the rivers Broom, Cuileig and Droma, known locally as 'The Valley of The Broom'. Stop at the large observation car park just before the A835. It is a staggering view down into the junction of the three valleys, the steep wooded banks ablaze with colour in the autumn. Less than a mile (1.5km) further on, a sign on the left marks the Corrieshalloch Gorge and the Falls of Measach. It is only a short walk from the road and there is an alternative approach from round the corner, where there is another car park and signs, on the A835.

Corrieshalloch

Corrieshalloch is unforgettable: a mile-long (1.5km) box canyon, 200 feet (60m) deep, its sheer rock sides festooned with ferns and mosses, saxifrage, sorrel, tufts of grasses and wood-millet. Miraculously rooted wych elm, birch, hazel, sycamore, Norway maple and beech trees cling to the sides, with goat-willow, bird-cherry and guelder-rose. There is an observation platform from which to look back at the Falls of Measach, a single cascade of 150 feet (46m) that seems to hang in the air like smoke. There is an even better view from the suspension bridge that spans the gorge, but this is not for vertigo sufferers. The deep pools below are rich in trout, and, above the roar of the falls, the angry 'pruk' of the ravens can be heard, as they nest on a ledge opposite the viewing platform.

The drive back to Inverness from here is attractive, through open moor, past lochs and glens. See the Inverness to Durness section for things to look at on the way.

Where to Stay

moderate

Gairloch Hotel, © 0445 2001, is a huge Victorian pile overlooking the sea, open from April to October. You expect to see pitchers and bowls in the bedrooms but actually it is reasonably modern and comfortable and, rare in this part of the world, all 66 bedrooms are en suite. **Shieldaig Lodge Hotel**, near Gairloch, © 044583 250, is a Victorian country house, right by the water and backed by trees, with good food. **Kinlochewe Hotel**, ✆ 0445 84253, is cheaper and reasonably comfortable. **Pool House Hotel**, at Poolewe, ✆ 044586 272, is a small family-run hotel by the bridge where Loch Maree pours out into Loch Ewe, within walking distance of Inverewe Garden. **Loch Torridon Hotel**, ✆ 0445 791242, is a Victorian mansion with lovely views in 56 acres, open April to October. **Ocean View Hotel** at Sand, ✆ 0445 731385, has a marvellously friendly atmosphere.

inexpensive

Aultbea Hotel, ✆ 0445 731201, is a small hotel on the eastern shore of Loch Ewe, quiet and comfortable with good food. **Drumchork Lodge Hotel** close by, ✆ 0445 731242, is slightly bigger, slightly more expensive, with the same stunning views. **Badachro Inn**, ✆ 044583 255, is a whitewashed inn with a small garden on the edge of the bay. It has two bedrooms only, and one bathroom. The food is unpretentious and very cheap.

Inverness to Durness

The first part of the drive to Durness goes through farmland backed by hills, rapidly turning to moor and rugged mountain as the road crosses to the west. From Loch Broom north it is all mountains and vistas of loch, mountain and sea.

Beauly is 10 miles (16km) west of Inverness at the head of the Beauly Firth. This is Lovat country. The Lovat family came to Britain with the Normans and it was their French influence that inspired the name Beauly, *Beau Lieu*. (Romantics prefer to attribute the name to Mary, Queen of Scots, fresh from her French chateau, exclaiming '*Ah, quelle beau lieu!*')

The centre of Beauly is a widening of the main road, making an attractive rectangular market place with the ruin of Beauly Priory (open daily: free) at the north end, beyond the old cross. Founded in 1230 for Valliscaulian monks, the priory is now a roofless shell. In the south wall are three fine triangular windows embellished with trefoils dating from the original building. It fell into ruin after the Reformation.

The monument in the Square commemorates the raising of the Lovat Scouts for service in South Africa, by Simon Joseph, 16th Lord Lovat. Perhaps the most colourful member of the family was Simon, Lord Lovat, born in about 1667. His many notorious escapades included the attempted abduction of a nine-year-old heiress and his subsequent marriage by force to her mother, a deed that left him convicted of high treason and outlawed. Having come into the title, by devious means, he became a Jacobite agent, involved in conveying false information to the enemy. Outlawed once more, he turned government man and received a full pardon. Swearing loyalty to the Crown, he sent his son to fight for Prince Charles in 1745. He was beheaded, finally, in London, meeting his end with humorous dignity. 'You'll get that nasty head of yours chopped off, you ugly old Scotch dog,' taunted a Cockney woman in the crowd. 'I believe I shall, you ugly old English bitch,' he replied. Hogarth painted a portrait of him in hideous old age, just before he was helped up the steps to the scaffold—bloated, villainous, with satanic eyebrows and a cruel mouth, wracked by gout. Known as 'The Old Fox of the '45', he was indisputably a rogue, traitor and hypocrite. Alternative, more kindly, reports also credit him with intelligence, charm and Celtic wit.

Internationally known, **Campbells of Beauly** faces on to the Square. This shop is a treasure-trove of tweeds, woollens, tartans and all possible Highland accessories, ready made or custom built. Visitors return, year after year, tempted by the remarkable range and quality of the products, efficiently served by the Campbell family.

Moniack Castle Winery and Wine Bar (open on weekdays) is an excellent staging post a few miles southeast of Beauly. They serve their own home-produced country wines, meads and a variety of delicious jellies, in converted out-buildings in an ancestral setting. The food is excellent and the wine is for sale.

In 1990, a number of idealists organized a sponsored 'Poethon' to raise money to establish a Writers Centre, Moniack Mhor, in outbuildings on the Moniack estate. For 24 hours, at various venues in London, 144 people recited contemporary poetry from memory, with the help of such celebrated poets as James Fenton and Wendy Cope. They raised a lot of money, and the centre is now a going concern.

Before continuing north, it is worth making a detour to visit the glens of Farrar, Glass, Beauly, Cannich and Affric. From Beauly, take the A831 southwest down Strathglass to Glen Affric, through wooded glens following the River Beauly and then the River Glass. The remains of two Iron Age forts lie off to the right from **Kilmorack**, 2 miles (3km) from Beauly. Here, and at **Aigas,** 3 miles (4.5km) further on, are hydroelectric dams where visitors can watch salmon being 'lifted' on their way upstream to breed. **Tomich** is an attractive estate village built in the late 19th century. The home farm up on the hill has been converted as a holiday centre with swimming pool, accommodation and some chalets.

There are lovely walks in this area where the three glens of the Farrar, Glass and Beauly meet; the scenery is gentler than that of the western Highlands but just as magnificent, enhanced rather than spoiled by the hydroelectric developments that have changed the landscape. Steep, pine-clad rocks rise from peaty lochs in broad, green valleys.

At **Glassburn,** look out for the **Holy Well of St Ignatius,** beside the road: an intriguing old headstone in a modern cairn, with ingravings that include references to: saints Columba 563, Bean 1015, and Margaret 1070, as well as Pope Leo XIII. There is also a poem which could be the marching song of the Temperance League:

> *'Water bright water, pure water for me,*
> *the drink of the wise, the wine of the free . . .'*

and a lot more in that vein.

Stop off at the chapel of St Mary's, in **Eskadale,** a mile (1.5km) beyond Aigas. This pretty, early Victorian church was once the main Catholic centre for this area. In the graveyard is a memorial to an almost-forgotten episode in Scotland's history: the graves of the 'Sobieski Stuarts'. These two brothers, John Sobieski Stolberg Stuart, 1795–1872, and Charles

Edward Stuart, 1799–1880, conned Victorian society into accepting them as grandsons of Prince Charles Edward Stuart. They claimed that their father, Lieutenant Thomas Allen, Royal Navy, was Prince Charles's son. They called themselves Counts d'Albanie and there is a splendid book, *The Sobieski Stuarts*, by H. Beveridge, about them. They lived at Eskadale House, further down the valley, and at Eilan Aigas House, where they kept deer hounds and invented several tartans with which further to impress their gullible friends.

More lovely scenery is at Cannich, 17 miles (27km) southwest of Beauly, where the River Glass meets up with the Rivers Affric and Cannich. There is a youth hostel here. About 3 miles (4.5km) southeast, the Corrimony Cairn is a Stone and Bronze Age burial cairn, its passage still roofed and surrounded by a stone circle.

Although it is far nicer to walk, it is possible to drive the 12 miles (19km) up Glen Farrar to Loch Monar; it is a private road so permission must first be asked. A road runs 8miles (13km) up Glen Cannich to Cozac Lodge, and another up Glen Affric (one of the most beautiful glens in Scotland) to a car park, 2 miles (3km) short of Affric Lodge. Each glen has its own charm, with tumbling burns, lichen-hung trees, glinting sheets of water, all sheltered by hills. From Affric Lodge there is a good hike, 10 miles (16km) west, to the youth hostel at Alltbeath. Another 10 miles (16km) or so reaches Loch Duich. It cannot be emphasized too often that anyone walking and climbing here, and anywhere else in the Highlands, should be fit, sensibly equipped, and should carry and know how to use a map and compass. They should also make sure it isn't the stalking season.

Contin, 11 miles (17.5km) north of Beauly, has an old coaching inn, on the west side of the River Blackwater, from which passengers used to depart on the tortuous journey west to Poolewe and Ullapool, after the roads were built in the 18th century. Telford built the first bridge here, later swept away by flood water. Dealers used to come up from England to the Contin Horse Fair, to buy sturdy Highland ponies for work in the coal mines. Fair days were festive occasions, drawing people in from far afield, to jostle and gossip over the braziers, among the peddlers' stalls and animal pens.

Strathpeffer

Strathpeffer, a couple of miles northeast of Contin, was a famous spa town until the First World War. People came from overseas, including foreign royalty, to the sulphur and chalybeate springs. The springs were used as early as 1770, but it was not until the first pump room (now derelict) was built in 1820 that Strathpeffer's fame spread over the border. Lying in a sheltered hollow among wooded hills, the town is a popular holiday centre, with plenty for the visitor to do, including climbing Ben Wyvis, the great bulk a few miles to the north. Houses and hotels rise in neat terraces from the heart of the town, whose gently refined atmosphere has won it the title 'Harrogate of the North'.

Strathpeffer Highland Games are held in the grounds of Castle Leod in early August, with all the traditional events such as tossing the caber, putting the shot, piping and dancing.

The **Eagle Stone** stands 3 feet (1m) high on a hillock to the east of Strathpeffer, reached by a lane near Eaglestone House. It is a Pictish symbol stone with an engraved angel and a horseshoe and was the subject of one of the Brahan Seer's prophecies. If the stone should fall three times, he said, then ships would tie up to it. Setting aside a tidal wave, this seems improbable. However, the seer had an uncanny eye and it is said that the stone has already fallen twice (hence its having been cemented into place and surrounded by wire) and that on the second occasion the Cromarty Firth flooded up to the old county buildings in Dingwall.

Strathpeffer Craft and Visitor Centre (open in the summer: free) has craftsmen and women at work in what was the Victorian station.

Highland Museum of Childhood, in the Old Station (open daily Feb–Nov except closed Mon in Mar and Nov; closed Dec–Jan: adm), brings to life the story of childhood in the Highlands.

At the **Water Sampling Pavilion** in The Square (open daily, Easter–Oct: adm), you can hold your nose and sample the sulphur waters that made Strathpeffer famous as a Victorian spa.

To the south, on a ridge called **Druim Chat**, meaning 'cat's back', there is a well-preserved vitrified fort, **Knockfarrel**, one in a line of three great Pictish defence sites, the other two being at Craig Phadrig in Inverness and Ord Hill in Kessock. You can see the foundations clearly—a vast place, extending to some 810 feet (250m). This is believed to have been a stronghold of Fingal and his warriors, and many are the legends told about it.

A terrible clan battle took place to the southwest, at **Kinellan**, between the Macdonalds and the Mackenzies, in the 16th century. The Macdonalds, seeking vengeance after an alleged insult, lost the fight and were later punished by James IV who deposed them as Lords of the Isles.

Rogie Falls are just over 2 miles (3km) northwest of Contin, well signposted and only a short walk from the car park. It is a delightful picnic spot among birches, rowans and gnarled old oaks, carpeted in heather, bracken and mossy crags. It is possible to watch salmon leaping up a series of falls, from a suspension bridge over the river. They often achieve astonishing heights.

Five miles (8km) on, the road divides, beyond **Garve**. The A832 to the left goes southwest along attractive Strath Bran, past Loch Luichart (where there is an excellent knitwear shop) and out to Achnasheen, a lonely, scattered hamlet where the railway widens to provide a passing place for trains. Here the road divides again, southwest to Loch Carron and Applecross (see p.419) or northwest to Loch Maree (see p.420).

Ullapool

Ullapool is 32 miles (51km) northwest of Garve, a pleasant drive through moorland and river-filled glens, backed by hills including massive Beinn Dearg, 3547 feet (1090m), to the north. The **Lael Forest Garden Trail** is further on, with over 150 different species of trees and shrubs, all labelled. There are good views across Loch Broom, fringed with beaches and nice picnic spots. The town is a popular holiday resort as well as an important fishing port and the ferry terminus for boats to Stornoway in Lewis. Freshly painted houses line the sea front, their upper windows sharply gabled, looking down on the jumble of quays and slipways, cluttered with small boats and fishing gear, creels, spars, nets and fish boxes. The town was developed as a fishing port by the British Fishery Society in 1788, Loch Broom providing an excellent deep-water anchorage for the boats. There are often east European and Russian fishing boats at anchor in the bay in the anchorage, usually scruffy looking tubs, bringing a gabble of foreign languages to the streets. It is not unknown to find a female skipper in Soviet boats. Locals will tell intriguing tales of shady people coming and going from the boats with very little interference: splendid material for a spy thriller. The town has a good range of shops, boutiques, restaurants, cafés, bars and every sort of accommodation. Some of the street names are written in Gaelic.

The Loch Broom Highland Museum (open daily except Sun, April–Oct: free) gives insight into the history of Wester Ross, the life of a fishing village and the story of the Clearances. It also has displays of geology, wildlife, military and farming history.

Ullapool Museum, in West Argyle Street, (open weekdays, April-Oct: adm), tells the life of the community over the past 200 years, including crofting, fishing, education, religion and emigration.

The tourist information office will give information on sea fishing, boating, pony trekking and cruises. There is a youth hostel and the surrounding countryside is perfect for walking.

Drumrunie is about 8 miles (13km) beyond Ullapool on the A835. Turn left here on to a minor road that skirts the **Coigach** peninsula, winding through land and sea-lochs in some of Scotland's loveliest and wildest scenery. **Achiltibuie**, about 13 miles (21km) round, well signposted, is a honeymooners' paradise and a perfect holiday base. Boats run to the Summer Isles, scattered a few miles off the Coigach Peninsula.

Horticulturists should visit the **Hydroponicum**, at the **Summer Isles Hotel**, in Achiltibuie (open daily, March–Oct: adm). Created by Robert Irvine, it has 'hi-tech soilless growing houses'—an amazing place, with three distinct climates: Hampshire, Bordeaux and the Canaries. Strawberries are picked fresh every day from April to October and bananas flourish. Figs, lemons, passion fruit, vines, vegetables, flowers and herbs all grow luxuriantly without soil. One-hour lecture tours are given in the summer; these include information on the use of solar energy. It is often featured on television. For details © 085482 202.

At **Achiltibuie Smokehouse** (open weekdays, Oct–April; daily except Sun, May–Sept: free), the process of curing and smoking of meat, fish and game can be watched and there is a retail shop. For details © 085482 353.

Back on the A835, the road runs northwards through the Inverpolly National Nature Reserve, a remote, lonely stretch of moorland dotted with lochs, burns and great jagged red sandstone peaks. These include Stac Polly, 2009 feet (618m), Cul Beag, 2523 feet (776m) and Sul Mor, 2786 feet (857m), all very popular with climbers. There is a Nature Conservancy Council visitor centre at Knockan, less than 5 miles (8km) up the road with full information about this area.

Ledmore is less than eight miles (13km) beyond Drumrunie. Here, an alternative route southeast runs 30 miles (48km) through Strath Oykel to Bonar Bridge, leaving the mountains and running through moorland and attractive wooded valleys.

Ardvreck Castle

Ardvreck Castle (always accessible: free), about 6 miles (9.5km) north of Ledmore, is a jagged fang of a ruin, three storeys high, on **Loch Assynt**. Dating from 1597, it was one of the few castles to be built in this area where lack of roads in the old days made it difficult to maintain large establishments. The Community Council is hoping to consolidate the ruin. It was a Macleod stronghold, and carries in its stones a poignant echo of the last days of Montrose. There are several conflicting stories but it is certain that gallant Montrose, fighting for Charles II, fled to Assynt in 1650 after his final defeat at Carbisdale, near Bonar Bridge. Some say he threw himself on the mercy of the Macleod laird of the time, who responded by selling him to the government for £25,000. Others say Macleod found him and took him prisoner honourably. Whatever the story, Montrose was imprisoned in this grim fortress, on its rocky peninsula jutting into the loch. From here he was taken ignominiously to Edinburgh, tied, back-to-front, on his horse, and abandoned by the king to whom he had given his loyalty.

Inchnadamph Caves, 2 miles (3km) south of Ardvreck, yielded evidence of occupation by early man and also bones of late Pleistocene animals, going back at least 10,000 years.

Lochinver is 10 miles (16km) to the west on the A837, along the north shore of Loch Assynt, a large-ish village and the only place of any size between Scourie and Ullapool. It is a delightful place on one of the most beautiful stretches of coastline in Scotland, with heart-stopping views all round. Two-hour wildlife cruises run from Lochinver, in the summer, with a chance to see some of the many birds and the colonies of seals basking on the rocks.

Dramatic sugar-loaf **Suilven**, 2,399 feet (738m), is 5 miles (8km) to the south in **Glencanisp Forest**, with **Canisp**, 2,779 feet (855m), 2 miles (3km) beyond to the east. Both are well worth climbing on a clear day. The coast road on round from Lochinver is another stunner, about 35 miles (56km) in all, back to join the A894 near **Kylestrome**, where a bridge replaces the small ferry that used to hold up traffic for hours in the holiday season. Boats run from Unapool, down Loch Glencoul to the southeast, to see Britain's highest waterfall, Eas-Coul-Aulin, a fantastic sight, 658 feet (202m) high in a wild, melancholy setting that seems appropriate for such a giddy cascade.

Yet another beautiful drive of nearly 10 miles (16km) reaches **Scourie**, a popular holiday village in a sheltered bay with a sandy beach and rocky pools. Several varieties of orchid thrive in the mild climate here; boats run to the nature reserve on **Handa Island**, a mile (1.5km) off the sandy beach north of Scourie. Here you will see a great variety of sea birds, including razorbills, guillemots, puffins, kittiwakes and skua.

The road north goes inland a few miles to **Laxford Bridge**. An alternative route goes southeast from here to **Lairg** (see p.437), through rocky mountains that tower threateningly over the road, with sharp turns and terrifying blind summits. On a sunny day, with the sparkling waters of Loch More, Loch Merkland, and Loch Shin, it can be beautiful, but on a grey, sullen day of mist and rain, it is an awe-inspiring route.

Four miles (6.5km) north of Laxford Bridge, at **Rhiconich**, a good new road goes 4 miles (6.5km) west to **Kinlochbervie**, on **Loch Inchard**, an important west-coast fishing port. Strong currents around the northern headland make swimming very dangerous here. For the most beautiful beach in Scotland, drive 5 miles (8km) on past Kinlochbervie to the end of the road and then walk on round the coast, about 4 miles (6.5km) over abandoned crofts, to **Sandwood Bay**. Entirely remote, it is outstandingly beautiful, with sand, cliffs and columns of rock rising from the sea.

The drive north from Rhiconich is through a bleak wilderness of rock-strewn glens, forbidding mountains and dark, sombre lochs.

Durness

Durness is about 15 miles (24km) northeast of Rhiconich, perched on the north coast, built to withstand the fury of the elements. It is a good base for exploring this northwestern corner and has plenty of places to stay. Durness Highland Gathering is in July.

Durness Old Church, on the bay and dating from 1619, is a roofless shell on the site of an older church. Look for the skull and crossbone carving on the wall; this is thought to mark the site of the grave of a notorious highwayman, Donald MacMurchov, who hoped to buy his way into the afterlife by making substantial contributions to the building of the church. The previous church on this site appears in records in the Vatican as having contributed to one of the Crusades in the 12th century. There was a summer palace for the Bishops of Caithness where the farmhouse now stands, opposite the church.

Smoo Cave is signposted from the road, about a mile (1.5km) to the east. This vast limestone cavern has three compartments, two of which are difficult to get to. The main chamber is 200 feet (61m) long and 120 feet (37m) high, with holes in the roof. Consult the Durness Information Centre for advice on how to reach the inner sections and the dramatic 80-foot (25m) waterfall, where the Alt Smoo River pours down from the cliffs into the caves.

Balnakeil Craft Village, in a former Ministry of Defence Early Warning Station camp, just along the track that runs west from Durness, stands on a lovely white sand bay. Sixteen or so non-local hippy-type craftsmen and women display and sell their astonishingly overpriced handiwork. The crafts include weaving, jewels, candles, rag dolls, bookbinding, painting, woodwork, pottery. In 1981 the Regional Council sold the buildings to the craftsmen and they then formed a Community Co-operative, which also runs the visitor centre.

Cape Wrath

A passenger boat runs across the Kyle of Durness in the summer to link up with a minibus that goes out to the Cape 10 miles (16km) northwest. Check times from local shops. It is worth walking one way, with binoculars and a good bird book: the promontory is an ornithologist's paradise.

Cape Wrath (pronounced 'Raath') got its name from the Viking word *hvarf* meaning 'turning place'. It was not named after the furious sea which pounds at the 523-foot-high (161m) cliffs. These cliffs have veins of rich pink pegmatite running through the gneiss. On a clear day you can see the Orkney Islands to the east, some 60 miles (96km) away, 45 miles (72km) west to the Butt of Lewis, and 80 miles (128km) southwest to Harris.

To the north lies the island of North Rona, with Stack Skerry and Skule Skerry further east. Turn your back on the great fort-like lighthouse and look across the bleak moor, **The Parbh**, that stretches away to the south. Wolves once roamed here in great numbers—an eerie thought as the mist comes creeping in across the desolate wasteland and you look around to make sure that the minibus hasn't left without you.

Where to Stay and Eating Out

See also Inverness.

expensive

Near Ullapool, the best is **Altnaharrie Hotel**, © 085483 230, an old drovers' inn on the shores of Loch Broom, reached by private launch from Ullapool. Small and very select, its bedrooms are pretty, and the food is sublime. This is the only place in Scotland to have been awarded two Michelin stars.

moderate

Unquestionably, the next two are the pick of the bunch. **Summer Isles Hotel**, Achiltibuie, © 085482 282, open Easter to October, is run by Mark and Geraldine Irvine and has been in the family since the 1960s. Wonderfully remote, in a spectacular setting overlooking the Summer Isles and beyond to the Hebrides, it is almost entirely self-sufficient. It has its own smokehouse, the Hydroponicum (see above) which provides fresh fruit and vegetables, and its own dairy, veal, quails, duck, fish, etc. There is everything here for lovers of solitude and beauty and it is exactly like going to stay with friends in a special place. In fact, once you've been there, that's what it becomes, except that you get a bill. It's worth every penny.

The other top choice is **Inchnadamph Hotel**, Loch Assynt, © 05712 202, known as the 'Anglers' Retreat'. This is another genuine Highland establishment where homely comfort is more important than double glazing, trouser presses and 'hospitality trays' in the bedroom. In the most glorious surroundings at the head of the loch, this hotel has been in the hands of the Morrison family for 71 years, which is probably why you feel completely at home the moment you arrive. It offers free fishing for salmon, grilse and brown trout, and excellent home-cooking.

Aigas Field Centre, Beauly, ✆ 0463 782443, is a Victorian-Gothic mansion on a working estate in a magnificent setting. Guests are offered optional field study programmes. Very friendly and ancestral, it's open April to October. **Contin House**, ✆ 0997 421920, is a Highland fishing lodge built in 1794, on a 35-acre island in the River Blackwater, in idyllic scenery surrounded by hills. They cater for parties of from six to ten, and it is like going to stay with very special old friends, except you don't do the washing up. **Coul House Hotel**, Contin, ✆ 0997 421487, is a splendid 19th-century pile looking across to the Strathconon hills, with an excellent reputation for good food. **Cozac Lodge**, Cannich, ✆ 04565 263, is an Edwardian shooting lodge in rugged Glen Cannich, furnished like a country house, warm and friendly with excellent food. **Ledgowan Hotel**, Achnasheen, ✆ 044588 252, was originally built as a private shooting lodge, but has been now converted into a comfortable country-house-type hotel. Open Easter to November. **Inchbae Lodge**, Garve, ✆ 09975 269, is a small country-house hotel with good food, quite comfortable. **Ben Wyvis Hotel**, Strathpeffer, ✆ 0997 421323, is a huge, rather daunting Victorian pile in six acres of attractive gardens, open from March to November. The food is patchy.

In Ullapool, **Royal Hotel** in Garve Road, ✆ 0854 612181, right on the shore of Loch Broom, is quite big, fairly sophisticated and has reasonable food. **Four Seasons Hotel**, also in Garve Road, ✆ 0854 612905, is a modern monster on the shores of Loch Broom; very friendly with good seafood.

Eddrachilles Hotel, Badcall Bay, Scourie, ✆ 0971 2080, is in a beautiful position overlooking the bay and islands, with good-ish food. Open March to October.

Scourie Hotel, ✆ 0971 2396, is comfortable with good home-cooking, and very friendly. Open March to October. **Kinlochbervie Hotel**, ✆ 097182 275, is highly recommended as a family hotel, with excellent food, overlooking Kinlochbervie harbour and Loch Clash. It's comfortable and friendly. **Cape Wrath Hotel**, Durness, ✆ 097181 274, is an easy-going, comfortable hotel on this far northern coast, open March to January.

inexpensive

The Ceilidh Place, in West Argyle Street, Ullapool, ✆ 0854 612103, is mildly eccentric, rather hearty, and fun (if you like that sort of thing), comprising: hotel, clubhouse, restaurant, coffee shop, bookshop, live shows of jazz, classical and folk music, and all sorts of other jollifications. You could do a lot worse, as long as you are gregarious. **Ferry Boat Inn** on Shore Street, Ullapool, ✆ 0854 612366, is a cosy, family-run inn looking across Loch Broom; it's rather noisy. **Morefield Motel**, also in Ullapool, ✆ 0854 612161, purpose-built in the middle of a housing estate, is not what you would expect from its appearance. It's seafood has been acclaimed—it was voted 'Fish Pub of the Year' by the *Good Pub Guide*. It's well worth a journey to eat here.

Kylesku Hotel, © 0971 2231, is a delightful little place on the loch at Kylesku in lovely scenery, with good seafood caught in their own boat. Open April to October. **Culag Hotel**, Lochinver, © 05714 270, is on the shore of Loch Inver with glorious views; an excellent place. **Parkhill Hotel**, Durness, © 097181 209, is a temperance hotel—and cheap.

Inverness to John o' Groats

The A9 north from Inverness crosses the Kessock Bridge, where the Beauly Firth meets the Moray Firth, in the lee of the Black Isle. Until 1982 this narrow neck of water was crossed in a small car ferry, known to side-slip in violent currents. The bridge, opened by the Queen Mother, won a design award. This east coast route to the top right-hand corner of Scotland crosses the fertile Black Isle and then hugs the coast almost all the way. The worst of the Highland Clearances took place in Sutherland and Caithness, and the scattered ruins of abandoned crofts can be found in deserted glens. Long straths run inland through vast tracts of moor and fen, linking the east with the north and west coasts. This, in Caithness, is the Flow Country, the biggest blanket bog in the world, coveted by forestry kings. Conservationists are struggling to stem the huge plantations already eating up this amazing concentration of wildlife. It is a fragile living surface of floating peat, with heather and sedges over a carpet of spagnum mosses. Among the threatened victims are 55 species of birds related to Arctic tundra, including 70 per cent of Britain's greenshanks, meadow pipits, red-throated divers with their primitive whale-like cries, peregrines and merlins. Among the many plants threatened is the rare insect-eating sundew. Dubh lochans, black from peat, speckle the land.

The Black Isle

The Black Isle is joined to the mainland between Beauly and Dingwall and has its own unique, soft, sing-song dialect. It is made up of rolling farmland, wildfowl beaches and attractive fishing villages. The new main road seems to rip through it in a few moments, showing little of its charms. It would be a pity to dash through it without noticing. Take the first turning right after the bridge to explore it properly—a hidden turning, easy to miss.

Munlochy Bay, about 3 miles (4.5km) up this twisting minor road, is vibrant with the cackle of geese in winter, targets for sportsmen who like to see their wildfowl at the end of a gun. **Avoch** (pronounced 'Auch'), about 4 miles (6.5km) further on, is a picturesque fishing village with a small harbour. There are miles of bracing walks on the tidal sandflats, with good views across the firth.

Fortrose, a couple of miles on, is a pleasant, no-nonsense resort town, sheltered by Chanonry Point and excellent for small boat sailing. **Fortrose Cathedral** (open daily:

free) is a mere fragment of the great church founded by King David I in the 12th century. All that remains is the south aisle of the nave and the sacristy. There are memorials here to Lord Seaforth and his family—an interesting confirmation of the Brahan Seer's prophecy about the downfall of the House of Seaforth (see p.53). In 1880, a hoard of silver coins was dug up from the green, dating from the reign of Robert III. Cromwell recycled much of the fabric of the cathedral for building a fort in Inverness. Look out for the memorial stone on **Chanonry Point** east of Fortrose. It marks the site where the Brahan Seer was burned in a barrel of tar.

Rosemarkie, a mile (1.5km) beyond the town on the northern side of Chanonry Point, is a popular beach in summer, with golden sand and rock pools. St Moluag founded a school and a church here in the 6th century, and tradition holds that he is buried below the Pictish stone in the churchyard.

Groam House Museum (open daily, June–Sept: adm) in Rosemarkie has local and archaeological exhibits: carved stones found in the vicinity of the church, indicating the importance of Rosemarkie in early Christian times; fragments of cross-slabs, and grave stones and a fine Pictish slab, all well displayed and explained. There is an audio-visual show and the curator is extremely knowledgeable.

Golf enthusiasts can enjoy an invigorating game within spitting distance of the sea on the 18-hole Fortrose and Rosemarkie golf course.

Cromarty

Cromarty, on the northeastern tip of the Black Isle, about 23 miles (37km) northeast of the Kessock Bridge, is an 18th-century fishing town and port, a Royal Burgh for seven centuries. Some of its old merchants' houses are important examples of domestic architecture of the period. Sheltered by the great headland of the South Sutor at the mouth of the Cromarty Firth, rows of terraced cottages stand gable-end-on to the street, hunched against the wind, forming rope walks where the fisherwomen used to stretch out the new ropes from the rope factory. The town was bought in 1772 by George Ross, some of whose descendants still live there. He built the harbour, founded a cloth factory, the rope factory, a nail and spade factory, a brewery, and a lace industry and built a Gaelic chapel for the Highlanders who came flocking to the town for employment. Cromarty has been skilfully and imaginatively restored. The old brewery is now Cromarty Arts Centre, with accommodation, and can be hired by groups for seminars and residential courses. Part of the old ropeworks is now housing and a restaurant. The sheltered bay was used as an anchorage for destroyer flotillas in the First World War.

Cromarty Courthouse (open daily: adm) is a visitor centre and museum, with video, animated figures, a reconstructed trial, cells, shop and displays.

Hugh Miller's Cottage (open daily, Easter–Sept, excluding Sun until June: adm), in Church Street, offers a nostalgic journey into the past. This long, low, thatched cottage with crow-stepped gables, its tiny upper windows half buried in the eaves, was built in 1711 by the great-grandfather of Hugh Miller (1802–56). He rose from simple beginnings to become a famous geologist, stonemason, naturalist, theologian and writer. (Among other things, he wrote about the Brahan Seer in *Scenes and Legends of the North of Scotland.*) Restored by the National Trust for Scotland, the cottage contains a museum devoted to collections of his writings, personal belongings, geological specimens, and such endearing memorabilia as the wooden chair in which his mother sat to nurse him.

In four restored cottages near the seafront, the work of resident craftsmen and women are displayed and sold: pottery, silver, printed hangings, jewellery, etc. There is also a small art gallery with exhibitions of local paintings.

North and South Sutors guard the entrance to the Firth like two massive sentinels: the view north, to the oil installations at Nigg, is rather marred these days, but there are foreshore walks and long expanses of sand lining Cromarty Bay. Charles II landed here on his way to be crowned at Scone in 1650. A car ferry runs between Cromarty and Nigg, one way of getting on to the north.

Continuing round the Black Isle, the B9163 runs down the coastal plain south of the firth 17 miles (27km) to **Conon Bridge** and across the neck of land that joins the Black Isle to the mainland, about 4 miles (6.5km) to **Muir of Ord**. The Black Isle Show is held just outside Muir of Ord in August.

To complete a circular tour of this attractive peninsula, a one-track road skirts the northern shore of the Beauly Firth, 10 miles (16km) back to the Kessock Bridge. It hugs the shore for the last stretch, where the tidal flats are rich in wildfowl, backed by blue-grey hills to the north. The ruined castle (private) behind a wall at the western end of the firth is Redcastle, originally built by William the Lion in 1178. The original castle, Edradour, is claimed to be the oldest inhabited house in Scotland and passed through several hands before it was annexed by the Crown after the fall from power of the notorious Douglas family. The Mackenzies held it for 200 years from 1570. According to stories they resorted to sorcery and human sacrifices in an attempt to save the land from a cattle plague. This illicit activity backfired, and the family was henceforth under a curse.

North Kessock, an attractive village straggling along the shore of the Beauly Firth, used to be the ferry terminal. Surnames such as Patience and Skinner are said to date from when Cromwell's soldiers were here. You get good bar lunches in the listed pub.

Dingwall

Dingwall, at the southwestern corner of the Cromarty Firth, is at the junction of several main routes. It is a busy little market town, its curious name being derived from the Norse words *thing* (parliament or council) and *volle* (place). Macbeth was born here, presumably in the castle that once stood in Castle Street. It is hard to believe that Dingwall was a thriving port, before the waterway at the mouth of the River Peffery became silted up. The canal at the end of Ferry Road was built by Telford, in an attempt to cut through the encroaching mudflats. Dingwall has always been an important cattle and livestock market, and even today it is just possible to hear a few exchanges in Gaelic, around the market square any Wednesday. The Dingwall Highland Gathering is in July.

The Town House (open Easter–Sept: adm), dating from 1730, is a museum. A special exhibition relates to General Sir Hector Macdonald (1853–1903), popularly known as 'Fighting Mac'—a local man who rose from the ranks to become a distinguished soldier. He served in the Second Afghan War, the Egyptian Police and the Egyptian Army and was given command of troops in Ceylon in 1902. He surpassed himself at the Battle of Omdurman. There is an impressive monument to him on Mitchell Hill, the local cemetery, a battlemented tower that serves as a landmark for miles around.

A few old stones are all that remain of the castle. Robert the Bruce's wife was held prisoner here, during part of his exile.

The surprising **Indian temple**, on the hill above Evanton, known as Fyrish Monument, was a folly erected by General Sir Hector Munro (1726–1805), as a philanthropic gesture, giving work to the unemployed in the area. It is modelled on the gateway to Negapatam, an Indian town captured by Sir Hector in 1781. It is clearly seen from the road, but much more fun close to and not an exacting climb.

The Tain Peninsula

Although the exploitation of North Sea oil fields has inevitably changed the character of the hammerhead peninsula jutting eastwards between Nigg Bay and Tain in the north, there are plenty of attractions to tempt the traveller to make a detour from the journey north.

Invergordon

Invergordon, 14 miles (22km) northeast of Dingwall, is a busy industrial centre on the western tip of Nigg Bay, dominated by all the surrealistic constructions built for the oil industry. The Cromarty Firth is one of the finest deep-water anchorages in the world and is now one of the most important European centres for the repair and maintenance of the exploration rigs. There is something curiously beautiful about some of these giant skeletons whose fragile-looking girders are built to withstand the full force of a North Sea gale. Inland, here and there, a lane or wood or farm is as peaceful as it was before the oil men came.

Fearn

Fearn, 11 miles (17.5km) northeast of Invergordon, is the hub of the peninsula, with cottages and pretty gardens grouped round a green. In restored 13th-century **Fearn Abbey**, the nave and choir are still used as the parish church. Fearn Abbey was the seat of the first martyr of the Scottish Reformation, Abbot Patrick Hamilton, who was burned at St Andrews for heresy, in 1528 (see St Andrews, p.297). The Reformation was responsible for the decay of the original abbey. In 1742, after it had been partly rebuilt to accommodate the parish church, the soaring voices of the parishioners had a disastrous effect on the stone-vaulted roof, which crashed down and killed 44 of them.

Tarbat Ness, about 9 miles (14.5km) beyond Fearn, on the northern tip of the peninsula, has one of the highest lighthouses in Britain, warning ships of the dangerous sandbanks threatening the entrance to the Dornoch Firth. The Norsemen called them Gizzen Briggs and were no doubt among their earliest victims. The views are stupendous and there are sometimes seals basking on the rocks below.

Portmahomack is a popular resort with a nine-hole golf course, a couple of miles (3km) south of the lighthouse. The small harbour once supported a fishing fleet.

Shandwick is halfway down the east coast, 8 miles (13km) south of the lighthouse. Fossil hunters may be rewarded if they search below the red sandstone cliffs and in the caves here. The 9-foot (3m) tall stone cross slab above the village was erected in memory of one of three Norse princes who were shipwrecked on one of the reefs.

Tain

Tain, like Dingwall, is derived from the Norse word *thing*—a meeting place or parliament. It is a sturdy town on the south side of the Dornoch Firth, 11 miles (17.5km) north of Invergordon. It is a holiday resort and market centre for the surrounding area and has an aura of antiquity.

St Duthus was born in Tain, in about 1000 and his bones were brought back here after his death in Ireland. **St Duthus Chapel** (always accessible) is an overgrown ruin in the cemetery between the town and the 18-hole golf course. It was built in the 11th century on the saint's birthplace and is the repository for his bones. It was built as a 'prayer cell' with the resident hermit guarding the sacred relics. Elizabeth de Burgh, wife of Robert the Bruce, and her children, took refuge here when fleeing to Orkney, relying on its status as a sanctuary for fugitives. This was violated by the Earl of Ross, who ignored the safety zone and captured her in 1307—an act Scotland did not forget. The chapel was burnt down by a smuggler, McNeill of Creich, in 1427, to destroy an enemy he had chased inside.

St Duthus Collegiate Church was built in 1360 on the site of an earlier church, traces of which can be seen in the chapter house. It is now a show place and memorial, no longer used for worship. When the chapel was burnt down, the relics of St Duthus were transferred to this church: they disappeared in 1560. James IV came on an annual pilgrimage for 20 years, but not entirely out of religious fervour. He liked to keep in touch with his subjects all over Scotland and he had established his favourite mistress, Flaming Janet Kennedy, in Darnaway Castle in Moray, giving him an excellent stopping-off place on the way. Don't miss the stained-glass windows, showing Malcolm Canmore and Queen Margaret bestowing a royal charter on the town, and an assembly of the Scottish parliament in 1560, adopting John Knox's Confessions of Faith.

Tain and District Museum (open Easter–Sept, Mon–Sat: donation box) in Castle Brae, off the High Street, is well worth a visit. It is full of a large variety of items: relics, manuscripts, photographs, archaeological remains, etc. The museum was founded as an exhibition for the visit of the Queen Mother in 1966, and became permanent. It includes details of St Duthus and of the patronage of James IV—though not of Flaming Janet—and good displays showing what life was like in 18th and 19th centuries in a thriving market town. This is also the Clan Ross Centre.

The Tolbooth is a fine example of many built in the 16th and 17th centuries, a tall, castellated keep with angle turrets and the original curfew bell of 1616.

The Highland Fine Cheeses Factory (open weekdays: free) shows how cheeses are made and allows sampling (℗ 0862 892034/892734). North of the town is the Glenmorangie Distillery, founded in 1843, where whisky is produced using water from the burn.

The A9 now sweeps across the **Dornoch Firth**, cutting the journey north considerably. The drive along the southern shore of the Firth to **Struie** is attractive but far the most scenic approach from the south is on the B9176 due north, 3 miles (4.5km) beyond Evanton. This road goes up over the moors and down to the Firth. Stop at Struie, at the **Stone Viewpoint**, about 10 miles (16km) up the road, for panoramic views over the **Kyles of Sutherland**. There is a view indicator, and a board explaining about the glacial action that created this beautiful spot. Windswept heather and pines fringe a road that zig-zags down through dramatic ravines.

Croick Church

Turn left at Ardgay (pronounced Ardguy as in Guy Fawkes), 14 miles (22.5km) west of Tain, at the head of the Firth. Drive 10 miles (16km) up Strath Carron, along a burn bordered by lichen, bracken and birches. Little **Croick Church** lies in a walled church-yard, surrounded by a few wind-bent trees in a pocket of desolate moorland. This is one of the most poignant places in Scotland. In the spring of 1845, families who had been evicted from their crofts in Glencalvie and who had nowhere to go camped here in an improvised shelter made of tarpaulin, rugs and plaids stretched over poles. They scratched memorials on the diamond panes of this simple kirk, which can still be read today: 'Glencalvie people was in the church here May 24 1845 . . .' 'Glencalvie people the wicked generation . . .' and one rather tart comment '. . . this place needs cleaning'. Inside, it is plain with unadorned walls, an iron stove, benches and table and a big pulpit. There is an interesting display board with contemporary newspaper cuttings from *The Times*.

Bonar Bridge

Bonar Bridge, a mile (1.5km) north of Ardgay, is so called after the bridge that spans the Kyle of Sutherland. It is a good base from which to explore Sutherland and has excellent fishing, walking and boating. Aspiring politicians and diplomats should visit MacKenzie Harris, where top-quality leather briefcases and luggage are made. They have supplied Margaret Thatcher and countless European diplomats: not cheap. **Carbisdale Castle Youth Hostel**, high above the river at **Invershin**, a couple of miles northwest, is near the site of Montrose's final disastrous battle, from which he fled to Assynt. This is a pleasant detour, up the River Shin, to Lairg. The **Falls of Shin**, on the way, are a popular beauty spot, complete with attendant café, gift shop, carpark and people.

Lairg, at the southern end of Loch Shin, is a fisherman's haven and a good base from which to explore the rugged hinterland of Sutherland. For those who don't want to spend their holiday on the end of a fishing rod, there are lovely walks.

Returning along the northern shore of the Dornoch Firth, the A949 passes several prehistoric remains: Dun Creich, a vitrified fort, on the promontory 3 miles (4.5km) out of Bonar Bridge; traces of a chambered cairn at Clashmore, west of the school; another cairn at Everlix; and a standing stone on the outskirts of Dornoch, 10 miles (16km) east of Bonar Bridge. These remains indicate what a large number of Pictish and Norse settlers populated this area.

Dornoch

Dornoch, isolated enough to retain its old world dignity, though more accessible with the new bridge, remains unspoiled by its popularity as a holiday resort, a charming, higgledy-piggledy town, full of character. Long famous as a golfing centre, its links have been played on since at least 1616. On the same latitude as Hudson Bay and Alaska, it is the most northerly first-class golf course in the world. Excavations have dated settlements here at least as far back as 1000 BC.

Dornoch Cathedral (always open: free) dates from 1224 when the town became a bishopric. It must be the cosiest cathedral in the country: small and cruciform with colourful windows illuminating its warm, mellow walls. It was burnt in a clan dispute between Murrays and Mackays in 1570, when only the tower and spire survived. Restored in 1616, it was then further, and tastelessly, restored in Victorian times. Mercifully, in 1924, it was again restored to celebrate its 700th anniversary. Much of the awful Victorian work was stripped away to reveal the original 13th-century stonework. It is now the parish church.

Dornoch Craft Centre and Town Jail (open daily, except winter weekends: free) is worth a visit. The restored jail gives a graphic example of what it would have been like to be imprisoned in the last century, and the crafts include the weaving of tartan on power looms, and kilt making. There is a book shop and coffee shop.

Dornoch is flanked by miles of clean sand, ideal for holidaymakers but not so good for the evicted crofters who, during the Highland Clearances, were expected to settle here and farm the infertile dune land. Small wonder so many of them emigrated.

Embo, about 3 miles (4.5km) north along the sands, has the remains of two Stone Age burial chambers dating from 2000 BC, at the entrance to the caravan site. When these were excavated it was discovered that two later cist tombs had been built into the original ones.

On the shore of **Loch Fleet**, a couple of miles (3km) further north, there is the scant ruin of 14th-century **Skelbo Castle** on a grassy mound. It was here, in an earlier, wooden castle, in 1290, that emissaries of Edward I waited to greet the little Princess Margaret, Maid of Norway, whose marriage to Edward's son was to solve the problem of sovereignty in Scotland. Whether it would have done so or not was never to be known, for it was here that they heard of the child's death caused by sea sickness on the voyage. This triggered off the Scottish Wars of Independence and Edward's ruthless hammering of the Scots.

Golspie, 9 miles (14.5km) north of Dornoch, is the farming centre for the area. There is an 18-hole golf course. Seventeenth-century St Andrew's Church has a splendid old canopied pulpit, some fine panelled walls and carvings. The great statue on Ben Vraggie, behind Golspie, is to the first Duke of Sutherland, a man who was, on the one hand, blamed for his harshness to crofters during the Clearances, and on the other, praised for sponsoring many social improvements in the area.

Dunrobin Castle

Dunrobin Castle (open daily, June–mid Sept: adm) stands high on a natural terrace overlooking the sea, a mile (1.5km) north of Golspie. Built in the 13th century on the site of an ancient broch, this seat of the Dukes of Sutherland was considerably restored in Victorian times. The huge white extravaganza, standing on a massive plinth, is more like a château than a castle. Its towers and turrets are a flamboyant pastiche of French and Scottish architecture. Formal gardens, bordering a long terrace, are a riot of colour in summer. The castle contains some fine paintings, including two Canalettos, as well as magnificent furniture, tapestries, and family heirlooms. There is also a museum in a summerhouse in the park, with archaeological exhibits, Victoriana, crafts and natural history.

Brora

Brora, 5 miles (8km) up the coast from Golspie, is a small tourist resort with good salmon fishing and an 18-hole golf course. The harbour, once used by fishing boats, is now a haven for pleasure craft. In the middle of the 19th century, crofters sailed from here to New Zealand, to start fresh lives away from the threat of eviction during the Clearances. **Hunter's of Brora** (open weekdays) are woollen mills, renowned for their yarn and tweed in many parts of the world.

There are two brochs, one either end of Brora, the best being about 3 miles (4.5km) north between the road and the sea. It has domed chambers in the walls and outworkings. Two headless skeletons were excavated from the site in 1880. There is hardly a hill or hummock in this area that is not crowned by some sort of fort or broch. As you go north, you will find fewer Gaelic-derived names and more with Nordic origins.

Helmsdale

Helmsdale, 10 miles (16km) north of Brora, is a fishing and holiday town where road and railway part company.

The ruin of 15th-century **Helmsdale Castle** (always accessible) overlooks the natural harbour. It was within these innocent-looking walls, in 1567, that Isobel Sinclair poisoned the Earl and Countess of Sutherland, so that her son might inherit the earldom. This somewhat drastic solution failed, however, because her son drank the poison and died with them.

The castle was rebuilt in the early 19th century by the Duke of Sutherland who, having evicted the crofters from his lands, tried to make amends by re-settling them. The streets are laid out in neat geometric parallels, named after the Duke's estates.

Timespan Heritage Centre (open daily, Easter–Sept: adm), left and left again off the main road into the village, is a gem. It traces the history of man in the Kildonan area from the stone circles, cairns and brochs of prehistory, through Norse invasion, the Clearances, herring fishing, gold rush and crofting to the present—including local celebrity Barbara Cartland, who has a holiday house in the area. It is extremely well done in film and animated tableaux and supplies many good aids to the imagination.

The River Helmsdale is rich in salmon and trout and there is a nine-hole golf course.

Suisgill

An alternative route north from Helmsdale goes inland on the A897, 38 miles (61km) up to Melvich on the north coast. This route through **Strath of Kildonan** is a windswept, treeless moorland, broken by delightful river valleys. Suisgill, 10 miles (16km) from Helmsdale, was the centre of a mini gold rush towards the end of the 19th century, and a considerable amount of gold was panned from the rivers. Ask in the Helmsdale Tourist Information Centre for details of the Goldrush Heritage Tour. Kildonan lost four-fifths of its population in the first half of the 19th century, during the Highland Clearances. Now it is sparsely populated with shooting lodges and sheep farms along the Helmsdale—one of Scotland's top fishing rivers. Several years ago, there was a bout of 'lodge burnings', thought to be the work of drunks or Scottish Nationalists, which left a number of smoking shells. Suisgill Lodge was one of the victims: all that is left is one end of the house while a complete wilderness replaces what was once a beautiful garden. **Strath Halladale**, running north from Strath Kildonan on this road, is green and fertile, fed by many rivers and burns—attractive farmland for the invading Vikings so many years ago.

Ord of Caithness

Going on up the A9 from Helmsdale, the scenery becomes more dramatic, with ravines and steep cliffs as the road climbs to a high plateau with spectacular views from the Ord of Caithness about 4 miles (6.5km) beyond Helmsdale. No superstitious Sinclair will cross the Ord on a Monday since that Monday in 1513 when the men of the clan passed this way to fight with James IV at Flodden, from which not one of them returned. There are often red deer up here, especially in the early morning or at dusk.

There is a broch at Ousdale, a couple of miles beyond the Ord, where the main road runs inland for a while. Take the track out to the old hamlet of Badbea, 2 miles (3km) east on the cliffs. Crofters took refuge here during the Clearances and stories are told of the beasts and the children having to be tethered to prevent them being blown into the sea.

The 15th-century castle visible from the road at **Dunbeath**, 5 miles (8km) north (private), was captured by Montrose in 1650. Six miles (9.5km) to the west, at **Braemore**, a monument was erected after the air crash here that killed the Duke of Kent in 1942. The Dunbeath Highland Games are held in July.

Laidhay Croft Museum, 2 miles (3km) north of Dunbeath (open daily Easter–Sept: adm), shows a typical Victorian croft house, looking cosier, perhaps, than it was in reality.

These interiors are excellent for displaying domestic detail, but not so good at conveying the damp, cold, smoky atmosphere, when rats ran around the floor and animals shared the living space. There is also a collection of farm implements in an outhouse, some of which, like the peat-cutters, are still used today.

Clan Gunn Museum and Heritage Centre (open June–Sept, Mon–Sat: adm) is in the old parish church, a couple of miles further north, beyond **Latheron** with its picturesque harbour. The A895 is an alternative but less spectacular route north to Thurso, which goes inland from Latheron.

Turn off the broad thoroughfare, flanked by sturdy, dignified houses, in **Lybster**, 4 miles (6.5km) north of Latheron. Dip down to the harbour, scooped out of rock to provide a perfect haven for the large fishing fleet that once plied from here in the 19th century. The fleet is reduced now to a few lobster boats and a number of pleasure craft, but the atmosphere is still very much that of a fishing community, with piles of creels and fishing gear, and the salty tang of the sea.

Inland from Lybster a minor road joins the A895 north to Thurso. A few miles further on is the **Achavanich Standing Stone Circle**. This ritual site in the form of an unusual truncated oval may once have contained as many as 60 stones. Less than a mile (1.5km) west of here, on the main road up from Latheron, is Rangag Broch, dating from 150 BC, once 40 or 50 feet (12–15m) high.

Five miles (8km) to the east, on the minor road north from **Clyth**, beyond Lybster, the **Grey Cairns of Camster** date from around 2500 BC. They have been restored and there are explanation boards. The smoothly rounded cairn is one of the best of its kind on the mainland. Its original entrance passage is still intact. Both animal and human remains were excavated from this site.

A couple of miles' (3km) walk to the east reaches the **Hill o' Many Stanes**, dating from the early Bronze Age. This fan of stones has ribs, each containing about eight or more stones, numbering some 200 in all. This could have been a ritual site for burials, like other henges, or some form of astronomical calculator, lined up with the stars. Whatever its purpose, it is eerie to stand on this lonely, windswept moor and try to picture how it must have been for those early settlers, once so numerous in this northern corner.

In **Ulbster**, 7 miles (11km) up the A9 from Lybster, a flight of 365 stone steps twists steeply down the cliff to the old harbour. Now disused and overgrown, it was once used by fishing fleets to moor and unload their catches, among the cheerful bustle and raucous banter of the fishermen and the teams of women working at the gutting. The steps are only for the sure-footed; they can be extremely slippery.

Wick

Wick, so called from the Viking word *vik* meaning 'bay or creek', is a substantially built seaport and tourist centre, stretching round the sweep of Wick Bay, 15 miles (24km) northeast of Lybster. There is a harbour, airport and railway terminal. Norse pirates were drawn to Wick by the shelter of its bay at the mouth of the river and by the magnet of the rich farmland that beckoned from the west. Created a Royal Burgh in 1140, it was only properly developed in the 19th century, by the British Fisheries Society, who commissioned Telford to design a model village for them at Pulteneytown. It is difficult to believe, now, that 1,122 herring boats once plied from the complex of three harbour basins, before the decline of the herring stock and the development of vast factory ships. White fish trawlers still use the harbour.

The Heritage Museum (open Mon–Sat, June–Sept: adm), near the harbour, tells the fishing story of Wick. Its collections include a fishing boat, working lighthouse, kippering kilns, blacksmith shop, coopering shop and fishing gear.

Carnegie Library has a small museum (open during library hours: admission by donation) displaying the history of the area, with its domestic and farming life.

Caithness Glass Factory (open daily, Easter–Oct: free) is on the north side of the town. Visitors can watch craftsmen fashioning molten glass, shaping it and engraving it. This factory was established in the slump of the herring industry to offer alternative employment for the fishermen. It is interesting to notice that in this land so full of echoes of the Norse occupation, the designs of the glass are distinctively Scandinavian.

Also south of the town is the shell of **Old Wick Castle** (always accessible), three storeys high on a rock promontory, and known to seamen as the 'Auld Man o' Wick'. Having no water supply, the castle was unable to withstand lengthy sieges and was abandoned in the 16th century.

Look out for the **Brig o' Trams** nearby, a spectacular natural rock arch formed by the erosion of sea and weather.

There are more spectacularly shaped rocks 3 miles (4.5km) to the north along the cliffs, at **Noss Head**. It is possible to drive but it is also a glorious walk, buffeted by the wind.

From the point it isn't far to walk to **Sinclair and Girnigoe Castles** (always accessible). These two dramatic ruins extend from a keep and were lived in as one dwelling by the Sinclairs, Earls of Caithness, for 200 years. The eastern part is 15th century, the western, 17th century. The jagged ruin seems to grow up out of horizontally layered rock on a cliff above a sheltered cove. Ghosts lurk in these history-soaked walls: in 1570 the 4th Earl of Caithness, suspecting his son of plotting to kill him, imprisoned him in the dungeons for seven years till he died of 'famine and vermine'.

The great sandy sweep of **Sinclair's Bay** leads north along coastland believed to be among the earliest inhabited in Scotland. Excavations revealed that Middle Stone Age man existed here in large numbers, on the fertile hinterland.

Less than 8 miles (13km) north of Wick, a detour left goes to **Lyth**, where, in a tiny community, you will find an 'arts centre'. The old school house has been converted, and there is a not always outstanding range of paintings, ceramics, sculpture, photography, etcetera. on show.

The tall, slender tower on top of the cliff at **Keiss**, 8 miles (13km) north of Wick, is all that remains of Keiss Castle, home of William Sinclair, founder of the first Baptist church in Scotland.

Northlands Viking Centre (open daily, June–Sept: adm), in the former schoolhouse at **Auckengill**, beyond the north arm of Sinclair's Bay, deals with the fascinating archaeology of this area.

The ruin of 12th-century **Bucholie Castle**, a mile (1.5km) north, was the stronghold of Sweyn Aslefson, a Norse pirate whose name features often in the old Norse sagas. A 10th-century Viking settlement is in the process of excavation, a mile (1.5km) further north at **Freswick**.

John o' Groats

Although it is neither the most northerly nor the most easterly tip of Britain, John o' Groats, 17 miles (27km) north of Wick, is loosely accepted as the northeastern extremity, linked diagonally to Lands End, 876 miles (1402km) away in the southwest, which is in fact neither the most southerly, nor the most westerly tip of the country.

Stop on the summit of the final curve of the moor and look down. It is a bleak, scattered village, washed by the Pentland Firth whose islands sometimes appear so close you could almost jump the gap. It is a marvellous vista—the edge of the world. But it has to be said that John o' Groats itself is often a disappointment to tourists—little more than an uninspiring coach park, a few ugly buildings and a flat, dreary landscape.

The small settlement, given over to supplying the needs of the dozens of tourists who come here, got its curious name from a Dutchman, Jan de Groot, who established a ferry link with the newly acquired Orkney, in 1496, under the rule of James IV. There are several explanations for the octagonal house he built, with eight doors, no longer standing but represented by the octagonal tower on the hotel which is believed to stand on the site of de Groot's house. One explanation is that he wanted to provide shelter from every point of the fierce wind for his waiting passengers. A nicer theory is that when his eight sons squabbled over who should take precedence at the dinner table, he decided to settle the dispute by having an octagonal table and eight doors, so that each son had his own entrance and no one, or everyone, sat at the head of the table.

Duncansby Head

Boat trips run from the harbour to Duncansby Head, 2 miles (3km) east, the true 'top right-hand corner' where many different species of seabirds throng the dramatic cliffs. A road runs out to the lighthouse on the cliffs, from which the only limit to the view over the Pentland Firth, in clear weather, is the keenness of your eye. The 12-knot tide rip here is a notorious hazard to shipping: over 400 wrecks have been recorded in only the last 150 years. Going back to the days of Viking longboats, the total number of wrecks must be enormous.

Once away from the inoffensive blemishes of tourism, this coastline is perfect for those who like wild and lonely places and extremes of weather.

moderate

Ord House Hotel, Muir of Ord, ✆ 0463 870492, is an old family house, a listed building in 20 acres of garden and woodland. It's hospitable, comfortable and friendly. **Marine Hotel**, Rosemarkie, ✆ 0381 20253, overlooks the sea with terraced lawns running down to a sandy beach.

Royal Hotel, Tain, ✆ 0862 2013, right in the middle of the town, is quite comfortable, though the decor in some of the public rooms is a bit overpowering. The food is quite good. **Morangie Hotel**, Tain, ✆ 0862 2281, has a good reputation for comfort and is more secluded.

Dornoch Hotel, Dornoch, ✆ 0862 810351, is an imposing seaside hotel overlooking the golf course; solid, old-fashioned and comfortable. **Dornoch Castle**, ✆ 0862 810261, is very special. This 400-year-old castle was formerly the Bishop's Palace and reeks of history. Its restaurant is one of the best in the area and the cellar is good. There is a sunny terrace and formal garden, and a 16th-century panelled bar overlooking the Square. **Royal Golf Hotel**, Dornoch, ✆ 0862 810283, is on the golf course; large and comfortable, with reasonable food.

Links Hotel, Brora, ✆ 0408 21225, is close to the golf course, serves decent food and is comfortable.

Forsinard Hotel, ✆ 06417 221, perhaps the most remote hotel in Britain, right in the heart of the Flow Country, is a haven of peace and a paradise for nature lovers. Comfortable and relaxed, it is open mid-April to mid-October.

inexpensive

Royal Hotel, Fortrose, ✆ 0381 20236, stands prominently on the corner of Union Street. It's rather central but the food is all right and the staff are friendly. **Royal Hotel** in Dingwall, ✆ 0349 62130, is not very peaceful but the comfort and service are reasonable. **Conon Hotel**, Conon Bridge, ✆ 0349 61500, is an attractive inn by the River Conon, renowned for its fishing. The staff are friendly and obliging and the food isn't bad.

Castle Hotel, Portmahomack, ✆ 086287 263, is a friendly hotel with panoramic views over the Dornoch Firth. **Bridge Hotel**, Bonar Bridge, ✆ 08632 204, is friendly.

Burghfield House Hotel, Dornoch, ✆ 0862 810212, has been run by the same family since 1946. It is known for its good food. **Golf Links Hotel**, Golspie, ✆ 04083 3408, is another good refuge for golfers. It's right on the golf course, and only 300 yards (275m) from the beach.

John o' Groats House Hotel, ✆ 095581 203, is the most northerly hotel on the mainland. What it lacks in sophistication, it makes up for in fresh air.

Portland Arms Hotel, Lybster, ✆ 05932 208/255, is early 19th-century, attractive and comfortable, with friendly staff and good food.

Eating Out

If you want a meal out on the Black Isle, **Le Chardon** in Cromarty, ✆ 03817 471, is a gourmet restaurant with a bistro-style atmosphere. Very reasonable.

John o' Groats to Durness

This is an end-of-the-world highway, with detours into great tracts of barren wasteland to the south.

Castle of Mey, 7 miles (11km) west of John o'Groats, was built around the middle of the 16th century for the Earl of Caithness and bought by the Queen Mother in 1956. The gardens are open on certain days in the summer in aid of charity.

Dunnet Head, 9 miles (14.5km) further on, is the most northerly point of Scotland's mainland. Walk out to the tip on a carpet of pink thrift, laced with tormentil, trefoils, wild thyme, yellow saxifrage, purple butterwort and many other wild flowers. You'll see lots of puffins, those endearing birds with comic tuxedo garb and vivid striped beaks, burrowing in the turf. The view from Dunnet Head is memorable particularly at sunrise or sunset. The village is a scattering of houses near the vast sweep of Dunnet Bay.

The tower of the charming little white church, with its saddle-backed roof, dates from the 14th century, a pre-Reformation survivor adding continuity to a place where nothing seems to have changed much over the years.

The fishing is good, both sea, river and loch. A halibut weighing 210lbs (93kg) was caught here with rod and line in 1975.

Castlehill Harbour, 6 miles (9.5km) south of Dunnet Point, was the main centre for the Caithness flagstone industry. Some stone is still produced today but a major scheme is under way for the renovation of the harbour and the construction of an Interpretive Museum and Heritage Trail, based on the flagstone industry.

Thurso

Thurso, 20 miles (32km) west of John o' Groats, is a large, thriving holiday resort and an important fishing port, built on the River Thurso. Elegant 18th-century houses built of brown sandstone surround a central square, with a long, narrow harbour. The name stems from the Norse *Thorsa*—meaning 'river of the God Thor'. This important Viking stronghold reached its zenith in the 11th century under Thorfinn, who defeated King Duncan's nephew in 1040 in a mighty battle at Thurso. The town was the chief trading port between Scotland and Scandinavia in the Middle Ages.

Thurso Folk Museum (open June–Sept, daily except Sun: adm), in the High Street, has a good collection of exhibits of local interest, including a reconstruction of a croft house kitchen, whose homely equipment was often just as efficient as its modern counterparts. The Pictish 'Ulbster Stone' is in the museum, with intricate carved symbols.

St Peter's Church, near the harbour, dates from the 12th or 13th century. It was restored in the 17th century and used for worship until 1862. Some of the original stone can be seen in the curious choir—a semicircular apse within a square end.

Harald Tower, just over a mile's walk along the coast to the northeast, was built in the early 19th century as a burial place for the Sinclairs. It stands on the grave of Harald, Earl of Caithness, a mighty war lord who ruled over half Caithness and Orkney and was killed in battle nearby in 1196.

There are good shops in the town, plenty of places to stay, an 18-hole golf course, and splendid walks all around.

Scrabster Harbour, 2 miles (3km) round the bay, is the terminal for the car ferry, *St Ola*, to Stromness in Orkney. It is an invigorating two-hour trip and on Mondays and Thursdays in the summer it links with special bus tours to make a pleasant day excursion, returning to Scrabster in the evening.

St Mary's Chapel, at **Crosskirk**, 6 miles (9.5km) to the west, dates from the 12th century, a simple little kirk with its chancel linked to the nave by a small doorway.

Dounreay

The tourist office in Thurso arranges tours of Britain's prototype Fast Reactor Power Station at Dounreay, 8 miles (13km) west of Scrabster. There is a visitor exhibition here for anyone with a scientific turn of mind. In a strange way this vast modern complex is not offensive to the eye in a land of such contrasts.

A few miles west, the A897 branches off south back to Helmsdale through Strath Halladale and Strath of Kildonan, into the heart of the Flow Country.

Just outside **Melvich**, a couple of miles (3km) on round the coast, is the **Split Stone of Melvich**. An old woman was returning from a shopping trip when she was chased by the devil. She ran round and round this stone and escaped: the devil was so furious he split it in two. Parts of **Portskerra Fort**, a mile (1.5km) or so beyond Melvich on the point, rise 80 feet (25m) sheer from the shore.

At **Strathy Point**, 12 miles (19km) west of Dounreay, the sea has carved fabulous arches and caverns in the cliffs. The variety of the coastal scenery is amazing; there are many types of rock, sandy beaches, sheltered bays and the restless sea, licking the feet of the cliffs. There is good birdwatching here and lots of wild flowers.

To the west is **Armadale Bay**, with a lovely sandy beach, and between the next two points, **Ardmore** and **Kirtomy**, the sea has carved out a natural tunnel from the cliffs. On **Farr Point**, 3 miles (4.5km) west, **Borve Castle** was a stronghold of the Clan Mackay in medieval times. It was destroyed by the Earl of Sutherland's army in 1515.

Bettyhill

Bettyhill, 10 miles (16km) on, named after Elizabeth, first Duchess of Sutherland, is at the top of Strath Naver. The **Strath Naver Museum** (open June–Sep, daily except Sun: donation) is in a converted church. It gives a fascinating insight to the Strath Naver chapter of the Highland Clearances (see Topics). The museum is extremely well laid out, and it is interesting to think that the minister may have read out eviction notices from his pulpit here.

The B873, to the south, runs through **Strath Naver**, where many croft houses went up in flames during those troubled times and where people died of exposure, huddled against the ruins of their homes. This too is Flow Country. About 5 miles (8km) down and accessible only on foot, there is a particularly attractive wooded gorge.

Invernaver National Nature Reserve, 2 miles (3km) south of Bettyhill, is a gold mine for nature lovers. It is situated around the mouth of the River Naver, with the finest collection of mountain and coastal plants in the north. Among the rarer birds that breed here are greenshank, ring ouzel and twite. On the edge of the reserve, on a plateau, is **Baile Marghait**, once a Neolithic community, with graves, hut circles and a broch.

Tongue

Tongue, 12 miles (19km) west of Bettyhill, is held by some to be the most attractive place on this northern coast; it has a very special charm. The ruin of **Castle Varrich** dominates the town, once a Norse stronghold in the days when the Vikings occupied these lands.

The **Kyle of Tongue**, crossed by a causeway, is a long, shallow inlet from the wild sea outside, so shallow that at low tide you can walk out to Rabbit Island at its mouth. The lane up the west side winds among sandy bays, cliffs, weirdly shaped rocks and islands, remote and lovely.

The **North Coast Adventure Centre** in Tongue organizes watersports and hill walking. This includes climbing Ben Loyal, 2504 feet (770m) high, its four jagged peaks dominating the skyline 5 miles (8km) to the south.

From Tongue, the A836 goes south through the heart of the Flow Country, past Loch Loyal, 38 miles (61km) to Lairg.

Loch Eriboll, 10 miles (16km) west of Tongue, is a sea loch running 10 miles inland, very deep and beautiful. This was one of the subjects of a prophecy by the Brahan Seer, early in the 17th century. He named Loch Eriboll as a place where a war would end one day. In 1945, German submarines came into the loch to surrender, at the end of the Second World War.

There are the remains of several ancient settlements around here. About a mile north of Laid School on the west side of the loch, there is a souterrain, complete and untouched, with curved steps leading down to a round chamber. You need a torch for this earth house, which floods after heavy rain.

Durness is the gateway to Cape Wrath and the top left-hand corner (see p.430).

moderate

Farr Bay Inn, Bettyhill, ✆ 06412 230, is an early 19th-century inn with good views and near a sandy beach. **Borgie Lodge Hotel**, Skerray, ✆ 06412 332, is a well-established fishing hotel in a nice old family house in attractive grounds. **Tongue Hotel**, ✆ 084755 206/7, is a family-run Victorian hotel which has kept its original character, including a paucity of bathrooms. Nice views and reasonable food.

inexpensive

Northern Sands Hotel, Dunnet, ✆ 084785 270, is on the coast, five minutes from the sandy beach and friendly. Each of the nine rooms has a bathroom. **Ulbster Arms Hotel**, Halkirk, ✆ 084783 206, stands on Thurso River, 5 miles (8km) south of Thurso in Flow Country. The bad news is that there are only five public bathrooms between 31 bedrooms. The staff are amiable and it's beautifully remote. A bit more expensive, **Forss Hotel**, ✆ 084786, about 5 miles (8km) west of Thurso is quite nice, in extensive woodland overlooking the river. **Berriedale Arms Hotel**, Mey, ✆ 084785 244, is an attractive old inn near the Queen Mother's castle, with one bathroom between four bedrooms. **Royal Hotel**, Traill Street, Thurso, ✆ 0847 63191, is in the town centre, and not over-endowed with style. However, it offers game and sea fishing and the staff are obliging.

Bettyhill Hotel, ✆ 06412 202, has panoramic views of the sea and the hills, and wonderfully old-fashioned hospitality. Bathrooms are scarce, but it is a lovely place. **Ben Loyal Hotel**, Tongue, ✆ 084755 216, overlooks Kyle of Tongue and Ben Loyal. The staff are very pleasant.

The Islands

There are hundreds of islands off the coast of Scotland, but this chapter only deals with the main inhabited ones, served by public transport. For the rest you need your own boat, a good knowledge of seamanship and navigation and many years of leisure. Each one has its own, special magic, each one is 'intire of it selfe'. (See also 'Strathclyde Islands', pp.217–38.) A native of Eriskay can feel homesick living a mile away across the sound in South Uist. Until recently almost untouched by the distractions and bright lights of an increasingly materialistic world, islanders tended to build their lives around God and the Church—a Church that varies, depending on the island, from Catholic to extreme Presbyterian. Today, with improved communications, the younger generations are more in tune with the modern world.

The Western Isles

From the lone shieling on the misty island
Mountains divide us, and a waste of seas
Yet still the blood is strong, the heart is Highland
And we, in dreams, behold the Hebrides.

Canadian Boat Song

Skye and the Small Isles lie close to the west coast between Ardnamurchan Point and Gairloch. They are separated from the Outer Hebrides by the Sea of the Hebrides and the Minch, a notoriously capricious channel treated with respect by prudent mariners.

First known to be populated around 3800 BC, the Hebrides are rich in archaeological sites, many of which are yet to be dug. Mesolithic man gave way to Neolithic, who came in boats made of animal hide, bringing skills and culture and leaving burial cairns as evidence of his existence. Gaelic immigrants from Europe arrived, with Celtic arts, building brochs and stone circles, practising a Druid religion and worshipping nature gods, until the first Christian missionaries arrived from Ireland early in the 6th century. The Norsemen arrived at the end of the 8th century and remained until the defeat of King Haakon by Alexander III at Largs in 1263. After this the islands were ceded to the Scottish Crown. But stronger than the authority of the Crown was the Lordship of the Isles. Chiefs as powerful as kings paid no heed to a government which ruled from the east of mainland Scotland.

A succession of Stewart kings tried to whip in the arrogant clans of the Western Isles, but they clung to their own traditions. A patriarchal clan system existed, with every member of the clan family being independent and equal in status, looking to their chief for guidance and justice but not for oppression. This was the foundation of that proud independence that still endures in Hebrideans today, a truly classless pride that endured even the suppression of the clans after Culloden, and, in the 19th century, the appalling depopulation of the Highland Clearances.

The islands to the south of Benbecula rejected the Reformation, in favour of the Gaelic-speaking monks who came over from Ireland and who kept the faith alive. They reconverted, with the help of the Clanranalds, Macneils and Macleods of Skye, who had political influence (the Macleods later defaulted). These islands are now almost entirely Catholic. North Uist, Harris and Lewis, and Skye embraced the Reformed Church with such enthusiasm that even today visitors must be careful not to offend their strong Sabbatarianism.

Most island families have their own croft, or smallholding, their tenancy carefully controlled by the Crofters Commission, brought about in 1886 as a result of public indignation after the Highland Clearances. But crofting is a hard life in the islands. With only a few acres, poor markets and expensive freight, few can exist solely on its returns. Crofting is therefore usually an auxiliary occupation, during weekends and days off from more lucrative employment such as building, fishing, and public works.

The old thatched croft houses have mostly been replaced by modern houses, but some are still occupied. In the old 'black houses', the byre was usually part of the dwelling, with the peat fire on a raised platform in the middle of the room, its smoke escaping through a hole in the roof. Black houses are only seen now as folk museums, restored and authentic in design, but probably misleadingly cosy in atmosphere. No museum can duplicate the reality: the vermin, the pervading damp, the smell from the byre and heavy pall of smoke.

Electricity transformed living conditions, but it brought with it the television, which has effectively killed the *céilidh* tradition. In the old days, when a crofting township was totally communal, the day's work was done on a co-operative basis and in the evenings communities gathered together round the fire in one of the black houses, to listen to music and poetry and to tell the old sagas. Attempts have been made to capture some of this ancient folklore and imprison it on paper, but it was a living thing, passed verbally from generation to generation, embroidered and altered year by year; its true spirit cannot be appreciated except by ear. Gaelic is still the first language for most people in the Outer Hebrides, but an influx of non-Gaelic speakers means that the children of today are growing up speaking English.

Those who go to the islands for their holidays enjoy outdoor life: walking, climbing, bird-watching, wild flowers, boating, fishing. Whatever the weather, and it is often good, each day is an adventure. Walk 5 miles (8km) to an isolated beach, collect driftwood and make a fire using dried heather twigs as kindling. Cook sausages on the stones and wash them down with peat-coloured water from a burn. Collect mussels from rocks below the high tide and rake cockles out of the white sand. Have a quick swim, diving into deep water as clear as glass (whatever people may say about the proximity of the Gulf Stream, the waters of the Minch are icy). Pick wild mushrooms from the grassy hillsides.

In the outer isles, there are few smart shops, only general foodstores which stock most things from boots to butter. There are a few craft shops and weavers, and a post office here and there. Portree and Stornoway have more sophisticated shops, but on the whole, people who enjoy shopping tend to stay on the mainland. For public entertainment, in the outer isles, there may be a local *céilidh* or concert in the village halls to mark a particular occasion, and there are games in the summer on most of the islands. Otherwise, evenings are spent in front of a peat fire with a good book, or the television, or listening to the tales of local people, who can still tell much of the old folklore, and who will often make music for you, or in the pub. Skye, being more accessible, has a much more modern culture.

Speed bonny boat, like a bird on the wing,
'Onward' the sailors cry;
Carry the lad that's born to be king
Over the sea to Skye.

from the 'Skye Boat Song' by Sir H.E. Boulton

On the map, Skye looks like a great, misshapen lobster claw, its pincers being lumpy peninsulas, separated by fiord-like inlets, surrounded by many islands. From the distance, Skye's outline is dominated by the Cuillins in the middle, a massive range of pointed peaks, training ground for international climbers, and by Macleod's Tables, two distinctive, flat-topped hills further north. It contains unique geographical features such as the Quiraing and the Old Man of Storr.

Skye is the most touristy of the Western Isles because of its accessibility, but tourism has not yet spoiled it. However, in 1991 the Scottish Office approved a long-disputed plan to build a half-mile (700m) toll bridge between Kyle of Lochalsh and Kyleakin—the longest single-span bridge outside Australia. This is due to open in 1994 and will improve communications dramatically for the locals. Whether they will appreciate this in a few years' time, when Skye has become a Bonnie Prince Charlie Theme Park, remains to be seen. Off the main road there are still rural communities quite untouched by the influx of knapsacks and campers. Gaelic is no longer the first language, though it is still spoken, and road signs are bilingual. Attempts are made in certain parts to revive the old language, with Gaelic teaching, a Gaelic College in Sleat and Gaelic playgroups opening all over the island. Portree is the only town on the island, a lively little place, busy in the summer. The island now has arts centres, theatre shows, opera, traditional music and even reasonable restaurants.

Getting to Skye

by sea

There is a 24-hour ferry service from Kyle of Lochalsh to Kyleakin, taking only a few minutes to cross. There is a summer ferry service from Mallaig to Armadale, taking half an hour, and a limited service from Glenelg to Kylerhea. Ferries also run from Uig to the Outer Isles.

by train

Trains run from Inverness to Kyle of Lochalsh—the Kyle Line, one of the most beautiful in Britain. Just as scenic is the West Highland Line, from Glasgow to Mallaig, connecting with the ferry to Armadale.

by road

Once on the island, there is a limited bus service and you can hire cars at Broadford and Portree. Broadford has a 24-hour petrol station.

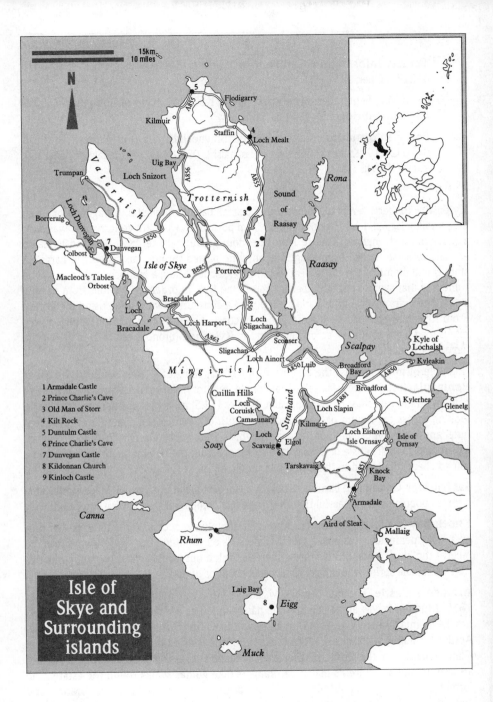

Isle of
Skye and
Surrounding
islands

15km
10 miles

N

Flodigarry
5
Kilmuir
Staffin
4 Loch Mealt

Uig Bay
Loch Snizort
Trumpan
V a t e r n i s h
Borreraig
Loch Dunvegan
7 Dunvegan
Colbost
Macleod's Tables
Orbost

T r o t t e r n i s h
3
Sound
of
Raasay
2

Rona

Raasay

Isle of Skye
B885 Portree

Bracadale
A850
Loch
Bracadale
Loch Harport
Loch
Sligachan

Scalpay
Kyle of
Lochalsh

Loch
Sligachan
Sconser
A863
Sligachan
Loch Ainort
A850 Luib
Broadford
Bay

Kyleakin

M i n g i n i s h
Cuillin Hills
Loch
Coruisk
Camasunary
Loch
Scavaig

S t r a t h a i r d
Loch Slapin
Kilmaric

Broadford
A881
Kylerhea
Glenelg

Elgol
6
Tarskavaig
Loch Eishort
Isle Ornsay
Isle of
Ornsay

Soay
Knock
Bay
1
Armadale

Canna
Aird of Sleat
Mallaig

Rhum 9

1 Armadale Castle
2 Prince Charlie's Cave
3 Old Man of Storr
4 Kilt Rock
5 Duntulm Castle
6 Prince Charlie's Cave
7 Dunvegan Castle
8 Kildonnan Church
9 Kinloch Castle

Laig Bay
8 Eigg

Muck

453

Tourist Information Centre, Meall House, **Portree**, Isle of Skye, © 0478 612137. Open all year.

Open May–September: **Broadford**: © 0471 822361; **Kyle of Lochalsh**: © 0599 4276; **Shielbridge**: © 0599 81 264.

Ferry Information: Caledonian MacBrayne Ltd, Uig (for Western Isles), © 047042 219; Kyleakin (for Kyle of Lochalsh), 0599 4482; Armadale (for Mallaig), © 047 14248.

Kyleakin, the ferry terminal, stands round a small bay overlooked by a fragment of a ruin on a knoll; a jagged double tooth, familiar from postcards. The 12th-century relic was once a Mackinnon stronghold: **Castle Maol** or Moil, or Dunnakyne. (Kyleakin and Dunakin are said to be so named from King Haakon, who passed through on his way to Largs.) A story is told of one of the castle's earliest inmates, Saucy Mary, a Norwegian princess, who somehow managed to stretch a barrier across the Kyle in order to levy tolls from passing ships. There are several hotels and a shop, and a constant flow of traffic using the ferries. From Kyleakin, the road runs west along the coast. About 4 miles (6.5km) along, a very minor road leads southeast across moorland to **Kylerhea** (pronounced 'Kile-ray') and the ferry back to Glenelg.

A couple of miles on past the turning to Kylerhea, the A851 leads south to the **Sleat Peninsula** (pronounced 'slate'), Macdonald territory. **Isleornnsay** is an attractive hamlet, on the east coast of the peninsula, 9 miles (14.5km) across heather-carpeted moor, looking across the Sound of Sleat into the mouth of Loch Hourn. There is an excellent hotel and a bar, whose landlord encourages his staff to speak Gaelic. There is also an art gallery and shop. The Isle of Ornsay is just offshore from the hotel with a lighthouse and a ruined chapel dedicated to the Columban monk, Oran.

Sabhal Mór Ostaig (big barn of Ostaig) is a Gaelic college in a former Macdonald home farm, so popular and successful that they have just completed a great new extension.

Knock Bay is 3 miles (4.5km) on. Knock Castle (always accessible), an overgrown ruin on a rocky peninsula, was held by the Macdonalds on condition they were always ready to receive the king or one of his representatives. Watch out for the *glaisrig* who haunts this ruin—a female sprite who graciously accepts libations of milk.

Armadale Castle, another 3 miles (4.5km) south, was built by Gillespie Graham in 1815. Much of it was demolished, some has been left as a 'sculptured ruin' and the rest has been imaginatively restored. It is now the **Clan Donald Centre** (open daily, April–Oct: adm), with an excellent Museum of the Isles exhibition, telling the story of Clan Donald and the Lords of the Isles. It stands in lovely grounds with a mature arboretum and a children's play area. Rangers take guided walks round the estate. The former coach house/stable block has won prestigious awards for its restoration and conversion to a well-stocked book and gift shop, and a restaurant.

A ferry runs from Armadale Pier to Mallaig, in the summer, taking half an hour: book ahead through Caledonian MacBrayne. Look out for **Ragamuffin** by the Armadale quay, an unprepossessing looking hut that is an Aladdin's Cave of hand- and machine-knitted woollen garments. Also in Armadale, visit **Skye Batiks** for original hand-made clothes, including some lovely silks.

The road goes on another 5 miles (8km) to **Aird of Sleat** with glorious views across the sound. A couple of miles' walk reaches the lighthouse on the southern tip of the peninsula where there is a sandy beach and more good views. Returning on the same road, take the narrow, twisting lane to the west, a mile (1.5km) north of Armadale. It runs for 5 miles (8km) through woodland and moor, past lochans and mossy glades among silver birches, out to the west coast of Sleat.

Tiny settlements cluster round coves and sandy beaches. The road goes north from **Tarskavaig** about 2 miles (3km) to **Dunsgiath Castle** (always accessible). This is one of the oldest fortified headlands in the Hebrides, home of the Macdonalds until the late 16th century. Little remains now but stacks of stones on a rock 40 feet (12m) high, overlooking Loch Eishort. Celtic legend tells of Scathac the Wise, Queen of Skye in the Dark Ages, who held court here and preached the arts of peace and war to Cuchullin, an Ossianic hero. Cuchullin went off to a foreign land to practise his newly learned arts, leaving his beautiful wife, Bragela, weeping in vain at Dunsgiath, on 'The Isle of Mist'. He never returned.

Another 2 miles (3km) north, at **Ord**, the views, particularly of the Cuillins across Loch Eishort, and southwest to the Isle of Rum, are magnificent, especially at sunset.

From here, it is 15 miles (24km) or so to **Broadford**, rejoining the road a couple of miles short of Isleornsay. Broadford, a straggling settlement, is a busy place on a crossroads. It has hotels, shops and, inevitably, groups of people bowed under knapsacks. A new baker attached to the General Store makes delicious bread and cakes. Other shops include Skye Jewellers, a candlemaker and several craft shops.

Take the narrow, cul-de-sac road 14 miles (22.5km) southwest to Elgol. **Elgol** is a scattered village with more splendid views and from here you can get a boat across Loch Scavaig to **Loch Coruisk**. This was a popular stop for Victorian tourist steamers and was painted by Turner. A half-hour stop gives time to walk across ice-smooth rocks to the inland loch, long, deep and dark, surrounded by the peaks of the Cuillins. In the evening, the sun goes down behind the hills sending up great shafts of colour, made more dramatic by the proximity of the hills. For the energetic, another way is out along the Camasunary track, from **Kilmarie**, about 3 miles (4.5km) before Elgol. It is an easy walk over stony ground through bracken and heather, with just one tricky bit—The Bad Step—where care is needed.

Anyone fortunate enough to be exploring by boat should put into the perfect natural harbour on the island of **Soay** off the entrance to Loch Scavaig. The remains of a shark factory can be seen on the quay, established after the Second World War by the author Gavin Maxwell. His subsequent book, *Harpoon at a Venture*, is a compelling read, telling about these waters in the days when sharks and whales were so plentiful in the Minch that at times the water was literally black with them.

Continuing round the island from Broadford, the road follows the coast, looping round long inlets, zig-zagging up the hills. In a thatched cottage at **Luib**, 7 miles (11km) north-west on Loch Ainort, **Old Skye Crofter's House** is a folk museum (open daily except Sun, Easter–Sept: adm) furnished in the style of a croft house 100 years ago, with an 'on the trail of Bonnie Prince Charlie' exhibition. From Luib there is an easy 4-mile (6.5km) walk due south following the river along Strath Mor, between the rounded paps of the red Cuillins and mighty Blaven, an isolated black Cuillin.

Continuing north, the main hazard for golfers on the nine-hole course at **Sconser**, 6 miles (9.5km) further on, is sheep. The ferry for **Raasay** sails from here, five times a day.

The Cuillins

> Beyond the lochs of the blood of the children of men,
> beyond the frailty of plain and the labour of the mountain,
> beyond poverty, consumption, fever agony,
> beyond hardship, wrong, tyranny, distress,
> beyond misery, despair, hatred, treachery,
> beyond guilt and defilement; watchful
> heroic, the Cuillin is seen
> rising on the other side of sorrow.

> This is the final lyric from 'The Cuillin', by Somhairle Macgill-Eain (Sorley MacLean), Skye's greatest contemporary poet.

There is a delightful hotel at the head of **Loch Sligachan**, 5 miles (8km) west of Sconser. It sits on the junction of the east and west routes to the north and is popular with fishermen and anyone planning to climb in the Cuillins. Here, surrounded by the sound of falling water, the Cuillins reign supreme. Whether capped with snow, their lower slopes mottled and smeared like camouflage jackets; or elusive and eerie in mist; or shrouded by swirling cloud; or brilliant against a postcard-blue sky, they always present a challenge. Only experienced climbers, with proper equipment, should attempt to conquer these mountains, which have claimed many lives over the years.

The road up the east coast, 9 miles (14.5km) from Sligachan to Portree, runs through valleys, pine woods and moorland past fast-flowing rivers and burns. Just south of Portree, a minor road goes out to Braes overlooking the Sound of Raasay, with lovely views and sheltered bays below the cliffs.

Portree is a busy little tourist resort. During the summer, bus excursions run from here to many of the island's beauty spots. It is an attractive town, built round a natural harbour with the houses rising steeply from the water's edge, neat and brightly painted. The name Portree is derived from the Gaelic for King's Port, after a visit by James V in 1540 when he came to subdue the Islanders.

Coming into Portree from the south you will see **Aros Heritage Centre** (open daily:

adm) with exhibitions of life in Skye from the 18th century, an excellent audio-visual display and commentary in six languages. Don't pass this one by. There is also a restaurant, a shop and forest walks from the car park.

It was in a room in what is now the Royal Hotel that Prince Charles took his leave of Flora Macdonald. He repaid her the half-a-crown she had lent him, gave her a miniature of himself, and said: 'For all that has happened, I hope, Madam, we shall meet in St James yet.' He bowed and kissed her hand—a fugitive with a bundle of clean shirts, a chicken, a bottle of whisky and a bottle of brandy tied at his waist, and £30,000 reward on his head. Such is the romance of Scotland.

Portree is the stage for Skye Week, in June, with every sort of Scottish entertainment both indoors and out": the Portree Show in July, Portree Folk Festival in mid-August, the Skye Highland Games also in August, and the Portree Fiddlers Rally in September.

The Skye Woollen Mill has excellent cashmere and lambswool products at reduced prices, as well as a coffee lounge. Fishermen should visit **North West Fishermen**, down by the pier, for fishing tackle, flies and fishing permits.

Going northeast from Portree, up the **Trotternish Peninsula**, Prince Charles' Cave is about 3 miles (4.5km) north, out on the coast—one of the more doubtful of the Prince's alleged hiding places.

The Old Man of Storr

The Old Man of Storr is about 7 miles (11km) north of Portree, to the west of the road and is another of those landmarks made familiar by cameras. Geographically part of Quiraing or Trotternish Ridge, the easiest walk up is through the forestry woods along maintained paths, rather than up the steep, southerly grass slopes. The Old Man is the tallest of a group of mighty towers and pinnacles of basaltic rock. He is over 180 feet (55m) high and 40 feet (12m) in diameter: a great weathered stack, undercut and pointed at the top, like a giant fir cone.

In 1891, on the shore below the Old Man of Storr, a hoard of treasure was unearthed—a remarkable collection of silver neck rings, brooches, bracelets and beaten ingots, together with many 10th-century coins, some from Samarkand. It is believed they must have been left there by a Norseman, who presumably died before he could return to claim them. These treasures are now in the Antiquities part of the Royal Museum of Scotland, in Edinburgh.

There is good trout fishing in the stocked **Storr Lochs**, from bank or boat.

Loch Mealt

The road twists and turns up the east coast, with views across the islands of Rona and Raasay, to the Highland skylines of Dundonnel, Torridon and Applecross on the mainland, south to the Cuillins and west to the Quiraing ridge. Stop at the car park at Loch Mealt, 7 miles (11km) north of the Old Man of Storr where the road comes to the brink of the cliff.

The loch drains in a sheer 300-foot (92m) white cascade, plummeting into the cobalt sea. Extreme care should be taken here and vertigo sufferers should not think of approaching the edge even though it is fenced. **Kilt Rock**, on the north side of Loch Mealt, has vertical columns of basalt over horizontal strips of grey and white oolite like the pleats and pattern of a kilt.

The Quiraing is 2 miles (3km) west of Staffin and you must scramble up quite a slope to get into it through a steep narrow gorge in the rocks. Great pillars of basaltic rock surround an emerald-green grass amphitheatre, like a surreal Gothic cathedral. Cattle used to be driven here for safety during raids in the old days. It is hard to find and difficult to get to, but once there it is a magical place with stunning views.

Flodigarry, about 3 miles (4.5km) north of Staffin, is where Flora Macdonald lived for eight years, after her marriage to Captain Allan Macdonald of Kingsburgh in 1751. Five of her seven children were born here. **Flora Macdonald's Cottage** is adjacent to the Flodigarry Country House Hotel which has a Moorish-style bar in what was probably the billiard room of the house.

Duntulm Castle

This is a jagged ruin, less than 5 miles (8km) to the west. The castle, with a water gate, stands in an easily defended position on a precipitous cliff on the northwest coast. Built on the site of an earlier fortress, it was a stronghold of the Macdonalds of Sleat, under the authority of James VI during his attempts to discipline the Hebridean chiefs at the turn of the 16th century. Sir Donald Gorme Macdonald was ordered to maintain his fortress in good condition, to restrict his household to six gentlemen, to limit his consumption of wine to four tuns (1008 gallons) a year, and to produce three of his kinsmen, annually, as surety for his good behaviour. The family left the castle after a nursemaid dropped the laird's infant son out of a window into the sea. The luckless nursemaid was punished for her carelessness by being cast adrift in an open boat full of holes.

Kilmuir

One of Scotland's most endearing heroines, Flora Macdonald is buried below a simple white Celtic cross in the windswept churchyard at **Kilmuir**, a couple of miles further south. They say her shroud is a sheet on which Prince Charles slept when he was hidden at Kingsburgh House. Flora smuggled the Prince, disguised as her maid Betty Burke, from Loch Uskavagh in Benbecula to Skye. For this act of courage she was briefly imprisoned. She lived with her family in North Carolina for some years but returned to Kingsburgh for the last decade of her life, dying at the age of 68. A portrait of her by Allan Ramsay shows a woman with large eyes and a calm, fine-boned face of classic Scottish beauty. Dr Johnson, who was a guest of Flora and her husband at Kingsburgh in 1773, wrote of her: 'Flora Macdonald, a name that will be mentioned in history, and if courage and fidelity be virtues, mentioned with honour. She is a woman of middle stature, soft features, gentle manners and elegant presence.'

From the churchyard you can look westwards across the entrance to Loch Snizort, to where Flora and the Prince came on their daring voyage. Kilmuir has a popular agricultural show in August.

The Skye Cottage Museum (open daily except Sun, April–Sept: adm) is close to the churchyard. It consists of a group of cottages with a 'black house', farming and domestic implements and a collection of documents and photographs, giving a good idea of what life was like in the old days of crofting. The green plain stretching away to the south is known as the Granary of Skye and was once a loch until drained by the Macdonalds.

Monkstadt House

Monkstadt House, 4 miles (6.5km) south of Kilmuir, is now virtually a ruin, though the owner plans to restore it. This was the home of Sir Alexander Macdonald of Sleat who supported the Hanoverian cause. Flora and Prince Charles landed here while the house was occupied by Hanoverian troops. Fortunately Macdonald was away ingratiating himself with the Duke of Cumberland at Fort Augustus and his wife, Lady Margaret, was a staunch Jacobite. The Prince hid in the grounds where he was served by Macdonald of Kingsburgh who brought him food and wine under the noses of the soldiers. (Sir Alexander is reputed to have made a fast buck by shipping Highlanders to the Caribbean as slaves but in fact he seems to have been honest, if naive, and only sanctioned the removal of undesirables such as thieves from his lands. He certainly resisted attempts to cook the books to disguise the fact that some of the 'criminals' were small children. It is said that Macleod of Dunvegan and Macdonald of Boisdale were much more deeply involved.)

Uig Bay

Uig Bay, 3 miles (4.5km) to the south, lies below a green amphitheatre of hills, its long pier cutting across it like an outflung arm. The hamlet of Uig is busy with ferry traffic, for this is the terminal for the steamer to the Outer Isles. If you are lucky, one of the fishing boats that use the pier may have berthed with a load of scampi and may agree to sell a bagful, scooped up off a great pile on deck. Anyone with a portable camping stove should boil these for just a few moments and eat them while still warm, accompanied by a slice of locally baked brown bread from the village shop.

Loch Snizort Beag

At Borve, 11 miles (17.5km) south of Uig, take the right turn (west) and stop in **Skeabost**, about 3 miles (4.5km) along, a pretty hamlet at the head of Loch Snizort Beag. Below the stone bridge the river branches round an island, now reached by a bridge. (Take the road to the village hall; by the stone bridge on the right, a path leads to the new bridge.) This was the site of an ancient Christian settlement, probably founded by St Columba, whose name it bears, with the ruin of a Celtic chapel and a collection of old gravestones carved with effigies. This was a burial place around the Cathedral Church of the Bishops of the Isles, certainly from 1079 (except for about 60 years when it was transferred to St Germain's on the Isle of Man) until the bishopric moved to the Benedictine Monastery of Iona in 1498 after the eclipse of its patrons, the Lords of the Isles. The small cruciform church dates from the 13th century and the 16th-century mortuary chapel is said to contain the remains of 28 Nicolson chiefs. Information plaques give some of the history of this site. **Skeabost Hotel** offers salmon fishing and lays on an excellent eat-as-much-as-you-want buffet lunch.

Annait

Annait is the site of the oldest Christian settlement in these parts. The wall and foundations of a small chapel and the monks' cells are scattered across a green promontory between two deep gulleys. In this wild and lonely place the only sounds are the piping of skylarks, the chatter of running water and the wind.

At **Trumpan**, the scant remains of a church have an unholy history. In 1579, the Macleods were attending a service in the church when they were attacked by their bitter enemies, the Macdonalds of South Uist, who massacred them, setting fire to the church and burning the congregation. One woman, cutting off a breast in order to escape through a window, managed to get away and warn the remainder of the Macleod clan. When the Macdonalds returned to their boats they were massacred by the alerted Macleods.

Dunvegan

From the road south towards Dunvegan, the outline of Macleod's Tables dominates, the horizon 10 miles (16km) away to the southwest. It is said that when Alasdair Crottach Macleod went to the court of King James V at Holyrood in Edinburgh in the 16th century, he was asked somewhat patronizingly whether he was impressed by the grandeur of the palace. He replied that he saw nothing to compare for grandeur with his own domain in Skye. When James V then visited Skye, trying to rally support from the Hebridean clans, Macleod gave an open-air banquet for him, on the lower of the two 'tables', lit by his kilted clansmen, each holding aloft a flaming torch. 'My family candlesticks', he told the king, with a sweep of his hand. One can only hope it was a fine day and that the monarch was supplied with a good horse or some stout walking shoes.

Dunvegan Castle (open daily, Easter–mid-Oct; winter by arrangement: adm) is 5 miles (8km) southwest of the Fairy Bridge. Seat of the Macleods since at least 1200, it is a massive castle on a rock, with Georgian sash windows added later which soften its otherwise fortress-like appearance. From every angle it seems to show a different face, each one grey, formidable and impressive. Today it is approached by a bridge over a ravine which once formed a dry moat. In the old days the only way in was from the sea through a water-gate on to the rocks.

The Fairy Flag

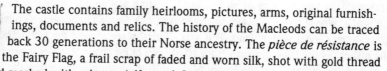
The castle contains family heirlooms, pictures, arms, original furnishings, documents and relics. The history of the Macleods can be traced back 30 generations to their Norse ancestry. The *pièce de résistance* is the Fairy Flag, a frail scrap of faded and worn silk, shot with gold thread and marked with crimson 'elf spots'. Legend tells of the Macleod who fell in love with a fairy, hundreds of years ago. The lovers were forced to part (at Fairy Bridge, to the north) and the fairy left the flag as a coverlet for their child. This flag

had the power to save the Macleod Clan from destruction three times, but only if waved in a genuine crisis. It has been used twice: once at Trumpan (see above), helping the Macleods to massacre the marauding Macdonalds of South Uist, and once during a famine, caused by cattle plague.

Boat cruises run from the jetty below the castle to the little islands where seals bask on the rocks. Dunvegan has a Gala Day in August and the Dunvegan Show, also in August. Look out for the excellent craft shop just outside Dunvegan on the Portree road.

Drive a few miles on past the castle to see seal colonies and swan lochs. At Claigan, follow the path to the coral beaches—don't be put off by the Aberdeen Angus bull who rarely bothers people.

The Durinish Peninsula

The Durinish Peninsula, topped by Macleod's Tables, stretches away west of Loch Dunvegan. Macleod's Maidens, only visible if you walk or go by sea, are off the southern tip 8 miles (13km) south of Dunvegan. These three basalt stacks are called after the wife and daughters of a Macleod, who drowned here in a shipwreck.

The Orbost Art Gallery

The Orbost Art Gallery, 3 miles (4.5km) south of Dunvegan on the east side of the peninsula, has modern exhibitions in the summer. Five miles (8km) further north, the **Colbost Folk Museum** (open daily except Sun, Easter–Sept: adm) is a thatched 'black house' with peat fire in the middle of the room and all the implements and furnishings of the 19th century. There is also an illicit whisky still, once common all over the Highlands. The museum includes a watermill, 3 miles (4.5km) to the west at Glendale. Also on this road, 2 miles (3km) north of Colbost, is the Piping Centre at Borreraig. Here, a cairn marks the site of the piping school where the hereditary pipers to the Macleods, the MacCrimmons of Durinish, lived and taught piping for 300 years.

Carry on west to Loch Pooltiel, with its sheltered anchorage, and then on to **Neist Point**, the most westerly point in Skye. Park at the top and walk down to the lighthouse.

Going south on the main road from Dunvegan, after about 8 miles (13km) look carefully up to the left as you drop down into Bracadale. **Dun Beag** (always accessible), one of the best brochs in Skye, seems to grow out of the hillside and would be easy to miss. It is only a few minutes' climb over springy turf and stones to this 2000-year-old relic, which once stood 40 or 50 feet (12–15m) high. This refuge, once used by farmers and herdsmen, has double walls braced by a honeycomb of chambers and galleries, with cells, passages and stairways and traces of outbuildings.

To complete a circular tour of Skye, take the road that runs southeast along the northern edge of the Cuillins, dappled with brown, tan, grey, blue and ochre, 14 miles (22.5km) back to Sligachan and the route to the mainland.

A detour west from Drynoch takes you to **Talisker**, home of Skye's malt whisky, with daily tours on weekdays. To the south are glorious sands and coastal and hill walks at **Glen Brittle**. This is the base for exploring the Cuillins and there is a campsite and a hostel here.

Raasay

The island of Raasay can be reached by ferry from Sconser. It is a 15-mile (24km) strip, sheltered and fertile, once the hiding place of the fugitive Prince Charles, who spent a couple of nights in a shepherd's hut. Dr Johnson visited the island during his tour of the Hebrides with Boswell and was lavishly entertained at Raasay House, built by the Macleods in 1746. The house and land were badly neglected by an absentee landlord in the 1970s, giving rise to much publicity and local outrage. It now houses the Raasay Outdoor Centre.

Castle Brochel

Castle Brochel—Caisteal Bhrochail—(always accessible) is a ruin on a rock on the eastern shore overlooking a bay, with the hills of Torridon massing on the eastern horizon. The danger notices are justified. Boswell, exploring this ruin, discovered that it contained a privy—a convenience that was sadly lacking in Raasay House where they were staying. He pointed this out to their host: 'You take very good care of one end of a man, but not of the other.'

There are two carved Celtic crosses within easy walking distance of Kilmaluag.

The island has a ruined chapel dedicated to St Moluag of Lismore, with a carved Celtic cross, and the remains of a ruined broch, Dun Borodale. A nice walk goes up the Inverarish Burn to the flat-topped volcano-like Dunn Caan, then west along the track to join the coastal road.

Where to Stay and Eating Out

moderate

Broadford Hotel, Broadford, ℂ 04712 204/5, is on the edge of the village. The food isn't too bad.

Cuillin Hills Hotel, ℂ 0478 2003, overlooks Portree Bay. **Portree Hotel,** Somerled Square, ℂ 0478 2511, has three crowns. **Rosedale Hotel,** Portree, ℂ 0478 2531, is on the waterfront overlooking the harbour. **Royal Hotel,** Portree, ℂ 0478 2525, is not quite as it was the day Prince Charles took his leave of Flora Macdonald in one of its parlours, but the older part has plenty of character. **Viewfield House Hotel,** ℂ 0478 2217, is on the outskirts of Portree as you come in from the south. Run by the family for whom it has always been home, it still feels more like a welcoming, comfortable country house than a hotel. Open from May to mid-October, it is not expensive.

Sconser Lodge Hotel, ℂ 047852 333, was a Victorian shooting lodge, at the mouth of Loch Sligachan, looking across to Raasay. **Kinloch Lodge,** Isleornsay, ℂ 04713 214/333, is another Victorian shooting lodge overlooking the sea, owned and run by Lord and Lady Macdonald. The magic touch of Lady Macdonald, who writes cookery books, is very evident. Open from March to

January. **Hotel Eilean Iarmain**, Isle Oronsay, © 04713 332, is right on the water. It is a lively place and has art exhibitions in the adjoining Céilidh Hall.

Torvaig House Hotel, Knock Bay, Sleat, © 04713 231, is on the bay, and serves good food.

Isle of Raasay Hotel, © 047862 222/226, overlooking the Sound of Raasay, is comfortable. **Uig Hotel**, © 047042 205, is highly recommended—especially for its breakfasts.

inexpensive

Duntulm Castle Hotel, © 047052 213, stands high above Score Bay, looking across to the Outer Isles. Open April to October. **Dunringell Hotel**, Kyleakin, © 0599 4180, is reasonably comfortable.

The Isles Hotel in Somerled Square, Portree, © 0478 2129, has three crowns. You might also try: **Bosville Hotel & Restaurant**, Bosville Terrace, © 0478 2846; **Kings Haven**, Bosville Terrace, © 0478 2290, two crowns; and **Tongadale Hotel**, Wentworth Street, © 0478 2115.

Flodigarry Country House Hotel, at Staffin, © 047 052 203, is cheapish and historic (see above), beneath the Quiraing, with fine views across to the Ross-shire coast and an 'eastern-style' bar. The food is excellent. **Sligachan Hotel**, © 047852 204, is easy-going, ideally placed for the Cuillins. **Ferry Inn Hotel**, Uig, © 047042 242, is a charming old inn with a great atmosphere and not too many frills.

Of the many **bed and breakfast** places, two are specially recommended. Mrs Flora Cumming, Eilean Dubh, Edinbane, © 047082 218, is so welcoming and hospitable it is like going to stay with an old friend. At Mrs B. La Trobe's house in Fiordham, Ord, © 04715 226, the sea laps below the dining room whose picture windows look west to the setting sun. Take your own wine if you want dinner.

One of the nicest **self-catering** houses is at Braes, high above the Narrows of Raasay south of Portree. This is a cosy, family house, sleeping six to seven people, looking across Isle of Raasay to the mainland and is very reasonable. Book c/o Mrs Bengough, White Lodge, Church Street, Sidbury, Devon EX10 0SB, © 03957 214.

The Small Isles: Rum, Eigg, Canna and Muck

Getting There

Caledonian MacBrayne run a seasonal service to all four islands from Mallaig. For details write to Caledonian MacBrayne, The Ferry Terminal, Gourock, Renfrewshire, PA19 1QP, © 0475 34531. Murdo Grant runs regular cruises from Arisaig at Easter and from May to September, less frequently out of season. His boat, *MV Shearwater*, is fast and comfortable and takes 130 people. He will also charter; © 06875 224.

Fort William and Lochaber Tourist Board, Cameron Square, **Fort William**, ℭ 0397 3781.

Rum

Rum is a squashed-diamond-shaped island, rising to a series of peaks; an unmistakable landmark for sailors, 8 miles (13km) west of Sleat in Skye. Inhabited since the Stone Age, its population of over 400 was reduced to one family in 1826, to make way for one sheep farm of 8000 sheep. Deer were then introduced and it became a private sporting estate until the Nature Conservancy acquired it in 1957. It is now an 'outdoor laboratory', trying to discover how the Hebrides can best support wildlife and human beings.

The name Rum is thought to come from the Greek *rhombos*, referring to the rhomboid shape. The 'h' that sometimes creeps into the spelling of Rum was added by the Bulloughs, see below, who hoped thus to give a Gaelic flavour to the name, not realising that in Gaelic, 'r' is never aspirated. The island's chief interest is its geology: special permission must be obtained from the Scottish Natural Heritage warden to visit most places.

The half-wild golden-brown ponies on Rum are said to be descended from the survivors of a Spanish galleon which was part of the Armada wrecked off these coasts in 1588. There are also wild goats, golden eagles and plenty of red deer.

The red sandstone castle that looks across the bay is Kinloch Castle, built in 1901 by the owners of the estate, the Bulloughs of Lancashire. So bitten by the Scottish bug were the Bulloughs that it is said they offered extra wages to employees who would work in kilts, despite the fact that Rum is notorious for its midges. It is now a hotel with the atmosphere of a baronial seat and all the original furnishings. The hotel is owned by Scottish Natural Heritage and gets written up in quality magazines. One of the features is the extremely rare electric 'orchestrarian', a Heath Robinson contraption whose parts represent a full orchestra, activated by a vast library of pre-set cylinders, each programmed with a well-known tune. All the working components can be seen in action, in a huge glass chamber in the hall.

For further information about the Kinloch Castle Hotel, ring 9687 2037.

Eigg

Eigg, privately owned, is an idyllic holiday island about 4 miles (6.5km) southeast of Rum, with chalets and cottages to let. Shaped like an upturned boat, or a crouching lion, surrounded by clear, sparkling water, it is a magic place, both in sunshine, or in storm. About 6 miles by 4, (9.5 by 6.5km), it is dominated by the huge black hump of the Sgurr.

Walk up from the little harbour in the southeast, east round the bay to the ancient burial ground at Kildonnan Church. This is the resting place of Macdonalds, who were once holders of the island. A broken Celtic cross, a scattering of grave stones and a roofless ruin are all that remain.

An aura of tragedy still hangs over *Uamh Fhraing*, a cave southwest of the pier, easily reached by a path from Galmisdale—torch advised. In 1577 some Macleods were forced to shelter from storm on Eigg. Owing to constant feuding over disputed land, the Macdonalds were not hospitable. The Macleods left and returned later to take revenge. The Macdonalds took shelter in this cave and the landing party found one old woman, whose life they spared. But as they were putting out to sea, they saw a scout, sent from the cave to see if they had gone. They rushed back, found the cave and lit a fire in the mouth of it, suffocating the 398 inhabitants. Sir Walter Scott is said to have found bones here in 1814 and taken a souvenir away with him. Several people have seen ghosts here.

Palm trees and flame trees thrive on this paradise island in the garden surrounding the lodge and there are lovely walks. Go up to the northwest corner, the glorious Bay of Laig, with 'Singing Sands'. The sands make a curious keening sort of song in certain conditions. Cattle wander on the beach and the views across to Rum are glorious on a clear day.

Where to Stay

inexpensive

Both the following are friendly and hospitable: **Laig Farm Guest House**, ✆ 0687 82437, is a farmhouse overlooking Rum and Skye near the Singing Sands, and **Seaview Guest House**, ✆ 0687 82433, is a working croft overlooking the Sgurr and Laig Bay. For information about self-catering places, write to: Eigg Holiday Bookings, Maybank, Udny, Ellon, Aberdeenshire, ✆ 06513 2367.

The café on the pier is the meeting place for the island, there being no pub. Locals and visitors mingle and enjoy delicious home cooking and exchange island news.

Canna

Sometimes called 'the Garden of the Hebrides', Canna lies less than 5 miles (8km) off the west coast of Rum. The highest point of this long thin island is only 690 feet (212m) above sea level. Compass Hill, 458 feet (141m), in the north, is so called because of the magnetic rock in it that can distort the true readings of a ship's compass. Canna is charming—serene and lonely, with a good harbour. The remains of a Celtic nunnery that once flourished here can still be seen. The ruined tower near the harbour was owned by a Lord of the Isles, who is reputed to have imprisoned his beautiful wife in it, suspecting her of infidelity. Canna is owned by the National Trust for Scotland. A tiny fragile Hebridean community survives here—just.

Where to Stay

The National Trust for Scotland has a guest house on the island; members get priority. Apply to National Trust for Scotland, 5 Charlotte Square, Edinburgh, EH2 4DU, ✆ 031 226 5922.

Muck

Muck, 7 miles (11km) south of Rum, is the smallest of the group known as the Small Isles, its strange name being derived from the Gaelic *muc*, a pig. It is a green, pretty little island with lovely sandy beaches. Bed and breakfast can be had from Mrs Martin, Godag House, © 0687 2371.

The Outer Hebrides

Of all Scotland's islands, the Western Isles seem to evoke the deepest nostalgia; its exiles suffer the strongest pangs of homesickness. There is no specific explanation. The distinctive tang of peat-smoke, the Gaelic, the wild flowers on the machair, the cry of the curlew, the fundamental faith, the humour; these and many other things cast an unbreakable spell.

The Western Isles run about 130 miles (208km) from the Butt of Lewis in the north, down to Barra Head in the south. The main islands include Lewis and Harris, Berneray, North Uist, Benbecula, South Uist, Eriskay, Barra, Scalpay, Vatersay and Mingulay.

Each is unique, with dialects that differ even between the moorlands of Lewis and the mountains of Harris. Gaelic still lives, the first language for many and fighting to remain so. North of Benbecula the islanders are almost entirely Presbyterian, and south almost entirely Catholic. The islanders are famous for the warm hospitality and friendliness they offer to strangers.

The scenery is made up of miles of white sand; acres of machair, rich in wild flowers; rugged hills and moorland carpeted with heather. The east coast is indented by long sea lochs that provide shelter for boats in bad weather. An aerial photograph reveals a land broken up by a vast number of lochs and lochans, which once provided waterways throughout the islands. The climate is unpredictable.

Tourists should note that all road signs are now only in Gaelic, except in Benbecula where they are bilingual, and are often difficult for strangers to pronounce and to translate into the more familiar Anglicized version. For example, if you saw *Taobh a Deas Loch Aineort*, you might not realize you had reached South Locheynort. In this guide, the Gaelic translation is given where it differs from the Anglicized name. The Western Isles Tourist Board have published an excellent leaflet with all the names in both English and Gaelic, well worth arming yourself with.

Getting to the Outer Hebrides

by sea

Ferries run from Ullapool to Stornoway in Lewis; from Uig in Skye to Tarbert in Harris and Lochmaddy in North Uist; from Oban to Castlebay in Barra and Lochboisdale in South Uist. A ferry is planned soon from Mallaig to Lochboisdale. The timetable changes for winter and summer and is constantly under review. Apply to Caledonian Macbrayne, The Ferry Terminal, Gourock PA19 1QP, © 0475 34531. Local boats run between the smaller islands. Their timetables are

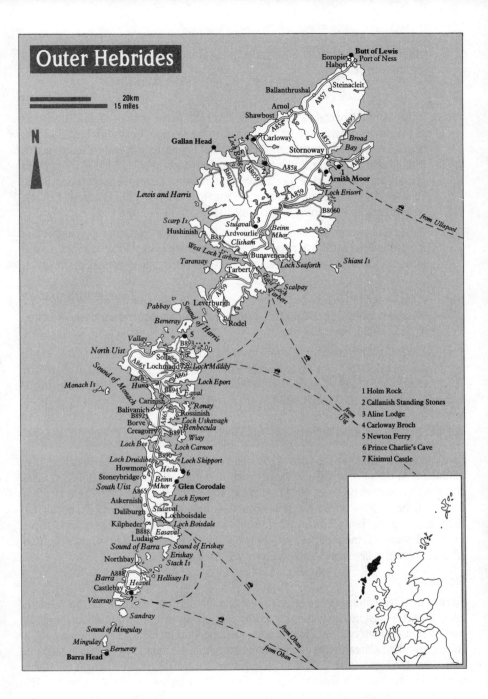

Outer Hebrides

20km
15 miles

N

Butt of Lewis
Eoropie Port of Ness
Habost
Steinacleit
Ballanthrushal
Arnol
Shawbost
Carloway
Gallan Head
Stornoway
Broad
Bay
1
Arnish Moor
Loch Erisort
Lewis and Harris
B8060
from Ullapool
Scarp Is
Hushinish
Stulaval **3**
Ardvourlie Beinn
Clisham Mhor
West Loch Tarbert
Taransay
Bunaveneader
Loch Seaforth
Shiant Is
Tarbert
Scalpay
Loch
Tarbert
Leverburgh
Pabbay
Berneray
Rodel
Valley
5
North Uist
B893
Sollas
Lochmaddy Loch Maddy
Monach Is
Loch
Huna
Loch Eport
Carinish
Egval
Balivanich
Ronay
Borve
Rossinish
Creagorry
Loch Uskavagh
Benbecula
Wiay
Loch Bee
Loch Carnon
Loch Druidibeg
Loch Skipport
Howmore
Hecla **6**
Stoneybridge
Beinn
South Uist
Mhor **Glen Corodale**
Askernish
Loch Eynort
Daliburgh
Stulaval
Lochboisdale
Kilpheder
Loch Boisdale
Easaval
Ludaig
Sound of Barra Sound of Eriskay
Northbay
Eriskay
Stack Is
Barra
Heaval Hellisay Is
Castlebay
Vatersay
Sandray
Sound of Mingulay
Mingulay
Berneray
Barra Head

Sound of Harris

Sound of Monach

from Uig

from Oban
from Oban

1 Holm Rock
2 Callanish Standing Stones
3 Aline Lodge
4 Carloway Broch
5 Newton Ferry
6 Prince Charlie's Cave
7 Kisimul Castle

Loch Roag

Loch Bhrollum

B801

B8059

A857

A858

A859

A866

A865

A861

A894

A863

A888

467

sometimes subject to tides and sometimes they do extra runs to connect with other services. Details of these times are available locally and through the tourist information centres.

British Airways operate a daily service (except Sundays) from Glasgow/Inverness to Stornoway, Lewis, and from Glasgow to Benbecula. Apply to British Airways, Buchanan Street, Glasgow, ✆ 041 889 1311. Loganair operate a daily service from Glasgow to Barra, and a Glasgow to Stornaway service, Mon–Fri. They also operate an inter-island service between Stornoway, Lewis, Benbecula and Barra. Charter flights can be arranged. Write to Loganair Ltd, Glasgow Airport, Abbotsinch, Renfrewshire, ✆ 041 889 1311.

Public transport in the islands is operated through local garages, supplemented by the post office Post Bus Service. For visitors wanting to explore at random, a car is essential. Cars can be hired locally; consult the tourist office for more information.

Tourist Information

Western Isles Tourist Board, 26 Cromwell Street, **Stornoway**, Isle of Lewis, ✆ 0851 3088, open all year.

The following offices are open from Easter–September: **Barra**: Main Street, Castlebay, ✆ 0871 810336; **Harris**: Pier Road, Tarbert, ✆ 0859 502011; **North Uist**: Pier Road, Lochmaddy, ✆ 0876 500321; **South Uist**: Pier Road, Lochboisdale, ✆ 0878 700286.

Lewis (Eilean Leòdhas)

Lewis and Harris are joined to form one island. Lewis, the largest of all the outer isles, has mountains in the southwest, undulating moor in the middle, thousands of lochs, especially in the southeast, green fertile croftland and many fine beaches. There is still a flourishing network of tweed weavers throughout both Lewis and Harris. To qualify for the stamp of pure Harris Tweed the cloth has to be woven in the home of an islander from local wool. It is then sent to a factory in Stornoway to be processed. Visitors can stop off at the houses where most of the weavers will have a small shop.

Stornoway

Stornoway (Steòrnabhagh), the largest town and administrative centre for the Western Isles, is on the east coast. It forms a sturdy metropolis with a busy harbour, brightly painted houses, reasonable shops and plenty of amenities including a swimming pool, a college and the Laintear, with national and international exhibitions—Europie Teampul Mor. After the First World War, the rich industrialist Lord Leverhulme bought the island and tried to develop it in order to improve the economy for the benefit of the people. His motives were entirely philanthropic but came to nothing. Economic recession caused failure of the herring markets, particularly in Europe and Lord Leverhulme did not understand the importance of letting crofters have their own plots of land. He offered to give the island to the people, having lost a considerable sum of money trying to establish a strong fishing industry, but they refused to accept his gift. Stornoway Town Council, however, accepted the land of the Stornoway Parish, including croftland, the town itself, Lews Castle and grounds. The Stornoway Trust was formed, a unique form of land ownership in the Highlands. It is administered by elected trustees so that the crofters are at the same time their own landlords and tenants of the Stornoway Trust, which is democratically administered by themselves.

The picturesque harbour, with fishing boats and all the clutter of the waterfront, is the focus of the town. The grounds of **Lews Castle** are now a public park and golf course. The castle is closed, awaiting decisions on its future from the local authority, Comhairle nan Eilean. The original Lews Castle, near the present ferry terminal, was the stronghold of the Macleods and was destroyed by Cromwell.

Museum nan Eilean—Western Isles Museum (open daily except Sunday; afternoons only in winter: free) is in the Old Town Hall, with good local history displays. Also in the town hall, open daily except Sunday, is the award-winning **An Lanntair Gallery**, with exhibitions by local artists and themes of local interest.

About 4 miles (6.5km) south of the castle, on the edge of Arnish Moor, a cairn commemorates the night Prince Charles spent here, while trying to negotiate for a boat during his fugitive days after Culloden. (Such was rumour in those days that when one of his three companions, Donald Macleod, went ahead of him into Stornoway to make arrangements, he found large numbers of armed Mackenzies preparing to fight off the Prince and an estimated army of 500 Highlanders.)

On New Year's Day 1919, a troop ship, the *Iolaire*, hit Holm Rock on the other side of the harbour and sank, drowning 200 men returning from the war.

East of Stornoway, past the airport, a narrow neck of land connects **Point** (an Rubha) to the rest of Lewis. It is also called the Eye (or Ui) Peninsula, after a Norse word meaning narrow ford or isthmus. The 14th-century **St Columba's Church**, at the western end of Point, is the burial ground of the Macleod chiefs. There is some fine carving in the church which was last used in 1828.

North of Stornoway, **Back** (Am Bac) and **North Tolsta** (Tolastadh) have fertile croft land, steep cliffs and large white beaches, unique on the east coast of the Western Isles. At the end of the road is Lord Leverhulme's 'bridge to nowhere', the beginning of the road he hoped to build between Tolsta and Ness to complete the coastal road.

The Butt of Lewis (Rubha Robhanais) is a bleak headland on the northern tip of the island, 27 miles (43km) from Stornoway by road, and topped by a lighthouse. This is a birdwatcher's dreamland: shags, cormorants, puffins, razorbills, guillemots, terns, kittiwakes, fulmars, gulls, oystercatchers, plovers, redshanks, greenshanks are just a few of the birds whose calls echo among the cliffs.

The 'Ness' (Nis) district just to the south has a hotel, a tearoom (open in the summer), and a very active football and social club. There are good beaches here, particularly the one near the harbour at Port of Ness. On the road out to the lighthouse, the old *feannagan* or inappropriately named lazy beds can be seen clearly, characteristic of the old type of agriculture practised throughout the islands. There was nothing lazy about the hard work that went into digging these strips and fertilizing them with seaweed carted from the shore in heavy creels.

At **Eoropie** (Eoropaidh), the hamlet southwest of the lighthouse, is the restored 12th-century **St Moluag's Chapel**, known as Teamphull Mholuidh and built on the site of an early Christian chapel. The key for this charming little place is in the shop. Episcopal services are held occasionally and there is a strong feeling of the simple, uncomplicated faith that keeps such a remote church alive.

About 10 miles (16km) down the A857, the 20-foot (12m) monolith, the **Thrushel Stone** (Clach an Truiseil), is the largest single stone in Scotland, a relic from prehistoric settlers. This and the burial cairn within a stone circle surrounded by bleak moorland at **Steinacleit**, about a mile (1.5km) or so away, have a marvellously primal atmosphere.

About 8 miles (13km) further on, at **Arnol**, there is the **Black House Museum** (open daily except Sun: adm). It illustrates how crofting families lived until as recently as the Second World War. At **Bragar**, a mile (1.5km) beyond Arnol, look for a gateway beside the road made of the massive jaw bone of an 80-foot (24.5m) blue whale that came ashore in the bay here in 1920. It had been harpooned and the harpoon hangs from the centre of the arch.

Shawbost (Siabost) Folk Museum (open daily except Sun: donation box) is a couple of miles further on. Here there is an exhibition covering the old way of life in Lewis. It includes a restored Norse watermill about a mile (1.5km) to the west. The entire museum was set up by pupils of the school. There is a modern Harris Tweed Mill, open to visitors, in Shawbost.

Between Shawbost and Carloway (Carlabhagh), there are beautiful sheltered beaches at **Dalbeg** (Dail Beag) and **Dalmore** (Dail Mor), down two turnings off the A857.

In **Carloway**, 5 miles (8km) southwest of Shawbost, drive out to the end of the Gearrannan road. Here is a typical village street of black houses in traditional style, one of which has been renovated and is a Gatliff Trust Hostel. Stop on the way to watch John MacGregor at work in his weaving shed and buy a length of his Harris tweed.

Carloway Broch, on the northern shore of East Loch Roag, a couple of miles south of the village overlooking the sea, is the best-preserved broch in the Hebrides. Its only rival for age and quality of preservation is Mousa Broch in Shetland. Part of it rises to about 30 feet (15m), forming a reassuring shelter for those families who 2000 years ago crowded inside the massive walls to take refuge from invaders.

Callanish (Calanais) Standing Stones

The Callanish Standing Stones are 5 miles (8km) southeast of Carloway along the northern shore of East Loch Roag. They rank in importance with Stonehenge, being one of the most complete prehistoric sites in Britain. The stones are laid out to depict a Celtic cross with a burial cairn at the centre, approached from north and south by avenues of pillars. Traces of cremated bones were found in the cairn. The central pillar casts its shadow along the entrance passage into the grave only at sunset on the days of the equinox. It is a dramatic place, in moorland overlooking the loch. It stirs the imagination, conjuring up the burial of some priest-king with the elaborate ritual practised in the centuries before Christianity. A mini-museum, open in the summer, gives details of the stones. There is also a tea room in a converted thatched house. On a clear day the **Flannan Islands** lighthouse can be seen, 15 miles (24km) to the west. In 1900 a gale raged at Christmas and all three of the lighthouse-keepers vanished without trace.

After Callanish, the B8011 branches south at **Garynahine** (Gearraidh Na H-Aibhne) for **Bernera** (Bearnaraigh) and **Uig**. The island of Bernera is reached by a 'bridge over the Atlantic', built in 1953.The men of Bernera were agitators in the period leading up to the 1886 crofters' revolt, when they marched with their grievances to the landlord, Sir James Matheson, in his castle in Stornoway. **Bosta Beach**, on the northern tip, is well worth a visit. Go on down the B8011 and explore the district around Uig, which has some of the most beautiful scenery in the islands.

The famous **Lewis Chessmen**, made of walrus ivory, were discovered in 1831, in the sands of **Ardroil** (Eadar Dha Fhadhail), a few miles south of Gallan Head. Of Norse origin, they are thought to have been buried here to save them from plunder by nuns living in a Benedictine convent at Brenish at the end of the road. Replicas can be bought all over the islands. The original chessmen are divided between the British Museum and the Scottish National Museum.

This is grand walking country—along the coast to the Uig Hills and south to the hills of Harris.

Going south from Stornoway towards Harris, the road goes through the 'Lochs' area and a detour east on the B8060 leads down to **Lemreway** (Leumrabhagh). The land is split by deep sea lochs and masses of little lochans, surrounded by heathery hills.

Harris (Na Hearadh)

Aline Lodge, at the head of Loch Seaforth (Shiophoirt), marks the boundary between Harris and Lewis. Harris is divided into north and south by a narrow isthmus at Tarbert (Tairbeart), between East and West Loch Tarbert. North Harris has outstanding mountain scenery and the west coast of South Harris has machair and huge white sandy beaches. The east coast of South Harris is a complete contrast, with a rugged landscape so rocky you could be on the moon. Although geographically one island, Lewis and Harris are effectively divided by the high range of hills along the border and are always referred to as separate islands. The inhabitants are conscious of their very different Gaelic dialects and marked character differences.

The moors of Lewis give way to the hills of Harris, dominated by Clisham, at 2600 feet (800m) the highest mountain in the Western Isles. Although not as impressive as the mainland Munros, these hills and their glens offer wonderful walks. There is a controversial plan to form a huge quarry in one of the hills, virtually removing it entirely, for rock infill by Redlands Quarrys. It will provide much needed employment and Harris can easily spare one rocky mountain, but it could bring less welcome developments.

Tarbert (An Tairbeart)

Tarbert, Harris's main village, at the head of East Loch Tarbert on the east coast, is a thriving centre with good shops and the ferry terminal for Skye and North Uist. It is a good base for fishermen, both for salmon, sea trout and trout, and for sea fishing. There are local tweed suppliers who welcome visitors to watch Harris Tweed being woven.

Scalpay (Scalpaigh), at the entrance to East Loch Tarbet, was where Prince Charles stayed whilst trying to arrange a boat from Stornoway. He and his three companions spent four nights here as guests of the tenant, Donald Campbell. It was here that the only recorded attempt to betray the Prince for the £30,000 reward offered for his capture was made. John Macaulay (grandfather of the historian Lord Macaulay) was the Presbyterian minister in South Uist. A zealous Whig on a Catholic island, he sent word to his father, Aulay MacAulay, who was minister in Harris. He warned him of the Prince's arrival and urged him to contact Colin Mackenzie, the minister in Stornoway, and arrange to have the fugitive arrested. A boatload of armed men led by Aulay duly landed on Scalpay 'with a determined resolution to seize the Chevalier and secure the bribe offered by the Government'. They reckoned without Donald Campbell who, although not a Jacobite, was deeply aware of his obligations as a Highlander and a host. He refused the offered bribe and dismissed the invaders with bitter scorn; they slunk away, ashamed. Donald Campbell's house is now the Free Church Manse.

The footpath east from Tarbert to Scalpay road was until now the only access by land to the little village of Rhenigadale (Reinigeadal). The new road down from Maraig will transform the lives of this community.

When weather permits, boat cruises run from Tarbert to the **Shiant Islands**, 12 miles (19km) to the east, a wild cliff-land with a natural sea arch and a huge colony of puffins as well as other sea birds. Compton Mackenzie wrote some of his books here.

North of Tarbert is **Ardvourlie Castle**, once a shooting lodge and now a guest house, on the west side of the loch. It was here that Prince Charles Edward Stuart landed to walk the rest of the way to Arnish.

The road to the west from Tarbert runs through 14 miles (22.5km) of lovely scenery with views out to sea, among hills sliced by burns and carpeted in heather. There was a whaling station along this road, at **Bunavoneadar** (Bun Abhainn Eadarra), built by Norwegians in 1912, when whales were plentiful in these waters. About 8 miles (13km) further on, you can see literally hundreds of salmon jostling about in the sea, waiting to jump the falls where Loch Leosaidh pours down a cliff into the sea. **Abhainnsuidhe**—pronounced Avensooey—is a jewel of a castle on the road into the village, built in 1868 by the Earl of Dunmore. James Barrie began his novel *Mary Rose* here. The beaches at **Hushinish** (Huisinis), another 5 miles (8km) on, at the end of the road, are magnificent. **Scarp**, the island off the tip at Hushinish, is best known because in 1934 it was to be the recipient of a very advanced method of postal delivery: mail was to be sent by rocket. A special stamp was issued, coveted by philatelists, and the first rocket was fired. Unfortunately it exploded, as rockets tend to, destroying the mail and the project.

The roads down the east and west coasts of South Harris are so different it is fun to travel them both. The east coast road is a tortuous single track through a bleak, stony landscape. The tiny cultivated patches were painstakingly nurtured by people evicted from the fertile west coast who were forced to live here and try to make a living from fishing. Many of the inhabitants are now Harris Tweed weavers. Stop at **Plocrapool** (Plocrabol) to see Marion Campbell spinning and handweaving tweed in the old way. There is a youth hostel at Stockinish (Stocinis), open in the summer, and a guest house halfway down at **Lickisto** (Liceasto).

At **Rodel** (Roghadal), on the southern tip, the Church of St Clement's dates from the 12th century and is the best piece of architecture in the outer isles, with some intriguing carved kilted figures on its tower. It was restored in the 19th century. Among the tombs there is one of Alastair Crotach, the Macleod chief from Dunvegan who entertained James V at Macleod's Tables (p.460). The 18th-century harbour is wonderfully secluded, overlooked by the **Rodel Hotel**, part of which is now closed and dilapidated, although the atmospheric bar still operates.

On the main road round the west side, the first expanse of coast is the huge **Luskintyre Beach** (Losgaintir)—one of the most beautiful beaches in Britain—and from here on there are beaches and sea views all the way down to Leverburgh.

Leverburgh (An T-ob/Tob), on the south coast, a couple of miles northwest of Rodel, was developed by Lord Leverhulme after his plans for Stornoway had collapsed. He put a great deal of money into improving the harbour, building a large pier, houses, kippering sheds, roads and lighthouses. But he died a year after the local fishing industry began to flourish and with him died the drive and energy needed to keep things going as he had planned.

A passenger ferry runs from Leverburgh to North Uist and Berneray.

Berneray (Eilean Bhearnaraigh)

As well as the ferry from Leverburgh, a car ferry runs to Berneray from Newton Ferry in North Uist. It is a lovely, fertile island, its people living by crofting and fishing. The Prince of Wales escapes here to stay with a crofter and mix with the locals as one of the community. He is accepted as a friend and no fuss is made. They have a lively Community Centre and tea and snacks are served in the Community Hall.

Where to Stay in Lewis:

moderate

Caberfeidh Hotel, Manor Park, Stornoway, ✆ 0851 2604, is modern and purpose-built, at the upper end of the price range; comfortable if characterless. **Seaforth Hotel**, Stornoway, ✆ 0851 2740, is a bit cheaper, friendly and comfortable.

inexpensive

Baile-Na-Cille, Timsgarry, Uig, ✆ 0851 672242, is a converted 18th-century manse in a superb position overlooking Uig Sands. Closed in January, it is simple but very comfortable with good country cooking. **Cross Inn**, Ness, ✆ 085181 378, is an attractive old inn with lovely views, very cheap and friendly.

For a recommended bed and breakfast, try Mrs C. Mackay, Blackburn, 109 Newmarket, Stornoway, ✆ 0851 705232.

Where to Stay in Harris:

expensive

Scarista House, Scarista, ✆ 0859 550238, is a Georgian manse backed by hills and overlooking a sandy beach. This is unquestionably the pick of the bunch. It is very comfortable, with peat fires and a good library, interesting food and an extensive wine list.

inexpensive

Harris Hotel, Tarbert, ✆ 0859 2154, is a comfortable, friendly and relaxed place. **Ardvourlie Castle Guest House**, ✆ 0859 2307, is a splendid, rather gaunt house overlooking the loch where Prince Charles landed after his narrow escape from the avaricious minister, Macaulay, on Scalpay.

North Uist (Uibhist a Tuath)

North Uist is about 17 miles (27km) long and 13 miles (21km) wide and a great deal of it is water. Wild peat moors cover the eastern side and the centre, with gentler green farmland to the west and glorious sandy beaches.

Lochmaddy (Loch Na Madadh) is the island port, a sprawling village with a sheltered harbour. It has a court house, hospital, church, several shops, a bank, hotel, and guest houses. Some say the three rocks at the harbour entrance look like crouching dogs and, indeed, the port's name comes from the Gaelic for dog—*madadh.*

Uist Outdoor Centre, on the outskirts of Lochmaddy, is a new adventure training establishment where groups or individuals can indulge in sub-aqua diving, watersports of all kinds, climbing, walking, wildlife watching, environmental and field studies— and a lot more. The accommodation is good. For details contact Niall Johnson, Uist Outdoor Centre, Cearn Dusgaidh, Lochmaddy, Isle of North Uist, PA82 5AE, © 08763 480.

A road circles the island, an attractive drive through a series of crofting and fishing communities. Peat bogs flank the road with rows of neatly stacked peat bricks waiting to be transported to the houses. Almost all the outer isles use this free fuel, each croft having its own 'hag', supplemented by gas and, in recent years, electricity. The peat is cut in spring and stacked on the site until dry enough to cart. It is then built into piles beside the houses and used both on open fires and in stoves for the rest of the year.

There are several prehistoric remains to look at round the island. About 3 miles (4.5km) west from Lochmaddy going anti-clockwise, there are three standing stones on the slope of **Blashaval** (Blathaisbhal). These are known as the Three False Men, said to be three men from Skye who were turned to stone by a witch as punishment for deserting their wives.

Five miles (8km) west of Lochmaddy, a small road goes 4 miles (6.5km) north to **Newton Ferry** (Port Nan Long). In a loch on the right of this road, just before its end, is a well-preserved fortress, **Dun-an-Sticir**, reached by a causeway and occupied as late as 1601. A car ferry runs from Newton Ferry to Berneray and a passenger ferry to Harris.

Back on the circular road, **Eilean-an-Tighe** is a rocky islet in Loch-nan-Geireann, 2 miles (3km) west. It was the site of a Neolithic potters' workshop, the oldest to be excavated in western Europe. The pottery found here was of a very high quality, better than that of later times and there was so much of it that the factory must have supplied a large area.

In **Sollas** (Solas), 3 miles (4.5km) west, a medieval settlement is being excavated. This district was the scene of one of the episodes of the Highland Clearances. In 1849 Lord Macdonald, 4th Baron of the Isles, was faced with debts of around £200,000, due mainly to the decline of the kelp industry. Among other schemes to find money to pay off his creditors, he decided to evict some 600 people from the overcrowded, uneconomic area around Sollas and rent the land to sheep farmers. Since the potato famine in 1846, the people had been living well below subsistence level. However, they loved their land and resisted eviction physically during some extremely unfortunate skirmishes with the Sheriff's officers and police. Eventually they were forced to give in, but for various reasons there was a three-year delay before they were shipped off to Canada—in a frigate carrying smallpox germs below decks.

Vallay (Bhalaigh), pronounced Varlie, is an island at the entrance to a wide, shallow bay running north and west from Sollas. Here stands a big Edwardian house sadly dying of neglect, inhabited only by birds and the occasional dead sheep. There are also the remains of an earlier house and outbuildings. You can walk out to Vallay at low tide but watch out for the flood tide: it is very easy to get cut off.

Follow the road about 4 miles (6.5km) round the coast westwards to **Huna**. Here, a footpath goes 2 miles (3km) east across the moor, to a chambered cairn on **Clettraval.** This was built before peat covered the land, in the days when birchwood copses grew here. A fort was built over it in the Iron Age, from which pottery was excavated and found to be the same as that made in the factory at Eilean-an-Tighe.

At **Balranald** (Baile Raghaill), stretching out to the most westerly tip of the island at **Aird an Runair**, there is an important RSPB reserve supporting one of the highest densities of breeding waders in Britain. Altogether, 183 species of bird have been recorded on the reserve. Visitors are asked to report to the RSPB cottage on arrival.

Unival is a hill north of the road, 6 miles (9.5km) southeast of Huna. Walk across the moor, up its eastern flank, on the west side of Loch Huna to another chambered burial cairn with a small cist.

A couple of miles further down, the road forks, south to the right and northeast to the left. The left-hand road completes the circuit of the island and takes in two of its greatest treasures.

Pobull Fhinn

Two miles (3km) along this road back to Lochmaddy, a track to the right is signposted to Langlass Lodge Hotel, less than a mile (1.5km) away. Park at the hotel and take the footpath up behind it, a 10-minute climb through heather, bracken and bog-myrtle. On the hillside is an oval of standing stones called Pobull Fhinn (Finn's People), a prehistoric site deeply overlaid with mysticism. It is believed this may have been one of the sites where, hundreds of years before Christ, an annual ritual included the ceremonial sacrifice of the king.

Barpa Langass

Back on the road, continue less than a mile northeast. On the shoulder of Ben Langass on the right there is a grey lump, obviously man-made, shaped like a squashed beehive. This is Barpa Langass—a truly magnificent and amazingly well-preserved burial cairn, the tomb of a chieftain, thought to date from about 1000 BC. Visitors are asked not to crawl through the tunnel into the cairn, both for their own safety and for the preservation of the site. Great stone slabs line the interior and there are traces of where other cells may have led off the main chamber.

From here it is about 6 miles (9.5km) on to Lochmaddy, to complete the circuit of the island. Going back southwest to the fork, go left. **Carinish** (Cairinis) is 2 miles (3km) down the road, with some of the most interesting, though by no means the oldest, remains in North Uist.

Teampull-na-Trionaid (Trinity Temple) is a ruin on the top of a knoll on the Carinish promontory at the southern end of the island. A large building with a detached side chapel reached by a vaulted passage, this early 13th-century church was regarded as an important seat of learning for the training of priests.

The last battle to be fought in Scotland using just swords and bows and arrows was the Battle of Carinish, in 1601, between the Macdonalds of Uist and the Macleods of Harris. The cause of the battle appears to have been the insulting behaviour of one of the Macdonalds, who divorced his Macleod wife and sent her home. The Macleods descended on Carinish in a wild frenzy, but in the furious battle that ensued all but two of them were killed. **Feith-na-Fala** (The Field of Blood) marks the site of the battle, which is just north of the Carinish Inn.

Ben Lee, 896 feet (276m) high, southeast of Lochmaddy, gives a marvellous view of the island with its mass of lochs and great expanses of moorland, peat and hill.

Where to Stay

inexpensive

Langlass Lodge Hotel, Locheport, ✆ 0876 580285, is a converted shooting lodge overlooking Loch Langlass, remote and peaceful. The food is first class. **Lochmaddy Hotel**, ✆ 0876 500331, is convenient for the ferry terminal; a comfortable, old-established fishing hotel with friendly staff.

There are also quite a few bed and breakfast and self-catering places, listed in the tourist information brochure.

Benbecula (Beinn Na Faoghla)

Benbecula is linked to the south of North Uist by over 3 miles (4.5km) of causeway. The low-tide route across North Ford by foot, once the only way, is extremely dangerous for those who don't know the path. Locals tell hair-raising stories of lost travellers and quicksands. Rocky bays and inlets surround the causeway, washed by the ever-changing tides.

The Gaelic name means 'the mountain of the fords'. The only mountain is Rueval in the east, a small round hillock only 409 feet (126m) high, but with good views from the top. The island is flat and waterlogged, with a fertile strip on the west side. The main road cuts through the middle with minor roads off to the east and a circular road round the west coast to the airport.

Benbecula has an army base which runs the rocket range to the south. In the northwest corner there is a large army camp—a rash of utility buildings not designed to please the eye. The airport is just beside the army camp, at **Balivanich**. In contrast to the ugly military buildings there are white beaches and spectacular views and a landscape dotted with old stone houses.

Near the airfield are the remains of St Columba's Chapel, dating from early Christian times. There is a well close by, now marked by a cairn, where people came to drink the holy water.

Benbecula was part of the patrimony of the Macdonalds of Clanranald from the 13th to 19th centuries, when the lands were sold off to pay impatient creditors. Most of the ruins are of Clanranald origin.

At **Nunton**, 2 miles (3km) south of Balivanich, there is a ruined chapel which belonged to a nunnery whose nuns were brutally massacred when the building was destroyed during the Reformation. The stones of a large-ish farmhouse by the road came from the nunnery. This is Nunton House, L-plan with a pavilion on each side of the entrance to a courtyard.

Borve Castle, a gaunt ruined keep near the road 4 miles (6.5km) south of Balivanich, was a Clanranald stronghold and scene of many a bloody skirmish. The scant remains of the castle chapel can still be seen nearby.

Wiay, an island off the southeast tip of Benbecula, is a bird sanctuary supporting snipe, duck, geese and swans.

It was from **Rossinish**, on the northeast corner, that Prince Charlie sailed 'over the sea to Skye' disguised as gawky Betty Burke, the servant of Flora Macdonald.

In 1988 a new Community School was built at **Liniclate** on the southern end of the island. It is a huge place with a swimming pool, superb sports facilities, restaurant, library and museum, serving children throughout the islands, some of whom previously had to board on the mainland for their education. It is also open to the public, and has been the cause of dispute between Presbyterians and Catholics over Sunday opening.

Keen shoppers must visit **D. MacGillivray and Co**, at Balivanich opposite the high cone-shaped water tank at the airport. Inside the unpretentious building is an Aladdin's Cave of tweed and woollen products, including some fantastic bargains. It's the sort of place you pop into to buy a pair of socks and stagger out of laden with parcels.

Where to Stay

inexpensive

Creagorry Hotel, Creagorry, ✆ 0870 602024, is an old inn with a newish extention, known for its convivial bar. **Dark Island Hotel**, Liniclate, ✆ 0870 602414/602283, is a modern hotel with very obliging staff and reasonable food. Prices range from cheap to moderate. **Inchyra Guest House**, also at Liniclate, ✆ 0870 602176, is comfortable and gives a very warm welcome.

There is a self-catering bungalow, sleeping six, at Liniclate; apply to Mrs Shepherd, Heisker, Liniclate, ✆ 0870 602235.

South Uist (Uibhist a Deas)

A straight causeway links Benbecula with South Uist, less than half a mile (0.8km) across South Ford, a white strand that yields an abundant harvest of cockles at low tide. When the tide is out there is usually at least one stooped figure scooping the molluscs into a bucket.

South Uist is about 20 miles (32km) long and 7 (9.5km) wide at its widest point, with mountains and long sea lochs to the east, sand and machair to the west, peat bog and moorland in between. Ben Mhor, less than halfway down in the east, is the highest peak at 2034 feet (626m). A roadside shrine to the Virgin Mary, just south of the causeway, seems to be a gentle reminder that you have left the Presbyterian north and are on the threshold of the Catholic south.

In **Iochdar**, just down the road to the west, look out for Mrs Johnson's amazing bus, completely decorated with shells, and her partly shell-covered house. The main road runs straight from north to south, part single track and part fast, new highway—this is somewhat unnerving as it narrows abruptly and often without warning, back to the old road. Lateral roads branch off like the veins of a leaf and lead to the many crofting townships that scatter the island.

The first road to the east, a mile (1.5km) south of the causeway, goes out 2 miles (3km) to **Loch Carnan**, a beautiful fiord-type sea loch with a pier for large boats.

Three miles (4.5km) to the south, the main road becomes a causeway and crosses **Loch Bee**, one of the largest swan reserves in Britain. The area of marshland to the east is a nature reserve, the breeding ground of many wildfowl including greylag geese. The hill on the left, just south of Loch Bee, is another **Rueval**, crested by a futuristic contraption which is an army range head. Rocket targets can often be seen off the west coast, and you will hear the muffled bang of firing.

On the western slope of Rueval, clearly seen from the road, there is a classically beautiful statue by Hew Lorimer of Our Lady of the Isles. Carved from white granite, it stands high on the hillside, the Child held up on His mother's shoulder. The clean-cut simplicity of the statue seems to embody the deep faith that exists in these islands.

The next road east, a mile (1.5km) south, runs 4 miles (6.5km) out to **Loch Skipport** (Loch Sgioport), another fiord-like sea loch where there is a deep-water anchorage, a salmon farm and a skeleton pier which used to be the main one for the island.

Less than 2 miles (3km) further south on the main road, beyond the road west to **Drimisdale** (Dreumasdal), there is a small loch with an island and a ruined castle. A submerged causeway runs out to the island. Beware! Some of its wobbly stones have been known to topple the unwary into the dark peaty water of the loch. The ruined castle is **Caisteal Bheagram**, a 15th- or 16th-century keep that was once a mighty Clanranald stronghold. Some years ago the present Captain of Clanranald tried to map out the original layout of the castle and discovered that its foundations cover almost all the island.

A mile south, the side road runs west a mile to **Howmore** (Tobha Mor), where there is an ancient burial ground and early Christian stones. The Church of Scotland still has its old central communion pew here.

Ormaclete Castle (Ormacleit) (always accessible), attached to a later farmhouse now being restored, is 3 miles (4.5km) to the south on the western machair between the main road and the sea. The castle was finished in 1704. It was built for Allan Macdonald of Clanranald whose wife Penelope refused to live there until a new house was built, since even her father's hens were better housed. Only eleven years after its completion it was accidentally burnt down, on the day of the Battle of Sheriffmuir in which the chief was killed.

Hecla, 1988 feet (612m), and **Beinn Mhor**, 2034 feet (626m), rise to the east of the road from which they can be approached over a wasteland of bog. The summits are dangerous in high winds, especially the sharp serrated edge of Beinn Mhor, with dizzying drops off the east side.

To the south a road runs east to Loch Eynort (Loch Aineort), another sea loch, cutting deep into the east coast and a starting point for good walks over the remote moorland between it and Loch Skipport. Beinn Mhor can also be reached from here, as can **Glen Corodale**, about 4 miles (6.5km) northeast of the end of the road. This wild country north of Loch Eynort, among the hills and glens surrounding Ben Mhor and Hecla, was where Prince Charles took refuge for a while in a forester's hut in a shieling, hiding in a cave when discovery seemed likely. The cave is not the one marked on the map, by a group of ruined houses by a burn. The real one is difficult to find, up on the rock face. This whole area is only accessible on foot or by boat. In the summer of 1980 Hercules the bear, star of several television advertisements, went for a swim with his owner off this coast. Freedom went to his head and he escaped. He was missing for three weeks, during which time frantic bear-hunting went on. He was finally recaptured, weighing a mere fraction of his normal weight, having been too domesticated to cope with life in the wild.

Three miles (4.5km) south of the turning to Loch Eynort, a road runs west, signposted to **Milton** (Gearraidh Bhailteas) where a cairn marks the place where Flora Macdonald was born in 1722. Flora's father was a tacksman. She was tending her brother's cattle in the shieling about 3 miles from here when the Prince was brought to her in need of her help.

Askernish (Aisgernis), a mile (1.5km) south, has a nine-hole golf course on the machair where players must dodge sheep and plovers' nests among the dunes. The South Uist Games take place on the golf course in July, usually followed by a dance or a concert in the church hall. Everyone on the island turns out for the games, where, as well as piping, dancing and all the traditional sports, there are jovial gatherings of spectators among the parked cars and in the beer tent.

Daliburgh (Dalabrog) is a village on the crossroads west of Lochboisdale. There are three shops and a post office, a hospital and an old people's home The road to the west leads to the parish church of St Peter's, a large, simple building dating from the 1860s, weathered and unadorned. This is the living heart of the island, filled to capacity at every Sunday Mass and well attended throughout the week, as indeed are the other churches that support it to the north and south.

Northwest of St Peter's is what must be one of the most beautiful, lonely burial grounds in the country, on the edge of the machair, overlooking the wild Atlantic.

The road east from Daliburgh goes 3 miles (4.5km) to the port of **Lochboisdale** (Loch Baghasdail), with a hotel, bank, police station and harbour. It is at its busiest early in the morning and late at night, for then the Caledonian MacBrayne ferry comes and goes, turning the quay into a bustling place, with a babble of Gaelic voices. A few visiting yachts anchor in the small bay in the summer and the hotel overlooking the harbour, with its reputation for fishing and for food, attracts many visitors. Towering over the northern shore of Loch Boisdale is **Beinn Ruigh Choinnich**. There is a challenging race to its summit every year for the young men of the area, who may take whatever route they choose to the top.

A mile (1.5km) south of Daliburgh a small road runs about 2 miles (3km) west to **Kilpheder** (Cille Pheadair), from where a track leads out on to the machair to an Iron Age Pictish wheel house. This is a communal dwelling with a central hearth with cells radiating from it like the spokes of a wheel, elaborate drainage systems and storage places sunk into the floor.

Two miles (3km) south of Daliburgh, a road runs east for 2 miles, through **South Lochboisdale** (Taobh A Deas Loch Baghasdail), to a parking bay. From here a map is needed to follow a faint track over hills and moor, along lochs Kerrsinish, Marulaig and Moreef, a total of 5 miles (8km) southwest to the coast. **Bun Sruth** is a loch joined to the sea by a narrow passage of sheer rock, surrounded by hills. It is inaccessible except by boat or on foot, peopled only by sheep and birds and the ghosts of the people who once lived in the now-ruined croft houses that lie scattered over the valley. When the tide is out, the loch is higher than the sea, draining over a shelf of rock in the entrance passage and marooning boats until the next tide, which comes in through the passage fast and hard. Golden eagles can be seen, gliding on the wind above the hills north of Loch Marulaig.

All this southeastern foot of the island is good walking country, and the views from the summits of the hills are spectacular. On a clear day you can see Ardnamurchan Point on the mainland. The road out to the west, opposite that to South Lochboisdale, leads to a white beach with the gloomy remains of a once-flourishing seaweed factory, a ghostly shell of flapping corrugated iron and scrap. A few years ago any islander could cut seaweed—a laborious job—and sell it to this factory, where it was processed into alginates for use in a large number of products ranging from soap to cosmetics. Now, any seaweed that is harvested is collected in lorries and shipped to factories on the mainland. The white beach runs for miles in great sweeps of sand where keen eyes will spot tiny pink cowrie shells. The wide fringe of machair is famous for its carpet of wild flowers in the summer. Opposite the seaweed factory there is a small conical island called **Orosay**, accessible at low tide, with lovely views. In westerly gales, spray has been known to break over its top.

The road south climbs to the modern wedge-shaped church at **Garrynamonie** (Gearraidh Na Monadh), built in 1963 and rather bizarre in its setting. It has an enamelled mosaic behind the side altar and Stations of the Cross designed by a priest from Barra, Father Calum McNeil. Here, as in the other churches, you can hear Mass in Gaelic, with a haunting chant from the choir.

At the end of the road, 5 miles (8km) south of Daliburgh, is the **Pollachar Inn** (Pol A Charra) overlooking one of the most beautiful views in Scotland, across the sound to Barra and east to Eriskay. The inn used to be a great place for local atmosphere and stories of the past. It is now being enlarged and altered, not necessarily to its advantage, but you can still sit outside and enjoy your drink overlooking a standing stone and the Sound of Eriskay, across to the heart-shaped hills of Barra.

Ludag is a couple of miles east along the south coast, and ferries run from the pier here to

Eriskay (cars) and Barra (passengers only). A lovely sandy bay beyond at **South Glendale** dries out at low tide and makes an excellent picnic spot, sheltered all round by turf-covered rocks. East of the bay, along the rocky shore and below the water, lies part of the wreck of the *Politician*, immortalized as the *Cabinet Minister* by Compton Mackenzie in his book, *Whisky Galore*. The true story was only slightly embroidered in the novel. The ship was carrying 20,000 cases of whisky to America in 1941, at a time when whisky was scarce in the islands. Magnetic minerals in the rocks distorted the compass readings and she went off course, riding over Hartamul, the rock at the entrance to the Sound of Eriskay, and finishing up against the cliff. The islanders made a valiant attempt to 'rescue' the whisky, thwarted by the bureaucracy of the customs and excise department, and not a few families still own a much-valued 'Polly bottle'. Stories are still told, with a twinkle and a knowing shake of the head, of animals reeling down the road, and of bottles dug up on the machair that had been buried for years. Recently the last of the bottles went up for auction and fetched nearly £100 each.

South Uist is littered with places where Prince Charles is said to have sheltered. He certainly hid for a time in the jagged, ruined castle on Calvay Island, at the entrance to Loch Boisdale, clearly seen from the ferry.

Eriskay (Eiriosgaigh)

For some, the island of Eriskay is the jewel of them all. A car ferry runs from Ludag in South Uist but as the road is barely 2 miles (3km) long it is hardly worth taking a car across. The boat runs a mile across the sound to **Haun** (Haunn), a smiling village of freshly painted white cottages with roofs of bright blue, pink, green and red, sheltered by hills. The church, perched high above the harbour, is the heart of the island. It was built in 1903 by Father Allan MacDonald who wrote down the folklore and many of the songs of the Hebrides and was a distinguished poet. The altar is shaped like the prow of a ship, worshipped at by a community whose existence has always been shaped by the sea. The ship's bell outside, beyond the church, was rescued from the *Derflinger*, one of the German ships that sank in Scapa Flow in 1919.

Just beyond the village on the western shore there is a crescent of sand called Prince Charlie's Bay. This was where the prince landed from France on 23 July 1745 and where he spent his first night on Scottish soil. The black house he stayed in was only pulled down in 1902. Its smoky interior drove him out into the fresh air several times during the night, drawing reproofs from his host. It was a simple place like all the others of its kind, with cupboard beds, hens running over the earth floor and wooden trunks holding the family possessions. The pink convolvulus called Prince Charlie's Rose, in the machair round Prince Charlie's Bay, is said to have been introduced here from a seed dropped from his shoe.

The **Stack Islands** lie just off the southern tip of Eriskay. There is a rock creek on the main island where boats can moor in calm weather. It is then a scramble to climb the precipitous cliff to the Weaver's Castle at the top. Here a notorious Macneil lived, a much-feared wrecker and pirate. He built the castle as a hideout, and stole a girl from a shieling in South Uist to be his wife and the mother of a large number of sure-footed children.

Where to Stay

inexpensive

Borrodale Hotel, Daliburgh, South Uist, ✆ 0878 700444, stands on the cross-roads in Daliburgh and provides the centre of island life. It is comfortable and friendly and the food is good. **Lochboisdale Hotel**, South Uist, ✆ 0878 700332, looks over Loch Boisdale by the ferry terminal. It has always been a popular fishing hotel and has a reputation for good food. The 17th-century **Pollachar Inn**, Kilbride, South Uist, ✆ 0878 700215, has one of the best views in Scotland, and has a convivial bar. (Five bedrooms share one bathroom.) It is open from April to October. **The Grianaig Guest House**, Garryhallie, South Uist, ✆ 0878 700406, is just north of Daliburgh, not far from the golf course. It is a comfortable, modern house, well run with good food. At the north end of the island there is **Orasay Inn**, Lochcarnan, ✆ 0870 700298, a small, family-run hotel with good food.

A number of houses offer bed and breakfast, listed in the brochure.

For those who prefer the freedom of self-catering, **Boisdale House**, South Lochboisdale, is good value—a family holiday house by the water, sleeping 12; ✆ 09856 219.

Barra (Barraigh)

Barra, 4 miles (6.5km) south of South Uist at the nearest point, is ringed by a number of smaller islands. One road circles the main part of the island, with an arm running north to the airport and Scurrival Point. Beaches, croftland and a hilly interior make up this compact haven which took its name from St Barr of Cork, who converted its people to Christianity. Barra has seascapes and landscapes that have inspired many artists, writers and musicians.

No one arriving in the ferry forgets their first sight of Castlebay (Bagh A Chaisteil). **Kisimul Castle** (open May–Sept, Wed and Sat afternoons: adm) stands on a rock in the middle of the harbour. Some people claim that it originates from 1060 and is one of Scotland's oldest castles but there is no firm evidence that it existed before the 15th century. It is a splendid sight in any weather but most romantic when silhouetted against a half-dark sky on a summer night. The Macneils acquired the castle as a reward for fighting for Robert the Bruce at Bannockburn. This clan was famous for its lawlessness, piracy and arrogance: a clansman from Barra is said to have declared, 'The reason there was no Macneil on Noah's Ark is that the Macneil had a boat of his own.' Kisimul was virtually destroyed by fire at the end of the 18th century. It remained in ruins until the 45th chief of the Macneil clan, returning from his adopted homeland in America, restored it to its present excellent condition in this century.

Neat shops and houses line the road that climbs from the harbour in **Castlebay**, overlooked by a statue of the Blessed Virgin and Child, high on the southern shoulder of **Heaval**—at 1260 feet (388m), Barra's highest peak. The Virgin stands, the Child on her shoulder holding a star. The statue, carved from Carrara marble, was erected in 1954, to celebrate the Marian Year and in memory of the 58 men from Barra who died in the Second World War, mostly in the Atlantic convoys. This is another symbol of the deep faith that governs the lives of these islands.

Like all the islands, Barra has its ancient remains. Going clockwise, 2 miles (3km) west from Castlebay, the standing stones beside the road past the Isle of Barra Hotel are said to mark the grave of a Norse pirate. A mile (1.5km) inland from the chapel at **Gariemore**, a mile further north, is **Dun Bharpa**, a large chambered cairn beyond the hamlet, surrounded by standing stones.

On the eastern side of the peninsula at the north end of the island, 4 miles (6.5km) beyond Gariemore and past North Bay, the great sweep of white sand is the landing strip for the daily Loganair air service. Two square miles (5 sq km) of dazzling cockle-shell strand, the **Tràigh Mhór** is washed twice a day by the tide and provides a firm touchdown for the little plane that comes droning in like a bumblebee, its timetable tied to the tide.

The house at the end of this great strand was the home of Compton Mackenzie, the writer who caught the spirit of the Highlands more perceptively than anyone. He attracted a lively community of writers and Gaelic scholars when he lived here. He is buried in the graveyard at **Eoligarry** (Eolaigearraidh), just to the north. Here among the ruins of a chapel are burial slabs said to have arrived from Iona as ballast in an ancient galley.

Another famous name can be seen in the cemetery: that of John Macpherson, better known to lovers of Gaeldom as 'The Coddy', who died here on his native island in 1955. *Tales from Barra*, recorded in both Gaelic and English, is a large collection of folk tales told by the Coddy in his inimitable voice—a delight for exiled Scots all over the world and well worth getting.

A grassy mound is all that remains of Eoligarry House, a three-storey house built by the Macneils after Kisimul Castle burned down in 1795. It was a substantial ruin until recently.

Isle of Vatersay (Bhatarsaigh), just off the south of Barra, is now linked by causeway. The other islands off Barra are each a delight for anyone with access to a boat. Golden eagles and a number of black rabbits greet visitors to **Hellisay**, off the east coast. The birds are magnificent, the wild flowers a delight, the sea so clear that the bottom seems no more than a few inches away.

Where to Stay

moderate

Castlebay Hotel, ✆ 0871 810223, is comfortable and friendly, with prices from cheap to moderate. **Isle of Barra Hotel**, Tangusdale, ✆ 0871 810383, is purpose built overlooking a crescent of white sand. It is comfortable and has good food, an easy-going atmosphere and self-contained apartments.

Clachan Beag Hotel, Castlebay, ✆ 0871 810279, is full of local atmosphere, with a friendly staff. **Craigard Hotel**, Castlebay, ✆ 0871 810200, serves nice food and the staff are obliging.

There are a number of bed and breakfast and self-catering places, listed in the brochure.

St Kilda

St Kilda, consisting of four islands and a few great rock stacks, is the most westerly of the British Isles apart from Rockall. These lonely islands are owned by the National Trust for Scotland. A small detachment of gunners man a missile tracking-station, but otherwise they are unpopulated. **Outer Hebrides Yachts**, 33 Cromwell St, Stornoway, operate regular trips to St Kilda.

The islands' history is one of decline brought about by isolation in a world increasingly obsessed by centralization and conformity. There is evidence of human occupation as far back as the Iron Age with the remains of a pottery and earth house. A small, patriarchal, strongly Presbyterian society subsisted here, paying its rent with meat, feathers and oil from seabirds. They were often cut off by storms. The population of about 200 in the 18th and 19th centuries remained fairly constant, except for a smallpox epidemic in 1727, kept in check by puerperal fever. The introduction of money and visitors from the mainland reduced their self-reliance and many of the younger ones left. In 1930 the able members of the community, attracted by the lure of the outside world and dragged down by hardship, persuaded the older ones they should move to the mainland, and a mass emigration took place.

Some of the houses, at Village Bay on Hirta, have been preserved, with their cleits— beehive-shaped cells of rough stone that served as larders and storerooms. The careful design of these cleits allowed air and wind to circulate inside and preserve the meat of the sea birds. It also kept clothes and gear dry. *The Life and Death of St Kilda* by Tom Steel gives an excellent account of the islands' history.

The Northern Isles

Although separated by 60 miles (96km) or so of ocean and very different in character, Orkney and Shetland have a common history and tend to be bracketed together. Norsemen called them the 'Nordereys'.

Both groups—about 70 Orkney islands, and 100 Shetland islands—were inhabited in the Stone Age. The Picts colonized them in the 1st century AD and were subjected to continual harassment from the Vikings for centuries until the Norse King Harold Harfagri annexed them in 875. When Harold succeeded to the throne of Norway in about 860, large parts of his kingdom didn't recognize the authority of the Crown—like the Lords of the Scottish Isles. Harold was in love with a Princess Gyda, daughter of one of the rebel 'kings', and she refused to marry him until he had conquered all Norway. He vowed that he would not cut his hair or his beard until he'd done this. He claimed his bride 10 years later. All the dispossessed *jarls*, or minor kings, took refuge in Orkney and Shetland and from here proceeded to harass Norway with wild Viking raids. King Harold, exasperated, collected up a fleet and sailed down to put an end to their antics. He landed at what is now Haraldswick in Unst, Shetland, and declared all the islands to be a 'Jarldom'. The Norse occupation of these islands is recorded in romantic stirring sagas, handed down over the years. *The Orkneyinga Saga* is one of the best known.

By the 13th century, although still under Norse rule, the islands were presided over by Scots' earls. When Princess Margaret of Norway and Denmark became betrothed to James III of Scotland, her father, King Christian I, pledged the islands to Scotland as part of her dowry in 1468. They were formally annexed in 1472 and since then they have been part of Scotland.

Norse placenames still predominate and the people of these northern islands are a blend of Norse and Scots, very different in character to the dreamy Celts of the Hebrides. They are extremely friendly, extrovert and stolid, industrious and mainly Presbyterian. Their accent is sing-song; the old 'Norn' language disappeared during the 18th century, although some phrases have remained, and when the Islanders talk among themselves they use many words more akin to Norwegian than English.

The coming of the oil boom struck hard at established roots, bringing innovations that were not always popular and making Shetland relatively rich compared to the rest of Scotland. However, on the whole the Islanders managed to retain their old way of life.

Orkney

Orkney's 70 or so islands are 6 miles (9.5km) off the north coast of Scotland on a level with Leningrad. They extend 53 miles (85km) from north to south and about 23 (37km) from west to east: Oslo is closer than London. Nineteen of them are inhabited, and when an Orcadian talks of the Mainland, he means Mainland Orkney—the big island. (The Mainland of Scotland is 'the sooth'.) Orkney means 'seal islands', the *ey* being Norse for islands: no one talks of the Orkneys, just Orkney.

First impressions are of emerald green plateaux of turf above sheer rock cliffs and sandy beaches, fertile farmland and a sparkling sea. Apart from Hoy, nothing is higher than 900 feet (278m). A great dome of clear sky seems to shed an ethereal greenish light. Sunsets in May and June are fantastic. At midsummer the sun is above the horizon for 18 hours and it is possible to read a book outside all through the night. This Midsummer Twilight is called 'Grimlins', from the Norse word *Grimla*, to glimmer or twinkle.

St Magnus Festival in Kirkwall in June is a week of music, drama and art, rapidly growing in popularity and attracting companies from many countries. The standard is

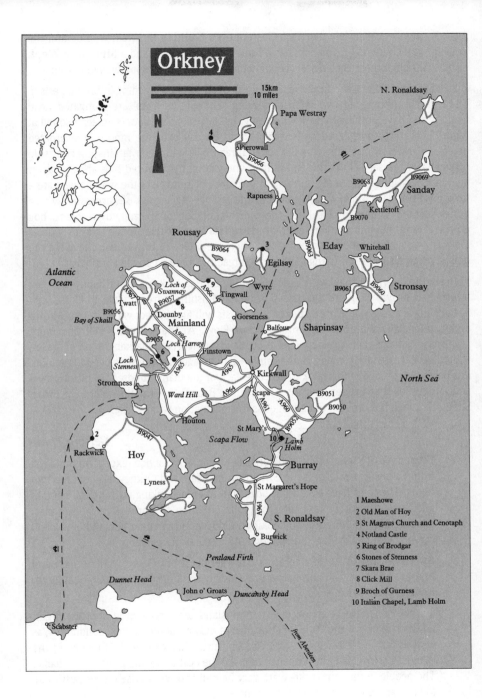

Orkney

15km
10 miles

N

Atlantic Ocean

North Sea

N. Ronaldsay

Papa Westray

Pierowall

B9066

Rapness

4

B9068   B9069

Sanday

Kettletoft

B9070

Rousay

B9064   **3**

Egilsay

Eday   Whitehall

B9063

Loch of Swannay

A966

Tingwall

Wyre   B9061   B9060   Stronsay

Twatt   B9057   **8**

B9056

Dounby

Bay of Skaill   Mainland

A986

Gorseness

Balfour   Shapinsay

7   B9055

Loch Harray   **6**   **1**   Finstown

Loch Stenness   **5**

A965   Kirkwall

Stromness

Ward Hill   A964   Scapa   B9051

A961   A960   B9050

Houton

St Mary's

Scapa Flow   **10**   Lamb Holm

2   B9047

Rackwick   Hoy

Lyness   Burray

St Margaret's Hope

9

Scabster

Dunnet Head

John o' Groats   Duncansby Head

Pentland Firth

A961

S. Ronaldsay

Burwick

from Aberdeen

1 Maeshowe
2 Old Man of Hoy
3 St Magnus Church and Cenotaph
4 Notland Castle
5 Ring of Brodgar
6 Stones of Stenness
7 Skara Brae
8 Click Mill
9 Broch of Gurness
10 Italian Chapel, Lamb Holm

high. For two weeks in July there is a **Craftsmen's Guild** in Kirkwall, with demonstrations of local craftwork. Stromness has a **Folk Festival** in May and a **Shopping Week** in July. Although there is plenty of accommodation, it is wise to book well in advance.

Birdwatching is almost compulsive. One in six of all seabirds breeding in Britain nests in Orkney. The long-eared owl is an endearing resident; its 'ears' are elongated head feathers and have nothing to do with hearing. Its low, moaning hoot is an eerie sound at night. There are short-eared owls, which hunt by day over the moors; red-throated divers, so graceful until they come in to land; razorbills with their fascinating courtship displays and refusal to build nests; puffins, whose brightly coloured bills are a weapon and a spade with which to dig burrows in the turf. For **botanists** the wild flowers are a joy: tiny Primula scotica, a survivor from the last Ice Age; grass of Parnassus, whose honey-scented white flowers litter the marshland; bog pimpernel, oysterplant, bog asphodel, and many more. For general **naturalists** there is the unique Orkney vole to look out for, a sweet little round ball of fur. There are otters—Kirkwall must be about the only town to display a red triangular road sign reading: 'Otters Crossing 100 yds'.

Fishermen leave Orkney with enough fishing stories to keep them happy till they return. The brown trout are the best in Britain and fishing is free, thanks to Norse law. Sea angling is also good. **Water sports** enthusiasts will find perfect waters for **sub-aqua** diving, especially wreck-diving around Scapa Flow. **Archaeologists** will find more prehistoric remains than anwhere else in Scotland, some in a remarkable state of preservation: brochs, standing stones, burial cairns—an average of three sites per square mile. It is beyond the scope of this book to describe each of the many hundreds of historic sites and antiquities that pepper Orkney. The Tourist Board's information office, in Broad Street, Kirkwall, has brought out a first-class free booklet on what to see.

Getting There

By sea: P&O operate a daily roll-on, roll-off car ferry service (except on Sundays) from Scrabster near Thurso to Stromness on Mainland Orkney; sailing time two hours. They also have a Saturday boat from Aberdeen taking eight hours. Thomas and Bews run passenger boats from John o' Groats to Burwick in the summer; crossing time 45 minutes, no bookings. Orkney Ferries run a new roll-on, roll-off car ferry from Gill's Bay; crossing time 45 minutes, no bookings.

By air: British Airways operate a daily service from Glasgow, Inverness and Aberdeen to Kirkwall. Loganair operate a daily service from Glasgow, Edinburgh, Inverness and Wick.

On arrival, there is an excellent inter-island air service (the shortest flight, between Westray and Papa Westray, taking only a minute in good conditions), as well as ferries. It is easy to hire cars and there are causeways to some of the islands. Careful planning is needed to make the best use of the transport available. The people in the tourist office are very helpful and will advise on the best tours to take, and give up-to-date opening times.

Orkney Tourist Board Information Centre, Broad Street, **Kirkwall**, ✆ 0856 2856.

Ferry Terminal, Stromness, ✆ 0856 850716 (limited hours Oct–April).

Mainland

Kirkwall is the capital of Orkney and one of the earliest established Norse trading towns. It is referred to in *The Orkneyinga Saga* as Kirkjuvagr, 'Church-bay-of-the-Vikings', indicating that the Norsemen found an Early Christian church here when they arrived. It is an ideal centre from which to explore these fascinating islands.

The Ba' Game

Kirkwall has its own unique 'Ba' Game', loosely described as football. It is played on Christmas and New Year's Day, between the 'trsuppies' and 'trsdoonies' and often involves as many as 150 men from either end of the town. If the ball finishes up in the harbour, it is victory for the 'trsuppies': if it reaches the goal at the old castle, then the 'trsdoonies' win. The game can last all day and dates from Norse times.

St Magnus Cathedral (open daily except Sun when it is only open for worship: free) dominates the town, though it is not in fact as large as its clever proportions suggest. This cruciform building founded in 1137 was built up of alterating stripes of local red sandstone and yellow stone and looks more continental than British. St Magnus, who was murdered in 1116 and whose canonization may have been more political than spiritual, was the uncle of Jarl Rognvald Kilson, the founder of the cathedral. The bones of both these men now lie below the columns of the central bay of the choir. They were discovered, hidden in chests, during repair work in this century. The cathedral has been carefully restored; the rose window is modern but the east window dates from 1511. Although it is still called a cathedral, the services are Church of Scotland.

The old part of the town clusters round the cathedral, with the ruin of the 12th-century **Bishop's Palace** (open daily except Fri afternoons and Sat in winter: adm) next door to it. It was here that poor old King Haakon of Norway died, having struggled back this far from his defeat by Alexander III at Largs in 1263.

Across the road from the Bishop's Palace is the ruin of the **Earl's Palace** (open daily except Fri afternoons and Sat in winter: adm), built by forced labour for a much-loathed tyrant, Earl Patrick Stewart, at the beginning of the 17th century. The palace is L-shaped, with attractive angle-turrets, once described as 'the most mature and accomplished piece of Renaissance architecture in Scotland'. Earl Patrick was Steward of Orkney and Shetland and entirely corrupt. He was finally executed for his awful crimes against humanity, having been granted a week's reprieve so that he could learn the Lord's Prayer.

Tankerness House Museum (open daily except Sun: adm) is in a very well-restored

16th-century merchant's townhouse, with an attractive courtyard and garden. The history of Orkney over 4000 years is displayed here.

The Library (open daily except Sun: free), founded in 1683, is the oldest public library in Scotland and has an excellent Orkney Room for anyone wanting to go more deeply into the history of the island.

Among the other things to visit in the town are the **Silver Works** and the two malt whisky distilleries, the **Highland Park Distillery** and **Scapa Distillery**, both of which welcome visitors, free, on weekdays.

Stromness, about 17 miles (27km) west of Kirkwall, is the only other proper town in Orkney. This pretty place, with a sheltered harbour and steep winding cobbled streets, has houses dating from 1716. It was once a principal port on the sailing route round the north of Scotland and base for the Hudson Bay Company ships. Many local men went to do contract work in Canada. The houses, many of them with their own jetties, seem to jostle each other aside, to get the best position along the mile of waterfront. Stromness is the terminal for the car ferry from Scrabster. There is a traditional Folk Festival in May and a Shopping Week in July, when all the shops compete for your custom and offer many good bargains.

Pier Arts Centre (open daily except Mon: free) is housed in well-restored 18th-century buildings and puts on exhibitions of modern paintings.

Stromness Natural History Museum (open daily except Thurs afternoons and Sun: small fee) has collections of birds, fossils, shells and butterflies. There are also exhibitions covering whaling, fishing, the Hudson Bay Company, Scapa Flow and the German fleet.

Scapa Flow is a great inlet to the south of Mainland, surrounded by protective islands. This perfect deep-water anchorage, up to 10 miles (16km) wide, was adopted as the main base of the Grand Fleet in 1912. At the end of the First World War, the German Navy sailed their fleet into Scapa, having surrendered. Then, on 21 June 1919, on the order of Rear Admiral Ludwig von Reuter, the whole fleet of 74 warships was scuttled. At the beginning of the Second World War a German U-boat crept through the defences and sank the *Royal Oak*, after which the Churchill Barriers were erected, making the anchorage almost impregnable.

Scapa is popular with sub-aqua divers and its clear water offers great scope for wreck diving. There are good supplies of air obtainable locally.

The following is a small selection of the many historic and prehistoric antiquities to be seen in Orkney. Consult the tourist office in Broad Street, Kirkwall, for more detailed information and advice as to how best to fit in as much as possible.

Maes Howe

Maes Howe (open daily: adm) is 10 miles (16km) west of Kirkwall, just off the main road to Stromness. It is a huge Stone Age burial cairn, unquestionably the most outstanding in Britain. The passage into the cairn, made of huge single slabs of stone, is so aligned that a shaft of sunlight pierces its 36-foot (11m) length into the chamber on only one day of the year, that of the winter solstice. Burial cells lead off the main chamber, which has massive stone buttresses in each corner.

When Maes Howe was first excavated, in 1861, the cells were found to be empty and this fact, together with runic Viking inscriptions on the walls, misled archaeologists into thinking the tomb was Norse. Then it became obvious that the structure dates back many centuries before that and probably to around 3500 BC. The Vikings came much later, sacking the tombs and leaving their graffiti on the walls.

In fact the graffiti are just as fascinating as the much older cairn. There are references to treasure and to the Crusades, and a collection of sex slogans that are as modern as any today: 'Thorny was bedded, Helgi says so,' reads one; 'Ingigerd is the best of them all,' says another. There is an excellent guidebook on sale at the site. Beside the car park is **Tormiston Mill**, a restored 19th-century water mill with a restaurant and a craft centre.

The Ring of Brodgar

The Ring of Brodgar (always accessible) is on the narrow neck of land between Harray and Stenness Lochs, 4 miles (6.5km) northwest of Maes Howe. From the original 60 stones, 36 remain. They are precisely set, being 6° apart, with a surrounding ditch cut from bedrock, as much as 9 feet (2.75m) deep and 27 feet (8m) wide, crossed by two causeways. These stones date from about 1560 BC and are believed to be some sort of lunar observatory, a splendid reminder that those Stone Age men may have been primitive but they certainly weren't stupid.

The Stones of Stenness

The Stones of Stenness (always accessible) date from around the third millennium BC, and only four stones remain of the original circle. Excavations uncovered an almost square setting of horizontal stones, scattered with fragments of cremated bones, charcoal and shards of pottery, indicating that this must have been some sort of cremation and burial site. The two outlying stones, the Barnhouse and the Watch Stone, were probably associated with this circle, as must have been the many cists and cairns that have been unearthed in this area.

Skara Brae

Skara Brae (open daily: adm) is 5 miles (8km) northwest of the Stones of Stenness, on the west coast and on the southern arm of the sandy sweep of **Bay of Skaill**. This was a Stone Age settlement, hit by a massive storm that buried it in sand for about 4000 years. Another storm then blew away some of the sand to reveal the village to archaeologists. It is unique, giving an insight into the whole way of life of those prehistoric tribes, rather than just revealing a burial cairn, which only tells a fraction of their story. Careful excavation has uncovered about six of the original ten one-roomed houses, and a workshop, with covered passages from one to another and a communal paved courtyard.

Lack of wood meant they used stone for their furniture and the old bed platforms, cupboards, hearths, fish tanks and tables can still be seen, as well as a fascinating collection of tools and implements. Recent progress in carbon-dating means that more and more information is coming to light about those mysterious settlers and there is an excellent guide book with up-to-date findings. A small museum gives more details. Midden (rubbish heap) excavations have revealed that the inhabitants of this earliest fishing village in Scotland were also farmers.

The only surviving **Click Mill** is beyond Dounby, about 8 miles (12.5km) northeast of Skara Brae (always accessible). It is a horizontal water wheel, built in about 1800 from an earlier design and so called from the noise it makes as it turns. It is preserved in working order, although the pond has been drained.

Gurness

On the wild, windswept headland at **Gurness,** 5 miles (8km) northeast of the Click Mill, there is the best broch in Orkney (open daily: adm). A booklet describes the very complicated layout of the site. It was built as a broch and then added to over the centuries by the Norsemen, and includes many domestic buildings, Norse longhouses, partitioned chambers and a well.

Islands South of Mainland

Lamb Holm, linked by a mile (1.5km) of causeway, south of Mainland, has a heart-stirring little chapel, called **The Italian Chapel**. It was created out of two Nissen huts, corrugated iron, plasterboard, paint and cement by Italian prisoners of war during the Second World War. They were building the Churchill Barrier after the sinking of the *Royal Oak* and made the chapel in their spare time. It is a miracle of faith, with delicate wrought-iron tracery and frescoes. The artist, Dominico Chiocchetti, returned in 1960 to restore the original work.

South Ronaldsay, joined to Lamb Holm by 4 miles (6.5km) of causeway across Burray, has a picturesque village with a poignant memory—St Margaret's Hope. In 1290 the seven-year-old Princess Margaret, Maid of Norway, died of sea sickness in the ship bringing her from Norway to marry Prince Edward of England. (The marriage had been planned as a way of uniting Britain with Norway.) The ship, bearing the wasted body of the little princess, put in to St Margaret's Hope.

Hoy, the largest island apart from Mainland, about 3 miles (4.5km) south of Stromness, is the only one that is not flat. Its hills provide a good backdrop to views over the flat green farmland wherever you are in these islands. Ward Hill rises to 1500 feet (460m). **The Old Man of Hoy** is a rock stack, 450 feet (138m) high, on a

Old Man of Hoy

promontory above the sea. This is a favourite challenge to serious rock climbers, a towering pinnacle of horizontally layered rock. **St John's Head**, on northwest Hoy, is part of a 1140-foot (350m) vertical cliff, teeming with seabirds and many rare plants. **Melsetter House**, not open to the public but visible from the road, was built on to an older house in 1898 by W. R. Lethaby for Thomas Middlemore, who inherited a fortune from a Birmingham leather business. New and old are kept distinct but the scale and materials used blend nicely into the Orkney landscape

Islands North of Mainland

Birsay and **Brough of Birsay** are less than a mile off northwest Mainland and it is possible to walk out at low tide. Here there are the remains of early Christian and Norse settlements.

Rousay, a couple of miles (3km) northeast of Mainland, has a burial cairn at **Midhowe**. This cairn has a long chamber, 76 feet (23m) by 7 feet (2m), with 24 burial cells leading off it, in which the remains of 25 human bodies were found. Another tomb on Rousay, **Taversoe Tuick**, is unusual because it is two-storied. One tomb sits on top of the other, each with its own entrance passage. Rousay also has also a well-preserved broch, with a complex of cells, cubicles, passages, stairs and doorways, and outbuildings.

Wyre, a mile (1.5km) southeast of Rousay, has the ruin of a 12th-century stone castle, one of the oldest in Scotland, known as **Cubbie Roo's Castle** and probably the stronghold of a Norse robber baron. There is also a ruined 12th-century chapel, St Mary's.

Egilsay is 2 miles (3km) east of Rousay. **St Magnus' Cenotaph** marks the site of the murder of Jarl Magnus in 1116, after whom the cathedral in Kirkwall is named. The ruin of St Magnus' Church dominates this small, low-lying island, with a tall, tapering round tower at the west end. This design is of Irish origin, indicating close contact between Ireland and Orkney during Viking times. It was probably built in the 12th century, and its walls still stand to their full height. The tower, nearly 50 feet (15m) high, was once taller still and it seems to beckon from all round. Magnus was killed on the order of his rival, Earl Haakon, who wanted sole power over Orkney. Egilsay has a large proportion of southerners in its small population.

On **Eday**, 4 miles (6.5km) to the east of Egilsay, there are chambered tombs and an Iron Age dwelling that was once a roundhouse with radial divisions inside, dating from several centuries BC.

Westray, 7 miles (11km) north of Rousay, has the formidable ruin of **Noltland Castle**. This was built in 1560 by Gilbert Balfour who was implicated in the murder of Cardinal Beaton and served on a French galley beside John Knox in punishment. He was later Master of the Household for Mary, Queen of Scots. Its design is Z-plan, with all-round visibility and an extravagant provision of gun loops. It was burned by Covenanters in 1650.

Papa Westray, 2 miles (3km) off the northeast tip of Westray, is so called from the hermits who lived in the cells here. This island was part of an important Norse family estate in the 11th and 12th centuries and archaeologists discovered the remains of Neolithic settlements which have provided valuable clues to the lifestyle of those ancient inhabitants.

North Ronaldsay is the most northern island of Orkney, 15 miles (24km) east of Papa Westray and 32 miles (51km) northeast of Kirkwall. It is surrounded by a sea dyke designed to keep the unique breed of sheep off the grass, so that they feed from the rich seaweed on the shore. The meat of these small, sturdy animals has a distinctive flavour.

Where to Stay

moderate

Ayre Hotel, Ayre Road, Kirkwall, ℂ 0856 3001, is on the waterfront overlooking Kirkwall Bay near the main shopping area. It is comfortable and friendly. **Kirkwall Hotel**, Harbour Street, ℂ 0856 2232, overlooks the harbour in the town centre and has good food.

inexpensive

Barony Hotel, Birsay, ℂ 085672 327, is on the shores of Boardhouse Loch, with views of the village and the Brough of Birsay. Open from May to September, it has free trout fishing. **Merkister Hotel**, Harray, is on the edge of Loch Harray, specializes in trout fishing holidays and is open April to October. **Merry Dancers Inn**, Eday, ℂ 08572 221, is a cottage overlooking Calfsound and Calf of Eday. It only has three bedrooms and one bathroom, but it is cosy and has a licence and is ridiculously cheap.

There are plenty more, and dozens of bed and breakfast and self-catering places, all detailed in the brochure. For something a bit different, try **Wildabout**, Inner Urrigar, Costa, Evie, ℂ 0856 75 307. Michael and Jenny Hartley run week-long 'Wildlife, Environmental' Holidays with every day planned to take you round the sights of Orkney.

Shetland

Sixty miles (96km) north of Orkney and halfway to Norway, Shetland has its own character, very different from that of Orkney although they share much of their history. In spite of being on the same latitude as Greenland, Shetland's climate is mild, because of the Gulf Stream, with plenty of sunshine in early summer and less rain than the Western Isles. Of the 100 islands in the archipelago, only 15 are continuously inhabited.

According to Tacitus, when the Romans sailed round the north coast of Scotland and

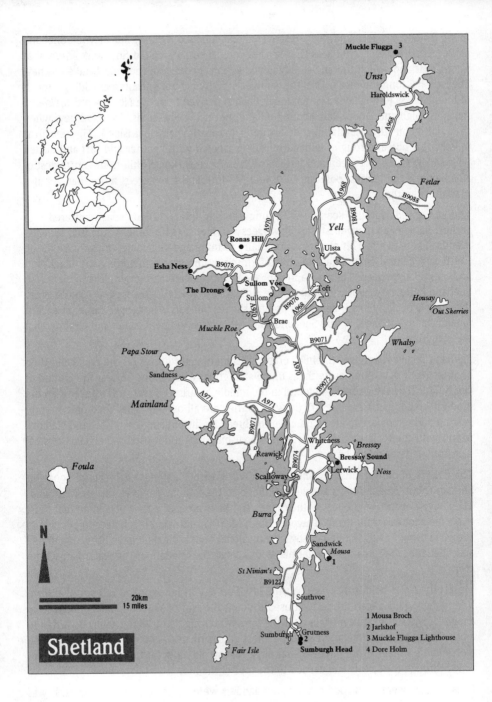

Shetland

20km
15 miles

1 Mousa Broch
2 Jarlshof
3 Muckle Flugga Lighthouse
4 Dore Holm

found Britain was an island, they 'discovered and subdued' Orkney but they left Shetland alone because of the wild seas that lay between them. He called Shetland *Thule*, that mythical island which the ancients believed lay on the edge of the world. Like Orkney, Shetland has long summer nights, the 'simmer dim' twilight of midsummer adding a touch of timelessness to holidays. The name Shetland is derived from the Norse word *hjaltland*, meaning Highland. Locals talk about Shetland, never the Shetlands. As in Orkney, when they talk about the Mainland, they are referring to the principal island. The terrain is mostly peat bog and rough highland hillside, carpeted with heather and turf and dotted with small lochs—not green and fertile as it is in Orkney. Ronas Hill, to the northwest of Mainland, is the highest point at 1475 feet (454m), and nowhere is more than 3 miles (4.5km) from the sea.

There is wonderful cliff scenery with long winding inlets, called 'voes', battered into arches, fissures and jagged stacks. Few trees survive the gale-force winds that lash the islands. There is a fair bit of agriculture: dairy farming and vegetable crops thrive in the south and central Mainland and sheep-farming is important, including the black and brown Shetland sheep. The Shetland cabbage is salt resistant and grown as a fodder crop. Shetland knitwear is world famous. In the old days the wool was plucked, or 'roo'ed' from the sheep's neck by hand, being too fine for shears, but this is no longer common except for some show animals. A true Shetland shawl should be so fine it can be pulled through a wedding ring.

Shetland ponies roam over the hills, originally mini draught horses on the crofts and then bred for work in coal mines, with 'as much strength as possible and as near the ground as can be got'. The skeleton of one found in the middle of Jarlshof Broch was smaller than the modern breed. They are not strictly wild as they are all owned. They feed on common grazing and efforts are made to improve the breed by introducing good Shetland stallions to run with them. Their tail hair was used as fishing line and it used to be illegal to steal hair from another man's horse.

The old life of crofting, fishing and knitting was greatly changed when the oil boom hit Shetland, but the oil depots are well confined to the Sullom Voe area on the Mainland. They have not spoiled the rest of the islands and have brought a new prosperity that must make life a lot easier for many. The poet Hugh MacDiarmid said: 'It is indeed impossible to eke out a decent living in Shetland by crofting alone. That is the difference between Orkney and Shetland: the Orcadian is a farmer with a boat, the Shetlander is a fisherman with a croft.'

Up-Helly-Aa is held in Lerwick, on the last Tuesday in January and is a survival from Viking days. This pagan fire festival used to mark the end of Yuletide and symbolize the desire for the sun to appear again after the long winter nights. A Viking galley is carried to a park in the centre of the town amidst a forest of blazing torches and set alight while 'The Norseman's Home' is sung as a funeral dirge. In the old days, blazing barrels of tar were rolled through the streets and carried to the tops of the hills.

Because they were such good seamen, Shetlanders were vulnerable to press gangs. It was not unknown for a whole community of able-bodied young men to be snatched away in a furtive raid from the sea. The fiddle tune 'Jack is yet alive' was composed for a Shetlander who had been press-ganged, served his time and returned to a family who had written him off long ago. Fiddle music is still very popular throughout the islands.

The seascapes are unforgettable: sudden glimpses of an island-dotted sea with dramatic rocks, cliffs and beaches, suffused by an extraordinary clarity of light. The colours must have influenced the natural shades used in the knitwear, particularly those in the Fair Isle designs.

For **ornithologists**, there are vast colonies of sea birds, both northern and migrant. Among the many hundred species to be seen is the Shetland wren, 'stinkie', even smaller than her more common cousin. As if to make up for her stature, her formal name is *Troglodytes troglodytes shetlandicus*. Fair Isle, halfway to Orkney, has an observation station and is famous as a staging post for migrants.

For **botanists** the wild flowers are marvellous, with around 500 species of plants to discover. Because much of the pasture is untreated, many that have become rare elsewhere have survived, including the rather hideous large Australian daisy. There are Arctic flowers, the American mondey flower, and the tiny blue Caucasus from Asia Minor.

For **naturalists** there are vast quantities of seals to watch, basking on the rocks, known locally as 'selkies' (too many of them, in fact, due to culling restrictions). Otters can be seen, around small rocks and skerries in the remoter coastal areas. Whales, killer whales, sharks, dolphins and porpoises can all be seen off the coast.

Trout fishing is excellent in the lochs, of which there are more than 300, and there are some salmon. **Sea angling** is first class and fishermen catch cod, halibut and many other white fish. Porbeagle shark of up to 450lbs (200kg) have been caught in local waters and the current European record of a 226.5 lb (100kg) skate is held by Shetland. There is a wealth of prehistoric remains for **archaeologists**.

Getting There

By air: British Airways operate four flights a day from Aberdeen. These connect with flights to and from Glasgow, Edinburgh, Manchester, Birmingham, Belfast and London. They also operate a daily service from Inverness, via Orkney. Loganair run daily flights from Edinburgh and Glasgow.

By sea: P&O Scottish Services operate a passenger and car ferry service, overnight, five times a week from Aberdeen to Lerwick, including a weekend crossing via Orkney. From June to August, the Tuesday night boat also goes via Orkney. For information and booking write or phone P&O Ferries, PO Box 5, Jamieson's Quay, Aberdeen, © 0224 572615. P&O Scottish Ferries also operate from the middle of June to the end of August, between Norway and Shetland, and Smyril Line operates during the same period between Denmark, Faroe and Shetland.There are good bus and taxi services from the airport, as well as plenty of hire cars. Shetland roads are good and the inter-island ferries are excellent. The ferries between Mainland and Yell, North Yell and Unst, Unst and Fetlar, Mainland and Whalsay are all roll-on, roll-off. There is also a good inter-island air service.

Mainland

Mainland is by far the biggest of the islands, its chief town being **Lerwick**, Britain's most northerly town, so called from the Norse *leir-vik* meaning 'clay creek'. Looking over sheltered Bressay Sound, Lerwick has always been a refuge for seafarers. In spite of its geographical isolation, it is a lot more up-to-date and cosmopolitan than many of the towns in the Highland region of Scotland. It was a stopping-off port for Norsemen: King Haakon reprovisioned his fleet here on the way to defeat at Largs in 1263.

Lerwick has always been important for fishing: the home waters are productive and it lies on the edge of the valuable northern fishing fields. Dutch fishing fleets were based here in the 17th century and by the 18th century the export of salt fish was thriving. In the 17th century the town became important as a base for the British Navy. Fort Charlotte was built in 1665 to protect the Sound of Bressay from the Dutch.

The buildings that grew up round the port were sturdy and compact, designed to withstand violent storms. Many of them were the town houses of Scottish lairds who succeeded the Norsemen and found winter conditions rather bleak in the outlying countryside.

The *Dim Riv* is a replica Norse longship, over 40 feet (12m) long, and she takes visitors on trips round the harbour in the summer. The harbour is a lively, bustling place with a picturesque waterfront, and charmingly haphazard, flagstoned Commercial Street, straggling up behind. This is the main shopping centre of the town, and the steep, narrow lanes around it are said to cover a network of secret tunnels and passages used by smugglers in the past. Boat trips run from Victoria Pier, to cruise round the coast in the summer. Look out for the distinctive Shetland sailing dinghy, a local design with the elegant double-prow effect of the Viking longboats. They can be seen in most of the harbours around Shetland and are raced in local regattas.

Fort Charlotte (open daily: free), built by Cromwellian troops, was partly burned by the Dutch in 1673. It was repaired and restored in 1781 and garrisoned during the Napoleonic wars. It is the only Cromwellian military building still intact in Scotland.

The **Town Hall** above Commercial Street in Hillhead is a Victorian-Gothic building, partly resembling a church with tower and rose window, four corner turrets, a central oriel window and stained-glass windows on the upper floor. These enclose the main hall and depict the history of Shetland, beginning with the Scandinavian conquest in 870. There are full-length figures of Norway's King Harald Harfagri, the conqueror of the islands, and Rognvald, Jarl of More, to whom Harald offered the first earldom. The windows cover all the main events in Shetland's story and include one of the Maid of Norway, who died at sea nearby.

The **Shetland Museum** (open daily except Sun: free) is opposite the town hall. It has four galleries devoted to the history of man in Shetland, from prehistoric times to the present. Look for the **Papil Stone**, dating from the 7th century, showing a procession of papas, or priests, one of whom is on a horse. Other exhibits include the history of Shetland knitting and the history of the islands' marine and fishing past. There are also replicas of the treasure found on St Ninian's Isle.

These beautiful islands are an inspiration to artists and there are exhibitions of local art and crafts in the **Shetland Workshop Gallery** (open daily: free) in Burns Lane.

Clickhimin Broch (always accessible) is on the western outskirts of the town, on an island in a loch, reached by a causeway. It is 65 feet (20m) in diameter, its walls 18 feet (5.5m) thick and 15 feet (4.5m) high, on a massive stone platform. Excavations on this site suggest that it may have been a late Bronze Age settlement.

A frequent car ferry crosses to the island of **Bressay** just east of Lerwick, and from here a boat crosses the 200 yards (185m) to the bird sanctuary on **Noss**. (It is only open to the public from mid-May to the end of August.)

Scalloway is Mainland's other town, in an attractive bay 7 miles (11km) west of Lerwick. It was the capital until 200 years ago and is still an important fishing port. It is much older than Lerwick and retains a quiet, old-fashioned atmosphere. There is a small local **museum** in the middle of the town, which has, among other things, a detailed history of the Shetland Bus. During the Second World War, small Norwegian fishing boats crossed to Nazi-occupied Norway to carry out sabotage or to land secret agents and bring back refugees. 'To take the Shetland Bus' meant to escape from Norway. **Lunna House**, in northeast Mainland, now a guest house, was the original headquarters of this Norwegian Resistance Movement, before it was transfered to Scalloway where more facilities were available. *The Shetland Bus* by David Howarth, recently reprinted, gives a good account of the operation.

Scalloway Castle (always accessible) dominates the town, a forbidding ruin built by Earl Patrick Stewart in 1600. Stewart was the notorious despot who tyrannized Orkney and Shetland until he was executed. Built in medieval style, the roofless shell, with corner turrets and gables, stands on a narrow promontory by the water. The Earl is said to have hung his victims from an iron ring in one of the chimneys. The castle was, not surprisingly, left to rot after the Earl's death.

There are bridges across to the islands of **Tronda** and **Burra** just to the south. Scalloway is at the southern end of the agricultural valley of **Tingwall**, so called after the site of the old Norse parliament, or *thing*, at the north end of **Tingwall Loch**, reached by stepping stones.

At **Whiteness,** 7 miles (11km) north of Scalloway, the **Hjaltasteyn Workshop** (open weekdays: free) produces handmade jewellery, in silver, gold and enamel. Not far north, at **Weisdale, Shetland Jewellery** also make high-quality Celtic- and Viking-design jewellery.

South of Lerwick

Mousa Broch (open daily: free, with a fee for ferry), on **Mousa Island**, is one of Shetland's main archaeological treasures. The boat runs, weather permitting, from

Sandwick, 11 miles (17.5km) south of Lerwick. Mousa Island, a mile (1.5km) offshore, is inhabited only by sheep and ponies and its broch is the best preserved in existence. It is a thrilling experience to climb its steps, walking in the footsteps of its Pictish builders 2000 years ago. Over 50 feet (15m) in diameter, 45 feet (14m) high, with walls that taper from 12 feet (3.5m) to 7 feet (2m) in thickness, this was one of the smallest of the brochs and probably one of the latest. Galleries honeycomb its double walls and stairways lead to a parapet round the top. This broch illustrates clearly how the builders tapered the walls inwards to within about 10 feet (3m) of the top and then sloped them outwards, making it impossible for invaders to climb up.

Mousa appears romantically in two of the old sagas. In 1150, the Norwegian Prince Erland abducted a famous beauty and held her in the broch until her son, a Jarl, unable to storm the impregnable fortress, had to consent to their marriage. Another saga tells of a young man called Bjorn, who brought Thora, whom he had seduced, to Mousa in 900 and here they set up home together.

St Ninian's Isle is 4 miles (6.5km) southwest of Sandwick, off the west coast of Mainland. You can walk to it along a white crescent of sand, called a 'tombolo', that forms a causeway. Here are the foundations of a 12th-century chapel, buried by sand for many hundreds of years. In 1958, Aberdeen University began excavating the site and discovered not only the foundations of the chapel, but also a Bronze Age burial ground and the remains of a pre-Norse church.

Under a stone slab in the chapel nave they found a hoard of 8th-century Celtic silver, now in the Royal Museum of Scotland, in Edinburgh, with a replica collection in the museum in Lerwick. It is believed that this wonderful hoard was buried by the monks who lived here, probably during an invasion threat from Vikings. The treasure includes silver bowls, delicate brooches and a Communion spoon. Lengthy litigation followed the finding, it being disputed whether the Crown could claim treasure in a land where Udal law still applies.

The Shetland Croft Museum (open daily, 1 May–30 Sept: adm) is at **Boddam** on the east coast of Mainland, 5 miles (8km) south of Sandwick. The museum is a restored croft house, typical of the mid-19th century. Inside the cottage is the original driftwood furniture and all the domestic utensils, giving a picture of how crofters lived in the last century. There is also the old watermill, down the hill by the burn. Recently restored **Quendale Mill** (open daily except Monday, May-Sept: adm) gives the history of a working 19th-century watermill.

Sumburgh, with the airport, is at the southern tip of Mainland, 27 miles (43km) south of Lerwick. The modern, clean-cut buildings at the airport present a remarkable contrast to the antiquity of Jarlshof, nearby.

Jarlshof (site always accessible: free; visitor centre open daily, April–Sept: adm) was a name invented by Sir Walter Scott in *The Pirate*. He visited the island in 1814, was impressed by the laird's hall and wrote his story around it. He was not to know how misleading this name was to prove because it was not until 1905 that a violent storm revealed that this was a site that had been occupied for over 3000 years, by seven distinct civilizations of which the Norse Jarls were by far the most recent.

The remains of these village settlements, from Bronze Age to Viking, are sprawled over a low green promontory by the sea. The first house dates from the early or middle part of the second millennium BC. It would be impossible to sort out the various ages and purposes of the conglomeration of stones without the excellent explanations displayed, and the very helpful guide book. The Bronze Age huts include cattle stalls and a metal workshop; the Iron Age settlement has two earth houses and a broch. The three 8th-century wheel-houses are thought to be family dwellings consisting of a number of individual recesses separated as if by the spokes of a wheel, all around a central hearth. A confusion of long-houses is all that is left of the Norse occupation. It was the now-ruined medieval farmhouse that Sir Walter used as his setting. A museum exhibits some of the artefacts that have been dug from the site as well as a good ground plan and an interpretive display showing the history of Jarlshof.

North of Lerwick

Sandness is about 25 miles (40km) northwest of Lerwick and boats run from West Burrafirth, nearby, to **Papa Stour**, a couple of miles off the coast. The boats go four times a week and day trips are possible on Fridays and Saturdays. The sea caves are believed to be the finest in Britain, but you will need to hire a boat locally to see them properly. The scent from the wild flowers on Papa Stour was said to be so strong that fishermen could fix their position from it if caught in fog out at sea.

Lunna is about 18 miles (29km) north of Lerwick as the crow flies, out on the east coast. When Lunna House, now a small hotel, was the original headquarters of the Norwegian Resistance, the barns and outhouses were used as an arsenal. Lunna Kirk is one of the oldest Shetland churches still in use. Built in 1753, it is a charming old building with a leper squint, through which lepers could listen to the service and receive Communion.

At **Brae**, about 23 miles (37km) north of Lerwick, a narrow neck of land called **Mavis Grind** prevents the northwest corner of Mainland from being an island. You can stand on this 'anchor cable' of land and throw a stone one way into the Atlantic and the other way into the North Sea.

Sullom Voe Oil Terminal (pronounced Soolem), with its complex of buildings and jetties, is on the peninsula of **Calback Ness**, 7 miles (11km) northeast of Brae, joined to Mainland by reclaimed land. The terminal is tucked away so discreetly that you are hardly aware of it, though you cannot miss the ugly buildings that house the oil workers—incongruous against the bleak landscape. **Firth**, nearby, was built to house the oilmen. **Toft** is 4 miles (6.5km) east of Sullom Voe and from here the car ferry crosses to **Yell**, 3 miles (4.5km) northeast.

This northern part of Mainland is dominated by **Ronas Hill**, Shetland's highest point, 1475 feet (454m) high, 10 miles (16km) north of Brae, and well worth climbing for marvellous views.

Muckle Flugga Lighthouse Unst Shetland

Eshaness, on the coast of Mainland, 15 miles (24km) northwest of Brae, has precipitous cliffs and breathtaking views of the **Drongs**, a collection of weird stacks carved by the force of the ocean. These stacks include a huge natural arch called the **Dore Holm**.

The island of **Yell**, to the north, is mostly peat moor. It was described by Eric Linklater as 'dull and dark and one large peat bog'. Although the second-largest of the Shetland islands, it has suffered from depopulation and can be rather depressing. It is one of the best places in Britain to see otters.

A Minister of the Kirk once said: 'Yell is Hell, but Unst—Oh! Unst!' **Unst** is Britain's most northern island, with the **Muckle Flugga** lighthouse on a rock just off its northern tip. The lighthouse was built by Robert Louis Stevenson's father and while he was designing and building it, his son stayed on Unst, dreaming up the story of *Treasure Island*. Unst supports a number of Shetland ponies and it has wonderful cliff scenery. Philatelists can get a special frank on their letters at Britain's most northerly post office in **Haroldswick**, in northeast Unst, the place where Harald Harfagri landed from Norway to subdue the troublesome Vikings.

Fetlar, east of Yell and much smaller, derives its name from the Norn name for 'fat land' and is the most fertile of the islands, with a large number of birds. Snowy owls bred on Fetlar until 1975, when the resident male died. Now, although they no longer breed there, visiting females can still be seen. They have a buzzard-like flight and distinctive white plumage. Another of Fetlar's rare visitors is the red-necked phalarope with a long, needle-like beak, which spins round on the water to stir up insects. The whimbrel, rather like a smaller curlew, usually a coastal migrant, nests on Fetlar and can be seen combing the shore for molluscs and worms with its long curved beak.

Whalsay, a couple of miles off northeast Mainland, is important for fishing and fish processing. On the pier there is a 17th-century Hanseatic trading booth. The Hanseatic League merchants came from northern Germany to Shetland to trade, buying fish and salting it for export, until salt tax was introduced in 1712. The traders set up booths like this one, from which they offered fine cloth, fishing tackle, exotic foods, tobacco, fruit and gin at a farthing a pint, in exchange for fish, butter, wool and fish oil. It is intriguing to look at this quiet, peaceful place and picture what it was like when the merchants haggled and bartered from their booths.

Whalsay has two prehistoric sites: the **Standing Stones**, at Yoxie, and the **Benie Hoose**, thought to have been the dwelling for the Druid priests who were responsible for the ceremonies performed around the standing stones.

Foula is an island 27 miles (43km) west of Mainland, with dramatic cliff scenery and a colony of skuas. Still inhabited, it is often cut off in bad weather. This was the last place where Norn was spoken, in the 19th century.

Fair Isle

Fair Isle is 24 miles (38km) southwest of Sumburgh on Mainland, and boats run to it from Grutness Pier, on Sumburgh Head. These aren't day trips: there is a three-day stay on the island before the next boat back. Alternatively, Loganair operate two flights from Tingwall Airport on Mondays, Wednesdays and Fridays, making a day's outing possible. Fair Isle, the 'Far Isle' of the Vikings, halfway between Orkney and Shetland, is a buffer between the Atlantic and the North Sea. It must be the most gale-battered island in Britain, presenting a tough challenge to the 60-odd people who live there. The bird population is enormous, preserved by the warden of the **Observatory**. Over 300 species have been recorded on Fair Isle; as well as resident colonies, it is a regular staging post for many migratory birds.

Although bleak, Fair Isle is magnificent, with needle-sharp rocks pounded by ferocious seas and sheer cliffs topped by green turf and wild flowers. Paying guests can stay at the Observatory in the summer.

Fair Isle knitting is internationally renowned. There is an island co-operative of men and women who work machines and hand finish 200 orders of Fair Isle jumpers, scarves, hats and gloves a year. These are only sold on the island. Each jersey takes seven hours to finish by hand. The designs date back to Viking times, possibly influenced by the Moorish patterns learnt from the survivors of a Spanish Armada shipwreck, in 1588, who were given shelter by the islanders.

expensive

Kveldsro House Hotel, Lerwick, ℂ 0595 2195, is highly recommended with four crowns, overlooking the harbour. **Lerwick Hotel**, ℂ 0595 2166, 10 minutes' walk from the town centre, is a hideous modern building with a glorious view over Breiwick Bay and Bressay Island. What it lacks in style and character, however it makes up for in comfort and service and it has four crowns. **Shetland Hotel**, Holmsgarth Road, ℂ 0595 5515, is another modern horror, opposite the ferry terminal. It is comfortable and well run with a friendly staff and has five crowns.

Busta House, Busta, ℂ 080622 506, is a large old country house, full of character, with four crowns, good food and wine and a selection of 120 malt whiskies.

moderate

Queens Hotel, ℂ 0595 2826, with three crowns, is right on the water in Commercial Street, picturesque, old fashioned and comfortable, at the top of the price range. **Grand Hotel**, ℂ 0595 2826, is in Commercial Street in the centre of the town, with an imposing castellated tower. It has three crowns and Shetland's only nightclub.

Sumburgh Hotel, ℂ 0950 60201, close to the airport and next to Jarlshof, is an old laird's house, with lots of character and very friendly, with four crowns.

inexpensive

Westings Hotel, Wormdale, Whiteness, ℂ 059584 242, is a family-run hotel with gorgeous sea views. It's easy-going and friendly, with three crowns. **St Magnus Bay Hotel**, Hillswick, ℂ 080623 372/3, is a charming Norwegian-style hotel overlooking the bay, comfortable and hospitable.

For a really cosy, friendly bed and breakfast, try Mrs W. J. Hutchison, Orablaa, 3 Twageos Road, Lerwick, ℂ 0595 3417.

Fair Isle Bird Observatory Lodge, ℂ 03512 258, is idyllic. The building itself is modern and unbeautiful but it offers the perfect island/wildlife holiday for anyone interested in birds, nature and hospitality. Open from April to October, its 12 bedrooms share one bathroom, its staff are relaxed and friendly and its outlook sublime. It offers full board.

83	Defeat of Picts at battle of Mons Graupius by Roman Agricola.
141–2	Building of Antonine Wall.
397	Founding of Christian church at Whithorn by St Ninian.
410	Departure of Romans from Britain.
500	Invasion of Scotland by Irish Scots, settlement of Dalriada.
563	Landing of St Columba in Iona, conversion of Picts to Christianity begins.
794	Invasion of Hebrides by Norsemen.
844–60	Kenneth Macalpine unites Picts and Scots.
1034	Whole of Scotland united into one kingdom under Duncan I.
1040	Duncan I murdered by Macbeth who is in turn murdered by Malcolm Canmore.
1057–93	Anglicizing of Scotland under Queen Margaret.
1102	Western Isles granted to Magnus of Orkney.
1124–53	David I founds many abbeys and burghs, grants land to Normans.
1174	William the Lion forced to acknowledge supremacy of Henry II.
1214	Alexander II, Golden Age of Scottish history.
1263	Battle of Largs, defeat by Alexander III of King Haakon of Norway. Annexation of the Hebrides.
1286	Death of Alexander III, succeeded by Margaret of Norway.
1290	Death of Maid of Norway at sea on her way to Scotland.
1291	Edward I arbitrates between Robert the Bruce and John Balliol. Balliol gets crown.
1296	Balliol renounces his crown in favour of Edward I. Scottish nobility agree to treaty of mutual assistance with Philip IV of France—the beginning of the Auld Alliance.
1297–98	William Wallace stirs up resistance, defeats Edward at Stirling Bridge, and is defeated at Falkirk. Goes into hiding.
1305	Capture and execution of William Wallace.
1306	Robert Bruce slays John Comyn and is crowned at Scone.
1307	Edward I dies.

Chronology

1314	Battle of Bannockburn, Bruce defeats English.
1320	Declaration of Arbroath.
1326	First Scottish Parliament at Cambuskenneth.

1328	By treaty of Edinburgh England recognizes Robert the Bruce as king of independent Scotland
1346	Battle of Neville's Cross. David II taken prisoner by English.
1371	Robert Stewart crowned Robert II, first Stewart King.
1406	James I captured, Duke of Albany become guardian of Scotland.
1414	Foundation of St Andrews, Scotland's first university.
1450–5	Struggle for supremacy between Stewarts and Douglases. Douglases crushed by James II.
1469	Orkney and Shetland pledged to James III as part of dowry of his wife, Margaret of Denmark.
1476	Overthrow of Lords of the Isles.
1488	James III defeated and killed by rebels at Sauchieburn
1491	Perkin Warbeck claims English throne, encouraged by James IV.
1503	James IV marries Margaret Tudor, daughter of Henry VII.
1513	Battle of Flodden, death of James IV.
1528	Burning of Patrick Hamilton, proto–martyr of Reformation.
1538	Marriage of James V to Marie de Guise-Lorraine.
1542	Defeat of Scots at Solway Moss, death of James V, accession of his infant daughter, Mary.
1544	Rough Wooing, devastation of Lowland Scotland by Henry VIII.
1546	Burning of George Wishart, murder of Cardinal Beaton.
1554	Regency of Marie de Guise.
1557	Signing of first Protestant Covenant.
1558	Marriage of Mary to Dauphin of France, later Francis II.
1559	John Knox returns to Scotland. Reformers destroy the abbey church at Scone.
1561	Mary, Queen of Scots returns to Scotland
1565	Marriage of Mary to Darnley. Moray's rebellion is suppressed.
1566	Murder of Rizzio. Birth of James VI.
1567	Murder of Darnley, marriage of Mary to Bothwell, defeat, imprisonment and abdication.
1568	Mary escapes to England and is imprisoned by Elizabeth.
1570	Moray is assassinated and Lennox becomes regent of Scotland.
1582	James VI is abducted in the Ruthven raid.
1587	Mary, Queen of Scots is executed.

1603	Accession of James VI to English throne making him James VI/I (VI of Scotland, I of England). Establishment of Episcopacy in Scotland.
1637	Riots of Edinburgh against Charles I's new prayer book.
1638	Signing of National Covenant to uphold Presbyterian worship.
1643	Signing of Solemn League and Covenant recognized by English Parliament.
1645	Battle of Philiphaugh. Defeat of Royalist Montrose by Covenanters under Leslie.
1646	Charles surrenders to the Scots.
1647	The Scots give Charles to the English.
1649	Execution of Charles I, Charles II proclaimed King in Scotland.
1650	Signing of Covenants by Charles II. Invasion of Scotland by Cromwell.
1660	Restoration of Monarchy.
1662	Renunciation of Covenants by Charles II and re-establishment of Episcopacy.
1666	Start of the Killing Times, persecution of Covenanters.
1688	James VII/II tries to restore Catholicism. He is deposed in favour of William and Mary.
1689	Highlanders, under Claverhouse, Bonnie Dundee, defeat King's army at Killiecrankie.
1692	Massacre of Glencoe.
1695	Bank of Scotland founded and Company of Scotland established to colonize Darien coast.
1699	Darien colony evacuated.
***c.*1700– *c.*1800**	The Age of Enlightenment
1707	Union of Parliaments.
1715	Rebellion in favour of the Old Pretender.
1736	The Porteous Riots, Scots rebel against English domination.
1745/6	Final Jacobite rebellion. Defeat of Prince Charles Edward Stuart at Battle of Culloden. Repression of Highlands. Soon followed by the beginning of the Highland Clearances which lasted for over 100 years and depopulated the Highlands.
1760	Carron Ironworks starts production.
1845/6	Irish potato famine spreads to Scotland causing starvation and terrible hardship.
1947	Founding of Edinburgh International Festival, putting Scotland back on the cultural map.
1970s	North Sea oil industry developed.
1979	Scotland rejected devolution in a referendum.

Kenneth Macalpine: 843–58

Donald: 858–62

Constantine I: 862–77

Aed: 877–8

Eochaid and Giric (joint kingship): 878–89

Donald II: 889–900

Constantine II: 900–43

Malcolm I: 943–54

Indulf: 954–62

Dubh: 962–6

Culen: 966–71

Kenneth II: 971–95

Constantine III: 995–7

Kenneth III: 997–1005

Malcolm II: 1005–34

Duncan I: 1034–40

Macbeth: 1040–57

Lulach: 1058

Malcolm III, Canmore: 1058–93

Donald III Bane: 1093–4 (six months)

Duncan II: 1094 (six months)

Donald III Bane: 1094–7

Edgar: 1097–1107

Alexander I: 1107–24

David I: 1124–53

Malcolm IV, the Maiden: 1153–65

William I, the Lion: 1165–1214

Alexander II: 1214–49

Alexander III. 1249–86

Margaret, Maid of Norway: 1286–90

John Balliol: 1292–6

Interregnum: 1296–1306

Robert I (the Bruce): 1306–29

David II: 1329–71

Stewarts

Robert II: 1371–90

Robert III: 1390–1406

James I: 1406–37

James II: 1437–60

James III: 1460–88

James IV: 1488–1513

James V: 1513–42

Mary: 1542–67

James VI/I: 1567–1625

Charles I: 1625–49

The Commonwealth: 1649–60

Charles II: 1660–85

James VII/II: 1685–8

William and Mary: 1689–94

William (alone): 1694–1702

Anne: 1702–1714

Hanoverians

George I: 1714–27

George II: 1727–60

George III: 1760–1820

George IV: 1820–30

William II/IV: 1830–7

Saxe-Coburg-Gotha

Victoria: 1837–1901

Edward I/VII: 1901–10

Windsors

George V: 1910–36

Edward II/VIII: 1936

George VI: 1936–52

Elizabeth I/II: 1952–

Adam, William and his four sons, John, Robert, James and William. Renowned Scottish-born architects, Robert, 1728–92 being the best known.

Adamnan, Saint. *c.* 624–704. Ninth Abbot of Iona and biographer of St Columba.

Barrie, Sir James. 1860–1937. Novelist and playwright. Born in Kirriemuir which he renamed Thrums in a series of novels. *Peter Pan* is one of his best-known works. Belonged to the Kailyard school of writers who sentimentalized small-town life in Scotland.

Bean, Sawney. Apocryphal 17th-century cannibal who lived with his incestuously bred family in a cave in Ayrshire, existing on the flesh and gold of unwary travellers.

Beaton, David. (?)1494–1546. Cardinal and Archbishop of St Andrews. Notorious for persecution of Reformers. Burned George Wishart for heresy and was murdered in revenge in St Andrews Castle.

Beaton, James. 1470–1539. Uncle of the above. Archbishop of Glasgow, then St Andrews. Opponent of the Reformation and responsible for death of Patrick Hamilton, proto-martyr.

Boswell, James. 1740–95. Scottish lawyer, writer and admirer of prominent people. Met Dr Johnson in 1763 and toured Hebrides with him in 1773. Wrote *Life of Samuel Johnson*. A volatile, promiscuous man given to fits of depression. Of great value to anyone visiting Scotland is to read his *Journal of a Tour of the Hebrides*, in conjunction with Dr Johnson's account.

Bothwell, James Hepburn, Earl of. *c.* 1535–78. Powerful and ambitious. Closely involved in murder of Mary, Queen of Scots' husband, Darnley. Abducted Mary, and married her after quick divorce from his wife. Escaped when Mary was deposed. Imprisoned in Denmark where he died insane.

Brahan Seer. Coinneach Odhar. 17th century. Given gift of second sight after falling asleep on a fairy hill. Made astonishing prophecies, many of which have been fulfilled; some of which may yet be. Murdered by Countess of Seaforth having told her of her husband's infidelity.

Bridie, James. 1888–1951. Pseudonym of Osborne Henry Mavor, dramatist. Born in Glasgow, qualified as a doctor and served in RAMC in both world wars. His plays include *The Anatomist, Dr Angelus* and *A Sleeping Clergyman*. Amusing, extravagant, thought-provoking and entertaining.

Bryce, David. 1803–76. Edinburgh architect whose speciality was Scottish Baronial, most evident in Fettes College.

Burns, Robert. 1759–96. Born at Alloway in Ayrshire of humble parents and rose to become lionized as Scotland's greatest vernacular poet. Renowned almost as much for his enthusiastic love life and 'joi de vie' as for his verse. Among the many classics he wrote were 'Tam o' Shanter', 'My Love is like a Red, Red Rose', 'A Man's a Man, for a' That' and 'Auld Lang Syne'.

Biographical Notes

The names in this section are mentioned in the text but are not necessarily explained.

Columba, Saint. *c.* 521–97. Of royal Irish blood, he was exiled from Ireland for ecclesiastical plagiarism, settled in Iona in 563 and founded a religious community, launching-pad for missionaries who then converted Scotland to Christianity.

Cromwell, Oliver. 1599–1658. Led Parliamentarians in England's civil war and was responsible for execution of Charles I.

Cromwell, Thomas. 1485–1540. *Malleus monachorum*, Hammer of the Monks. Rose from humble beginnings with help from Cardinal Wolsey. Ingratiated himself with Henry VIII, encouraging his first divorce and promising to make him rich. Very active in suppression and dissolution of monasteries; served in many high offices before losing favour by encouraging marriage to Anne of Cleves whom Henry disliked. Sent to the tower and beheaded.

Cumberland, William Augustus, Duke of. 1721–65. Fat son of George II, defeated Prince Charles at Culloden 1746, winning nickname of Butcher Cumberland for his brutality.

Douglas. Ancient Scottish family, often so powerful that they were a threat to the Crown. Divided into the Black Douglases and the Red Douglases, they appear for better or worse throughout Scottish history. The Black Douglases were finally subdued by James II. The Red Douglases, who 'rose upon the ruins of the Black', held considerable power until deposed by James V.

Duns Scotus, Johannes. *c.* 1265–1308. One of the greatest of the medieval scholars, joined Franciscans, studied and lectured on philosophy and theology in Oxford, Paris and Cologne.

Fingal, or Fionn MacCumhail. *c.* 3rd century. Legendary Irish warrior and hunter, dominating Gaelic sagas. His band of men were the original Fenians, defending Ireland against invasion. Traditionally father of Ossian.

Graham of Claverhouse, John, Viscount ('Bonnie Dundee'). 1648–89. Royalist and notorious persecutor of Covenanters. Led early Jacobite rebellion after James VII/II was deposed, and was killed defeating William's army at Killiecrankie.

Hamilton, Patrick. 1502–28. Proto-martyr of Scottish Reformation, influenced by Erasmus and Luther. He returned to his native Scotland and was burned for heresy by Archbishop James Beaton at St Andrews. In spite of his youth, he was titular Abbot of Ferne.

Hertford, Edward Seymour, Earl of. 1506–52. Leading aggressor in Henry VIII's 'Rough Wooing' of Scotland, to punish them for cancelling marriage between Mary, Queen of Scots, and Henry's son, Edward. He was responsible for appalling destruction to many of Scotland's finest Lowland buildings, including the Border abbeys.

Hogg, James. 1770–1835. Protégé of Sir Walter Scott, known as the 'Ettrick Shepherd'. Prolific poet and novelist.

Johnson, Samuel. 1709–84. English lexicographer, critic and poet, whose reputation as a man and a conversationalist is as great as his literary fame. Dogmatic, unreasonable, humble, pious and loveable, his account of his tour of the Hebrides with James Boswell, in 1773, makes marvellous reading and is full of acute observations on life in the Highlands after Culloden and the Act of Proscription.

Jones, John Paul. 1747–92. Born in Kirkcudbrightshire, son of a gardener. He received commission in American Navy and returned to harass the English, but always with honour. Stories are told of his chivalrous treatment of his victims.

Knox, John. *c*. 1502–72. Leading Scottish reformer. Spent 19 months as French galley-slave, returning to preach fiery iconoclastic sermons in Perth and St Andrews in 1559 which led to destruction of monasteries. Minister of St Giles in Edinburgh, during which time he tangled with Mary, Queen of Scots. The phrase 'monstrous regiment of women' was coined from his pamphlet called: 'The First Blast of the Trumpet Against the Monstrous Regiment of Women'. Although dogmatic, he had a keen sense of humour. As a 51-year-old-widower, he married a girl of 16.

Lauder, Sir Harry. 1870–1950. Mill boy and miner who became a much-loved writer and interpreter of Scottish songs, including 'The Road to the Isles'.

Leslie, David. 1601–82. Scottish Covenanter and General. Defeated Montrose at Battle of Philiphaugh. Supported Charles II in 1650 and was defeated by Cromwell at Dunbar. Imprisoned in Tower of London till Restoration of Monarchy, and then made Lord Newark.

Lorimer, Sir Robert. 1864–1929. Architect responsible for Thistle Chapel in St Giles Cathedral, Scottish War Memorial in Edinburgh Castle, and restoration of many castles and abbeys as well as important houses and buildings.

Macdonald, Flora. 1722–90. Born in South Uist. Tacksman father died when she was two. Adopted at 13 by Lady Clanranald, wife of chief of clan, and brought up in Skye. She smuggled Prince Charles from Benbecula to Skye, disguised as her maid, Betty Burke, thus helping to save his life. Was imprisoned for a year on a troopship. Married son of Macdonald of Kingsburgh and entertained Dr Johnson during his tour of Hebrides in 1773. Emigrated with family to North Carolina where her husband became a brigadier-general in American War of Independence. Returned to Scotland in 1779 and died at Kingsburgh.

MacGregor, Rob Roy. 1671–1734. Known as Rob Roy (Red Robert) from colour of his hair. Romanticized by Walter Scott as philanthropic Robin Hood, he was in fact a cattle-raider and smuggler. Died peacefully, having been imprisoned in London and pardoned.

Mackintosh, Charles Rennie. 1868–1928. Architect, born in Glasgow. He made the 'Glasgow style' famous and exercised considerable influence on European design. His style was simple and uncluttered. The best example of his work is the Glasgow School of Art.

Macpherson, James. 1736–96. Scottish poet who 'translated' the Ossianic poems. Many believed that these works were genuine and they were certainly of great value, but others, including Dr Johnson, doubted their authenticity and it is now believed that Macpherson collected a quantity of Gaelic material and composed his own poems from them. In their own right, whatever the source, they are a valuable and beautiful contribution to Gaelic past.

Monk, George. 1608–69. Parliamentary General in Scotland, fighting for Cromwell at Dunbar and then Governor of Scotland in 1653–8. When Cromwell died he saw that the only way to heal the turmoil in Britain was to restore the Monarchy and he was instrumental in bringing Charles II back to the throne.

Monmouth, Duke of. 1649–85. Bastard son of Charles II by Lucy Waters, he claimed that his parents had been married and raised a revolt against James VII/II, for which he was executed.

Moray, James Stuart. Regent. 1531–70. Bastard son of James V, half-brother to Mary, Queen of Scots. Sided with Lords of the Congregation and became Regent on Mary's abdication. Shot while riding through Linlithgow.

Ossian. 3rd-century Gaelic bard, possibly son of Fingal, chief of the Fenians, semi-mythical military body said to have been raised for defence of Ireland against Norse. Countless tales told. (See Macpherson, above.)

Queensberry 'Old Q', 4th Duke of. 1724–1810. Notorious gambler, despoiled many tree plantations in Scotland, to pay his debts.

Ramsay, Allan. 1686–1758. Scottish poet, best known for 'The Gentle Shepherd'.

Ramsay, Allan. 1713–84. Son of above. Famous portrait painter.

Scott, Sir Walter. 1771–1832. Prolific poet and novelist. Remarkable for his efforts to pay off debts of £130,000 after collapse of his publisher, hence the amazing volume of his work. He also did much for Scotland after the despair that followed Culloden. It was he who organized the search for the Scottish Regalia, and he who organized the State Visit of George IV.

Stevenson, Robert. 1772–1850. Scottish engineer responsible for many important lighthouses, including Bell Rock.

Stevenson, Robert Louis. 1850–94. Grandson of above and son of another engineer. Prolific writer, best known for *Treasure Island*, *Kidnapped*, *The Master of Ballantrae*, and *Dr Jekyll and Mr Hyde*.

Telford, Thomas. 1757–1834. Scottish engineer famous for his bridges, many of which still exist, his roads and his canals including the Caledonian Canal.

Thomas the Rhymer. *c.* 1220–97. Thomas Learmont of Erceldoune (Earlston), Scottish seer and poet, many of whose prophecies were fulfilled. Said to have lived with the Fairy Queen for three years in the Eildon Hills. He foretold the death of Alexander III at his wedding feast.

Wade, George. 1673–1748. British general, Irish by birth, sent to Scotland in 1724 to try to bring the Highlands under control. Built a system of metalled roads and bridges that opened up the north.

Warbeck, Perkin. c. 1474–1499. Claimed to be one of the Princes in the Tower. Put forward by English Yorkists as rightful king. Made three futile 'invasions', was caught and executed. He was in fact the son of a Flemish boatman.

Wishart, George. *c.* 1513–46. Scottish reformer, burned by Cardinal David Beaton in St Andrews, for which the cardinal was later murdered.

Wolf of Badenoch. died 1394. Bastard son of Robert II, Alexander Stewart, Earl of Buchan. Also known as 'Big Alastair, Son of the King'. Brutal and merciless, terrorizing the countryside from his castles of Ruthven and Lochindorb. Excommunicated by Bishop of Elgin in 1390 for which he destroyed Elgin Cathedral and much else.

Clans and Families

The Gaelic *clann* means offspring, family, stock, race, derived from Latin *planta*—meaning 'sprout' or 'scion'.

When Robert the Bruce released Scotland from the English yoke in 1314, he opened the field for tremendous power struggles between the leading clans. Some became too powerful, others sank into obscurity. Many families, too weak to survive alone, sought the protection of stronger neighbours; some of these took the name of their adopted chief, others retained their own names. Thus many clans have 'septs' and dependants. Clans amalgamated for strength: the Clan Chattan Confederation consisted of a large number of clans who joined forces under Mackintosh hegemony. The chiefs of the Highland clans ruled with total disregard for the authority of the Crown, as did the powerful Border families. The final Jacobite rebellion, in 1745–56, resulted in the death of the old clan system. (See also 'Clans and Tartans', in 'Topics'.)

Today, although all that is left is the clan name, many still live in the area traditionally associated with their clan and there remains a pride and sense of loyalty so strong that people come from all over the world to visit the land of their ancestors. This is a list of the main clans and families, with the address (where there is one) of the clan secretary, or clan centre, who will send more information if required. Names not included will be those of septs, or clan branches. Anyone seriously seeking their roots should get hold of *The Clan Almanac*, by Charles Maclean, published by Lochar, a comprehensive little book which lists, among other things, the septs and dependants of the main clans: thus if you are called Abbot, for instance, you will find you are part of the Macnab clan. Mac and Mc mean son of, as of course does any name ending in son.

Anderson: son of Andrew, Highland version MacAndrew. They came from Badenoch and their motto is 'Stand Sure'. In the 15th century they were part of the Clan Chattan Confederation. Clan Chattan Secretary, Dyunmaglash, Westhill, Inverness-shire.

Armstrong: the original, armour-bearer to a King of Scots, saved his king, fallen in a battle, by lifting him on to his horse. He was given land as a reward and named Strong-arm. They were Borderers and their motto *Invictus maneo* means 'I remain unvanquished'. Clan Secretary, Brieryshaw, Langholm, Dumfriesshire.

Baird: from an old Scots word meaning sumptuous dress. They came from Aberdeenshire and their motto *Dominus fecit* means 'The Lord made'.

Barclay: derived from the Berkeley family who came over with William the Conqueror. They settled in Aberdeenshire and Kincardineshire and their motto *Aut agere aut mori*, means 'Either action or death'.

Blair: from Gaelic *blar*—field, battlefield; motto: *Amo Probos*—'I love the righteous'. An ancient family, one branch having roots in Renfrew, Ayr and Wigtown; and another in Perth, Fife and Angus. The Barony of Blair, in Ayrshire, was granted by William the Lion in the 12th century. When the two branches competed for chieftainship, James VI settled the dispute by appointing the oldest man in either family to be chief. Thus the honour alternates, depending upon seniority. Clan Secretary, 15 Brompton Terrace, Perth.

Brodie: from their Norman ancestor, de Brothie. They settled in Morayshire and their motto is 'Unite'. Clan Secretary, Brodie Castle, Forres, Moray.

Bruce: from the French town Brix—Adam de Brus came over with William the Conqueror. They lived in Annandale, Clackmannan and Elgin and their motto, *Fuimus*, means 'We have been'. Robert the Bruce won independence for Scotland at the Battle of Bannockburn in 1314; Thomas Bruce, 7th Earl of Elgin and 11th Earl of Kincardine, 1766–1841, rescued the decorated sculptures on the Parthenon from vandalism and installed them in the British Museum.

Buchanan: from Gaelic *mac-a-Chanonaich*—son of the canon. They lived around Loch Lomond and their motto is *Clarior hinc honos*—'Brighter hence the honour'. Clan secretary, Brechin Robb, 24 George Square, Glasgow.

Cameron: from Gaelic *cam-shron*—crooked nose. They lived in Northern Argyll and Locheil. Their mottos, translated from Gaelic, are: 'Unite'; 'For King and Country'; and 'Sons of the hounds come here and get flesh'. The Cameron Highlanders, now amalgamated with the Seaforth Highlanders to become the Queen's Own Highlanders, were raised by Sir Alan Cameron in 1793. Their Clan Centre is at Aberchalder, Loch Eil, and the new Clan Cameron Museum is at Achnacarry. Clan Secretary, 78 Milton Road West, Edinburgh.

Campbell: from Gaelic *cam-beul*—crooked mouth. They came from Argyll, Cawdor, Loudoun and Breadalbane. Their various mottos are: 'Forget not'; 'Follow me'; 'Be mindful'; 'I byde my tyme'. The Duke of Argyll is their chief and the clan centre is Inverary Castle, Argyll.

Chisholm: means a water meadow which produces milk good for cheese-making. They lived in Roxburghshire and Berwickshire and later moved to Inverness-shire. Their motto *Feros ferio* means 'I am fierce with the fierce'. Clan Secretary, 21 Blytheswood Square, Glasgow.

Colquhoun (pronounced *k'hoon*): the name comes from the Barony, in Dunbartonshire and they lived around Loch Lomond. Their motto, *Si je puis*—'If I can', was said by one of their ancestors, to James I, when ordered to capture Dumbarton Castle. (He did.)

Cumming: derived from the herb cummin, which is their emblem. They come from Roxburghshire, Buchan, Badenoch and Altyre and their motto is 'Courage'. The Comyns came to Scotland during the reign of Malcolm Canmore in the 11th century, and it was Sir John Comyn—'The Red Comyn', who was murdered by Robert the Bruce in order to gain the Crown. Clan Secretary, House of Altyre, Forres.

Douglas: from Gaelic *dubh glais*—black water. They lived in Lanarkshire, Galloway, Dumfriesshire and Angus and were as powerful as kings in the Middle Ages. Their motto, *Jamais arrière*, means 'Never behind'. Archibald Douglas became known as Bell-the-cat, from his undertaking to kill the much-despised favourites of James III. Sir James Douglas was killed in 1330, while honouring his promise to take Robert the Bruce's heart to the Holy Land.

Drummond: derived from Drymen, near Stirling. They came from Perthshire and their motto is 'Gang (go) warily'.

Duncan: more properly Clan Donnachaidh—Brown Warriors. They came from Atholl and Lundie in Fife and their motto is *Disce parti*—'Learn to suffer'. Donnaichaidh Clan Secretary, 127 Rose Street, South Lane, Edinburgh.

Elliot (there are different spellings): probably derived from Old English *Aelfwald*—Elf Ruler, which became the Christian name Elward. They were one of the strongest of the Border families and their mottos are *Soyez sage*—'Be wise', and *Fortiter et Recte*—'With Strength and Right'. Clan Secretary, Redheugh, Newcastleton, Roxburghshire.

Erskine: from the Barony of Erskine in Renfrewshire. They lived around Alloa and their motto is *Je pense plus*—'I think more'. John Erskine, 11th Earl of Mar, was known as Bobbing John during the Jacobite rebellions because he kept changing sides.

Farquharson: the Gaelic *fearchar* means dear one, and they came from Aberdeenshire and Invercauld. Their motto is *Fide et Fortitudine*—'By Fidelity and Fortitude'. They were part of the Clan Chattan Confederation. Clan Chattan Secretary, Dyunmaglash, Westhill, Inverness-shire.

Ferguson: Fergus founded the Scottish kingdom of Dalriada and they inhabited the lands of Argyll, Perthshire, Dumfries, Galloway and Raith. Their motto is *Dulcius ex asperis*—'Sweeter after difficulties'. They are one of the oldest clans of Scotland. Clan Secretary, Pendle Cottage, Dunigoyne, Glasgow.

Forbes: from Gaelic *forba*—field or district. They were powerful in Aberdeenshire and their motto is 'Grace me guide'. Clan Secretary, Balforbes, Lonach, Donside, Aberdeenshire.

Fraser: of Norman derivation, from *fraises*—strawberry flowers. Originally they were in East Lothian, then Aberdeenshire. Their motto is *Je suis prest*—'I am ready'. Clan Secretary, Balblair House, Beauly, Black Isle, Ross-shire.

Gordon: from Gordon in Berwickshire, where they settled, as Anglo-Normans, in the 12th century. They became very powerful in the northeast in Strathbogie, Deeside and around Aberdeen, and their chief was called Cock of the North. Their mottos are *Animo non Astutia*—'By Courage, not Craft'; and *Bydand*—'Remaining'. Clan Secretary, Harlaw House, Harlaw Hill, Prestonpans, East Lothian.

Graham: Anglo-Saxon origin—*graeg ham*, meaning grey home. William de Graham came to Scotland with David I, who gave him lands and the family became prominent in the Wars of Independence. Their lands included those north of Glasgow,

Loch Katrine, part of Perthshire, and around Dundee and Montrose. Their motto is *Ne Oublie*—'Do not forget'. Among their greatest ancestors were Montrose, that gallant Royalist, and Graham of Claverhouse (Bonnie Dundee), hero of Killiecrankie in 1689. Clan Secretary, 23 Ardmillan Terrace, Edinburgh.

Grant: derived from the French *grand*—'great'. Their origins are disputed: some say the first Grant was a Nottinghamshire squire married into an Inverness-shire family, some that they are descended from Kenneth MacAlpine, some that they are descended from MacGregors. Their lands were Strathspey, Rothiemurchas, Glen Moriston and Loch Ness and their motto is 'Stand fast'. Clan Secretary, 18 Great Stewart Street, Edinburgh.

Gunn: possibly from Gunni, in the Norse sagas, or from Gaelic *guineach*, meaning fierce, or of Pictish descent. Their lands were in Caithness and Sutherland and their motto is *Aut Pax Aut Bellum*—'Either Peace or War'. Clan Secretary, 22 Muirhouse Gardens, Edinburgh.

Hamilton: derived from Hameldone, meaning crooked hill', in England, whence came Walter Fitz-Gilbert to lands in Renfrewshire and Arran during the Wars of Independence. Their motto is 'Through'. Patrick Hamilton, 1498–1528, was the protomartyr of the Scottish Reformation. Clan Secretary, Lennoxlove, Haddington, East Lothian.

Hay: derived from La Haye, in Normandy, which stemmed from *haie*, meaning hedge. Their lands were Aberdeenshire and Tweedale and their motto is *Serva jugum*—'Keep the yoke'. Clan Secretary, 12 St Peter's Place, Edinburgh. Clan Centre, Delgatie Castle, Turriff, Grampian.

Henderson: in Gaelic, this clan is MacEanraig, anglicized as MacKendrick. Their lands were Caithness and Glencoe and their motto is *Sola Virtus nobilitat*—'Virtue alone ennobles'.

Home (pronounced Hume): derived from Gaelic *uamh*—cave. Their lands were the Borders and their motto is 'A Home, a Home!' Among their scions were David Hume, the great philosopher of the Scottish Enlightenment and Sir Alec Douglas-Home, Prime Minister of Britain.

Innes: meaning 'greens'. Innes was a town in Morayshire for which the family received a royal charter in the 12th century. Their motto is *Be traist*—'Be faithful'. Clan Secretary, 35 East Clarmont Street, Edinburgh.

Johnstone: derived from John's *toun*—homestead; the Gaelic for John is Iain, giving MacIain. There are various spellings but Johnson is uncommon in Scotland. They were a powerful Border family and also had lands in Aberdeenshire. Their mottos are *Numquam non paratus*—'Never unprepared', and 'Light thieves all'.

Keith: from the town of Keith in Banffshire. Their lands stretched from East Lothian to Caithness and they held the hereditary office of Great Marischal of Scotland from the 12th to the 18th centuries. Their motto is *Veritas vincit*—'Truth conquers'. Clan Secretary, North Dykes, Kilbirnie, Ayrshire.

Kennedy: from Gaelic *ceann éitigh*—grim-headed—or possibly from *ceann dubh*—black-headed. Their lands were in Ayrshire, Lochaber and Skye and their motto is *Avise la Fin*—'Consider the end'. The seat of their chief, the Marquess of Ailas, is Culzean Castle.

Kerr: pronounced *kar*, the name is derived from the Norse *kjarr* meaning 'brushwood'. They were an Anglo-Norman family who came to Scotland in the 12th century. Their lands were Roxburghshire and their motto is *Sero sed serio*—'Late but in earnest'. Legend has the Kerrs left-handed so they reversed the spiral of their stair-cases to allow space for the left sword-arm.

Lamont: derived from Lawman, Lawgiver; MacKeracher is the Highland version. Their lands were in Argyll and Cowal and their motto is *Nec parcas nec spernas*—'Neither spare nor dispose'. Clan Secretary, 17 Broomhall Loan, Edinburgh.

Leslie: taken from the barony of Leslie in Aberdeenshire which they adopted in the reign of William the Lion. Their motto is 'Grip fast'.

Lindsay: Lindsey means Linden (lime tree) Island. They came to Scotland with David I and became very powerful, with lands in the Borders and in Angus. Their motto is *Endure Fort*—'Endure with Strength'. Clan Secretary, 112 Corsebar Road, Paisley.

Livingstone: from Livingstone in West Lothian where they held land, as well as in the Trossachs and Lorne. Their motto is *Si je puis*—'If I can'. Clan Secretary, Bachuil, Isle of Lismore, Oban, Argyll.

Logan or **MacLennan**: Logan is in Lothian, with MacLennan as the Highland version. Their lands were in Lothian, Berwickshire and Easter Ross and their motto is 'The Ridge of Tears'.

MacAlister: son of Alasdair, Gaelic for Alexander, who was descended from the great Somerled. Their lands were Kintyre, Arran and Bute and their motto is *Fortiter*—'Boldly'. Clan Centre, Glenbarr Abbey, Kintyre, Strathclyde.

MacAlpin: Alpins claim descent from 9th-century King Alpin and Dunstaffnage was their traditional home, though the race had no land. Their motto is *Cuimhnich bas Ailpein*—'Remember the death of Alpin'.

MacArthur: the MacArthurs were the senior branch of the Campbell clan, taking their name from Arthur Campbell in the 14th century. Their lands were Argyll, Cowal and Skye and their mottos are *Fide et Opera*—'By Fidelity and Work' and *Eisd! O eisd!*—'Listen! O listen!' Clan Secretary, 14 Hill Park Road, Edinburgh.

MacAulay: son of Olaf, who was King of Man and the Isles in the 13th century. Their lands were Dunbartonshire, Isle of Lewis, Sutherland and Ross. Their motto is *Dulce Periculum*—'Danger is sweet'. Clan Secretary, Cameron Loch Lomond Ltd, Alexandria, Dumbartonshire.

MacBean: son of Beathan, or from the Gaelic *bian*—fair skin—or from King Donald Ban, from whom they claim descent. Donald Ban was the son of Duncan, murdered by Macbeth. Their lands were in Inverness-shire and their motto is 'Touch not the catt bot a targe' (without a shield). At Culloden, gallant Gillies MacBean breached a gap in a wall with his enormous body and killed 14 Hanoverians before he was himself slain.

MacBeth: derived from the Gaelic for 'Son of Life'. Their lands were in Morayshire and Perthshire and their most famous ancestor, King MacBeth 1040–57, was very different from Shakespeare's character: a wise, generous, pious ruler, the last of the Gaelic kings.

MacCallum: *calaman* is Gaelic for dove, implying a disciple of St Columba whose emblem was the Dove of Peace. Their lands were in Argyll and their mottos are *In ardua petit*—'He has tried difficult things' and *Deus refugium nostrum*—'God is our refuge'.

Macdonald: *Dòmhnall* is Gaelic for world ruler. Donald of Islay was grandson of Somerled, Lord of the Isles and Ragnhildis, daughter of King Olaf of Man. Clan Donald was the largest and most powerful of the clans, with a number of branches, reigning supreme in the northwest Highlands and Islands. There are a variety of spellings, including MacDonnell. (Mac was not used in the surname until the 16th century.) It is the commonest Mac name in Scotland. The main branches were: Sleat in Skye, Clanranald in Moidart, Glengarry, Keppoch in Lochaber, and Glencoe. They were staunch Jacobites and Royalists, fiercely claiming their position on the right wing of any battle, given them by Robert the Bruce at Bannockburn and still held at Culloden. Their mottos include: *Per mare per terras*—'By land and by sea'; *Fraoch eilean*—'The heathery isle'; 'My hope is constant in thee'; *Dh'aindeoin co'theireadh e*—'Gainsay who dare'; *Creag an fitheach*—'the Raven's Rock'; and *Dia's naomh Aindrea*—'God and St Andrew'. Clan Centre, Armadale Castle, Sleat, Skye. Clan Secretary, Ceadach, 39 Redford Road, Edinburgh.

MacDougal: from the Gaelic *dubh gall,* meaning 'dark stranger'. Their lands were Lorne and their motto is *Buaidh no bàs*—'To conquer or die'. They fought against Robert the Bruce in the Wars of Independance, and with the Hanoverians at Culloden. Clan Secretary, Dunollie Castle, Oban, Argyll.

MacDuff: from the Gaelic *mac dubh*—son of the dark one. Their lands were in Fife, Lothian, Strathbran and Strathbogie and their motto is *Deus juvat*—'God assists'. The MacDuffs spawned a number of other clans: a MacDuff earl was known as *Mac an tòiseach*—son of the chief, which became MacIntosh, for example. Clan Secretary, 5 Sidlaw Road, Glasgow.

MacEwan: son of Ewan, who flourished in the 13th century. Their lands were Cowal, Lennox and Galloway and their motto is *Reviresco*—'I grow strong'.

MacFarlane: son of Partholon, whose father, Sear, took over Ireland after the Flood. Their lands were around Loch Lomond, Tarbert and Arrochar and their motto is *Loch Sloigh*—'Loch Sloy'.

MacFie: derived from the Gaelic *Dubhsìth*, meaning 'peaceful dark one', the MacFies are a branch of the Clan Alpine. Their lands were Colonsay and their motto is *pro rege*—'for the king'. Clan Secretary, 120 Cockburn Crescent, Balerno, Midlothian.

MacGillivray: *gille breth* is Gaelic for 'servant of judgement' and the clan belonged to the Clan Chattan Confederation. Their lands were in Mull, Lochaber and Morven, and later in Inverness-shire. Their motto is Dunmaghlas, the name of the chief's castle. MacGillivray of Dunmaglass led the Clan Chattan at Culloden. Clan Secretary, Dunlichty, 7 Cramond Park, Edinburgh.

MacGregor: *Grioghair* is Gaelic for Gregory and they claim descent from Griogar, son of 8th-century King Alpin. Some prefer to claim Pope Gregory the Great as their forefather. Whatever the truth, they all claim royal descent. Their lands were in Argyll and Perthshire and their motto is *S'rìoghail mo drèam*—'Royal is my race'. Their name was first proscribed 'under pain of death' after a bloodthirsty massacre of the Colhuhouns in 1603, and again by William III. Many changed their names. Clan Secretary, 14 Lockharton Avenue, Edinburgh.

MacInnes: *aontaghais* is Gaelic for 'unique choice' and they were an ancient Celtic clan. Their lands were Morven and Ardnamurchan and their motto is *Irid Ghibht dhe Agus an Righ*—Through the Grace of God and the King. Clan Secretary, 35 East Claremont Street, Edinburgh.

MacIntosh: see **Mackintosh** and **MacDuff**.

MacIntyre: *an-t-saor* is Gaelic for 'son of a carpenter' and the clan is said to have taken this name from one who chopped off his thumb to stop a leak in a Macdonald chief's galley. Their lands were Kintyre, Glenoe and Badenoch and they were part of the Clan Chattan Confederation. Their motto is *Per ardua*—'Through difficulties'. Clan Chattan Secretary, Dyunmaglash, Westhill, Inverness-shire.

MacKenzie: *coinnich* is Gaelic for 'fair' or 'bright' and was a popular Celtic forename, anglicized as Kenneth. MacKenzie lands were in Ross and Cromarty and the Isle of Lewis. Their mottos include *Luceo no uro*—'I shine, not burn'; *Tulach Ard*—'The High Hillock'; and *Cuidich 'n righ*—'Save the King'. Traditionally they provided most of the men in the Seaforth Highlanders, now amalgamated with the Cameron Highlanders to form The Queen's Own Highlanders. Clan Secretary, 1b Downie Place, Musselburgh, Midlothian.

MacKinnon: Kinnon derives from 13th-century Fingan and the MacKinnons were the family of St Columba, part of the Clan Alpin. Their lands were Iona and North Mull; then Skye and Arran and their mottos are *Audentes fortuna iuvat*—'Fortune favours the brave'; and *Cùimhnich bas Ailpein*—'Remember the death of Alpin'. Clan Secretary, 222 Darnley Street, Pollockshiels, Glasgow.

MacKintosh: *toiseach* is Gaelic for 'tribal leader' or thane and the clan descended from the MacDuffs, originally the leading family of the Clan Chattan Confederation. Their lands were Inverness-shire and their motto is 'Touch not the cat bot (without) a glove'. Brave, beautiful, Jacobite Lady Anne MacKintosh, known as Colonel Anne, masterminded the Rout of Moy, ousting 1500 of Cumberland's troops with a mere five men. Clan Secretary, Moy Hall, Moy, Inverness-shire.

MacLachlan: Lachlan was a Celtic forename derived from Lochlann, the Gaelic for Norway, and the clan claims descent from Niall of the Nine Hostages, High King of Ireland, who won land in Argyllshire. They later spread to Lochaber, Perthshire and Stirlingshire. Their motto is *Fortis et Fidis*—'Brave and Trusty'. MacLachlan of MacLachlan, Prince Charles' ADC, died at Culloden in 1746. Clan Secretary, Tigh-na-Croft, Enochdhu, Blairgowrie, Angus.

MacLaine of Lochbuie: *gille Eoin* is Gaelic for 'servant of John' and they claim descent from Lachlans and MacLeans. Their lands were Lochbuie and their motto is *Vincere vel mori*—'conquer or die'.

MacLaren: from the Gaelic, 'son of Lawrence'. Their lands were Strathearn and Balquhidder and their motto is 'The Boar's Rock'. Clan Secretary, 1 Inverleith Place, Edinburgh.

Maclean: *gille Eoin* is Gaelic for 'servant of John' and they claim descent from the Kings of Dalriada. Their lands were Morvern, Mull, Coll and Tiree and their mottos are *Bas no Beatha*—'death or life'; and *Fear eile airson Eachairn*—'Another for Hector'. Clan Secretary, 12 Elie Street, Glasgow.

Macleod: *liotr* was old Norse for 'ugly'; *leod* was Saxon for 'prince.' They claim descent from Olaf the Black, King of Man and the Islands in the 13th century, and their lands were Skye, Lewis and Harris. 'Hold fast' is their motto. Clan Secretary, 38 Ravelston Gardens, Edinburgh.

MacMillan: *maoilein* means 'bald one', meaning tonsured and therefore priest, so their origins were ecclesiastical. Their lands were Lochaber, Argyll and Galloway and their motto is *Miseris succurrere disco*—'I learn to succor the distressed'. John MacMillan 1670–1753, founded the Reformed Presbyterian Church. Clan Centre, Finlaystone, Langbank, Renfrewshire. Clan Secretary, 21 Huntley Gardens, Edinburgh.

MacNab: from *aba* meaning 'abbot', the MacNabs are descended from the Abbot of Glendochart, in the time of David I. Their lands were Glendochart and Loch Tay and their motto is *Timor omnis abesto*—'Let fear be far from all'. Raeburn's magnificent painting of *The MacNab*, was of the 12th chief, Francis, 1734–1816, a remarkable eccentric, described by one as 'a herculean Highlander'. Clan Secretary, Finlarig, Killin, Perthshire.

MacNaughton/MacNachtan: *neachdainn* is Gaelic for 'pure one' and they can be traced back to Pictish royalty. Their lands were Strathtay, Lewis and Argyll and their motto is 'I hope in God'. The Clan Centre is at Dunderaive Castle, near Inveraray. Clan Secretary, 2 Douglas Crescent, Edinburgh.

MacNeil: descended from the O'Neills who were High Kings of Ireland. Their lands were Barra, Gigha, Knapdale and Colonsay and their motto is *Vincere vel mori*—'To conquer or die'. Clan Secretary, 34 Craigleith Hill Avenue, Edinburgh.

MacNicol or **Nicholson:** son of Nicol, tracing their ancestry back to the dark ages. Their lands were Sutherland, Skye and Argyll and their motto is *Sgorra Bhreac*— Skorrybreck.

MacPherson: *phearsain* was Gaelic for 'parson'. They were part of the Clan Chattan Confederation and trace their ancestry to Ferchar, King of Lorne, who died in 697. Staunch Jacobites, they arrived too late for the Battle of Culloden. Their land was Badenoch and their motto is 'Touch not the cat bot (without) a glove'. Clan Secretary, 39 Swanson Avenue, Edinburgh.

MacQuarrie: *guardhre* is Gaelic for 'noble one' and they trace their roots to the Clan Alpine and Saint Columba's family. Their lands were Ulva and their motto, *An t-arm breac dearg*, means 'the red tartaned army'.

MacQueen: from the Norse *sweyne*, or Gaelic *siubhne*, meaning 'good going'. They were strong members of the Clan Chattan Confederation, with close Macdonald connections. Their lands were Skye, Lewis, Argyll and Lanarkshire and their motto is 'Constant and faithful'. Clan Chattan Secretary, Dyunmaglash, Westhill, Inverness-shire.

MacRae: means 'son of grace', probably of ecclesiastical origin. Known as the 'Wild MacRaes' and also as 'MacKenzies Coat of Mail,' they were hereditary Constables of Eilan Donan Castle for the MacKenzies of Kintail, now restored by one of their descendants. Their lands were Beauly and Kintail and their motto is *Fortitudine*— 'With Fortitude'. Clan Secretary, 6 Gardiners Crescent, Edinburgh.

Malcolm: followers of St Columba. Their lands were in Argyll, Fife, Lochore and Dumfriesshire. Their motto was *Deus refugium nostrum*—'God is our refuge', and is now *In ardua petit*—'He aims at difficult things'. Clan Secretary, Duntrune Castle, Kilmelford, Lochgilphead, Argyll.

Matheson: *math-ghamhainn* is Gaelic for 'bear' and, traditionally, the Clan of the Bear helped Kenneth MacAlpin against the Picts in 843. Their lands were Lochalsh and Sutherland and their motto is *Fac et Spera*—'Do and hope'. Clan Secretary, Burnside, Duirnish, Kyle of Lochalsh, Ross-shire.

Maxwell: from Maxwell on the River Tweed, derived from Maccus's Wiel, they were a powerful Border family descended either from 11th-century Maccus, King of Man and the Isles, or from Norman settlers. Their lands were in Nithsdale and their motto is *Reviresco*—'I flourish again'.

Menzies (correctly pronounced *mingiz*): from Mesnières in Normandy. Although of Anglo-Norman origin they became Gaelicized. Their lands were Atholl, Weem, Aberfeldy and Glendochart and their mottos are *Vil God I Zal*—'Will God I shall'; and *Geal 'us dearg a suas*—'Up with the white and red'. Clan Secretary, 1 Belford Place, Edinburgh. Clan Museum, Castle Menzies, Aberfeldy, Tayside.

Moncreiffe: from Gaelic *monadh craobhe*—tree on the moor, descended from Maldred, brother of King Duncan. Their lands were in Perthshire and their lairds were traditionally archers of the sovereign's bodyguard. Clan Secretary, Easter Moncreiffe, Perthshire.

Montgomery: from Montgomerie, in Normandy, the family are descended from Anglo-Norman Robert de Montgomery, who came to Scotland in the 12th century. Their lands were Eglinton, Ardrossan and Kintyre and their motto is *Gardez bien*—'Look well'. Clan Secretary, c/o P.O. Box 6, Saltcoats, Ayrshire.

Morrison: *gille Mhoire* is Gaelic for 'servant of Mary', presumably of ecclesiastical origin, and they trace their ancestors to the MacLeods of Dunvegan in 13th century. Their lands were Lewis, Sutherland, Skye and Harris. Hebridean Morrisons are well-known pipers today. Clan Secretary, Ruchdi, by Loch Maddy, Isle of North Uist.

Munro: from the Gaelic *Rothach*—man from Ro, thought to be from the River Roe in Ireland. Their lands were in Easter Ross, their motto is 'Dread God' and their war-cry, 'Castle Foulis Ablaze!', refers to the beacon that used to be lit on the chief's castle to summon the clan to arms. They were Whigs, supporting the Government against the Jacobites.

Murray: from Moray, the placename meaning 'settlement by the sea'. They are descended from Pictish Mormaers, with lands in Morayshire and Perthshire. Their motto is *Tout pret*—'All ready'. Andrew Murray, who died in 1338, was Regent of Scotland; Lord George Murray was a Jacobite general, believed by some to have been a traitor at Culloden. Clan Secretary, 204 Bruntsfield Place, Edinburgh.

Napier: descended from the ancient earls of Lennox; legend has it that one, having been particularly brave in battle, was ordered by his King to change his name to 'Nae peer'! Their lands were Gosford, Fife and Midlothian and their mottos are *Sans tache*—'Without stain'; and *To vincula frange*—'To break bones'.

Ogilvie: from Brythonic *ocel fa*—'high plain'. Ogilvie Earls of Airlie descend directly from the Earls of Angus, and were granted lands in Angus by William the Lion. Their motto is *A fin*—'To the finish'. St John Ogilvie, 1579–1615, was a Scottish Jesuit martyr, canonized in 1976.

Ramsay: meaning 'wild-garlic island'. The family is descended from an Anglo-Norman, Simund de Ramesie, who was granted lands in Lothian by David I. Their lands were Dalhousie and Perthshire, and their motto is *Ora et labor*—'Pray and work'.

Robertson: the eponymous Robert was Robert Riabhach (Grizzled Robert) Duncanson, 4th Chief of Clan Donnachaidh, and the Robertsons of Struan are one of the earliest known families in Scotland. Struan was their land and their mottos are: *Virtutis Gloria Merces*—'Glory is the reward of valour'; and *Garg'n uair dhuis gear*—'Fierce when raised'. Clan Secretary, 29 Lauriston Gardens, Edinburgh.

Rose: descended from the Norman family de Rose and first recorded in Scotland in the reign of Alexander II. Their lands were Strathnairn and Ross-shire and their motto is 'Constant and true'. Clan Secretary, Kilravock Castle, Nairnshire.

Ross: the Gaelic *ros* means 'headland'; Brythonic *ros* means 'moor'. They are descended from Fearchar Mac-an-t-Sagairt of Applecross, created Earl of Ross in 1234. Their lands were Ross-shire, Ayrshire and Renfrewshire and their motto is *Spem successus alit*—'Success nourishes hope'. Clan Secretary, 57 Barnton Park View, Edinburgh.

Scott: the Scoti were the Irish tribe who gave Scotland its name. The family descend from

Uchtred, *filius Scoti*—'son of a Scot'—in the 12th century, and were one of the most powerful Border families. Their lands were in the Borders and Fife and one of their best-known scions is Sir Walter, the 19th-century writer.

Scrymgeour: from French *eskermisor*—sword-fencer or skirmisher. Their ancestor Alexander 'Schyrmeschar' was royal banner-bearer, hanged by Edward I in 1306. Their lands were in Argyll and Fife and their motto is 'Dissipate'. Clan Secretary, 21 Braid Farm Road, Edinburgh.

Shaw: possibly derived from the Gaelic *seaghdha*—pithy. Principal members of the Clan Chattan Confederation, they were probably descended from 14th-century Shaw Macduff, founder of the MacIntosh clan. Their land was Strathspey and their motto is *Fide et Fortitudine*—'By Fidelity and Fortitude'. Clan Secretary, Tordarroch House, Tordarroch, Inverness-shire.

Sinclair: from the French St Clair sur Elle, in Normandy, whence came William de Sancto Claro in the 12th century, receiving the barony of Roslin. Their lands were in Midlothian, Orkney and Caithness, and they were jarls of Orkney in 14th century. Their motto is 'Commit thy work to God'. Clan Secretary, 2 Shandon Road, Edinburgh.

Skene: from Skene in Aberdeenshire, they are descended from Robertsons of Struan. Their lands were in Aberdeenshire, granted by the king in 11th century. Their motto is *Virtutis regia merces*—'A palace the reward of bravery'.

Stewart: derived from High Steward. Walter Fitz-Allan, an Anglo-Norman, came to Scotland in the 12th century and was given land and the greatest office in the realm—Steward of Scotland. The family provided Scotland with 14 sovereigns, five of whom also reigned in England. Stuart was the French form of the name, adopted in England. Their lands were Renfrewshire, Teviotdale, Lauderdale, Appin and Ardshiel and their motto is *Virescit vulnere virtus*—'Courage grows strong at a wound'. Probably the best-known Stuart was the one who never got to the throne, Prince Charles Edward, 1720–88. Clan Secretary, 48 Castle Street, Edinburgh.

Sutherland: Sudrland was the Norman name for Sutherland, to the south of Caithness. The clan is descended from early inhabitants of Sutherland, which was granted to them in 1228. Clan Secretary, Donrobin Castle, Golspie, Sutherland.

Urquhart: derived from Brythonic *air cairdean*—at the woods, the name of the district where the family originated. William of Urquhart was hereditary sheriff of Cromarty during the reign of Robert the Bruce. Their lands were in Ross-shire and Inverness-shire and their motto is 'Mean, speak and do well'. Thomas Urquart, 1611–60, who claimed descent from Adam, was a brilliant translator of Rabelais and is said to have died of laughter, on hearing of the Restoration. Clan Secretary, Bigram, Port of Monteith, Stirlingshire.

Wallace: derived from Wallenses, the mediaeval word for the Welsh who peopled Strathclyde, from whom the Wallaces are descended. Their lands were Ayrshire and Renfrewshire and their motto is *Pro Libertate*—'For Liberty'. William Wallace fought for Scottish independence, paving the way for Robert the Bruce.

Scotland is proud of the seven regiments that make up the Scottish Division. Perhaps because of their war-like ancestors, Scots have always had the reputation for being the bravest in battle, their war-memorials the longest. On parade, with their colourful uniforms, pipes and drums, Scottish regiments draw the largest crowds. Within the Scottish Division, administered from Edinburgh, each regiment is a close-knit family, retaining its separate identity, uniform, traditions and customs.

The Royal Scots (The Royal Regiment) recruit mainly in Lothian, Edinburgh and Tweeddale. The oldest infantry regiment in the British Army, the Royal Scots were raised by Sir John Hepburn in 1633, for service under Louis XIII in France. They claimed and won precedence over all others in the French Service, challenged by the Regiment of Picardy, who declared that they had been on duty on the night of the Crucifixion. 'If we had been on guard', retorted the colonel of the Royal Scots, 'we should not have slept at our posts', thus gaining the regiment its famous nickname 'Pontius Pilate's Bodyguard'.

The Royal Highland Fusiliers (Princess Margaret's Own Glasgow and Ayrshire Regiment). In 1678, Charles Erskine, 5th Earl of Mar, raised the Earl of Mar's Regiment to subdue the fanatical Covenanters in the southwest shires of Scotland. They became the Scots Fusiliers in 1695 and gained their present title in 1959 when they were amalgamated with the Highland Light Infantry.

The King's Own Scottish Borderers recruit across the south of Scotland. They were raised in 1689 by David Earl of Leven, when the citizens of Edinburgh were alarmed at the Jacobite threat. They fought at Killiecrankie, Sheriffmuir and Culloden. They are also one of six infantry regiments to have 'gained immortal glory' at the Battle of Minden in 1759, and now wear red roses on 1 August, Minden Day, to commemorate the tradition that the soldiers picked roses as they advanced through gardens during the battle.

The Black Watch (the Royal Highland Regiment) recruits from Angus, Perthshire, Fife and Dundee. The Black Watch was originally raised as six independent companies to police the Highlands after the first Jacobite rebellions, and was then formed into one regiment with the addition of four more companies, in 1739. Their name comes from the dark colour of their tartan (compared to the red coats and white trousers of the other regiments of that period), and from their duty to 'Watch the Highlands'. They were busy 'watching' on the Continent, in 1745, which may have contributed to Bonnie Prince Charlie's early success in raising an army of Jacobites to his father's standard and marching south as far as Derby. They wear a plume of red feathers in their bonnets—the red hackle—said to originate from recapturing guns lost to the enemy.

The Queen's Own Highlanders (Seaforth and Camerons) recruit from the Northern and Western Highlands and the Islands. They are descended from three Highland

Scottish Regiments

regiments raised in the late 18th century for service in the American and French Revolutionary Wars. The 72nd and 78th Highlanders were raised by Chiefs of Clan MacKenzie, mainly from Ross-shire and Lewis, and became the Seaforth Highlanders. The 79th Cameron Highlanders were raised by Alan Cameron of Erracht, mainly from Lochaber and North Argyll, and were honoured with the title Queen's Own by Queen Victoria in 1873. The regiments amalgamated to become the Queen's Own Highlanders in 1961.

Owing to defence cuts there are plans to amalgamate the Queen's Own Highlanders and the Gordon Highlanders late in 1994. Both regiments are strongly opposed to such an unwieldy marriage.

The Gordon Highlanders recruit in Grampian. They were raised by the Duke of Gordon in 1794 with the help of his wife Jean, who donned a regimental jacket and bonnet and toured her husband's estates, placing a guinea between her lips and kissing each man who came forward to enlist: she was 47 at the time and known to her contemporaries as 'well run'. They wear black buttons on their spats in tribute to Sir John Moore who was killed in the moment of victory at the battle of Corunna in 1809. One of their achievements was capturing the Heights of Dargai on the Northwest Frontier of India in 1897, driven on by the skirl of the pipes played by Piper Findlater, who, shot through both ankles, continued to play the regimental march 'The Cock of the North' throughout the battle.

The Argyll and Sutherland Highlanders (Princess Louise's) recruit in Argyllshire and eastwards. They were formed in 1881 by the amalgamation of two Highland regiments, the 91st and 93rd, which had been raised at the end of the 18th century for foreign service. They earned the nickname 'The Thin Red Line' at Balaklava in 1854. The 93rd Sutherland Highlanders were ordered to the Heights above the town by Sir Colin Campbell and commanded to form a line against the full might of the Russian cavalry. 'There is no retreat from here, you must die where you stand,' they were told. They advanced, fired two volleys and routed the Russians, suffering only two casualties. They won glory in Aden in 1967 and later conducted a successful campaign to avoid disbandment.

Further Reading

Non-fiction

A Concise History of Scotland, Fitzroy Maclean

Scotland's Story, Tom Steel

A History of the Scottish People 1560–1830, T. C. Smout

A Century of the Scottish People, 1830–1950

The Lion in the North, John Prebble

Mary, Queen of Scots, Antonia Fraser

Bonnie Prince Charlie, Fitzroy Maclean (Beautifully written and entirely unbiased.)

The Prince in the Heather, Eric Linklater (Prince Charlie's escape after Culloden.)

In Search of Scotland, H. V. Morton

In Scotland Again, H. V. Morton (These two were written in 1929 and 1933 and are as fresh and readable today as then.)

A Description of the Western Islands of Scotland, M.Martin (James Thin reprinted a facsimile of this 1716 gem.)

A Hundred Years in the Highlands, Osgood Mackenzie

The Life and Death of St Kilda, Tom Steel

A Companion to Scottish Culture, David Daiches

The Highland Clans, Sir Iain Moncreiffe of that Ilk (Not quite so readable but an erudite book of great value.)

A Journey to the Western Islands, Samuel Johnson

Journal of a Tour to the Hebrides, James Boswell

(These two can be obtained in one volume and should be read together. They are fascinating to read as you visit the places they went to.)

The Drove Roads of Scotland, A. R. B. Haldane

Highland Drove, John Keay (An account of droving cattle today using the old methods and routes. Good descriptions.)

Highland Folk Ways, I. F. Grant

Memoires of a Highland Lady, Elizabeth Grant

The Fringe of Gold, Charles MacLean (Wonderful collection of anecdotes about the fishing villages of the east coast.)

The Islands of Western Scotland, W. H. Murray

The Prophecies of the Brahn Seer, Alexander Mackenzie

A Macdonald for the Prince, Alasdair Maclean (The story of Neil MacEachen, native of Uist and father of Napoleon's Marshal Macdonald.)

Tales of a Grandfather, Walter Scott (The history of Scotland as told by Walter Scott to his young grandson. Delightful.)

Edinburgh: A Travellers' Companion, (ed) David Daiches (Excellent new anthology of historical accounts of the city, its life and customs.)

Scotland: An Anthology, Paul Harris (Delightful, idiosycratic literary collection covering all aspects of Scotland.)

The Sobieski Stuarts, H. Beveridge

The House of Elrig, Gavin Maxwell (About his childhood in Galloway). Also *Harpoon at a Venture; Ring of Bright Water; The Rocks Remain; Raven Seek Thy Brother.* (All describe Maxwell's fascinating life in the Western Highlands.)

The Discovery of the Hebrides, Elizabeth Bray

The Highlands, Calum I. Maclean (Charming reminiscenses, recently reprinted to include an introduction by his brother Sorley, the poet, with outstanding photographs by his nephew, Cailean.)

Reflections on Scotland, Ian Wallace (A traveller's scrap-book, by the well-known Scottish singer.)

Scottish Highland Estate: Preserving an Environment, Michael Wigan

Novels

Whisky Galore, and anything else by Compton Mackenzie

Walter Scott's vast output includes: *Waverley*, his first novel, about Jacobites; *Redgauntlet*, about how Prince Charlie returned to Scotland to try his luck once more; *Fair Maid of Perth*, set in Perth at the end of the 14th century; *Old Mortality*, about Covenanters; and *Rob Roy*.

The Song of the Forest, Colin Mackay (A beautiful piece of contemporary writing, giving a picture of life in the Dark Ages.)

The Sound of the Sea, also by Colin Mackay and equally well written

Consider the Lilies, Iain Crichton Smith (Charming, sad story about the Clearances .)

No Mean City, A. MacArthur (Brilliant description of slum life in the Gorbals.)

Shetland Bus, David Howarth

King Hereafter, Dorothy Dunnet

A Scots Quair, Lewis Grassic Gibbon

Lanark, Alasdair Gray

The Inn at the Edge of the World, Alice Thomas Ellis

Sea Music, David Profumo

Kidnapped, Robert Louis Stevenson, and *Catriona* (Based on the story of the Appin murder.)

John Macnab, The Thirty-Nine Steps, etc, John Buchan

Poetry

Poems and Songs of Robert Burns, edited and introduced by James Barke

From Wood to Ridge, Sorley Maclean (A collection of his haunting poems, in Gaelic and English.)

Poetic Gems Selected From the Works of William McGonagall, Poet and Tragedian (Scotland's worst poet—compulsive reading.)

Anything by Hugh MacDiarmid

Anthology of Poetry, Norman McCaig

Light Relief

The Old Man of Lochnagar, HRH The Prince of Wales

1. Aberfoyle   ? Cameron House
2. Aberfeldy (Moness)
3. Dalmally

? 2000

Aber—mouth of: confluence of (rivers)

Advocate—barrister

Aird—point, promontory

Allt—stream

An—of the

Aros—dwelling

Athole brose—delicious drink made from whisky, honey, oatmeal and cream, left to soak and squeezed through a cloth: once tasted, never forgotten

Auch—a field

Auld—old

Aye—yes

Bairn—child

Bal—town, home

Ban—fair

Bannock—oatmeal pancake-ish scone-ish cake

Bap—bread roll

Bard—poet

Barr—crest

Beag—small

Bealach, balloch—mountain pass

Bean—woman

Ben, beinn—mountain

Bhlair—plain

Blether—talk nonsense

Bogle—frightening ghost

Bothy—rough hut, temporary accommodation

Brae—hill

Bramble—blackberry

Branks—bridle, halter

Braw—fine

Breeks—trousers

Bridie—pie made with circle of pastry folded over filling of meat, onions, vegetables, etc.

Brig—bridge

Broch—prehistoric round stone tower with hollow walls, enclosing cell-like galleries, and stairways, often built round a well, purpose only guessed at, probably dwelling for chief and refuge for clan in times of danger

Burn—stream

Byre—barn

Cadger—pedlar

Cailleach—old woman

Cairn—stone monument

Callan(t)—youth

Cam—crooked

Canny—prudent

Caolas—firth

Capercailzie—wood-grouse

Car—curve

Ceann—head

Ceilidh—informal social gathering among neighbours, often with spontaneous singing, music, story telling, etc.

Chanter—double-reeded pipe on which bagpipe tune is played

Cil—church

Clach—stone

Cladach—beach

Clarty—dirty

Claymore—sword

Cleg—horsefly

Close—shared entry to tenement, enclosure, courtyard

Glossary

Cnoc—hillock

Collie—sheepdog, wood

Corbie—crow

Corrie—hollow

Crack—conversation

Craig—rock

Crannog—small man-made island dating from Iron Age. Stones piled on wooden base with easily defended single dwelling on top, often reached by a sunken causeway

Creel—pannier-type basket, also lobster pot

Croft—smallholding

Crowdie—soft cheese

Cuddy—donkey

Cul—recess

Cutty—short (cutty sark, short petticoat; cutty stool, stool of repentance)

Dal—field

Dalr—valley

Damph—deer, steer

Daunder—saunter

Ding—knock, beat

Dominie—schoolmaster

Doo—dove

Doo'cot—dovecot

Dour—dry, humourless

Douse—sweet, gentle

Dram—officially one-eighth fluid ounce: commonly generous tot of whisky

Dreich—dreary, boring

Drochit—bridge

Dross—coal dust

Drove road—tracks used for herding (droving) cattle or sheep to market, often long distances

Druim, drum—ridge

Dubh—dark, black

Dun—hillfort

Dux—best pupil

Dyke—wall of stones or turf

Dysart—hermit's retreat, desert

Eaglais—church

Eas—waterfall, gorge

Eilean—island

Ey—island

Factor—land agent, usually of private estate

Fada—long

Fail—rock

Fank—sheepfold

Fash—trouble, upset, 'dinna fash yersel'—don't trouble yourself

Fear—man

Feu—feudal tenure of land with rent paid in kind or money

Fey—susceptible to supernatural influence

Fillebeg—kilt

Fionn—gleaming, white

Firth—wide mouth of river, estuary

Flit—remove, move house

Fou—full (of drink)

Fraoch—heather

Gearr—short

Geodha—chasm

Gil—ravine

Girdle—iron baking tray

Glass—grey

Glen—valley

Gleo—mist

Gobha—blacksmith

Gorm—blue, green

Gowk—fool

Greet—cry

Grieve—farm manager

Harling—rough-cast facing to walls

Haver—talk nonsense

Heugh—hillock

Hog—unshorn lamb

Hogmanay—New Year's Eve

Holm—low ground by river, islet in river

Hope—bay

How—burial mound

Howe—low-lying ground, hollow

Howff—meeting place, refuge, burial ground

Howk—dig

Ilk—same, of that ilk—surname and name of property the same

Inch—island

Inver—mouth of river

Jougs—iron neck collar used as instrument of public punishment

Kail—cabbage

Kailyard—cabbage patch, back yard

Keek—peep

Kelpie—water-sprite, water-horse

Ken—know

Kenspeckle—easily recognizable, conspicuous

Kil—burial place, church

Kin—head (of loch, river)

Kirk—church

Knock, knowe—knoll, hillock

Kye—cattle

Kyle—strait, narrow channel between two points of land

Lag, laggan—hollow, dip

Laird—owner of estate

Land—tenement

Larach—site of ruin

Larig, learg—mountain pass

Law—round hill

Leac—flagstone

Leana—plain

Liath—grey

Links—dunes

Linn, linne—pool

Lis—garden on site of fortress

Loan—lane

Loch, lochan—lake, small lake

Lug—ear

Lum—chimney

Machair—sand-peat lowland bordering seashore

Maol—bare headland

Manse—minister's house (ecclesiastical)

March—boundary

Meikle—large

Mon—moor

Mor—great

Moy—plain

Muc, muic—sow

Muckle—large

Mull—promontory

Na, nam, nan—of the

Neeps—turnips (bashed neeps—mashed turnips). Turnips in Scotland refer to English swedes

Neuk—nose

Ob, oba, oban—bay

Ochter—high

Pit—dip

Plenishing—furniture, domestic equipment

Ploy—activity

Poke—bag

Policies—grounds within an estate

Poll—pool

Provost—mayor

Puddock—frog

Quaich—shallow, two-handled drinking bowl

Rath—fort

Reek—smoke

Reidh—smooth

Rig—ridge

Ross—peninsula

Roup—auction

Ru, rhu, row, rubha—point

Sark—shift, shirt

Saugh—willow

Scunner—dislike

Selkie—seal

Sgeir, skerry—sea, rock

Sgor, scuir, sgurr—sharp rock

Sheiling—hut for summer pasture

Sherrif—county court judge

Shinty—hockey

Siccar—certain

Siller—silver (money)

Slochd—hollow, grave

Sonsie—bonnie

Soutar—cobbler

Spittal—hospice

Stob—stake, point

Strath—broad valley

Strone—nose, promontory

Struan, struth—stream

Swither—vacillate

Syne—ago

Tarbert, tarbet—isthmus

Tassie—cup

Thing—parliament, council

Thole—endure

Thrang—thronged

Thrawn—awkward

Tigh—house

Tir—land

Tobar—well

Tocher—dowry

Tod—fox

Toom—empty

Tom—hillock

Torr—hill

Tow—rope

Tulloch, tilly, tully—knoll

Uachdar—upper, high

Uamh—cave

Uig—sheltered bay

Uisge, esk—water

Uisge beatha—water of life (whisky)

Unco—strange, very

Usquebaugh—whisky

Vennel—alley

Voe—narrow bay, fiord

Wean—child

Weems—caves

Whaup—curlew

Whinn—gorse

Wick, vik—bay

Wight—strong

Wynd—alley

Yett—gate

Notes: The most significant pages for a particulat entry are **emboldened**. Maps have *italicised* page numbers.

Index